THE HISTORY

OF THE

BUCCANEERS OF AMERICA;

CONTAINING DETAILED ACCOUNTS OF THOSE

BOLD AND DARING FREEBOOTERS;

CHIEFLY ALONG THE

SPANISH MAIN, IN THE WEST INDIES,

AND IN THE GREAT SOUTH SEA,

SUCCEEDING THE CIVIL WARS IN ENGLAND.

NEW EDITION;

WITH SOME INTRODUCTORY NOTICES OF PIRACIES ON THE COAST OF NEW ENGLAND, TO THE YEAR 1724.

BOSTON:
SANBORN, CARTER AND BAZIN.
PORTLAND:
SANBORN & CARTER.
1856.

PREFACE

TO THE EDITION OF 1699.

It would be superfluous to say much by way of Preface to the following work, since a great part of it has some years ago been exposed to public view with a general applause; and indeed the wondrous actions and daring adventures therein related, are such as could not but transport the most stupid minds into an admiration of them, though many times they were not attended with that justice and regularity that becomes civilized men, or men of any pretensions to morality; but because we have here gathered up all that ever has been written in any language upon the subject of *buccaneering*, and that in a successive order down to the present time, [1700,] it will be necessary to enumerate the particulars thereof for the better information and satisfaction of the reader.

First, then, we have all the expeditions and exploits of the buccaneers of Jamaica and Tortuga, both English and French, set forth at large; and more especially what was transacted under the conduct of Sir Henry Morgan, by sacking of Puerto Velo, burning of Panama, &c., in the West Indies, written originally in the Dutch tongue; whereunto there are added the no less bold attempts and performances of men of the same stamp under the command of Captains Sharp, Sawkins, Coxon, and others, on the coasts of the South Seas; the whole being intermixed with vast variety of adventures and discoveries, and written by Mr. Basil Ringrose, who kept a journal of the said voyage, as being personally present at all the transactions, and is said by Mr. Dampier to be very exact.

But let nobody be surprised that he doth not find both these relations printed verbatim, as in the former edition has been done, since the matter is much improved; for whereas the style before was loose and uncouth in divers parts thereof, the same is now rectified, and made more correct, throughout the whole body of it, which cannot but add a new life and relish thereunto. And if this may be presumed upon, how much more may be expected from the succeeding journal of a voyage made into the South Sea by the *American Freebooters*, commencing the year 1684, (about which time the other terminated,) and ending at 1689, which was written in French by the SIEUR RAVENEAU DE LUSSAN, an ensign amongst them, and now first put into an English dress, and so consequently new to us; and, indeed the particulars are all as novel as they are stupendous and amazing, that men should run such extreme hazards, and hardships for money, and make such ill use of it when they have got it; and, for my own part, I must ingenuously confess, that since my first perusal I could never yet think of them without the greatest astonishment imaginable; especially seeing the whole contexture and narrative is so plain and simple, that to me it seems to carry an evidence of truth in every part of it.

I will not take upon me to apologize for many of the actions done, and here related, since even in the most regular troops and best disciplined armies, daily enormities are committed which the strictest vigilance cannot prevent. However, it is very remarkable, that in such a lawless body as these buccaneers seem to be, in respect to all others, that yet there should be such an economy (if I may so say) kept, and regularity practised amongst themselves, so that every one seemed to have his property as much secured to himself, as if he had been a member of the most civilized community in the world; though at the same time, when I consider of some of their laws, such as those against drunkenness and the like immoralities, I believe I have a great deal of reason to remain suspicious of their sincerity. But, be these things as they will, a bolder race of men, both as to personal valor and conduct, certainly never yet appeared on the liquid element or dry land; and I hope it will be taken neither for any affront nor a compliment to say, the English were always the leading and prevailing party amongst them.

What closes up the whole is an account of the adventures of Capt. Montauban on the coast of Africa, in the last years of the war between us and France, to whom, though the character of *privateer* doth more properly belong than that of *buccaneer* or *freebooter*, yet his actions, fight with the English guard ship, blowing up, strange escape, subsequent wanderings and hazards, are of so surprising a nature, and have so much likeness and affinity to the foregoing relations, that they could not without injustice to our design be omitted, and without which the whole would appear to be lame and imperfect.

INTRODUCTION.

It is very common at this day, and probably always was so, for even apparently thoughtful and considerate people to lament over the degenerate times in which they live, and to assert confidently that "the world is going on from bad to worse;" but it is a great mistake to suppose this — nothing can be farther from the truth. The following treatise is sufficient to set every individual who shall peruse it, right on this question. If there be any who entertain doubts as to the propriety of making this class of works public, we say to them, "Read the following pages, and compare the state and transactions of the world at the times on which it treats with those of the present." If, when they have done this, they are not satisfied that the general character of mankind has been greatly ameliorated within the last three centuries, nothing, it is thought, would satisfy them of the fact.

Within the period just stated there has been a complete revolution of the seas. Sea-kings are no longer known or acknowledged. Their dark and dismal reign has passed away forever. But we need not go back to the times of the desperate and bloody Vikingr of the north; it is only necessary to survey our own American coast within the space of two hundred years after its settlement by Europeans, to learn what terrors awaited all those who attempted voyages by sea.

In no very remote period, the European states were often glad to make the best terms they could with pirates, and merchants were subjected to heavy tribute when permitted to pursue their voyages. Pirates hovered upon every coast, and often sent challenges on shore to the kings of the countries. It is said to be no fable, that one of the dreaded sea rovers, while sweeping up and down the coast of England, sent to the king this bravado : —

> "Go tell the king of England, go tell him thus from me,
> Though he reigns king o'er all the land, I will reign king at sea."

Those rovers went sometimes in considerable fleets, and it was very common for one piratical fleet to attack another. Such fights often resulted in the entire destruction of the vanquished party. Sometimes one would chase another into the very harbor of a populous place, to the great terror of its inhabitants, and there carry on their bloody work.

To judge of the actors of those times, their barbarous condition must be considered. They bore as fair a relation to the civilization of their times as the rougher part of the community of later days do to theirs. For a long period Scandinavia was the nursery of Sea-kings, in other words, pirates; it was a period when the law of nations was the law of the strongest; an age when every male child was born for war as surely as he arrived at an age to enable him to wield a battle-axe; an age when it was thought the most inglorious thing that could happen to a man was not to die in war. War was the great and grand business of life.

Coming down to a later period, the sixteenth century, something of that fierceness had worn away; civilization had spread its influence far into the north, and though pirates infested every sea where commerce was found, yet they had gradually lost their preëminence on the ocean. Those who retaliated for their losses were not considered pirates, though those who suffered from retaliation had often no hand in the cause of such reprisal. This relict of the ancient Vikingr disgraces the annals of our own times; the hand of friendship is to this hour extended to those who have made themselves rich by their robberies on the ocean; they even fill places of honor and profit as a reward for their crimes — crimes they are, though sanctioned by law, as much so as though they had happened in another age, and even more.

The stories of the pirates that have infested the American seas, since the time of Capt. William Kidd, would make a large volume, and one of exceeding great interest. We have space to advert to but few of them. In the year 1689, two noted pirates, *Thomas Hawkins* and *Thomas Ponnd,* cruised upon the coast of New England, and committed many depredations with great boldness. The colony of Massachusetts Bay came to the determination to attempt their capture, and accordingly fitted out a sloop called the Mary, Samuel Pease commander, which sailed on the 4th of October of that year. Having received information that the piratical vessel was in or about Tarpaulin Cove, Capt. Pease made for that harbor. When off Wood's Hole he had certain intelligence of the object of his search, and making all the sail he could, he soon found himself within hailing distance of the outlaw. When he was ordered to heave to, the pirate ran up a red flag, whereupon Pease fired a shot athwart his forefoot, and ordered him to strike his colors. As the Mary came down upon him, she sent another shot under his forefoot, and again ordered him to strike; but Ponnd, stationed upon his quarterdeck, brandished his naked sword, bid them "Come on, you dogs, and I will strike you!" Meantime, his men standing ready with their guns pointed, discharged a volley upon the Mary, whose men returned it in earnest. The fight, thus commenced, for some time raged fiercely, no quarter being expected on either side. At length, laying the pirate on board, Capt. Pease compelled him to strike, though not till himself had received many wounds, and several of his men were wounded also; but how many, our accounts do not state, nor what damage the pirates received before they surrendered. But the conquest was dearly bought by the victors, as the wounds of Capt. Pease proved mortal five days after the battle.

For the next quarter of a century and more, the records of our admiralty courts are full of trials of pirates, with the most revolting accounts of their cruelties, and their executions. The following will probably be read with much interest, as it brings to our notice the immediate ancestor of our present chief magistrate of the United States, who, being taken by a pirate, effected his own deliverance in the most heroic and extraordinary manner.

Every body has probably read of a noted pirate of the name of Phillips, who, for some time previous to 1724, roved where he listed, making spoil where he could, and shedding innocent blood as it were for sport. At the same time there was living at Ipswich, in the colony of Massachusetts Bay, a certain *John Fillmore*, aged twenty-one years, he having been born in the year 1702. His father, also named John, had followed the seas, but had died in the West Indies several years before his son's majority, from the effects of cruel treatment while a prisoner there with the French. John Fillmore, the son, shipped on a fishing voyage for the Grand Banks, in the sloop Dolphin of Cape Ann, Mark Haskell skipper, in the spring of 1723. Having pursued their business of fishing till the autumn of the same year, Haskell and his company were fallen in with by Phillips, and all made prisoners. Plunder was not the object of their capture, but men to join the pirates in their nefarious enterprises. It was soon apparent that they intended to take only such of the fishermen as were stout and able-bodied. Accordingly, Fillmore was made choice of, and his captain was ordered to send him on board. There was no alternative, and Fillmore was compelled to join the pirates, though to their sad cost, as in the sequel will appear.

"When I first went on board the pirate," says Fillmore, "their crew consisted of ten men, including the captain, and the whole of them, I think, as stout, hardy-looking fellows as ever I saw together." The great reluctance which Fillmore discovered on entering the service of his new master caused Phillips to promise him his liberty if he would serve him faithfully two months. He was probably as sincere, when he made this promise, as Fillmore was in his intention of serving him faithfully. The two months soon ran away, and little or no booty fell into the pirate's hands, which caused him to treat his men roughly; and when at the end of that time Fillmore reminded him of his promise, he said *upon his honor* he would let him go after three months more. As before, there was no escape, and he submitted to his fate as well as he could. But the next three months were as unprofitable as the preceding two, only the pirate made an accession to his crew of several able men, whom, from time to time he had, as in the case of Fillmore, forced from other vessels into his service. At or near the expiration of seven months, they took a merchant ship, Capt. Harridon, of Boston, returning from a voyage to the West Indies. Harridon was a young man, only about twenty-two years of age.

Meantime, when Fillmore ventured again to claim his liberty, the pirate captain sneered a most fiendish grin, and among unutterable oaths roared out, "*Set you at liberty! Damn ye — you'll be set at liberty when I'm damned, and not before!*"

Phillips's rage was heightened against Fillmore, because the latter had all along refused to sign the ship's piratical articles. The others of the forced crew who had not signed them were

Capt. *Harridon*, *James Cheesman*, a ship carpenter, and a *Spanish Indian*, who was taken with Harridon. Seeing now that he had no chance of escape left, or not until his captain was "damned," as he himself expressed it, he was not long in making up his mind to have him *put into that state* whenever it could be attempted with a slight prospect of success.

So tyrannical had Phillips become, that even his own regular pirates hated him, and the more so, as they knew he had not a shadow of honor, and they had daily evidences of his bad faith even with them. About this time he put one of his men on board a prize, and ordered him to keep company. This man attempted to escape with the prize, but being overtaken by Phillips, he surrendered on assurances of good quarter. But as soon as he reached the deck of the pirate ship, Phillips run him through with his sword.

So watchful and jealous were Phillips and his companions, that it was with much difficulty and extreme hazard that Fillmore and his few friends, Cheesman, Harridon and the Indian, could form a plan for the effecting of their design. At length, however, after about nine months' captivity, a plan was laid and successfully carried into execution. But not long before its maturity, the authors were suspected by Phillips, and one of their company was in the most barbarous manner put to death by him by running him through the body with his sword, as he had his brother pirate before mentioned. This man, thus cold-bloodedly murdered (whose name is not mentioned) belonged to New England, and what aggravates his case is the fact, that he knew nothing of the conspiracy. Fillmore and the others intended to enlist him in it, but had not yet found a suitable opportunity. He also suspected Fillmore, and attempted his life by snapping his pistol against his breast, which missed fire. It however went off on the second attempt, which was immediately made; but Fillmore at the moment of the discharge struck the pistol so much aside that its contents missed him. For some unexplained or unexplainable cause the murderer made no further attempt upon his life, but "*damned him, and bid him go about his business.*"

It was not long after this that the pirates had a carousal, some of them got beastly drunk, and all got exhausted, and this was an opportunity not to be lost. The day before, Cheesman, the carpenter, had been ordered to make some repairs on deck, and he took care to leave his broadaxe and other tools there. In the dead of night, when the carousal had ceased, all things were arranged. Fillmore was to split out the brains of Capt. Phillips, Cheesman was to seize the master and throw him headlong into the sea, the Indian was to stand ready to act according to circumstances, while Harridon was so overcome with fear that nothing was allotted to him to perform in the tragedy. And although the Indian stood to the post assigned him, yet, as Fillmore in his narrative expresses it, he was so terrified that "he became near as white as any of us." And, as to himself, he says, that as he stood ready to seize the broadaxe, "his knees fairly smote together."

The pirate crew seems now to have consisted of ten men, and none can wonder that trepidation should seize upon the three that were to attack them. The three chief pirates were on deck at about twelve o'clock in the day — that day which was to seal the destiny of one or the other party. The fatal moment having arrived, Cheesman seized his man, and at the same breath Fillmore brought down the broadaxe upon the head of the boatswain, splitting it in twain; and before Phillips could draw his sword, the axe fell upon his head also.

The quartermaster was in the cabin, who, hearing the bustle, rushed out upon Cheesman and was prevented dealing a deadly blow upon him by the Indian, who was stationed at the companionway. He seized him by the arms, and in a moment more, Fillmore, with another blow of his broadaxe, nearly severed his head from his body. The rest of the crew surrendered at discretion, and with the captured vessel the victors arrived in Boston on the 3d of May, 1724.

Such was the end of the piratical enterprise of the famous and much dreaded Capt. John Phillips. Three of the pirates were tried, condemned and executed, and hung in chains on Bird Island, in Boston harbor. The other three, with the ship, were sent to England, with whom went Cheesman and the Indian also. The three pirates were soon after hung at Execution Dock, and Cheesman and the Indian were suitably rewarded.

It will be interesting, probably, to the reader to learn, that the *John Fillmore*, who was so conspicuous in the desperate enterprise here related, was the great-grandfather of MILLARD FILLMORE, President of the United States.

THE

BUCCANEERS OF AMERICA.

CHAPTER I.

The Introduction. — The Author * sets forth for the Western Islands, in the Service of the West India Company of France. — They meet with an English Frigate, and arrive at the Island of Tortuga.

As the Buccaneers in the West Indies have been so formidable and numerous that they have interrupted the trade of Europe into those parts, and our English merchants, in particular, have suffered more by their depredations than by the united force of France and Spain, in the late war, we do not doubt but the world will be curious to know the origin and progress of these desperadoes, who were the terror of the trading part of the world.

But before we enter upon their particular history, it will not be amiss, by way of introduction, to show, by some examples drawn from history, the great mischief and danger which threaten kingdoms and commonwealths from the increase of these sort of robbers; when, either by the troubles of particular times, or the neglect of governments, they are not crushed before they gather strength.

It has been the case heretofore, that when a single pirate has been suffered to range the seas, as not being worth the notice of a government, he has by degrees grown so powerful, as to put them to the expense of a great deal of blood and treasure, before he was suppressed. We shall not examine how it came to pass that our Buccaneers in the West Indies have continually increased till of late. This is an inquiry which belongs to the legislature.

I shall therefore speak of the pirates infesting the West In-

* Joseph Esquemeling, in company with Le Grand, Lolonois, Roche Brasilino, Bat, the Portuguese, &c.

dies, where they are more numerous than in any other part of the world, on several reasons.

First. Because there are so many uninhabited little islands and keys, with harbors convenient and secure for cleaning their vessels, and abounding with what they often want, provision: I mean water, sea-fowl, turtle, shell and other fish; where, if they carry in but strong liquor, they indulge a time, and become ready for new expeditions, before any intelligence can reach to hurt them.

It may here, perhaps, be no unnecessary digression to explain what they call keys in the West Indies. These are small sandy islands, appearing a little above the surface of the water, with only a few bushes or weeds upon them, but abound (those most at any distance from the main) with turtle, amphibious animals, that always choose the quietest and most unfrequented place for laying their eggs, which are to a vast number in the seasons, and would seldom be seen, but for this, (except by pirates.) Then vessels from Jamaica and the other governments make voyages, called turtling, for supplying the people; a common and approved food with them. I am apt to think these keys, especially those nigh islands, to have been once contiguous with them, and separated by earthquakes (frequently there) or inundations; because some of them that have been within continual view, as those nigh Jamaica, are observed within our time to be entirely wasted away and lost, and others daily wasting. They are not only of the use above taken notice of to pirates, but, it is commonly believed, were always, in buccaneering, piratical times, the hiding-places for their riches, and oftentimes a shelter for themselves, till their friends on the main had found means to obtain indemnity for their crimes; for you must understand, when acts of grace were more frequent, and the laws less severe, these men continually found favors and encouragers at Jamaica, and perhaps they are not all dead yet. I have been told many of them, still living, have been of the same trade, and left it off only because they can live as well honestly, and gain now at the hazard of others' necks.

Second. Another reason why these seas are chose by pirates is the great commerce thither by French, Spaniards, Dutch, and especially English ships. They are sure, in the latitude of these trading islands, to meet with prizes, booties of provision, clothing, and naval stores, and sometimes money; there being great sums remitted this way to England; (the returns of the Assiento, and private slave-trade to the Spanish West Indies;) and, in short, by some one or other, all the riches of Potosi.

A third reason is the inconvenience and difficulty of being pursued by the men-of-war; the many small inlets, lagoons, and harbors, on these solitary islands and keys, are a natural security.

It is generally here that the pirates begin their enterprises, setting out at first with a very small force; and, by infesting these seas, and those of the continent of North America, in a year's time, if they have good luck on their sides, they accumulate such strength as enables them to make foreign expeditions. The first is usually to Guinea, taking the Azores and Cape de Verd Islands in their way, and then to Brazil and the East Indies, where, if they meet with prosperous voyages, they set down at Madagascar, or the neighboring islands, and enjoy their ill-gotten wealth, among their elder brethren, with impunity. But that I may not give too much encouragement to the profession, I must inform my maritime readers that the far greater part of these rovers are cut short in the pursuit, by a sudden precipitation into the other world.

The rise of these rovers, since the peace of Utrecht, or, at least, the great increase of them, may justly be imputed to the Spanish settlements in the West Indies, the governors of which, being often some hungry courtiers, sent thither to repair or make a fortune, generally countenance all proceedings that bring in profit. They grant commissions to great numbers of vessels of war, on pretence of preventing an interloping trade, with orders to seize all ships or vessels whatsoever, within five leagues of their coasts, which our English ships cannot well avoid coming, in their voyage to Jamaica. But if the Spanish captains chance to exceed this commission, and rob and plunder at discretion, the sufferers are allowed to complain, and exhibit a process in their court, and, after great expense of suit, delay of time, and other inconveniences, obtain a decree in their favor; but then, when the ship and cargo come to be claimed, with costs of suit, they find, to their sorrow, that it has been previously condemned, and the plunder divided among the crew. The commander that made the capture, who alone is responsible, is found to be a poor, rascally fellow, not worth a groat, and, no doubt, is placed in that station for the like purposes.

The frequent losses sustained by our merchants abroad, by these pirates, was provocation enough to attempt something by way of reprisal; and a fair opportunity offering itself in the year 1716, the traders to the West Indies took care not to slip it over, but made the best use of it their circumstances would permit.

It was about two years before, that the Spanish galleons, or Plate fleet, had been cast away in the Gulf of Florida; and several vessels from the Havana were at work, with diving engines, to fish up the silver that was on board the galleons.

The Spaniards had recovered some millions of dollars, or pieces of eight, and had carried it all to the Havana; but they had at present about three hundred and fifty thousand pieces of eight, then, upon the spot, and were daily taking up more. In the mean time, two ships and three sloops, fitted out from Jamaica, Barbadoes, &c., under Captain Henry Jennings, sailed to the gulf, and found the Spaniards there upon the wreck; the money before spoken of was left on shore, deposited in a storehouse, under the government of two commissaries, and a guard of about sixty soldiers.

The rovers came directly upon the place, bringing their little fleet to an anchor, and, in a word, landing three hundred men, they attacked the guard, who immediately ran away; and thus they seized the treasure, which they carried off, making the best of their way to Jamaica.

In their way, they unhappily met with a Spanish ship, bound from Porto Bello to the Havana, with a great many rich goods, viz., bales of cochineal, casks of indigo, and sixty thousand pieces of eight more, which, their hands being in, they took, and having rifled the vessel, let her go.

They went away to Jamaica with their booty, and were followed in view of the port by the Spaniards, who, having seen them thither, went back to the governor of the Havana, with the account of it, who immediately sent a vessel to the governor of Jamaica, to complain of this robbery, and to reclaim the goods.

As it was in full peace, and contrary to all justice and right, that this fact was committed, they were soon made sensible that the government at Jamaica would not suffer them to go unpunished, much less protect them. Therefore they saw a necessity of shifting for themselves; so, to make bad worse, they went to sea again, though not without disposing of their cargo to good advantage, and furnishing themselves with ammunition, provisions, &c.; and being thus made desperate, they turned pirates, robbing not the Spaniards only, but their own countrymen, and any nation they could lay their hands on.

It happened about this time that the Spaniards, with three or four small men-of-war, fell upon our logwood-cutters in the Bay of Campeachy and Honduras; and after they had made them prizes, they gave the men belonging to them three sloops, to carry them home; but these men, being made desperate by their misfortunes, and meeting with the pirates, they took on with them, and so increased their number.

Not to detain the reader any longer with these particulars, I shall proceed to give an account of our voyage from Havre de Grace, in France, from whence we set sail in a ship called St. John, May 2, 1666. Our vessel was equipped with twenty-eight guns, twenty mariners, and two hundred and twenty passengers, including those whom the Company sent as free passengers. Soon after we came to an anchor under the Cape of Barfleur, there to join seven other ships of the same West India Company, which were to come from Diep, under convoy of a man-of-war, mounted with thirty-seven guns, and two hundred and fifty men. Of these ships, two were bound for Senegal, five for the Caribbee Islands, and ours for Tortuga. Here gathered to us about twenty sail of other ships, bound for Newfoundland, with some Dutch vessels going for Nantz, Rochelle, and St. Martin's, so that in all we made thirty sail. Here we put ourselves in a posture of defence, having notice that four English frigates, of sixty guns each, waited for us near Aldernay. Our admiral, the Chevalier Sourdis, having given necessary orders, we sailed thence with a favorable gale, and some mists arising, totally impeded the English frigates from discovering our fleet. We steered our course as near as we could to the coast of France, for fear of the enemy. As we sailed along, we met a vessel of Ostend, who complained to our admiral that a French privateer had robbed him that very morning; whereupon, we endeavored to pursue the said pirate; but our labor was in vain, not being able to overtake him.

Our fleet, as we sailed, caused no small fears and alarms to the inhabitants of the coasts of France, these judging us to be English, and that we sought some convenient place for landing. To allay their fright, we hung out our colors; but they would not trust us. After this, we came to an anchor in the Bay of Conquet, in Brittany, near Ushent, there to take in water. Having stored ourselves with fresh provisions here, we prosecuted our voyage, designing to pass by the Ras of Fontenau, and not expose ourselves to the Sorlingues, fearing the English that were cruising thereabouts. This River Ras is of a current very strong and rapid, which, rolling over many rocks, disgorges itself into the sea, on the coast of France, in 48° 10′ latitude; so that this passage is very dangerous, all the rocks, as yet, being not thoroughly known.

Here I shall mention the ceremony which, at this passage, and some other places, is used by the mariners, and by them called *baptism*, though it may seem little to our purpose. The master's mate clothed himself with a ridiculous sort of garment, that reached to his feet, and on his head he put a suitable cap, made very burlesque; in his right hand he had a naked wooden sword, and in his left a pot full of ink. His face was horribly blacked with soot, and his neck adorned with a collar, of many little pieces of wood. Thus apparelled, he commanded every one to be called who had never passed through that dangerous place before; and then causing them to kneel down, he made the sign of the cross on their foreheads with ink, and gave every one a stroke on the shoulders with his wooden sword. Meanwhile the bystanders cast a bucket of water upon each man's head, and so ended the ceremony. But that done, each of the baptized must give a bottle of brandy, placing it nigh the mainmast, without speaking a word — even those who have no such liquor not being excused. If the vessel never passed that way before, the captain is obliged to distribute some wine among the mariners and passengers; but, as for other gifts, which the newly-baptized frequently offer, they are divided among the old seamen, and of them they make a banquet among themselves.

The Hollanders, likewise, not only at this passage, but also at the rocks called Berlingues, nigh the coast of Portugal, in 39° 40′, (being a passage very dangerous, especially by night, when, in the dark, the rocks are not distinguishable, the land being very high,) they use some such ceremony, but their manner of baptizing is very different from that of the French; for he that is to be baptized is fastened, and hoisted up thrice at the main-yard's end, as if he were a criminal. If he be hoisted the fourth time, in the name of the Prince of Orange, or of the captain of the vessel, his honor is more than ordinary. Thus every one is dipped several times in the main ocean; but he that is dipped first has the honor of being saluted with a gun. Such as are not willing to fall must pay twelve pence for ransom; if he be an officer, two shillings; and if a passenger, at their own pleasure. If the ship never passed that way before, the captain is to give a small runlet of wine, which, if he denies, the mariners may cut off the stem of the vessel. All the profit accruing by this ceremony is kept by the master's mate, who, after reaching their port, usually lays it out in wine, which is drank amongst the ancient seamen. Some say this ceremony was instituted by the Emperor Charles V., though it is not amongst his laws. But here I leave these sea customs, and return to our voyage.

Having passed the Ras, we had very good weather, till we came to Cape Finisterre; here a sudden tempest surprised us, and separated our ship from the rest that were in our company. This storm continued eight days, in which time it would move compassion to see how miserably the passengers were tumbled to and fro, on all sides of the ship; insomuch, that the mariners, in the performance of their duty, were compelled to tread upon them. This boisterous weather being over, we had very favorable gales again, till we came to the tropic of Cancer. This tropic is an imaginary circle which astronomers have invented in the heavens, limiting the progress of the sun towards the north pole. It is placed in latitude 23° 30′. Here we were baptized a second time, as before. The French always perform this ceremony at the tropic of Cancer, as also under the tropic of Capricorn. In this part of the world we had very favorable weather, at which we were very glad, because of our great want of water; for that element was so scarce with us, that we were stinted to two half pints a man, every day.

About the latitude of Barbadoes, we met an English frigate, or privateer, who first began to give us chase; but finding herself not to exceed us in force, presently got away. Hereupon, we pursued her, firing several guns, eight pounders, at her; but at length she escaped, and we returned to our course. Soon after, we came within sight of Martinico. We were bent to the coast of the Isle of St. Peter, but were frustrated by a storm which took us hereabouts. Hence we resolved to steer to Guadalupe, yet we could not reach this island, by reason of the said storm; so that we directed our course to the Isle of Tortuga, being the very same land we were bound to. We passed along the coast of Punta Rica, which is extremely agreeable and delightful to the sight, being adorned with beautiful woods, even to the tops of the mountains. Then we discovered Hispaniola, (of which I shall give a description,) and we coasted about it till we came to Tortuga, our desired port. Here we anchored July 7, in the same year, not having lost one man in the voyage. We landed the goods that belonged to the West India Company, and, soon after, the ship was sent to Cal de Sac, with some passengers.

CHAPTER II.

A Description of Tortuga, and of the Fruits and Plants there. — How the French first settled there, at two several Times, and forced out the Spaniards. — The Author twice sold in the said Island.

The Island of Tortuga is situate on the north side of Hispaniola, in latitude 20° 30′. Its just extent is threescore leagues about. The Spaniards, who gave name to this island, called it so from the shape of the land, in some manner resembling a great sea-tortoise, called by them *Tortuga-de-mar*. The country is very mountainous, and full of rocks, and yet thick of lofty trees, that grow upon the hardest of those rocks, without partaking of a softer soil. Hence it comes that their roots, for the greatest part, are seen naked, entangled among the rocks like the branching of ivy against our walls. That part of this island which stretches to the north is totally uninhabited. The reason is, first, because it is incommodious and unhealthy; and, secondly, for the ruggedness of the coast, that gives no access to the shore, unless among rocks almost inaccessible. For this cause, it is peopled only on the south part, which has only one port, indifferently good. Yet this harbor has two entries, or channels, which afford passage to ships of seventy guns, the port itself being without danger, and capable of receiving a great number of vessels. The inhabited parts, of which the first is called the Lowlands, or Low Country; this is the chief among the rest, because it contains the port aforesaid. The town is called Cayona, and here live the chiefest and richest planters of the island. The second part is called the Middle Plantation; its soil is yet almost new, being only known to be good for tobacco. The third is named Ringot, and is situate towards the west part of the island. The fourth, and last, is called the Mountain, in which place were made the first plantations upon this island.

As to the wood that grows here, we have already said that the trees are exceedingly tall, and pleasing to the sight, whence no man will doubt but they may be applied to several uses. Such is the yellow saunder, which by the inhabitants is called *bois de chandel*, or, in English, candle-wood, because it burns like a candle, and serves them with light while they fish by night. Here grows, also, *Lignum Sanctum*, or Guaiacum. Its virtues are very well known, more especially to those who observe not the seventh commandment, and are given to impure copulations! — physicians drawing hence, in several compositions, the greatest antidote for venereal diseases, as also for cold and viscous humors. The trees, likewise, which afford *gummi elemi*, grow here in great abundance, as doth *radix Chinæ*, or China root. Yet this is not so good as that of other parts of the western world. It is very white and soft, and serves for pleasant food to the wild boars, when they can find nothing else. This island, also, is not deficient in aloes, nor an infinite number of the other medicinal herbs, which may please the curiosity of such as are given to their contemplation. Moreover, for building of ships, or any other sort of architecture, here are found several sorts of timber. The fruits, likewise, which grow here abundantly, are nothing inferior, in quantity or quality, to what other islands produce. I shall name only some of the most ordinary and common. Such are magniot, potatoes, abajou apples, yannas, bacones, paquays, carosoles, mamayns, annananes, and divers other sorts, which I omit to specify. Here grow, likewise, in great numbers, those trees called palmettoes or palmites, whence is drawn a certain juice, which serves the inhabitants instead of wine, and whose leaves cover their houses, instead of tiles.

In this island aboundeth, also, the wild boar. The governor hath prohibited the hunting of them with dogs, fearing lest, the island being but small, the whole race of them, in a short time, should be destroyed. The reason why he thought convenient to preserve these wild beasts, was, that, in case of any invasion, the inhabitants might sustain themselves with their food, especially were they once constrained to retire to the woods and mountains. Yet this sort of game is almost impeded by itself, by reason of the many rocks and precipices, which, for the greatest part, are covered with little shrubs, very green and thick, whence the huntsmen have oftentimes fallen, and left us the sad remembrance of many a memorable disaster.

At a certain time of the year there resort to Tortuga large flocks of wild pigeons, and then the inhabitants feed on them very plentifully, having more than they can consume, and leaving totally to their repose all other sorts of fowl, both wild and tame; that so, in the absence of the pigeons, these may supply their place. But as nothing in the universe, though never so pleasant, can be found, but what hath something of bitterness with it, the very symbol of this truth we see in the aforesaid pigeons; for these, the season being past, can scarce be touched with the tongue, they become so extremely lean, and bitter, even to admiration. The reason of this bitterness is attributed to a certain seed, which they eat about that time, even as bitter as gall. About the sea-shores, every where, are found great multitudes of crabs, both of land and sea, and both sorts very big. These are good to feed servants and slaves, whose palates they please, but are very hurtful to the sight; besides, being eaten too often, they cause great giddiness in the head, with much weakness of the brain, so that, very frequently, they are deprived of sight for a quarter of an hour.

The French, having settled in the Isle of St. Christopher, planted there a sort of trees, of which, at present, there possibly may be greater quantities, with the timber whereof they made longboats and hoys, which they sent thence westward, well manned and victualled, to discover other islands. These, setting sail from St. Christopher, came within sight of Hispaniola, where they arrived with abundance of joy. Having landed, they marched into the country, where they found large quantities of cattle, such as cows, bulls, horses, and wild boars; but finding no great profit in these animals, unless they could enclose them, and knowing, likewise, the island to be pretty well peopled by the Spaniards, they thought it convenient to enter upon and seize the Island of Tortuga. This they performed without any difficulty, there being upon the island no more than ten or twelve Spaniards to guard it. These few men let the French come in peaceably, and possess the island for six months, without any trouble. Meanwhile, they passed and repassed, with their canoes, to Hispaniola, from whence they transported many people, and at last began to plant the whole Island of Tortuga. The few Spaniards remaining there, perceiving the French to increase their number daily, began at last to repine at their prosperity, and grudge them the possession. Hence they gave notice to others of their nation, their neighbors, who sent several boats, well armed and manned, to dispossess the French. This expedition succeeded according to their desires; for the new possessors, seeing the great number of Spaniards, fled, with all they had, to the woods, and hence, by night, they wafted over with canoes to the Island of Hispaniola. This they the more easily performed, having no women or children with them, nor any great substance to carry away. Here they also retire into the woods, both to seek for food, and from thence, with secrecy, to give intelligence to others of their own faction; judging for certain, that within a little while they should be in a capacity to hinder the Spaniards from fortifying in Tortuga.

Meanwhile, the Spaniards of the great island ceased not to seek after their new guests, the French, with intent to root them out of the woods, if possible, or cause them to perish with hunger; but this design soon failed, having found that the French were masters both of good guns, powder, and bullets. Here, therefore, the fugitives waited for a certain opportunity, wherein they knew the Spaniards were to come from Tortuga, with arms and a great number of men, to join with those of the greater island, for their destruction. When this occasion offered, they, in the mean while deserting the woods where they were, returned to Tortuga, and dispossessed the small number of Spaniards that remained at home. Having so done, they fortified themselves the best they could, thereby to prevent the return of the Spaniards, in case they should attempt it. Moreover, they sent immediately to the governor of St. Christopher's, craving his aid and relief, and demanding of him a governor, the better to be united among themselves, and strengthened on all occasions. The governor of St. Christopher's received their petition with much satisfaction, and, without delay, sent Monsieur Le Passeur to them, in quality of a governor, together with a ship full of men, and all necessaries for their establishment and defence. No sooner had they received this recruit, but the governor commanded a fortress to be built upon the top of a high rock, from whence he could hinder the entrance of any ships, or other vessels, to the port. To this fort no other access could be had, than by almost climbing through a very narrow passage, that was capable only of receiving two persons at once, and those not without difficulty. In the middle of this rock was a great cavity, which now serves for a storehouse. Besides, here was great convenience for raising a battery. The fort being finished, the governor commanded two guns to be mounted, which could not be done without great toil and labor; as, also, a house to be built within the fort; and afterwards the narrow way, that led to the said fort, to be broken and demolished, leaving no other ascent thereto than by a ladder. Within the fort gushes out a plentiful fountain of pure fresh water, sufficient to refresh a garrison of a thousand men. Being possessed of these conveniences, and the security these things might promise, the French began to people the island, and each of them to seek their living, some by hunting, others by planting tobacco, and others by cruising, and robbing upon the coasts of the Spanish islands, which trade is continued by them to this day.

The Spaniards, notwithstanding, could not behold, but with jealous eyes, the daily increase of the French in Tortuga, fearing lest, in time, they might by them be dispossessed also of Hispaniola. Thus taking an opportunity, (when many of the

French were abroad at sea, and others employed in hunting,) with eight hundred men, in several canoes, they landed again in Tortuga, almost without being perceived by the French; but finding that the governor had cut down many trees, for the better discovery of any enemy, in case of an assault, as also that nothing of consequence could be done without great guns, they consulted about the fittest place for raising a battery. This place was soon concluded to be the top of a mountain which was in sight, seeing that from thence alone they could level their guns at the fort, which now lay open to them since the cutting down of the trees by the new possessors. Hence they resolved to open a way for the carriage of some pieces of ordnance to the top. This mountain is somewhat high, and the upper part thereof plain, from whence the whole island may be viewed. The sides thereof are very rugged, by reason a great number of inaccessible rocks do surround it; so that the ascent was very difficult, and would always have been the same, had not the Spaniards undergone the immense labor and toil of making the way before mentioned, as I shall now relate.

The Spaniards had with them many slaves and Indians, laboring men, whom they call *matades*, or, in English, half-yellow men. These they ordered with iron tools to dig a way through the rocks. This they performed with the greatest speed imaginable, and through this way, by the help of many ropes and pullies, they at last made shift to get up two pieces of ordnance, wherewith they made a battery next day, to play on the fort. Meanwhile the French, knowing these designs, prepared for a defence, (while the Spaniards were busy about the battery,) sending notice every where to their companions, for help. Thus the hunters of the island all joined together, and with them all the pirates, who were not already too far from home. These landed by night at Tortuga, lest they should be seen by the Spaniards; and under the same obscurity of the night, they all together, by a back way, climbed the mountain where the Spaniards were posted, which they did the more easily, being acquainted with these rocks. They came up at the very instant that the Spaniards, who were above, were preparing to shoot at the fort, not knowing in the least of their coming. Here they set upon them at their backs, with such fury, as forced the greatest part to precipitate themselves from the top to the bottom, and dash their bodies in pieces. Few or none escaped; for if any remained alive, they were put to the sword. Some Spaniards did still keep the bottom of the mountain; but these, hearing the shrieks and cries of them that were killed, and believing some tragical revolution to be above, fled immediately towards the sea, despairing ever to regain the Island of Tortuga.

The governors of this island behaved themselves as proprietors, and absolute lords thereof, till 1664, when the West India Company of France took possession thereof, and sent thither, for their governor, Monsieur Ogeron. These planted the colony for themselves by their factors and servants, thinking to drive some considerable trade from thence with the Spaniards, even as the Hollânders do from Curasao. But this design did not answer; for with other nations they could drive no trade, by reason they could not establish any secure commerce, from the beginning, with their own; forasmuch as, at the first institution of this company in France, they agreed with the pirates, hunters, and planters, first possessors of Tortuga, that these should buy all their necessaries from the said company upon trust. And though this agreement was put in execution, yet the factors of the company soon after found that they could not recover either moneys or returns from those people, that they were constrained to bring some armed men into the island, in behalf of the company, to get in some of their payments. But neither this endeavor, nor any other, could prevail towards the settling a second trade with those of the island. Hereupon the company recalled their factors, giving them orders to sell all that was their own, in the said plantation, both the servants belonging to the company, (which were sold, some for twenty, others for thirty pieces of eight,) as also all other merchandises and properties. And thus all their designs fell to the ground.

On this occasion I was also sold, being a servant under the said company, in whose service I left France. But my fortune was very bad, for I fell into the hands of the most cruel and perfidious man that ever was born, who was then governor, or rather lieutenant-general, of that island. This man treated me with all the hard usage imaginable, yea, with that of hunger, with which I thought I should have perished inevitably. Withal, he was willing to let me buy my freedom and liberty, but not under the rate of three hundred pieces of eight, I not being master of one at a time in the world. At last, through the manifold miseries I endured, as also affliction of mind, I was thrown into a dangerous sickness. This misfortune, added to the rest, was the cause of my happiness; for my wicked master, seeing my condition, began to fear lest he should lose his moneys with my life. Hereupon he sold me a second time to a surgeon, for seventy pieces of eight. Being with this second master, I began soon to recover my health, through the good usage I received, he being much more humane and civil than my first patron. He gave me both clothes and very good food, and after I had served him but one year, he offered me my liberty, with only this condition, that I should pay him one hundred pieces of eight, when I was in a capacity so to do, which kind proposal of his I could not but accept with infinite joy and gratitude.

Being now at liberty, though like Adam when he was first created, that is, naked and destitute of all human necessaries, not knowing how to get my living, I determined to enter into the order of the pirates or robbers at sea. Into this society I was received with common consent, both of the superior and vulgar sort, where I continued till 1672. Having assisted them in all their designs and attempts, and served them in many notable exploits, of which, hereafter, I shall give the reader a true account, I returned to my own native country. But before I begin my relation, I shall say something of the Island of Hispaniola, which lies towards the western part of America, as also give my reader a brief description thereof, according to my slender ability and experience.

CHAPTER III.

A Description of Hispaniola.

The large and rich island called Hispaniola is situate from latitude 17° to 19°; the circumference is three hundred leagues; the extent from east to west, one hundred and twenty; its breadth almost fifty, being broader or narrower at certain places. This island was first discovered by Christopher Columbus, A. D. 1492, he being sent for this purpose by Ferdinand, king of Spain, from which time to this present the Spaniards have been continually possessors thereof. There are upon this island very good and strong cities, towns, and hamlets, as well as a great number of pleasant country-houses and plantations, the effects of the care and industry of the Spaniards, its inhabitants.

The chief city and metropolis hereof is Santo Domingo, being dedicated to St. Dominick, from whom it derives its name. It is situate towards the south, and affords a most excellent prospect, the country round about being embellished with innumerable rich plantations, as also verdant meadows and fruitful gardens, all which produce plenty and variety of excellent, pleasant fruits, according to the nature of those countries. The governor of the island resides in this city, which is, as it were, the storehouse of all the cities, towns, and villages, which hence export and provide themselves with all necessaries for human life; and yet hath it this particularity above many other cities, that it entertains no commerce with any nation but its own, the Spaniards. The greatest part of the inhabitants are rich and substantial merchants or shopkeepers.

Another city of this island is San Jago, or St. James, being consecrated to that apostle. This is an open place, without walls or castle, situate in latitude 19°. The inhabitants are generally hunters and planters, the adjacent territory and soil being very proper for the said exercises. The city is surrounded with large and delicious fields, as much pleasing to the view as those of Santo Domingo; and these abound with beasts, both wild and tame, yielding vast numbers of skins and hides, very profitable to the owners.

In the south part of this island is another city, called *Nuestra Sennora de Alta Gracia.* This territory produces great quantities of cocoa, whereof the inhabitants make great store of the richest chocolate. Here grow, also, ginger and tobacco, and much tallow is made of the beasts which are hereabouts hunted.

The inhabitants of this beautiful Island of Hispaniola often resort in their canoes to the Isle of Savona, not far distant, where is their chief fishery, especially of tortoises. Hither those fish constantly resort in great multitudes, at certain seasons, there to lay their eggs, burying them in the sands of the shoal, where, by the heat of the sun, which in those parts is very ardent, they are hatched. This Island of Savona has little or nothing that is worthy consideration, being so very barren by reason of its sandy soil. True it is, that here grows some small quantity of *Lignum Sanctum*, or guaiacum, of whose use we say something in another place.

Westward of Santo Domingo is another great village, called *El Pueblo de Aso*, or the town of Aso. The inhabitants thereof drive great traffic with those of another village, in the very middle of the island, and is called *San Juan de Goave*, or St. John of Goave. This is environed with a magnificent prospect of gardens, woods, and meadows. Its territory extends above twenty leagues in length, and grazes a great number of wild bulls and cows. In this village scarce dwell any other than hunters and butchers, who flay the beasts that are killed. These are for the most part a mongrel sort of people, some of which are born of white European people and negroes, and called mulattoes; others of Indians and white people, and termed mesticoes. But others come of negroes and Indians, and are called alcatraces. Besides which sorts of people, there are several other species and races, both here and in other places of the West Indies, of whom this account may be given: that the Spaniards love better the negro women in those western parts, or the tawny Indian females, than their own white European race; when as, peradventure, the negroes and Indians have greater inclinations to the white women or those that come near them, the tawny, than their own. From the said village are exported yearly vast quantities of tallow and hides, they exercising no other traffic. For as to the lands in this place, they are not cultivated, by reason of the excessive dryness of the soil. These are the chiefest places that the Spaniards possess in this island, from the Cape of Lobos towards St. John de Goave, unto the Cape of Samana, nigh the sea, on the north side, and from the eastern part towards the sea, called *Punta de Espada.* All the rest of the island is possessed by the French, who are also planters and hunters.

This island hath very good ports for ships from the Cape of Lobos to the Cape of Tiburon, on the west side thereof. In this space there are no less than four ports, exceeding in goodness, largeness, and security, even the very best of England. Besides these, from the Cape of Tiburon to the Cape of Donna Maria, there are two very excellent ports, and from this cape to the Cape of St. Nicholas there are no less than twelve others. Every one of these ports hath also the confluence of two or three good rivers, in which are great plenty of several sorts of fish, very pleasing to the palate. The country hereabouts is well watered with large and deep rivers and brooks, so that this part of the land may easily be cultivated without any great fear of droughts, because of these excellent streams. The sea coasts and shores are also very pleasant, to which the tortoises resort in large numbers, to lay their eggs.

This island was formerly very well peopled on the north side, with many towns and villages; but these, being ruined by the Hollanders, were at last, for the greatest part, deserted by the Spaniards.

CHAPTER IV.

Of the Fruits, Trees, and Animals of Hispaniola.

THE spacious fields of this island commonly are five or six leagues in length, the beauty whereof is so pleasing to the eye, that, together with the great variety of their natural productions, they captivate the senses of the beholder. For here, at once, they not only, with diversity of objects, recreate the sight, but with many of the same do also please the smell, and with most contribute delights to the taste; also they flatter and excite the appetite, especially with the multitudes of oranges and lemons here growing, both sweet and sour, and those that participate of both tastes, and are only pleasantly tartish. Besides, here abundantly grow several sorts of fruit; such are citrons, toronjas, and limas, in English not improperly called crab-lemons. True it is, that the lemons exceed not here the bigness of a hen's egg, which smallness distinguishes them from those of Spain, most frequently used in these our northern countries. The date-trees, which here cover very spacious plains, are exceeding tall, which, notwithstanding, doth not offend, but delight the view. Their height is from one hundred and fifty to two hundred feet, being destitute of branches to the very tops. Within it is a certain pleasant white substance, like that of white cabbage, whence the branches and leaves sprout, in which the seeds or dates are contained. Every month one of those branches falls, and at the same time another sprouts out; but the seed ripens not but once a year. The dates are food extremely coveted by the hedgehogs. The white substance at the top of the tree is used by the Spaniards as cabbage, in Europe, they cutting it in slices, and boiling it in their ollas, with all sorts of meat. The leaves of this date tree are seven or eight feet long, and three or four broad, being very fit to cover houses, for they defend from rain equally with the best tiles, though never so rudely huddled together. They use them, also, to wrap up smoked flesh, and to make buckets to carry water in, though not durable for above six, seven, or eight days. These cabbages, for so we shall call them, are greenish on the outside, though inwardly very white, whence may be separated a rind, very like to parchment, being fit to write on, as we do on paper. The bodies of these trees are of a huge thickness, which two men can hardly compass with their arms; and yet they cannot properly be termed woody, but only three or four inches deep in thickness, all the rest of the internal part being very soft ; so that, paring off those three or four inches of woody substance, the remaining part may be sliced like new cheese. They wound them three or four feet above the root, and, making an incision in the body, from thence gently distils a liquor, which, in a short time fermenting, becomes as strong as the richest wine, and which easily inebriates, if not used with moderation. The French call these palm-trees Frank-palms, and they only grow here, or elsewhere in saltish grounds.

Besides these palm-trees which we have mentioned, there are in Hispaniola four other species of palms, distinguished by the names of *latanier*, *palma espinosa*, or prickle palm, *palma a chapelet*, or rosary palm. The *latanier* palm is not so tall as the wine palm, but almost of the same shape, only the leaves are like the fans our women use. They grow mostly in gravelly and sandy ground, their circumference being of seven feet, more or less. The body hath many prickles or thorns, half a foot long, very sharp and pungent. It produces its seed, like as that above mentioned, which serves for food to the wild beasts.

The prickle palm, so called because it is infinitely full of prickles, from the root to the very leaves, much more than the precedent. With these prickles, the barbarous Indians use to torment the prisoners they take in battle. They tie them to a tree, then taking these thorns, they put them into little pellets of cotton, dipped in oil, and stick them into the sides of the miserable prisoners, as thick as the bristles of a hedgehog, which cause an incredible torment to the patient. Then they set them on fire, and if the tormented prisoner sing in the midst of his torments, he is esteemed a courageous soldier, who neither fears his enemies nor their torments ; but if, on the contrary, he cries out, they esteem him a coward, and unworthy of any memory. This custom was told me by an Indian, who said he had used his enemies thus oftentimes. The like cruelties to these many Christians have seen, while they lived among those barbarians. But returning to the prickle palm, I shall only tell you that this palm-tree in this only differs from the *latanier*, that the leaves are like those of the Frank-palm ; its seed is like that of the other palm-trees, being only much bigger and rounder, and full of little kernels, as pleasing to the taste as our walnuts in Europe. This tree grows for the most part in the marshes and low grounds of the sea-coast.

The wine palm is so called from the abundance of wine

gathered from it. This palm grows in high and rocky mountains, not exceeding the height of forty or fifty feet, but yet of an extraordinary shape or form. For from the root up half way, it is only three or four inches thick; but upwards, something above two thirds of its height, it is as big and as thick as an ordinary bucket or milk-pail; within it is full of a certain matter, very much like the tender stalk of a white cabbage, which is very juicy, of a liquor very pleasing to the palate. This liquor, after fermentation and settling of the grounds, becomes very good and clear wine, without any great pains; for, having wounded the tree with a hatchet, they make a square incision or orifice in it, through which they bruise the said matter till it may be squeezed out, or expressed with the hands, they needing no other instrument. With the leaves they make vessels, not only to settle and purify the said liquor, but also to drink it. It bears its fruit like to other palms, but very small, being like cherries. The taste is very good, but dangerous to the throat, causing extreme pains, which produce malignant quinsies.

The *palm a chapelet*, or rosary palm, so called by the French and Spaniards, because its seed is very fit to make rosaries or beads to say prayers upon, they being small, hard, and easily bored. This fourth species grows on the tops of the highest mountains, and is of an excessive tallness, very straight, and hath very few leaves.

Here grows, also, a certain sort of apricot-trees, whose fruit equals in bigness that of our ordinary melons. The color is like ashes, and the taste the very same with that of ours in Europe; the stones of this fruit being as big as a hen's egg. On these the wild boars feed very deliciously, and fatten to admiration.

The trees called caremites are very like to our pear-trees, whose fruits resemble our Damascene plums, or prunes of Europe, being of a very pleasant and agreeable taste. This fruit is black on the inside, and the kernels thereof sometimes only two, sometimes three or four, as big as a lupine. This plum affords no less pleasant food to the wild boars than the apricots above mentioned, only it is not so commonly found, nor in such quantities.

The genipa-trees are all over this island, being like our cherry-trees, though the branches are more dilated. The fruit thereof is ash-colored, as big as two fists, which is full of many prickles or points, involved under a thin membrane or skin, which, if not taken away at the time of eating, causes great obstructions and gripings of the belly. Before this fruit grows ripe, if pressed, it affords a juice as black as ink, being fit to write withal, but the letters disappear within nine days, the paper remaining as white as if it never had been written on. The wood of this tree is very strong, solid, and hard, good to build ships, seeing it lasts many years in the water without putrefaction.

Besides these, divers other sorts of trees are natives of this island, producing very excellent and pleasant fruits. Of these I shall omit to name several, knowing there are learned authors who have described and searched them with greater attention and curiosity; but I shall mention some few more, in particular. Such are the cedars, which this part of the world produces in prodigious quantities. The French call them *acajou*, and they find them useful for building ships and canoes. These canoes are like little wherry boats, being made of only one tree, hollowed, and fitted for the sea. They are so swift, that they may be well called Neptune's post-horses. The Indians make these canoes without any iron instruments, by only burning the trees nigh the root, and then so governing the fire, as nothing is burnt more than what they would have. Some have hatchets of flint, with which they scrape or pare off whatsoever is burnt too far; and thus, by fire only, they give them that shape which renders them capable of navigating sixty or eighty leagues, with ordinary security.

As to medicinal productions, here is to be found the tree that affords the gum elemi, used in our apothecary shops, likewise guaiacum or lignum sanctum, lignum aloes, aloe wood, cassia lignea, China roots, with several others. The tree mapou, besides that it is medicinal, is also used for making canoes, being very thick; yet it is much inferior to the acajou, or cedar, being somewhat spongy, sucking in much water, which renders it dangerous in navigation. The tree called acoma hath its wood very hard and heavy, and of the color of palm, which renders it very fit to make oars for the sugar mills. Here are, also, in great quantities, brasilete, or brasil wood, and that which the Spaniards call manchanilla.

Brasil wood is now very well known in Holland and the Low Countries. It is called, also, by the Spaniards, *lenna de peje palo.* It serves only, or chiefly, for the trade of dyers. It grows abundantly along the sea-coasts, especially in two places, called Jacmel and Jaquina. These are two commodious ports, or bays, capable of receiving ships of the greatest bulk.

The tree called manchanilla, or dwarf apple-tree, grows near the sea-shore, being naturally so low that its branches, though never so short, always touch the water. It bears a fruit somewhat like a sweet-scented apple, which yet is of a very venomous quality; for these apples being eaten by any person, he instantly changes color, and such a thirst seizes him as all the water of the Thames cannot quench, he dying, raving mad, within a little while. But what is more strange, the fish that eat, as it often happens, of this fruit, are also poisonous. This tree affords a liquor, thick and white, like the fig-tree, which, if touched by the hand, raises blisters, and these are as red as if it had been scalded. One day, being hugely tormented with mosquitoes or gnats, and being as yet unacquainted with the nature of this tree, I cut a branch, to serve me for a fan; but all my face was swelled the next day, and filled with blisters, as if it were burnt, to such a degree that I was blind for three days.

Yaco is another sort of tree, so called by the Spaniards, growing by the river sides. This bears a fruit like our bullace, or damson plums, which, when ripe, is extremely coveted by the wild boars, with which they fatten as much as our hogs do with the sweetest acorns of Spain. These trees love a sandy ground, yet are so low, that their branches being very large, they take up a great circumference, almost couching on the ground. The trees named abelcoses bear fruit of like color with the yacos above mentioned, of the bigness of melons, the seeds, or kernels, being as big as eggs. The substance of this fruit is yellow, and of a pleasant taste, which the poorest among the French eat instead of bread, the wild boars not caring at all for it. These trees grow very tall and thick, being somewhat like our largest pear-trees.

As to the insects of this island, I shall only remark three sorts of flies, which excessively torment all human bodies, but especially such as were never or but little acquainted with these countries. The first sort are as big as our common horse flies in Europe, and these, darting themselves upon men's bodies, there stick, and suck their blood till they can fly no longer. Their importunity obliges to make almost continual use of branches of trees to fan them away. The Spaniards in those parts call them musquitoes, or gnats, but the French call them maranguines. The second sort is no bigger than a grain of sand; these make no buzzing noise, as the preceding species do, so are less avoidable, being able also, through their smallness, to penetrate the finest linen, or cloth. The hunters are forced to anoint their faces with hog's grease, to defend themselves from their stings. By night, in their huts or cottages, they constantly burn the leaves of tobacco, without which smoke they could not rest. True it is, in the day-time they are not very troublesome, in case any wind be stirring, for this, though never so little, dissipates them. The gnats of the third species exceed not the bigness of a grain of mustard; their color is red. These sting not at all, but bite so sharply as to create little ulcers, whence it often happens that the face swells, and is rendered frightful to the view. These are chiefly troublesome by day, even from morning till sunset, after which they take their rest, and permit human bodies to do so. The Spaniards call these rojados, and the French, calarodes.

The insects which the Spaniards call cochinillas, and the English, glow-worms, are also to be found here. These are very much like those of Europe, but somewhat bigger, and longer. They have two little specks on their heads, which by night give so much light, that three or four of them together, upon a tree, seem at a distance like a bright, shining fire. I had once three of these cochinillas in my cottage, which continued there till past midnight, shining so brightly, that, without any other light, I could easily read in any book, of never so small a print. I attempted to bring some of them to Europe, but as soon as they came into a colder climate, they died. They lost, also, their shining, upon the change of air, before their deaths. This shining is so great that the Spaniards, with great reason, call them *moscas de fuego*, that is, fire-flies.

There are, also, in Hispaniola, a great number of grillones, or crickets. These are of an extraordinary magnitude, if compared to ours, and so noisy that they are ready to burst themselves with singing, if any person comes near them. Here is not a less number of reptiles, as serpents, &c., but by a particular providence of the Creator, these have no poison, neither do they any other harm than catch fowls, but more especially pullets, pigeons, and the like. Oftentimes these serpents or snakes are useful in houses, to clear them of rats and mice; for with great cunning they counterfeit their shrieks, and hereby deceive and catch them at their pleasure. Having taken them, they only suck their blood at first; then, throwing away the guts, they swallow almost entire the rest of the body, which they readily digest into soft excrements. Another sort of reptiles of this island is called *cazadores de moscas*, or fly-catchers. This name was given to this reptile by the Spaniards, by reason they never could experiment that it lived upon any other food than flies. Hence it cannot be said that this creature causes any harm to the inhabitants, but rather benefit, seeing it consumes the vexatious and troublesome flies.

Here are, also, many land tortoises. These breed mostly in mud, and fields overflowed with water. The inhabitants eat them, as very good food. But here are a sort of very hideous spiders; these are as big as an ordinary egg, and their feet as long as those of the biggest sea-crabs. They are very hairy withal, and have four black teeth, like a rabbit's both in bigness and shape; but their bitings are not venomous, though they can bite very sharp, and do very commonly. They breed mostly in the roofs of houses. In this island, also, is the insect called, in Latin, *millepes*, and in Greek, *scolopendria*, or many feet, and likewise scorpions. Yet, by the providence of Nature, neither the one nor the other are poisonous; for though they often bite, yet the wounds require not any medicament for their cure; and though their bitings cause some inflammation and swelling at first, yet these symptoms disappear of their own accord. Thus in Hispaniola no venomous animal is found.

After the insects, I shall say something of that terrible beast called cayman. This is a species of the crocodile, wherewith this island abounds. Among these caymans, some are found to be very large and horrible to the sight. Some have been seen no less than seventy feet long, and twelve broad. Yet more marvellous than their bulk is their cunning and subtilty. Being hungry, they place themselves nigh the sides of rivers, especially at the fords where cattle come to drink, or wade over. Here they lie without any motion, resembling an old tree fallen into the river, floating upon the waters. Yet they go not far from the banks, but continually lurch in the same place, till some wild boar or cow come to drink or refresh themselves; and then, with great activity, they seize on them with no less fierceness, and, dragging the prey into the water, stifle it. But what is more admirable, is, that three or four days before the caymans go upon this design, they eat nothing at all, but, diving into the river, they swallow a hundred weight or two of stones; with these they render themselves heavier than before, and add to their natural strength, (which is very great,) thereby to make their assault the more terrible and secure. The prey thus stifled, they let it lie four or five days under the water, untouched, for they cannot eat the least bit unless it is half rotten; but when it is so much putrified as is most pleasing to their palates, they devour it with great appetite and voracity. If they can light on any hides of beasts, placed by the inhabitants in the fields for drying, they drag them into the water, leaving them for some days, well loaded with stones, till the hair falls off; then they eat them with no less appetite than they would the animals themselves. I have seen myself, many times, like things to these I write; but beside my own experience, many writers of natural things have made entire treatises of these animals, describing their shape, magnitude, voracity, and other qualities. A certain person, of good credit, told me that one day he was by a river-side, washing his baraca, or tent. As soon as he began his work, a cayman fastened upon the tent, and dragged it under water. The man, desirous to save his tent, pulled, on the contrary, with all his strength, having in his mouth a butcher's knife, (with which, as it happened, he was scraping the canvas,) to defend himself, in case of necessity. The cayman, angry at this, vaulted upon him out of the river, and drew him with great celerity into the water, endeavoring with his weight to stifle him. He, finding himself in the greatest extremity, almost crushed to death by that huge animal, with his knife he gave the cayman several wounds in the belly, with which he suddenly expired. Being thus delivered from danger, he drew the cayman out of the water, and opened the body, to satisfy his curiosity. In his stomach he found near a hundred weight of stones, each stone being almost as big as his fist.

The caymans are ordinarily busied in catching flies, which they eagerly devour. The occasion is, because close to their skin they have little scales, which have a sweet scent, somewhat like musk. This aromatic odor the flies love, and here they come to repose themselves, and sting. Thus they both persecute each other continually, with an incredible hatred and antipathy. Their manner of procreating and hatching their young is thus: they approach the sandy banks of some river exposed to the south sun; among these sands they lay their eggs, which afterwards they cover with their feet; and here they find a young generation, hatched only by the heat of the sun. These, as soon as they are out of the shell, by natural instinct run to the water. Many times these eggs are destroyed by birds, that find them as they scrape among the sands. Hereupon the female caymans, when they fear the coming of any flocks of birds, oftentimes, by night, swallow these their eggs, and keep them in their stomachs till the danger is over, and then they bury them again, and, as I have told you, bring them forth again out of their bellies, till the season is come of their being hatched; then, if the mother be nigh, they run to her, and play with her, as little whelps do with their dams. In this sort of sport, they will often run in and out of their mother's belly, even as rabbits into their holes. I myself have often spied them thus at play with their dams, over the water, upon the contrary banks of some river, and have disturbed their sport by throwing a stone that way, causing them on a sudden to creep into the mother's bowels for fear. The manner of procreating of these animals is always such as I have related, and at the same time of the year; for they meddle not with one another but in May. They call them in this country *crocodiles*, though in other places of the West Indies they go under the name of *caymans*.

CHAPTER V.

Of all the Sorts of Quadrupeds and Birds of this Island: as also a Relation of the French Buccaneers.

Beside the fruits which this island produces, whose plenty, as is said, surpasses all the islands of America, it abounds also with all sorts of quadrupeds, as horses, bulls, cows, wild boars, and others, very useful to mankind, not only for food, but for cultivating the ground, and the management of commerce.

Here are vast numbers of wild dogs; these destroy yearly many cattle; for no sooner hath a cow calved, or a mare foaled, but these wild mastiffs devour the young, if they find not resistance from keepers and domestic dogs. They run up and down the woods and fields, commonly fifty, threescore, or more, together; being withal so fierce, that they will often assault an entire herd of wild boars, not ceasing to worry them till they have fetched down two or three. One day a French Buccaneer showed me a strange action of this kind: being in the fields a hunting together, we heard a great noise of dogs, which had surrounded a wild boar. Having tame dogs with us, we left them to the custody of our servants, being desirous to see the sport. Hence my companion and I climbed up two several trees, both for security and prospect. The wild boar, all alone, stood against a tree, defending himself with his tusks from a great number of dogs that enclosed him; killed with his teeth, and wounded several of them. This bloody fight continued about an hour, the wild boar, meanwhile, attempting many times to escape. At last flying, one dog leaping upon his back, fastened on his testicles, which at one pull he tore in pieces. The rest of the dogs, perceiving the courage of their companion, fastened likewise on the boar, and presently killed him. This done, all of them, the first only excepted, laid themselves down upon the ground about the prey, and there peaceably continued, till he, the first and most courageous of the troop, had eat as much as he could. When this dog had left off, all the rest fell in to take their share, till nothing was left. What ought we to infer from this notable action, performed by wild animals, but this: that even beasts themselves are not destitute of knowledge, and that they give us documents how to honor such as have deserved well; even since these irrational animals did reverence and respect him that exposed his life to the greatest danger against the common enemy?

The governor of Tortuga, Monsieur Ogeron, finding that the wild dogs killed so many of the wild boars, that the hunters of that island had much ado to find any, fearing lest that common sustenance of the island should fail, sent for a great quantity of poison from France to destroy the wild mastiffs. This was done A. D. 1668, by commanding horses to be killed and empoisoned, and laid open at certain places where the wild dogs used to resort. This being continued for six months, there were killed an incredible number; and yet all this could not exterminate and destroy the race, or scarce diminish them; their number appearing almost as large as before. These wild dogs are easily tamed among men, even as tame as ordinary house dogs. The hunters of those parts, whenever they find a wild bitch with whelps, commonly take away the puppies, and bring them home; which being grown up, they hunt much better than other dogs.

But here the curious reader may perhaps inquire how so many wild dogs came here. The occasion was, the Spaniards having possessed these isles, found them peopled with Indians, a barbarous people, sensual and brutish, hating all labor, and only inclined to killing and making war against their neighbors; not out of ambition, but only because they agreed not with themselves in some common terms of language; and perceiving the dominion of the Spaniards laid great restrictions upon their lazy and brutish customs, they conceived an irreconcilable hatred against them; but especially because they saw them take possession of their kingdoms and dominions. Hereupon they made against them all the resistance they could, opposing every where their designs, to the utmost: and the Spaniards finding themselves cruelly hated by the Indians, and nowhere secure from their treacheries, resolved to extirpate and ruin them, since they could neither tame them by civility, nor conquer them with the sword. But the Indians, it being their custom to make the woods their chief places of defence, at present made these their refuge, whenever they fled from the Spaniards. Hereupon those first conquerors of the New World made use of dogs to range and search the intricatest thickets of woods and forests for those implacable and unconquerable enemies;

thus they forced them to leave their old refuge, and submit to the sword, seeing no milder usage would do it; hereupon they killed some of them, and, quartering their bodies, placed them in the highways, that others might take warning from such a punishment; but this severity proved of ill consequence, for instead of frighting them and reducing them to civility, they conceived such horror of the Spaniards, that they resolved to detest and fly their sight forever; hence the greatest part died in caves and subterraneous places of the woods and mountains, in which places I myself have often seen great numbers of human bones. The Spaniards, finding no more Indians to appear about the woods, turned away a great number of dogs they had in their houses, and they, finding no masters to keep them, betook themselves to the woods and fields to hunt for food to preserve their lives; thus by degrees they became unacquainted with houses, and grew wild. This is the truest account I can give of the multitudes of wild dogs in these parts.

But besides these wild mastiffs, here are also great numbers of wild horses every where all over the island. They are but low of stature, short-bodied, with great heads, long necks, and big or thick legs. In a word, they have nothing handsome in their shape. They run up and down, commonly in troops of two or three hundred together, one going always before to lead the multitude. When they meet any person travelling through the woods or fields, they stand still, suffering him to approach till he can almost touch them; and then suddenly starting, they betake themselves to flight, running away as fast as they can. The hunters catch them only for their skins, though sometimes they preserve their flesh likewise, which they harden with smoke, using it for provisions when they go to sea.

Here would be also wild bulls and cows in great number, if by continual hunting they were not much diminished; yet considerable profit is made to this day by such as make it their business to kill them. The wild bulls are of a vast bigness of body, and yet they hurt not any one except they be exasperated. Their hides are from eleven to thirteen feet long.

The diversity of birds of this island is so great, that I should be troublesome if I should attempt to muster up their species; so that I shall content myself to mention some few of the chief. Here is a certain species of pullets in the woods which the Spaniards call *pintadas*, which the inhabitants find to be as good as those bred in houses. Every body knows that the parrots we have in Europe are brought from these parts, whence may be inferred, that seeing such a number of these talkative birds are preserved among us, notwithstanding the diversity of climates, much greater multitudes are to be found where the air and temperament is natural to them. The parrots make their nests in holes of palmetto trees, which holes are before made by other birds; for they are not capable of excavating any wood, though never so soft, having their own bills too crooked and blunt; hence provident Nature hath supplied them with the labor of other birds, called carpenters. These are no bigger than sparrows, yet have such hard and piercing bills, that no iron instrument can be made fitter to excavate any tree, though never so solid and hard; and these holes the parrots getting possession of, build in them their nests. There are pigeons of all sorts, which are very useful to the inhabitants. Those of this island observe the same seasons we mentioned before, speaking of Tortuga. Betwixt the pigeons of both islands is little or no difference, only that these of Hispaniola are something fatter and bigger. Another sort of small birds here are called *cabreros*, or goat-keepers; these are very like others called *heronsetas*, and chiefly feed upon crabs of the sea. In these birds are found seven distinct bladders of gall, and their flesh is as bitter as aloes. Crows or ravens, more troublesome than useful, do here make a hideous noise through the whole island. Their ordinary food is the flesh of wild dogs, or the carcasses of those beasts the Buccaneers kill and throw away. These clamorous birds no sooner hear the report of a fowling-piece or musket, but they gather from all sides in flocks, and fill the air and woods with their unpleasant notes; they are nothing different from those of Europe.

It is now time to speak of the French who inhabit a great part of this island. We have already told how they came first into these parts; we shall now only describe their manner of living, customs, and ordinary employments. The callings or professions they follow are generally but three, either to hunt or plant, or else to rove the seas as pirates. It is a constant custom among them all to seek out a comrade or companion, whom we may call partner in their fortunes, with whom they join the whole stock of what they possess towards a common gain. This is done by articles agreed to and reciprocally signed. Some constitute their surviving companion absolute heir to what is left by the death of the first. Others, if they be married, leave their estates to their wives and children; others, to other relations. This done, every one applies himself to his calling, which is always one of the three afore mentioned.

The hunters are again subdivided into two sorts; for some of these only hunt wild bulls and cows, others only wild boars. The first of these are called Buccaneers, and not long ago were about 600 on this island, but now they are reckoned about 300. The cause has been the great decrease of wild cattle, which has been such, that, far from getting, they now are but poor in their trade. When the Buccaneers go into the woods to hunt for wild bulls and cows, they commonly remain there a twelvemonth or two years without returning home. After the hunt is over, and the spoil divided, they commonly sail to Tortuga, to provide themselves with guns, powder, and shot, and other necessaries for another expedition; the rest of their gains they spend prodigally, giving themselves to all manner of vices and debauchery, particularly to drunkenness, which they practise mostly with brandy; this they drink as liberally as the Spaniards do water. Sometimes they buy together a pipe of wine; this they stave at one end, and never cease drinking till it is out. Thus sottishly they live till they have no money left, and as freely gratify their lusts, for which they find more women than they can use; for all the tavern-keepers and strumpets wait for these lewd Buccaneers, just as they do at Amsterdam for the arrival of the East India fleet. The said Buccaneers are very cruel and tyrannical to their servants, so that commonly they had rather be galley-slaves, or saw Brazil wood in the rasp-houses of Holland, than serve such barbarous masters.

The second sort hunt nothing but wild boars; the flesh of these they salt, and sell it so to the planters. These hunters have the same vicious customs, and are as much addicted to debauchery as the former; but their manner of hunting is different from that in Europe; for these Buccaneers have certain places designed for hunting, where they live for three or four months, and sometimes a whole year. Such places are called *Deza Boulan;* and in these, with only the company of five or six friends, they continue all the said time in mutual friendship. The first Buccaneers many times agree with planters to furnish them with meat all the year at a certain price; the payment hereof is often made with two or three hundred weight of tobacco in the leaf; but the planters commonly into the bargain furnish them with a servant, whom they send to help. To the servant they afford sufficient necessaries for the purpose, especially of po der and shot to hunt withal.

The planters began to cultivate and plant the Isle of Tortuga A. D. 1598. The first plantation was of tobacco, which grew to admiration, being likewise very good; but by reason of the smallness of the island they could plant but little, there being many pieces of land there that were not fit to produce it. They attempted likewise to make sugar, but by reason of the great expenses they could not bring it to any effect; so that the greatest part of the inhabitants, as we said before, betook themselves to hunting, and the remaining part to piracy. At last the hunters finding themselves unable to subsist by that profession, began to seek out lands fit for culture, and in these they also planted tobacco. The first land they chose was *Cal de Sac*, towards the south part of the island. This ground they divided into several quarters, which were called *the great Amea*, *Niep*, *Rochelois*, *the Little Grave*, *the Great Grave*, and the *Augame*. Here they increased so, that now there are above 2000 planters. At first they endured much hardship, because while they were busied about their husbandry, they could not go out of the island for provisions. This hardship was increased by the necessity of grubbing, cutting down, burning and digging, to extirpate the innumerable roots of shrubs and trees; for when the French possessed themselves thereof, it was overgrown with woods very thick, and these only inhabited by wild boars. The method they took was to divide themselves into small companies of two or three persons together, and these companies to separate far enough from each other, provided with a few hatchets and some coarse provision. Thus they used to go into the woods, and there to build huts only of a few rafters and boughs of trees. They first rooted up the shrubs and little trees, then cut down the great ones; these they heaped up, and then set on fire; but they were constrained to grub and dig up the roots as well as they could. The first seed they sowed was beans; these in those countries ripen and dry always in six weeks.

The second fruit necessary to human life, which here they tried, was potatoes; these come not to perfection in less than four or five months. On these they most commonly make their breakfasts; they dress them only by boiling them in a kettle with fair water, then they cover them with cloth for half an hour, whereby they become as soft as boiled chestnuts. Of the said potatoes also they make a drink called maiz; they cut them into small slices, and cover them with hot water; when they are well imbibed, they press them through a coarse cloth, and the liquor that comes, though something thick, they keep in vessels made for that purpose; here, after setting two or three days, it works, and having thrown off its lees, is fit for drink. They use it with great delight; and though the taste is somewhat sour, yet it is very pleasant, substantial, and wholesome. The invention of this is owing to the Indians, as well as of many other things, which those barbarians found out for the preservation and pleasure of life.

The third fruit the newly cultivated land afforded was mandioca, which the Indians call *cazave;* this root comes not to perfection till after eight or nine months, or perhaps a year; being thoroughly ripe, it may be left in the ground for eleven or twelve months without fear of corruption; but this time past, they must be used one way or other, otherwise they rot. Of these roots is made a sort of granulous flour or meal, dry and white, which supplies the want of common bread of wheat, whereof the fields are altogether barren. For this purpose they have certain graters, made either of copper or tin, wherewith they grate these roots, just as they do *mirio* in Holland. By the by, let me tell you, *mirio* is a root of a very biting taste, like strong mustard, wherewith they make sauces for some sorts of fish. When they have grated as much *cazave* roots as will serve the turn, they put the gratings into bags or sacks of coarse linen, and press out all the moisture; then they sieve the gratings, leaving them very like saw-dust. The meal, thus prepared, they lay on planches of iron made very hot, on which it is converted into very thin cakes; these are placed in the sun, on the tops of houses, to be thoroughly dried, and, lest they should lose any part of their meal, what did not pass the sieve is made up in rolls, five or six inches thick; these are placed one upon another, and left so till they begin to corrupt. Of this they make a liquor called *veycou,* which they find very excellent, and certainly is not inferior to our English beer.

Bananas are another fruit, of which is made excellent liquor, which, in strength and pleasantness of taste, may be compared to the best wines of Spain; but this liquor easily causes drunkenness, and frequently inflames the throat, and produces dangerous diseases in that part. *Guineas agudos* is also another fruit whereof they make drink, but not so strong as the precedent. Howbeit, one and the other are frequently mixed with water to quench thirst.

After they had cultivated these plantations with all sorts of roots and fruits necessary for human life, they began to plant tobacco for trade, the manner whereof is thus: they make beds of earth twelve feet square; these they cover with *palmite* leaves, that the rays of the sun may not reach the earth; they water them when it doth not rain, as we do our gardens in Europe; being grown about the bigness of young lettuce, they transplant it into straight lines in spacious fields, setting every plant three feet distant from each other. The fittest season of the year for these things is from January till the end of March, these being the months wherein most rains fall. Tobacco must be weeded very carefully, seeing the least root of any other herb coming near it hinders its growth. When it is grown to the height of about one foot and a half, they cut off the tops, to hinder the stalks and leaves from shooting up too high, that the whole plant may receive greater strength from the earth. When it comes to full perfection, they prepare certain apartments of fifty or sixty feet long, and thirty or forty broad; these they fill with poles and rafters, and on them lay the green tobacco to dry. When it is thoroughly dried, they strip the leaf from the stalks, and cause it to be rolled up by certain people, who are employed in this work and no other; to these they afford for their labor the tenth part of what they make up. This property is peculiar to tobacco, which I shall not omit, — that if, while it is in the ground, the leaf be pulled off from the stalk, it sprouts again no less than four times a year. Here I would also give an account of the manner of making sugar, indigo, and gimbes; but seeing these things are not planted in those parts, I pass them over.

The French planters of Hispaniola have always been subject to the governors of Tortuga, but not without much reluctancy and grudging. In 1644, the West India Company of France laid the foundations of a colony in Tortuga, under which the planters of Hispaniola were comprehended as subjects. This decree disgusted the said planters, they taking it very ill to be reputed subjects to a private company of men who had no authority to make them so, especially being in a country which belonged not to the king of France. Hereupon they resolved to work no longer for the said company; and this resolution was sufficient to compel the company to a total dissolution of the colony. But at last the governor of Tortuga, who was pretty well stocked with planters, conceiving he could more easily force them than the West India Company, found an invention to draw them to his obedience: he promised them he would put off their merchandise, and cause such returns to be made from France as they should like; withal, he dealt with the merchants underhand, that all ships should come consigned to him, and no persons should correspond with those planters of Hispaniola, thinking thereby to avoid many inconveniences, and compel them through want of all things to obey. Thus he not only obtained the obedience he designed, but some merchants, who had promised to deal with them and visit them no longer, did it.

Notwithstanding what hath been said, A. D. 1669 two ships from Holland arrived at Hispaniola with all sorts of merchandise: with these, presently, the planters resolved to deal, and with the Dutch nation for the future, thinking hereby to withdraw their obedience from the governor of Tortuga, and by frustrating his designs, revenge themselves of what they had endured under his government. Not long after the arrival of the Hollanders, the governor of Tortuga came to visit the plantation of Hispaniola, in a vessel very well armed; but the planters not only forbid him to come ashore, but with their guns forced him to retire faster than he came. Thus the Hollanders began a trade with these people; but such relations and friends as the governor had in Hispaniola used all the endeavors they were capable of, to impede the commerce. This being understood by the planters, they sent them word, that in case they laid not aside their artifices for the hinderance of the commerce which was begun with the Hollanders, they should every one assuredly be torn in pieces. Moreover, to oblige further the Hollanders, and contemn the governor and his party, they gave greater ladings unto the two ships than they could desire, with many gifts and presents unto the officers and mariners, whereby they sent them very well contented to their own country. The Hollanders came again very punctually, according to their promise, and found the planters under a greater indignation than before against the governor, either because of the great satisfaction they had already conceived of this commerce with the Dutch, or that by their means they hoped to subsist by themselves, without any further dependence from the French nation. However it was, suddenly after they set up another resolution more strange than the precedent; the tenor whereof was, that they would go unto the Island of Tortuga, and cut the governor in pieces. Hereupon they gathered together as many canoes as they could, and set sail from Hispaniola, with design not only to kill the governor, but also to possess themselves of the whole Island. This they thought they could not but easily perform, by reason of all necessary assistance, which they believed would at any time be sent them from Holland; by which means, they were ready determined, in their minds, to erect themselves into a new commonwealth, independent of the crown of France. But no sooner had they begun this great revolution of their little state, when they received news of a war declared between the two nations in Europe. This wrought such a consternation in their minds, as caused them to give over that enterprise, and retire, without attempting any thing.

In the mean time, the governor of Tortuga sent into France for aid towards his own security, and the reduction of those people unto their former obedience. This was granted him, and two men-of-war were sent unto Tortuga, with orders to be at his command. Having received such a considerable support, he sent them, very well equipped, to the Island of Hispaniola. Being arrived at that place, they landed part of the forces, with a design to force the people to the obedience of those whom they hated in their hearts. But the planters, seeing the arrival of these two frigates, and not being ignorant of their design, fled into the woods, abandoning their houses and many of their goods, which they left behind. These were immediately rifled and burned by the French, without compassion, not sparing the least cottage. Afterwards the governor began to relent, and let them know that, if they would return to his obedience, he would hearken to an accommodation. Hereupon the planters, finding they could expect no relief, surrendered to the governor, upon articles made and signed on both sides. But these were not strictly observed, for he commanded two of the chief of them to be hanged. The residue were pardoned, and withal he gave them free leave to trade with any nation for whatsoever they found necessary. With this liberty, they began to recultivate their plantations, which yielded a great quantity of very good tobacco, they selling yearly to the sum of twenty or thirty thousand rolls.

The planters here have but very few slaves, for want of which, themselves and their servants are constrained to do all the drudgery. These servants commonly bind themselves to their masters for three years; but their masters, having no consciences, often traffic with their bodies, as with horses at a fair, selling them to other masters as they sell negroes. Yea, to advance this trade, some persons go purposely into France (and likewise to England and other countries) to pick up young men or boys, whom they inveigle and transport; and having once got them into these islands, they work them like horses, the toil imposed on them being much harder than what they enjoin the negroes, their slaves; for these they endeavor to preserve, being their perpetual bondmen. But for their white servants, they care not whether they live or die, seeing they are to serve them no longer than three years. These miserable kidnapped people are frequently subject to a disease, which in these parts is called coma, being a total privation of their senses. This distemper is judged to proceed from their hard usage, and the change of their native climate; and there being often among these some of good quality, tender education, and soft constitutions, they are more easily seized with this disease, and others of those countries, than those of harder bodies and laborious lives. Beside the hard usage in their diet, apparel, and rest, many times they beat them so cruelly that they fall down dead under the hands of their cruel masters. This I have often seen, with great grief. Of the many instances, I shall only give you the following history, it being very remarkable in its circumstances.

A certain planter of these countries exercised such cruelty towards one of his servants, as caused him to run away. Having absconded for some days, in the woods, at last he was taken, and brought back to the wicked Pharaoh. No sooner had he got him, but he commanded him to be tied to a tree; here he gave him so many lashes on his naked back, as made his body run with an entire stream of blood; then, to make the smart of his wounds the greater, he anointed him with lemon-juice, mixed with salt and pepper. In this miserable posture he left him tied to the tree for twenty-four hours, which being past, he began his punishment again, lashing him, as before, so cruelly, that the miserable wretch gave up the ghost, with these dying words: "I beseech the Almighty God, Creator of heaven and earth, that he permit the wicked spirit to make thee feel as many torments before thy death as thou hast caused me to feel before mine." A strange thing, and worthy of astonishment and admiration! Scarce three or four days were past, after this horrible fact, when the Almighty Judge, who had heard the cries of that tormented wretch, suffered the evil one suddenly to possess this barbarous and inhuman homicide, so that those cruel hands which had punished to death his innocent servant were the tormenters of his own body; for he beat himself and tore his flesh after a miserable manner, till he lost the very shape of a man, not ceasing to howl and cry, without any rest by day or night. Thus he continued raving mad, till he died. Many other examples of this kind I could rehearse; but these not belonging to our present discourse, I omit them.

The planters of the Carribee Islands are rather worse, and more cruel to their servants, than the former. In the Isle of St. Christopher dwells one named Bettesa, well known to the Dutch merchants, who has killed above a hundred of his servants with blows and stripes. The English do the same with their servants, and the mildest cruelty they exercise towards them is, that when they have served six years of their time, (they being bound among the English for seven,) they use them so cruelly as to force them to beg of their masters to sell them to others, though it be to begin another servitude of seven years, or at least three or four. And I have known many who have thus served fifteen or twenty years, before they could obtain their freedom. Another law, very rigorous in that nation, is, if any man owes another above twenty-five English shillings, if he cannot pay it he is liable to be sold for six or eight months. Not to trouble the reader any longer with relations of this kind, I shall now describe the famous actions and exploits of the greatest pirates of my time, during my residence in those parts; these I shall relate without the least passion or partiality, and assure my reader that I shall give him no stories upon trust or hearsay, but only those enterprises to which I was myself an eye-witness.

CHAPTER VI.

Of the original of the most famous Pirates of the Coasts of America. — A famous Exploit of Pierre Le Grand.

I HAVE told you, in the preceding chapters, how I was compelled to adventure my life among the pirates of America, which sort of men I name so, because they are not authorized by any sovereign prince; for the kings of Spain, having on several occasions sent their ambassadors to the kings of England and France, to complain of the molestations and troubles those pirates often caused on the coasts of America, even in the calm of peace; it hath always been answered, that such men did not commit those acts of hostility and piracy as subjects to their majesties; and, therefore, his Catholic majesty might proceed against them as he should think fit. The king of France added, that he had no fortress nor castle upon Hispaniola, neither did he receive a farthing of tribute from thence. And the king of England rejoined, that he had never given any commissions to those of Jamaica, to commit hostilities against the subjects of his Catholic majesty. Nor did he only give this bare answer, but out of his royal desire to pleasure the court of Spain, recalled the governor of Jamaica, placing another in his room; all which could not prevent these pirates from acting as heretofore. But before I relate their bold actions, I shall say something of their rise and exercises, as also of the chiefest of them, and their manner of arming themselves before they put to sea.

The first pirate that was known upon Tortuga was Pierre Le Grand, or Peter the Great. He was born at Diep, in Normandy. That action which rendered him famous, was his taking the vice-admiral of the Spanish flota, near the Cape of Tiburon, on the west side of Hispaniola. This he performed with only one boat and twenty-eight men. Now, till that time the Spaniards had passed and repassed, with all security, through the Channel of Bahama; so that Pierre Le Grand, setting out to sea by the Caycos, he took this great ship with all the ease imaginable. The Spaniards they found aboard they set ashore, and sent the vessel to France. The manner how this undaunted spirit attempted and took this large ship, I shall give you out of the journal of the author, in his own words: "The boat," says he, "wherein Pierre Le Grand was with his companions, had been at sea a long time without finding any prize worth his taking; and their provisions beginning to fail, they were in danger of starving. Being almost reduced to despair, they spied a great ship of the Spanish flota, separated from the rest. This vessel they resolved to take, or die in the attempt. Hereupon they sailed towards her, to view her strength; and though they judged the vessel to be superior to theirs, yet their covetousness, and the extremity they were reduced to, made them venture. Being come so near that they could not possibly escape, they made an oath to their captain, Pierre Le Grand, to stand by him to the last. 'Tis true, the pirates did believe they should find the ship unprovided to fight, and thereby the sooner master her. It was in the dusk of the evening they began to attack; but before they engaged, they ordered the surgeon of the boat to bore a hole in the sides of it, that, their own vessel sinking under them, they might be compelled to attack more vigorously, and endeavor more hastily to board the ship. This was done accordingly, and without any other arms than a pistol in one hand and a sword in the other, they immediately climbed up the sides of the ship, and ran altogether into the great cabin, where they found the captain, with several of his companions, playing at cards. Here they set a pistol to his breast, commanding him to deliver up the ship. The Spaniards, surprised to see the pirates aboard their ship, cried, 'Jesus bless us! are these devils, or what are they?' Meanwhile, some of them took possession of the gun-room, and seized the arms, killing as many as made any opposition; whereupon the Spaniards presently surrendered. That very day, the captain of the ship had been told, by some of the seamen, that the boat which was in view, cruising, was a boat of pirates; whom the captain slightly answered, 'What then, must I be afraid of such a pitiful a thing as that is? No, though she were a ship as big and as strong as mine is.' As soon as Pierre Le Grand had taken this rich prize, he detained in his service as many of the common seamen as he had need of, setting the rest ashore, and then set sail for France, where he continued, without ever returning to America again."

The planters and hunters of Tortuga had no sooner heard of the rich prize those pirates had taken, but they resolved to follow their example. Hereupon many of them left their employments, and endeavored to get some small boats, wherein to exercise piracy; but not being able to purchase or build them at Tortuga, they resolved to set forth in their canoes, and seek them elsewhere. With these they cruised at first upon Cape de Alvarez, where the Spaniards used to trade from one city to another in small vessels, in which they carry hides, tobacco, and other commodities, to the Havana, and to which the Spaniards from Europe do frequently resort.

Here it was that those pirates at first took a great many boats, laden with the aforesaid commodities. These they used to carry to Tortuga, and sell the whole purchase to the ships that waited for their return, or accidentally happened to be there. With the gains of these prizes they provided themselves with necessaries wherewith to undertake other voyages, some of which were made to Campeachy, and others towards New Spain, in both which the Spaniards then drove a great trade. Upon those coasts they found great numbers of trading vessels, and often ships of great burden. Two of the biggest of these vessels, and two great ships which the Spaniards had laden with plate in the port of Campeachy, to go to the Caraccas, they took in less than a month's time, and carried to Tortuga, where the people of the whole island, encouraged by their success, especially seeing in two years the riches of the country so much increased, they augmented the number of pirates so fast, that in a little time there were, in that small island and port, above twenty ships of this sort of people. Hereupon the Spaniards, not able to bear their robberies any longer, equipped two large men-of-war, both for the defence of their own coasts and to cruise upon the enemies.

CHAPTER VII.

How the Pirates arm their Vessels, and regulate their Voyages.

Before the pirates go to sea, they give notice to all concerned of the day on which they are to embark, obliging each man to bring so many pounds of powder and ball as they think necessary. Being all come aboard, they consider where to get provisions, especially flesh, seeing they scarce eat any thing else, and of this the most common sort is pork. The next food is tortoises, which they salt a little. Sometimes they rob such or such hog-yards, where the Spaniards often have a thousand heads of swine together. They come to these places in the night, and having beset the keeper's lodge, they force him to rise, and give them as many heads as they desire, threatening to kill him if he refuses or makes any noise. And these menaces are oftentimes executed on the miserable swine-keepers, or any other person that endeavors to hinder their robberies.

Having got flesh sufficient for their voyage, they return to their ship. Here they allow, twice a day, every one as much as he can eat, without weight or measure; nor does the steward of the vessel give any more flesh, or any thing else, to the captain, than to the meanest mariner. The ship being well victualled, they deliberate whither they shall go to seek their desperate fortunes, and likewise agree upon certain articles, which are put in writing, which every one is bound to observe; and all of them, or the chiefest part, do set their hands to it. Here they set down distinctly what sums of money each particular person ought to have for that voyage, the fund of all the payments being what is gotten by the whole expedition; for otherwise it is the same law among these people as with other pirates: *no prey, no pay.* First, therefore, they mention how much the captain is to have for his ship; next, the salary of the carpenter, or shipwright, who careened, mended, and rigged the vessel. This commonly amounts to one hundred or one hundred and fifty pieces of eight, according to the agreement. Afterwards, for provisions and victualling, they draw out of the same common stock about two hundred pieces of eight; also a salary for the surgeon, and his chest of medicaments, which usually is rated at two hundred or two hundred and fifty pieces of eight. Lastly, they agree what rate each one ought to have that is either wounded or maimed in his body, suffering the loss of any limb; as, for the loss of a right arm, six hundred pieces of eight, or six slaves; for the left arm, five hundred pieces of eight, or five slaves; for a right leg, five hundred pieces of eight, or five slaves; for the left leg, four hundred pieces of eight, or four slaves; for an eye, one hundred pieces of eight, or one slave; for a finger, the same as for an eye; all which sums are taken out of the common stock of what is gotten by their piracy, and a very exact and equal dividend is made of the remainder. They have also regard to qualities and places. Thus the captain, or chief, is allotted five or six portions to what the ordinary seamen have; the master's mate only two, and other officers proportionably to their employ; after which, they draw equal parts, from the highest to the lowest mariner, the boys not being omitted, who draw half a share; because, when they take a better vessel than their own, it is the boys' duty to fire their former vessel, and then retire to the prize.

They observe among themselves very good orders; for in the prizes which they take, it is severely prohibited, to every one, to take any thing to themselves. Hence all they take is equally divided, as hath been said before. Yea, they take a solemn oath to each other, not to conceal the least thing they find among the prizes; and if any one is found false to the said oath, he is immediately turned out of the society. They are very civil and charitable to each other, so that if any one wants what another has, with great willingness they give it one to another. As soon as these pirates have taken a prize, they immediately set ashore the prisoners, detaining only some few, for their own help and service; whom, also, they release after two or three years. They refresh themselves at one island or another, but especially at those on the south of Cuba. Here they careen their vessels, while some hunt, and others cruise in canoes for prize. Many times they take the poor tortoise fishermen, and make them work during their pleasure.

In the several parts of America are found four distinct species of tortoises. The first are so great, that they weigh two or three thousand pounds. The scales are so soft, that they may be cut with a knife. But these are not good to eat. The second sort is of an indifferent bigness, and of a green color; their scales are harder than the first, and of a very pleasant taste. The third is little different in size from the second, only the head something bigger. It is called by the French, cavana, and is not good meat. The fourth is named caret, being very like those of Europe. This sort keeps commonly among the rocks, whence they crawl out for their food, which is generally sea-apples; those other above mentioned feed on grass, which grows in the water on the sandy banks; these banks or shelves, for their pleasant green, resemble the delightful meadows of the United Provinces. Their eggs are almost like those of the crocodile, but without any shell, being only covered with a thin film; they are found in such prodigious quantities along the shores, that were they not frequently destroyed by birds, the sea would abound with tortoises.

These creatures have certain places where they lay their eggs every year; the chief are the three islands called Caymanes, in 20° 15′, lat., being 45 leagues north of Cuba.

It is worth considering how the tortoises find these islands; for the greatest part come from the Gulf of Honduras, 150 leagues off, and many times the ships having lost their altitude, from the darkness of the weather, steer only by the noise the tortoises make in swimming, and reach those isles. When the season of hatching is past, they retire to Cuba, which affords them good food; but while they are at the Caymanes, they eat little or nothing. When they have been a month in the seas of Cuba, and are grown fat, the Spaniards fish for them, being then to be taken in such abundance, that they furnish their cities, towns, and villages with them. The way they take them is, by making with a great nail a kind of dart; this they fix at the end of a long pole, with which they kill the tortoises whenever they appear above the water.

The inhabitants of New Spain and Campeachy lade their best merchandise in ships of great bulk: the vessels from Campeachy sail in the winter to Caraccas, Trinity Isles, and that of Margarita, and return back again in the summer. The pirates knowing these seasons, (being very diligent in their inquiries,) always cruise between the places above mentioned; but in case they light of no considerable booty, they commonly undertake some more hazardous enterprises, one remarkable instance of which I shall here give you. A certain pirate called *Pierre François*, or *Peter Francis*, waiting a long time at sea with his boat and twenty-six men, for the ships that were to return from Maracaibo to Campeachy, and not being able to find any prey, at last he resolved to direct his course to Rancheiras, near the River de la Plata, in 12° and a half north latitude. Here lies a rich bank of pearl, to the fishery whereof they yearly sent from Carthagena twelve vessels with a man-of-war for their defence. Every vessel has at least two negroes in it, who are very dexterous in diving to the depth of six fathoms, where they find good store of pearls. On this fleet, called the pearl-fleet, Pierre François resolved to venture, rather than to go home empty:

Bartholomew Portugues.

they then rode at anchor at the mouth of the River de la Harha, the man-of-war scarce half a league distant from the small ships, and the wind very calm. Having spied them in this posture, he presently pulled down his sails and rowed along the coast, feigning to be a Spanish vessel come from Maracaibo; but no sooner was he come to the pearl-bank, when suddenly he assaulted the vice-admiral of eight guns and sixty men, commanding them to surrender. The Spaniards made a good defence for some time, but at last were forced to submit. Having thus taken the vice-admiral, he resolved to attempt the man-of-war, with which addition he hoped to master the rest of the fleet: to this end he presently sunk his own boat, putting forth the Spanish colors, and weighed anchor with a little wind which then began to stir, having with threats and promises compelled most of the Spaniards to assist him. But so soon as the man-of-war perceived one of his fleet to sail, he did so too, fearing lest the mariners designed to run away with the riches they had on board. The pirate on this immediately gave over the enterprise, thinking themselves unable to encounter force to force. Hereupon they endeavored to get out of the river and gain the open seas, by making as much sail as they could; which the man-of-war perceiving, he presently gave them chase; but the pirates having laid on too much sail, and a gust of wind suddenly rising, their mainmast was brought by the board, which disabled them from escaping.

This unhappy event much encouraged those in the man-of-war, they gaining upon the pirates every moment, and at last overtook them; but they finding they had twenty-two sound men, the rest being either killed or wounded, resolved to defend themselves as long as possible; this they performed very courageously for some time, till they were forced by the man-of-war, on condition that they should not be used as slaves to carry stones, or be employed in other labors for three or four years, as they served their negroes, but that they should be set safe ashore on free land. On these articles they yielded with all they had taken, which was worth, in pearls alone, above one hundred thousand pieces of eight, besides the vessel, provisions, goods, &c. All which would have made this a greater prize than he could desire, which he had certainly carried off, if his mainmast had not been lost, as we said before.

Another bold attempt like this, nor less remarkable, I shall also give you. A certain pirate of Portugal, thence called *Bartholomew Portugues*, was cruising in a boat of thirty men and four small guns from Jamaica, upon the Cape de Corriente, in Cuba, where he met a great ship from Maracaibo and Carthagena, bound for the Havana, well provided with twenty great guns and seventy men, passengers and mariners; this ship he presently assaulted, which they on board as resolutely defended. The pirate escaping the first encounter, resolved to attack her more vigorously than before, seeing he had yet suffered no great damage: this he performed with so much resolution, that at last, after a long and dangerous fight, he became master of it. The Portuguese lost only ten men, and had four wounded; so that he had still remaining twenty fighting men, whereas the Spaniards had double the number. Having possessed themselves of the ship, the wind being contrary to return to Jamaica, they resolved to steer to Cape St. Anthony, (which lies west of Cuba,) there to repair and take in fresh water, of which they were then in great want.

Being very near the cape above said, they unexpectedly met with three great ships coming from New Spain, and bound for the Havana; by these, not being able to escape, they were easily retaken, both ship and pirates, and all made prisoners, and stripped of all the riches they had taken but just before. The cargo consisted in one hundred and twenty thousand weight of cocoa nuts, the chief ingredient of chocolate, and seventy thousand pieces of eight. Two days after this misfortune, there arose a great storm, which separated the ships from one another. The great vessel, where the pirates were, arrived at Campeachy, where many considerable merchants came and saluted the captain; these presently knew the Portuguese pirate, being infamous for the many insolencies, robberies, and murders he had committed on their coasts, which they kept fresh in their memory.

The next day after their arrival, the magistrates of the city sent to demand the prisoners from on board the ship, in order to punish them according to their deserts; but fearing the captain of the pirates should make his escape, (as he had formerly done, being their prisoner once before,) they judged it safer to leave him guarded on shipboard for the present, while they erected a gibbet to hang him on the next day, without any other process than to lead him from the ship to his punishment; the rumor of which was presently brought to Bartholomew Portugues, whereby he sought all possible means to escape that night. With this design he took two earthen jars, wherein the Spaniards carry wine from Spain to the West Indies, and stopped them very well, intending to use them for swimming, as those unskilled in that art do corks or empty bladders. Having made this necessary preparation, he waited when all should be asleep; but not being able to escape his sentinel's vigilance, he stabbed him with a knife he had secretly purchased, and then threw himself into the sea with the earthern jars before mentioned; by the help of which, though he never learned to swim, he reached the shore, and immediately took to the woods, where he hid himself for three days, not daring to appear, eating no other food than wild herbs.

Those of the city next day made diligent search for him in the woods, where they concluded him to be. This strict inquiry Portugues saw from the hollow of a tree, wherein he lay hid; and upon their return he made the best of his way to Del Golpho Triste, forty leagues from Campeachy, where he arrived within a fortnight after his escape; during which time, as also afterwards, he endured extreme hunger and thirst, having no other provision with him than a small calabaca with a little water, besides the fears of falling again into the hands of the Spaniards. He ate nothing but a few shell fish, which he found among the rocks near the sea-shore; and being obliged to pass some rivers, not knowing well how to swim, he found at last an old board, which the waves had driven ashore, wherein were a few great nails; these he took, and with no small labor whetted on a stone, till he had made them like knives, though not so well; with these, and nothing else, he cut down some branches of trees, which with twigs and osiers he joined together, and made as well as he could a boat to waft him over the rivers. Thus arriving at the Cape of Golpho Triste, as was said, he found a vessel of pirates, comrades of his own, lately come from Jamaica.

To these he related all his adversities and misfortunes, and withal desired they would fit him with a boat and twenty men, with which company alone he promised to return to Campeachy, and assault the ship that was in the river, by which he had been taken fourteen days before. They presently granted his request, and equipped him a boat accordingly. With this small company he set out to execute his design, which he bravely performed eight days after he left Golpho Triste; for being arrived at Campeachy, with an undaunted courage, and without any noise, he assaulted the said ship. Those on board thought it was a boat from land that came to bring contraband goods, and so were in no posture of defence; which opportunity the pirates laying hold of, assaulted them so resolutely, that in a little time they compelled the Spaniards to surrender.

Being masters of the ship, they immediately weighed anchor and set sail from the port, lest they should be pursued by other vessels. This they did with the utmost joy, seeing themselves possessors of so brave a ship; especially Portugues, who by a

Roche Brasiliano.

second turn of fortune was become rich and powerful again, who was so lately in that same vessel a prisoner, condemned to be hanged: with this purchase he designed greater things, which he might have done, since there remained in the vessel so great a quantity of rich merchandise, though the plate had been sent to the city. But while he was making his voyage to Jamaica, near the Isle of Pinos, on the south of Cuba, a terrible storm arose, which drove against the Jardines Rocks, where she was lost; but Portugues with his companions escaped in a canoe, in which he arrived at Jamaica, where it was not long ere he went on new adventures, but was never fortunate after.

Nor less considerable are the actions of another pirate who now lives at Jamaica, who on several occasions has performed very surprising things. He was born at Groninghen, in the United Provinces. His own name not being known, his companions gave him that of Roche Brasiliano, by reason of his long residence in Brazil; hence he was forced to fly, when the Portuguese retook those countries from the Dutch, several nations then inhabiting at Brazil (as English, French, Dutch, and others) being constrained to seek new fortunes.

This person fled to Jamaica, where being at a stand how to get his living, he entered himself into the society of pirates, where he served as a private mariner for some time, and behaved himself so well, that he was beloved and respected by all. One day some of the mariners quarrelled with their captain, to that degree, that they left the boat. Brasiliano following them, was chose their leader, who having fitted out a small vessel, they made him captain.

Within a few days after, he took a great ship coming from New Spain, which had a great quantity of plate on board, and carried it to Jamaica. This action got him a great reputation at home, and though in his private affairs he governed himself very well, he would oftentimes appear brutal and foolish when in drink, running up and down the streets, beating or wounding those he met, no person daring to make any resistance.

To the Spaniards he was always very barbarous and cruel, out of an inveterate hatred against that nation; of these he commanded several to be roasted alive on wooden spits, for not showing him hog-yards, where he might steal swine. After many of these cruelties, as he was cruising on the coasts of Campeachy, a dismal tempest surprised him so violently, that his ship was wrecked upon the coasts, the mariners only escaping with their muskets, and some few bullets and powder, which were the only things they could save. The ship was lost between

Campeachy and the Golpho Triste: here they got ashore in a canoe, and marching along the coast with all the speed they could, they directed their course towards Golpho Triste, the common refuge of the pirates. Being upon his journey, and all very hungry and thirsty, as is usual in desert places, they were pursued by a troop of one hundred Spaniards. Brasiliano perceiving their imminent danger, encouraged his companions, telling them they were better soldiers, and ought rather to die under their arms, fighting as it became men of courage, than surrender to the Spaniards, who would take away their lives with the utmost torments. The pirates were but thirty, yet seeing their brave commander oppose the enemy with such courage, resolved to do the like; hereupon they faced the troop of Spaniards, and discharged their muskets on them so dexterously, that they killed one horseman almost with every shot. The fight continued for an hour, till at last the Spaniards were put to flight: they stripped the dead and took from them what was most for their use; such as were also quite dead, they dispatched with the ends of their muskets.

Having vanquished the enemy, they mounted on horses they found in the field, and continued their journey; Brasiliano having lost but two of his companions in this bloody fight, and had two wounded. Prosecuting their way, before they came to the port they spied a boat at anchor from Campeachy well manned, protecting a few canoes that were lading wood; hereupon they sent six of their men to watch them, who next morning, by a wile, possessed themselves of the canoes. Having given notice to their companions, they boarded them, and also took the little man-of-war, their convoy. Being thus masters of this fleet, they wanted only provisions, of which they found little aboard those vessels; but this defect was supplied by the horses which they killed and salted with salt, which by good fortune the woodcutters had brought with them, with which they supported themselves till they could get better.

They took also another ship going from New Spain to Maracaibo, laden with divers sorts of merchandise and pieces of eight, designed to buy cocoa-nuts for their lading home; all these they carried to Jamaica, where they safely arrived, and, according to custom, wasted all in a few days in taverns and stews, giving themselves to all manner of debauchery. Such of these pirates will spend two or three thousand pieces of eight in a night, not leaving themselves a good shirt to wear in the morning. I saw one of them give a common strumpet five hundred pieces of eight to see her naked. My own master would buy sometimes a pipe of wine, and placing it in the street, would force those that passed by to drink with him, threatening also to pistol them if they would not. He would do the like with barrels of beer or ale, and very often he would throw these liquors about the streets, and wet people's clothes, without regarding whether he spoiled their apparel.

Among themselves, these pirates are very liberal. If any one has lost all, which often happens in their manner of life, they freely give him of what they have. In taverns and ale-houses, they have great credit; but at Jamaica they ought not to run very deep in debt, seeing the inhabitants there easily sell one another for debt. This happened to my patron, to be sold for a debt of a tavern, wherein he had spent the greatest part of his money. This man had, within three months before, three thousand pieces of eight in ready cash, all which he wasted in that little time, and became as poor as I have told you.

But to return. Brasiliano, after having spent all, was forced to go to sea again to seek his fortune. He set forth towards the coast of Campeachy, his common rendezvous. Fifteen days after his arrival, he put himself into a canoe, to espy the port of that city, and see if he could rob any Spanish vessel; but his fortune was so bad, that both he and all his men were taken and carried before the governor, who immediately cast them into a dungeon, intending to hang them every one; and doubtless he had done so, but for a stratagem of Brasiliano, which saved their lives. He wrote a letter to the governor, in the names of other pirates that were abroad at sea, telling him, "He should have a care how he used those persons he had in custody; for if he hurt them in the least, they swore they would never give quarter to any Spaniard that should fall into their hands."

These pirates having been often at Campeachy, and other places of the West Indies in the Spanish dominions, the governor feared what mischief their companions abroad might do, if he should punish them. Hereupon he released them, exacting only an oath on them, that they would leave their exercise of piracy forever; and withal he sent them, as common mariners in the galleons, to Spain. They got in this voyage, all together, five hundred pieces of eight; so that they tarried not long there, after their arrival. Providing themselves with necessaries, they returned to Jamaica, from whence they set forth again to sea, committing greater robberies and cruelties than before, but especially abusing the poor Spaniards who fell into their hands with all sorts of cruelty.

The Spaniards, finding they could gain nothing on these

people, or diminish their number, daily resolved to lessen the number of their trading ships. But neither was this of any service; for the pirates, finding few ships at sea, began to gather into companies, and to land on their dominions, ruining cities, towns, and villages; pillaging, burning, and carrying away as much as they could.

The first pirate who began these invasions by land was Lewis Scot, who sacked the city of Campeachy, which he almost ruined, robbing and destroying all he could; and after he had put it to an excessive ransom, he left it. After Scot, came another, named Mansvelt, who invaded Granada, and penetrated even to the South Sea, till at last, for want of provision, he was forced to go back. He assaulted the Isle of St. Catherine, which he took, with a few prisoners. These directed him to Carthagena, a principal city in Nueva Granada. But the bold attempts and actions of John Davis, born at Jamaica, ought not to be forgotten, being some of the most remarkable; especially his rare prudence and valor showed in the fore-mentioned kingdom of Granada. This pirate, having long cruised in the Gulf of Pocatauro, on the ships expected to Carthagena, bound for Nicaragua, and not meeting any of them, resolved at last to land in Nicaragua, leaving his ship hid on the coast.

This design he soon executed; for, taking eighty men out of ninety which he had in all, and the rest he left to keep the ship, he divided them equally into three canoes. His intent was to rob the churches, and rifle the houses of the chief citizens of Nicaragua. Thus, in the dark night, they entered the river leading to that city, rowing in their canoes. By day they hid themselves and boats under the branches of trees, on the banks, which grow very thick along the river-sides in those countries, and along the sea-coast. Being arrived at the city the third night, the sentinel, who kept the post of the river, thought them to be fishermen that had been fishing in the lake; and most of the pirates understanding Spanish, he doubted not, as soon as he heard them speak. They had in their company an Indian, who had run away from his master, who would have enslaved him unjustly. He went first ashore, and instantly killed the sentinel; this done, they entered the city, and went directly to three or four houses of the chief citizens, here they knocked softly. These, believing them to be friends, opened the doors, and the pirates, suddenly possessing themselves of the houses, stole all the money and plate they could find. Nor did they spare the churches, and most sacred things, all which were pillaged and profaned, without any respect or veneration.

Meanwhile, great cries and lamentations were heard of some who had escaped them; so that the whole city was in an uproar, and all the citizens rallied in order to a defence, which the pirates perceiving, they instantly fled, carrying away their booty and some prisoners. These they led away, that if any of them should be taken by the Spaniards, they might use them for ransom. Thus they got to their ship, and with all speed put to sea, forcing the prisoners, before they let them go, to procure them as much flesh as was necessary for their voyage to Jamaica. But no sooner had they weighed anchor, when they saw a troop of about five hundred Spaniards, all well armed, at the sea-side. Against these they let fly several guns, wherewith they forced them to quit the sands and retire, with no small regret to see these pirates carry away so much plate of their churches and houses, though distant at least forty leagues from the sea.

These pirates got, on this occasion, above four thousand pieces of eight in money, besides much plate and many jewels, in all to the value of fifty thousand pieces of eight, or more. With all this, they arrived at Jamaica soon after. But this sort of people being never long masters of their money, they were soon constrained to seek more by the same means; and Captain John Davis, presently after his return, was chosen admiral of seven or eight vessels, he being now esteemed an able conductor for such enterprises. He began his new command by directing his fleet to the north of Cuba, there to wait for the fleet from New Spain; but missing his design, they determined for Florida. Being arrived there, they landed their men and sacked a small city named St. Augustine of Florida. The castle had a garrison of two hundred men, but could not prevent the pillage of the city, they effecting it without the least damage from the soldiers or townsmen.

Thus we have spoken, in the first part of this book, of the constitution of Hispaniola and Tortuga, their properties and inhabitants, as also of the fruits. In the second part, we shall describe the actions of the two most famous pirates, who committed many horrible crimes and inhumanities upon the

Francis Lolonois.

CHAPTER VIII.

Of the Origin of Francis Lolonois, and the Beginning of his Robberies.

Francis Lolonois was a native of that territory in France which is called *Les Sables d'Olone*, or The Sands of Olone. In his youth he was transported to the Caribbee Islands, in quality of servant, or slave, according to custom, of which we have already spoken. Being out of his time, he came to Hispaniola. Here he joined for some time with the hunters, before he began his robberies upon the Spaniards, which I shall now relate, till his unfortunate death.

At first he made two or three voyages as a common mariner, wherein he behaved himself so courageously, as to gain the favor of the governor of Tortuga, Monsieur de La Place; insomuch that he gave him a ship, in which he might seek his fortune, which was very favorable to him at first, for in a short time he got great riches. But his cruelties against the Spaniards were such, that the fame of them made him so well known through the Indies, that the Spaniards in his time would choose rather to die or sink fighting, than surrender, knowing they should have no mercy at his hands. But fortune, being seldom constant, after some time turned her back; for in a huge storm he lost his ship on the coast of Campeachy. The men were all saved, but, coming upon dry land, the Spaniards pursued them, and killed the greatest part, wounding also Lolonois. Not knowing how to escape, he saved his life by a stratagem. Mingling sand with the blood of his wounds, with which besmearing his face, and other parts of his body, and hiding himself dexterously among the dead, he continued there till the Spaniards quitted the field.

They being gone, he retired to the woods, and bound up his wounds as well as he could. These being pretty well healed, he took his way to Campeachy, having disguised himself in a Spanish habit. Here he enticed certain slaves, to whom he promised liberty, if they would obey him and trust to his conduct. They accepted his promises, and, stealing a canoe, they went to sea with him. Now the Spaniards, having made several of his companions prisoners, kept them close in a dungeon, while Lolonois went about the town, and saw what passed. These were often asked, "What is become of your captain?" to whom they constantly answered, "He is dead;" which rejoiced the Spaniards, who made bonfires, and, knowing nothing to the contrary, gave thanks to God for their deliverance from such a cruel pirate. Lolonois, having seen these rejoicings for his death, made haste to escape, with the slaves above mentioned, and came safe to Tortuga, the common refuge of all sorts of wickedness, and the seminary, as it were, of pirates and thieves. Though now his fortune was low, yet he got another ship with craft and subtlety, and in it twenty-one men. Being well provided with arms and necessaries, he set forth for Cuba, on the south whereof is a small village, called De los Cayos. The inhabitants drive a great trade in tobacco, sugar, and hides, and all in boats, not being able to use ships, by reason of the little depth of that sea.

Lolonois was persuaded he should get here some considerable prey; but by the good fortune of some fishermen who saw him, and the mercy of God, they escaped him. For the inhabitants of the town despatched immediately a messenger over land to the Havana, complaining that Lolonois was come to destroy them, with two canoes. The governor could very hardly believe this, having received letters from Campeachy that he was dead. But, at their importunity, he sent a ship to their relief, with ten guns, and ninety men, well armed, giving them this express command, that they should not return into his presence, without having totally destroyed those pirates. To this effect, he gave them a negro to serve for a hangman, and orders that they should immediately hang every one of the pirates, excepting Lolonois, their captain, whom they should bring alive to the Havana. This ship arrived at Cayos, of whose coming the pirates were advertised beforehand, and instead of flying, went to seek it in the river Estera, where she rode at anchor. The pirates seized some fishermen, and forced them by night to show them the entry of the port, hoping soon to obtain a greater vessel than their two canoes, and thereby to mend their fortune. They arrived, after two in the morning, very nigh the ship, and the watch on board the ship asking them, "Whence they came, and if they had seen any pirates aboard?" they caused one of the prisoners to answer, "They had seen no pirates, nor any thing else;" which answer made them believe that they were fled upon hearing of their coming.

But they soon found the contrary, for about break of day the pirates assaulted the vessel on both sides, with their two canoes, with such vigor, that, though the Spaniards behaved themselves as they ought, and made as good defence as they could, making some use of their great guns, yet they were forced to surrender, being beaten by the pirates, with sword in hand, down under the hatches. From hence Lolonois commanded them to be brought up, one by one, and in this order caused their heads to be struck off. Among the rest came up the negro, designed to be the pirates' executioner. This fellow implored mercy at his hands very dolefully, telling Lolonois he was constituted hangman of that ship, and if he would spare him, he would tell him faithfully all that he should desire. Lolonois, making him confess what he thought fit, commanded him to be murdered with the rest. Thus he cruelly and barbarously put them all to death, reserving only one alive, whom he sent back to the governor of the Havana, with this message in writing: "I shall never henceforward give quarter to any Spaniard whatsoever; and I have great hopes I shall execute on your own person the very same punishment I have done upon them you sent against me. Thus I have retaliated the kindness you designed to me and my companions. The governor, much troubled at this sad news, swore, in the presence of many, that he would never grant quarter to any pirate that should fall into his hands. But the citizens of the Havana desired him not to persist in the execution of that rash and rigorous oath, seeing the pirates would certainly take occasion from thence to do the same, and they had a hundred times more opportunity of revenge than he; that, being necessitated to get their livelihood by fishery, they should hereafter always be in danger of their lives. By these reasons he was persuaded to bridle his anger, and remit the severity of his oath.

Now Lolonois had got a good ship, but very few provisions and people in it; to purchase both which he resolved to cruise from one port to another. Doing thus for some time without success, he determined to go to the port of Maracaibo. Here he surprised a ship laden with plate, and other merchandises, outward bound to buy cocoa-nuts. With this prize he returned to Tortuga, where he was received with joy by the inhabitants, they congratulating his happy success, and their own private interest. He stayed not long there, but designed to equip a fleet sufficient to transport five hundred men and necessaries. Thus provided, he resolved to pillage both cities, towns, and villages, and, finally, to take Maracaibo itself. For this purpose he knew the Island of Tortuga would afford him many resolute and courageous men, fit for such enterprises. Besides, he had in his service several prisoners well acquainted with the ways and places designed upon.

CHAPTER IX.

Lolonois equips a Fleet to land upon the Spanish Islands of America, with intent to rob, sack, and burn whatsoever he met with.

Of this design, Lolonois giving notice to all the pirates, whether at home or abroad, he got together in a little while above four hundred men, beside which, there was then in Tortuga another pirate, named Michael de Basco, who, by his piracy, had got riches sufficient to live at ease, and go no more abroad, having, withal, the office of major of the island. But seeing the great preparations that Lolonois made for this expedition, he joined him, and offered him, that if he would make him his chief captain by land, (seeing he knew the country very well, and all its avenues,) he would share in his fortunes, and go with him. They agreed upon articles, to the great joy of Lolonois, knowing that Basco had done great actions in Europe, and had the repute of a good soldier. Thus they all embarked in eight vessels, that of Lolonois being the greatest, having ten guns of indifferent carriage.

All things being ready, and the whole company on board, they set sail together about the end of April, being in all six hundred and sixty persons. They steered for that part called Bayala, north of Hispaniola. Here they took into their company some French hunters, who voluntarily offered themselves; and here they provided themselves with victuals and necessaries for their voyage.

From hence they sailed again the last of July, and steered directly to the eastern cape of the isle called Punta d'Espada. Hereabouts espying a ship from Puerto Rico, bound for New Spain, laden with cocoa-nuts, Lolonois commanded the rest of the fleet to wait for him near Savona, on the east of Cape Punta d'Espada, he alone intending to take the said vessel. The Spaniards, though they had been in sight full two hours, and knew them to be pirates, yet would not flee, but prepared to fight, being well armed and provided. The combat lasted three hours, and then they surrendered. This ship had sixteen guns, and fifty fighting men aboard. They found in her one hundred and twenty thousand weight of cocoa, forty thousand pieces of eight, and the value of ten thousand more in jewels. Lolonois sent the vessel presently to Tortuga to be unladed, with orders to return as soon as possible to Savona, where he would wait for them. Meanwhile the rest of the fleet being arrived at

Savona, met another Spanish vessel coming from Coman, with military provisions to Hispaniola, and money to pay the garisons there. This vessel they also took, without any resistance, though mounted with eight guns. In it were seven thousand weight of powder, a great number of muskets, and like things, with twelve thousand pieces of eight.

These successes encouraged the pirates, they seeming very lucky beginnings, especially finding their fleet pretty well recruited in a little time: for the first ship arriving at Tortuga, the governor ordered it to be instantly unladen, and soon after sent back, with fresh provisions, and other necessaries, to Lolonois. This ship he chose for himself, and gave that which he commanded to his comrade, Anthony du Puis. Being thus recruited with men, in lieu of them he had lost in taking the prizes, and by sickness, he found himself in a good condition to set sail for Maracaibo, in the province of Nueva Venezuela, in the latitude of 12° 10′ north. This island is twenty leagues long, and twelve broad. To this port also belong the islands of Onega and Monges. The east side thereof is called Cape St. Roman, and the western side Cape of Caquibacoa. The gulf is called, by some, the Gulf of Venezuela, but the pirates usually called it the Bay of Maracaibo.

At the entrance of this gulf are two islands extending from east to west; that towards the east is called Isla de las Vigilias, or the Watch Isle; because in the middle is a high hill, on which stands a watch-house; the other is called Isla de la Palomas, or the Isle of Pigeons. Between these two islands runs a little sea, or rather lake of fresh water, sixty leagues long, and thirty broad; which disgorging itself into the ocean, dilates itself about the said two islands. Between them is the best passage for ships, the channel being no broader than the flight of a great gun, of about eight pounds. On the Isle of Pigeons standeth a castle, to impede the entry of vessels, all being necessitated to come very nigh the castle, by reason of two banks of sand on the other side, with only fourteen foot water. Many other banks of sand there are in this lake; as that called El Tablazo, or the Great Table, no deeper than ten foot, forty leagues within the lake. Others there are, that have no more than six, seven, or eight foot in depth; all are very dangerous, especially to mariners unacquainted with them. West hereof is the city of Maracaibo, very pleasant to the view, its houses being built along the shore, having delightful prospects all round: the city may contain three or four thousand persons, slaves included, all which make a town of a reasonable bigness. There are judged to be about eight hundred persons able to bear arms, all Spaniards. Here are one parish church, well built and adorned, four monasteries, and one hospital. The city is governed by a deputy-governor, substituted by the governor of the Caraccas. The trade here exercised is mostly in hides and tobacco. The inhabitants possess great numbers of cattle, and many plantations which extend thirty leagues in the country, especially towards the great town of Gibraltar, where are gathered great quantities of cocoa-nuts, and all other garden-fruits, which serve for the regale and sustenance of the inhabitants of Maracaibo, whose territories are much drier than those of Gibraltar. Hither those of Maracaibo send great quantities of flesh, they making returns in oranges, lemons, and other fruits; for the inhabitants of Gibraltar want flesh, their fields not being capable of feeding cows or sheep.

Before Maracaibo is a very spacious and secure port, wherein may be built all sorts of vessels, having great convenience of timber, which may be transported thither at little charge. Nigh the town lies also a small island called Borrica, where they feed great numbers of goats, which cattle the inhabitants use more for their skins than their flesh or milk; they slighting these two, unless while they are tender and young kids. In the fields are fed some sheep, but of a very small size. In some islands of the lake, and in other places hereabouts, are many savage Indians, called, by the Spaniards, *bravoes*, or wild: these could never be reduced by the Spaniards, being brutish and untamable. They dwell mostly towards the west side of the lake, in little huts built on trees growing in the water; so to keep themselves from the innumerable mosquitoes, or gnats, which infest and torment them night and day. To the east of the said lake are whole towns of fishermen, who likewise live in huts built on trees, as the former. Another reason of this dwelling, is the frequent inundations; for after great rains, the land is often overflown for two or three leagues, there being no less than twenty-five great rivers that feed this lake. The town of Gibraltar is also frequently drowned by these, so that the inhabitants are constrained to retire to their plantations.

Gibraltar, situate at the side of the lake, about forty leagues within it, receives its provisions of flesh, as has been said, from Maracaibo. The town is inhabited by about fifteen hundred persons, whereof four hundred may bear arms; the greatest part of them keep shops, wherein they exercise one trade or other. In the adjacent fields are numerous plantations of sugar and cocoa, in which are many tall and beautiful trees, of whose timber houses may be built, and ships. Among these are many handsome and proportionable cedars, seven or eight foot about, of which they build boats and ships, so as to bear one only great sail; such vessels being called *periagues*. The whole country is well furnished with rivers and brooks, very useful in droughts, being then cut into many little channels to water their fields and plantations. They plant also much tobacco, well esteemed in Europe, and, for its goodness, is called there *tobacco de sacerdotes*, or *priests' tobacco*. They enjoy nigh twenty leagues of jurisdiction, which is bounded by very high mountains, perpetually covered with snow. On the other side of these mountains is situate a great city called Merida, to which the town of Gibraltar is subject. All merchandise is carried hence to the aforesaid city on mules, and that but at one season of the year, by reason of the excessive cold in those high mountains. On the said mules returns are made in flour of meal, which comes from towards Peru, by the way of Estaffe.

Thus far I thought good to make a short description of the Lake of Maracaibo, that my reader might the better comprehend what I shall say concerning the actions of pirates in this place, as follows.

Lolonois arriving at the Gulf of Venezuela, cast anchor with his whole fleet out of sight of the Vigilia or Watch Isle; next day very early he set sail thence with all his ships for the Lake of Maracaibo, where they cast anchor again; then they landed their men, with design to attack first the fortress that commanded the bar, therefore called De la Barra. This fort consists only of several great baskets of earth placed on a rising ground, planted with sixteen great guns, with several other heaps of earth round about for covering their men. The pirates having landed a league off this fort, advanced by degrees towards it; but the governor having espied their landing, had placed an ambuscade to cut them off behind, while he should attack them in front. This the pirates discovered, and getting before, they defeated it so entirely, that not a man could retreat to the castle. This done, Lolonois, with his companions, advanced immediately to the fort, and after a fight of almost three hours, with the usual desperation of this sort of people, they became masters thereof, without any other arms than swords and pistols. While they were fighting, those who were the routed ambuscade, not being able to get into the castle, retired into Maracaibo in great confusion and disorder, crying, "The pirates will presently be here with two thousand men and more." The city having formerly been taken by this kind of people, and sacked to the uttermost, had still an idea of that misery; so that upon these dismal news they endeavored to escape towards Gibraltar in their boats and canoes, carrying with them all the goods and money they could. Being come to Gibraltar, they told how the fortress was taken, and nothing had been saved, nor any persons escaped.

The castle thus taken by the pirates, they presently signified to the ships their victory, that they should come farther in without fear of danger: the rest of that day was spent in ruining and demolishing the said castle. They nailed the guns, and burnt as much as they could not carry away, burying the dead, and sending on board the fleet the wounded. Next day, very early, they weighed anchor, and steered all together towards Maracaibo, about six leagues distant from the fort; but the wind failing that day, they could advance little, being forced to expect the tide. Next morning they came in sight of the town, and prepared for landing under the protection of their own guns, fearing the Spaniards might have laid an ambuscade in the woods: they put their men into canoes, brought for that purpose, and landed where they thought most convenient, shooting still furiously with their great guns. Of those in the canoes, half only went ashore, the other half remained aboard; they fired from the ships as fast as possible towards the woody part of the shore, but could discover nobody; then they entered the town, whose inhabitants, as I told you, were retired to the wood and Gibraltar, with their wives, children, and families. Their houses they left well provided with victuals, as flour, bread, pork, brandy, wines, and poultry. With these the pirates fell to making good cheer, for in four weeks before they had no opportunity of filling their stomachs with such plenty.

They instantly possessed themselves of the best houses in the town, and placed sentinels wherever they thought convenient; the great church served them for their main-guard. Next day they sent out one hundred and sixty men to find out some of the inhabitants in the woods thereabouts; these returned the same night, bringing with them twenty thousand pieces of eight, several mules laden with household goods and merchandise, and twenty prisoners, men, women, and children. Some of these were put to the rack, to make them confess where they had hid the rest of their goods; but they could extort very little from them. Lolonois, who valued not murdering, though in cold blood, ten or twelve Spaniards, drew his cutlass, and hacked one to pieces before the rest, saying, "If you do not confess and declare where you have hid the rest of your goods, I will do the like to all your companions." At last, amongst these horrible cruelties and inhuman threats, one promised to show the place where the rest of the Spaniards were hid; but those that were fled, having intelligence of it, changed place, and buried the remnant of their riches under ground, so that the pirates could not find them out, unless some of their own party should reveal them; besides, the Spaniards flying from one place to another every day, and often changing woods, were jealous even of each other, so as the father durst scarce trust his own son.

After the pirates had been fifteen days in Maracaibo, they resolved for Gibraltar; but the inhabitants having received intelligence thereof, and that they intended afterwards to go to Merida, gave notice of it to the governor there, who was a valiant soldier, and had been an officer in Flanders. His answer was: He would have them take no care, for he hoped in a little while to exterminate the said pirates. Whereupon he came to Gibraltar with four hundred men well armed, ordering at the same time the inhabitants to put themselves in arms, so that in all he made eight hundred fighting men. With the same speed he raised a battery towards the sea, mounted with twenty guns, covered with great baskets of earth; another battery he placed in another place, mounted with eight guns. This done, he barricadoed a narrow passage to the town through which the pirates must pass, opening at the same time another through much dirt and mud into the wood, totally unknown to the pirates.

The pirates, ignorant of these preparations, having embarked all their prisoners and booty, took their way towards Gibraltar. Being come in sight of the place, they saw the royal standard hanging forth, and that those of the town designed to defend their houses. Lolonois, seeing this, called a council of war what they ought to do, telling his officers and mariners, "that the difficulty of the enterprise was very great, seeing the Spaniards had had so much time to put themselves in a posture of defence, and had got a good body of men together, with much ammunition; but notwithstanding," said he, "have a good courage; we must either defend ourselves like good soldiers, or lose our lives with all the riches we have got. Do as I shall do who am your captain. At other times we have fought with fewer men than we have in our company at present, and yet we have overcome greater numbers than there possibly can be in this town; the more they are, the more glory, and the greater riches, we shall gain." The pirates supposed that all the riches of the inhabitants of Maracaibo were transported to Gibraltar, or at least the greatest part. After this speech, they all promised to follow and obey him. Lolonois made answer, "'Tis well; but know ye, withal, that the first man who shall show any fear, or the least apprehension thereof, I will pistol him with my own hands."

With this resolution they cast anchor nigh the shore, neai three quarters of a league from the town: next day, before sunrising, they landed three hundred and eighty men well provided, and armed every one with a cutlass and one or two pistols, and sufficient powder and bullet for thirty charges. Here they all shook hands in testimony of good courage, and began their march, Lolonois speaking thus: "Come, my brethren, follow me, and have good courage." They followed their guide, who, believing he led them well, brought them to the way which the governor had barricadoed. Not being able to pass that way, they went to the other newly made in the wood, among the mire, which the Spaniards could shoot into at pleasure; but the pirates, full of courage, cut down the branches of trees, and threw them on the way, that they might not stick in the dirt. Meanwhile, those of Gibraltar fired with their great guns so furiously, they could scarce hear nor see for the noise and smoke. Being past the wood, they came on firm ground, where they met with a battery of six guns, which immediately the Spaniards discharged upon them, all loaded with small bullets and pieces of iron; and the Spaniards, sallying forth, set upon them with such fury as caused the pirates to give way, few of them caring to advance towards the fort, many of them being already killed and wounded. This made them go back to seek another way; but the Spaniards having cut down many trees to hinder the passage, they could find none, but were forced to return to that they had left. Here the Spaniards continued to fire as before, nor would they sally out of their batteries to attack them any more. Lolonois and his companions not being able to grimp up the baskets of earth, were compelled to use an old stratagem, wherewith at last they deceived and overcame the Spaniards.

Lolonois retired suddenly with all his men, making show as if he fled. Hereupon the Spaniards, crying out, "They flee, they flee, let us follow them," sallied forth, with great disorder, to the pursuit. Being drawn to some distance from the batteries, which was the pirates' only design, they turned upon them unexpectedly, with sword in hand, and killed above two hundred men; and thus fighting their way through those who remained, they possessed themselves of the batteries. The Spaniards that remained abroad, giving themselves over for lost, fled to the woods; those in the battery of eight guns surrendered themselves, obtaining quarter for their lives. The pirates being now become masters of the town, pulled down the Spanish colors and set up their own, taking prisoners as many as they could find. These they carried to the great church,

Capture of Gibraltar.

where they raise a battery of several great guns, fearing lest the Spaniards that were fled should rally, and come upon them again; but next day, being all fortified, their fears were over. They gathered the dead to bury them, being above five hundred Spaniards, besides the wounded in the town, and those that died of their wounds in the woods. The pirates had also above one hundred and fifty prisoners, and nigh five hundred slaves, many women and children.

Of their own companions, only forty were killed, and almost eighty wounded, whereof the greatest part died through the bad air, which brought fevers and other illness. They put the slain Spaniards into two great boats, and carrying them a quarter of a league to sea, they sunk the boats; this done, they gathered all the plate, household stuff, and merchandise they could, or thought convenient to carry away. The Spaniards who had any thing left had hid it carefully; but the unsatisfied pirates, not contented with the riches they had got, sought for more goods and merchandise, not sparing those who lived in the fields, such as hunters and planters. They had scarce been eighteen days on the place, when the greatest part of the prisoners died for hunger; for in the town were few provisions, especially of flesh, though they had some, but no sufficient quantity of flour of meal, and this the pirates had taken for themselves, as they also took the swine, cows, sheep, and poultry, without allowing any share to the poor prisoners; for these they only provided some small quantity of mules' and asses' flesh; and many, who could not eat of that loathsome provision, died for hunger, their stomachs not being accustomed to such sustenance; only some women were allowed better cheer, because they served their sensual delights, to which those robbers are much given. Among these, some had been forced, others were volunteers, though almost all rather submitted through poverty and hunger, than any other cause. Of the prisoners, many also died under the torment they sustained to make them discover their money or jewels; and of these, some had none, nor knew of none, and others, denying what they knew, endured such horrible deaths.

Finally, after having been in possession of the town four entire weeks, they sent four of the prisoners to the Spaniards that were fled to the woods, demanding of them a ransom for not burning the town. The sum demanded was ten thousand pieces of eight, which if not sent, they threatened to reduce it to ashes. For bringing in this money, they allowed them only two days; but the Spaniards not having been able to gather so punctually such a sum, the pirates fired many places of the town; whereupon the inhabitants begged them to help quench the fire, and the ransom should be readily paid. The pirates condescended, helping as much as they could to stop the fire; but, notwithstanding all their best endeavors, one part of the town was ruined, especially the church belonging to the monastery was burned down. After they had received the said sum, they carried aboard all the riches they had got, with a great number of slaves which had not paid the ransom; for all the prisoners had sums of money set upon them, and the slaves were also commanded to be redeemed. Hence they returned to Maracaibo, where, being arrived, they found a general consternation in the whole city, to which they sent three or four prisoners, to tell the governor and inhabitants, "they should bring them thirty thousand pieces of eight aboard their ships, for a ransom of their houses, otherwise they should be sacked anew and burned."

Among these debates, a party of pirates came on shore, and carried away the images, pictures, and bells of the great church, aboard the fleet. The Spaniards who were sent to demand the sum aforesaid, returned, with orders to make some agreement, who concluded with the pirates to give for their ransom and liberty twenty thousand pieces of eight, and five hundred cows, provided that they should commit no further hostilities, but depart thence presently after payment of money and cattle. The one and the other being delivered, the whole fleet set sail, causing great joy to the inhabitants of Maracaibo, to see themselves quit of them. But three days after they renewed their fears with admiration, seeing the pirates appear again, and re-enter the port with all their ships. But these apprehensions vanished upon hearing one of the pirates' errand, who came ashore from Lolonois, "to demand a skilful pilot, to conduct one of the greatest ships over the dangerous bank that lieth at the very entry of the lake;" which petition, or rather command, was instantly granted.

They had now been full two months in those towns, wherein they committed those cruel and insolent actions we have related. Departing thence, they took their course to Hispaniola, and arrived there in eight days, casting anchor in a port called *Isla de la Vacca*, or Cow Island. This island is inhabited by French Buccaneers, who mostly sell the flesh they hunt to pirates and others who now and then put in there to victual or trade. Here they unloaded their whole *cargazon* of riches, the usual storehouse of the pirates being commonly under the shelter of the Buccaneers. Here they made a dividend of all their prizes and gains, according to the order and degree of every one, as has been mentioned before. Having made an exact calculation of all their plunder, they found in ready money two hundred and sixty thousand pieces of eight. This being divided, every one received for his share in money, as also in silk, linen, and other commodities, to the value of above one hundred pieces of eight. Those who had been wounded received their first part, after the rate mentioned before, for the loss of their limbs. Then they weighed all the plate uncoined, reckoning ten pieces of eight to a pound. The jewels were prized differently, either too high or too low, by reason of their ignorance. This done, every one was put to his oath again, that he had not smuggled any thing from the common stock. Hence they proceeded to the dividend of the shares of such as were dead in battle, or otherwise. These shares were given to their friends, to be kept entire for them, and to be delivered in due time to their nearest relations, or their apparent lawful heirs.

The whole dividend being finished, they set sail for Tortuga. Here they arrived a month after, to the great joy of most of the island; for as to the common pirates, in three weeks they had scarce any money left, having spent it all in things of little value, or lost it at play. Here had arrived, not long before them, two French ships, with wine and brandy, and such like commodities, whereby these liquors, at the arrival of the pirates, were indifferent cheap. But this lasted not long, for soon after they were enhanced extremely, a gallon of brandy being sold for four pieces of eight. The governor of the island bought of the pirates the whole cargo of the ship laden with cocoa, giving for that rich commodity scarce the twentieth part of its worth. Thus they made shift to lose and spend the riches they had got, in much less time than they were purchased. The taverns and stews, according to the custom of pirates, got the greatest part; so that soon after they were forced to seek more by the same unlawful means they had got the former.

CHAPTER X.

Lolonois makes new Preparations to take the City of St. James de Leon, as also that of Nicaragua, where he miserably perishes.

Lolonois had got great repute at Tortuga, by this last voyage, because he brought home such considerable profit: and now he need take no great care to gather men to serve under him, more coming in voluntarily than he could employ, every one reposing such confidence in his conduct, that they judged it very safe to expose themselves, in his company, to the greatest dangers. He resolved, therefore, a second voyage to the parts of Nicaragua, to pillage there as many towns as he could.

Having published his new preparations, he had all his men together at the time, being about seven hundred. Of these he put three hundred aboard the ship he took at Maracaibo, and the rest in five other vessels of lesser burthen, so that they were in all six ships. The first port they went to was Bayaha, in Hispaniola, to victual the fleet, and take in provisions; which done, they steered their course to a port called Matamana, on the south side of Cuba, intending to take here all the canoes they could, these coasts being frequented by the fishers of tortoises, who carry them hence to the Havana. They took as many of them, to the great grief of those miserable people, as they thought necessary, for they had great use for these small bottoms, by reason the port they designed for had not depth enough for ships of any burthen. Hence they took their course towards the Cape Gracias à Dios, on the continent, in latitude 15° north, one hundred leagues from the Island de los Pinos. Being at sea, they were taken with a sad and tedious calm, and, by the agitation of the waves alone, were thrown into the Gulf of Honduras. Here they labored hard in vain to regain what they had lost, both the waters and the winds being contrary; besides, the ship wherein Lolonois was embarked could not follow the rest, and, what was worse, they wanted provisions. Hereupon, they were forced to put into the first port they could reach, to revictual. So they entered, with their canoes, into the River Xagua, inhabited by Indians, whom they totally destroyed, finding great quantities of millet, and many hogs and hens, not contented with which, they determined to remain there till the bad weather was over, and to pillage all the towns and villages along the coast of the gulf. Thus they passed from one place to another, seeking still more provisions, with which they were not sufficiently supplied. Having searched and rifled many villages, where they found no great matter, they came at last to Puerto Cavallo. Here the Spaniards have two store-houses, to keep the merchandises that are brought from the inner parts of the country, till the arrival of the ships. There was then in the port a Spanish ship of twenty-four guns and sixteen pedreros, or mortar-pieces. This ship was immediately seized by the pirates, and then drawing nigh the shore, they landed and burned the two storehouses with all the rest of the houses there. Many inhabitants, likewise, they took prisoners, and committed upon them the most inhuman cruelties that ever heathens invented, putting them to the cruellest tortures they could devise. It was the custom of Lolonois, that having tormented persons not confessing, he would instantly cut them in pieces with his hanger, and pull out their tongues, desiring to do so, if possible, to every Spaniard in the world. It often happened, that some of these miserable prisoners, being forced by the rack, would promise to discover the places where the fugitive Spaniards lay hid, which being not able afterwards to perform, they were put to more cruel deaths than they who were dead before.

The prisoners being all dead but two, (whom they reserved to show them what they desired,) they marched hence to the town of San Pedro, or St. Peter, ten or twelve leagues from Puerto Cavallo, being three hundred men, whom Lolonois led, leaving behind him Moses Van Vin, his lieutenant, to govern the rest in his absence. Being come three leagues on their way, they met with a troop of Spaniards, who lay in ambuscade for their coming. These they set upon with all the courage imaginable, and at last totally defeated. Howbeit, they behaved themselves very manfully at first, but not being able to resist the fury of the pirates, they were forced to give way and save themselves by flight, leaving many pirates dead in the place, some wounded, and some of their own party maimed, by the way. These Lolonois put to death without mercy, having asked them what questions he thought fit for his purpose.

There were still remaining some few prisoners not wounded. These were asked by Lolonois if any more Spaniards did lie farther on in ambuscade? They answered, there were. Then being brought before him, one by one, he asked if there was no other way to the town but that? This he did to avoid, if possible, those ambuscades. But they all constantly answered him, they knew none. Having asked them all, and finding they could show him no other way, Lolonois grew outrageously passionate, so that he drew his cutlass, and with it cut open the breast of one of those poor Spaniards, and, pulling out his heart, began to bite and gnaw it with his teeth, like a ravenous wolf, saying to the rest, "I will serve you all alike, if you show me not another way."

Hereupon those miserable wretches promised to show him another way; but, withal, they told him it was extremely difficult, and laborious. Thus, to satisfy that cruel tyrant, they began to lead him and his army; but finding it not for his purpose, as they had told him, he was forced to return to the former way, swearing, with great choler and indignation, *Mort Dieu, les Espagnols me le payeront.* By God's death, the Spaniards shall pay me for this.

Next day he fell into another ambuscade, which he assaulted with such horrible fury, that in less than an hour's time he routed the Spaniards, and killed the greatest part of them. The Spaniards thought by these ambuscades better to destroy the pirates, assaulting them by degrees; and for this reason had posted themselves in several places. At last he met with a third ambuscade, where was placed a party stronger, and more advantageously, than the former. Yet, notwithstanding, the pirates, by continually throwing little fire-balls in great numbers, for some time, forced this party as well as the former to flee, and this with so great loss of men, that before they could reach the town, the greatest part of the Spaniards were either killed or wounded. There was but one path which led to the town, very well barricadoed with good defences; and the rest of the town round was planted with shrubs called *raqueltes*, full of thorns very sharp-pointed. This sort of fortification seemed stronger than the triangles used in Europe, when an army is of necessity to pass by the place of an enemy; it being almost impossible for the pirates to traverse those shrubs. The Spaniards posted behind the said defences, seeing the pirates come, began to ply them with their great guns; but these perceiving them ready to fire, used to stoop down, and when the shot was made, to fall upon the defendants with fire-balls, and naked swords, killing many of the town. Yet, notwithstanding, not being able to advance any farther, they retired for the present. Then they renewed the attack, with fewer men than before, and observing not to shoot till they were very nigh, they gave the Spaniards a charge so dexterously, that with every shot they killed an enemy.

The attack continuing thus eager on both sides till night, the Spaniards were compelled to hang forth a white flag, and desired to come to a parley. The only conditions they required were, that the pirates should give the inhabitants quarter for two hours. This little time they demanded, with intent to carry away and hide as much of their goods and riches as they could, and to fly to some other neighboring town. Granting this article, they entered the town, and continued there the two hours, without committing the least hostility on the inhabitants; but no sooner was that time past, than Lolonois ordered that the inhabitants should be followed, and robbed of all they had carried away; and not only their goods, but their persons likewise to be made prisoners; though the greatest part of their merchandise and goods were so hid, as the pirates could not find them, except a few leathern sacks, filled with anil, or indigo.

Having staid here a few days, and, according to their custom, committed most horrid insolencies, they at last quitted the place, carrying away all they possibly could, and reducing the town to ashes. Being come to the sea-side, where they left a party of their own, they found these had been cruising upon the fishermen thereabouts, or who came that way from the River of Guatemala: in this river was also expected a ship from Spain. Finally, they resolved to go towards the islands on the other side of the gulf, there to cleanse and careen their vessels; but they left two canoes before the coast, or rather the mouth of the River of Guatemala, in order to take the ship, which, as I said, was expected from Spain.

But their chief intent in going hither was to seek provisions, knowing the tortoises of those places are excellent food. Being arrived, they divided themselves, each party choosing a fit post for that fishery. They undertook to knit nets with the rinds of certain trees called *macoa*, whereof they make also ropes and cables; so that no vessel can be in need of such things, if they can but find the said trees. There are also many places where they find pitch in so great abundance, that running down the sea-coasts, being melted by the sun, it congeals in the water in great heaps, like small islands. This pitch is not like that of Europe, but resembles, both in color and shape, that froth of the sea called bitumen. But, in my judgment, this matter is nothing but wax mixed with sand, which stormy weather, and the rolling waves of great rivers, hath cast into the sea. For in those parts are great quantities of bees, who make their honey in trees, to the bodies of which the honey-comb being fixed, when tempests arise, they are torn away, and by the fury of the winds carried into the sea, as is said. Some naturalists say, that the honey and the wax are separated by the salt water, whence proceeds the good amber. This opinion seems the more probable, because the said amber tastes as wax doth.

But to return to my discourse. The pirates made in those islands all the haste they possibly could to equip their vessels, hearing that the Spanish ship was come which they expected. They spent some time cruising on the coasts of Yucatan, where inhabit many Indians, who seek for the said amber in those seas. And I shall here, by the by, make some short remarks on the manner of living of the Indians, and their religion.

They have now been above one hundred years under the Spaniards, to whom they performed all manner of services; for whensoever any of them needed a slave, or servant, they sent for these to serve them as long as they pleased. By the Spaniards they were initiated in the principles of the Christian faith and religion, and they sent them every Sunday and holiday a priest to perform divine service among them. Afterwards, for reasons not known, but certainly through temptations of the father of idolatry, the devil, they suddenly cast off the Christian religion, abusing the priest that was sent them. This provoked the Spaniards to punish them, by casting many of the chief into prison. Every one of those barbarians had, and hath still, a god to himself, whom he serves and worships. It is a matter of admiration how they use a child newly born. As soon as it comes into the world, they carry it to the temple; here they make a hole, which they fill with ashes only, on which they place the child naked, leaving it there a whole night alone, not without great danger, no body daring to come near it: meanwhile the temple is open on all sides, that all sorts of beasts may freely come in and out. Next day, the father and relations of the infant return to see if the track or step of any animal appears in the ashes: not finding any, they leave the child there till some beast has approached the infant, and left behind him the marks of his feet. To this animal, whatsoever it be, they consecrate the creature newly born, as to its god, which he is bound to worship all his life, esteeming the said beast his patron and protector. They offer to their gods sacrifices of fire, wherein they burn a certain gum, called by them *copal,* whose smoke smells very deliciously. When the infant is grown up, the parents thereof tell him who he ought to worship, serve, and honor as his own proper god. Then he goes to the temple, where he makes offerings to the said beast. Afterwards, if in the course of his life any one injure him, or any evil happen to him, he complains to that beast and sacrifices to it for revenge. Hence it often comes, that those who have done the injury of which he complains, are bitten, killed, or otherwise hurt by such animals.

After this superstitious and idolatrous manner live those miserable and ignorant Indians that inhabit the islands of the Gulf of Honduras; as also many of them on the continent of Yucatan, in the territories whereof are most excellent ports, where those Indians most commonly build their houses. These people are not very faithful to one another, and use strange ceremonies at their marriages. Whensoever any one pretends to marry a young damsel, he first applies himself to her father or nearest relation. He examines him nicely about the manner of cultivating their plantations, and other things at his pleasure.

Having satisfied the questions of his father-in-law, he gives the young man a bow and arrow, with which he repairs to the young maid, and presents her with a garland of green leaves and sweet-smelling flowers; this she is obliged to put on her head, and lay aside that which she wore before, it being the custom for virgins to go perpetually crowned with flowers. This garland being received and put on her head, every one of the relations and friends go to advise with others, whether that marriage will be like to be happy or not; then they meet at the house of the damsel's father, where they drink of a liquor made of maize, or Indian wheat; and here, before the whole company, the father gives his daughter in marriage to the bridegroom. Next day the bride comes to her mother, and in her presence pulls off the garland, and tears it in pieces with great cries and lamentations. Many other things I could relate of the manner of living and customs of those Indians, but I shall follow my discourse.

Our pirates, therefore, had many canoes of the Indians in the Isle of Sambale, five leagues from the coasts of Yucatan. Here is great quantity of amber, but especially when any storm arises from towards the east; whence the waves bring many things, and very different. Through this sea no vessels can pass, unless very small, it being too shallow. In the lands that are surrounded by this sea, is found much Campeachy wood, and other things that serve for dyeing, much esteemed in Europe, and would be more, if we had the skill of the Indians, who make a dye or tincture that never fades.

The pirates having been in that gulf three months, and receiving advice that the Spanish ship was come, hastened to the port where the ship lay at anchor unlading his merchandise, with design to assault her as soon as possible; but first, they thought convenient to send away some of their boats to seek for a small vessel also expected, very richly laden with plate, indigo, and cochineal. Meanwhile, the ship's crew having notice that the pirates designed upon them, prepared all things for a good defence, being mounted with forty-two guns, well furnished with arms and other necessaries, and one hundred and thirty fighting men. To Lolonois all this seemed but little, for he assaulted her with great courage, his own ship carrying but twenty-two guns, and having no more than a small *saety*, or fly-boat, for help. But the Spaniards defended themselves so well, as they forced the pirates to retire; but the smoke of the powder continuing thick, as a dark fog or mist, with four canoes well manned, they boarded the ship with great agility, and forced the Spaniards to surrender.

The ship being taken, they found not in her what they thought, being already almost unladen. All they got was only fifty bars of iron, a small parcel of paper, some earthen jars of wine, and other things of small importance.

Then Lolonois called a council of war, and told them he intended for Guatamala. Hereupon they divided into several sentiments, some liking the proposal, and others disliking it, especially a party of them who were but raw in those exercises, and who imagined at their setting forth from Tortuga, that pieces of eight were gathered as easily as pears from a tree; but finding most things contrary to their expectation, they quitted the fleet and returned; others affirmed they had rather starve than return home without a great deal of money.

But the major part judging the propounded voyage little to their purpose, separated from Lolonois and the rest. Of these, one Moses Vanclein was ringleader, captain of the ship taken at Puerto Cavallo: this fellow steered for Tortuga, to cruise to and fro in these seas. With him joined another comrade of his, by name Pierre le Picard, who seeing the rest leave Lolonois, thought fit to do the same. These runaways having thus parted company, steered homewards, coasting along the continent till they came to Costa Rica; here they landed a strong party nigh the River Veraguas, and marched in good order to the town of the same name; this they took and totally pillaged, though the Spaniards made a strong resistance. They brought away some of the inhabitants as prisoners, with all that they had, which was of no great importance, by reason of the poverty of the place, which exerciseth no other trade than working in the mines, where some of the inhabitants constantly attend, while none seek for gold, but only slaves. These they compel to dig and wash the earth in the neighboring rivers, where often they find pieces of gold as big as peas. The pirates gaining in this adventure but seven or eight pound weight of gold, they returned, giving over the design to go to the town of Nata, situate on the coasts of the South Sea, whose inhabitants are rich merchants, and their slaves work in the mines of Veraguas; being deterred by the multitude of Spaniards gathered on all sides to fall upon them, whereof they had timely advice.

Lolonois, thus left by his companions, remained alone in the Gulf of Honduras. His ship being too great to get out at the reflux of those seas, there he sustained great want of provisions, so as they were constrained to go ashore every day to seek sustenance, and not finding any thing else, they were forced to kill and eat monkeys, and other animals, such as they could find.

At last, in the latitude of the Cape of Gracias a Dios, near a certain little island called De las Pertas, his ship struck on a bank of sand, where it stuck so fast, as no art could get her off again, though they unladed all the guns, iron, and other weighty things as much as they could. Hereupon they were forced to break the ship in pieces, and with planks and nails build themselves a boat to get away; and while they are busy about it, I shall describe the said isles and their inhabitants.

The Islands De las Pertas are inhabited by savage Indians, not having known or conversed with civil people. They are tall and very nimble, running almost as fast as horses; at diving, also, they are very dexterous and hardy. From the bottom of the sea I saw them take up an anchor of six hundred weight, tying a cable to it with great dexterity, and pulling it from a rock. Their arms are made of wood, without any iron point; but some instead thereof use a crocodile's tooth. They have no bows nor arrows, as the other Indians have, but their common weapon is a sort of lance, a fathom and a half long. Here are many plantations, surrounded with woods, whence they gather abundance of fruits, as potatoes, bananas, racoven, ananas, and many others. They have no houses to dwell in, as at other places in the Indies. Some say they eat human flesh, which is confirmed by what happened when Lolonois was there. Two of his companions, one a Frenchman and the other a Spaniard, went into the woods, where, having straggled a while, a troop of Indians pursued them. They defended themselves as well as they could with their swords, but at last were forced to flee. The nimble Frenchman escaped; but the Spaniard, being not so swift, was taken and heard of no more. Some days after, twelve pirates set forth very well armed to seek their companion, among whom was the Frenchman, who conducted them, and showed them the place where he left him; here they found that the Indians had kindled a fire, and at a small distance they found a man's bones well roasted, with some pieces of flesh ill-scraped off the bones, and one hand, which had only two fingers remaining, whence they concluded they had roasted the poor Spaniard.

They marched on, seeking for Indians, and found a great number together, who endeavored to escape, but they overtook some of them, and brought aboard their ships five men and four women; with these they took much pains to make themselves be understood, and to gain their affections, giving them trifles, as knives, beads, and the like; they gave them also victuals and drink, but nothing would they taste. It was also observable, that while they were prisoners, they spoke not one word to each other; so that seeing these poor Indians were much afraid, they presented them again with some small things and let them go. When they parted, they made signs they would come again, but they soon forgot their benefactors, and were never heard of more; neither could any notice afterwards be had of these Indians, nor any others in the whole island, which made the pirates suspect that both those that were taken and all the rest of the islanders swam away by night to some little neighboring islands, especially considering they could never set eyes on any Indian more, nor any boat or other vessel. Meanwhile the pirates were very desirous to see their long-boat finished out of the timber that struck on the sands; yet considering their work would be long, they began to cultivate some pieces of ground: here they sowed French beans, which ripened in six weeks, and many other fruits. They had good provision of Spanish wheat, bananas, racoven, and other things; with the wheat they made bread, and baked it in portable ovens, brought with them. Thus they feared not hunger in those desert places, employing themselves thus for five or six months; which past, and the long-boat finished, they resolved for the River of Nicaragua, to see if they could take some canoes, and return to the said islands for their companions that remained behind, by reason the boat could not hold so many men together. Hereupon, to avoid disputes, they cast lots, determining who should go or stay.

The lot fell on one half of the people of the lost vessel, who embarked in the long-boat and on the skiff which they had before, the other half remaining ashore. Lolonois having set sail, arrived in few days at the River of Nicaragua. Here that ill fortune assailed him which of long time had been reserved for him, as a punishment due to the multitude of horrible crimes committed in his licentious and wicked life. Here he met with both Spaniards and Indians, who jointly setting upon him and his companions, the greatest part of the pirates were killed on the place. Lolonois, with those that remained alive, had much ado to escape aboard their boats; yet, notwithstanding this great loss, he resolved not to return to those he had left at the Isle of Pertas, without taking some boats, such as he looked for. To this effect he determined to go on to the coasts of Carthagena; but God Almighty, the time of his divine justice being now come, had appointed the Indians of Darien to be the instruments and executioners thereof. These Indians of Darien are esteemed as bravoes, or wild savage Indians, by the neighboring Spaniards, who never could civilize them. Hither Lolonois came (brought by his evil conscience, that cried for punishment) thinking to act his cruelties; but the Indians within a few days after his arrival took him prisoner, and tore him in pieces alive, throwing his body limb by limb into the fire, and his ashes into the air, that no trace or memory might remain of such an infamous, inhuman creature. One of his companions gave me an exact account of this tragedy, affirming, that himself had escaped the same punishment with the greatest difficulty; he believed also that many of his comrades, who were taken in that renconter by those Indians, were, as their cruel captain, torn in pieces and burnt alive. Thus ends the history, the life, and miserable death of that infernal wretch Lolonois, who, full of horrid, execrable, and enormous deeds, and debtor to so much innocent blood, died by cruel and butcherly hands, such as his own were in the course of his life.

Those that remained in the Island De las Pertas, waiting for the return of them who got away only to their great misfortune, hearing no news of their captain nor companions, at last embarked on the ship of a certain pirate, who happened to pass that way. This fellow came from Jamaica, with intent to land at Gracias a Dios, and from thence to enter the river with his canoes, and take the city of Carthagena. These two crews of pirates being now joined, were infinitely glad at the presence and society of one another. Those, because they found themselves delivered from the miseries, poverty, and necessities wherein they had lived ten entire months; — these, because they were now considerably strengthened, to effect with greater satisfaction their designs. Hereupon, as soon as they were arrived at Gracias a Dios, they all put themselves into canoes, and entered the river, being five hundred men, leaving only five or six persons in each ship to keep them. They took no provisions, being persuaded they should find every where sufficient; but these their hopes were found totally vain, not being grounded on Almighty God; for he ordained it so, that the Indians, aware of their coming, all fled, not leaving in their houses or plantations, which for the most part border on the sides of rivers, any necessary provisions or victuals. Hereby, in a few days after they had quitted the ships, they were reduced to most extreme necessity and hunger; but their hopes of making their fortunes very soon animating them for the present, they contented themselves with a few green herbs, such as they could gather on the banks of the river.

Yet all this courage and vigor lasted but a fortnight, when their hearts, as well as bodies, began to fail for hunger; insomuch as they were forced to quit the river, and betake themselves to the woods, seeking out some villages where they might find relief, but all in vain; for having ranged up and down the woods for some days, without finding the least comfort, they were forced to return to the river, where being come, they thought convenient to descend to the sea-coast where they had left their ships, not having been able to find what they sought for. In this laborious journey they were reduced to such extremity, that many of them devoured their own shoes, the sheaths of their swords, knives, and other such things, being almost ravenous, and eager to meet some Indians, intending to sacrifice them to their teeth. At last they arrived at the sea-coast, where they found some comfort and relief to their former miseries, and also means to seek more; yet the greatest part perished through faintness and other diseases contracted by hunger, which also caused the remaining part to disperse, till at last, by degrees, many or most of them fell into the same pit that Lolonois did: of whom, and of whose companions, having given a compendious narrative, I shall continue with the actions and exploits of Capt. Henry Morgan, who may deservedly be called the second Lolonois, not being unlike or inferior to him, either in achievements against the Spaniards, or in robberies of many innocent people.

CHAPTER XI

The Origin and Descent of Captain Henry Morgan; his Exploits, and the most remarkable Actions of his Life.

Capt. Henry Morgan was born in Great Britain, in the principality of Wales; his father was a rich yeoman, or farmer, of good quality, even as most who bear that name in Wales are known to be. Morgan, when young, had no inclination to the calling of his father, and therefore left his country, and came towards the sea-coasts to seek some other employment more suitable to his aspiring humor; where he found several ships at anchor, bound to Barbadoes. With these he resolved to go in the service of one, who, according to the practice of those parts, sold him as soon as he came ashore. He served his time at Barbadoes, and obtaining his liberty, betook himself to Jamaica, there to seek new fortunes. Here he found two vessels of pirates ready to go to sea; and being destitute of employment, he went with them, with intent to follow the exercises of that sort of people. He soon learned their manner of living, so exactly, that having performed three or four voya-

Sir Henry Morgan.

ges with profit and success, he agreed with some of his comrades, who had got by the same voyages a little money, to join stocks and buy a ship. The vessel being bought, they unanimously chose him captain and commander.

With this ship he set forth from Jamaica to cruise on the coasts of Campeachy, in which voyage he took several ships, with which he returned triumphant. Here he found an old pirate, named Mansvelt, (whom we have already mentioned,) busied in equipping a considerable fleet, with design to land on the continent, and pillage whatever he could. Mansvelt seeing Capt. Morgan return with so many prizes, judged him to be a man of courage, and chose him for his vice-admiral in that expedition. Thus having fitted out fifteen ships, great and small, they sailed from Jamaica with 500 men, Walloons and French. This fleet arrived not long after at the Isle of St. Catherine, near the continent of Costa Rica, latitude 12° 30′, and distant 35 leagues from the river Chagre. Here they made their first descent, landing most of their men, who soon forced the garrison that kept the island to surrender all the forts and castles thereof; which they instantly demolished, except one, wherein they placed one hundred men of their own party, and all the slaves they had taken from the Spaniards; with the rest of their men they marched to another small island, so near St. Catherine's, that, with a bridge they made in a few days, they passed thither, taking with them all the ordnance they had taken on the great island. Having ruined with fire and sword both the islands, leaving necessary orders at the said castle, they put to sea again with their Spanish prisoners; yet these they set ashore not long after, on the Firm Land, near Puerto Velo. Then they cruised on Costa Rica, till they came to the river Colla, designing to pillage all the towns in those parts, thence to pass to the village of Nata, to do the same.

The governor of Panama, on advice of their arrival, and of the hostilities they committed, thought it his duty to meet them with a body of men. His coming caused the pirates to retire suddenly, seeing the whole country was alarmed, and that their designs were known, and consequently defeated at that time. Hereupon, they returned to St. Catherine's, to visit the hundred men they had left in garrison there. The governor of these men was a Frenchman, named Le Sieur Simon, who behaved himself very well in that charge, while Mansvelt was absent, having put the great island in a very good posture of defence, and the little one he had caused to be cultivated with many fertile plantations, sufficient to revictual the whole fleet, not only for the present, but also for a new voyage.

Mansvelt was very much bent to keep these two islands in perpetual possession, being very commodiously situated for the pirates; being so near the Spanish dominions, and easily defended, as I shall represent in the third part of this history at large, in a copper plate.

Hereupon, Mansvelt determined to return to Jamaica, to send recruits to St. Catherine's, that in case of an invasion the pirates might be provided for a defence. As soon as he arrived, he propounded his intentions to the governor there, who rejected his propositions, fearing to displease his master, the king of England; besides that, giving him the men he desired, and necessaries, he must of necessity diminish the forces of that island, whereof he was governor. Hereupon, Mansvelt, knowing that of himself he could not compass his designs, went to Tortuga; but there, before he could put in execution what was intended, death surprised him, and put a period to his wicked life, leaving all things in suspense till the occasion I shall hereafter relate.

Le Sieur Simon, governor of St. Catherine's, receiving no news from Mansvelt, his admiral, was impatiently desirous to know the cause thereof. Meanwhile, Don John Perez de Guzman, being newly come to the government of Costa Rica, thought it not convenient for the interest of Spain for that island to be in the hands of the pirates. Hereupon, he equipped a considerable fleet, which he sent to retake it; but before he used violence, he wrote a letter to Le Sieur Simon, telling him, that if he would surrender the island to his Catholic majesty, he should be very well rewarded; but in case of refusal severely punished, when he had forced him to do it. Le Sieur Simon, seeing no probability of being able to defend it alone, nor any emolument that by so doing could accrue either to him or his people, after some small resistance delivered it up to its true lord and master, under the same articles they had obtained it from the Spaniards; a few days after which surrender there arrived from Jamaica an English ship, which the governor there had sent under-hand, with a good supply of people, both men and women. The Spaniards from the castle having espied this ship, put forth English colors, and pursuaded Le Sieur Simon to go aboard, and conduct the ship into a port they assigned him. This he performed, and they were all made prisoners. A certain Spanish engineer has published in print an exact relation of the retaking of this isle by the Spaniards, which I have thought fit to insert here.

A true relation and particular account of the Victory obtained by the arms of his Catholic Majesty against the English Pirates, by the direction and valor of Don John Perez de Guzman, Knight of the Order of St. James, Governor and Captain-General of Terra Firma and the Province of Veraguas.

The kingdom of Terra Firma, which of itself is sufficiently strong to repel and destroy great fleets, especially the pirates of Jamaica, had several ways notice imparted to the governor thereof, that fourteen English vessels cruised on the coasts belonging to his Catholic majesty. July 14, 1665, news came to Panama that they were arrived at Puerto de Naos, and had forced the Spanish garrison of the Isle of St. Catherine, whose governor was Don Esteven del Campo, and possessed themselves of the said island, taking prisoners the inhabitants, and destroying all that they met. About the same time, Don John Perez de Guzman received particular information of these robberies from some Spaniards who escaped out of the island, (and whom he ordered to be conveyed to Puerto Velo) that the said pirates came into the island May 2, by night, without being perceived; and that the next day, after some skirmishes, they took the fortresses, and made prisoners all the inhabitants and soldiers that could not escape. Upon this, Don John called a council of war, wherein he declared the great progress the said pirates had made in the dominions of his Catholic majesty, and propounded, "that it was absolutely necessary to send some force to the isles of St. Catherine, sufficient to retake it from the pirates, the honor and interest of his majesty of Spain being very narrowly concerned herein; otherwise the pirates by such conquests might easily, in course of time, possess themselves of all the countries thereabouts." To this some made answer, "that the pirates, not being able to subsist in the said island, would of necessity consume and waste themselves, and be forced to quit it, without any necessity of retaking it: that consequently it was not worth the while to engage in so many expenses and troubles as this would cost." Notwithstanding which, Don John being an expert and valiant soldier, ordered that provisions should be conveyed to Puerto Velo for the use of the militia, and transported himself thither, with no small danger of his life. Here he arrived July 2, with most things necessary to the expedition in hand, where he found in the port a good ship, and well mounted, called the St. Vincent, that belonged to the company of the negroes, which he manned and victualled very well, and sent to the Isle of St. Catherine, constituting Capt. Joseph Sanchez Ximenez, major of Puerto Velo, commander thereof. He carried with him two hundred and seventy soldiers, and thirty-seven prisoners of the same island, beside thirty-four Spaniards of the garrison of Puerto Velo, twenty-nine mulattoes of Panama, twelve Indians, very dextrous at shooting with bows and arrows, seven expert and able gunners, two lieutenants, two pilots, one surgeon, and one religious, of the order of St. Francis, for their chaplain.

Don John soon after gave orders to all the officers how to behave themselves, telling them that the governor of Carthagena would supply them with more men, boats, and all things else, necessary for that enterprise, to which effect he had already written to the said governor. July 24, Don John setting sail with a fair wind, he called before him all his people, and made them a speech, encouraging them to fight against the enemies of their country and religion, and especially against those inhuman pirates, who had committed so many horrid cruelties upon the subjects of his Catholic majesty; withal, promising every one most liberal rewards, especially to such as should behave themselves well in the service of their king and country. Thus Don John bid them farewell, and the ship set sail under a favorable gale. The 22d they arrived at Carthagena, and presented a letter to the governor thereof from the noble and valiant Don John, who received it with testimonies of great affection to the person of Don John, and his majesty's service. And seeing their resolution to be conformable to his desires, he promised them his assistance, with one frigate, one galleon, one boat, and one hundred and twenty-six men; one half out of his own garrison, and the other half mulattoes. Thus being well provided with necessaries, they left the port of Carthagena August 2, and the 10th they arrived in sight of St. Catherine's, towards the western point thereof; and though the wind was contrary, yet they reached the port, and anchored within it, having lost one of their boats by foul weather, at the rock called Quita Signos.

The pirates, seeing our ships come to an anchor, gave them presently three guns with bullets, which were soon answered in the same coin. Hereupon, Major Joseph Sanchez Ximenez sent ashore to the pirates one of his officers, to require them, in the name of the Catholic king his master, to surrender the island, seeing they had taken it in the midst of peace between the two crowns of Spain and England; and that if they would be obstinate, he would certainly put them all to the sword. The pirates made answer, that the island had once before belonged unto the government and dominions of the king of England, and that, instead of surrendering it, they preferred to lose their lives.

On Friday the 13th three negroes, from the enemy, came swimming aboard our admiral; these brought intelligence that all the pirates upon the island were only seventy-two in number, and that they were under a great consternation, seeing such considerable forces come against them. With this intelligence, the Spaniards resolved to land, and advance towards the fortresses, which ceased not to fire as many great guns against them as they possibly could; which were answered in the same manner on our side, till dark night. On Sunday the 15th, the day of the assumption of our Lady, the weather being very calm and clear, the Spaniards began to advance thus: the ship St. Vincent, riding admiral, discharged two whole broadsides on the battery called the Conception; the ship St. Peter, that was vice-admiral, discharged likewise her guns against the other battery named St. James. Meanwhile, our people landed in small boats, directing their course towards the point of the battery last mentioned, and thence they marched towards the gate called Cortadura. Lieutenant Francis de Cazeres, being desirous to view the strength of the enemy, with only fifteen men, was compelled to retreat in haste, by reason of the great guns, which played so furiously on the place where he stood; they shooting, not only pieces of iron, and small bullets, but also the organs of the church, discharging in every shot three score pipes at a time.

Notwithstanding this heat of the enemy, Captain Don Joseph Ramirez de Leyva, with sixty men, made a strong attack, wherein they fought on both sides very desperately, till at last he overcame, and forced the pirates to surrender the fort.

On the other side, Captain John Galeno, with ninety men, passed over the hills, to advance that way towards the castle of St. Teresa. Meanwhile Major Don Joseph Sanchez Ximenes, as commander-in-chief, with the rest of his men, set forth from the battery of St. James, passing the port with four boats, and landing in despite of the enemy. About this same time, Captain John Galeno began to advance with the men he led to the fore-mentioned fortress; so that our men made three attacks on three several sides, at one and the same time, with great courage; till the pirates seeing many of their men already killed, and that they could in no manner subsist any longer, retreated towards Cortadura, where they surrendered themselves, and the whole island, into our hands. Our people possessed themselves of all, and set up the Spanish colors, as soon as they had rendered thanks to God Almighty for the victory obtained on such a signalized day. The number of dead were six men of the enemy's, with many wounded, and seventy prisoners. On our side was only one man killed, and four wounded.

There were found on the island eight hundred pounds of powder, two hundred and fifty pounds of small bullets, with many other military provisions. Among the prisoners were taken also two Spaniards, who had bore arms under the English against his Catholic majesty. These were shot to death the next day, by order of the major. The 10th day of September arrived at the isle an English vessel, which being seen at a great distance by the major, he ordered Le Sieur Simon, who was a Frenchman, to go and visit the said ship, and tell them that were on board, that the island belonged still to the English. He performed the command, and found in the said ship only fourteen men, one woman and her daughter, who were all instantly made prisoners.

The English pirates were all transported to Puerto Velo, excepting three, who by order of the governor were carried to Panama, there to work in the castle of St. Jerom. This fortification is an excellent piece of workmanship, and very strong, being raised in the middle of the port, of a quadrangular form, and of very hard stone; its height is eighty-eight geometrical feet, the wall being fourteen, and the curtains seventy-five feet diameter. It was built at the expense of several private persons, the governor of the city furnishing the greatest part of the money, so that it cost his majesty nothing.

CHAPTER XII.

Of the Island of Cuba. — Captain Morgan attempts to preserve the Isle of St. Catherine as a refuge to the nest of Pirates, but fails of his design. — He arrives at, and takes the Village of, El Puerto del Principe.

Capt. Morgan seeing his predecessor and Admiral Mansvelt were dead, used all the means that were possible to keep in possession the Isle of St. Catherine, seated near Cuba. His chief intent was to make it a refuge and sanctuary to the pirates of those parts, putting it in a condition of being a convenient receptacle of their preys and robberies. To this effect he left no stone unmoved, writing to several merchants in Virginia and New England, persuading them to send him provisions and necessaries, towards putting the said island in such a posture of defence, as to fear no danger of invasion from any side. But all this proved ineffectual, by the Spaniards retaking the said island; yet Captain Morgan retained his courage, which put him on new designs. First, he equipped a ship, in order to gather a fleet as great and as strong as he could. By degrees he effected it, and gave orders to every member of his fleet to meet at a certain port of Cuba, there determined to call a council, and deliberate what was best to be done, and what place first to fall upon. Leaving these preparations in this condition, I shall give my reader some small account of the said Isle of Cuba, in whose port this expedition was hatched, seeing I omitted to do it in its proper place.

Cuba lies from east to west, in north latitude, from twenty to twenty-three degrees; in length, one hundred and fifty German leagues, and about forty in breadth. Its fertility is equal to that of Hispaniola; besides which, it affords many things proper for trading and commerce; such as hides of several beasts, particularly those that in Europe are called hides of Havana. On all sides it is surrounded with many small islands, called the *Cayos:* these little islands the pirates use as ports of refuge. Here they have their meetings, and hold their councils, how best to assault the Spaniards. It is watered on all sides with plentiful and pleasant rivers, whose entries form both secure and spacious ports; beside many other harbors for ships, which along the calm shores and coasts adorn this rich and beautiful island; all which contribute much to its happiness, by facilitating trade, whereto they invited both natives and aliens. The chief of these ports are San Jago, Byame, Santa Maria, Espiritu Santo, Trinidad, Zagoa, Cabo de Corientes, and others, on the south side of the island. On the north side are, La Havana, Puerto Mariano, Santa Cruz, Mata Ricos, and Barracoa.

This island hath two chief cities, to which all the towns and villages thereof give obedience. The first is Santa Jago, or St. James, seated on the south side, and having under its jurisdiction one half of the island. The chief magistrates hereof are a bishop and a governor, who command the villages and towns of the said half. The chief of these are, on the south side, Espiritu Santo, Puerto del Principe, and Bayame. On the north it has Barracoa, and De los Cayos. The greatest part of the commerce driven here comes from the Canaries, whither they transport much tobacco, sugar, and hides, which sort of merchandise are drawn to the head city from the subordinate towns and villages. Formerly this city of Santa Jago was miserably sacked by the pirates of Jamaica and Tortuga, though it is defended by a considerable castle.

The city and port De la Havana lies between the north and west side of the island. This is one of the strongest places of the West Indies; its jurisdiction extends over the other half of the island; the chief places under it being Santa Cruz on the north side, and La Trinidad on the south. Hence is transported huge quantities of tobacco, which is sent to New Spain and Costa Rica, even as far as the South Sea, besides many ships laden with this commodity that are consigned to Spain and other parts of Europe, not only in the leaf but in rolls. This city is defended by three castles, very great and strong; two of which lie towards the port, and the other is seated on a hill that commands the town. It is esteemed to contain about ten thousand families. The merchants of this place trade in New Spain, Campeachy, Honduras, and Florida. All ships that come from the parts before mentioned, as also from Caraccas, Carthagena, and Costa Rica, are necessitated to take their provisions in at Havana, to make their voyage for Spain; this being the necessary and straight course they must steer for the south of Europe, and other parts. The plate-fleet of Spain, which the Spaniards call *flota*, being homeward bound, touches here yearly to complete their cargo with hides, tobacco, and Campeachy wood.

Captain Morgan had been but two months in these ports of the south of Cuba, when he had got together a fleet of twelve sail, between ships and great boats, with seven hundred fighting men, part English and part French. They called a council, and some advised to assault the city of Havana in the night, which they said might easily be done, if they could but take any few of the ecclesiastics; yea, that the city might be sacked before the castles could put themselves in a posture of defence. Others propounded, according to their several opinions, other attempts; but the former proposal was rejected, because many of the pirates, who had been prisoners at other times in the said city, affirmed nothing of consequence could be done with less than fifteen hundred men. Moreover, that with all these people, they ought first to go to the Island De los Pinos, and land them in small boats about Matamona, fourteen leagues from the said city, whereby to accomplish their designs.

Finally, they saw no possibility of gathering so great a fleet, and hereupon, with what they had, they concluded to attempt some other place. Among the rest, one propounded they should assault the town of El Puerto del Principe. This proposition he persuaded to, by saying he knew that place very well, and that being at a distance from sea, it never was sacked by any pirates, whereby the inhabitants were rich, exercising their trade by ready money, with those of Havana, who kept here an established commerce, chiefly in hides. This proposal was presently admitted by Captain Morgan and the chief of his companions. Hereupon they ordered every captain to weigh anchor and set sail, steering towards that coast nearest to El Puerto del Principe. Here is a bay, named by the Spaniards El Puerto de Santa Maria. Being arrived at this bay, a Spaniard, who was prisoner aboard the fleet, swam ashore by night to the town of El Puerto del Principe, giving an account to the inhabitants of the design of the pirates, which he overheard in their discourse, while they thought he did not understand English. The Spaniards upon this advice began to hide their riches, and carry away their movables; the governor immediately raised all the people of the town, freemen and slaves, and with part of them took a post by which of necessity the pirates must pass, and commanded many trees to be cut down and laid cross the ways to hinder their passage, placing several ambuscades strengthened with some pieces of cannon to play upon them on their march. He gathered in all about eight hundred men, of which detaching part into the said ambuscades, with the rest he begirt the town, drawing them up in a spacious field, whence they could see the coming of the pirates at length.

Captain Morgan with his men, now on the march, found the avenues to the town unpassable; hereupon they took their way through the wood, traversing it with great difficulty, whereby they escaped divers ambuscades; at last they came to the plain, from its figure, called by the Spaniards *La Savanna*, or the *Sheet*. The governor seeing them come, detached a troop of horse to charge them in the front, thinking to disperse them, and to pursue them with his main body; but this design succeeded not, for the pirates marched in very good order, at the sound of their drums, and with flying colors: coming near the horse they drew into a semicircle, and so advanced towards the Spaniards, who charged them valiantly for a while; but the pirates being very dexterous at their arms, and their governor, with many of their companions, being killed, they retreated towards the wood, to save themselves with more advantage; but, before they could reach it, most of them were unfortunately killed by the pirates. Thus they left the victory to these new-come enemies, who had no considerable loss of men in the battle, and but very few wounded. The skirmish lasted four hours. They entered the town not without great resistance of such as were within, who defended themselves as long as possible, and many seeing the enemy in the town, shut themselves up in their own houses, and thence made several shots upon the pirates; who thereupon threatened them, saying, "If you surrender not voluntarily, you shall soon see the town in a flame, and your wives and children torn in pieces before your faces." Upon these menaces the Spaniards submitted to the discretion of the pirates, believing they could not continue there long.

As soon as the pirates had possessed themselves of the town, they enclosed all the Spaniards, men, women, children, and slaves, in several churches, and pillaged all the goods they could find; then they searched the country round about, bringing in daily many goods and prisoners, with much provision. With this they fell to making great cheer, after their old custom, without remembering the poor prisoners, whom they let starve in the churches, though they tormented them daily and inhumanly to make them confess where they had hid their goods, money, &c., though little or nothing was left them, not sparing the women and little children, giving them nothing to eat, whereby the greatest part perished.

Pillage and provisions growing scarce, they thought convenient to depart and seek new fortunes in other places. They told the prisoners, "they should find money to ransom themselves, else they should be all transported to Jamaica; and beside, if they did not pay a second ransom for the town, they would turn every house in ashes." The Spaniards hereupon nominated among themselves four fellow-prisoners to go and seek for the above-mentioned contributions; but the pirates, to the intent they should return speedily with those ransoms, tormented several cruelly in their presence, before they departed. After a few days, the Spaniards returned, telling Captain Morgan, "We have ran up and down, and searched all the neighboring woods and places we most suspected, and yet have not been able to find any of our own party, nor consequently any fruit of our embassy; but if you are pleased to have a little longer patience with us, we shall certainly cause all that you demand to be paid within fifteen days;" which Captain Morgan granted. But not long after, there came into the town seven or eight pirates who had been ranging in the woods and fields, and got considerable booty. These brought, amongst other prisoners, a negro whom they had taken with letters. Captain Morgan having perused them, found they were from the governor of Santa Jago, being written to some of the prisoners, wherein he told them, "they should not make too much haste to pay any ransom for their town or persons, or any other pretext; but, on the contrary, they should put off the pirates as well as they could with excuses and delays, expecting to be relieved by him in a short time, when he would certainly come to their aid.

Upon this intelligence Captain Morgan immediately ordered all their plunder to be carried aboard; and withal, he told the Spaniards, that the very next day they should pay their ransoms, for he would not wait a moment longer, but reduce the whole town to ashes, if they failed of the sum he demanded.

With this intimation, Captain Morgan made no mention to the Spaniards of the letters he had intercepted. They answered, "that it was impossible for them to give such a sum of money in so short a space of time, seeing their fellow-townsmen were not to be found in all the country thereabouts." Captain Morgan knew full well their intentions, but thought it not convenient to stay there any longer, demanding of them only five hundred oxen or cows, with sufficient salt to powder them, with this condition, that they should carry them on board his ships. Thus he departed with all his men, taking with him only six of the principal prisoners as pledges. Next day the Spaniards brought the cattle and salt to the ships, and required the prisoners; but Captain Morgan refused to deliver them, till they had helped his men to kill and salt the beeves. This was performed in great haste, he not caring to stay there any longer, lest he should be surprised by the forces that were gathering against him; and having received all on board his vessels, he set at liberty the hostages. Meanwhile there happened some dissensions between the English and the French. The occasion was as follows: a Frenchman being employed in killing and salting the beeves, an English pirate took away the marrow-bones, he had taken out of the ox, which these people esteem much; hereupon they challenged one another. Being come to the place of duel, the Englishman stabbed the Frenchman in the back, whereby he fell down dead. The other Frenchmen, desirous of revenge, made an insurrection against the English; but Captain Morgan soon appeased them, by putting the criminal in chains to be carried to Jamaica, promising he would see justice done upon him; for though he might challenge his adversary, yet it was not lawful to kill him treacherously, as he did.

All things being ready, and on board, and the prisoners set at liberty, they sailed thence to a certain island, where Captain Morgan intended to make a dividend of what they had purchased in that voyage; where, being arrived, they found nigh the value of fifty thousand pieces of eight in money and goods. The sum being known, it caused a general grief to see such a small purchase, not sufficient to pay their debts at Jamaica. Hereupon Captain Morgan proposed they should think on some other enterprise and pillage before they returned. But the

French not being able to agree with the English, left Captain Morgan with those of his own nation, notwithstanding all the persuasions he used to induce them to continue in his company. Thus they parted with all external signs of friendship, Captain Morgan reiterating his promises to them, that he would see justice done on that criminal. This he performed, for being arrived at Jamaica, he caused him to be hanged, which was all the satisfaction the French pirates could expect.

CHAPTER XIII.

Captain Morgan, resolving to Attack and Plunder the City of Puerto Bello, Equips a Fleet, and with little Expense and small Forces take it.

Some may think that the French, having deserted Captain Morgan, the English alone could not have sufficient courage to attempt such great actions as before. But Captain Morgan, who always communicated vigor with his words, infused such spirit into his men, as put them instantly upon new designs; they being all persuaded that the sole execution of his orders would be a certain means of obtaining great riches, which so influenced their minds, that with inimitable courage they all resolved to follow him, as did also a certain pirate of Campeachy, who on this occasion joined with Captain Morgan, to seek new fortunes under his conduct. Thus Captain Morgan in a few days gathered a fleet of nine sail, either ships or great boats, wherein he had four hundred and sixty military men.

All things being ready, they put forth to sea, Captain Morgan imparting his design to nobody at present; he only told them on several occasions that he doubted not to make a good fortune by that voyage, if strange occurrences happened not. They steered towards the continent, where they arrived in a few days near Costa Rica, all their fleet safe. No sooner had they discovered land, but Captain Morgan declared his intentions to the captains, and presently after to the company. He told them he intended to plunder Puerto Bello by night, being resolved to put the whole city to the sack. And to encourage them, he added, "this enterprise could not fail, seeing he had kept it secret, without revealing it to any body, whereby they could not have notice of his coming." To this proposition some answered, "they had not a sufficient number of men to assault so strong and great a city." But Captain Morgan replied, "If our number is small, our hearts are great; and the fewer persons we are, the more union and better shares we shall have in the spoil." Hereupon, being stimulated with the hope of those vast riches they promised themselves from their success, they unanimously agreed to that design. Now, that my reader may better comprehend the boldness of his exploits, it may be necessary to say something beforehand of the city of Puerto Bello.

This city is in the province of Costa Rica, ten degrees north latitude, fourteen leagues from the Gulf of Darien, and eight westward from the ports called Nombre de Dios. It is judged the strongest place the king of Spain possesses in all the West Indies, except Havana and Carthagena. Here are two castles almost impregnable, that defend the city, situate at the entry of the port, so that no ship or boat can pass without permission. The garrison consists of three hundred soldiers, and the town is inhabited by about four hundred families. The merchants dwell not here, but only reside a while, when the galleons come from or go for Spain, by reason of the unhealthiness of the air, occasioned by vapors from the mountains; so that though their chief warehouses are at Puerto Bello, their habitations are at Panama, whence they bring the plate upon mules, when the fair begins, and when the ships belonging to the company of negroes arrive to sell slaves.

Captain Morgan, who knew very well all the avenues of this city and the neighboring coasts, arrived in the dusk of the evening at Puerto de Naos, ten leagues to the west of Puerto Bello. Being come hither they sailed up the river to another harbor called Puerto Pontin, where they anchored. Here they put themselves into boats and canoes, leaving in the ships only a few men to bring them next day to the port. About midnight they came to a place called Estera longa Lemos, where they all went on shore, and marched by land to the first post of the city. They had in their company an Englishman, formerly a prisoner in those parts, who now served them for a guide. To him and three or four more they gave commission to take the sentinel if possible, or kill him on the place; but they seized him so cunningly, as he had no time to give warning with his musket, or make any noise, and brought him with his hands bound to Captain Morgan, who asked him how things went in the city, and what forces they had, with other circumstances he desired to know. After every question, they made him a thousand menaces to kill him, if he declared not the truth. Then they advanced to the city, carrying the said sentinel bound before them: having marched about a quarter of a league, they came to the castle near the city, which presently they closely surrounded, so that no person could get either in or out.

Being posted under the walls of the castle, Captain Morgan commanded the sentinel, whom they had taken prisoner, to speak to those within, charging them to surrender to his discretion; otherwise they should be all cut in pieces, without quarter. But they regarding none of these threats, began instantly to fire; which alarmed the city; yet notwithstanding, though the governor and soldiers of the said castle made as great resistance as could be, they were forced to surrender. Having taken the castle, they resolved to be as good as their words, putting the Spaniards to the sword, thereby to strike a terror into the rest of the city. Whereupon, having shut up all the soldiers and officers as prisoners into one room, they set fire to the powder, (whereof they found a great quantity,) and blew up the castle into the air, with all the Spaniards that were within. This done, they pursued the course of their victory, falling upon the city, which, as yet, was not ready to receive them. Many of the inhabitants cast their precious jewels and money into wells and cisterns, or hid them in places under ground, to avoid, as much as possible, being totally robbed. One party of the pirates, assigned to this purpose, ran immediately to the cloisters, and took as many religious men and women as they could find. The governor of the city, not being able to rally the citizens, through their great confusion, retired to one of the castles remaining, and thence fired incessantly at the pirates; but these were not in the least negligent either to assault him, or defend themselves; so that amidst the horror of the assault they made very few shots in vain; for aiming with great dexterity at the mouths of the guns, the Spaniards were certain to lose one or two men every time they charged each gun anew.

This continued very furious from break of day till noon; yea, about this time of the day the case was very dubious which party should conquer, or be conquered. At last, the pirates perceiving they had lost many men, and yet advanced but little towards the gaining either this or the other castles, made use of fire-balls, which they threw with their hands, designing to burn the doors of the castle: but the Spaniards from the walls let fall great quantities of stones, and earthen pots full of powder, and other combustible matter, which forced them to desist. Captain Morgan seeing this generous defence made by the Spaniards, began to despair of success. Hereupon, many faint and calm mediations came into his mind; neither could he determine which way to turn himself in that strait. Being thus puzzled, he was suddenly animated to continue the assault, by seeing English colors put forth by one of the lesser castles, then entered by his men; of whom he presently after spied a troop coming to meet him, proclaiming victory with loud shouts of joy. This instantly put him on new resolutions of taking the rest of the castles, especially seeing the chiefest citizens had fled to them, and had conveyed thither great part of their riches, with all the plate belonging to the churches and divine service.

To this effect, he ordered ten or twelve ladders to be made in all haste, so broad, that three or four men at once might ascend them: these being finished, he commanded all the religious men and women, whom he had taken prisoners, to fix them against the walls of the castle. This he had before threatened the governor to do, if he delivered not the castle; but his answer was, "he would never surrender himself alive." Captain Morgan was persuaded the governor would not employ his utmost force, seeing the religious women, and ecclesiastical persons, exposed in front of the soldiers to the greatest danger. Thus the ladders, as I have said, were put into the hands of religious persons of both sexes, and these were forced, at the head of the companies, to raise and apply them to the walls; but Captain Morgan was fully deceived in his judgment of this design; for the governor, who acted like a brave soldier in performance of his duty, used his utmost endeavors to destroy whosoever came near the walls. The religious men and women ceased not to cry to him, and beg of him by all the saints of heaven to deliver the castle, and spare both his and their own lives; but nothing could prevail with his obstinacy and fierceness. Thus many of the religious men and nuns were killed before they could fix the ladders; which, at last, being done, though with great loss of the said religious people, the pirates mounted them in great numbers, and with not less valor, having fire-balls in their hands, and earthen pots full of powder; all which things, being now at the top of the walls, they kindled and cast in among the Spaniards.

This effort of the pirates was very great, insomuch that the Spaniards could no longer resist nor defend the castle, which was now entered. Hereupon, they all threw down their arms, and craved quarter for their lives; only the governor of the city would crave no mercy, but killed many of the pirates with his own hands, and not a few of his own soldiers, because they did not stand to their arms. And though the pirates asked him if he would have quarter; yet he constantly answered, "By no means; I had rather die as a valiant soldier, than be hanged as a coward." They endeavored as much as they could to take him prisoner, but he defended himself so obstinately, that they were forced to kill him, notwithstanding all the cries and tears of his own wife and daughter, who begged him on their knees to demand quarter, and save his life. When the pirates had possessed themselves of the castle, which was about night, they enclosed therein all the prisoners, placing the women and men by themselves, with some guards; the wounded were put in an apartment by itself, that their own complaints might be the cure of their diseases, for no other was afforded them.

This done, they fell to eating and drinking, as usual; that is, committing in both all manner of debauchery and excess: these two vices were immediately followed by many insolent actions of rape and adultery, committed on many very honest women, as well married as virgins; who, being threatened with the sword, were constrained to submit their bodies to the violence of those lewd and wicked men. Thus they gave themselves up to all sorts of debauchery, that fifty courageous men might easily have retaken the city, and killed all the pirates. Next day, having plundered all they could find, they examined some of the prisoners, (who had been persuaded by their companions to say they were the richest of the town,) charging them severely to discover where they had hid their riches and goods. Not being able to extort any thing from them, they not being the right persons, it was resolved to torture them. This they did so cruelly, that many of them died on the rack, or presently after. Now the president of Panama being advertised of the pillage and ruin of Puerto Bello, he employed all his care and industry to raise forces to pursue and cast out the pirates thence; but these cared little for his preparations, having their ships at hand, and determined to fire the city, and retreat. They had now been at Puerto Bello fifteen days, in which time they had lost many of their men, both by the unhealthiness of the country, and their extravagant debaucheries.

Hereupon they prepared to depart, carrying on board all the pillage they had got, having first provided the fleet with sufficient victuals for the voyage. While these things were doing, Captain Morgan demanded of the prisoners a ransom for the city, or else he would burn it down, and blow up all the castles; withal he commanded them to send speedily two persons, to procure the sum, which was one hundred thousand pieces of eight. To this effect two men were sent to the president of Panama, who gave him an account of all. The president having now a body of men ready, set forth towards Puerto Bello, to encounter the pirates before their retreat; but they hearing of his coming, instead of flying away, went out to meet him at a narrow passage, which he must pass: here they placed one hundred men, very well armed, which at the first encounter put to flight a good party of those of Panama. This obliged the president to retire for that time, not being yet in a posture of strength to proceed farther. Presently after, he sent a message to Captain Morgan, to tell him, "that if he departed not suddenly with all his forces from Puerto Bello, he ought to expect no quarter for himself, nor his companions, when he should take them, as he hoped soon to do." Captain Morgan, who feared not his threats, knowing he had a secure retreat in his ships, which were at hand, answered, "he would not deliver the castles before he had received the contribution money he had demanded; which if it were not paid down, he would certainly burn the whole city, and then leave it, demolishing beforehand the castles, and killing the prisoners."

The governor of Panama perceived by this answer that no means would serve to mollify the hearts of the pirates, nor reduce them to reason. Hereupon, he determined to leave them, as also those of the city whom he came to relieve, involved in the difficulties of making the best agreement they could. Thus in a few days more the miserable citizens gathered the contribution required, and brought one hundred thousand pieces of eight to the pirates for a ransom of their cruel captivity: but the president of Panama was much amazed to consider that four hundred men could take such a great city, with so many strong castles, especially having no ordnance wherewith to raise batteries; and what was more, knowing the citizens of Puerto Bello had always great repute of being good soldiers themselves, and who never wanted courage in their own defence. This astonishment was so great, as made him send to Captain Morgan, desiring some small pattern of those arms wherewith he had taken with such vigor so great a city. Captain Morgan received this messenger very kindly and with great civility; and gave him a pistol, and a few small bullets, to carry back to the president his master; telling him, withal, "he desired him to accept that slender pattern of the arms wherewith he had taken Puerto Bello, and keep them for a twelvemonth; after which time he promised to come to Panama, and fetch them away." The governor returned the present very soon to Captain Morgan, giving him thanks for the favor of lending him such weapons as he needed not; and, withal, sent him a ring of gold, with this message, "that he desired him not to give himself the labor of coming to Panama, as he had done to Puerto Bello; for he did assure him, he should not speed so well here as he had done there.

After this, Captain Morgan (having provided his fleet with all necessaries, and taken with him the best guns of the castle, nailing up the rest) set sail from Puerto Bello with all his ships, and arriving in a few days at Cuba, he sought out a place wherein he might quickly make the dividend of their spoil. They found in ready money two hundred and fifty thousand pieces of eight, besides other merchandises; as cloth, linen, silks, &c. With this rich purchase they sailed thence to their common place of rendezvous, Jamaica. Being arrived, they passed here some time in all sorts of vices and debaucheries, according to their custom; spending very prodigally what others had gained with no small labor and toil.

CHAPTER XIV.

Captain Morgan takes the City of Maracaibo, on the coast of Neuva Venezuela. — Piracies committed in those Seas. — Ruin of three Spanish Ships, sent forth to hinder the robberies of the Pirates.

Not long after their arrival at Jamaica, being that short time they needed to lavish away all the riches above mentioned, they concluded on another enterprise to seek new fortunes. To this effect, Captain Morgan ordered all the commanders of his ships to meet at De la Vacca, or the Cow Isle, south of Hispaniola, as is said. Hither flocked to them great numbers of other pirates, French and English; the name of Captain Morgan being now famous in all the neighboring countries for his great enterprises. There was then at Jamaica an English ship newly come from New England, well mounted with thirty-six guns: this vessel, by order of the governor of Jamaica, joined Captain Morgan to strengthen his fleet, and give him great courage to attempt mighty things. With this supply, Captain Morgan judged himself sufficiently strong; but there being in the same place another great vessel of twenty-four iron guns, and twelve brass ones, belonging to the French, Captain Morgan endeavored also to join this ship to his own; but the French not daring to trust the English, denied absolutely to consent.

The French pirates belonging to this great ship had met at sea an English vessel; and being under great want of victuals, they had taken some provisions out of the English ship, without paying for them, having, perhaps, no ready money aboard; only they gave them bills of exchange, for Jamaica and Tortuga, to receive money there. Captain Morgan having notice of this, and perceiving he could not prevail with the French captain to follow him, resolved to lay hold on this occasion, to ruin the French and seek his revenge. Hereupon he invited, with dissimulation, the French commander, and several of his men, to dine with him on board the great ship that was come to Jamaica, as is said. Being come, he made them all prisoners, pretending the injury aforesaid done to the English vessel.

This unjust action of Captain Morgan was soon followed by divine punishment, as we may conceive; the manner I shall instantly relate. Captain Morgan, presently after he had taken these French prisoners, called a council to deliberate what place they should first pitch upon in this new expedition. Here it was determined to go to the Isle of Savona, to wait for the flota then expected from Spain, and take any of the Spanish vessels straggling from the rest. This resolution being taken, they began aboard the great ship to feast one another for joy of their new voyage, and happy council, as they hoped. They drank many healths, and discharged many guns, the common sign of mirth among seamen. Most of the men being drunk, by what accident is not known, the ship suddenly was blown up, with three hundred and fifty Englishmen, besides the French prisoners in the hold; of all which, there escaped but thirty men, who were in the great cabin, at some distance from the main force of the powder. Many more, it is thought, might have escaped, had they not been so much overtaken with wine.

This loss brought much consternation of mind upon the English; they knew not whom to blame, but at last the accusation was laid on the French prisoners, whom they suspected to have fired the powder of the ship out of revenge, though with the loss of their own lives; hereupon they added new accusations to their former, whereby to seize the ship and all that was in it, by saying the French designed to commit piracy on the English. The grounds of this accusation were given by a commission from the governor of Barracoa, found aboard the French vessel, wherein were these words, "That the said governor did permit the French to trade in all Spanish ports, &c., as also to cruise on the English pirates in what place soever they could find them, because of the multitude of hostilities which they had committed against the subjects of his Catholic majesty in time of peace betwixt the two crowns. This commission for trade was interpreted as an express order to exercise piracy and war against them, though it was only a bare license for coming into the Spanish ports; the cloak of which permission were those words, "That they should cruise upon the English. And though the French did sufficiently expound the true sense of it, yet they could not clear themthemselves to Captain Morgan, nor his council; but in lieu thereof, the ship and men were seized and sent to Jamaica. Here they also endeavored to obtain justice, and the restitution of their ship, but all in vain; for instead of justice, they were long detained in prison, and threatened with hanging.

Eight days after the loss of the said ship, Captain Morgan commanded the bodies of the miserable wretches who were blown up to be searched for, as they floated on the sea; not to afford them Christian burial, but for their clothes and attire; and if any had gold rings on their fingers, these were cut off, leaving them exposed to the voracity of the monsters of the sea. At last they set sail for Savona, the place of their assignation. There were in all fifteen vessels, Captain Morgan commanding the biggest, of only fourteen small guns; his number of men was nine hundred and sixty. Few days after they arrived at the Cabo de Lobos, south of Hispaniola, between Cape Tiburon and Cape Punta de Espada; hence they could not pass by reason of contrary winds for three weeks, notwithstanding all the utmost endeavors Captain Morgan used to get forth; then they doubled the cape, and spied an English vessel at a distance. Having spoken with her, they found she came from England, and bought of her for ready money some provisions they wanted.

Captain Morgan proceeded in his voyage till he came to the port of Ocoa; here he landed some men, sending them into the woods to seek water and provisions, the better to spare such as he had already on board. They killed many beasts, and among others some horses. But the Spaniards, not well satisfied at their hunting, laid a stratagem for them, ordering three or four hundred men to come from Santo Domingo not far distant, and desiring them to hunt in all the parts thereabout near the sea, that so, if the pirates should return, they might find no subsistence. Within few days the same pirates returned to hunt, but finding nothing to kill, a party of about fifty straggled farther on into the woods. The Spaniards, who watched all their motions, gathered a great herd of cows, and set two or three men to keep them. The pirates having spied them, killed a sufficient number; and though the Spaniards could see them at a distance, yet they would not hinder them at present; but as soon as they attempted to carry them away, they set upon them furiously, crying, *mata, mata*, i. e. kill, kill. Thus the pirates were compelled to quit the prey, and retreat to their ships; but they did it in good order, retiring by degrees, and when they had opportunity, discharging full vollies on the Spaniards, killing many of their enemies, though with some loss.

The Spaniards seeing their damage, endeavored to save themselves by flight, and carry off their dead and wounded companions. The pirates perceiving them flee, would not content themselves with what hurt they had already done, but pursued them speedily into the woods, and killed the greatest part of those that remained. Next day Captain Morgan, extremely offended at what had passed, went himself with two hundred men into the woods to seek for the rest of the Spaniards, but finding nobody, he revenged his wrath on the houses of the poor and miserable rustics that inhabit those scattering fields and woods, of which he burnt a great number: with this he returned to his ships, somewhat more satisfied in his mind for having done some considerable damage to the enemy, which was always his most ardent desire.

The impatience wherewith Captain Morgan had waited a long while for some of his ships not yet arrived, made him resolve to sail away without them, and steer for Savona, the place he always designed. Being arrived, and not finding any of his ships come, he was more impatient and concerned than before, fearing their loss, or that he must proceed without them; but he waited for their arrival a few days longer, and having no great plenty of provisions, he sent a crew of one hundred and fifty men to Hispaniola to pillage some towns near Santo Domingo; but the Spaniards, upon intelligence of their coming, were so vigilant, and in such good posture of defence, that the pirates thought not convenient to assault them, choosing rather to return empty handed to Captain Morgan, than to perish in that desperate enterprise.

At last Captain Morgan, seeing the other ships did not come, made a review of his people, and found only about five hundred men; the ships wanting were seven: he had only eight in his company, of which the greatest part were very small. Having hitherto resolved to cruise on the coasts of Caraccas, and to plunder the towns and villages there, finding himself at present with such small forces, he changed his resolution by advice of a French captain in his fleet. This Frenchman having served Lolonois in the like enterprises, and at the taking of Maracaibo, knew all the entries, passages, forces, and means how to put in execution the same again in company of Captain Morgan; to whom having made a full relation of all, he concluded to sack it the second time, being himself persuaded, with all his men, of the facility of the Frenchmen propounded. Hereupon they weighed anchor, and steered towards Curasao. Being come within sight of it, they landed at another island near it, called Ruba, about twelve leagues from Curasao, to the west. This island, defended by a slender garrison, is inhabited by Indians subject to Spain, and speak Spanish, by reason of the Roman Catholic religion, here cultivated by a few priests sent from the neighboring continent.

The inhabitants exercise commerce of trade with the pirates that go and come this way. They buy of the islanders sheep, lambs, and kids, which they exchange for linen, thread, and like things. The country is very dry and barren, the whole substance thereof consisting in those three things, and in a little indifferent wheat. This isle produces many venomous insects, as vipers, spiders, and others. These last are so pernicious, that a man bitten by them dies mad; and the manner of recovering such, is to tie them very fast both hands and feet, and so to leave them twenty-four hours, without eating or drinking any thing. Captain Morgan, as was said, having cast anchor before this island, bought of the inhabitants sheep, lambs, and wood, for all his fleet. After two days, he sailed again in the night, to the intent that they might not see what course he steered.

Next day they arrived at the Sea of Maracaibo, taking great care not to be seen from Vigilia, for which reason they anchored out of sight of it. Night being come, they set sail again towards the land, and next morning, by break of day, were got directly over against the bar of the said lake. The Spaniards had built another fort since the action of Lolonois, whence they now fired continually against the pirates, while they put their men into boats to land. The dispute continued very hot, being managed with great courage from morning till dark night. This being come, Captain Morgan, in the obscurity thereof, drew nigh the fort, which having examined, he found nobody in it, the Spaniards having deserted it not long before. They left behind them a match lighted near a train of powder, to have blown up the pirates and the whole fortress as soon as they were in it. This design had taken effect, had not the pirates discovered it in a quarter of an hour; but Captain Morgan snatching away the match, saved both his own and his companions' lives. They found here much powder, whereof he provided his fleet, and then demolished part of the walls, nailing sixteen pieces of ordnance, from twelve to twenty-four pounders. Here they also found many muskets and other military provisions.

Next day they commanded the ships to enter the bar, among which they divided the powder, muskets, and other things found in the fort; then they embarked again to continue their course towards Maracaibo; but the waters being very low, they could not pass a certain bank at the entry of the lake. Hereupon they were compelled to go into canoes and small boats, with which they arrived next day before Maracaibo, having no other defence than some small pieces which they could carry in the said boats. Being landed, they ran immediately to the fort De la Barra, which they found as the precedent, without any person in it, for all were fled into the woods, leaving also the town without any people, unless a few miserable folks, who had nothing to lose.

As soon as they had entered the towns, the pirates searched every corner to see if they could find any people that were hid, who might offend them unawares; not finding any body, every party as they came out of their several ships chose what houses they pleased. The church was deputed for the common *corps du guard*, where they lived after their military manner, very insolently. Next day after they sent a troop of one hundred men to seek the inhabitants and their goods; these returned next day, bringing with them thirty persons, men, women, and children, and fifty mules loaded with good merchandise. All these miserable people were put to the rack, to make them confess where the rest of the inhabitants were and their goods. Among other tortures, one was to stretch their limbs with cords, and then to beat them with sticks and other instruments. Others had burning matches placed betwixt their fingers, which were thus burnt alive. Others had slender cords or matches twisted about their heads, till their eyes burst out. Thus all inhuman cruelties were executed on those innocent people. Those who would not confess, or who had nothing to declare, died under the hands of those villains. These tortures and racks continued for three whole weeks, in which time they sent out daily parties to seek for more people to torment and rob, they never returning without booty and new riches.

Captain Morgan having now gotten into his hands about one hundred of the chief families, with all their goods, at last resolved for Gibraltar, as Lolonois had done before; with this design he equipped his fleet, providing it sufficiently with all necessaries. He put likewise on board all the prisoners, and weighing anchor, set sail with resolution to hazard a battle. They had sent before some prisoners to Gibraltar, to require the inhabitants to surrender, otherwise Captain Morgan would certainly put them all to the sword, without any quarter. Arriving

10*

before Gibraltar, the inhabitants received him with continual shooting of great cannon bullets; but the pirates, instead of fainting hereat, ceased not to encourage one another, saying, "We must make one meal upon bitter things, before we come to taste the sweetness of the sugar this place affords."

Next day, very early, they landed all their men, and being guided by the Frenchman abovesaid, they marched towards the town; not by the common way, but crossing through woods, which way the Spaniards scarce thought they would have come; for at the beginning of their march, they made as if they intended to come the next and open way to the town, hereby to deceive the Spaniards; but these, remembering full well what Lolonois had done but two years before, thought it not safe to expect a second brunt, and hereupon all fled out of the town as fast as they could, carrying all their goods and riches, as also all the powder, and having nailed all the great guns, so as the pirates found not one person in the whole city, but one poor innocent man who was born a fool. This man they asked whither the inhabitants were fled, and where they had hid their goods; to all which questions and the like, he constantly answered, "I know nothing, I know nothing;" but they presently put him to the rack, and tortured him with cords, which torments forced him to cry out, "Do not torture me any more, but come with me, and I will show you my goods and my riches." They were persuaded, it seems, he was some rich person disguised under those clothes so poor, and that innocent tongue; so they went along with him, and he conducted them to a poor miserable cottage, wherein he had a few earthen dishes and other things of no value, and three pieces of eight, concealed with some other trumpery under ground. Then they asked him his name, and he readily answered, "My name is Don Sebastian Sanchez, and I am brother unto the governor of Maracaibo." This foolish answer, it must be conceived, these inhuman wretches took for truth; for no sooner had they heard it, but they put him again upon the rack, lifting him up on high with cords, and tying huge weights to his feet and neck. Besides which, they burnt him alive, applying palm-leaves burning to his face.

The same day they sent out a party to seek for the inhabitants, on whom they might exercise their cruelties. These brought back an honest peasant with two daughters of his, whom they intended to torture as they used others, if they showed not the places where the inhabitants were hid. The peasant knew some of those places, and seeing himself threatened with the rack, went with the pirates to show them; but

take the governor. This gentleman was retired to a small island in the middle of the river, where he had built a little fort, as well as he could, for his defence; but hearing that Captain Morgan came in person with great forces to seek him, he retired to the top of a mountain not far off, to which there was no ascent, but by a very narrow passage, so straight, that whoever did attempt to gain the ascent, must march his men one by one. Captain Morgan spent two days before he arrived at this little island, whence he designed to proceed to the mountain where the governor was posted, had he not been told of the impossibility of ascent, not only for the narrowness of the way, but because the governor was well provided with all sorts of ammunition; besides, there was fallen a huge rain, whereby all the pirates' baggage and powder was wet. By this rain, also, they lost many men at the passage over a river that was overflown; here perished likewise some women and children, and many mules laden with plate and goods, which they had taken from the fugitive inhabitants; so that things were in a very bad condition with Captain Morgan, and his men much harassed, as may be inferred from this relation; whereby, if the Spaniards, in that juncture, had had but fifty men well armed, they might have entirely destroyed the pirates. But the fears the Spaniards had at first conceived were so great, that the leaves stirring on the trees they often fancied to be pirates. Finally, Captain Morgan and his people, having upon this march sometimes waded up to their middles in water for half or whole miles together, they at last escaped, for the greatest part; but the women and children, for the major part, died.

Thus twelve days after they set forth to seek the governor, they returned to Gibraltar, with many prisoners; two days after, arrived also the two settees that went to the river, bringing with them four boats, and some prisoners; but the greatest part of the merchandise in the said boats they found not, the Spaniards having unladed and secured it, having intelligence of their coming; who designed also, when the merchandise was taken out, to burn the boats; yet the Spaniards made not so much haste to unlade these vessels, but that they left in the ship and boats great parcels of goods, which the pirates seized, and brought a considerable booty to Gibraltar. Thus, after they had been in possession of the place five entire weeks, and committed an infinite number of murders, robberies, rapes, and such like insolences, they concluded to depart; but first they ordered some prisoners to go forth into the woods and fields, and collect a ransom for the town, otherwise they would certainly burn it down to the ground. These poor afflicted men went as they were sent, and having searched the adjoining fields and woods, returned to Captain Morgan, telling him, they had scarce been able to find any body, but that to such as they had found, they had proposed his demands; to which they had answered, that the governor had prohibited them to give any ransom for the town, but they beseeched him to have a little patience, and among themselves they would collect five thousand pieces of eight; and for the rest, they would give some of their own townsmen as hostages, whom he might carry to Maracaibo, till he had received full satisfaction.

Captain Morgan having now been long absent from Maracaibo, and knowing the Spaniards had had sufficient time to fortify themselves, and hinder his departure out of the lake, granted their proposition, and made as much haste as he could for his departure: he gave liberty to all the prisoners, first putting every one to a ransom; yet he detained the slaves. They delivered him four persons agreed on for hostages of what money more he was to receive, and they desired to have the slave mentioned above, intending to punish him according to his deserts; but Captain Morgan would not deliver him, lest they should burn him alive. At last they weighed anchor, and set sail in all haste for Maracaibo. Here they arrived in four days, and found all things as they had left them; yet here they received news from a poor distressed old man, whom alone they found sick in the town, that three Spanish men-of-war were arrived at the entry of the lake, waiting the return of the pirates; moreover, that the castle at the entry thereof was again put into a good posture of defence, well provided with guns, and men, and all sorts of ammunition.

This relation could not choose but disturb the mind of Captain Morgan, who now was careful how to get away through the narrow entry of the lake. Hereupon, he sent his swiftest boat to view the entry, and see if things were as they had been related. Next day the boat came back, confirming what was said, assuring him they had viewed the ships so nigh, that they had been in great danger of their shot; hereunto they added, that the biggest ship was mounted with forty guns, the second with thirty, and the smallest with twenty-four. These forces being much beyond those of Captain Morgan, caused a general consternation in the pirates, whose biggest vessel had not above fourteen small guns. Every one judged Captain Morgan to despond, and to be hopeless, considering the difficulty of passing safe with his little fleet amidst those great ships and the fort, or he must perish. How to escape any other way, by sea or land, they saw no way. Under these necessities, Captain Morgan resumed new courage, and, resolving to show himself still undaunted, he boldly sent a Spaniard to the admiral of those three ships, demanding of him a considerable ransom for not putting the city of Maracaibo to the flames. This man (who was received by the Spaniards with great admiration of the boldness of those pirates) returned two days after, bringing to Captain Morgan a letter from the said admiral, as follows:—

"*The Letter of Don Alonso del Campo y Espinosa, Admiral of the Spanish Fleet; to Captain Morgan, Commander of the Pirates:*—

"Having understood, by all our friends and neighbors, the unexpected news, that you have dared to attempt and commit hostilities in the countries, cities, towns, and villages belonging to the dominions of his Catholic majesty, my sovereign lord and master, I let you understand, by these lines, that I am come to this place, according to my obligation, near that castle which you took out of the hands of a parcel of cowards; where I have put things into a very good posture of defence, and mounted again the artillery which you had nailed and dismounted. My intent is, to dispute with you your passage out of the lake, and follow and pursue you every where, to the end you may see the performance of my duty. Notwithstanding, if you be contented to surrender with humility all that you have taken, together with the slaves and all other prisoners, I will let you freely pass, without trouble or molestation, on condition that you retire home presently to your own country. But if you make any resistance or opposition to what I offer you, I assure you I will command boats to come from Caraccas, wherein I will put my troops, and, coming to Maracaibo, will put you every man to the sword. This is my last and absolute resolution. Be prudent, therefore, and do not abuse my bounty with ingratitude. I have with me very good soldiers, who desire nothing more ardently than to revenge on you and your people all the cruelties and base, infamous actions you have committed upon the Spanish nation in America. Dated on board the royal ship named the Magdalen, lying at anchor at the entry of the Lake of Maracaibo, this 24th of April, 1669.

"DON ALONSO DEL CAMPO Y ESPINOSA."

As soon as Captain Morgan received this letter, he called all his men together in the market-place of Maracaibo, and after reading the contents thereof, both in French and English, asked their advice and resolution on the whole matter, and whether they had rather surrender all they had got, to obtain their liberty, than fight for it.

They answered all, unanimously, they had rather fight to the last drop of blood, than surrender so easily the booty they had got with so much danger of their lives. Among the rest, one said to Captain Morgan, "Take you care for the rest, and I will undertake to destroy the biggest of those ships with only twelve men. The manner shall be, by making a brulot, or fire-ship, of that vessel we took in the River of Gibraltar; which, to the intent she may not be known as a fire-ship, we will fill her decks with logs of wood, standing with hats and montera caps, to deceive their sight with the representation of men. The same we will do at the port-holes that serve for the guns, which shall be filled with counterfeit cannon. At the stern we will hang out English colors, and persuade the enemy she is one of our best men-of-war going to fight them." This proposition was admitted and approved by every one; howbeit, their fears were not quite dispersed.

For, notwithstanding what had been concluded there, they endeavored the next day to come to an accommodation with Don Alonso. To this effect, Captain Morgan sent to him two persons, with these propositions: First. That he would quit Maracaibo, without doing any damage to the town, or exacting any ransom for the firing thereof. Secondly. That he would set at liberty one half of the slaves and all the prisoners without ransom. Thirdly. That he would send home freely the four chief inhabitants of Gibraltar, which he had in his custody as hostages for the contributions those people had promised to pay. These propositions were instantly rejected by Don Alonso, as dishonorable; neither would he hear of any other accommodation, but sent back this message: "That if they surrendered not themselves voluntarily into his hands, within two days, under the conditions which he had offered them by his letter, he would immediately come and force them to do it."

No sooner had Captain Morgan received this message from Don Alonso, than he put all things in order to fight, resolving to get out of the lake by main force, without surrendering any thing. First, he commanded all the slaves and prisoners to be tied, and guarded very well, and gather all the pitch, tar, and brimstone they could find in the whole town, for the fire-ship above mentioned; then they made several inventions of powder and brimstone with palm-leaves, well anointed with tar. They covered very well their counterfeit cannon, laying under every piece many pounds of powder; besides, they cut down many out-works of the ship, that the powder might exert its strength the better; breaking open, also, new port-holes, where, instead of guns, they placed little drums used by the negroes. Finally, the decks were handsomely beset with many pieces of wood, dressed up like men with hats, or monteras, and armed with swords, muskets, and bandeleers.

The fire-ship being thus fitted, they prepared to go to the entry of the port. All the prisoners were put into one great boat, and in another of the biggest they placed all the women, plate, jewels, and other rich things; into others they put the bales of goods and merchandise, and other things of bulk; each of these boats had twelve men aboard, very well armed; the Brulot had orders to go before the rest of the vessels, and presently to fall foul with the great ship. All things being ready, Captain Morgan exacted an oath of all his comrades, protesting to defend themselves to the last drop of blood, without demanding quarter; promising withal, that whosoever behaved himself thus, should be very well rewarded.

With this courageous resolution, they set sail to seek the Spaniards. On April 30, 1669, they found the Spanish fleet riding at anchor in the middle of the entry of the lake. Captain Morgan, it being now late, and almost dark, commanded all his vessels to an anchor, designing to fight, even all night, if they forced him to it. He ordered a careful watch to be kept aboard every vessel till morning, they being almost within shot, as well as within sight of the enemy. The day dawning, they weighed anchor, and sailed again, steering directly towards the Spaniards; who seeing them move, did instantly the same. The fire-ship sailing before the rest, fell presently upon the great ship, and grappled her; which the Spaniards (too late) perceiving to be a fire-ship, they attempted to put her off, but in vain; for the flame seizing her timber and tackling, soon consumed all the stern, the fore part sinking into the sea, where she perished. The second Spanish ship perceiving the admiral to burn, not by accident, but by industry of the enemy, escaped towards the castle, where the Spaniards themselves sunk her, choosing to lose their ship rather than to fall into the hands of those pirates. The third, having no opportunity to escape, was taken by the pirates. The seamen that sunk the second ship near the castle, perceiving the pirates come towards them to take what remains they could find of their shipwreck, (for some part was yet above water,) set fire also to this vessel, that the pirates might enjoy nothing of that spoil. The first ship being set on fire, some of the persons in her swam towards the shore; these the pirates would have taken up in their boats, but they would not ask or take quarter, choosing rather to lose their lives, than receive them from their hands, for reasons which I shall relate.

The pirates being extremely glad at this signal victory so soon obtained, and with so great an inequality of forces, conceived greater pride than they had before, and all presently ran ashore, intending to take the castle. This they found well provided with men, cannon, and ammuniton, they having no other arms than muskets, and a few hand granadoes; their own artillery they thought incapable, for its smallness, of making any considerable breach in the walls. Thus they spent the rest of the day, firing at the garrison with their muskets till the dusk of the evening; when they attempted to advance nearer the walls, to throw in their fire-balls; but the Spaniards resolving to sell their lives as dear as they could, fired so furiously at them, that they having experimented the obstinacy of the enemy, and seeing thirty of their men dead, and as many more wounded, they retired to their ships.

The Spaniards believing the pirates would next day renew the attack with their own cannon, labored hard all night to put things in order for their coming; particularly, they dug down, and made plain, some little hills and eminences, when possibly the castle might be offended.

But Captain Morgan intended not to come again, busying himself next day in taking prisoners some of the men who still swarm alive, hoping to get part of the riches lost in the two ships that perished. Among the rest, he took a pilot, who was a stranger, and who belonged to the lesser ship of the two, of whom he inquired several things; as, What number of people those three ships had in them? Whether they expected any more ships to come? From what port they set forth last, when they came to seek them out? He answered, in Spanish:—

"Noble sir, be pleased to pardon and spare me, that no evil be done to me, being a stranger to this nation I have served, and I shall sincerely inform you of all that passed till our arrival at this lake. We were sent, by orders from the supreme council of state in Spain, being six men of war well equipped, into these seas, with instructions to cruise upon the English pirates, and root them out from these parts, by destroying as many of them as we could.

"These orders were given, upon the news brought to the court of Spain of the loss and ruin of Puerto Bello, and other places; of all which damages and hostilities committed here by the English, dismal lamentations have often been made to the Catholic king and council, to whom belongs the care and preservation of this new world. And though the Spanish court hath many times by their ambassadors complained hereof to the king of England, yet it has been the constant answer of his majesty of Great Britain, that he never gave any letters patent, nor commissions, for acting any hostility against the subjects of the king of Spain. Hereupon the Catholic king resolved to revenge his subjects, and punish these proceedings; commanded six men of war to be equipped, which he sent under the command of Don Augustine de Bustos, admiral of the said fleet. He commanded the biggest ship, named N. S. de la Soleda, of forty-eight great guns, and eight small ones. The vice-admiral was Don Alonzo del Campo y Espinosa, who commanded the second ship called La Conception, of forty-four great guns, and eight small ones; beside four vessels more, whereof the first was named the Magdalen, of thirty-six great guns, and twelve small ones, with two hundred and fifty men. The second was called St. Lewis, with twenty-six great guns, twelve small ones, and two hundred men. The third was called La Marquesa, of sixteen great guns, eight small ones, and one hundred and fifty men. The fourth and last, N. S. del Carmen, with eighteen great guns, 8 small ones, and one hundred and fifty men.

"Being arrived at Carthagena, the two greatest ships received orders to return to Spain, being judged too big for cruising on these coasts. With the four ships remaining, Don Alonso del Campo y Espinosa departed towards Campeachy to seek the English. We arrived at the port there, where, being surprised by a huge storm from the north, we lost one of our ships, being that which I named last. Hence we sailed for Hispaniola, in sight of which we came in a few days, and steered for Santo Domingo: here we heard that there had passed that way a fleet from Jamaica, and that some men thereof had landed at Alta Gracia; the inhabitants had taken one prisoner, who confessed their design was, to go and pillage the city of Caraccas. On this news, Don Alonso instantly weighed anchor, and crossing over to the continent, we came in sight of the Caraccas; here we found them not, but met with a boat, which certified us they were in the Lake of Maracaibo, and that the fleet consisted of seven small ships, and one boat.

"Upon this we came here, and arriving at the entry of the lake, we shot off a gun for a pilot from the shore. Those on land perceiving we were Spaniards, came willingly to us with a pilot and told us the English had taken Maracaibo, and that they were now at the pillage of Gibraltar. Don Alonso, on this news, made a handsome speech to his soldiers and mariners, encouraging them to their duty, and promising to divide among them all they should take from the English. He ordered the guns we had taken out of the ship that was lost to be put into the castle, and mounted for its defence, with two eighteen pounders more out of his own ship. The pilots conducted us into the port, and Don Alonso commanded the people on shore to come before him, whom he ordered to repossess the castle, and reinforce it with one hundred men more than it had before its being taken. Soon after, we heard of your return from Gibraltar to Maracaibo, whither Don Alonso wrote you a letter, giving you an account of his arrival and design, and exhorting you to restore what you had taken. This you refusing, he renewed his promises to his soldiers and seamen; and having given a very good supper to all his people, he ordered them not to take or give any quarter; which was the occasion of so many being drowned, who dared not to crave quarter, knowing themselves must give none. Two days before you came against us, a negro came aboard Don Alonso's ship, telling him, "Sir, be pleased to have great care of yourself, for the English have prepared a fire-ship, with design to burn your fleet." But Don Alonso not believing this, answered "How can that be? Have they, peradventure, wit enough to build a fire-ship? Or what instruments have they to do it withal?"

This pilot having related so distinctly these things to Captain Morgan, was very well used by him, and after some kind proffers made to him, remained in his service. He told Captain Morgan, that in the ship which was sunk there was a great quantity of plate, to the value of forty thousand pieces of eight; which occasioned the Spaniards to be often seen in boats about it. Hereupon, Captain Morgan ordered one of his ships to remain there, to find ways of getting out of it what plate they could. Meanwhile, himself, with all his fleet, returned to Maracaibo, where he refitted the great ship he had taken, and chose it for himself, giving his own bottom to one of his captains.

Then he sent a messenger to the admiral, who was escaped ashore, and got into the castle, demanding of him a ransom of fire for Maracaibo; which being denied, he threatened entirely to consume and destroy it. The Spaniards considering the ill luck they had all along with those pirates, and not knowing how to get rid of them, concluded to pay the said ransom, though Don Alonso would not consent.

Hereupon, they sent to Captain Morgan, to know what sum he demanded. He answered, that on payment of thirty thousand pieces of eight, and five hundred beeves, he would release the prisoners, and do no damage to the town. At last they agreed on twenty thousand pieces of eight, and five hundred beeves to victual his fleet.. The cattle were brought the next day, with one part of the money; and while the pirates were busied in salting the flesh, they made up the whole twenty thousand pieces of eight, as was agreed.

But Captain Morgan would not presently deliver the prisoners, as he had promised, fearing the shot of the castle at his going forth out of the lake. Hereupon he told them he intended not to deliver them till he was out of that danger, hoping thus to obtain a free passage. Then he set sail with his fleet in quest of the ship he had left, to seek for the plate of the vessel that was burnt. He found her on the place, with fifteen thousand pieces of eight got out of the work, besides many pieces of plate, as hilts of swords, and the like; also a great quantity of pieces of eight, melted and run together by the force of the fire.

Captain Morgan scarce thought himself secure, nor could he contrive how to avoid the shot of the castle; hereupon he wished the prisoners to agree with the governor to permit a safe passage to his fleet, which, if he should not allow, he would certainly hang them all up in his ships. Upon this, the prisoners met, and appointed some of their fellow-messengers to go to the said governor, Don Alonso. These went to him, beseeching and supplicating him to have compassion on those afflicted prisoners, who were, with their wives and children, in the hands of Captain Morgan; and that to this effect he would be pleased to give his word to let the fleet of pirates freely pass, this being the only way to save both the lives of them that came with this petition, as also of those who remained in captivity; all being equally menaced with the sword and gallows, if he granted them not this humble request. But Don Alonso gave them for answer a sharp reprehension of their cowardice, telling them, "If you had been as loyal to your king in hindering the entry of these pirates, as I shall do their going out, you had never caused these troubles neither to yourselves, nor to our whole nation, which hath suffered so much through your pusillanimity. In a word, I shall never grant your request, but shall endeavor to maintain that respect which is due to my king, according to my duty."

Thus the Spaniards returned with much consternation, and no hopes of obtaining their request, telling Captain Morgan what answer they had received. His reply was, "If Don Alonso will not let me pass, I will find means how to do it without him."

Hereupon he presently made a dividend of all they had taken, fearing he might not have an opportunity to do it in another place, if any tempest should rise and separate the ships, as also being jealous that any of the commanders might run away with the best part of the spoil, which then lay more in one vessel than another. Thus they all brought in according to their laws, and declared what they had, first making oath not to conceal the least thing. The accounts being cast up, they found to the value of twenty-five thousand pieces of eight in money and jewels, besides the huge quantity of merchandise and slaves, all which purchase was divided to every ship or boat, according to their share.

The dividend being made, the question still remained how they should pass the castle, and get out of the lake. To this effect they made use of a stratagem, as follows. The day before the night wherein they determined to get forth, they embarked many of their men in canoes, and rowed towards the shore, as if they designed to land. Here they hid themselves under branches of trees that hang over the coast a while, laying themselves down in the boats; then the canoes returned to the ships, with the appearance of only two or three men rowing them back, the rest being unseen at the bottom of the canoes; thus much only could be perceived from the castle, and this false landing of men, for so we may call it, was repeated that day several times. This made the Spaniards think the pirates intended at night to force the castle, by scaling it. This fear caused them to place most of their great guns on the land side, together with their main force, leaving the side towards the sea almost destitute of defence.

Night being come, they weighed anchor, and by moonlight, without setting sail, committed themselves to the ebbing tide, which gently brought them down the river, till they were near the castle; being almost over against it, they spread their sails with all possible haste. The Spaniards perceiving this, transported with all speed their guns from the other side, and began to fire very furiously at them; but these having a very favorable wind, were almost past danger before those of the castle could hurt them; so that they lost few of their men, and received no considerable damage in their ships. Being out of the reach of the guns, Captain Morgan sent a canoe to the castle with some of the prisoners, and the governor thereof gave them a boat to return to their own homes; but he detained the hostages from Gibraltar, because the rest of the ransom for not firing the place was yet unpaid. Just as he departed, Captain Morgan ordered seven great guns with bullets to be fired against the castle, as it were to take his leave of them, but they answered not so much as with a musket shot.

Next day after, they were surprised with a great tempest, which forced them to cast anchor in five or six fathom water; but the storm increasing, compelled them to weigh again, and put to sea, where they were in great danger of being lost; for if they should have been cast on shore, either into the hands of the Spaniards or Indians, they would certainly have obtained no mercy. At last, the tempest being spent, the wind ceased, to the great joy of the whole fleet.

While Captain Morgan made his fortune by these pillagings, his companions, who were separated from his fleet at the Cape de Lobos, to take the ship spoken of before, endured much misery, and were unfortunate in all their attempts. Being arrived at Savona, they found not Captain Morgan there, nor any of their companions, nor had they the fortune to find a letter which Captain Morgan at his departure left behind him in a place where in all probability they would meet with it. Thus, not knowing what course to steer, they concluded to pillage some town or other. They were in all about four hundred men, divided into four ships and one boat. Being ready to set forth, they constituted an admiral among themselves, being one who had behaved himself very courageously at the taking of Puerto Bello, named Captain Hansel. This commander attempted the taking of the town of Commana, on the continent of Caraccas, nigh sixty leagues to the west of the Isle de la Trinidad. Being arrived there, they landed their men, and killed some few Indians near the coast; but approaching the town, the Spaniards having in their company many Indians, disputed the entry so briskly, that, with great loss and confusion, they were forced to retire to the ships. At last they arrived at Jamaica, where the rest of their companions who came with Captain Morgan mocked and jeered them for their ill success at Commana, often telling them, "Let us see what money you brought from Commana, and if it be as good silver as that which we bring from Maracaibo."

CHAPTER XV.

Captain Morgan goes to Hispaniola to equip a new Fleet, with Intent to pillage again on the Coast of the West Indies.

Captain Morgan perceived now that Fortune favored him, by giving success to all his enterprises, which occasioned him, as is usual in human affairs, to aspire to greater things, trusting she would always be constant to him. Such was the burning of Panama, wherein Fortune failed not to assist him, as she had done before, though she had led him thereto through a thousand difficulties. The history hereof I shall now relate, being so remarkable in all its circumstances, as peradventure nothing more deserving memory will be read by future ages.

Captain Morgan arriving at Jamaica, found many of his officers and soldiers reduced to their former indigency, by their vices and debaucheries; hence, they perpetually importuned him for new exploits, thereby to get something to expend still in wine and strumpets, as they had already done what they got before. Captain Morgan, willing to follow Fortune's call, stopped the mouths of many inhabitants of Jamaica, who were creditors to his men for large sums, with the hopes and promises of greater achievements than ever, by a new expedition. This done, he could easily levy men for any enterprise, his name being so famous through all those islands, as that alone would readily bring him in more men than he could well employ. He undertook therefore to equip a new fleet, for which he assigned the south side of Tortuga as a place of rendezvous, writing letters to all the expert pirates there inhabiting, as also to the governor, and to the planters and hunters of Hispaniola, informing them of his intentions, and desiring their appearance, if they intended to go with him. These people upon this notice flocked to the place assigned, in huge numbers, with ships, canoes, and boats, being desirous to follow him. Many who had not the convenience of coming by sea, traversed the woods of Hispaniola, and with no small difficulties arrived there by land. Thus all were present at the place assigned, and ready against October the 24th, 1670.

Captain Morgan was not wanting to be there punctually, coming in his ship to port Couillon, over against the Island de la Vaca, the place assigned. Having gathered the greatest part of his fleet, he called a council to deliberate about finding provisions for so many people. Here they concluded to send four ships, and one boat with four hundred men, to the continent, in order to rifle some country towns and villages for all the corn and maize they could gather. They set sail for the continent towards the River de la Hacha, designing to assault the village called La Rancheria, usually best stored with maize of all the parts thereabouts. Meanwhile Captain Morgan sent another party to hunt in the woods, who killed a huge number of beasts, and salted them; the rest remained in the ships, to clean, fit, and rig them, that, at the return of their fellows, all things might be in readiness to weigh anchor and follow their designs.

CHAPTER XVI.

What happened in the River de la Hacha.

THESE four ships setting sail from Hispaniola, steered for the River de la Hacha, where they were suddenly overtaken with a tedious calm. Being within sight of land becalmed for some days, the Spaniards inhabiting along the coasts, who had perceived them to be enemies, had sufficient time to prepare themselves, at least to hide the best of their goods, that without any care of preserving them, they might be ready to retire, if they proved unable to resist the pirates, by whose frequent attempts on those coasts they had already learned what to do in such cases. There was then in the river a good ship, come from Carthagena to load with maize, and now almost ready to depart. The men of this ship endeavored to escape, but not being able to do it, both they and their vessel fell into their hands. This was a fit purchase for them, being good part of what they came for. Next morning, about break of day, they came with their ships ashore, and landed their men, though the Spaniards made good resistance from a battery they had raised on that side, where, of necessity, they were to land; but they were forced to retire to a village, whither the pirates followed them. Here the Spaniards rallying, fell upon them with great fury, and maintained a strong combat, which lasted till night; but then perceiving they had lost a great number of men, which was no less on the pirates' side, they retired to secret places in the woods.

Next day the pirates seeing them all fled, and the town left empty of people, they pursued them as far as they could, and overtook a party of Spaniards, whom they made prisoners, and exercised with most cruel torments, to discover their goods: some were forced by intolerable tortures to confess; but others, who would not, were used more barbarously. Thus in fifteen days that they remained there, they took many prisoners, much plate and movables, with which booty they resolved to return to Hispaniola; yet not content with what they had got, they dispatched some prisoners into the woods to seek for the rest of the inhabitants, and to demand a ransom for not burning the town. They answered, they had no money, nor plate; but if they would be satisfied with a quantity of maize, they would give as much as they could. The pirates accepted this, it being then more useful to them than ready money, and agreed they should pay four thousand *hanegs*, or bushels of maize. These were brought in three days after, the Spaniards being desirous to rid themselves of that inhuman sort of people. Having laded them on board with the rest of their purchase, they returned to Hispaniola, to give account to their leader, Captain Morgan, of all they had performed.

They had now been absent five weeks on this commission, which long delay occasioned Captain Morgan almost to despair of their return, fearing lest they were fallen into the hands of the Spaniards; especially considering the place whereto they went could easily be relieved from Carthagena and Santa Maria, if the inhabitants were careful to alarm the country. On the other side, he feared lest they should have made some great fortune in that voyage, and with it have escaped to some other place: but seeing his ships return in greater numbers than they departed, he resumed new courage, this sight causing both in him and his companions infinite joy, especially when they found them full laden with maize, which they much wanted, for the maintenance of so many people, from whom they expected great matters under such a commander.

Captain Morgan having divided the said maize, as also the flesh which the hunters brought, among his ships, according to the number of men, he concluded to depart; having viewed beforehand every ship, and observed their being well equipped and clean. Thus he set sail, and stood for Cape Tiburon, where he determined to resolve what enterprise he should take in hand. No sooner were they arrived, but they met some other ships, newly come to join them, from Jamaica; so that now their fleet consisted of thirty-seven ships, wherein were two thousand fighting men, beside mariners and boys. The admiral hereof was mounted with twenty-two great guns, and six small ones of brass; the rest carried some twenty, some sixteen, some eighteen, and the smallest vessel at least four; besides which, they had great quantities of ammunition and fire-balls, with other inventions of powder.

Captain Morgan having such a number of ships, divided the whole fleet into two squadrons, constituting a vice-admiral, and other officers of the second squadron, distinct from the former; to these he gave letters patent, or commissions, to act all manner of hostilities against the Spanish nation, and take of them what ships they could, either abroad at sea, or in the harbors, as if they were open and declared enemies (as he termed it) of the king of England, his pretended master. This done, he called all his captains and other officers together, and caused them to sign some articles of agreement betwixt them, and in the name of all. Herein it was stipulated, that he should have the hundredth part of all that was gotten to himself; that every captain should draw the shares of eight men, for the expenses of his ship, besides his own. To the surgeon, besides his pay, two hundred pieces of eight, for his chest of medicaments; to every carpenter, above his salary, one hundred pieces of eight. The rewards were settled in this voyage much higher than before: as for the loss of both legs, fifteen hundred pieces of eight, or fifteen slaves, the choice left to the party: for the loss of both hands, eighteen hundred pieces of eight, or eighteen slaves: for one leg, whether right or left, six hundred pieces of eight, or six slaves: for a hand, as much as for a leg; and for the loss of an eye, one hundred pieces of eight, or one slave. Lastly, to him that in any battle should signalize himself, either by entering first any castle, or taking down the Spanish colors, and setting up the English, they allotted fifty pieces of eight, for a reward; all which extraordinary salaries and rewards to be paid out of the first spoil they should take, as every one should occur to be either rewarded or paid.

This contract being signed, Captain Morgan commanded his vice-admirals and captains to put all things in order, to attempt one of these three places; either Carthagena, Panama, or Vera Cruz. But the lot fell on Panama, as the richest of all three, though this city being situate at such a distance from the North Sea, as they knew not well the approaches to it, they judged it necessary to go before hand to the Isle of St. Catherine, there to find some persons for guides in this enterprise: for in the garrison there are commonly many banditti and outlaws, belonging to Panama and the neighboring places, who are very expert in the knowledge of that country. But before they proceeded, they published an act through the whole fleet, promising if they met with any Spanish vessel, the first captain who should take it should have for his reward the tenth part of what should be found in her.

CHAPTER XVII.

Captain Morgan leaves Hispaniola, and goes to St. Catherine's, which he takes.

Captain Morgan and his companions weighed anchor from the Cape of Tiburon, December 16, 1670. Four days after, they arrived in sight of St. Catherine's, now in possession of the Spaniards again, as was said before, to which they commonly banish the malefactors of the Spanish dominions in the West Indies. Here are huge quantities of pigeons, at certain seasons. It is watered by four rivulets, whereof two are always dry in summer. Here is no trade or commerce exercised by the inhabitants, neither do they plant more fruits than what are necessary for human life, though the country would make very good plantations of tobacco, of considerable profit, were it cultivated.

As soon as Captain Morgan came near the island, with his fleet, he sent one of his best sailing vessels to view the entry of the river, and see if any other ships were there, who might hinder him from landing ; as also fearing lest they should give intelligence of his arrival to the inhabitants, and prevent his designs.

Next day, before sunrise, all the fleet anchored near the island, in a bay called Aguade Grande. On this bay the Spaniards had built a battery, mounted with four pieces of cannon. Captain Morgan landed about one thousand men in divers squadrons, marching through the woods, though they had no other guides than a few of his own men, who had been there before, under Mansvelt: the same day they came to a place where the governor sometimes resided; here they found a battery called the Platform, but nobody in it, the Spaniards having retired to the lesser island, which, as was said before, is so near the great one, that a short bridge only may conjoin them.

This lesser island was so well fortified with forts and batteries round it, as might seem impregnable: hereupon, as soon as the Spaniards perceived the pirates approach, they fired on them so furiously, that they could advance nothing that day, but were content to retreat, and take up their rest in the open fields, which was not strange to these people, being sufficiently used to such kind of repose. What most afflicted them was hunger, having not ate any thing that whole day. About midnight, it rained so hard, that they had much ado to bear it, the greatest part of them having no other clothes than a pair of seaman's trowsers, or breeches, and a shirt, without shoes or stockings. In this great extremity, they pulled down a few thatched houses to make fires withal; in a word, they were in such a condition, that one hundred men, indifferently well armed, might easily that night have torn them all in pieces. Next morning, about break of day, the rain ceased, and they dried their arms, and marched on; but soon after it rained afresh, rather harder than before, as if the skies were melted into waters; which kept them from advancing towards the forts, whence the Spaniards continually fired at them.

The pirates were now reduced to great affliction and danger, through the hardness of the weather, their own nakedness, and great hunger; for a small relief hereof, they found in the fields an old horse, lean, and full of scabs and blotches, with galled back and sides: this they instantly killed and flayed, and divided in small pieces among themselves, as far as it would reach, (for many could not get a morsel,) which they roasted and devoured without salt or bread, more like ravenous wolves than men. The rain not ceasing, Captain Morgan perceived their minds to relent, hearing many of them say they would return on board. Among these fatigues of mind and body, he thought convenient to use some sudden remedy: to this effect, he commanded a canoe to be rigged in haste, and colors of truce to be hung out. This canoe he sent to the Spanish governor, with this message: "That if within a few hours he delivered not himself and all his men into his hands, he did by that messenger swear to him, and all those that were in his company, he would most certainly put them to the sword, without granting quarter to any."

In the afternoon the canoe returned with this answer: "That the governor desired two hours time to deliberate with his officers about it, which being past, he would give his positive answer." The time being elapsed, the governor sent two canoes with white colors, and two persons, to treat with Captain Morgan; but before they landed, they demanded of the pirates two persons as hostages. These were readily granted by Captain Morgan, who delivered them two of his captains for a pledge of the security required: with this the Spaniards propounded to Captain Morgan, that the governor, in a full assembly, had resolved to deliver up the island, not being provided with sufficient forces to defend it against such an *armada:* but, withal, he desired Captain Morgan would be pleased to use a certain stratagem of war, for the better saving of his own credit, and the reputation of his officers both abroad and at home, which should be as follows: That Captain Morgan would come with his troops by night, to the bridge that joined the lesser island to the great one, and there attack the fort of St. Jerom: that at the same time all his fleet would draw near the castle of Santa Teresa, and attack it by land, landing in the mean while more troops, near the battery of St. Matthew: that these troops being nearly landed, should by this means intercept the governor as he endeavored to pass to St. Jerom's fort, and then take him prisoner; using the formality, as if they forced him to deliver the castle; and that he would lead the English into it, under color of being his own troops. That on both sides, there should be continual firing, but without bullets, or at least into the air, so that no side might be hurt. That thus having obtained two such considerable forts, the chiefest of the isle, he need not take care for the rest, which must fall, of course, into his hands.

These propositions were granted by Captain Morgan, on condition they should see them faithfully observed; otherwise they should be used with the utmost rigor: this they promised to do, and took their leave, to give account of their negotiation to the governor. Presently after, Captain Morgan commanded the whole fleet to enter the port, and his men to be ready to assault that night the castle of St. Jerom. Thus the false battle began, with incessant firing from both the castles, against the ships, but without bullets, as was agreed: then the pirates landed, and assaulted by night the lesser island, which they took, as also both the fortresses; forcing the Spaniards, in appearance, to fly to the church. Before this assault, Captain Morgan sent word to the governor, that he should keep all his men together in a body; otherwise, if the pirates met any straggling Spaniards in the streets, they should certainly shoot them.

This island being taken by this unusual stratagem, and all things put in order, the pirates made a new war against the poultry, cattle, and all sorts of victuals they could find, for some days; scarce thinking of any thing else than to kill, roast, and eat, and make what good cheer they could. If wood was wanting, they pulled down the houses, and made fires with the timber, as had been done before in the field. Next day they numbered all the prisoners they had taken upon the island, which were found to be in all four hundred and fifty-nine persons, men, women and children, viz.: one hundred and ninety soldiers of the garrison; forty inhabitants, who were married; forty-three children; thirty-four slaves, belonging to the king; with eight children; eight banditti; thirty-nine negroes, belonging to private persons; with twenty-seven female blacks, and thirty-four children. The pirates disarmed all the Spaniards, and sent them out immediately to the plantations to seek for provisions, leaving the women in the church, to exercise their devotions.

Soon after they reviewed the whole island, and all the fortresses thereof, which they found to be nine in all, viz.: the Fort of St. Jerom, next the bridge, had eight great guns, of twelve, six, and eight pounds carriage, with six pipes of muskets, every pipe containing ten muskets. Here they found still sixty muskets, with sufficient powder, and other ammunition. The second fortress, called St. Matthew, had three guns, of eight pounds each: the third, and chiefest, named Santa Teresa, had twenty great guns, of eighteen, twelve, eight, and six pounds; with ten pipes of muskets, like those before, and ninety muskets remaining, besides other ammunition. This castle was built with stone and mortar, with very thick walls, and a large ditch round it, twenty feet deep, which, though it was dry, yet was very hard to get over. Here was no entry, but through one door, to the middle of the castle. Within it was a mount almost inaccessible, with four pieces of cannon at the top; whence they could shoot directly into the port: on the seaside it was impregnable, by reason of the rocks round it, and the sea beating furiously upon them: to the land it was so commodiously seated on a mountain, as there was no access to it but by a path three or four feet broad. The fourth fortress was named St. Augustine, having three guns of eight and six pounds. The fifth, named La Plattaforma de la Conception, had only two guns, of eight pounds. The sixth, by name San Salvador, had likewise no more than two guns. The seventh, called Plattaforma de los Artilleros, had also two guns. The eighth, called Santa Cruz, had three guns. The ninth, called St. Joseph's Fort, had six guns, of twelve and eight pounds, besides two pipes of muskets, and sufficient ammunition.

In the storehouses were above thirty thousand pounds of powder, with all other ammunition, which was carried by the pirates on board: all the guns were stopped and nailed, and the fortresses demolished; except that of St. Jerom, where the pirates kept guard and resistance. Captain Morgan inquired for any banditti from Panama or Puerto Bello, and three were brought him, who pretended to be very expert in the avenues of those parts. He asked them to be his guides, and show him the securest ways to Panama, which if they performed, he promised them equal shares in the plunder of that expedition, and their liberty when they arrived in Jamaica. These propositions the banditti readily accepted, promising to serve him very faithfully, especially one of the three, who was the greatest rogue, thief, and assassin among them, and who had deserved rather to be broken alive on the wheel, than punished with serving in a garrrison : this wicked fellow had a great ascendant over the other two, and domineered over them as he pleased, they not daring to disobey his orders.

Captain Morgan commanded four ships and one boat to be equipped, and provided with necessaries, to go and take the Castle of Chagre, on the river of that name ; neither would he go himself with his whole fleet, lest the Spaniards should be jealous of his further design on Panama. In these vessels he embarked four hundred men, to put in execution these his orders: meanwhile, himself remained in St. Catherine's, with the rest of the fleet, expecting to hear of their success.

CHAPTER XVIII.

Captain Morgan takes the Castle of Chagre, with Four Hundred Men sent to this Purpose from St. Catherine's.

Captain Morgan sending this little fleet to Chagre, chose for vice-admiral thereof one Captain Brodely, who had been long in those quarters, and committed many robberies on the Spaniards, when Mansvelt took the Isle of St. Catherine, as was before related ; and therefore was thought a fit person for this exploit, his actions likewise having rendered him famous among the pirates, and their enemies the Spaniards. Captain Brodely being made commander, in three days after his departure arrived in sight of the said castle of Chagre, by the Spaniards called St. Lawrence. This castle is built on a high mountain, at the entry of the river, surrounded with strong palisadoes, or wooden walls, filled with earth, which secures them as well as the best wall of stone or brick. The top of this mountain is, in a manner, divided into two parts, between which is a ditch thirty feet deep. The castle hath but one entry, and that by a draw bridge over this ditch. To the land it has four bastions, and to the sea two more. The south part is totally inaccessible, through the cragginess of the mountain; the north is surrounded by the river, which here is very broad. At the foot of the castle, or rather, mountain, is a strong fort, with eight great guns, commanding the entry of the river. Not much lower are two other batteries, each of six pieces, to defend likewise the mouth of the river. At one side of the castle are two great storehouses of all sorts of warlike ammunition and merchandise, brought thither from the inland country: near these houses is a high pair of stairs hewn out of the rock, to mount to the top of the castle. On the west is a small port, not above seven or eight fathoms deep, fit for small vessels, and of very good anchorage; besides, before the castle, at the entry of the river is a great rock, scarce to be descried but at low tides.

No sooner had the Spaniards perceived the pirates, but they fired incessantly at them with the biggest of their guns. They came to an anchor in a small port, about a league from the castle. Next morning, very early, they went ashore, and marched through the woods to attack the castle on that side. This march lasted till two of the clock in the afternoon, before they could reach the castle, by reason of the difficulties of the way, and its mire and dirt; and though their guides served them very exactly, yet they came so nigh the castle at first, that they lost many of their men by its shot, they being in an open place, without covert. This much perplexed the pirates, not knowing what course to take; for on that side, of necessity, they must make the assault, and being uncovered from head to foot, they could not advance one step without danger: besides that, the castle, both for its situation and strength, made them much doubt of success. But to give it over they dared not, lest they should be reproached by their companions.

At last, after many doubts and disputes, resolving to hazard the assault and their lives desperately, they advanced towards the castle with their swords in one hand and fire-balls in the other. The Spaniards defended themselves very briskly, ceasing not to fire at them continually; crying withal, "Come on, ye English dogs, enemies to God and our king; and let your other companions that are behind come on too, ye shall not go to Panama this bout." The pirates making some trial to climb the walls, were forced to retreat, resting themselves till night. This being come, they returned to the assault, to try by the help of their fire-balls to destroy the pales before the wall; and while they were about it, there happened a very remarkable accident, which occasioned their victory. One of the pirates being wounded with an arrow in his back, which pierced his body through, he pulled it out boldly at the side of his breast, and winding a little cotton about it, he put it into his musket, and shot it back to the castle; but the cotton being kindled by the powder, fired two or three houses in the castle, being thatched with palm-leaves, which the Spaniards perceived not so soon as was necessary; for this fire meeting with a parcel of powder, blew it up, thereby causing great ruin, and no less consternation to the Spaniards, who were not able to put a stop to it, not having seen it time enough.

The pirates perceiving the effect of the arrow, and the misfortunes of the Spaniards, were infinitely glad; and while they were busied in quenching the fire, which caused a great confusion, for want of water, the pirates took this opportunity, setting fire likewise to the palisadoes. The fire thus seen at once in several parts about the castle, gave them great advantage against the Spaniards, many breaches being made by the fire among the pales, great heaps of earth falling into the ditch. Then the pirates climbing up, got over into the castle, though those Spaniards, who were not busy about the fire, cast down many flaming pots full of combustible matter, and odious smells, which destroyed many of the English.

The Spaniards, with all their resistance, could not hinder the palisadoes from being burnt down before midnight. Meanwhile the pirates continued in their intention of taking the castle; and though the fire was very great, they would creep on the ground, as near as they could, and shoot amidst the flames against the Spaniards on the other side, and thus killed many from the walls. When day was come, they observed all the movable earth that lay betwixt the pales to be fallen into the ditch; so that now those within the castle lay equally exposed to them without, as had been on the contrary before; whereupon the pirates continued shooting very furiously, and killed many Spaniards; for the governor had charged them to make good those posts, answering to the heaps of earth fallen into the ditch, and caused the artillery to be transported to the breaches.

The fire within the castle still continuing, the pirates from abroad did what they could to hinder its progress, by shooting incessantly against it: one party of them was employed only for this, while another watched all the motions of the Spaniards. About noon the English gained a breach, which the governor himself defended with twenty-five soldiers. Here was made a very courageous resistance by the Spaniards, with muskets, pikes, stones, and swords; but through all these the pirates fought their way till they gained the castle. The Spaniards, who remained alive, cast themselves down from the castle into the sea, choosing rather to die thus (few or none surviving the fall) than to ask quarter for their lives. The governor himself retreated to the *corps de garde*, before which were placed two pieces of cannon; here he still defended himself, not demanding any quarter, till he was killed with a musket shot in the head.

The governor being dead, and the *corps de garde* surrendering, they found remaining in it alive thirty men, whereof scarce ten were not wounded; these informed the pirates that eight or nine of their soldiers had deserted, and were gone to Panama, to carry news of their arrival and invasion. These thirty men alone remained of three hundred and fourteen wherewith the castle was garrisoned, among which not one officer was found alive. These were all made prisoners, and compelled to tell whatever they knew of their designs and enterprises. Among other things, that the governor of Panama had notice sent him three weeks ago from Carthagena, that the English were equipping a fleet at Hispaniola, with a design to take Panama; and besides, that this had been discovered by a deserter from the pirates at the River de la Hacha, where they had victualled. That upon this, the governor had sent one hundred and sixty-four men to strengthen the garrison of that castle, with much provision and ammunition; the ordinary garrison whereof was only one hundred and fifty men, but these made up two hundred and fourteen men, very well armed. Besides this, they declared that the governor of Panama had placed several ambuscades along the river of Chagre; and that he waited for them in the open fields of Panama with three thousand six hundred men.

The taking of this castle cost the pirates excessively dear, in comparison to what they were wont to lose, and their toil and labor was greater than at the conquest of the Isle of St. Catherine; for numbering their men, they had lost above one hundred, besides seventy wounded. They commanded the Spanish prisoners to cast the dead bodies of their own men from the top of the mountain to the sea-side, and to bury them. The wounded were carried to the church, of which they made a hospital, and where also they shut up the women. Thus it was likewise turned into a place of prostitution, the pirates ceasing not to defile the bodies of those afflicted widows with all manner of insolent actions and threats.

Captain Morgan remained not long behind at St. Catherine's, after taking the castle of Chagre, of which he had notice presently; but before he departed, he embarked all the provisions could be found, with much maize, or Indian wheat, and cazave, whereof also is made bread in those parts. He transported great store of provisions to the garrison of Chagre, whencesoever they could be got. At a certain place they cast into the sea all the guns belonging thereto, designing to return, and leave that island well garrisoned to the perpetual possession of the pirates; but he ordered all the houses and forts to be fired, except the castle of St. Teresa, which he judged to be the strongest and securest wherein to fortify himself at his return from Panama. He carried with him all the prisoners of the island, and then sailed for Chagre, where he arrived in eight days. Here the joy of the whole fleet was so great, when they spied the English colors on the castle, that they minded not their way into the river, so that they lost four ships at the entry thereof, Captain Morgan's being one; yet they saved all the men and goods. The ships, too, had been preserved, if a strong northerly wind had not risen, which cast them on the rock at the entry of the river.

Captain Morgan was brought into the castle with great acclamations of all the pirates, both of those within and those newly come. Having heard the manner of the conquest, he commanded all the prisoners to work, and repair what was necessary, especially to set up new palisadoes round the forts of the castle. There were still in the river some Spanish vessels, called *chatten*, serving for transportation of merchandise up and down the river, and to Puerto Bello and Nicaragua. These commonly carry two great guns of iron, and four small ones of brass. These vessels they seized, with four little ships they found there, and all the canoes. In the castle they left a garrison of five hundred men, and in the ships in the river one hundred and fifty more. This done, Captain Morgan departed for Panama at the head of twelve hundred men. He carried little provisions with him, hoping to provide himself sufficiently among the Spaniards, whom he knew to lie in ambuscade bv the way.

CHAPTER XIX.

Captain Morgan departs from Chagre, at the Head of Twelve Hundred Men, to take the City of Panama.

Captain Morgan set forth from the castle of Chagre, towards Panama, August 18, 1670. He had with him twelve hundred men, five boats laden with artillery, and thirty-two canoes. The first day they sailed only six leagues, and came to a place called De los Bracos. Here a party of his men went ashore, only to sleep and stretch their limbs, being almost crippled with lying too much crowded in the boats. Having rested a while, they went abroad to seek victuals in the neighboring plantations; but they could find none, the Spaniards being fled, and carrying with them all they had. This day, being the first of their journey, they had such scarcity of victuals, as the greatest part were forced to pass with only a pipe of tobacco, without any other refreshment.

Next day, about evening, they came to a place called Cruz de Juan Gallego. Here they were compelled to leave their boats and canoes, the river being very dry for want of rain, and many trees having fallen into it.

The guides told them, that about two leagues farther the country would be very good to continue the journey by land; hereupon they left one hundred and sixty men on board the boats, to defend them, that they might serve for a refuge in necessity.

Next morning, being the third day, they all went ashore, except those who were to keep the boats. To these Captain Morgan gave order, under great penalties, that no man, on any pretext whatever, should dare to leave the boats, and go ashore; fearing lest they should be surprised by an ambuscade of Spaniards in the neighboring woods, which appeared so thick, as to seem almost impenetrable. This morning beginning their march, the ways proved so bad, that Captain Morgan thought it more convenient to transport some of the men in canoes (though with great labor) to a place farther up the river, called Cedro Bueno. Thus they reëmbarked, and the canoes returned for the rest; so that about night they got all together at the said place. The pirates much desired to meet some Spaniards or Indians, hoping to fill their bellies with their provisions, being reduced to extremity and hunger.

The fourth day the greatest part of the pirates marched by

land, being led by one of the guides; the rest went by water farther up, being conducted by another guide, who always went before them, to discover, on both sides the river, the ambuscades. These had also spies, who were very dexterous to give notice of all accidents, or of the arrival of the pirates, six hours, at least, before they came. This day, about noon, they came near a post, called Torna Cavallos; here the guide of the canoes cried out, that he perceived an ambuscade. His voice caused infinite joy to all the pirates, hoping to find some provisions to satiate their extreme hunger. Being come to the place, they found nobody in it, the Spaniards being fled, and leaving nothing behind but a few leathern bags, all empty, and a few crums of bread, scattered on the ground, where they had eaten. Being angry at this, they pulled down a few little huts which the Spaniards had made, and fell to eating the leathern bags, to allay the ferment of their stomachs, which was now so sharp, as to gnaw their very bowels. Thus they made a huge banquet upon these bags of leather, divers quarrels arising concerning the greatest shares. By the bigness of the place, they conjectured about five hundred Spaniards had been there, whom, finding no victuals, they were now infinitely desirous to meet, intending to devour some of them, rather than perish.

Having feasted themselves with those pieces of leather, they marched on, till they came about night to another post, called Torna Munni: here they found another ambuscade, but as barren as the former. They searched the neighboring woods, but could not find any thing to eat, the Spaniards having been so provident, as not to leave, any where, the least crum of sustenance; whereby, the pirates were now brought to this extremity. Here, again, he was happy that had reserved since noon any bit of leather, to make his supper of, drinking after it a good draught of water, for his comfort. Some, who never were out of their mothers' kitchens, may ask, how these pirates could eat and digest those pieces of leather, so hard and dry. Whom I answer, that could they once experiment what hunger, or rather famine, is, they would find the way as the pirates did. For these first sliced it in pieces, then they beat it between two stones, and rubbed it, often dipping it in water, to make it supple and tender: lastly, they scraped off the hair, and broiled it. Being thus cooked, they cut it into small morsels, and ate it, helping it down with frequent gulps of water, which, by good fortune, they had at hand.

The fifth day, about noon, they came to a place called Barbaco: here they found traces of another ambuscade, but the place totally as unprovided as the former. At a small distance were several plantations, which they searched very narrowly, but could not find any person, animal, or other thing, to relieve their extreme hunger. Finally, having ranged about, and searched a long time, they found a grot, which seemed to be but lately hewn out of a rock, where were two sacks of meal, wheat, and like things, with two great jars of wine, and certain fruits called *platanoes*. Captain Morgan, knowing some of his men were now almost dead with hunger, and fearing the same of the rest, caused what was found to be distributed among them who were in greatest necessity. Having refreshed themselves with these victuals, they marched anew with greater courage than ever. Such as were weak were put into the canoes, and those commanded to land that were in them before. Thus they prosecuted their journey till late at night; when coming to a plantation, they took up their rest, but without eating any thing; for the Spaniards, as before, had swept away all manner of provisions.

The sixth day they continued their march, part by land and part by water: howbeit, they were constrained to rest very frequently, both for the ruggedness of the way, and their extreme weakness, which they endeavored to relieve by eating leaves of trees and green herbs, or grass; such was their miserable condition. This day, at noon, they arrived at a plantation, where was a barn full of maize: immediately they beat down the doors, and ate it dry, as much as they could devour; then they distributed a great quantity, giving every man a good allowance. Thus provided, and prosecuting their journey for about an hour, they came to another ambuscade. This they no sooner discovered, but they threw away their maize, with the sudden hopes of finding all things in abundance: but they were much deceived, meeting neither Indians nor victuals, nor any thing else: but they saw, on the other side of the river, about one hundred Indians, who all fleeing, escaped. Some few pirates leaped into the river to cross it, and try to take any of the Indians, but in vain; for being much more nimble than the pirates, they not only baffled them, but killed two or three with their arrows; hooting at them, and crying, "*Ha! perros, à la savana, à la savana.*" "Ha! ye dogs, go to the plain, go to the plain."

This day they could advance no farther, being necessitated to pass the river, to continue their march on the other side. Hereupon they reposed for that night, though their sleep was not profound; for great murmurings were made at Captain Morgan, and his conduct; some being desirous to return home, while others would rather die there than go back a step from their undertaking: others, who had greater courage, laughed and joked at their discourses. Meanwhile, they had a guide, who much comforted them, saying, it would not now be long before they met with people from whom they should reap some considerable advantage.

The seventh day, in the morning, they made clean their arms, and every one discharged his pistol, or musket, without bullet, to try their fire-locks: this done, they crossed the river, leaving the post where they had rested, called Santa Cruz, and at noon they arrived at a village called Cruz. Being yet far from the place, they perceived much smoke from the chimneys: the sight hereof gave them great joy, and hopes of finding people, and plenty of good cheer. Thus they went on as fast as they could, encouraging one another, saying, "There is smoke comes out of every house; they are making good fires, to roast and boil what we are to eat;" and the like.

At length they arrived there, all sweating and panting, but found no person in the town, nor any thing eatable to refresh themselves, except good fires, which they wanted not; for the Spaniards, before their departure, had every one set fire to his own house, except the king's storehouses and stables.

They had not left behind them any beast, alive or dead, which much troubled their minds, not finding any thing but a few cats and dogs, which they immediately killed, and devoured. At last, in the king's stables, they found, by good fortune, fifteen or sixteen jars of Peru wine, and a leathern sack, full of bread. No sooner had they drank of this wine, when they fell sick, almost every man: this made them think the wine was poisoned, which caused a new consternation in the whole camp, judging themselves now to be irrecoverably lost. But the true reason was, their want of sustenance, and the manifold sorts of trash they had eaten. Their sickness was so great, as caused them to remain there till the next morning, without being able to prosecute their journey in the afternoon. This village is seated in nine degrees two minutes north latitude, distant from the River Chagre twenty-six Spanish leagues, and eight from Panama. This is the last place to which boats or canoes can come; for which reason they built here storehouses for all sorts of merchandise, which to and from Panama are transported on the backs of mules.

Here Captain Morgan was forced to leave his canoes, and land all his men, though never so weak; but lest the canoes should be surprised, or take up too many men for their defence, he sent them all back to the place where the boats were, except one, which he hid, that it might serve to carry intelligence. Many of the Spaniards and Indians of this village having fled to the near plantations, Captain Morgan ordered that none should go out of the village, except companies of one hundred together, fearing lest the enemy should take an advantage upon his men. Notwithstanding one party contravened these orders, being tempted with the desire of victuals: but they were soon glad to fly into the town again, being assaulted with great fury by some Spaniards and Indians, who carried one of them away prisoner. Thus the vigilancy and care of Captain Morgan were not sufficient to prevent every accident.

The eighth day in the morning, Captain Morgan sent two hundred men before the body of his army, to discover the way to Panama, and any ambuscades therein; the path being so narrow, that only ten or twelve persons could march abreast, and often not so many. After ten hours' march, they came to a place called *Quebrada Obscura;* here, all on a sudden, three or four thousand arrows were shot at them, they not perceiving whence they came, or who shot them; though they presumed it was from a high rocky mountain, from one side to the other, whereon was a grot capable of but one horse, or other beast laded. This multitude of arrows much alarmed the pirates, especially because they could not discover whence they were discharged. At last, seeing no more arrows, they marched a little farther, and entered a wood: here they perceived some Indians to fly as fast as they could, to take the advantage of another post, thence to observe their march; yet there remained one troop of Indians on the place, resolved to fight, and defend themselves, which they did with great courage, till their captain fell down wounded; who, though he despaired of life, yet his valor being greater than his strength, would ask no quarter, but endeavoring to raise himself, with undaunted mind laid hold of his *azagayo*, or javelin, and struck at one of the pirates; but before he could second the blow, he was shot to death. This was, also, the fate of many of his companions, who, like good soldiers, lost their lives with their captain, for the defence of their country.

The pirates endeavored to take some of the Indians prisoners, but they being swifter than the pirates, every one escaped, leaving eight pirates dead, and ten wounded: yea, had the Indians been more dexterous in military affairs, they might have defended that passage, and not let one man pass. A little while after, they came to a large champaign, open, and full of fine meadows: hence they could perceive at a distance before them some Indians, on the top of a mountain, near the way by which they were to pass: they sent fifty men, the nimblest they had, to try to catch any of them, and force them to discover their companions; but all in vain; for they escaped by their nimbleness, and presently showed themselves in another place, hallooing to the English, and crying, "*A la savana, a la savana, cornudos, perros Ingleses:*" that is, "To the plain, to the plain, ye cuckolds, ye English dogs." Meanwhile the ten pirates, that were wounded, were dressed and plastered up.

Here was a wood, and on each side a mountain. The Indians possessed themselves of one, and the pirates of the other. Captain Morgan was persuaded the Spaniards had placed an ambuscade there, it lying so conveniently: hereupon he sent two hundred men to search it. The Spaniards and Indians, perceiving the pirates descend the mountain, did so too, as if they designed to attack them; but being got into the wood, out of sight of the pirates, they were seen no more, leaving the passage open.

About night fell a great rain, which caused the pirates to march the faster, and seek for houses to preserve their arms from being wet; but the Indians had set fire to every one, and driven away all their cattle, that the pirates, finding neither houses nor victuals, might be constrained to return: but, after a diligent search, they found a few shepherds' huts, but in them nothing to eat. These not holding many men, they placed in them, out of every company, a small number, who kept the arms of the rest: those who remained in the open field endured much hardship that night, the rain not ceasing till morning.

Next morning, about break of day, being the ninth of this tedious journey, Captain Morgan marched on while the fresh air of the morning lasted; for the clouds, hanging yet over their heads, were much more favorable than the scorching rays of the sun, the way being now more difficult than before. After two hours' march, they discovered about twenty Spaniards, who observed their motions: they endeavored to catch some of them, but could not, they suddenly disappearing, and absconding themselves in caves among the rocks, unknown to the pirates. At last, ascending a high mountain, they discovered the South Sea. This happy sight, as if it were the end of their labors, caused infinite joy among them; hence they could descry, also, one ship and six boats, which were set forth from Panama, and sailed towards the islands of Tovago and Tovagilla. Then they came to a vale where they found much cattle, whereof they killed good store: here, while some killed and flayed cows, horses, bulls, and chiefly asses, of which there were most, others kindled fires, and got wood to roast them: then cutting the flesh into convenient pieces, or gobbets, they threw them into the fire, and half carbonadoed or roasted, they devoured them, with incredible haste and appetite; such was their hunger, as they more resembled cannibals than Europeans, the blood many times running down from their beards to their waists.

Having satisfied their hunger, Captain Morgan ordered them to continue the march. Here, again, he sent before the main body fifty men to take some prisoners, if they could; for he was much concerned, that in nine days he could not meet one person to inform him of the condition and forces of the Spaniards. About evening they discovered about two hundred Spaniards, who hallooed to the pirates, but they understood not what they said. A little while after they came in sight of the highest steeple of Panama; this they no sooner discovered, but they showed signs of extreme joy, casting up their hats into the air, leaping and shouting, just as if they had already obtained the victory, and accomplished their designs. All their trumpets sounded, and drums beat, in token of this alacrity of their minds. Thus they pitched their camp for that night, with general content of the whole army, waiting with impatience for the morning, when they intended to attack the city. This evening appeared fifty horse, who came out of the city, on the noise of the drums and trumpets, to observe, as it was thought, their motions; they came almost within musket shot of the army, with a trumpet that sounded marvellously well. Those on horseback hallooed aloud to the pirates, and threatened them, saying, "*Perros! nos veremos;*" that is, "Ye dogs! we shall meet ye." Having made this menace, they returned to the city, except only seven or eight horsemen, who hovered thereabouts to watch their motions. Immediately after the city fired, and ceased not to play their biggest guns all night long against the camp, but with little or no harm to the pirates, whom they could not easily reach. Now also the two hundred Spaniards, whom the pirates had seen in the afternoon, appeared again, making a show of blocking up the passages, that no pirates might escape their hands. But the pirates, though in a manner besieged, instead of fearing their blockades, as soon as they had placed sentinels about their camp, opened their satchels, and, without any napkins or plates, fell to eating, very heartily, the pieces of bulls' and horses' flesh which they had reserved since noon. This done they laid themselves down to sleep on the grass, with great repose and satisfaction, expecting only, with impatience, the dawning of the next day.

The tenth day, betimes in the morning, they put all their men in order, and, with drums and trumpets sounding, marched directly towards the city; but one of the guides desired Captain Morgan not to take the common highway, lest they should find in it many ambuscades. He took his advice, and chose another way through the wood, though very irksome and difficult. The Spaniards, perceiving the pirates had taken another way they scarce had thought on, were compelled to leave their stops and batteries, and come out to meet them. The governor of Panama put his forces in order, consisting of two squadrons, four regiments of foot, and a huge number of wild bulls, which were driven by a great number of Indians, with some negroes, and others to help them.

The pirates, now upon their march, came to the top of a little hill, whence they had a large prospect of the city and champaign country underneath. Here they discovered the forces of the people of Panama, in battle array, to be so numerous, that they were surprised with fear, much doubting the fortune of the day. Yea, few or none there were but wished themselves at home, or at least free from the obligation of that engagement, it so nearly concerning their lives. Having been some time wavering in their minds, they at last reflected on the straits they had brought themselves into, and that now they must either fight resolutely, or die; for no quarter could be expected from an enemy on whom they had committed so many cruelties. Hereupon, they encouraged one another, resolving to conquer, or spend the last drop of blood. Then they divided themselves into three battalions, sending before two hundred Buccaneers, who were very dexterous at their guns. Then descending the hill, they marched directly towards the Spaniards, who in a spacious field waited for their coming. As soon as they drew nigh, the Spaniards began to shout and cry, "*Viva el rey!*" "God save the king!" and immediately their horse moved against the pirates. But the fields being full of quags, and soft under foot, they could not wheel about as they desired. The two hundred Buccaneers, who went before, each putting one knee to the ground, began the battle briskly with a full volley of shot; the Spaniards defended themselves courageously, doing all they could to disorder the pirates. Their foot endeavored to second the horse, but were constrained by the pirates to leave them. Finding themselves baffled, they attempted to drive the bulls against them behind, to put them into disorder; but the wild cattle ran away, frighted with the noise of the battle; only some few broke through the English companies, and only tore the colors in pieces, while the Buccaneers shot every one of them dead.

The battle having continued two hours, the greatest part of the Spanish horse was ruined, and almost all killed; the rest fled, which the foot seeing, and that they could not possibly prevail, they discharged the shot they had in their muskets, and throwing them down, fled away, every one as he could. The pirates could not follow them, being too much harassed and wearied with their long journey. Many, not being able to fly whither they desired, hid themselves, for that present, among the shrubs of the sea-side, but very unfortunately; for most of them, being found by the pirates, were instantly killed, without any quarter. Some religious men were brought prisoners before Captain Morgan; but he, being deaf to their cries, commanded them all to be pistolled, which was done. Soon after, they brought a captain to him, whom he examined very strictly; particularly, wherein consisted the forces of those of Panama. He answered, their whole strength consisted in four hundred horse, twenty-four companies of foot, each of one hundred men complete; sixty Indians, and some negroes, who were to drive two thousand wild bulls upon the English, and thus, by breaking their files, put them into a total disorder. Besides that, in the city they had made trenches, and raised batteries in several places, in all which they had placed many guns; and that at the entry of the highway, leading to the city, they had built a fort, mounted with eight great brass guns, defended by fifty men.

Captain Morgan, having heard this, gave orders instantly to march another way; but first he made a review of his men, whereof he found both killed and wounded a considerable number, and much greater than had been believed. Of the Spaniards were found six hundred dead on the place, besides the wounded and prisoners. The pirates, nothing discouraged, seeing their number so diminished, but rather filled with greater pride; perceiving what huge advantage they had obtained against their enemies, having rested some time, prepared to march courageously towards the city, plighting their oaths to one another, that they would fight till not a man was left alive. With this courage they recommenced their march, either to conquer or be conquered; carrying with them all the prisoners.

They found much difficulty in their approach to the city, for within the town the Spaniards had placed many great guns, at several quarters, some charged with small pieces of iron, and others with musket bullets. With all these they saluted the pirates at their approaching, and gave them full and frequent broadsides, firing at them incessantly; so that unavoidably they lost at every step great numbers of men. But these manifest dangers of their lives, nor the sight of so many as dropped continually at their sides, could deter them from advancing, and gaining ground every moment on the enemy. And though the Spaniards never ceased to fire, and act the best they could for their defence, yet they were forced to yield, after three hours' combat. And the pirates having possessed themselves, killed and destroyed all that attempted in the least to oppose them. The inhabitants had transported the best of their goods to more remote and occult places; howbeit, they found in the city several warehouses well stocked with merchandise, as well silks and cloths, as linen, and other things of value. As soon as the first fury of their entrance was over, Captain Morgan assembled his men, and commanded them, under great penalties, not to drink or taste any wine; and the reason he gave for it was, because he had intelligence that it was all poisoned by the Spaniards. Howbeit, it was thought he gave these prudent orders to prevent the debauchery of his people, which he foresaw would be very great at the first, after so much hunger sustained by the way; fearing, withal, lest the Spaniards, seeing them in wine, should rally, and falling on the city, use them as inhumanly as they had used the inhabitants before.

CHAPTER XX.

Captain Morgan sends Canoes and Boats to the South Sea. — He fires the City of Panama. — Robberies and Cruelties committed there by the Pirates, till their Return to the Castle of Chagre.

Captain Morgan, as soon as he had placed necessary guards at several quarters, within and without the city, commanded twenty-five men to seize a great boat, which had stuck in the mud of the port, for want of water at a low tide. The same day, about noon, he caused fire privately to be set to several great edifices of the city, nobody knowing who were the authors thereof, much less on what motives Captain Morgan did it, which are unknown to this day. The fire increased so, that before night the greatest part of the city was in a flame. Captain Morgan pretended the Spaniards had done it, perceiving that his own people reflected on him for that action. Many of the Spaniards, and some of the pirates, did what they could, either to quench the flame, or by blowing up houses with gunpowder, and pulling down others, to stop it, but in vain; for in less than half an hour it consumed a whole street. All the houses of this city were built with cedar, very curious and magnificent, and richly adorned, especially with hangings and paintings, whereof part were before removed, and another great part were consumed by fire.

There were in this city (which is the see of a bishop) eight monasteries, seven for men, and one for women; two stately churches, and one hospital. The churches and monasteries were all richly adorned with altar pieces and paintings, much gold and silver, with other precious things, all which the ecclesiastics had hidden. Besides which, here were two thousand houses of magnificent building, the greatest part inhabited by merchants vastly rich. For the rest of less quality, and tradesmen, this city contained five thousand more. Here were also many stables for the horses and mules, that carry the plate of the king of Spain, as well as private men, towards the North Sea. The neighboring fields are full of fertile plantations and pleasant gardens, affording delicious prospects to the inhabitants all the year.

The Genoese had in this city a stately house for their trade of negroes. This likewise was by Captain Morgan burnt to the very ground. Besides which building, there were consumed two hundred warehouses, and many slaves, who had hid themselves therein, with innumerable sacks of meal; the fire of which continued four weeks after it had begun. The greatest part of the pirates still encamped without the city, fearing and expecting the Spaniards would come and fight them anew, it being known they much outnumbered the pirates. This made them keep the field, to preserve their forces united, now much diminished by their losses. Their wounded, which were many, they put into one church which remained standing, the rest being consumed by the fire. Besides these decreases of their men, Captain Morgan had sent a convoy of one hundred and fifty men to the castle of Chagre, to carry the news of his victory to Panama.

They saw often whole troops of Spaniards run to and fro in the fields, which made them suspect their rallying, which they never had the courage to do. In the afternoon Captain Morgan reëntered the city with his troops, that every one might take up their lodgings, which now they could hardly find, few houses having escaped the fire. Then they sought very carefully among the ruins and ashes for utensils of plate or gold, that were not quite wasted by the flames. And of such they found no small number, especially in wells and cisterns, where the Spaniards had hid them.

Next day Captain Morgan despatched away two troops of one hundred and fifty men each, stout and well armed, to seek for the inhabitants who were escaped. These having made several excursions up and down the fields, woods, and mountains adjacent, returned after two days, bringing above two hundred prisoners, men, women, and slaves. The same day returned also the boat which Captain Morgan had sent to the South Sea, bringing three other boats which they had taken. But all these prizes they could willingly have given, and greater labor into the bargain, for one galleon, which miraculously escaped, richly laden with all the king's plate, jewels and other precious goods of the best and richest merchants of Panama. On board which were also the religious women of the nunnery, who had embarked with all the ornaments of their church, consisting in much gold, plate, and other things of great value.

The strength of this galleon was inconsiderable, having only seven guns, and ten or twelve muskets, and very ill provided of victuals, necessaries, and fresh water, having no more sails than the uppermost of the mainmast: this account the pirates received from some, who had spoken with seven mariners belonging to the galleon, who came ashore in the cock-boat for fresh water. Hence they concluded they might easily have taken it, had they given her chase, as they should have done; but they were impeded from following this vastly rich prize, by their lascivious exercises with women, which they had carried and forced on board their boat. To this vice were also joined those of gluttony and drunkenness, having plentifully debauched themselves with several rich wines they found ready, choosing rather to satiate their lusts and appetites, than to lay hold on such huge advantage; since this only prize would have been of far greater value than all they got at Panama and the places thereabout. Next day, repenting of their negligence, being weary of their vices and debaucheries, they set forth another boat well armed, to pursue with all speed the said galleon, but in vain, the Spaniards who were on board, having had intelligence of their own danger one or two days before, while the pirates were cruising so near them; whereupon they fled to places more remote and unknown.

The pirates found in the ports of the Island of Tavoga and Tavogilla several boats laden with very good merchandise; all which they took, and brought to Panama, where they made an exact relation of all that had passed to Captain Morgan. The prisoners confirmed what the pirates said, adding, that they undoubtedly knew where the galleon might then be, but that it was very probable they had been relieved before now, from other places. This stirred up Captain Morgan, anew, to send forth all the boats in the port of Panama, to seek the said galleon, 'till they could find her. These boats, being in all four, after eight days' cruising to and fro, and searching several ports and creeks, lost all hopes of finding her: hereupon, they returned to Tavoga and Tavogilla; here they found a reasonable good ship newly come from Payta, laden with cloth, soap, sugar, and biscuit, with twenty thousand pieces of eight: this they instantly seized, without the least resistance, as also a boat, which was not far off, on which they laded great part of the merchandises from the ship, with some slaves. With this purchase they returned to Panama, somewhat better satisfied; yet, withal, much discontented that they could not meet with the galleon.

The convoy which Captain Morgan had sent to the castle of Chagre returned much about the same time, bringing with them very good news: for while Captain Morgan was on his journey to Panama, those he had left in the castle of Chagre had sent forth two boats to cruise. These met with a Spanish ship, which they chased within sight of the castle: this being perceived by the pirates in the castle, they put forth Spanish colors, to deceive the ship that fled before the boats; and the poor Spaniards, thinking to take refuge under the castle, were caught in a snare, and made prisoners. The cargo on board the said vessel consisted in victuals and provisions, than which, nothing could be more opportune for the castle, where they began already to want things of this kind.

This good luck of those of Chagre caused Captain Morgan to stay longer at Panama, ordering several new excursions into the country round about; and while the pirates at Panama were upon these expeditions, those at Chagre were busy in piracies on the north sea. Captain Morgan sent forth, daily, parties of two hundred men, to make inroads into all the country round about; and when one party came back, another went forth, who soon gathered much riches, and many prisoners. These being brought into the city, were put to the most exquisite tortures, to make them confess both other people's goods and their own. Here it happened that one poor wretch was found in the house of a person of quality, who had put on, amidst the confusion, a pair of taffety breeches of his master's, with a little silver key hanging out; perceiving which, they asked him for the cabinet of the said key. His answer was, he knew not what was become of it, but that, finding those breeches in his master's house, he had made bold to wear them. Not being able to get any other answer, they put him on the rack, and inhumanly disjointed his arms; then they twisted a cord about his forehead, which they wrung so hard, that his eyes appeared as big as eggs, and were ready to fall out. But with these torments, not obtaining any positive answer, they hung him up by the testicles, giving him many blows and stripes, under that intolerable pain and posture of body. Afterwards they cut off his nose and ears, and singed his face with burning straw, till he could not speak, nor lament his misery any longer: then, losing all hopes of any confession, they bade a negro run him through, which put an end to his life, and to their inhuman tortures. Thus did many others of those miserable prisoners finish their days, the common sport and recreation of these pirates being such tragedies.

They spared, in these their cruelties, no sex, nor condition; for as to religious persons, and priests, they granted them less quarter than others, unless they could produce a considerable sum sufficient for a ransom. Women were no better used, except they submitted to their filthy lusts; for such as would not consent, were treated with all the rigor imaginable. Captain Morgan gave them no good example in this point; for when any beautiful woman was brought prisoner to his presence, he used all means, both of rigor and mildness, to bend them to his lascivious pleasure. For confirmation of which, I shall give a short history of a lady, whose virtue and constancy ought to be transmitted to posterity.

Among the prisoners brought by the pirates from Tavoga and Tavogilla, was a gentlewoman of good quality, and no less virtue and chastity, wife to one of the richest merchants there. She was young, and so beautiful, as perhaps few in all Europe surpassed her, either in comeliness or honesty. Her husband then was from home, being gone as far as Peru, about his commerce and trade. This virtuous lady, hearing of the pirates' coming, had fled, with other friends and relations, to preserve her life from the cruelties and tyrannies of those hard-hearted enemies: but no sooner did she appear before Captain Morgan, but she was designed for his pleasure. Hereupon, he lodged her in an apartment by herself, giving her a negro, or black woman, to wait on her, and treated her with all the respect due to her quality. The poor afflicted lady begged, with many sobs and tears, to lodge among the other prisoners; her relations fearing that unexpected kindness of the commander might be a design on her chastity. But Captain Morgan would by no means hearken to her, but commanded she should be treated with more particular care than before, and have her victuals from his own table.

This lady had formerly heard very strange reports concerning the pirates, as if they were not men, but, as they said, heretics, who did neither invoke the blessed Trinity, nor believe in Jesus Christ. But now she began to have better thoughts of them, upon these civilities of Captain Morgan; especially hearing him many times swear by God, and Jesus Christ, in whom she thought they did not believe. Nor did she think them to be so bad, or to have the shapes of beasts, as had been related. As to the name of robbers, or thieves, commonly given them, she wondered not much at it, seeing, among all nations of the universe, there were wicked men, covetous to possess the goods of others. Like this was the opinion of another woman of weak understanding, at Panama, who used to say, before the pirates came thither, she had a great curiosity to see a pirate; her husband having often told her they were not like other men, but rather irrational beasts. This silly woman happening to see the first of them, cried out, aloud, "Jesus bless me! these thieves are like us Spaniards."

This false civility of Captain Morgan towards this lady, as is usual to such as pretend, and cannot obtain, was soon changed into barbarous cruelty; for after three or four days he came to see her, and entertained her with lascivious discourses, desiring the accomplishment of his lust. The virtuous lady constantly denied him, with much civility, and many humble and modest expressions; but Captain Morgan still persisted in his base request, presenting to her much pearl, gold, and whatever he had that was precious and valuable: but the lady, not willing to consent, or accept his presents, showing herself like Susannah for constancy, he presently changed his note, and addressed her in another tone, threatening a thousand cruelties and hard usages, to all which she gave only this resolute and positive answer: "Sir, my life is in your hands; but as to my body, in relation to that which you would persuade me to, my soul shall sooner be separated from it, through the violence of your arms, than I shall condescend to your request." Captain Morgan understanding this her heroic resolution, commanded her to be stripped of the best of her apparel, and imprisoned in a darksome, stinking cellar: here she was allowed a small quantity of meat and drink, wherewith she had much ado to sustain her life.

Under this hardship, the virtuous lady prayed daily to God Almighty for constancy and patience: but Captain Morgan, now thoroughly convinced of her chaste resolutions, as also desirous to conceal the cause of her hard usage, since many of his companions compassionated her condition, pretended she held intelligence with the Spaniards, and corresponded with them, abusing his lenity and kindness. I, myself, was an eye-witness thereof, and could never have judged such constancy and chastity to be found in the world, if my own eyes and ears had not assured me thereof. But of this incomparable lady, I shall say something more, hereafter.

Captain Morgan, having now been at Panama full three weeks, commanded all things to be prepared for his departure. He ordered every company of men to seek so many beasts of carriage, as might convey the whole spoil to the river where his canoes lay. About this time there was a great rumor that a considerable number of pirates intended to leave Captain Morgan, and that, taking a ship then in the port, they determined to go and rob on the South Sea, till they had got as much as they thought fit, and then return homewards, by way of the East Indies. For which purpose, they had gathered much provisions, which they had hid in private places, with sufficient powder, bullets, and all other ammunition: likewise, some great guns belonging to the town, muskets, and other things, wherewith they designed not only to equip their vessel, but to fortify themselves in some island, which might serve them for a place of refuge.

This design had certainly taken effect, had not Captain Morgan had timely advice of it from one of their comrades. Hereupon, he commanded the mainmast of the said ship to be cut down and burnt, with all the other boats in the port: hereby the intentions of all, or most of his companions, were totally frustrated. Then Captain Morgan sent many of the Spaniards into the adjoining fields and country, to seek for money, to ransom, not only themselves, but the rest of the prisoners, as likewise the ecclesiastics. Moreover, he commanded all the artillery of the town to be nailed and stopped up. At the same time he sent out a strong company of men to seek for the governor of Panama, of whom intelligence was brought, that he had laid several ambuscades in the way by which he ought to return: but they returned soon after, saying, that they had not found any sign of any such ambuscades. For confirmation whereof, they brought some prisoners, who declared that the said governor had had an intention of making some opposition by the way, but that the men designed to effect it were unwilling to undertake it; so that, for want of means, he could not put his design in execution.

February 24, 1671, Captain Morgan departed from Panama, or rather, from the place where the city of Panama stood; of the spoils whereof he carried with him one hundred and seventy-five beasts of carriage, laden with silver, gold, and other precious things, beside about six hundred prisoners, men, women, children, and slaves. That day they came to a river, that passes through a delicious plain, a league from Panama. Here Captain Morgan put all his forces into good order, so as that the prisoners were in the middle, surrounded on all sides with pirates, where nothing else was to be heard but lamentations, cries, shrieks, and doleful sighs of so many women and children, who feared Captain Morgan designed to transport them all into his own country, for slaves. Besides, all those miserable prisoners endured extreme hunger and thirst, at that time, which misery Captain Morgan designedly caused them to sustain, to excite them to seek for money, to ransom themselves, according to the tax he had set upon every one. Many of the women begged Captain Morgan, on their knees, with infinite sighs and tears, to let them return to Panama, there to live with their dear husbands and children, in little huts of straw, which they would erect, seeing they had no houses till the rebuilding of the city. But his answer was, "he came not thither to hear lamentations, and cries, but to seek money; therefore they ought first to seek out that, wherever it was to be had, and bring it to him; otherwise, he would assuredly transport them all to such places whither they cared not to go."

Next day, when the march began, those lamentable cries and shrieks were renewed, so as it would have caused compassion in the hardest heart: but Captain Morgan, as a man little given to mercy, was not moved in the least. They marched in the same order as before, one party of the pirates in the van, the prisoners in the middle, and the rest of the pirates in the rear; by whom the miserable Spaniards were at every step punched and thrust in their backs and sides, with the blunt ends of their arms, to make them march faster. That beautiful and virtuous lady, mentioned before for her unparalleled constancy and chastity, was led prisoner by herself between two pirates. Her lamentations now pierced the skies, seeing herself carried away into captivity, often crying to the pirates, and telling them, "that she had given orders to two religious persons, in whom she had relied, to go to a certain place, and fetch so much money as her ransom did amount to; that they had promised faithfully to do it, but having obtained the money, instead of bringing it to her, they had employed it in another way, to ransom some of their own, and particular friends." This ill action of theirs was discovered by a slave, who brought a letter to the said lady. Her complaints, and the cause thereof,

being brought to Captain Morgan, he thought fit to inquire thereinto. Having found it to be true, especially hearing it confirmed by the confession of the said religious men, though under some frivolous excuses of having diverted the money but for a day or two, in which time they expected more sums to repay it, he gave liberty to the said lady, whom otherwise he designed to transport to Jamaica. But he detained the said religious men, as prisoners in her place, using them according to their deserts.

Captain Morgan arriving at the town called Cruz, on the banks of the River of Chagre, he published an order among the prisoners, that within three days every one should bring in their ransom, under the penalty of being transported to Jamaica. Meanwhile he gave orders for so much rice and maize, to be collected thereabouts, as was necessary for victualling his ships. Here some of the prisoners were ransomed, but many others could not bring in their money. Hereupon he continued his voyage, leaving the village on the fifth of March following, carrying with him all the spoil he could. Hence he likewise led away some new prisoners, inhabitants there, with those of Panama, who had not paid their ransoms: but the two religious men, who had diverted the lady's money, were ransomed three days after by other persons, who had more compassion for them than they had showed for her. About the middle of the way to Chagre, Captain Morgan commanded them to be mustered, and caused every one to be sworn that they had concealed nothing, not even to the value of sixpence. This done, Captain Morgan knowing those lewd fellows would not stick to swear falsely for interest, he commanded every one to be searched very strictly, both in their clothes and satchels, and elsewhere. Yea, that this order might not be ill taken by his companions, he permitted himself to be searched, even to his very shoes. To this effect, by common consent, one was assigned out of every company, to be searchers of the rest. The French pirates that assisted on this expedition disliked this new practice of searching; but being outnumbered by the English, they were forced to submit, as well as the rest. The search being over, they reëmbarked, and arrived at the Castle of Chagre on the ninth of March. Here they found all things in good order, excepting the wounded men, whom they had left at their departure; for of these, the greatest number were dead of their wounds.

From Chagre, Captain Morgan sent, presently after his arrival, a great boat to Puerto Bello, with all the prisoners taken at the Isle of St. Catherine, demanding of them a considerable ransom for the Castle of Chagre, where he then was, threatening otherwise to ruin it. To this those of Puerto Bello answered, they would not give one farthing towards the ransom of the said castle, and the English might do with it as they pleased. Hereupon, the dividend was made of all the spoil made in that voyage; every company, and every particular person therein, receiving their proportion, or rather, what part thereof Captain Morgan pleased to give them. For the rest of his companions, even of his own nation, murmured at his proceedings, and told him to his face, that he had reserved the best jewels to himself; for they judged it impossible that no greater share should belong to them than two hundred pieces of eight, *per capita*, of so many valuable plunders they had made; which small sum they thought too little for so much labor, and such dangers as they had been exposed to. But Captain Morgan was deaf to all this, and many other like complaints, having designed to cheat them of what he could.

At last, finding himself obnoxious to many censures of his people, and fearing the consequence, he thought it unsafe to stay any longer at Chagre, but ordered the ordnance of the castle to be carried on board his ship: then he caused most of the walls to be demolished, the edifices to be burnt, and as many other things ruined as could be done in a short time. This done, he went secretly on board his own ship, without giving any notice to his companions, and put out to sea, being only followed by three or four vessels of the whole fleet. These were such (as the French pirates believed) as went shares with Captain Morgan in the best part of the spoil, which had been concealed from them in the dividend. The Frenchmen could willingly have revenged themselves on Captain Morgan and his followers, had they been able to encounter him at sea; but they were destitute of necessaries, and had much ado to find sufficient provisions for their voyage to Jamaica, he having left them unprovided for all things.

CHAPTER XXI.

A Voyage made by the Author along the Coast of Costa Rica, at his Return towards Jamaica.—What happened most remarkable in the said Voyage.—Some Observations then made by him.

Captain Morgan left us all in such a miserable condition, as lively represented what reward attends wickedness in the end; whence we ought to have learned to regulate and amend our actions for the future. We were so reduced, that every company which was left, whether English or French, being compelled to help themselves, most of them separated from each other, and several companies took several courses at their return homewards. That party to which I did belong, steered along the coast of Costa Rica, to get provisions, and careen our vessel in some secure place or other; for our boat was grown foul, and unfit for sailing. In a few days we arrived at a great port, called Bocca del Toro, where are always multitudes of good eatable tortoises. It is about ten leagues in compass, surrounded with little islands, under which vessels may ride secure from violent winds.

These islands are inhabited by Indians, who never could be subdued by the Spaniards; and hence they call them *Indios bravos*, or wild Indians. They are divided, according to the variety of their language, into several people, whence it is that they are in perpetual wars. Towards the east side of this port are some who formerly did trade much with the pirates, selling them the flesh of divers animals which they hunt, as also all sorts of fruits; the exchange for which was iron instruments which the pirates brought, beads, and toys, whereof they made great account for wearing, more than of precious jewels, which they neither knew nor esteemed. But this commerce failed, the pirates committing many barbarities, killing their men, and taking away their women, to serve their lust; which put an end to all friendship and commerce between them.

We went ashore to seek provisions, our necessity being extreme; but we could find nothing but a few eggs of crocodiles, wherewith we were forced to be content. Hereupon we left those quarters, and steered eastward. Upon this tack we met three boats more of our own companions, who had been left behind by Captain Morgan. These told us, they had been able to find no relief for their extreme hunger, and that Captain Morgan himself and his people were reduced to such misery, as he could afford them no more than one short allowance a day.

Hearing thus that little or no good was to be expected by sailing farther eastward, we changed our course westward. Here we found a vast many tortoises more than we needed to victual our boats, though for a long time. Being provided with this sort of victuals, the next thing we wanted was fresh water. There was enough to be had in the neighboring islands, but we scarce dared to land, by reason of the enmity abovesaid, between the pirates and Indians. But, necessity having no law, we were forced to do as we could, not as we desired. Hereupon we went all of us together to one of the islands. Being landed, one party of our men ranged the woods, while another filled the barrels with water. Scarce an hour was past, when suddenly the Indians came upon us, and one of our men cried, "Arm, arm." We presently began to fire at them, as hot as we could. This stopped them, and, in a short time, put them to flight, sheltering themselves in the woods. We pursued them, but not far, desiring rather to get in our water, than any advantage on the enemy. Coming back, we found two Indians dead on the shore: the habiliments of one showed him to be a person of quality among them, for he had about his body a girdle, or sash, richly woven; and on his face he wore a beard of massy gold, I mean a small planch of gold hung down at his lips, by two strings, which run through two little holes, made there on purpose, that covered his beard, or served instead thereof. His arms were made of sticks of palmite-trees, very curiously wrought; at one end whereof was a kind of hook, which seemed to be hardened with fire. We should have spoke with some of these Indians, to reconcile them to us, and to renew the former trade, and obtain provisions, but it was impossible, through the savageness of their minds. However, we filled our barrels with water, and carried them aboard.

The night following, we heard from shore huge cries and shrieks among the Indians. These lamentations caused us to believe that they had called in many more people to their aid, and that they lamented the death of those two men. These Indians never came upon the sea, or ever built canoes, or any vessels for navigation, not so much as fisher-boats, of which art of fishery they are ignorant. At last, having nothing else to hope for in these parts, we resolved to depart for Jamaica. Being set forth, we met with contrary winds, which caused us to use our oars, and row to the river of Chagre. When we came near it, we perceived a ship, that began to give us chase; we feared it was a ship from Carthagena, sent to rebuild and retake possession of the Castle of Chagre, now the pirates had left it. Hereupon we set our sail, and ran before the wind, to make our escape. But the vessel being much swifter and cleaner than ours, easily got the wind of us, and stopped our course. Then approaching to us, we discovered them to be our former comrades in the expedition of Panama, but lately sent out from Chagre. Their design was to go to Nombre de Dios, and thence to Carthagena, to seek some purchase or other. But the wind being contrary, they concluded to go in our company to the place whence we came, called Boco del Toro.

This accident and encounter retarded our journey two days more than we could regain in a fortnight; this obliged us to return to our former station for a few days. Thence we directed our course for a place called Boca del Dragon, to get provisions of flesh, especially of an animal by the Spaniards called manentine, by the Dutch, sea-cow, because its head, nose, and teeth are very like those of a cow. They are found commonly where, under the depth of the waters, it is full of grass, on which it is thought they feed. They have no ears, but in place of them, two little holes as wide as one's little finger. Near the neck, they have two fins, under which they have two udders, like the breasts of a woman. The skin is very close, resembling the skin of a Barbary or Guinea dog. This skin on the back is two fingers thick, which, being dried, is as hard as whalebone, and may serve to make walking staffs. The belly is in all things like that of a cow, as far as the reins. Their manner of engendering is the same with that of a land cow, the male being every way like a bull. They conceive and breed but once. But what time they go with calf, I could not learn. These fishes have a very acute sense of hearing, so as in taking them, the fishermen make not the least noise, nor row, unless very slightly. For this reason they use certain instruments for rowing, by the Indians called *pagaros*, by the Spaniards, *canelettas*, with which they row without any noise to fright the fish. While they are fishing, they speak not one to another, only make signs. They dart them with a javelin as they do tortoises; but the point of the javelin somewhat differs, having two hooks at the end, and being longer. These fishes are from twenty to twenty-four feet long. Their flesh is good to eat, being like in color to that of a land cow; but in taste, to pork. It has much fat, or grease, which the pirates melt, and keep in earthern pots to use instead of oil.

Once, when we could not do any good at this fishery, some of our men going to hunt, and others to catch fish, we espied a canoe with two Indians: these no sooner discovered our vessels, but they rowed with all speed towards land, being unwilling to have any thing to do with us pirates. We followed them to the shore, but being naturally nimbler than us, they escaped into the woods. And, what was more, they drew ashore, and carried with them, their canoe into the wood, as easily as if it had been straw, though it weighed above two thousand weight; this we knew by the canoe itself, which we found afterwards, and had much ado to get into the water again, though we were in all eleven persons to pull at it.

We had then with us a pilot, who had been often in those parts; this man seeing this action of the Indians, told us, that some few years before, a squadron of pirates arriving at that place, they went in canoes to catch some little birds, which frequent the sea-coast, among very beautiful trees. While they were busied, certain Indians who had climbed the trees to view them, seeing the canoes underneath, suddenly leaped down into the sea, and seized some of the canoes and pirates, that kept them, both which they carried nimbly so far into the woods, that the prisoners could not be relieved by their companions. Hereupon the admiral of that squadron landed with five hundred men to rescue his men, but they saw such a number of Indians flock together to oppose them, as obliged them to retreat in haste to their ships, concluding, that if such forces as those could not do any thing towards the recovery of their companions, they ought to stay no longer there. Having heard this history, we came away, fearing some mischief, and bringing with us the canoe, in which we found nothing but a fishing net, not very large, and four arrows made of palm-trees, seven feet long each; these arrows, we believed to be their arms. The canoe we brought away was of cedar, but very roughly hewn, which made us think that those people have no instruments of iron.

Leaving that place, we arrived in twenty-four hours at another, called Rio de Zuera, where were some few houses belonging to Carthagena, inhabited by Spaniards, whom we resolved to visit, not being able to find any tortoises, nor any of their eggs. The inhabitants were all fled, leaving no victuals nor provisions, so we were forced to be content with a certain fruit they called platanoes; with these platanoes we filled our boats, and continued our voyage, coasting along the shore to find out some creek or bay, wherein to careen our vessel, which now was so very leaky, that night and day we were constrained to put several men, besides our slaves, to the pump. This voyage lasted a fortnight, all which time we were under continual fear of perishing. At last we arrived at a port called the Bay of Blevelt, so named from a pirate who used to resort thither as we did; here one party of our men went into the woods to hunt, while another undertook to refit and careen our vessel.

Our companions who went abroad to hunt found hereabouts porcupines of a monstrous bigness. But their chief exercise was killing of monkeys and birds, called by the Spaniards faisans, or pheasants; the toil of shooting seemed, at least to me, to be sufficiently compensated with the pleasure of killing the monkeys; for at these we usually made fifteen or sixteen shot, before we could kill three or four, so nimbly would they escape our hands and aim, even after being much wounded. Besides, it was diversion to see the female monkeys carry their little ones upon their backs, just as the negroes do their children. When any person passes under the trees where these monkeys are sitting, they will commonly squirt their excrements upon their heads and clothes; likewise, if, shooting at a parcel of them, one happen to be wounded, the rest flock about him, and lay their paws on the wound to hinder the blood from issuing forth; others gather moss from the trees, and thrust into the wound, and thereby stop the blood. At other times they gather such or such herbs, and, chewing them in their mouths, apply them as a poultice. All which caused in me great admiration, seeing such strange actions in those irrational creatures, which testified the fidelity and love they had for one another.

On the ninth day after our arrival, our women slaves being busied in ordinary employments of washing of dishes, sewing, drawing water out of wells, which we had made on the shore, and the like, one of them, who had seen a troop of Indians towards the woods, cried out, "Indians, Indians!" We ran presently to our arms, and their relief, but coming to the wood, we found no person there, but two of our women slaves killed upon the place with arrows. In their bodies we saw so many arrows sticking, as if they had been fixed there with particular care, for otherwise we know that one of them was sufficient to kill any man. These arrows were all of a rare shape, being eight feet long, and as thick as a man's thumb; at one end was a hook of wood, tied to the body of the arrow with a string, at the other end was a case or box, like the case of a pair of tweezers, in which we found little pebbles, or stones; the color was very red, very shining, as if they had been long locked up, all which we believed were the arms of their leaders. These arrows were all made without instruments of iron; for whatever the Indians make, they harden first artificially with fire, and then polish them with flints.

These Indians are of a very robust constitution, strong, and nimble at their feet. We sought carefully up and down the woods, but could find no track of them, nor any of their canoes nor floats which they use in fishing; hereupon we retired to our vessels, where, having embarked all our goods, we put off from shore, fearing lest, finding us there, they should return and overpower us.

CHAPTER XXII.

The Author departs towards the Cape of Gracias à Dios. — The Commerce of the Pirates with the Indians. — His Arrival at the Island de los Pinos. — And finally, his Return to Jamaica.

The great fear we had of those Indians, by reason of the death of our two women slaves, made us depart thence as fast as we could, directing our course towards the Cape Gracias à Dios, where we placed our last hopes of provisions; for thither usually resort many pirates, who friendly correspond with the Indians there. Being arrived at the said cape, we rejoiced and gave thanks to Almighty God, for having delivered us out of so many dangers, and brought us to this place of refuge, where we found people who showed us most cordial friendship, and provided us with all necessaries.

The custom here is, that when any pirates arrive, every one has liberty to buy himself an Indian woman, at the price of a knife, or any old axe, wood-bill, or hatchet. By this contract, the woman is obliged to remain with the pirate all the time he stays there. She serves him in the mean while with victuals of all sorts that the country affords. The pirate has liberty also to go when he pleases to hunt or fish, or about any other divertisement, but is not to commit any hostility or depredation on the inhabitants, seeing the Indians bring him in all that he needs or desires.

Through this frequent converse of these Indians with the pirates, they sometimes go to sea with them, and remain with them whole years, without returning home; so that many of them can speak English and French, and some of the pirates their Indian language. Being very dexterous at their javelins, they are useful to the pirates in victualling their ships, by the fishery of tortoises and manitas, a fish so called by the Spaniards. For one of these Indians is alone able to victual a vessel of one hundred men. We had in our crew two pirates who could speak the Indian language, by whose help I inquired into their customs, lives, and policy, whereof I shall give a brief account.

This island is about thirty leagues in circumference; it is governed as a little commonwealth, without any king, or sovereign prince; neither do they entertain any friendship or correspondence with other neighboring islands, much less with the Spaniards. They are in all but a small nation, whose number exceeds not sixteen or seventeen hundred persons. They have among them few negro slaves, who happened to arrive there, swimming after shipwreck made on that coast. For being bound for Terra Firma, in a ship that carried them to be sold there, they killed the captain and mariners, with design to return to their country, but being ignorant of navigation, they stranded their vessel hereabouts. Though, as I said, they make but a small nation, yet they are as it were two sorts of people; of which one sort cultivate the ground, and make plantations; but the other are so lazy, as they have no courage to build themselves huts, much less houses. They frequent chiefly the sea-coast, wandering up and down, without knowing or caring so much as to cover their bodies from the rains, (which are very frequent,) unless with a few palm-leaves; these they put on their heads, and keep their backs always to the wind. They use no other clothes than an apron, tied to their middle, coming down so as to hide their privities. Such aprons are made of the rinds of trees, which are strongly beat upon stones, till they are softened; the same they use for bed-clothes, except a few, who make them of cotton. Their usual arms are nothing but azagayas, or spears, which they make fit for use with points of iron, or teeth of crocodiles.

They know, after some manner, that there is a God, yet they live without any religion, or divine worship; and, as far as I can learn, they believe not in, nor serve, the devil, as many other nations of America do; hereby they are not so much tormented by him, as other nations are. Their ordinary food, for the most part, consists in several fruits; such as bananas, racoves, ananas, potatoes, cazave, as also crabs, and some few fish, which they kill in the sea with darts. They are pretty expert in making certain pleasant and delicate liquors; the commonest among them is called achioc. This is made of a certain seed of palm-tree, bruised and steeped in hot water, till it be settled at the bottom; this liquor being strained off, hath a pleasant taste, and is very nourishing. Other sorts of liquors they prepare, which I shall omit for brevity, only I shall say something of that made of platanoes; these they knead with hot water, and then put into great calabashes full of cold water, for eight days, during which it ferments as well as the best wine. This liquor they drink for pleasure, and as a great regale, so that when they invite their friends or relations, they cannot treat them better than with this pleasant drink.

They are very unskilful in dressing victuals, so that they seldom treat one another with banquets; but when they invite others, they desire them to come and drink of their liquors. Before the invited persons come to their house, those that expect them comb their hair very well, and anoint their faces with oil of palm, mixed with a black tincture, which renders them very hideous. The women also daub their faces with another sort of stuff, which makes them look as red as crimson, and such are their greatest ornaments and attire. Then he that invites takes his arms, which are three or four azagayas, and goes out of his cottage three or four hundred steps, to wait for and receive the invited persons. As soon as they draw nigh, he falls on the ground, lying flat on his face, without any motion, as if he was dead. Being thus prostrate, the invited friends take him up, and set him on his feet, and go all together to the hut. Here the persons invited use the same ceremony, falling down on the ground, as the inviter did before; but he lifts them up one by one, and giving them his hand, conducts them into his cottage, where he causes them to sit. The women on these occasions use few or no ceremonies.

Being thus brought into the house, they are presented every one with a calabash, of about four quarts, full of achioc, almost as thick as water gruel, or children's pap; these they are to drink off, and get down at any rate. The calabashes being emptied, the master of the house, with many ceremonies, goes about the room, and gathers his calabashes; and this drinking is reckoned but for one welcome. Afterwards, they drink of the achioc above mentioned, to which they are invited; then follow many songs, dances, and a thousand caresses, to the women; so that sometimes, for a testimony of their love, they take their darts, and with the points, pierce and wound their genital parts. This I could not believe, though often affirmed to me, till my own eyes were witnesses of these and the like actions; neither only on this occasion do they use this ceremony of piercing their genitals; but also when they make love to any woman, thereby they let them understand the greatness of their affection and constancy.

They marry not any young maid without the consent of her parents. If any one desires to take a wife, he is first examined by the damsel's father, concerning several points of good husbandry. These are commonly whether he can make azagayas, darts for fishing, or spin a certain thread, which they use about their arrows. Having answered to satisfaction, the examiner calls to his daughter for a little calabash full of achioc; of this he drinks first, then gives the cup to the young man, and he to the bride, who drinks it up, and with this only ceremony the marriage is made. When any one drinks to the health of another, the second person is to drink up the liquor left in the calabash. But in case of marriage, as was said, it is consumed only among them three, the bride obtaining the greatest share.

When the woman lies in, neither she nor her husband observe the time customary among the Caribbees. But as soon as the woman is delivered, she goes to the next river, brook, or fountain, and washes the new-born creature, swathing it up in certain rowlers, or swathbands, there called *cabalas*. This done, she goes about her ordinary labor. When the man dies, his wife buries him with all his azagayars, aprons, and ear jewels; and comes every day to her husband's grave, bringing him meat and drink for a whole year after. Their years they reckon by the moons, allowing fifteen to every year, which make their entire circle, as our twelve months do ours.

Some writers of the Caribbee Islands affirm that this ceremony of carrying victuals to the dead is general among them, and that the devil comes to the sepulchres, and carries away the meat and drink. But I know the contrary, having often myself taken away these offerings, and eaten them; knowing that the fruits used on these occasions were of the choicest, and the liquor of the best sort. The widow having completed her year, opens the grave, and takes out all her husband's bones; these she scrapes, and washes very well, and dries in the sun; then she ties them all together, and puts them into a cabalas, or satchel, and is obliged for another year to carry them upon her back by day, and sleep upon them by night, till the year is out; then she hangs up the bag and bones against the post of her own door, if she be mistress of a house; if not, she hangs them at the door of her next neighbors or relations.

The widows cannot marry the second time, according to their customs, till after two years' end. The men are bound to perform no such ceremonies for their wives; but if any pirate marry an Indian woman, she is bound to do in all things as if he were an Indian. The negroes on this island live in all respects according to their own customs. Now I shall continue the account of our voyage.

After we had refreshed and provided ourselves as well as we could at this island, we steered towards the Island de los Pinos. Here we arrived in fifteen days, and were constrained to refit our vessel, which now again was very leaky, and not fit for sailing any farther. Hereupon we divided ourselves as before, some to careening the ship, others to fishing. In this last we were so successful, as to take, in six or seven hours, fish sufficient for one thousand persons. We had with us some Indians from the Cape of Gracias a Dios, very dexterous both in hunting and fishing; with whose help we soon killed likewise, and salted, a huge number of wild cows, enough to satiate our hungry appetites, and to victual our vessel. These cows were formerly brought into this island by the Spaniards, that they might here multiply and stock the country. We salted also a vast number of tortoises, which are here very plentiful. These things made us forget the miseries we had lately endured, and we began to call one another again by the name of brothers, which was customary amongst us, but had been disused in our miseries.

While we continued here, we feasted ourselves very plentifully, without fear of enemies. For as to the Spaniards on the island, they were in friendship with us; only we were constrained to keep watch and ward every night for fear of the crocodiles, which swarm all over the island. For these, when they are hungry, will assault any man and devour him; as it happened to one of our companions, who being gone into the wood, in company with a negro, they chanced upon a crocodile, which with incredible agility assaulted the pirate, and, fastening upon his leg, cast him on the ground, the negro escaping by flight. Yet he, being a robust and a courageous man, drew forth a knife he had then about him, and after a dangerous combat, stabbed the crocodile, which done, himself, tired with the battle, and weakened with loss of blood, lay for dead on the place. Being so found by the negro, who returned to see what was become of him, he took him on his back, and brought him to the sea-side, though a whole league off, where we put him into a canoe, and conveyed him on board.

After this, none of our men dared to enter the woods without good company; and ourselves, desirous to revenge the disaster of our companion, went in troops next day to the woods, to find out crocodiles to kill. These animals would come every night to the sides of our ship, and offer to climb up into the vessel. One of these, one night, was seized with an iron hook; but he, instead of flying to the bottom, began to mount the ladder of the ship till we killed him with other instruments. After we had remained there some time, and refreshed ourselves, we set sail for Jamaica. Here we arrived in a few days, after a prosperous voyage, and found Captain Morgan got home before us;

but had seen, as yet, none of his companions whom he left behind, we being the first that arrived there after him.

He was then very busy in persuading and levying people to transport to the Isle of St. Catherine, which he designed to fortify, and hold for a common refuge to all pirates, especially of his own nation, as was said; but this design was soon hindered by the arrival of a man-of-war from England, which brought orders from his majesty of Great Britain, to recall the governor of Jamaica to the court of England, to give an account of his favoring the pirates in those parts, to the vast detriment of the subjects of the king of Spain; the said man-of-war bringing over also a new governor of Jamaica, in place of the precedent. This gentleman entering on the government of the island, presently gave notice to all the ports, by several boats sent forth to that intent, of the good correspondence the king of England resolved to maintain in those parts of the world towards his Catholic majesty, his subjects, and dominions; and that, for the future, he had received from his sacred majesty and privy council strict and severe orders not to permit any pirate to set forth from Jamaica, commit any hostility or depredation on the Spanish nation or dominions, or any other people of those neighboring islands.

These orders being sufficiently divulged, the pirates who were abroad at sea began to fear them, so as they dared not return to the said island, but kept the seas, and continued to act what hostilities they could. The same pirates took and ransacked a considerable town in the Isle of Cuba, called La Villa de los Calos, which we mentioned in the description of the said island. Here they committed again all sorts of inhuman and barbarous cruelties; but the new governor of Jamaica behaved himself so constant to his duty, and the orders he had from England, that he apprehended several of the chief actors, and caused them to be hanged. This severity made those remaining abroad take warning, and retire to the Island of Tortuga, lest they should fall into his hands. Here they joined with the French pirates, inhabitants there, in whose company they continue to this day.

CHAPTER XXIII.

The Relation of the Shipwreck which Monsieur Bertram Ogeron, Governor of Tortuga, suffered nigh the Isles of Guadanillas. — He and his Companions fall into the Hands of the Spaniards. — By what Arts he escaped their Hands, and preserved his Life. — The Enterprise against Puerto Rico to deliver his People, and its unfortunate Success.

After that expedition of Panama, the inhabitants of the French islands in America, in 1673, (while the war was so fierce in Europe between France and Holland,) gathered a considerable fleet to possess themselves of the islands belonging to the United Provinces in the West Indies. To this effect, their admiral raised all the pirates and volunteers that he could persuade; and the governor of Tortuga caused to be built a good strong man-of-war, which he named Ogeron, and provided very well with ammunition, and manned with five hundred Buccaneers, resolute men, being the vessel he designed for himself. Their first intention was to take the Isle of Curasao, belonging to the said States of Holland; but this design miscarried, by reason of a shipwreck.

Ogeron set sail from Tortuga, as soon as things were ready, to join the fleet, and pursue the said enterprise: being arrived on the west of St. John de Puerto Rico, he was suddenly surprised with a violent storm, to that degree, as shook his new frigate against the rocks, near the islands called Guadanillas, and broke it in a thousand pieces; yet being near the land of Puerto Rico, all his men saved their lives in their boats.

Next day, being got on shore, they were discovered by the Spaniards inhabiting the island, who, taking them to be French pirates, that meant to take the island anew, as they had done before, they alarmed the whole country, and, gathering their forces together, marched against them; and they found them, for want of arms, not able to make any defence, begging quarter for their lives, as the custom is. But the Spaniards, remembering the horrible cruelties those pirates had many times committed, would have no compassion on them; but answering them, "Ha! ye thievish dogs, here 's no quarter for you!" they assaulted them very furiously, and killed most of them. At last, perceiving they made no resistance, nor had any arms to defend themselves, they began to relent, taking prisoners as many as remained alive.

But, being still persuaded that those unfortunate people came with design to take again and ruinate the island, they bound them with cords, two and two, or three and three together, and drove them through the woods into the open fields. Being come thus far with them, they asked them what was become of their leader: they constantly made answer, he was drowned in the shipwreck, though they knew it was false. For Ogeron, being unknown to the Spaniards, behaved himself among them as an innocent fool, and in his actions mimicked the natural so well, that he was not tied as the rest of his companions, but let loose to serve the pleasure and laughter of the common soldiers. These, now and then, would give him scraps of bread and other victuals, whereas the rest of the prisoners had never sufficient to satisfy their hungry stomachs, their allowance from the Spaniards being scarce enough to preserve them alive.

There was among the French pirates a surgeon, who, having done some remarkable services to the Spaniards, was unbound and set at liberty to go freely up and down, even as Ogeron did. To this surgeon, Ogeron declared his resolution of attempting an escape from the cruelty and hard usage of those enemies, which they did by fleeing to the woods, there to make something or other wherein to transport themselves elsewhere, though they had nor could obtain no other thing in the world that could be serviceable in building of vessels, but one only hatchet. Thus they began their march towards the woods, nearest the sea-coast. Having travelled all day long, they came about evening to the sea-side, almost unexpectedly, but without any thing to eat, or any secure place to rest their wearied limbs. At last they perceived, nigh the shore, a huge quantity of fishes, called by the Spaniards, corladados. These frequently approach the sands of the shore, in pursuit of other little fishes that serve them for their food. Of these they took as many as they thought necessary, and by rubbing two sticks briskly together, they kindled fire, wherewith they made coals to roast them. Next day they began to cut down and prepare timber, to make a kind of small boat to pass over to the Isle of Santa Cruz, which belongs to the French.

While they were busied about their work, they discovered, at a great distance, a canoe steering directly towards the place where they were. This putting them in some fear, lest they should be found and taken again by the Spaniards, they retired into the woods, till they could discern what people were in the canoe. At last, perceiving them to be no more than two men, who seemed to be fishermen, they concluded to hazard their lives, and, overcoming them, to seize the canoe. Soon after, they perceived one of them, who was a mulatto, to go with calabashes hanging at his back, towards a spring not far off, to take in fresh water. The other, who was a Spaniard, staid behind him for his return. Seeing them divided, they assaulted the mulatto first, and, by a great blow on his head with the hatchet, they despatched him. The Spaniard, upon the noise, made towards the canoe, thinking to escape, but he was overtaken by the two, and killed. Having compassed their design, they fetched the corpse of the mulatto, and cast both into the middle of the sea, to be consumed by the fish, by this means to conceal this fact forever from the Spaniards.

This done, they took in as much fresh water as they could, and set sail thence to seek some place of refuge. That day they steered along the coasts of Puerto Rico, and came to Cabo Roxo. Hence they traversed directly to Hispaniola, where many of their own comrades and companions were to be found. The currents of the waters and winds were very favorable, so as in a few days they arrived at a place called Samana, in the said island, where they found a party of their own people.

Ogeron being landed at Samana, ordered the surgeon to levy all the people he could in those parts, while he departed to revisit his government of Tortuga; where being arrived, he used all his endeavors to gather vessels and men to his assistance; so that in a few days he got a good number of both, well equipped and disposed to follow him. These were to go to St. John de Puerto Rico, and deliver his fellows, whom he had left in the miserable condition as was said before. Having embarked all the people, which the surgeon had levied at Samana, he made them a speech, telling them, "You may all expect great spoil and riches from this enterprise, and therefore let all fear and cowardice be set aside; on the contrary, fill your hearts with courage and valor, for thus you will find yourselves soon satisfied, of what at present bare hopes do promise." Every one much relied on these promises of Ogeron, and from his words conceived no small joy in their minds. Thus they set sail from Tortuga, for the coasts of Puerto Rico. Being come within sight of land, they used only their lower sails, that they might not be discovered by the Spaniards, till they came near the place where they intended to land.

The Spaniards, notwithstanding this caution, having had intelligence of their coming, were prepared for a defence, having posted many troops of horse along the coasts to watch their descent. Ogeron, perceiving their vigilancy, ordered the vessels to draw near the shore, and shoot off many great guns, which forced the cavalry to retire within the woods: here lay concealed many companies of foot, prostrate on the ground. So the pirates made their descent at leisure, and began to enter among the trees, scarce suspecting any harm to be where the horsemen could do no service; but no sooner were they fallen into this ambuscade, than the Spaniards arose and assaulted them so courageously, that they soon destroyed great part of them. Thus leaving great numbers dead on the place, the rest very hardly escaped by flight to their ships.

Ogeron, though he escaped this danger, yet could willingly have perished in the fight, rather than suffer the shame which the ill success of this enterprise was like to bring upon his reputation: beside that, those that he had attempted to rescue were now cast into greater miseries. Hereupon they hastened back to Tortuga, the same way they came, with great confusion in their minds, much diminished in their number, and utterly disappointed of those spoils, the subject of their hopes, and of the promises of the unfortunate Ogeron. The Spaniards were very vigilant, and kept their posts near the sea-side till the fleet of pirates was out of sight. Meanwhile they made an end of killing such of their enemies as, being desperately wounded, could not escape by flight, and cut off several limbs from the dead bodies, to show them to the former prisoners, for whose rescue these others had crossed the seas.

The fleet being gone, the Spaniards made bonfires and great demonstrations of joy for their victory; but the French prisoners, who were there before, endured more hardship than ever. Of their misery and misusage, Jacob Binkes, governor at that time, in America, for the states general of the United Provinces, was an eye-witness; for he arriving in that juncture, at Puerto Rico, with some men-of-war, to buy provisions and other necessaries, he so pitied their misery, as to bring away by stealth five or six of them, which only exasperated the Spaniards; for soon after they sent the rest of the prisoners to the chief city of the island, to work and toil about the fortifications which then were making, forcing them to bring and carry stones, and all sorts of materials: these being finished, the governor transported them to Havana, where they employed them also in fortifying that city. Here they made them work by day, and at night they shut them up as close prisoners, lest they should enterprise upon the city; for of such attempts the Spaniards had had divers proofs, which gave them sufficient cause to use them so.

Afterwards, at several times, when ships arrived from New Spain, they transported them by degrees into Europe, and landed them at Cadiz; but notwithstanding this care of the Spaniards to disperse them, they soon after met almost all in France, and resolved to return to Tortuga, with the first opportunity.

To this effect they assisted one another very lovingly, with what necessaries they could, according to every one's condition; so that in a short while the greatest part had nested themselves again at Tortuga, their place of rendezvous. Here they equipped again a new fleet to revenge their former misfortunes on the Spaniards, under the conduct of one Le Sieur Maintenon, a Frenchman; with this fleet, he arrived at the Island de la Trinidad, between the Isle of Tabago and the coasts of Paria. This island they sacked, and after put to the ransom of one hundred thousand pieces of eight. Hence they departed with design to take and pillage the city of Caraccas, over against the Island of Curasao, belonging to the Hollanders.

CHAPTER XXIV.

Encounters at the Islands of Cayana and Tabago, between the Count d'Estrees, Admiral of France, in America, and the Heer Jacob Binkes, Vice Admiral of the United Provinces.

It is already known to the greatest part of Europe, that the prince of Courland began to establish a colony in the Island of Tobago, and that some time after his people, for want of timely recruits, abandoned the same, leaving it to the next occupant. Thus it fell into the hands of Adrian and Cornelius Lampesius, natives of Flissing, in Zealand, who, arriving there in 1654, they fortified it by the order of the states general, building a goodly castle, in a convenient situation, capable of hindering the assaults of any enemies.

The strength of this castle was afterwards sufficiently tried by Monsieur d'Estrees, as I shall relate, after I have first told you what happened before Cayana, in 1676. This year the states general sent the vice-admiral, Jacob Binkes, to the Island of Cayana, then in possession of the French, to repossess it. With these orders he set forth from Holland, March 16, in the said year, with a fleet of seven men-of-war, one fire-ship, and five other small vessels. This fleet arrived at Cayana, May 4, next following. Upon their arrival, the Heer Binkes landed nine hundred men, who, approaching the castle, summoned the governor to surrender at discretion. He answered, "he thought of nothing less than surrendering, but that he and his people were resolved to defend themselves to the utmost." The Heer Binkes having received this answer, presently commanded his troops to attack the castle on both sides at once: the assault was very furious, but at length the French, being very few, and overwhelmed with the multitude of their enemies, surrendered both their arms and the castle. In it were found thirty-seven pieces of cannon. The governor, named Monsieur Lesi, with two priests, were sent into Holland. The Heer Binkes lost in the combat fourteen men only, and had seventy-two wounded.

The French king no sooner understood this, but he sent in October following the Count d'Estrees, to retake the said island from the Hollanders. He arrived there in December, with a squadron of men-of-war, all well equipped and provided. Being come as far as the River Aperovaco, he met with a small vessel of Nantes, which had set forth from Cayana but a fortnight before, which gave him intelligence of the condition, wherein he might be certain to find the Hollanders at Cayana. They told him there were three hundred men in the castle, that all about it they had fixed strong palisadoes or empalements, and that within the castle were mounted twenty-six pieces of cannon.

Monsieur d'Estrees being enabled with this intelligence to take his own measures, proceeded on his voyage, and arrived at the port of the said island, three leagues from the castle: here he landed eight hundred men, in two several parties; one he placed under the Count de Blinac, and the other under Monsieur de St. Faucher. On board the fleet he left Monsieur Gabaret, with divers other principal troops, which he thought not necessary to be landed. The men being set on shore, the fleet weighed anchor, and sailed very slowly towards the castle, while the soldiers marched by land. These could not travel otherwise than by nights, by reason of the excessive heats and intolerable exhalations of the earth, which here is very sulphurous, and no better than a smoky and stinking oven.

October 19, the Count d'Estrees sent Monsieur de Lesi, (who had been governor of the island, as was said before,) demanding of them to deliver the castle to the obedience of the king his master, and to him in his sovereign's name. But those within resolved not to yield, but at the expense of their lives and blood; which answer they sent to Monsieur d'Estrees. Hereupon the French, the next night, stormed the castle on seven several sides at once. The defendants having done their duty, and fought with as much valor as possible, were at last forced to surrender, having thirty-eight persons killed, besides many wounded. All the prisoners were transported into France, where they were used with great hardship.

Monsieur d'Estrees having settled all things at the Isle of Cayana, departed thence for Martinico, where, being arrived, he was told that the Heer Binkes was then at the Island of Tobago, and his fleet lay at anchor in the bay. Upon this intelligence, Monsieur d'Estrees made no long stay there, but steered directly for Tobago. No sooner was he come nigh the island, but Vice Admiral Binkes sent his land forces with a good number of mariners on shore, to manage and defend the artillery there. These forces were commanded by the Captains Vander Graaf, Van Dongen, and Ciavone, who labored very hard all that night in raising batteries, and filling up the palisadoes of the fortress called Sterrschans.

Two days after, the French fleet came to an anchor in the Bay of Palmet, and immediately in eighteen boats they landed all their men. The Heer Binkes perceiving the French upon the hills, gave orders to burn all the houses near the castle, that the French might have no place to shelter themselves there. February 23, Monsieur d'Estrees sent a drum to the Hollanders to demand the surrendry of the fort, which was absolutely denied. Thus things continued till the 3d of March: on this day the French fleet came with full sail, and engaged the Dutch fleet, and the dispute was very hot on both sides: meantime, the land forces of the French being sheltered by the thickness of the woods, advanced towards the castle, and stormed it very briskly; but were repulsed by the Dutch with such vigor, as caused them after three several attacks to retire, with the loss of above one hundred and fifty men, and two hundred wounded; these they carried off, or rather, dragged away, with no small difficulty, by reason of their disorderly retreat.

All this while the two fleets continued the combat, and fought very desperately, till on both sides some ships were consumed between Vulcan and Neptune; of this number was Monsieur d'Estrees's own ship, mounted with twenty-seven guns of prodigious bigness, besides smaller pieces. The battle lasted from break of day till evening; a little before which time Monsieur d'Estrees quitted the bay with the rest of the ships to the Hollanders, except two, which were stranded under sail, having gone too high within the port, leaving the victory to the Hollanders, though with the loss of several ships that were burnt.

Monsieur d'Estrees finding himself under the shame of this defeat, and that he could expect no advantage for the present, over the Island of Tobago, set sail thence March 18, and June 21 he arrived at Brest, in France. Having given an account of himself to the king, he was commanded to undertake again the enterprise of Tabago. To this effect he ordered eight great men-of-war and eight smaller, to be equipped with all speed, with which Monsieur d'Estrees set sail from the said port of Brest, October 3 following, and arrived December 1 at Barbadoes. Having received some recruits from Martinico, he sent beforehand to review Tabago, and set sail directly for the same, where he arrived December 7, with all his fleet.

Immediately he landed five hundred men under Monsieur De Blinac, governor of the French islands in America. These were followed soon after by a thousand more. December 9, they approached within six hundred paces of a post called Le Cort, where they landed the artillery designed for this enterprise. On the 10th, Monsieur d'Estrees went in person to view the castle, and demanded of the Heer Binkes, by a messenger, the surrendry thereof, which was generously denied. Next day the French advanced towards the castle, and on the 12th the Dutch from within fired at them without intermission. The French began their attack by casting fire-balls into the castle with main violence: the very third ball that was cast in happened to fall in the pathway that led to the storehouse, where the powder and ammunition was kept; in this path was much powder scattered, through the negligence of those that carried it to and fro, for the necessary supply of the defendants, which by this means taking fire, it ran in a moment to the storehouse, which suddenly was blown up, and with it Vice Admiral Binkes himself, and all his officers, only captain Van Dongen remained alive. This mischance being perceived by the French, they instantly ran with five hundred men, and possessed themselves of the castle: here they found three hundred men alive, whom they took prisoners, and transported into France. Monsieur d'Estrees, after this, commanded the castle to be demolished, with other posts that might serve for any defence, as also all the houses standing upon the island: this done, he departed thence December 27, and arrived again in France, after a prosperous voyage.

CHAPTER XXV.

Captains Sharp, Coxon, Sawkins, and others, set sail for the Province of Darien, upon the Continent of America. — Their Designs to Pillage and Plunder in those Parts. — Number of their Ships, and strength of their Forces, by Sea and Land.

At a place called Bocca del Toro was the general rendezvous of the fleet, which lately had taken and sacked Puerto Bello the second time; that rich place having been taken once before, under the conduct of Sir Henry Morgan. At this place were two other vessels; the one belonging to Captain Peter Harris, the other to Captain Richard Sawkins, two English privateers. Here we had the news of a peace concluded between the Spaniards and the Indians of Darien, who were commonly at war one with the other. Also that, since the conclusion of the said peace, they had been found very faithful to Captain Bournano, a French commander, in an attempt upon a place called Chepo, nigh the South Sea. Further, that the Indians had promised to conduct him unto a great and very rich place, named Tocamora; whereupon Bournano promised them to return in three months with more ships and men. This made us agree to visit the said place, and in order thereto dispersed ourselves into several coves, (by the Spaniards called cuevas, i. e. hollow creeks under the coasts,) there to careen and fit our vessels for that purpose. Here, i. e. at Bocca del Toro, we found plenty of fat tortoises, the pleasantest meat in the world. Our vessels being refitted, we rendezvoused at an island called by us the Water-Key, and our strength was as followeth: —

	Tons.	Guns.	Men.
Capt. Coxon, in a ship of	80	8	97
Capt. Harris, in another of	150	25	107
Capt. Bournano,	90	6	86
Capt. Sawkins,	16	1	35
Capt. Sharp,	25	2	40
Capt. Cook,	35	00	43
Capt. Alleston,	18	00	24
Capt. Row,	20	00	25
Capt. Macket,	14	00	20

We sailed from thence March 23, 1679, and in our way touched at the islands called Zamblas. These islands reach eight leagues in length, lying fourteen leagues westward of the

River Darien. Being here at an anchor, many of the Indians, both men and women, came to see us; some brought plantain, others other fruits, and venison, to exchange with us for beads, needles, knives, or any trifling bauble whereof they stand in need; but they most covet axes and hatchets, for the felling of timber. The men here go naked, having only a sharp and hollow tip, made either of gold, silver, or bark, into which they thrust their privy members, which they fasten with a string about their middle. They wear as an ornament, in their noses, a gold or silver plate, in the form of a half-moon, which, when they drink, they hold up with one hand, while they lift the cup with the other. The men paint themselves sometimes with streaks of black, and the women with red: the women have in their noses a pretty thick ring of gold or silver, and cover themselves with a blanket only: they are generally well featured; among whom, I saw several fairer than the fairest of Europe, with hair as white as the finest flax: 'tis reported of them, that they see better in the dark than in the light.

These Indians misliked our design for Tocamora, and dissuaded us from it, asserting that it would prove too tedious a march, the way being so mountainous and uninhabited, that it would be extremely difficult to get provisions for our men. Withal, they proffered to guide us undescried, within a few leagues of the city of Panama, in case we were pleased to go thither, where we knew we should make a good voyage. Upon these, and other reasons which they gave us, we concluded to desist from the journey of Tocamora, and to proceed to Panama. These resolutions taken, Captain Bournano, and Captain Row's vessels separated from us, being all French, and not willing to go to Panama, they declaring themselves generally against a long march by land; so we left them at the Zamblas. From thence an Indian captain, or chief commander, named Andræas, conducted us to another island, called by the English the Golden Island, situated something to the westward of the mouth of the great River of Darien. At this island we met, being in all seven sail, April 3, 1680.

Here the Indians gave us notice of a town called Santa Maria, situate on a great river of the same name, which runs into the South Sea, by the Gulf of San Miguel; that in the town was kept a garrison of four hundred soldiers; and that from this place much gold was carried to Panama, which was gathered from the mountains thereabouts; that in case we should not find sufficient booty there, we might from thence proceed by sea to Panama, where we could not easily fail of our designs. This motion of the Indians we liked so well, that we landed three hundred and thirty-one men, April 5, 1680, leaving Captains Alleston and Macket, with a party of seamen, to guard our ships in our absence, with which we intended to return home.

These men that were landed had each of them three or four cakes of bread (called by the English doughboys) for their provision of victuals; and as for drink, the rivers afforded them enough. At our landing here, Captain Sharp was very faint and weak, having had a great fit of sickness, of which he was scarcely recovered. Our several companies that marched were distinguished as follows: first, Captain Bartholomew Sharp, with his company, had a red flag, with a bunch of white and green ribbons: the second division, led by Captain Richard Sawkins, with his men, had a red flag, striped with yellow: the third and fourth, which were led by Captain Peter Harris, had two green flags, his company marching in two distinct divisions. The fifth and sixth, led by Captain John Coxon, who had some of Alleston's and Macket's men joined unto his, made two divisions or companies, and had each of them a red flag: the seventh was led by Captain Edmund Cook, with red colors, striped with yellow, with a hand and sword for his device: all, or most of them, were armed with fuzee, pistol, and hanger.

CHAPTER XXVI.

They march towards the Town of Santa Maria, with a Design to take it. — The Indian King of Darien meeteth them. — Difficulties of this March.

Being landed on the coast of Darien, and divided into companies, as was mentioned in the preceding chapter, we began our march towards Santa Maria, the Indians serving us for guides in that unknown country: thus we marched at first through a small skirt of a wood, and then over a bay almost a league in length; after that, we went two leagues directly up a woody valley, where we saw here and there an old plantation, and had a very good path to march in: there we came to the side of a river, which in most places was dry, and built us houses, or rather, huts, to lodge in.

Here another Indian, who was a chief commander, a man of great parts, named Captain Antonio, joined us: this Indian officer mightily encouraged us to undertake the journey of Santa Maria, and promised to be our leader, saying, that he would have gone along with us presently, but that his child lay very sick; however, he was assured it would die by next day, and then he would most certainly follow and overtake us: withal, he desired we would not lie in the grass, for fear of monstrous adders, which are very frequent in those places. Breaking some of the stones that lay in the river, we found them shine like sparks of gold. These stones are driven down from the neighboring mountains in times of flood. This day four of our men tired, and returned back to the ships; so we remained, in all, three hundred and twenty-seven men, with six Indians to conduct us: that night, some showers of rain fell.

The next day of our march we mounted a very steep hill, and on the other side, at the foot thereof, we rested on the bank of the river, which Captain Andræas told us ran into the South Sea, being the same river on which the town of Santa Maria was situated. Hence, we continued our march until noon, and then ascended another mountain, far higher than the former. Here we were often, and in many places, in great danger, the mountain being so perpendicular, and the path so narrow, that but one man at a time could pass. We arrived in the evening on the other side of the mountain, and lodged again by the side of the same river, having marched that day, according to our reckoning, about eighteen miles: this night, likewise, some rain fell.

The next morning, being April 7, we marched all along the river afore mentioned, crossing it often, almost at every half mile, sometimes up to the knees, and at other times up to the middle, in a very swift current. About noon we came to a place where we found some Indian houses; these were very large and neat; the sides were built with cabbage-trees, and the roofs with wild canes, thatched with palmetto royal, but much neater than ours at Jamaica; they had many partitions, or distinct ground rooms, but no ascent by stairs. At this place were four of these houses together, within a stone's throw of one another, each of them having a large plantain walk before it. Half a mile from this place lived the king, or chief captain of these Indians of Darien, who came to visit us in royal robes, with his queen and family. His crown was made of small white reeds, curiously woven, having no other top than its lining, which was red silk. Round about the middle of it was a thin plate of gold, about two inches broad, laced behind, in which stuck two or three ostrich's feathers; about this plate went also a row of golden beads, which were bigger than ordinary peas, underneath which, the red lining of the crown was seen. In his nose he wore a large plate of gold, in form of a half-moon;

and in each ear a great gold ring, nigh four inches diameter, with a round, thin plate of gold, of the same breadth, having a small hole in the centre, by which it hung to the ring. He was covered with a thin, white cotton robe, reaching to the small of his legs, and round its bottom was a fringe of the same, three inches deep; so that, by reason of the length of this robe, we could see no higher than his naked ankles. In his hand he had a long, bright lance, as sharp as any knife. With him he had three sons, each of them having a white robe, and their lances in their hands, but standing bare-headed before him, as did eight or nine persons more of his retinue or guard. His queen wore a red blanket, which was closely girt about her waist, and another that came loosely over her head and shoulders, like our old-fashioned striped hangings: she had a young child in her arms, and two daughters walked by her, both marriageable, with their faces almost covered with stripes or streaks of red, and about their neck and arms almost loaden with small beads, of several colors. These Indian women of the Province of Darien are generally very free, airy, and brisk; yet withal very modest, and cautious in their husband's presence, of whose jealousy they stand in fear. With these Indians we made an exchange, or had a truck, as it is called, for knives, pins, needles, or any other such like trifles; but in our dealing with them we found them to be very cunning. Here we rested ourselves for the space of one day; and withal chose Captain Sawkins to lead the forlorn, unto whom, for that purpose, we gave the choice of fourscore men. The king ordered us each man to have three plantains, with suga canes to suck, by way of a present; but when these were consumed, if we would not truck, we must have starved, for the king himself did not refuse to deal for his plantains: this sort of fruit is first reduced to mash, then laid between leaves of the same tree, and so used with water, after which preparation they call it *miscelaw*.

April 9, we continued our march along the banks of the river above mentioned, finding in our way here and there a house. The owners of the said houses would most commonly stand at the door, and give, as we passed by, to every one of us, either ripe plantain, or some sweet cazove root. Some of them would count us, by dropping a grain of corn for each man that passed before them, for they know no greater number, nor can tell farther than twenty. That night we arrived at three great Indian houses, where we took up our lodgings, the weather being clear and serene all night.

The next day, Captain Sharp, Captain Coxon, and Captain

Cook, with about threescore and ten of our men, embarked themselves in fourteen canoes upon the river to glide down the stream: among this number I did also embark, and we had in our company our Indian Captain Andræas, of whom mention was made above; and two Indians more in each canoe, to pilot or guide us down the river: but if we were tired in travelling by land before, certainly we were in a worse condition now in our canoes; for at the distance of almost every stone's cast we were constrained to quit and get out of our boats, and haul them over either sands or rocks; at other times, over trees that lay cross and filled up the river, so that they hindered our navigation; yea, several times over the very points of land itself. That night we built ourselves huts, to shelter in upon the river side, and rested our wearied limbs till next morning.

The eleventh we prosecuted our journey all day long, with the same fatigue and toil as we had done the day before. At night came a tiger, and looked on us for some while, but we dared not to fire at the animal, fearing we should be descried by the sound of our fuzees; the Spaniards, as we were told, not being at much distance from that place.

But the next day, being April 12, our pain and labor was rather doubled than diminished, not only for the difficulties of the way, which were intolerable, but chiefly for the absence of our main body of men, from whom we had parted the day before: for now, hearing no news of them, we grew extremely jealous of the Indians, and their counsels, suspecting it a design of those people thus to divide our forces, and then betray us to the Spaniards, our implacable enemies. That night we rested ourselves by building of huts, as we had done, and hath been mentioned, before.

The next day, being Tuesday, we continued our navigation down the river, and arrived at a beachy point of land, where another arm joineth the same river: here, as we understood, the Indians of Darien did usually rendezvous, whensoever they drew up in a body with intention to fight their ancient enemies, the Spaniards. Here, also, we made a halt, and staid for the rest of our forces and company, the Indians having now sent to seek them, being themselves not a little concerned at our dissatisfaction and jealousies. In the afternoon our companions came up with us, and were very glad to see us, they having been in no less fear for us than we had been in for them: we continued and rested there that night also, with design to fit our arms for action, which now, as we were told, was nigh at hand.

We departed from thence early the next morning, which was

16 *

the last day of our march, being in all, now, the number of threescore and eight canoes, wherein were embarked three hundred and twenty-seven of us Englishmen, and fifty Indians, who served us for guides. To the point above mentioned, the Indians had hitherto guided our canoes with long poles, or sticks, but now we made ourselves oars and paddles, to row withal, and thereby made what speed we could: thus we rowed with all haste imaginable, and on the river happened to meet two or three Indian canoes, that were laden with plantains. About midnight we arrived, and landed at the distance of half a mile, or thereabouts, from the town of Santa Maria, whither our march was all along intended. The place where we landed was very muddy, insomuch that we were constrained to lay our paddles upon it, and withal, lift ourselves up by the boughs of the trees, to support our bodies from sinking: afterwards we were forced to cut our way through the woods for some space, where we took up our lodgings for that night, for fear of being discovered by the enemy, whom we were so near.

CHAPTER XXVII.

They take the Town of Santa Maria, with no loss of Men, but meet not with so much Booty as was expected. — Description of the Place, Country, and River adjacent. — They resolve to go and plunder, a Second Time, the City of Panama.

The next morning, which was Thursday, April 15, about break of day, we heard from the town a small arm discharged, and after that a drum beating a *reveille.* With this, we roused from our sleep, and taking to our arms, we put ourselves in order, and marched towards the town. As soon as we came out of the woods into the open ground, we were descried by the Spaniards, who had received beforehand intelligence of our coming, and were prepared to receive us, having already conveyed away all their treasure of gold, and sent it to Panama. They ran immediately into a large palisado fort, having each pale or post twelve feet high, and began to fire very briskly at us, as we came: but our vanguard ran up to the place, and pulling down two or three of their palisadoes, entered the fort instantly, and made themselves masters thereof. In this action there were not fifty of our men that came up, before the fort was taken: and on our side only two were wounded, and not one killed: notwithstanding, within the place were found two hundred and threescore men, besides which number, two hundred others were said to be absent, being gone up into the country, unto the mines, to fetch down gold, or rather, to convey away what was already in the town. This golden treasure cometh down another branch of this river unto Santa Maria, from the neighboring mountains, where are thought to be the richest mines of the Indies, or, at least, of all these parts of the western world. Of the Spaniards were killed in the assault twenty-six, and wounded to the number of sixteen more: but their governor, their priest, and all, or most, of their chief men made their escape by flight.

Having taken the fort, we expected to find here a considerable town belonging to it; but it proved to be only some wild houses made of cane, the place being chiefly a garrison, designed to keep the Indians in subjection, who bear a mortal hatred, and are often apt to rebel against the Spaniards. But as bad a place as it was, our fortune was much worse; for we came only three days too late, or else we had met with three hundred weight of gold, which was carried thence to Panama, in a bark, that is sent from thence twice or thrice every year, to fetch what gold is brought to Santa Maria from the mountains. This river, called by the name of the town, is hereabouts twice as broad as the River of Thames is at London, and floweth above threescore miles upwards, rising to the height of two fathom and a half, at the town itself. As soon as we had taken the place, the Indians who belonged to our company, and had served us for guides, came up to the town: for while they heard the noise of the guns, they were in a great consternation, and dared not approach the palisadoes, but had hid themselves so well in a small hollow ground, that the bullets, while we were fighting, flew over their heads.

Here we found and redeemed the eldest daughter of the king of Darien, of whom we made mention above: she had, as it should seem, been forced away from her father's house by one of the garrison, (which rape had greatly incensed him against the Spaniard,) and was with child by him. After the fight, the Indians destroyed as many more of the Spaniards as we had done in the assault, by taking them into the adjoining woods, and there stabbing them to death with their lances: but as soon as we understood this, their barbarous cruelty, we hindered them from taking any more out of the fort, where we confined them all prisoners. Captain Sawkins, with a small party of ten more, put himself into a canoe, and went down the river to pursue and stop, if it were possible, those that had escaped, who were the chief of the town and garrison. But now our great expectations of making a huge purchase of gold at this place being totally vanished, we were unwilling to come so far for nothing, or go back empty handed; especially, considering what vast riches were to be had at no great distance from thence. Hereupon we resolved to go for Panama, which place, if we could take, we were assured we should get treasure enough to satisfy our hungry appetite of gold and riches; that city being the receptacle of all the plate, jewels, and gold that is digged out of the mines of all Potosi and Peru. In order to it, therefore, and to please the humors of some of our company, we made choice of Captain Coxon to be our general, or commander-in-chief. Before our departure, we sent back what small booty we had taken here, by some prisoners, and these under the charge of twelve of our men, to convey it to the ships.

Thus we prepared to go forward on that dangerous enterprise of Panama. But the Indians who had conducted us, having gotten from us what knives, scissors, axes, needles, and beads they could obtain, would not stay any longer, but all, or the greatest part of them, returned to their home. Notwithstanding which, the king himself, Captain Andræas, Captain Antonio, the king's son, called by the Spaniards Bonete d'Oro, or King Golden Cap, as also his kinsman, would not be persuaded by their falling off to leave us, but resolved to go to Panama, out of the desire they had to see that place taken and sacked. Nay, the king promised, if there should be occasion, to join us with a very great number of men. Besides which promises, we had also another very considerable encouragement to undertake this journey; for the Spaniard who had forced away the king's daughter, as was mentioned above, fearing lest we should leave him to the mercy of the Indians, who would have had but little on him, having showed themselves so cruel unto the rest of his companions, for the safety of his life, had promised to lead us not only into the town, but even to the very door of the governor of Panama's bed-chamber, and that we should take him by the hand, and seize both him and the whole city, before we should be discovered by the Spaniards, either before or after our arrival.

CHAPTER XXVIII.

The Buccaneers leave the Town of Santa Maria, and proceed, by Sea, to take Panama.—The extreme Difficulties, with Sundry Accidents and Dangers of that Voyage.

Having been in possession of the town of Santa Maria only the space of two days, we departed from thence on Saturday, April 17, 1680. We embarked all in thirty-five canoes and a *periagua*, which we had taken here lying at anchor before the town. Thus we sailed, or rather, rowed, down the river, in quest of the South Sea, upon which Panama is seated, towards the Gulf of Belona, where we were to enter that ocean. Our prisoners, the Spaniards, begged very earnestly they might be permitted to go with us, and not be left abandoned to the mercy of the Indians, who would show them no favor, and whose cruelty they so much feared. But we had much ado to find a sufficient number of boats for ourselves, the Indians that left us having taken with them, either by consent or stealth, so many canoes. Yet, notwithstanding, they soon after either found bark-logs, or old canoes, and by that means shifted so well for their lives, as to come along with us. Before our departure, we burnt both the fort, the church, and the town, which was done at the request of the king, he being extremely incensed against it.

Among these canoes, it was my misfortune to have one that was very heavy, and consequently sluggish. By this means we were left behind the rest a little way, our number being only four men, besides myself, that were embarked therein. As the tide fell, it left several shoals of sand naked; and hence, not knowing the true channel amongst such variety of streams, we happened to steer within a shoal above two miles, before we perceived our error. Hereupon we were forced to lie by till high water; for to row in such heavy boats as those, against tide, is a thing totally impossible. As soon as the tide began to turn, we rowed away in prosecution of our voyage, and, withal, made what haste we could; but all our endeavors were in vain, for we neither could find nor overtake our companions. Thus about ten of the clock at night, it being low water, we stuck up an oar in the river, and slept, by turns, in our canoe; several showers of rain falling all night long, with which we were wet to the skin.

But the next morning, as soon as day appeared, we rowed

away down the river, as before, in pursuit of our people. Having rowed about two leagues, we were so fortunate as to overtake them; for they had lain that night at an Indian hut, or *embarcadero*, that is to say, landing-place, and had been filling of water till then in the morning. Being arrived at the place, they told us that we must not omit to fill our jars there with water, otherwise we should meet with none in the space of six days' time. Hereupon we went, every one of us, the distance of a quarter of a mile from the *embarcadero*, unto a little pond, to fill out water in calabazas, making withal what haste we could back to our canoe. But when we returned, we found not one of our men, they all being departed, and already got out of sight. Such is the procedure of these wild men, that they care not in the least whom they lose of their company or leave behind. We were now more troubled in our minds than before, fearing lest we should fall into the same misfortune we had so lately overcome.

Hereupon we rowed after them as fast as we possibly could, but all in vain. For here we found such huge numbers of islands, greater and lesser, as also keys about the mouth of the river, that it was not difficult for us, who were unacquainted with the river, to lose ourselves a second time amongst them. Yet, notwithstanding, though with much trouble and toil, we found at last that mouth of the river that is called by the Spaniards Bocca Chica, or the Little Mouth. But as it happened, it was now young flood, and the stream ran very violently against us; so that, though we were not above a stone's cast from the said mouth, and this was not a league broad, yet we could not by any means come near it. Hence we were forced to put ashore, which we did accordingly, till the time of high water. We hauled our canoe close by the bushes, and when we got out, we fastened our rope to a tree, which the tide had almost covered, for it flows here near four fathom deep.

As soon as tide began to turn, we rowed away from thence to an island, distant about a league and a half from the mouth of the river, in the Gulf of San Miguel. Here it went very hard with us, whensoever any wave dashed against the sides of our canoe; for it was almost twenty feet long, and yet not quite one foot and a half in breadth, where it was at the broadest; so that we had just room enough to sit down in her, and a little water would easily have both filled and overwhelmed us. At the island aforesaid, we took up our resting-place for that night, though for the loss of our company, and the great dangers we were in, the sorrowfullest night that, until then, I ever experimented in my whole life: for it rained impetuously all night long, insomuch that we were wet from head to foot, and had not one dry thread about us; neither, through the violence of the rain, were able to keep any fire, wherewith to warm or dry us. The tide ebbeth here a good half mile from the mark of high water, and leaveth bare wonderful high and sharp-pointed rocks. We passed this heavy and tedious night without one minute of sleep, being all very sorrowful to see ourselves so remote from the rest of our companions, as also totally destitute of all human comfort: for a vast sea surrounded us on one side, and the mighty power of our enemies, the Spaniards, on the other; neither could we descry at any hand the least thing to relieve us, all that we could see being the wide sea, high mountains, and rocks: meanwhile, ourselves were confined to an egg-shell instead of a boat, without so much as a few clothes to defend us from the injuries of the weather; for at that time none of us had a shoe to our feet. We searched the whole key, to see if we could find any water, but found none.

CHAPTER XXIX.

Shipwreck of Mr. Ringrose, the Author of this Narrative. — He is taken by the Spaniards, and miraculously by them preserved. — Several other Accidents and other Disasters which befel him after the Loss of his Companions, till he found them again. — Description of the Gulf of Vallona.

On Monday, April the 19th, at break of day, we hauled our canoe into the water again, and departing from the island afore mentioned, wet and cold as we were, we rowed towards the *Punta de San Lorenzo*, or Point S. Lawrence. In our way we met with several islands, which lie straggling thereabouts. But now we were so hard put to it by the smallness of our vessel, and being in an open sea, that it was become the work of one man, yea sometimes of two, to cast out the water which came in on all sides of our canoe. After struggling for some while with these difficulties, as we came near one of those islands, a sea came and overturned our boat, by which means we were all forced to swim for our lives: but we soon got to shore, and our canoe came tumbling after us. Our arms were fast lashed to the inside of the boat, and our locks as well cased and waxed down as was possible; so were also our cartouch boxes and powder horns; but all our bread and fresh water was utterly spoiled and lost.

Our canoe being tumbled on shore by the force of the waves, our first business was to take out and clean our arms. This we had scarcely done, but we saw another canoe run the same misfortune at a little distance to leward of us, amongst a great number of rocks that bounded the island. The persons that were cast away proved to be six Spaniards of the garrison of Santa Maria, who had found an old canoe, and had followed us to escape the cruelty of the Indians. They presently came to us, and made us a fire, on which we broiled our meat, and ate it amicably together. But we were in great want of water, or any other drink to our victuals, not knowing in the least where to get any. Our canoe was thrown up by the waves to the edge of the water, and there was no great fear of its splitting, as being full six inches on the sides thereof. But that in which the Spaniards came split itself against the rocks, as being old and slender, into a hundred pieces. Though we were thus shipwrecked and driven ashore, as I have related, yet at other times this Gulf of San Miguel is a mere mill-pond for smoothness of water.

My company was altogether for returning, aud to proceed no farther, but rather for living amongst the Indians, in case they could not reach the ships we had left behind us in the Northern Sea. But with much ado I prevailed with them to go forward, at least one day longer, and in case we found not our people the next day, that then I would be willing to do any thing which they should think fit. Thus we spent two or three hours of the day in consulting about our affairs, and withal keeping a man to watch and look out on all sides for fear of any surprisal by the Indians, or other enemies. About the time that we were come to a conclusion in our debates, our watchman, by chance, spied an Indian, who, as soon as he saw us, ran into the woods. I sent immediately two of my company after him, who overtook him, and found him to be one of our friendly Indians. He carried them to a place not far distant from thence, where seven more of his company were, with a great canoe which they had brought with them. They came to the place where I was with the rest of my company, and seemed to be glad to meet us on that island. I asked them, by signs, for the main body of our company, and they gave me to understand, that in case we would go with them in their canoe, which was much bigger than ours, we should be up with the party by next morning. This news, as may easily be supposed, not a little rejoiced our hearts.

Presently after this friendly invitation, they asked who the other six men were whom they saw in our company, for they easily perceived us not to be all of one and the same coat and *lingua.* We told them they were *Wankers,* which is the name they commonly give to the Spaniards. Their next question was, if they should kill them. But I answered them, "No, by no means; I would not consent to have it done;" with which answer they seemed to be satisfied for that present. But a little while after, my back being turned, my company thinking they should oblige the Indians thereby, beckoned to them to kill the Spaniards. With this, the poor creatures, perceiving the danger that threatened them, made a sad shriek and outcry, and I came time enough to save all their lives: but withal, I was forced to give my consent they should have one of them, to make him their slave. Hereupon I gave the canoe that I came in to the five Spaniards remaining, and bid them get away and shift for their lives, lest those cruel Indians should not keep their word, and they run again the same danger they had so lately escaped. Having sent them away, I rested myself a while, and took a survey of this gulf and the mouth of the river.

But now, thanks be to God, joining company with those Indians, we were got into a very large canoe, the which, for its bigness, was better able to carry twenty men, than our own, that we had brought, to carry five. The Indians had also fitted a very good sail to the said canoe; so that, having now a fresh and strong gale of wind, we set sail from thence, and made therewith brave way, to the infinite joy and comfort of our hearts, seeing ourselves so well accommodated, and so happily rid of the miseries we but lately had endured. We had now a smooth and easy passage, after such tedious and laborious pains as we had sustained in coming so far since we left Santa Maria. Under the point of St. Lawrence mentioned above, is a very great rippling of the sea, occasioned by a strong current which runneth hereabouts, and which, oftentimes, almost filled our boat with its dashes, as we sailed. This evening, after our departure from the island where we were cast away, it rained vehemently for several hours, and the night proved to be very dark. About nine of the clock that night, we descried two fires on the shore of the continent over against us. These fires were no sooner perceived by the Indians of our canoe, but they began to shout for joy, and cry out, Captain Antonio, Captain Andræas, the names of their Indian captains and leaders; and to affirm, they were assured those fires were made by their companions. Hence they made for the shore, towards those fires, as fast as they could drive; but as soon as our canoe came amongst the breakers, nigh the shore, out came from the woods above threescore Spaniards, with clubs and other arms, and laying hold on our canoe on both sides thereof, hauled it out of the water quite dry; so that by this means we were all suddenly taken and made their prisoners. I laid hold of my gun, thinking to make some defence for myself; but all was in vain; for they soon seized me between four or five of them, and hindered me from action. In the mean while, our Indians leaped overboard, and got away very nimbly into the woods. My companions standing amazed at what had happened, and the manner of our surprisal, I asked them, presently, if any of them could speak either French or English. But they answered, No. Hereupon, as well as I could, I discoursed to some of them who were more intelligent than the rest, in Latin, and by degrees came to understand their condition. These were Spaniards who had been turned here ashore by our English party, who left them upon this coast, lest by carrying them nearer to Panama any of them should make their escape, and discover our march towards the city. They had me, presently after I was taken, into a small hut which they had built, covered with boughs, and made there great shouts for joy, because they had taken us; designing in their minds to use us very severely for coming into those parts, and especially for taking and plundering their town of Santa Maria. But meanwhile the captain of those Spaniards was examining me, in came the poor Spaniard that was come along with us, and reported how kind I had been to him and the rest of his companions, by saving their lives from the cruelty of the Indians.

The captain having heard him, arose from his seat immediately and embraced me; saying, that we Englishmen were very friendly enemies, and good people, but that the Indians were very rogues, and a treacherous nation. Withal, he desired me to sit down by him, and to eat part of such victuals as our companions had left them when they were turned ashore. Then he told me, that for the kindness I had showed unto his countrymen, he gave us all our lives and liberties, which otherwise he would certainly have taken from us. And though he could scarcely be persuaded in his mind to spare the Indians' lives, yet for my sake he did pardon them all, and I should have them with me, in case I could find them. Thus he bid me likewise take my canoe, and go, in God's name; saying withal, he wished us as fortunate as we were generous. Hereupon I took my leave of him. I searched out, and at last found my Indians, who, for fear, had hid themselves in the bushes adjoining to the neighboring woods, where they lay concealed. Having found them, the captain led me very civilly down to the canoe, and bidding my companions and the Indians get in after me, as they at first hauled us ashore, so now again they pushed us off to sea, by a sudden and strange vicissitude of fortune. All that night it rained very hard, as was mentioned above; neither durst we put any more ashore at any place, it being all along such, as by mariners is commonly called an iron coast.

The next morning being come, we sailed and paddled, or rowed, till about ten of the clock; at which time we espied a canoe making towards us with all speed imaginable. Being come up with us, and in view, it proved to be one of our English company, who mistaking our canoe for a Spanish *periagua*, was coming in all haste to attack us. We were infinitely glad to meet them, and they presently conducted us to the rest of our company, who were at that instant coming from a deep bay, which lay behind a high point of rocks, where they had lain at anchor, all that night and morning. We were all mutually rejoiced to see one another again, they having given both me and my companions for lost.

CHAPTER XXX.

The Buccaneers prosecute their Voyage till they come within Sight of Panama. — They take several Barks and Prisoners by the Way. — Are descried by the Spaniards, before their Arrival. — They order the Indians to kill the Prisoners.

From the place where we rejoined our English forces, we all made our way towards a high hammock of land, as it appeared at a distance, but was nothing else than an island seven leagues distant from the bay afore mentioned. On the highest part of this island the Spaniards keep a watch, or look out, (for so it is termed by the seamen,) for fear of pirates, or other enemies. That evening we arrived at the island, and being landed, went up a very steep place, till we came to a little hut where the watchman lodged. We took by surprisal the old man who watched in the place, but happened not to see us, till we were got into his plantain walk, before the lodge. He told us in his examination, that we were not as yet descried by the Spaniards of Panama, or any others that he knew; which relation of the old man much encouraged us to go forwards with our design of surprising that rich city. This place, if I took its name right is called *Farol de Plantanos*, or, in English, Plantain Watch.

Here, a little before night, a certain bark came to an anchor, at the outside of the island, which was instantly descried by us. Hereupon we speedily manned out two canoes, who went under the shore, and surprised the said boat. Having examined the persons that were on board, we found she had been absent the space of eight days from Panama, and had landed soldiers at a point of land not far distant from this island, with intention to fight and curb certain Indians and Negroes, who had done much hurt in the country thereabouts. The bark being taken, most of our men endeavored to get into her, but more especially those who had the lesser canoes. Thus there embarked thereon to the number of one hundred and thirty-seven of our company, together with that sea artist, and valiant commander, Captain Bartholomew Sharp. With him went also on board Captain Cook, whom we mentioned at the beginning of this history. The remaining part of that night we lay at the key of the said island, with intent to prosecute our voyage the next day.

Morning being come, I changed my canoe and embarked myself in another, which, though it was something lesser than the former, yet was furnished with better company. Departing from this island, we rowed all day long over shoal water, at the distance of about a league from land, having sometimes not above four or five feet water, and white ground: in the afternoon we descried a bark at sea, and instantly gave her chase; but the canoe in which was Captain Harris happened to come up the first with her, who, after a sharp dispute, took her. Being taken, we put on board the said bark thirty men: but the wind would not suffer the other bark in chasing to come up with us. This pursuit of the vessel did so far hinder us in our voyage, and divide us asunder, that night coming on presently after, we lost one another, and could no longer keep in a body together; hereupon we laid our canoe ashore, to take up our rest for that night, at the distance of two miles, or thereabouts, from high-water mark, and about four leagues to leeward of the Island Chepillo, to which place our course was then directed.

The next morning, as soon as the water began to float us, we rowed away from the fore-mentioned Island Chepillo, where by assignation our general rendezvous was to be: in our way we espied a bark under sail, as we had done the day before. Captain Coxon's canoe was the first that came up with her, but a small breeze freshening at that instant, she got away from him after the first onset, killing in the said canoe one Mr. Bull, and wounding two others. We presently conjectured that this bark would get before us to Panama, and give intelligence of our coming to those of the town, all which happened accordingly. It was two of the clock that afternoon, before all our canoes could come together, and join one another, as was agreed at Chepillo. We took at that island fourteen prisoners, between negroes and mulattoes, also great stores of plantains, and good water, together with two fat hogs; but now, believing that ere this we had been descried at Panama, by the bark afore mentioned, we resolved among ourselves to waste no time, but to hasten away from the said island, to the intent we might at least be able to surprise and take their shipping, and by that means make ourselves masters of those seas, in case we could not get the town, which we now judged almost impossible to be done. At Chepillo, we took also a periagua, which we found at anchor before the island, and presently we put some men on board her. We staid here only a few hours, so that about four o'clock in the evening we rowed away from thence, designing to reach Panama before the next morning, it being only seven leagues between that city and Chepillo; but before we departed from Chepillo, it was judged convenient by our commanders, for certain reasons which I could not dive into, to rid their hands of the prisoners which we had taken, and hereupon orders were given to our Indians, who they knew would perform them very willingly to fight, or rather to murder and slay the said prisoners upon the shore, and that in the view of the whole fleet. This they instantly went about, being glad of this opportunity to revenge themselves upon their enemies, though in cold blood; but the prisoners, although they had no arms wherewith to defend themselves, forced their way through those barbarous Indians, in spite of their lances, bows, and arrows, and got into the woods of the island, only one man of them being killed. We rowed all night long, though much rain fell.

CHAPTER XXXI.

They arrive within sight of Panama; are encountered by three small Men-of-War: they fight them with only sixty-eight Men, and utterly defeat them, taking two of the said Vessels. — Description of that bloody Fight. — They take several Ships at the Isle of Perico, before Panama.

The next morning, which was April 23, 1680, that day being dedicated to St. George, our patron of England, we came before sunrise within view of the city of Panama, which makes a very pleasant prospect to the seaward; soon after we saw also the ships belonging to the said city, which lay at anchor at an island called Perico, distant only two leagues from Panama. On the aforesaid island are several storehouses built there, to receive the goods delivered out of the ships; at that time there rid at anchor at Perico five great ships, and three pretty big barks, called *barcos de la armadilla*, or little men-of-war; the word *armadilla* signifying a little fleet. These had been suddenly manned out, with design to fight us, and prevent any further attempts we should make upon the city or coasts of those seas. As soon as they espied us, they instantly weighed anchor, and got under sail, coming directly to meet us. Our two periaguas being heavy, could not row so fast as we that were in the canoes, so that we were got a pretty way before them. In our five canoes (for so many we were in company) we had only thirty-six men, and these but in a very unfit condition to fight, as being tired with so much rowing, and so few in number, in comparison of the enemy that came against us. They sailed towards us directly before the wind, insomuch that we feared lest they should run us down before it; hereupon we rowed up into the wind's eye, as the seamen term it, and got close to the windward of them. Meanwhile we were doing this, our lesser periagua came up with us, in which were thirty-two more of our company; so that we were in all sixty-eight men that were engaged in the fight of that day; the king himself being one of our number, who was in the periagua afore mentioned. In the vessel that was admiral of these three men-of-war were fourscore and six biscayners, who have the repute of being the best mariners, and also the best soldiers, amongst the Spaniards. These were all volunteers, who came designedly to show their valor, under the command of Don Jacinto de Barabona, who was high admiral of those seas. In the second were seventy-seven negroes, who were commanded by an old and stout Spaniard, a native of Andalusia in Spain, named Don Francisco de Peralta. In the third and last were sixty-five mestizos, or mulattoes, or tawny Moors, commanded by Don Diego de Carabaxal; so that they were in all two hundred and twenty-eight. The commanders had strict orders given them, and their resolutions were to give quarters to none of the pirates or buccaneers; but such bloody commands seldom prosper.

Captain Sawkin's canoe, and also that wherein I was, were much to leeward of the rest, so that the ship of Don Diego de Carabaxal came between us two, and fired presently on me to windward, and on him to leeward, wounding with these broadsides four men in his canoe, and one in that I was in, but he paid so dear for his passage between us, that he was not quick in coming about again, and making the same way; for we killed, with our first volley, several of his men upon the decks; thus we got also to windward, as the rest were before. The admiral of the armadilla, or little fleet, came up with us instantly, scarce giving us time to charge, thinking to pass by us all with as little damage as the first of his ships had done, but as it happened it fell out much worse with him, for we were so fortunate as to kill the man at the helm, so that his ship ran into the wind, and her sails lay a-back; by this means we had time to come all up under her stern, and firing continually into his vessel, we killed all that came to the helm; besides which slaughter, we cut asunder his main sheet and brace with our shot. Now also the third vessel, in which Captain Peralta was, was coming to the aid of their general; hereupon Captain Sawkins, who had changed his canoe, and was gone into the periagua, left the admiral to us four canoes, (for his own was quite disabled,) and met the said Peralta. Between him and Captain Sawkins the dispute was very hot, lying aboard each other, and both giving and receiving death as fast as they could charge. While we were thus engaged, the first ship tacked about, and came up to relieve the admiral; but we perceiving it, and foreseeing how hard it would go with us if we should be beaten from the admiral's stern, determined to prevent his design. Hereupon two of our canoes, to wit, Captain Springer's and my own, stood off to meet him. He made up directly towards the admiral, who stood upon the quarter-deck, waving unto him with a handkerchief so to do; but we engaged him so closely, in the middle of his way, that, had he not given us the helm, and made away from us, we had certainly been on board him. We killed so many of the men, that the vessel had scarce men enough left alive, or unwounded, to carry her off; yet the wind now blowing fresh, they made shift to get away from us, and save their lives.

The vessel which was to relieve the admiral being thus put to flight, we came about again upon the admiral, and all together gave a loud halloo, which was answered by our men in the periagua, though at a distance from us. At that time we came so close under the stern of the admiral that we wedged up the rudder, and withal, killed both the admiral himself and the chief pilot of his ship; so that now they were almost quite disabled and disheartened likewise, seeing what a bloody massacre we had made among them with our shot. Hereupon, two thirds of his men being killed, and many others wounded, they cried for quarter, which had several times been offered to them, and as stoutly denied till then. Captain Coxon boarded the admiral, and took with him Captain Harris, who had been shot through both his legs as he boldly adventured up along the side of the ship. This vessel being thus taken, we put on board her all our wounded men, and instantly manned two of our canoes to go and aid Captain Sawkins, who now had been three times beaten from on board Peralta, such valiant defence had he made. And, indeed, to give our enemies their due, no men in the world did ever act more bravely than these Spaniards.

Thus coming up close under Peralta's side, we gave him a full volley of shot, and expected to have the like return from him again; but on a sudden we saw his men blown up that were abaft the mast, some of them falling on the deck, and others into the sea. This disaster was soon perceived by their valiant Captain Peralta; but he leaped overboard, and, in spite of all our shot, got several of them into the ship again, though he was much burnt in both his hands himself. But as one misfortune seldom cometh alone, meanwhile he was recovering these men, to reinforce his ship withal, and renew the fight, another jar of powder took fire forward, and blew up several others upon the forecastle. Among this smoke, and under the opportunity thereof, Captain Sawkins laid them on board, and took the ship. Soon after they were taken, I went on board Captain Peralta, to see what condition they were in. And, indeed, such a miserable sight I never saw in my life; for there was not a man but was either killed, desperately wounded, or horribly burnt with powder, insomuch, that their black skins were turned white in several places, the powder having torn it from their flesh and bones. Having compassionated their misery, I went afterwards on board the admiral, to observe likewise the condition of his ship and men. Here I saw what did astonish me, and will scarcely be believed by any but ourselves who saw it. There were found on board this ship but twenty-five men alive, whose number before the fight had been four score and six, as was said above; so that three score and one, out of so small a number, were destroyed in the battle. But, what is more, of these twenty-five men, only eight were able to bear arms, all the rest being desperately wounded, and by their wounds totally disabled to make any resistance or defend themselves. Their blood ran down the decks in whole streams, and scarce one place in the ship was found that was free from blood.

Having possessed ourselves of these two armadilla vessels,

or little men-of-war, Captain Sawkins asked the prisoners how many men there might be on board the greatest ship that we could see from thence, lying in the harbor of the Island of Perico, above mentioned, as also in the others that were something smaller. Captain Peralta, hearing these questions, dissuaded him as much as he could from attempting them, saying, that in the biggest alone there were three hundred and fifty men, and that he would find the rest too well provided for defence against his small number. But one of his men, who lay dying upon the deck, contradicted him as he was speaking, and told Captain Sawkins there was not one man on board any of those ships that were in view; for they had all been taken out of them to fight us in these three vessels called the armadilla, or little fleet. Unto this relation we gave credit, as proceeding from a dying man; and, steering our course to the island, we went on board them, and found, as he had said, not one person there. The biggest of these ships, which was called La Santissima Trinidad, or the Blessed Trinity, they had set on fire, made a hole in her, and loosened her foresail. But we quenched the fire with all speed, and stopped the leak. This being done, we put our wounded men on board her, and made her for the present our hospital.

Having surveyed our own loss, we found eighteen of our men were killed in the fight, and twenty-two wounded. These three captains, against whom we fought, were esteemed by the Spaniards the valiantest in all the South seas. Neither was their reputation undeserved, as may easily be inferred from the relation we have given of this bloody engagement. As the third ship was running away from the fight, she met with two more coming out to their assistance; but withal, gave them so little encouragement, that they returned back, and dared not engage us. We began the fight about half an hour after sunrise, and by noon had finished the battle, and quite overcome them. Captain Peralta, while he was our prisoner, would often break out into admirations of our valor, and say, surely "we Englishmen were the valiantest men in the whole world, who designed always to fight open, whilst all other nations invented all the ways imaginable to barricade themselves, and fight as close as they could." And yet, notwithstanding, we killed more of our enemies than they of us.

Two days after our engagement we buried Captain Peter Harris, a brave and stout soldier, and a valiant Englishman, born in the county of Kent, whose death we very much lamented. He died of the wounds he received in the battle; and, besides him, only one man. All the rest of our wounded men recovered. Being now come before Panama, I inquired of Don Francisco de Peralta, our prisoner, many things concerning the state and condition of this city, and the neighboring country; and he satisfied me in manner following.

CHAPTER XXXII.

Description of the State and Condition of Panama, and the Parts adjacent. — What Vessels they took while they blocked up the said Port. — Captain Coxon, with seventy more, returns Home. — Sawkins is chosen in Chief.

The famous city of Panama is situate in the latitude of nine degrees north. It stands in a deep bay in the South Sea. It is round in form, excepting only that part where it runs along the sea-side. Formerly it stood four miles more easterly, when it was taken by Sir Henry Morgan. But being then burnt, and three times more since that accident, they removed it to the place where it now stands. Notwithstanding, there are some poor people still inhabiting the old town; and the cathedral church is still there, which makes a fair show at a distance, not unlike that of St. Paul's at London. This new city, of which I now speak, is much bigger than the old one was, and is built for the most part of brick, the rest being built of stone and tiled. As for the churches belonging thereto, they are not as yet finished. They are eight in number; the chief whereof is called Santa Maria. This city is better than a mile and a half in length, and above a mile in breadth. The houses, for the most part, are three stories high. It hath two gates belonging to it, and is well walled round, except only where a creek cometh into the city, which at high water letteth in barks, to furnish the inhabitants with all sorts of provisions and other necessaries. Here are always three hundred of the king's soldiers in garrison; besides which number, their militia of all colors are eleven hundred. But, when we arrived there, most of their soldiers were out of town; insomuch, that our coming put the rest into great consternation, they having had but one night's notice of our being in those seas. Hence we were induced to believe that had we gone ashore, instead of fighting their ships, we had certainly rendered ourselves masters of the place, especially considering that all their chief men were on board the admiral; I mean such as were undoubtedly the best soldiers. Round about the city, for the space of seven leagues, or thereabouts, all the adjacent country is *savanna*, as they call it in the Spanish language, that is to say plain and level ground, as smooth as a sheet; only here and there is to be seen a small spot of woody land. This level ground is full of *vaccadas*, or beef stations, where whole droves of cows and oxen are kept, which serve as so many look-outs, or watch-towers, to descry if an enemy is approaching by land. The ground whereon the city now stands is very damp and moist, which renders the place unhealthful. The water is also full of worms, which are very prejudicial to shipping; and this is the cause that the king's ships lie always at Lima, the capital of Peru, unless when they come down to Panama to bring the king's plate; which is only at such times as the fleet of galleons come from Old Spain to fetch and convoy it thither. Here, in one hour after our arrival, we found worms of three quarters of an inch in length, both in our bedclothes and other apparel.

At the islands of Perico above mentioned, we seized in all five ships: of these, the first and biggest was named, as was said before, the Trinidad, and was a great ship, of the burden of four hundred tons: her lading consisting of wine, sugar, sweetmeats, (whereof the Spaniards in those hot countries make infinite use,) skins, and soap. The second ship was of about three hundred tons burden, and not above half laden with bars of iron, which is one of the richest commodities that are brought into the South Sea. This vessel we burned with the lading in her, because the Spaniards pretended not to want that commodity, and therefore would not redeem it. The third was laden with sugar, being of the burden of one hundred and fourscore tons, or thereabouts. This vessel was given to Captain Cook. The fourth was an old ship of sixty tons, laden with flour, or meal. This ship we likewise burnt with her lading, esteeming both bottom and cargo at that time to be useless to us. The fifth was a ship of fifty ton, which, with a *periagua*, Captain Coxon took along with him when he left us.

Within two or three days after our arrival at Panama, Captain Coxon being much dissatisfied with some reflections cast upon him by our company, determined to leave us, and return back to our ships in the Northern seas, by the same way he came; and persuaded several of our company, who sided most with him, and had had the chief hand in his election, to fall off from us, and bear him company in his journey, or march over land. The main cause of those reflections was his backwardness in the last engagement with the armadilla; concerning which point some stuck not to brand him for a coward.

He drew off with him to the number of threescore and ten of our men, who all returned back with him in the ship and *periagua*, above mentioned, towards the mouth of the river of Santa Maria. In his company went also back the Indian king, Captain Antonio, and Don Andræas, who, being old, desired to be excused from staying any longer with us. However, the king desired we would not be less vigorous in annoying their enemy and ours, the Spaniards, than if he were personally present with us. And to the intent we might see how faithfully he did intend to deal with us, he at the same time recommended both his son and nephew to the care of Captain Sawkins, who was now our newly-chosen general, or commander-in-chief, in the absence of Captain Sharp. The two armadilla ships, which we took in the engagement, we burnt also, saving nothing of either of them but their rigging and sails. With them also we burnt a bark, that came into the port laden with fowls and poultry.

On Sunday, April the 25th, Captain Sharp with his bark and company came in and joined us again. His absence was occasioned by want of water, which forced him to bear up to the king's islands. Being there, he found a new bark, which he presently took, and burnt his old one. This vessel sailed excellently well. Within a day or two after the arrival of Captain Sharp, came in likewise the people of Captain Harris. These had also taken another bark, and cut down the masts of their old one by the board, and thus, without masts or sails, turned away the prisoners they had taken in her. The next day we took another bark, that came from Nata, being laden with fowls as before this. In this bark we turned away all the meanest prisoners we had on board us.

Having continued before Panama for the space of ten days, being employed in the affairs before mentioned, on May the 2d, we weighed from the Island of Perico, and stood off to another island, distant two leagues farther from thence, called Tavoga. On this island stands a town which bears the same name, and consists of a hundred houses, or thereabouts. The people of the town were all fled, seeing our vessels arrive. While we were here, some of our men being drunk, ashore, happened to set fire to one of the houses, the which consumed twelve houses more, before any could get ashore to quench it. To this island came several Spanish merchants, from Panama, and sold us what commodities we needed, buying also of us much of the goods we had taken in their own vessels: they gave us, likewise, two hundred pieces of eight, for each negro we could spare them, of such as were our prisoners. From this island we could easily see all the vessels that went out or came into the port of Panama; and here we took, likewise, several barks that were laden with fowls.

Eight days after our arrival at Tavago, we took a ship that was coming from Truxillo, and bound for Panama. In this vessel we found two thousand jars of wine, fifty jars of gunpowder, and fifty-one thousand pieces of eight. This money had been sent from that city, to pay the soldiers belonging to the garrison of Panama. From the said prize we had information given us that there was another ship coming from Lima, with one hundred thousand pieces of eight more; which ship was to sail ten or twelve days after them, and which they said could not be long before she arrived at Panama. Within two days after this intelligence, we took also another ship, laden with flour, from Truxillo, belonging to certain Indians, inhabitants of the same place, or thereabouts. This prize confirmed what the first had told us of that rich ship, and said, as the others had done before, that she would be there in the space of eight or ten days.

While we lay at Tavoga, the president, or governor of Panama, sent a message by some merchants to us, to know what we came for into those parts. To this message Captain Sawkins made answer, "That we came to assist the king of Darien, who was the true lord of Panama, and all the country thereabouts: and that since we were come so far, it was no reason but that we should have some satisfaction. So that if he pleased to send us five hundred pieces of eight for each man, and one thousand for each commander, and not any further to annoy the Indians, but suffer them to use their own power and liberty, as became the true and natural lords of the country, that then we would desist from further hostilities, and go away peaceably; otherwise that we should stay there, and get what we could, causing them what damage was possible." By the merchants also that went and came to Panama, we understood there lived then, as bishop of Panama, one who had formerly been bishop of Santa Martha, and who was prisoner to Captain Sawkins, when he took the said place, about four or five years past. The captain having received this intelligence, sent two loaves of sugar to the bishop, as a present. The next day the merchant who carried them, returning to Tavoga, brought the captain a gold ring, for a retaliation of his said present. And withal, he brought a message to Captain Sawkins, from the president above mentioned, to know further of him, since we were Englishmen, "from whom we had our commission, and to whom he ought to complain for the damages we had already done them." To this message, Captain Sawkins sent back foi an answer, "That, as yet, all his company were not come together; but that, when they were come up, we would come and visit him at Panama, and bring our commissions on the muzzles of our guns, at which time he should read them, as plain as the flame of gunpowder could make them."

At this Island of Tavoga, Captain Sawkins would fain have staid longer to wait for the rich ship above mentioned that was coming from Peru; but our men were so importunate for fresh victuals, that no reason could rule them, nor their own interest persuade them to any thing that might conduce to this purpose. Hereupon, May the 15th, we weighed anchor, and sailed from thence to the Island of Otoque. Being arrived there, we lay by it, while our boat went ashore, and fetched off fowls, hogs, and other things necessary for sustenance. Here I finished a draught, comprehending from Point Garachine to the Bay of Panama, &c. Of this, I may dare to affirm, that it is in general more correct and true than any the Spaniards have themselves. For which cause I have here inserted it, for the satisfaction of those that are curious in such things.

From Otoque we sailed to the Island of Cayboa, which is a place very famous for the fishery of pearl, thereabouts, and is at the distance of eight leagues from another place called Puebla Nueba, on the Main. In our way to this island we lost two of our barks, one whereof had fifteen men in her, and the other seven. Being arrived, we cast anchor at the said island.

CHAPTER XXXIII.

Captain Sawkins, chief Commander of the Buccaneers, is killed before Puebla Neuba. — They are repulsed from the Place. — Captain Sharp chosen to be their Leader. — Many more of their Company leave them, and return Home, over Land.

While we lay at anchor before Cayboa, our two chief commanders, Captain Sawkins and Captain Sharp, taking with them threescore men, or thereabouts, went in Captain Cook's ship to the mouth of the river, where Puebla Nueba is situated. The day of this action, as I find it quoted in my journal, was May 22, 1680. When they came to the river's mouth, they put themselves into canoes, and were piloted up the river, towards the town, by a negro, who was one of our prisoners. I was chosen to be concerned in this action, but happened not to land, being commanded to remain in Captain Cook's ship, while they went up to assault the town. But here the inhabitants were too well provided for the reception of our party; for, at the distance of a mile below the town, they had cut down great trees, and laid them across the river, with design to hinder the coming up of any boats. In like manner, on shore, before the town itself, they had raised three strong breastworks, and made other things for their defence. Here, therefore, Captain Sawkins, running up to the breastworks, at the head of a few men, was killed—a man who was as valiant and courageous as any could be, and likewise, next to Captain Sharp, the best beloved of all our company, or the most part thereof. Neither was this love undeserved by him; for we ought justly to attribute to him the greatest honor we gained in our engagement before Panama, with the Spanish armadilla. Especially, considering that, as hath been said above, Captain Sharp was, by accident, absent at the time of that great and bloody fight.

We that remained behind on board the ship of Captain Cook, carried her within the mouth of the River Puebla Nueba, and entered close by the east shore, which is crowned with a round hill. Within two stones cast of shore, we had four fathom water. Within the point opens a very fine and large river, which falls from a sandy bay, at a small distance from thence; but as we were getting in, being strangers to the place, we unwittingly ran our ship on ground, near a rock which lies on the westward shore, for the true channel of the said river is nearer to the east than west shore. With Captain Sawkins, in the unfortunate assault of this place, there died two men more, and three were wounded in the retreat, which they performed to the canoes in pretty good order. In their way down the river, Captain Sharp took a ship, whose lading consisted of indigo, otto, manteco, or butter and pitch; and likewise burnt two vessels more, as being of no value. With this he returned on board our ships, being much troubled in his mind, and grieved for the loss of so bold and brave a partner in his adventures as Sawkins had constantly showed himself to be. His death was much lamented, and occasioned another party of our men to mutiny, and leave us, returning, over land, as Captain Coxon and his company had done before.

Three days after the death of Captain Sawkins, Captain Sharp, who was now commander-in-chief, gave the ship which he had taken in the River of Puebla Nueba, and which was of the burthen of one hundred tons, or thereabouts, to Captain Cook, to command and sail in; ordering withal, that the old vessel which he had should go with those men that designed to leave us; their mutiny, and our distraction, being now grown very high. Hereupon Captain Sharp coming on board La Trinidad, the greatest of our ships, asked our men in full council, who of them were willing to go, or stay, and prosecute the design Captain Sawkins had undertaken, which was to remain in the South Sea, and there to make a complete voyage; after which he intended to go home round about America, through the Straits of Magellan; he added withal, that he did not as yet fear or doubt in the least but to make each man who should stay with him worth one thousand pounds, by the fruits he hoped to reap of that voyage. All those who had remained after the departure of Captain Coxon, for love of Captain Sawkins, and only to be in his company, and under his conduct, thinking thereby to make their fortunes, would stay no longer, but pressed to depart. Among this number I acknowledge myself to have been one, as being totally desirous in my mind to quit those hazardous adventures, and return homewards in company of those who were now going to leave us. Yet being much afraid and averse to trust myself among wild Indians any farther, I chose rather to stay, though unwillingly, and venture on that long and dangerous voyage; besides which danger of the Indians, I considered that the rains were now already up, and it would be hard passing so many gullies, which of necessity would then be full of water, and consequently create more than one single peril to the undertakers of that journey. Yet notwithstanding, sixty-three men of our company were resolved to encounter all these hardships, and to leave us; hereupon they took their leave of us and returned homewards, taking with them the Indian king's son, and the rest of the Indians for their guides over land. They had, as was said above, the ship wherein Captain Cook sailed to carry them; and out of our provision as much as would serve for treble their number.

On the last day of May they left us employed in taking in water, and cutting down wood, at the Island of Cayboa before mentioned, where this mutiny happened. Here we caught very good tortoise, and red deer; we killed also alligators of a very large size, some of them being above twenty foot in length. But we could not find but that they were very fearful of a man, and would fly from us very hastily when we hunted them. This island lieth south-south-east from the mouth of the river above mentioned. On the south-east side of the island is a shoal, or spit of sand, which stretched itself the space of a quarter of a league into the sea; here, therefore, just within this shoal, we anchored in the depth of fourteen fathom water. The island on this side thereof maketh two great bays, in the first of which we watered, at a certain pond not distant above the cast of a stone up from the bay. In this pond, as I was washing myself, and standing under a manzanilla tree, a small shower of rain happened to fall on the tree, and from thence dropped on my skin: these drops caused me to break out all over my body into red spots, of which I was well for the space of a week after. Here I eat very large oysters, the biggest that ever I eat in my life, insomuch that I was forced to cut them into four pieces, each quarter of them being a good mouthful.

Three days after the departure of the mutineers, Captain Sharp ordered us to burn the ship that I had hitherto sailed in, only out of design to make use of the iron-work belonging to the said vessel. Withal we put all the flour that was her lading into the last prize taken in the River of Puebla Nueba, and Captain Cook, as was said before, was ordered to command her; but the men belonging to his company would not sail any longer under his command. Hereupon he quitted his vessel, and came on board our admiral, the great ship above mentioned, called La Trinidad, determining to rule over such unruly company no longer. In his place was put John Cox, an inhabitant of New England, who forced kindred, as was thought, on Captain Sharp, out of old acquaintance, in this conjuncture of time, only to advance himself; thus he was made, as it were, vice-admiral to Captain Sharp. The next day three of our prisoners, viz., an Indian, who was captain of a ship, and two mulattoes, ran away from us, and made their escape.

After this it was thought convenient to send Captain Peralta prisoner in the admiral, on board Mr. Cox's ship; this was done to the intent he might not hinder the endeavors of Captain Juan, who was commander of the money ship we took, mentioned at the Island of Tavoga. For this man had promised to do great things for us, by piloting and conducting us to several places of great riches, but more especially to Guayaquil, where he said we might lay down our silver, and lade our vessel with gold. This design was undertaken by Captain Sawkins, and had not the headstrongness of his men brought him to the Island of Cayboa, where he lost his life, he had certainly effected it before now. That night we had such thunder and lightnings, as I never heard before in all my life; our prisoners told us, that in these parts it very often caused great damages, both by sea and land; and my opinion gave me to believe, that our mainmast received some damage on this occasion. The rainy season being now entered, the wind for the most part was at N. W., though not without some calms.

CHAPTER XXXIV.

They depart from the Island of Cayboa to the Isle of Gorgona, where they careen their Vessels. — Description of this Isle. — They resolve to go and plunder Arica, leaving their Design of Guayaquil.

Having got in all things necessary for sailing, we were now in a readiness to depart on Sunday, June 6, 1680. That day we had some rain fell, which now was very frequent in all those places. About five o'clock in the evening we set sail for the Island of Cayboa, with a small breeze, the wind being at S. S. W. Our course was E. S. by E. and S. E. after sailing two days, with little or no wind. On the third, about sunrising, we descried Quicara, which at that time bore N. W. by W. from us, at the distance of five leagues, or thereabouts.

These are two several islands, whereof the least is to the southward of the other. The land is a low table land; they are above three leagues in length.

Thursday, June 10, we saw many tortoises floating upon the sea; hereupon we hoisted out our boat, and came to one of them, who offered not to stir until she was struck, and even then not to sink to the bottom, but rather to swim away: the sea hereabouts is very full of several sorts of fish, as dolphins, bonites, albicores, mullets, and old wives, &c., which came swimming about our ship in whole shoals. The next day, which was Friday, our Spanish prisoners informed us we must not expect any settled wind until we came within the latitude of three degrees; for all along the western shore of these seas there is little wind, which is the cause that those ships that go from Acapulco to the islands called De las Philippinas, do coast along the shore of California, until they get into the height of forty-five degrees; yea, sometimes of fifty degrees latitude. As the wind varied, so we tacked several times, thereby to make the best of our way that was possible to the southward.

As our prisoners had informed us, so we found it by experience: for sailing two days with small wind, and much rain, June 17, about five in the morning we descried land, which appeared all along to be very low, and likewise full of creeks and bays. Our pilot not knowing what land it was, we called Mr. Cox on board us, who brought Captain Peralta with him: this gentleman being asked, presently told us the land we saw was the land of Barbacoa, being almost a wild country all over; withal, he informed us, that to the leeward of us, at the distance of ten leagues, or thereabouts, did lie an island called by the name of Gorgona; the which island, he said, the Spaniards did shun, and very seldom came near it, by reason of the incessant and continual rains there falling, scarce one day in the year being dry at that place. Captain Sharp having heard this information of Captain Peralta, judged the said island might be the fittest place for our company to careen at; considering, that if the Spaniards did not frequent it, we might in all probability lie there undescried, and our enemies, the Spaniards, in the mean time might think we were gone out of those seas. At this time it was that I seriously repented my staying in the South Seas, and that I did not return homewards in company of them that went before us: for I knew and could easily perceive that by these delays the Spaniards would gain time, and be able to send advice of our coming to every port all along the coast, so that we should be prevented in all, or most of our attempts and designs, wheresoever we came. But those of our company who had got money by the former prizes of this voyage, overswayed the others who had lost all their booty at gaming. Thus we bore away for the Island aforesaid of Gorgona.

On the main land, over against this Island of Gorgona, we were told by our prisoners, that up a great lake is an Indian town, where they have a large quantity of sand grains of gold: moreover, that five days' sail up a river belonging to the said lake dwell four Spanish superintendents, who have each of them the charge of overseeing fifty or sixty Indians, who are employed in gathering that gold which slippeth from the chief collectors, or finders thereof: these are at least threescore and ten, or fourscore Spaniards, with a great number of slaves belonging to them, who dwell higher up than these four superintendents, at the distance of twenty-five or thirty days' sailing on the said river. That once, every year, at a certain season, there comes a vessel from Lima, the capital city of Peru, to fetch the gold that is gathered here; and withal, to bring these people such necessaries as they want. By land, it is full six weeks' travel from thence to Lima. The main land to windward of this island is very low, and full of rivers: all along the coast it rains extremely: the island is distant from the continent only four leagues.

Captain Sharp gave this island the name of Sharp's Isle, by reason we careened at this place. We anchored on the south side of it, at the mouth of a very fine river, which there disgorges itself into the sea. There belong to this island about thirty rivers and rivulets, all which fall from the rocks on the several sides of the island: the whole circumference thereof is about three leagues and a half, being all high and mountainous land, excepting only on that side where we cast anchor. Here, therefore, we moored our ship in the depth of eighteen or twenty fathom water, and began to unrig the vessel: but we were four or five days' space before we could get our sails dry, so as to be able to take them from the yards, there falling a shower of rain almost every hour, day and night. The main land to the east of the island, and so stretching northwards, is extreme high and towering, and withal perpetually clouded, excepting only at the rising of the sun, when the tops of those hills are clear. From the south side of this island where we anchored, we could see the low land of the main, at least a point thereof, which lieth nearest to the island: the appearance it maketh is, as if it were trees growing out of the water.

Friday, July 2, as we were heaving down our ship, our mainmast happened to crack; hereupon our carpenters were obliged to cut out large fishes and fish it, as they term it.

The next day after the mischance of our mainmast, we killed a snake fourteen inches thick, and eleven feet long. About the distance of a league from this island runs a ledge of rocks, over which the water continually breaks; the ledge being about two miles, or thereabouts, in length. Had we anchored but half a mile more northerly, we had rid in much smoother water; for here the wind came in upon us in violent gusts. While we were there, from June 13 to July 3, we had dry weather, which was esteemed as a rarity by the Spaniards, our prisoners. Every day we saw whales and grampuses, who would often come and dive under our ship: we fired at them several times, but our bullets rebounded from their bodies. Our choice and best provisions here were Indian conies, monkeys, snakes, oysters, concks, periwinkles, with some other sorts of good fish, and a few small turtle. Here we also caught a sloth, a beast well deserving that name, given it by the Spaniards, by whom it is called *pereza*, from the Latin word *pigritia*.

At this island died Joseph Gabriel, a Spaniard, born in Chili, who was to have been our pilot to Panama; he was the same man who had stolen and married the Indian king's daughter, as was mentioned above: he had all along been very true and faithful to us, in discovering several plots and conspiracies of our prisoners, either to get away or destroy us. His death was occasioned by a calenture, or malignant fever, which killed him after three days' sickness, having lain two days senseless. During the time of our stay at this island, we lengthened our top-sail yards, and got up top-gallant masts: we made two stay-sails, and refitted our ship very well; but we wanted provisions extremely, as having nothing considerable of any sort, but flour and water. Being almost ready to depart, Captain Sharp, our commander, gave us to understand he had changed his resolution, concerning the design of going to Guayaquil, for he thought it would be in vain to go thither, considering, that in all this time we must of necessity have been descried; yet, notwithstanding he himself, before, had persuaded us to stay. Being very doubtful among ourselves what course we should take, a certain old man, who had a long time sailed among the Spaniards, told us he could carry us to a place called Arica, to which town, he said, all the plate was brought down from Potosi, Chuquisaca, and several other places within the land, where it was digged out of the mountains and mines; and that he doubted not but we might get there at least two thousand pound a man, by way of booty; for all the plate of the South Sea lay there as it were in store, being deposited at the said place till such time as the ships fetched it away. Being moved with these reasons, and having deliberated thereupon, we resolved in the end to go to the said place. At this Island of Gorgona afore mentioned, we likewise took down our round-house coach, and all the high carved work belonging to the stern of the ship: for when we took her from the Spaniards before Panama, she was as high as any third rate-ship in England.

CHAPTER XXXV.

The Buccaneers depart from the Isle of Gorgona, with Design to plunder Arica. — They lose one another by the Way. — They touch at the Isle of Plate, or Drake's Isle, where they meet again. — Description of this Isle. — Some Memoirs of Sir Francis Drake. — They sail as far in a Fortnight as the Spaniards usually do in three Months.

On Sunday, July 25, in the afternoon, all things being now in readiness for our departure, we set sail, and stood away from the Island of Gorgona, or Sharp's Isle, with a small breeze which served us at N. W., but as the sun went down, our breeze lessened by degrees into a perfect calm; yet we could perceive that our ship began to sail much better since the taking down her round-house, and the other alterations which we made in her.

The next day, about two o'clock in the morning, we had a land breeze to help us, which lasted for the space of six hours, and again in the evening we had another. This day the Spaniards, our prisoners, told us, in common discourse, that in most parts of this low land coast they find threescore fathom water. The third night, about ten o'clock, Captain Sharp ordered me to speak to Captain Cox to go about, and stand off from the shore, for he feared he would come too near it: but he replied, he knew well that he might stand in till two o'clock. The next morning, early, being cloudy and quite calm, we saw him not, and, notwithstanding at eight o'clock it cleared up, neither then could we get sight at him: from hence we concluded, and so it proved, that we had lost him in the dark, through his obstinacy in standing in too long, and not coming about when we spoke to him. Thus our admiral's ship was left alone, and we had not the company of Captain Cox again till we arrived at the Isle of Plate, where we had the good fortune to find him again, as shall be mentioned hereafter. The weather being clear this morning, we could see Gorgona, at the distance of at least fifteen or sixteen leagues to the east-north-east.

Thursday, July 29, 1680, about four in the afternoon, we came within sight of the Island del Gallo, which I guessed to be nigh twenty-eight leagues distant from that of Gorgona, the place of our departure, S. W.

The next day, being July 30, the wind blew very fresh and brisk, insomuch that we were in some fear for the heads of our low masts, as being very sensible that they were but weak. About three or four in the afternoon, we saw another island, six or seven leagues distant from Gallo, called Gorgonilla. All the main land hereabouts lieth very low and flat, and is in very many places overflown and drowned every high water. This day, and the night before it, we lost by our computation three leagues of our way, which I believe happened by reason we stood out too far from the land, as having stood off all night long.

August the 1st, which was Sunday, we had a very fresh wind, at W. S. W., with several small showers of rain. Meanwhile we got pretty well to windward, by making small trips to and fro; which we performed, most commonly, by standing in three glasses, and as many out.

The next day, August the 2d, in the morning, we came up to the high land of San Iago, where beginneth the high land of this coast. We kept at the distance of ten leagues from it, making continual short trips, as was mentioned before.

Wednesday, August the 4th, we continued still turning in

the wind's eye, as we had done for two days before. In the afternoon we discovered three hills at E. N. E. of our ship, which make the land of San Matteo. That evening, also, we saw the Cape of San Francisco.

Thursday, August the 5th, we being then about the cape, it looked very like Beachy Head, in England : it is full of white cliffs on all sides. The land turneth off here to the eastward of the south, and maketh a large and deep bay, the circumference whereof is full of pleasant hills. In the bite of the bay are two high and rocky islands, which represent exactly two ships with their sails full. We were now come out of the rainy countries into a pleasant and fair region, where we had for the most part a clear sky and dry weather; only now and then a small mist, which would soon vanish. Meanwhile a great dew used to fall every night, which supplied the defect of rain.

On Sunday, August the 8th, we came close under a wild and mountainous country, and saw Cape Passao, at the distance of ten leagues, or thereabouts, to windward of us. Ever since we came on this side Mangrove Point, we observed a windward current did run along as we sailed. Under shore, and lower towards the pitch of the cape, the land is full of white cliffs and groves.

The next day we had both a fair day and a fresh wind to help us on our voyage. We observed that Cape Passao maketh three points, between which are two bays; the leeward most of the two is three leagues long, and the other four. Adjoining to the bay is a pleasant valley. Our prisoners informed us, that northward of these capes live certain Indians who sell maize, and other provisions, to any ships that happen to come in there. The cape itself is a continued cliff, covered with several sorts of shrubs and low bushes. Under these cliffs lies a sandy bay, forty feet deep. The Spaniards say that the wind is always here between the S. S. W. and W. S. W.

Tuesday, August the 10th. This morning the sky was so thick and hazy, that we could not see the high land, though it were just before us; but as soon as it cleared up, we stood in towards the land, till we came within a mile of the shore.

August the 11th, we found ourselves N. N. W. from Monte de Christo, being a very high and round hill. From thence to windward is seen a very pleasant country, with spots here and there of woody land, which causes the country all over to look like so many enclosures of ripe corn-fields. To leeward of the said hill, the land is all high and hilly, with white cliffs at the sea-side. The coast runs S. W. till it reaches a point of land, within which is the port of Manta. This port is a settlement of the Spaniards and Indians together, where ships that want provisions put in, and are furnished with several necessaries. About six or seven leagues to windward of this port is Cape St. Lawrence, butting out into the sea, in form of the top of a church. As we sailed we saw multitudes of grampuses every day, as also water-snakes of divers colors. Both the Spaniards and Indians are very fearful of these snakes, as believing there is no cure for their bitings.

This day, before night, we came within sight of Manta. Here we saw the houses of the town belonging to the port, which were not above twenty or thirty Indian houses, lying under the windward and the mount. We were not willing to be descried by the inhabitants of the place, and hereupon we stood off to sea again.

On Thursday, August the 12th, in the morning, we saw the Island of Plate at S. W. at the distance of five leagues or thereabouts. It appeared to us to be a plain country. Having made this island, we resolved to go thither and refit our rigging, and get some goats which there run wild up and down the country. For, as was said before, at this time we had no other provision than flour and water. This day several great whales came up to us, and dived under our ship. One of these whales followed our ship, from two in the afternoon till dark night.

The next morning very early, about six of the clock, we came under the aforesaid Isle of Plate; and here unexpectedly, to our great joy, we found at anchor the ship of Captain Cox, with his whole company, whom he had lost at sea for the space of a whole fortnight before, who had arrived there four days before us, and were just ready to sail thence. About seven we came to an anchor, and then the other vessel sent us a live tortoise and a goat to feast upon that day; telling us, withal, of great store of tortoises to be found ashore upon the bays, and of much fish to be caught hereabouts. The island is very steep on all sides; insomuch that there is no landing, but only at the N. E. side thereof, where is a gully, near which we anchored in twelve fathom water. Here, at the distance of a furlong, or little more from the shore, is a cross still standing, erected at the first discovery of it by the Spaniards. No trees are to be found on the whole island, only low shrubs, on which the goats feed, which are here very numerous. The shore is bold and hard, neither is there any water to be found upon it, save only on the S. W. side, where it cannot be come at, being so environed by the rocks, and too great a sea hindering the approach by boats.

This island received its name from Sir Francis Drake, and his famous actions. For it is reported that he here made the dividend of that vast quantity of plate, which he took in the armada of this sea, distributing it to each man of his company by whole bowls full. The Spaniards affirm to this day, that he took at that time twelve score tons of plate, and sixteen bowls of coined money a man, his number being then forty-five men in all.; insomuch that they were forced to heave much of it overboard, because his ship could not carry it all. Hence this island was called by the Spaniards the Isle of Plate, from this great dividend, and by us Drake's Isle.

All along as we sailed, we found the Spanish pilots to be very ignorant of the coasts; but they pleaded in excuse for their ignorance, that the merchants either of Mexico, Lima, Panama, or other parts, who employ them, will not intrust one pennyworth of goods on that man's vessel that corks her, for fear she should miscarry. Here our prisoners told us likewise, that in the time of Oliver Cromwell, or the commonwealth of England, a certain ship was fitted out of Lima, with seventy brass guns, having on board her no less than thirty millions of dollars, or pieces of eight. All which vast sum of money was given by the merchants of Lima, and sent as a present to our gracious king (or rather, his father) who now reigneth, to supply him in his exile and distress. But that this great and rich ship was lost by keeping along the shore in the bay of Manta above mentioned, or thereabouts. The truth whereof is much to be questioned.

At this island we took out of Mr. Cox's ship the old Moor who pretended he would be our pilot to Arica. This was done lest we should have the misfortune of losing the company of Cox's vessel, as we had done before, our ship being the biggest in burden, and having the greatest number of men. Captain Peralta oftentimes admired that we were gotten so far to the windward in so little space of time; whereas they had been, he said, many times three or four months in reaching to this distance from our departure: but their long and tedious voyages, he added, were occasioned by their keeping at too great a distance from the shore. Moreover, he told us, that had we gone to the islands of Galapagos, as we were once determined to do, we had met with many calms and currents, in which many ships have been lost, and never heard of more. This Island of Plate is about two leagues in length, and very full of deep and dangerous bays, as also such as we call gullies in these parts.

We caught at this island, and salted good number, of goats and tortoises. One man standing here on a little bay, in one day turned seventeen tortoises; besides which number, our musquito strikers brought us in several more. Captain Sharp, our commander, showed himself very ingenious in striking them, he performing it as well as the tortoise strikers themselves. For these creatures have so little sense of fear, that they offer not to sink from the fishermen, but lie still till they are struck. But we found that the tortoises on this side were not so large nor so sweet to the taste as those on the north side of the island. Of goats we have taken, killed, and salted above a hundred in a day, and that with ease. While we staid here we made a square main-topsail yard. We cut also six foot of our boltsprit, and three foot more of our head. Most of the time we remained here we had hazy weather; only now and then the sun would happen to break out, and then shine so hot, that it burnt the skin off the necks of several of our men. As for me, my lips were burnt so that they were not well in a whole week after.

CHAPTER XXXVI.

Captain Sharp and his Company depart from the Island of Plate, in Prosecution of their Voyage towards Arica. — They take two Spanish Vessels by the Way, and get Intelligence from the Enemy. — Eight of their Company destroyed at the Isle of Gallo. — Tediousness of this Voyage, and great Hardship they endured.

Having taken in provisions and other necessaries we could get at the Isle of Plate, we set sail from thence, Tuesday the 17th of August, 1680, in prosecution of our voyage and designs above mentioned, to take and plunder the vastly rich town of Arica. This day we sailed so well, as we did likewise several days after, that we were forced to lie by several times, besides pressing our topsails, to keep our other ship company, lest we should lose her again.

Next morning, about break of day, we found ourselves at the distance of seven or eight leagues to the westward of the island, from whence we departed, standing W. by S., with a S. by W. wind. We were several times this day forced to stay for the other vessel belonging to our company.

The day following we continued likewise a west course all the day long. Hereabouts we observed very great ripplings of the sea.

August the 20th, we found still that we gained very much of the small ship, which did not a little both perplex and hinder us in our course.

The next day I finished two quadrants, each of which was two foot and a half radius. Here we had in like manner, as hath been mentioned on other days of our sailings, very many dolphins, and other sorts of fish swimming about our ship.

On the morning following we saw again the Island of Plate at N. E.

The same day, at the distance of six leagues, or thereabouts, from the said island, we saw another island called Solango. This isle lies close in by the main land. This day likewise we found that our lesser ship was still a great hinderance to our sailing, as being forced to lie by, and stay for her two or three hours every day. We found likewise, that the further from shore we were, the less wind we had all along; and that under the shore we were always sure of a fresh gale, though not so favorable as we could have wished. Hitherto we had used to stand off forty leagues, and yet notwithstanding, in the space of six days, we had not got above ten leagues on our voyage from the place of our departuae.

August 23d. This day, at S. by W. and about six leagues distance from us, we descried a long and even hill. I took it to be an island, and conjectured it might be at least eight leagues distant from the continent. But afterwards we found it was a point of land adjoining to the main, and is called Point St. Helen, being continued by a piece of land which lieth low, and in several places is almost drowned from the sight, so that it cannot be seen two leagues' distance. In this low land the Spaniards have convenience for making pitch, tar, salt, and some other things, for which purpose they have several houses here, and a friar, who serveth them as their chaplain. From Solango to this place, are reckoned eleven leagues, or thereabouts. The land is hereabouts indifferent high, and is likewise full of bays. We had this day very little wind to help us in our voyage, except now and then a blast. These sometimes would prove pretty fair to us, and allow us for some little while a south course. But our chiefest course was S. E. by S.

Here we found no great current of the sea to move any way. At the Isle of Plate before described, the sea ebbs and flows nigh thirteen foot perpendicular. About four leagues to leeward of this Point St. Helen is a deep bay, having a key at the mouth of it, which takes up the better part of its wideness. In the deepest part of the bay on shore, we saw a great smoke, which was at a village belonging to the bay, to which place the people were removed from the point above mentioned. Hereabouts it is all along a very bold shore. At three of the clock in the afternoon, we tacked about to clear ourselves of the point. Being now a little way without the point, we spied a sail, which we conceived to be a bark. Hereupon, we hoisted out our canoe, and sent it in pursuit of her, which made directly for the shore. But the sail proved to be nothing but a pair of bark-logs, which arriving on shore, the men spread their sails on the sand of the bay to dry. At the same time there came down upon the shore an Indian on horseback, who hallooed to our canoe which had followed the logs. But our men fearing to discover who we were, in case they went too near the shore, left the design, and returned back to us. In those parts the Indians have no canoes, nor any wood fit to make them of. Had we been descried by these poor people, they would in all probability have been very fearful of us: but they offered not to stir, which gave us to understand they knew us not. We could perceive from the ship a great path leading to the hills, so that we believed this place to be a lookout, or watch-place, for the security of Guayaquil. Between four and five we doubled the point, and then we descried the Point Chonday, at the distance of six leagues S. S. E. from this point.

Tuesday, August 24, at noon, we took the other ship wherein Captain Cox sailed, into a tow, she being every day a greater hinderance than other to our voyage. Thus about three in the afternoon we lost sight of land, in standing over for Cape Blanco: here we found a strong current move to the S. W., the wind was at S. W. by S., our course being S. by E. At the upper end of this gulf, which is framed by the two capes above mentioned, stands the city of Guayaquil, being a very rich place, and the *embarcadero*, or sea-port, to the great city of Quito. To this place, likewise, many of the merchants of Lima usually send the money they design for Old Spain, in barks, and by that means save the custom, that otherwise they should pay to the king, by carrying it on board the fleet. Hither comes much gold from Quito; and very good and strong broad-cloth, together with images for the use of churches, and several other things of considerable value; but more especially cocoa-nut, whereof chocolate is made, which is supposed here to be the best in the whole universe. The town of Guayaquil consists of about one hundred and fifty great houses, and twice as many little ones: this was the town to which Captain Sawkins intended to make his voyâge, as was mentioned above. When ships of greater burthen come into this gulf, they anchor without Lapina, and then put their lading into lesser vessels to carry it to town. Towards the evening of this day, a small breeze sprung up, varying from point to point; after which, about nine o'clock at night, we tacked about, and stood off at sea, W. by N.

As soon as we had tacked, we happened to spy a sail, N. N. E. from us ; hereupon, we instantly cast off our vessel, which we had in a tow, and stood round about after them. We came very near the vessel before they saw us, by reason of the darkness of the night ; as soon as they espied us they immediately clapped on a wind, and sailed very well before us ; insomuch, that it was a pretty while before we could come up with them, and within call. We hailed them in Spanish, by means of an Indian prisoner, and commanded them to lower their topsails. They answered, they would soon make us to lower our own. Hereupon, we fired several guns at them, and they as thick at us again with their harquebusses : thus they fought for the space of half an hour, or more, and would have done it longer, had we not killed the man at the helm ; after whom, none of the rest dared to be so hardy as to take his place. With another of our shot we cut in pieces and disabled their main-top-halliards ; hereupon they cried out for quarter, which we gave them, and entered their ship. Being possessed of the vessel, we found in her five and thirty men, of which number twenty-four were natives of Old Spain : they had one and thirty fire arms on board the ship for their defence. They had not fought us, as they declared afterwards, but only out of a bravado, having promised on shore so to do, in case they met us at sea. The captain of this vessel was a person of quality, and his brother, since the death of Don Jacinto de Barahona, killed in the engagement before Panama, was now made admiral of the sea armada : with him we took also, in this bark, five or six other persons of quality. They did us in this fight, though short, very great damage in our rigging, by cutting it in pieces. Besides which, they wounded two of our men ; and a third man was wounded by the negligence of one of our own men, occasioned by a pistol, which went off unadvisedly. About eleven o'clock this night, we stood off to the west.

The next morning, about break of day, we hoisted out our canoe, and went aboard the bark which we had taken the night before. We put on board our own ship more of the prisoners taken in the said vessel, and began to examine them, to get what intelligence we could from them. The captain of the vessel, who was a very civil and meek gentleman, satisfied our desires in this point very exactly, saying, "Gentlemen, I am now your prisoner of war by the overruling providence of fortune ; and moreover, am very well satisfied that no money whatsoever can procure my ransom, at least for the present, at your hands: hence I am persuaded, it is not my interest to tell you a lie; which if I do, I desire you to punish me as severely as you shall think fit. We heard of your taking and destroying our *armadilla*, aud other ships at Panama, about six weeks after that engagement, by two several barks which arrived here from thence; but they could not inform us whether you designed to come any further to the southward; but rather, desired we would send them speedily all the help by sea that we could. Hereupon, we sent the noise and rumor of your being in these seas to Lima, desiring they would expedite what succors they could send to join with ours. We had, at that time, in our harbor, two or three great ships, but all of them very unfit to sail; for this reason, at Lima, the viceroy of Peru pressed three great merchant ships, into the biggest of which he put fourteen brass guns; into the second, ten; and in the other, six; unto these he added two barks, and put seven hundred and fifty soldiers on board them all; of this number of men, they landed eightscore at Point St. Helen; all the rest being carried down to Panama, with design to fight you there; besides these forces, two other men-of-war, bigger than the afore mentioned, are still lying at Lima, and fitting out there with all speed to follow and pursue you. One of these men-of-war is equipped with thirty-six brass guns, and the other with thirty: these ships, besides their complement of seamen, have four hundred soldiers added to them by the viceroy. Another man-of-war belonging to this number, and lesser than the afore mentioned, is called the Patache; this ship carries twenty-four guns, and was sent to Arica to fetch the king's plate from thence; but the viceroy having received intelligence of your exploits at Panama, sent for this ship back from thence in such haste, that they came away and left the money behind them. Hence the Patache now lies at the port of Callao, ready to sail on the first occasion, or news of your arrival thereabouts; they having for this purpose sent to all parts very strict orders to keep a good look out on all sides, and all places along the coast; since this, from Manta they sent us word that they had seen two ships at sea pass by that place: and from the Goat Key also we heard, that the Indians had seen you, and that they were assured, that one of your vessels was the ship called La Trinidad, which you had taken before Panama, as being a ship very well known in these seas: from hence we concluded that your design was to ply and make your voyage thereabouts. Now this bark wherein you took us prisoners, being bound for Panama, the governor of Guayaquil sent us out before her departure, if possible, to discover you; which if we did, we were to run the bark on shore, and get away, or else to fight you with these soldiers and fire-arms, that you see. As soon as we heard of your being in these seas, we built two forts, the one of six guns, and the other of four, for the defence of the town: at the last muster taken in the town of Guayaquil, we had there eight hunred and fifty men, of all colors; but when we came out, we left only two hundred and fifty men that were actually under arms." Thus ended the relation of that worthy gentleman. About noon that day we unrigged the bark, which we had taken, and then sunk her. Then we stood S. S. E., and afterwards S. by W. and S. S. W. That evening we saw Point St. Helen at the north half east, at the distance of nine leagues, or thereabouts.

The next day, being August 26, in the morning we stood south. The next day we reckoned up all our pillage, and found it amounted to three thousand two hundred and seventy-six pieces of eight, which was accordingly divided into shares amongst us. We also punished a friar, who was chaplain to the bark afore mentioned, and shot him upon the deck, casting him overboard before he was dead. Such cruelties, though I abhorred very much in my heart, yet here was I forced to hold my tongue and not contradict them, as having no authority to oversway them. About ten o'clock this morning we saw land again, and the pilot said we were sixteen leagues to leeward of Cabo Blanco: hereupon we stood off and in, close under the shore, which appeared to be all barren land.

The morning following we had very little wind, so that we advanced but slowly all that day: to windward of us we could perceive the continent to be all high land, being whitish clay full of white cliffs. This morning, in common discourse, our prisoners acknowledged they had destroyed one of our little barks, which we lost in our way to the Island of Cayboa. They stood away, as it appeared by their information, for the Goat Key, thinking to find us there, as having heard Captain Sawkins say that he would go thither. On their way they happened to fall in with the Island of Gallo, and understanding its weakness by their Indian pilot, they ventured on shore, and took the place, carrying away three white women in their company. But after a small time of cruising, they returned again to the afore-mentioned island, where they staid the space of two or three days; after which they went to sea again. Within three or four days they came to a little key four leagues distant from this isle. But while they had been out and in thus, several times, one of their prisoners made his escape to the main, and brought off from thence fifty men with fire-arms. These

placing themselves in ambuscade, at the first volley of their shot, killed six of the seven men that belonged to the bark. The other man that was left took quarter of the enemy ; and he it was that discovered our design upon the town of Guayaquil. By an observation which was made this day, we found ourselves to be in the latitude of 3° 50′ S. At this time, our prisoners told us, there was an embargo laid on all the Spanish ships, commanding them not to stir out of the ports, for fear of falling into our hands.

Saturday, August 28. This morning we took out all the water, and most part of the flour, that was in Captain Cox's vessel: having done this, we made a hole in the vessel, and left her to sink, with a small old canoe at her stern. To leeward of Manta, a league from shore, in eighteen fathom water, there runs a great current outwards. About eleven in the forenoon, we weighed anchor, with wind at W. N. W., turning it out. Our number was now one hundred and forty men, boys, and fifty-five prisoners, all now in one and the same bottom. This day we got six or seven leagues in the wind's eye.

All the day following we had a very strong S. S. W. wind; insomuch that we were forced to sail with two reefs in our main-topsail, and one also in our fore-topsail. Here Captain Peralta told us, that the first place which the Spaniards settled in these parts, after Panama, was Tumbes, now to leeward of us. That there a priest went ashore with a cross in his hand, while ten thousand Indians gazed at him. Being landed, there came two lions out of the woods, and after them two tigers, on the backs of whom the priest having gently laid the cross, they fell down and worshipped it ; which gave such a testimony to the truth of the Christian religion, that the Indians soon embraced the same. About four in the evening we came abreast the cape, (Cape Blanco,) which is the highest part of all. The land thereabouts appeareth to be barren and rocky.

Were it not for a windward current which runs under the shore hereabouts, it were totally impossible for any ships to get about this cape, there being such a great current to the leeward in the offing. In the last bark which we took, of which we spoke in this chapter, we made prisoner one Nicholas Moreno, a Spaniard by birth, and who was esteemed to be a very good pilot of the South Sea. He was continually praising the sailing of our ship, which he said was especially occasioned by the alterations we made in her. As we went along, we observed many bays between this cape and Point Parina, of which we shall make mention hereafter.

In the night the wind came about to S. S. E., and we had a

very stiff gale; so that, by break of day, we found ourselves about five leagues to windward of the cape afore mentioned.

The next day likewise, being the last of August, the wind still continued S. S. E., as it had done the whole day before. This day we thought it convenient to stand further out to sea, for fear of being descried at Paita, which now was not very far distant from us. The morning proved hazy; but about eleven we spied a sail, which stood then just as we did, E. by S. Coming nearer by degrees, we found her to be nothing but a pair of bark-logs under sail. Our pilot advised us not to meddle with, or take any notice of them, for it was very doubtful whether we should be able to come up with them or not; and then, by giving chase to them, we should easily be descried and known to be English pirates, as they called us. These bark-logs sail excellently well for the most part, and some of them are so big as to carry two hundred and fifty packs of meal from the valleys to Panama, without wetting any of it. This day, by an observation made, we found ourselves in 4° 55′ latitude South: we saw Point Parina at N. E. by E., and at the distance of six leagues, or thereabouts.

At the same time La Silla de Paita bore from us S. E. by E., being distant only seven or eight leagues.

The town of Paita is situated in a deep bay about two leagues to the leeward of this hill. It serves for an *embarcadero*, or port town, to another great place which is distant from thence about thirteen leagues higher in the country, and is called Piura, seated in a very barren country.

On Wednesday, the first of September, our course was S. by W. The midnight before there sprung up a land wind.

That night as we sailed we saw something that appeared to us like a light; and the next morning we spied a sail, from whence we judged the light had come. The vessel was six leagues from us, in the wind's eye, and thereupon we gave her chase. She stood to windward, as we did. This day we had an observation, which gave us latitude 5° 30′ S. At night we were about four leagues to leeward of her; but so great a mist fell, that we suddenly lost sight of her. At this time the weather was as cold with us as in England in November. Every time we went about with our ship, the other did the like. Our pilot told us, that this ship set forth from Guayaquil eleven days before they were taken; and that she was laden with rigging, wollen, and cotton cloth, and other manufactures made at Quito. Moreover, that he had heard that they had spent a mast, and had put into Paita to refit it.

The night following, they showed us several lights through

their negligence, which they ought not to have done, for by that means we steered directly after them. The next morning she was above three leagues in the wind's eye from us. Had they suspected us, it could not be doubted, but they would have made towards the land; but they seemed not to fly nor stir for our chase. The land here all along is level, and not very high. The weather was hazy, so that about eleven that morning we lost sight of her. At this time we had been a whole week at an allowance of only two draughts of water a day, so scarce were provisions with us. That afternoon we saw the vessel again, and at night we were not full two leagues from her, and not above half a league to the leeward. We made short trips all that night.

On Saturday, September the 4th, about break of day, we saw the ship again at the distance of a league, or thereabouts, and not above a mile to windward of us. They stood out as soon as they espied us, and we stood directly after them. Having pursued them for several hours, about four in the afternoon we came up within half shot of our small arms, to windward of them. Hereupon they, perceiving who we were, presently, lowered all their sails at once, and we cast dice among ourselves for the first entrance. The lot fell to larboard, so that twenty men belonging to that watch entered her. In the vessel were found fifty packs of cocoa-nut, such as chocolate is made of, many packs of raw silk, Indian cloth, and thread stockings; these things being the principal part of her cargo. We stood out S. W. by S. all the night following.

Next day we put on board our ship the chief part of her lading. In her hold we found some rigging, as Nicholas Moreno, our pilot, taken in the former vessel of Guayaquil, told us; but the greatest part of it was full of timber. We took out of her also some osenbriggs, of which we made top-gallant sails, as shall be said hereafter. It was now nineteen days, as they told us, since they had set sail from Guayaquil; and then they had only heard there of our exploits before Panama, but did not so much as think of our coming so far to the southward, which did not give them the least suspicion of us, though they had seen us for the space of two or three days before at sea, and always steering after them; otherwise they had made for the land, and endeavored to escape our hands.

Next morning, likewise, we continued to take in the remaining part of what goods we desired out of our prize. When we had done, we sent most of our prisoners on board the said vessel, and left only their foremast standing, all the rest being cut down by the board. We gave them a foresail to sail withal, all their own water, and some of our flour to serve them for provision; and thus we turned them away, as not caring to be troubled or encumbered with their company. Notwithstanding we detained still several of the chief of our prisoners. Such were Don Thomas de Argandona, who was commander of the vessel taken before Guayaquil; Don Christoval and Don Baltazar, both gentlemen of quality taken with him; Captain Peralta, Captain Juan Moreno, the pilot, and twelve slaves, of whom we intended to make good use, to do the drudgery of our ship. At this time I reckoned we were about the distance of thirty-five leagues, or thereabouts, from land. By an observation made this day, we found latitude 7° 1′ S. Our plunder being over, and our prize turned away, we sold both chests, boxes, and several other things at the mast, by the voice of a crier.

The day following we stood S. S. W. and S. W. by S. all day long. This day one of our company died, named Robert Montgomery, being the same man that was shot by the negligence of one or two of our men with a pistol through the leg, at the taking of the vessel before Guayaquil, as was mentioned above. We had an observation also this day, by which we now found latitude 7° 26′ S. On the same day, likewise, we made a dividend, and shared all the booty taken in the last prize. This being done, we hoisted into our ship the launch which we had taken in her, as being useful to us. For several days past it was observed that we had every morning a dark cloud in the sky, which in the North Sea would certainly foretell a storm; but here it always blew over.

Wednesday, September 8th, in the morning, we drew our dead man above mentioned into the sea, and gave him three French volleys for his funeral ceremony. The night before we saw a light belonging to some vessel at sea. But we stood away from it, as not desiring to see any more sails to hinder us in our voyage towards Arica, whither now we were designed. This light was undoubtedly from some ship to leeward of us; but next morning we saw it not. Here I judged we had made a S. W. by S. way from Paita, and by an observation found 8° 0′ S.

CHAPTER XXXVII.

A Continuation of their long and tedious Voyage to Arica, with a Description of the Sailings thereunto. — Great Hardship for want of Water and other Provisions. — They are descried at Arica, and dare not land, the Country being all in Arms before them. — They retire from thence, and go to Puerto de Hilo, close by Arica. — Here they land, take the Town with little or no Loss on their Side, refresh themselves with Provisions; but in the End are cheated by the Spaniards, and forced shamefully to retreat from thence.

SEPTEMBER 9th, we continued still to make a S. W. by S. way, as we had done the day before. By a clear and exact observation taken the same day, we found now latitude 8° 12′ S. All the twenty-four hours last past afforded us but little on our voyage, and we were forced to tack about four or five hours.

Next day, by another observation taken, we found then latitude 9° 0′. Now the weather was much warmer than before; and with this warmth we had small and misty rains that frequently fell. That evening a strong breeze came up at south-east by east.

The night following, likewise, there fell a very great dew, and a fresh wind continued to blow. At this time we were all hard at work to make small sails of the ozenbrigs we had taken in the last prize, as being much more convenient for its lightness. The next morning, being Saturday, September 11th, we lay by to mend our rigging. These last twenty-four hours we had made a S. W. by W. way. And now we had an observation that gave us latitude 10° 9′ S. I supposed this day that we were west from Cosmey about the distance of eighty-nine leagues and a half.

September 12th. This day we reckoned a S. S. W. way, and that we had made thirty-four leagues and three quarters or thereabouts. Also that all our westing from Paita was eighty-four leagues. We supposed ourselves now to be in latitude 11° 40′ S. But the weather being hazy, no observation could be made.

September 13th. Yesterday, in the afternoon, we had a great eclipse of the sun, which lasted from one of the clock till three after dinner. From this eclipse I then took the true judgment of our longitude from the Canary Islands, and found myself to be 285° 35′; latitude 11° 45′ S. The wind was now so fresh that we took in our topsails, making a great way under our courses and spritsail.

September 14th, we had a cloudy morning, which continued

20

so all the first part thereof. About eight it cleared up, and then we set our fore-topsail; and, about noon, our main-topsail likewise. This was observable, that all this great wind precedent did not make any thing of a great sea. We reckoned this day that we had run by a S. W. by W. way twenty-six leagues and two thirds.

The next day we had close weather, as we had the morning before. Our reckoning was twenty-four leagues and two thirds by a S. W. by W. way. But by observation made, I found myself to be 23° south of my reckoning, as being in the latitude of 15° 17′ S.

On the 16th, we had but small and variable winds. For the twenty-four hours last past we reckoned twenty-four leagues and two thirds by a S. W. by S. way. By observation we had latitude 16° 41′. That evening we had a gale at E. S. E., which forced us to hand our topsails.

The 17th, likewise, we had many gusts of wind at several times, forcing us to hand our topsails often. But in the forenoon we set them, with a fresh gale at E. S. E. My reckoning this day was thirty-one leagues by a S. S. W. way. All day long we stood by our topsails.

The 18th, we made a S. by W. way. We reckoned ourselves to be in latitude 19° 32′ S. The weather was hazy, and the wind began to cease by degrees.

Next day, being the 19th, we had a very small wind. I reckoned thirteen leagues and a half by a S. W. by S. way; and our whole westing from Paita to be one hundred and sixty-four leagues in latitude 20° 6′ S. All the afternoon we had a calm, with drizzling rain.

Monday, September 20th. Last night we saw the Magellan clouds, so famous among mariners in the South seas. The least of these clouds was about the bigness of a man's hat. After this sight, the morning was very clear. We had run at noon at E. S. E. thirteen leagues and a half. And, by an observation then made, we found latitude 20° 15′ S. This day the wind began to freshen at W. by S., yet we had a very smooth sea.

Next morning the wind came about to S. W., yet slackened by degrees. At four this morning it came to S. by E., and at ten the same day to S. E. by S. We had this day a clear observation, and by it latitude 20° 25′ S. We stood now E. by N., with the wind at S. E.

September 22d. This morning the wind was at E. S. E. By a clear observation we found latitude 19° 30′ S., likewise on a N. E. by E. way, and two leagues and two thirds.

September 23d, we had a fresh wind, and a high sea. This morning early, the wind was at E., and about ten at E. N. E. From a clear observation we found our latitude to be 20° 25′ S. The way we made was S. by W. That morning we happened to split our spritsail.

Next morning the wind was variable and inconstant, and the weather but hazy. We reckoned a S. by E. way. This day we bent a new main-topsail, the old one serving for a fore-topsail. In the afternoon we had but little wind, whereupon we lowered our main-topsails, being a very smooth sea.

The following day being likewise calm and warm, we set up our shrouds both fore and aft. An observation taken this day afforded us latitude 21° 57′. That evening we bent a spritsail.

September 26th. An observation gave us latitude 22° 5′ S. At noon we had a breeze at N. N. E., our course being E. S. E. In the afternoon we set up a larboard topsail studden-sail. In the evening the wind came about at north pretty fresh.

Next day we had a smooth sea, and took in four studden-sails. For the day before, in the afternoon, we had put out, besides that above mentioned, another studden-sail, and two main studden-sails more. This day we had by observation 22° 45′ S, having made, by an E. S. E. way, thirty-five leagues and a half. Our whole meridian difference was sixty-eight leagues and a half.

September 28th, all the forenoon we had very little wind, and yet withal a great southern sea. By observation we had latitude 22° 40′ S.

September 29th. All the night past we had much wind, with three or four smart showers of rain. This was the first that we could call rain, ever since we left Cape Francisco above mentioned. This day our allowance was shortened, and reduced to three pints and a half of water for a day, and one cake of boiled bread to each man for a day. An observation this day gave us latitude 21° 59′ S. by a N. E. by E. way.

September 30th. We had a cloudy day, and the wind very variable, the morning being fresh. Our way was N. E. half N., wherein we made eighteen leagues.

October 1st. All the night past and this day, we had a cloudy sky, and not much wind. We made a N. E. by E. way, and by it seventeen leagues and two miles. This day we began at two pints and a half of water for a day.

October 2d. We made an E. N. E. way, and by it twenty-six leagues or thereabouts. Our observation this day gave us latitude 20° 29′ S. I reckoned now that we were ten leagues and a half to east of our meridian, the port of Paita; so that henceforward our departure was eastward. The wind was this day at S. E. by S.

October 3d, we had both a cloudy morning, a high sea, and drizzling weather. An observation which we had this day, gave us latitude 19° 45′ S. In the afternoon the wind blew so fresh, that we were forced to hand our topsails and spritsails.

October 4th, likewise, we had a high sea, and cold wind. At break of day, we set our topsails. An observation made, afforded us latitude 19° 45′ S. Here we supposed ourselves fifty-nine leagues D. M.

October 5th, we had still a great sea, and sharp and cold winds, forcing us to our low sails. By a N. E. by E. way, we reckoned this day twenty six leagues and a half.

But on the 6th, we had great gusts of wind; insomuch that this morning our ring-bolts gave way, which held our main stay, and had like to have brought our mainmast by the board. Hereupon we ran three or four glasses west before the wind. By an observation we found latitude 19° 4′ S.

October 7th, the wind was something fallen. We had both a cloudy day and variable winds.

The 8th of the said month we had again a smooth sea, and small whiffling winds. This morning we saw a huge shoal of fish, two or three water-snakes, and several seals.

Next day we had likewise a very smooth sea, and a cloudy day. Our course was east.

October 10th, we had also a cloudy day, with small and variable winds, and, as a consequent thereof, a smooth sea. Our way was S. by E. This day we spied floating upon the sea several tufts of sea-grass, which gave us good hopes that we were not far from shore. In the afternoon we had a S. E. by E. wind that sprang up: the night was very cold and cloudy.

October 11th, we had a fresh wind at S. E. and E. S. E., together with a cloudy day, such as we had experimented for several days before. We reckoned this day thirty-two leagues, by a N. E. by E. way. Our pilot told us, the sky is always hazy near the shore on these coasts.

October 12th, we had a clear day, and a north-east way.

October 13th, we had but little wind. This day we saw a whale, which we took for an infallible token that we were not far distant from land, which now we hoped to see in a few days. We made an E. S. E. way, and by it we reckoned nineteen leagues. All the evening was very calm.

Thursday, October 14th, we had both a calm and close day till afternoon; then the weather became very hot and clear.

This day we saw several land-fowls, being but small birds; concerning which our pilot said, that they used to appear about one or two days' sail from the land. Our reckoning was eleven leagues by an E. S. E. way. In the evening we thought we had seen land, but it proved to be nothing but a foggy bank.

October 15th. Both the night past, and this day, was very clear. We made an observation this day, which gave us latitude 18° 0′ south.

October 16th. Last night and this day were contrary to the former, both cloudy. Our way was N. E. by E.; whereof we reckoned thirteen leagues.

Sunday, October 17th, the wind blew very fresh, our course being E. N. E. About five that morning we saw land; but the weather was so hazy, that at first we could scarce perceive whether it was land or not. It was distant from us eight leagues, and appeared as a high and round hill, being in form like a sugar-loaf. We saw land afterwards all along to the S. E. by E. from it. In the evening, we being then within five leagues of the shore, the land appeared very high and steep.

October 18th. All the night last past we stood off to sea with a fresh wind. This morning we could just see land at N. N. E. We reckoned a S. E. by E. way; and by observation we found latitude 17° 17′ south.

Tuesday, October 19th, we had very cloudy weather, finding what our pilot had told us to be very true, concerning the haziness of this shore. We saw all along as we went very high land, covered with clouds, insomuch that we could not see its top.

Wednesday, October 20th, we had likewise cloudy weather, and for the most part calm, which continued so the next day.

Friday, October 22d. This morning we saw land before us. Our pilot being asked what land that was, answered, it was the Point of Hilo.

There is every morning and evening a brightness over the point, which lasts for two or three hours, being caused by the reflection of the sun on the barren land, as is supposed. This day we had but little wind, and the great want of water we were now under occasioned much disturbance among our men. As for my part, I must acknowledge, I could not sleep all night long through the greatness of my drought. We could willingly have landed here to seek for water, but the fear of being discovered, and making ourselves known, hindered us from so doing. Thus we unanimously resolved to endure our thirst a little longer. Hereabouts is a small current that runs under the shore. This morning we had but little wind at south, our course being E. S. E.

Our wind continued to blow not above six hours each day. We reckoned the difference of our meridian to be this day one hundred and eighty leagues. We were now hard put to it for want of water, having but half a pint a day to our allowance.

October 23d. This day we were forced to spare one measure of water, thereby to make it hold out the longer; so scarce it became with us.

About nine o'clock at night we had a land wind, and with it we stood S. E. by S. But all the night after we had but little wind.

October 24th. All the night past we had very cloudy and dark weather, with mizzling rain. The morning being come, cleared up; but all the land appeared covered with clouds.

This day we resolved 112 men should go ashore. And about eight this evening we sent our launch and four canoes, with 89 men, to take three or four fishermen at a certain river, close by Mora de Sama, called El Rio de Juan Diaz, with intent to gain what intelligence we could, how affairs stood at present on the coast and country thereabouts.

Monday, October 25th. Last night being about the distance of one league and a half from the shore, we sounded, and found forty-five fathom water, with hard ground at the bottom. This morning our people and canoes that were sent to take the fishermen returned, not being able to find either their houses or the river. They reported withal, they had had a very fresh wind all the night long under shore, whereas we had not one breath of wind all night on board.

Tuesday, October 26th. The evening before, about six o'clock, we left the ship to go to take Arica, resolved to land about the difference of a league to windward of the town. We were about six leagues from the town when we left the ship, whereby we were forced to row all night, that we might reach before day the place of our landing. Towards morning, the canoes left the launch, which they had all night in a tow, and wherein I was, and made all the speed they possibly could for the shore, with design to land before the launch could arrive. But being come near the place we designed to land at, we found, to our great disappointment, we were discovered; and that, all along the shore, and through the country, they had certain news of our arrival. Notwithstanding we would have landed, if we could by any means have found a place to do it in. But the sea ran so high, and with such a force against the rocks, that our boats must needs have been staved in a thousand pieces, and we in great danger of wetting our arms, if we should venture ashore. The bay all around was possessed by several par-

ties of horse, and likewise the tops of the hills; which seemed to be gathered there, by a general alarm, through the whole country, and that they waited only for our landing, with a design to make a strong opposition against us. They fired a gun at us, but we made them no answer, returning to our ship, till a fairer opportunity. The hill of Arica is very white, occasioned by the dung of the abundance of fowls that build their nests in the hollow thereof. To leeward of the said hill lies a small island, at about a mile from the shore. About half a league from that island, we could perceive six ships at anchor; four of which had their yards taken down from their masts, but the other two seemed ready to sail. We asked our pilot concerning these ships, and he told us, that one of them was mounted with six guns, and the other with only four. Being disappointed of our expectations at Arica, we now resolved to bear away from thence to the village of Hilo, there to take in water and other provisions, as also to learn what intelligence we could obtain. All that night we lay under a calm.

October 27, in the morning, we found ourselves about a league to windward of Mora da Sama. Notwithstanding the weather was quite calm, and we only drove with the current at leeward. The land between Hilo and Mora da Sama forms two several bays, and the coast runs along N. W. and S. E., as may appear by the following demonstration. Over the land we could see from our ship, as we drove, the coming or rising of a very high land, at a great distance far up in the country.

October 28. The night before we sent away our four canoes with fifty men in them, to seize and plunder the town of Hilo. All this day was very calm, as the day before.

The next morning, about break of day, we had a fair breeze spring up, with which we lay right in with the port. About one in the afternoon we anchored.

We cast anchor at the distance of two miles from the village: and then we perceived two flags, which our men had put out, having taken the town, and set up our English colors. The Spaniards were retreated to the hills, and there had done the same. Being come to an anchor, our commander, Captain Sharp, sent a canoe on board of us, and ordered that all the men our ship could spare should come ashore. Withal they told us, that those of our party that landed the morning before, were met by some horsemen on the shore, who only exchanged some few volleys of shot with our men, but were soon put to flight. That hereupon our forces had marched directly to the town, where the Spaniards, expecting we should have landed at first, made a breastwork thirty paces long, of clay and banks of sand. Here, in a small skirmish, we happened to kill an Indian, who told us before he died, that they had received news of our coming nine days ago, from Lima, and but one day before from Arica. Having taken the town, we found therein great quantity of pitch, tar, oil, wine, and flour, with several other sorts of provisions. We endeavored to keep as good a watch as the Spaniards did on the hills, fearing lest they should suddenly make any attempt to destroy us.

Next day, being October 30, we chose out threescore of our men who were fittest to march, and ordered them to go up and search the the valley belonging to the town. We found it very pleasant, being all overset with fig-trees, olive-trees, orange, lemon, and lime-trees, with many other agreeable fruits. About four miles up the valley we came to a sugar work, or *Ingenio de azucar*, as it is called by the Spaniards, where we found great store of oil and molasses; but most of the sugar the owners had hidden from us in the cane itself. As we marched up the valley, the Spaniards marched along the hills, and observed our motion. From the tops of the hills, they often tumbled great stones upon us, but with great care we endeavored to escape those dangers, and the report of one gun would make them all to hide their heads immediately. From this house, I mean the sugar work above mentioned, Mr. Cox, myself, and one Cannis, a Dutchman, (who was our interpreter,) went to the Spaniards with a flag of truce. They met us very civilly, and promised to give us fourscore beeves for the ransom of the sugar-work, upon condition that it should not be spoiled nor demolished. With them we agreed, that they should be delivered to us at the port, the next day at noon: hereupon Captain Sharp in the evening sent down to the port twenty men, with strict orders that our forces should offer no violence, in the least, to those that brought down the beeves.

Sunday, October 31. This day, being employed in casting up some accounts belonging to our navigation, I reckoned that Hilo was the eastward of Paita, one hundred and eighty-seven leagues. This morning the captain of the Spaniards came to our commander, Captain Sharp, with a flag of truce, and told him that sixteen beeves were already sent down to the port, and that the rest should certainly be there the next morning. Hereupon we were ordered to prepare ourselves to retreat, and march back to the port, and there embark ourselves on board our ship. My advice was to the contrary, that we should rather leave twenty men behind to keep the house of the sugar-work, and that others should possess themselves of the hills, thereby to clear them of the Spaniards and their lookout. But my counsel not being regarded, each man took away what burden of sugar he pleased, and thus we returned to our vessel. Being come there, we found no beeves had been brought down at all, which made us suspect some trick of the enemy.

The next morning, being November 1, our Captain went to the top of the hills before mentioned, and spoke with the Spaniards themselves, concerning the performance of their agreement. The Spaniards made answer, that the cattle would certainly come down this night; but in case they did not, that the master or owner of the sugar-work was now returned from Potosi, and we might go up and treat with him, and make, if we pleased, a new bargain for the preservation of his house and goods; whose interest it was, more than theirs, to save it from being demolished. With this answer our men returned, and we concluded to wait till the next day for the delivery of the beeves.

The day following, about eight in the morning, there came into us a flag of truce from the enemy, telling us, that the winds were so high, that they could not drive the cattle, otherwise they had been delivered before now. But withal, that by noon we should in no manner fail to have them brought to us. Noon being come, and no cattle appearing, we now having filled our water, and finished other concerns, resolved to be revenged on the enemy, and do them what mischief we could; at least, by setting fire on the sugar-work. Hereupon, threescore men of us marched up the valley, and burnt both the house, the canes, and the mill, belonging to the *Ingenio*. We broke likewise the coppers, coggs, and multitudes of great jars of oil, that we found in the house. This being done, we brought away more sugar, and returned to the port over the hills and mountains, the which we found very pleasant, smooth, and level, after once we had ascended them. It fell out very fortunately to us that we returned back the way we did, for otherwise our men at the sea-side had inevitably been cut off, and torn in pieces by the enemy, they being at that time dispersed, and straggling up and down by two and three in a party. For from the hills we spied coming from the northward of the bay above three hundred horsemen, all riding at full speed towards our men, who had not as yet descried them, and little thought of any such danger from the enemy so nigh at hand. Being alarmed with this sight, we threw down what sugar we had, and ran incontinently to meet them, thereby to give our other men time to rally, and put themselves into a posture of defence. We being in good rank and order, fairly proffered them battle upon the bay; but as we advanced to meet them, they retired and rode towards the mountains to surround us, and take the rocks from us if possibly they could. Hereupon, perceiving their intentions, we returned back and possessed ourselves of the said rocks, and also of the lower town; as the Spaniards themselves did of the upper town, (at the distance of half a mile from the lower,) the hills and the woods adjoining thereunto. The horsemen being now in possession of these quarters, we could perceive, as far as we could see, more and more men resort to them, so that their forces increased hourly to considerable numbers. We fired one at another as long as we could reach, and the day would permit. But in the mean while we observed that several of them rode to the watch-hill, and looked out often to the seaboard. This gave us occasion to fear that they had more strength and forces coming that way, which they expected every minute. Hereupon, lest we should speed worse than we had done before, we resolved to embark silently in the dark of the night, and go off from that coast where the enemy was so well provided for us. We carried off a great chest of sugar, whereof we shared seven pound weight and a half each man, thirty jars of oil, and great plenty of all sorts of garden herbs, roots, and most excellent fruit.

CHAPTER XXXVIII.

The Buccaneers depart from the Port of Hilo, and sail to that of Coquimbo. — They are descried before their Arrival; notwithstanding, they land. — Are encountered by the Spaniards, and put them to Flight. — They take, plunder, and fire the City of La Sarena. — A Description thereof. — A Stratagem of the Spaniards in endeavoring to fire their Ship discovered and prevented. — They are deceived again by the Spaniards, and forced to retire from Coquimbo, without any Ransom for the City, or considerable Pillage. — They release several of their chiefest Prisoners.

THE next morning, being Wednesday, November 3, 1680, about seven o'clock, we set sail from Hilo, standing directly off to sea, with a small land wind. Upon the shore we could not discover this morning above fifty men of our enemies' forces, which caused us to suspect the rest were run away from their colors, and had deserted in the dark of the night. If this were so, we were equally afraid of each other; and as we quitted the land being jealous of their multitudes, so they abandoned their stations for fear of our encounters. All the while we lay in the port of Hilo we had a fresh wind; but being come out thence, we found it almost stark calm. All along this coast runs a great sea, as we experimented at Arica, insomuch that there is no landing, except under the favor of some rock or other.

November 4th, in the morning, we saw the port of Hilo at E. N. E., at the distance of nine leagues, or thereabouts, from land. The white sand gives a bright reflection over the land, which we could see after we had lost the sight of the land itself.

The day following we had an indifferent fresh wind at S. S. E. We reckoned a S. W. half W. way, and by it, that we had made twenty leagues. The day was very fair and sunshiny, and the sea very smooth.

November 6th. We had a clear night the last past, and the day proved very fair and clear, like the former; we reckoned by a S. W. by W. way about twenty-one leagues. In the afternoon it was almost quite calm.

The day following we had no more than the last twenty-four hours. We were about this time many of us troubled with the scurvy. It proceeded, as we judged, from the great hardship and want of provisions, which we had endured for several months past, as having only bread and water, as was mentioned above—only at Hilo we killed a mule, which was looked upon by those that eat of it to be very good victuals, the Spaniards having swept away with them all other provisions of flesh. But we got there, as plunder, a small quantity of good chocolate, which the Spaniards have in great esteem; so now we had each morning a dish of pleasant liquor, containing almost a pint.

Next day, likewise, we had very little wind as before. We made an observation this day, and found latitude 20° 5′ S.

November 9th. We had still very little wind, and that variable. We took almost every hour an observation, and found ourselves to be in latitude 20° 18′ S.

November 10th, we had in like manner but little wind. We observed an E. S. E. current, or pretty near it, run hereabouts. This day we saw the homing of a very high land, which much surprised us, for at this time I conceived we could not be less than thirty-five or forty leagues from land. We supposed it to be Mora Tarapaca. That day we set up our shrouds.

Upon the 11th, an indifferent gale of wind sprang up at S. W. by S., by which we made twenty-five leagues and one third. We had now a great S. S. W. sea. In the night the wind, as we experimented, came one or two points from the land. This morning we saw the like homing of land, whereby we were made sensible it was no land we had seen the day before.

On the 12th, we had several mists of rain, with windy weather. We made by a S. S. W. half S. way twenty-five leagues and one third. We had likewise a great and rolling S. S. W. sea, as the day before.

November 13th, we had both cloudy and misty weather. We made a S. S. W. and one quarter S. way, by which we ran fifty leagues.

But the next day, fair and clear weather came about again. We had likewise an easy gale of wind, by which we made a S. W. way, and advanced twenty-two leagues and a half.

On the 15th of November we had also clear weather, and an indifferent gale of wind. Our way was S. W. by W., by which we reckoned eighteen leagues; likewise at our westing from Hilo, from whence we set forth, was one hundred and fourteen leagues and one third. Our latitude, by observation, we found to be 23° 25′ S. I took now the declination table used and made by the cosmographer at Lima.

Tuesday, November 16th. In the night last past we had a shower or two of rain. This day we made an observation, by which we found latitude 23° 35′ S.

November 17th, we made a S. W. by W. half S. way. By observation we found latitude 23° 46′ S., with very little wind.

November 18th, upon a S. W. by W. way we made twenty-one leagues. By observation we found latitude 23° 20′ S.

Friday, November 19th, 1680. This morning, about an hour before day, we observed a comet to appear a degree north from the bright star in Libra. The body thereof seemed dull, and its tail extended itself eighteen or twenty degrees in length, being of a pale color, and pointing directly N. N. W. Our prisoners hereupon told us that the Spaniards had seen very strange sights both at Lima, the capital city of Peru, Guayaquil, and other places much about the time of our coming into the South seas. I reckon this day we had run twenty leagues by a S. W. way.

The day following the appearance of the comet, we had many storms of wind at S. S. E. and E. S. E. Our reckoning by a S. W. way was twenty-two leagues.

Sunday, November 21st, likewise many gusts of wind, such as the day before, with frequent showers of rain. The wind varied to and fro, according as the clouds drew it here and there. We reckoned a S. S. W. way, and by it twenty-one leagues and a half. In all, west from Hilo, we judged ourselves to be one hundred and seventy-eight leagues and two thirds. We had this day a great S. W. sea, and cloudy weather. I supposed our latitude to be 26° 53′ S.

November 22d, we had in like manner cloudy weather, and now but little wind. We reckoned a south way, and fifty-one leagues.

November 23d, we had very little wind; and all storm, after the appearance of the comet, being now quite allayed, we reckoned we had made a S. E. by S. way, and found our latitude, by observation, to bear 27° 46′ S.

Wednesday, November 24th. For twenty-four hours past we had a N. W. wind. Our way was S. E. half S., by which we reckoned thirty-one leagues and one third.

November 25th. Last night the wind blew at W. S. W.; but this morning it came about again at N. W., as the day before. Our reckoning this day was a S. E. and one quarter E. way twenty-nine leagues and one third. Our latitude now, by observation, made this day, was 39° 57′ S. Our difference of meridian, one hundred and thirty-five and one third.

November 26th. In the night the wind started to S. S. W. But this day at noon we had little better than a calm. I reckoned an E. S. E. half E. way, and by it twenty-three leagues.

Saturday, November 27th. Yesterday, in the evening, the wind came to south. I reckoned an east and something southerly way, and by that twenty-three leagues, as the day before.

November 28th. For twenty-four hours past we had a fresh wind at S. S. E., having a high S. W. sea. Our reckoning was an E. by N. and half N. way, and withal twenty-four leagues. By observation we found latitude 30° 16′ S., and meridian distance eighty-eight leagues. At noon the wind came at S. half E.

On the 29th we had a very great S. W. sea, and withal cloudy weather. My reckoning was an E. one third S. way twenty leagues and one third. This day we happened to see two or three great fowls flying in the air, which our pilot told us used to appear seventy or eighty leagues off from the island called the Island of Juan Fernandez. The day before this, Captain Peralta, our prisoner, was taken very frantic, his distemper being occasioned, as we thought, through too much hardship and melancholy. Notwithstanding, this day he was indifferently well again.

The following day we had likewise cloudy weather. We made, according to our account, an E. half N. way, and by it sixteen leagues and two thirds. Our meridian difference fifty-two leagues.

The 1st of December we had hazy weather, and withal an indifferent good wind at S., yea, sometimes S. by W. Our way was E. by S., by which we reckoned twenty-two leagues. The night before, we sailed over white water-like banks, of a mile in length, or more. But these banks, upon examination, we found to be only great shoals of anchovies.

December 2d, very early in the morning, we spied land, which appeared to be very high. About noon this day we were at six leagues distance from it. All the preceding night we had so much wind, that we were forced to make use of a pair of courses. By an observation made this day, we found latitude 30° 35′ S. We went away largely, driving better than nine leagues every watch. With this wind we made all the sail we possibly could, designing by this means to get to Coquimbo, upon which coast we now were, before night. But the wind was so high, that sometimes we were forced to lower all our sails, it blowing now a mere fret of wind. Towards evening it abated by degrees, insomuch, that at midnight it was quite calm again. Then we hoisted out our launch and canoes, and putting into them one hundred men, we rowed away from the ship, with design to take by surprisal a considerable city near the coast, called by the Spaniards, *La Cividad de la Serena.*

Friday, December 3d, 1680. When we departed from the ship, we had about two leagues to row to the shore. But as it happened, the launch wherein I was rowed so heavy, in comparison of the canoes, that we could not keep pace with them. For this reason it was broad day before we got to a certain storehouse situated upon the shore ; our men having passed by it in the dark of the night without perceiving it. They being landed, immediately marched away from their canoes, towards the city before mentioned of La Serena. But we had not proceeded far on our march, when we found, to the great sorrow and chagrin of us all, that we were timely discovered here also, as we had been at the other two places before, Arica and Hilo. For as they marched in a body together, being but thirty-five men in all, who were all those that were landed out of the canoes, they were suddenly encountered and engaged by a whole troop of a hundred Spanish horse. We that were behind, hearing the noise of the dispute, followed them at their heels, and made all the haste we possibly could, to come up to their relief. But before we could reach the place of the battle, they had already routed the Spaniards, and forced them to fly towards the town.

Notwithstanding this rout, they rallied again, at the distance of about a mile from the place, and seemed as if they waited for us, and would engage us anew. But as soon as all our forces were come together, which were in all eighty-four, the rest being left to guard the boats, we marched towards them and offered them battle. As we came near unto them, we found plainly they designed no such thing ; for they instantly retired and rode away before us, keeping out of the reach of our guns. We followed them as they rode, being led by them designedly, clear out of the road that went to the town, that we might not reach nor find it so soon. In this engagement with the horse, our company had killed three of their chiefest men, and wounded four more, killing also four of their horses. When we found that we had been led by this stratagem of the enemy out of the way of the town, we left the bay, and crossed over the green fields to find it, wading oftentimes over several branches of water, which there serve to enclose each plat of ground. Upon this march we came to several houses, but found them all empty, and swept clean both of inhabitants and provisions. We saw likewise several horses and other heads of cattle in the fields, as we went along towards the city. This place of La Serena, our pilot had reported to us to be but a small town ; but being arrived there, we found in it no fewer than seven great churches and one chapel. Four of these churches were monasteries or convents, and each church had its organs for the performance of divine service. Several of the houses had their orchards of fruit, and gardens belonging to them ; both houses and gardens being as well and as neatly furnished as those in England. In these gardens we found strawberries as big as walnuts, and those very delicious to the taste. In a word, every thing in this city of La Serena was most excellent and delicate, and far beyond what we could expect in so remote a place. The town was inhabited by all sorts of tradesmen, and besides them, had its merchants, some of which were accounted very rich.

The inhabitants of La Serena, upon our approach, fled, carrying with them the best of their goods and jewels ; and what they could not carry away that was of value, they buried, having had time enough to do so, from the advice they received of our coming from Arica and other places. Notwithstanding, we took in the town one friar, and two Chilenos, or Spaniards, natives of the kingdom of Chili, which adjoins to that of Peru, towards the Straits of Magellan. These prisoners told us, that the Spaniards, when they heard of our coming, had killed most of their Chilian slaves, fearing they should revolt from them to us. Moreover, that we had been descried from their coasts four days before our landing ; all which time they had employed in carrying away their plate and goods. To this information they added, that for their defence they had received a supply of sixty men from Arica. Having taken possession of the town, that evening there came a negro to us, running away from the Spaniards. He informed us, that when we were before Panama, we had taken a negro, who was esteemed the best pilot in all the South Sea; but more especially for this place, and the coasts of Coquimbo. And further, that if the Spaniards had not sent all the negroes belonging to this city farther up into the country, out of our reach and communication, they would all undoubtedly have revolted to us.

That night, about twelve, our boatswain, accompanied by forty men, with a Chilian for their guide, went out of the town some miles into the country, with design to find out the places where the Spaniards lay concealed, and had hid their goods and plate. But before they came, the Spaniards had got intelligence thereof from some secret spies they had in the town, and both the men and their women were all fled to places that were more occult and remote. So that, by this search, they only found an old Indian woman and three children, but no gold nor plate. This morning our ship came to an anchor by the storehouse above mentioned, named Tortuga, at the distance of a furlong from shore, in the depth of seven fathom water.

Next morning, being Saturday, December 4th, came into the town a flag of truce from the enemy. Their message was to proffer a ransom for the town, to preserve it from burning; for now they began to fear we would set fire to it, as having found no considerable booty nor pillage therein. The chief commanders on both sides met about this point, and agreed betwixt them for the sum of ninety-five thousand pieces of eight, for the whole ransom. In the afternoon I was sent down to the Bay of Coquimbo, with a party of twenty men, to carry thither some goods we had taken in the town, as also provisions for the ship. It is two leagues and a half from the town to the port; one league on the bay, the rest being a very great road, which leads from the bay to the city. The Spaniards promised that the ransom should be collected and paid in by the next day. This day also there died one of our negro slaves, on board the ship.

The day following, in the morning, I came back to the town, with the men I had brought down the day before; only six of them I left behind, to look after our canoes at the end of the bay. When I came to the city, I found that the Spaniards had broken their promise, and had not brought in the ransom they had agreed for; but had begged time till to-morrow at eight in the forenoon. This evening, another party of our men went down to the ship to carry such goods as we had pillaged in the town. That night, about nine of the clock, happened an earthquake, the which we were very sensible of, as we were all together in the church of San Juan, where our chief rendezvous and *corps de garde* was kept. In the night the Spaniards opened a sluice, and let the water run in streams about the town, with intent either to overflow it, and thereby force us out of the place, or at least that they might the easier quench the flame, in case we should fire the town.

Next morning we set fire to the town, perceiving it to be overflown, and that the Spaniards had not performed, or rather, that they never designed to perform, their promise. We fired, as nigh as we could, every house in the whole town, to the end that it might be totally reduced to ashes. Thus we left La Serena, carrying with us what plunder we could find, having sent two parties before, loaded with goods to the ship, as was mentioned above. As we marched down to the bay, we beat up an ambuscade of two hundred and fifty horse, which lay hid in the way, with an intent to fall on our men, in case we had sent down any other party with goods to the ship. We received advice that the Spaniards had endeavored, by an unusual stratagem, to burn our ship, and thereby destroy us all. They blew up a horse's hide like a bladder, and upon this float a man ventured to swim from shore, and come under the stern of our ship. Being arrived there, he crammed oakum and brimstone, and other combustible matter, between the rudder and the sternpost. Having done this, he fired it with a match, so that in a small time our rudder was on fire, and all the ship in a smoke. Our men, both alarmed and amazed with this smoke, ran up and down the ship, suspecting the prisoners to have fired the vessel, thereby to get their liberty and destroy us. At last they found out where the fire was, and had the good fortune to quench it before its going too far. As soon as they had put it out, they sent the boat ashore, and found both the hide before mentioned, and the match burning at both ends, whereby they discovered the whole matter. When we came to the storehouse on the shore side, we set at liberty the friar our prisoner, and another gentleman, who was become our hostage for the performance of the ransom. And when we came aboard, we likewise set at liberty Captain Peralta, Don Thomas de Argandona, Don Baltazar, Don Christeval, Captain Juan, the pilot's mate, the old Moor, and several other of our chief prisoners. To this releasement of our prisoners we were moved, partly because we knew not well what to do with them, and partly because we feared that, by the example of this stratagem, they might be able to effect what the other had attempted with so much likelihood of success.

CHAPTER XXXIX.

The Buccaneers set sail from Coquimbo for the Isle of Juan Fernandez. — An exact Account of this Voyage. — Misery they endure, and great Dangers they escape there. — They mutiny among themselves, and choose Watling to be their chief Commander. — Description of the Island. — Three Spanish Men-of-War meet with the Buccaneers at the said Island: with what happened thereupon.

Being all embarked again, as was mentioned in the precedent chapter, the next morning, which was Tuesday, December 7th, twenty of us were sent ashore to observe the motions of the enemy. We went to the lookout, or watch-hill, but could learn nothing from thence. Hereupon, about noon we returned on board the ship, and at two in the afternoon we weighed anchor and set sail, directing our course for the Island of Juan Fernandez, not far from the coast of Coquimbo. At night, we were five leagues distant from thence, at N. W. by N. The southernmost island of those which are called *De los Paxaros*, or Islands of Birds, was then N. N. W. from us. Before our departure, I took a draught of the Bay of Coquimbo, and of the city of La Serena.

December 8th, we had but very little wind, and a leeward current here, which we could perceive heaved us to the northward. The afore-mentioned Island *De los Paxaros*, at three in the afternoon, bore N. E. of us, at the distance of three leagues, or thereabouts.

It is four leagues distant from the main continent, and from the next island of the same name, about two. The main is extremely high and mountainous hereabouts. At evening we were west from the said island five leagues. About eight or nine leagues to the windward of Coquimbo are certain white cliffs, which appear from the shore to those that are off at sea.

December 9th, we had likewise but little wind, as the day before. I supposed myself this day to be about thirteen leagues west from the island above mentioned. The weather was cloudy, with mizzling rain, so that no observation could be taken. However, this day it was thought convenient to come to an allowance of water, for we had taken in little or none at Coquimbo. The same weather, or very like it, we had the next day, being the 10th; that is to say, quite calm and cloudy.

December 11th, we had some small rain the fore part of the day; but in the afternoon it cleared up, so that the weather was very hot. We had still but little wind.

The next day, December 12th, we had very fair weather, and by a clear observation made this day, we found latitude 30° 6′ S.

December 13th. By a W. S. W. way, we made forty-two leagues. By observation, we found latitude 30° 45′ S. D. M. four leagues and two thirds.

The 14th, in the morning, we had a handsome shower of rain, which continued for some time. Then about eight o' clock there sprung up a S. S. W. breeze. My reckoning was by an E. S. E. way fourteen leagues; and, by observation, we found this day 30° 30′ S. In the afternoon died one of our men, whose name was William Cammock. His disease was occasioned by a surfeit, got by too much drinking on shore at La Serena, which produced a *calenture*, or malignant fever, and a hiccough. In the evening we buried him in the sea, according to the usual custom of mariners, giving him three French volleys for his funeral.

The day following we had an indifferent fresh wind on both tacks. Our way was W. S. W., and by it we reckoned thirty-four leagues. So, likewise, by an observation, we had latitude 30° 42′ S. All the afternoon blew a S. by W. wind, very fresh, with a short topping S. W. sea.

But the next day we had no small breezes, but rather hard gusts of wind. These grew so high, that they forced us to take in our topsails. We made a S. W. half S. way, and forty-five leagues.

On the 17th, we had likewise high winds, and withal a S. W. sea. Our way was W. by S. By an observation taken this day, we found latitude 30° 51′ S. In the afternoon we had a S. S. E. wind, our course being S. W.

December 18th. This day we had the same high winds as before, at S. S. E. We reckoned by a W. S. W. way forty-five leagues. At noon the wind was something fallen, and then we had some rain.

The 19th, we had both cloudy and windy weather. My reckoning was a S. W. by S. way, and hereupon fifty-eight miles. Yesterday we were assured by our pilot that we were now in the meridian of Juan Fernandez, whither our course was directed for the present. That which occasioned him to be so positive in this assertion, was the seeing of those great birds, of which we made mention in the foregoing chapter.

On the 20th, we had cloudy weather in the morning on both tacks. We made a S. W. and half S. way, and by it fifty-two leagues. By an observation, we found this day latitude 32° 30′ S. Difference of meridian was now one hundred and thirty-two leagues.

The next day, likewise, we had cloudy weather; yet, by an observation, we found a W. way. On the 22d, by observation, we found an E. way proved.

Thursday, December 23d. All the night past we had a fresh wind; but in the morning, from the topmast head, we descried a hammock of land. In the evening we saw it again. We found afterwards that what we had seen was the westernmost island of Juan Fernandez; which is nothing but a mere rock, there being no riding nor scarce landing near it.

Friday, December 24th. This morning we could descry the island itself of Juan Fernandez, S. by E., it being at sixteen leagues distance when we saw it the day before. At seven this morning, the island stood E., the wind being at N. W. by N.

Here my observation was, that I could neither fowl nor fish near this island; both which are usual about other islands. Having told my observation to our pilot, he answered me that he had made many voyages by this island, and yet never saw either fowl or fish. Our reckoning this day was an E. S. E. way, and hereby thirty-six leagues. Our latitude, by observation, was found to be 33° 30′ S.

Saturday, December 25th. The 24th, at three o'clock, we saw the other island, making two or three hammocks of land. This morning we were about eight leagues from it, the island bearing E. S. E. from us. At eight the same morning, we were right abreast with it. Here, therefore, are two islands together, the biggest whereof is three leagues and a half in length, nearest N. W. and S. E. The other, and lesser, is almost one league in circumference. At ten o'clock, we sent off from the ship one of our canoes to seek for the best landing and anchoring for our vessel. As we approached, both islands seemed to us but one entire heap of rocks. That which lies more to the north is the highest, though we could not see the tops thereof, for the clouds covered it; in most places it is so steep, that it becomes almost perpendicular.

This day, being Christmas day, we gave in the morning

early three volleys of shot, for solemnization of that great festival. I reckoned an E. by S. way. By a clear observation from the middle of the island, I found here latitude 33° 45′ S., and M. D. to be ninety-nine leagues. In the evening we came to an anchor at the south end of the island, in a stately bay, but which lies open to the south, and to the south-east winds. We anchored in the depth of eleven fathom water, and at the distance of only one furlong from the shore. Here we saw multitudes of seals, covering the bay every where, insomuch that we were forced to kill them before we could set foot on shore.

Sunday, December 26th. This day we sent a canoe to see if we could find any riding secure from the southerly winds, these being the most constant winds that blow on these coasts. The canoe being gone, our commander sent, likewise, what men we could spare on shore, to drive goats, whereof there is great plenty in this island. They caught and killed that day to the number of threescore, or thereabouts. The canoe returning to the ship, made report that there was good riding in another bay, situate on the north side of the island, in fourteen fathom water, and not above one quarter of a mile from the shore, and that there was much wood to be had; whereas, in the place where we first anchored, not one stick of wood, nor tuft of grass, was to be found.

The next day, being the 27th, between two and four in the morning, we had a tempest of violent winds, and fierce showers of rain. The same day we got in two hundred jars of water, bringing them a full league from the place of our riding. Meanwhile, others were employed to catch goats, as they had done the day before.

On the 28th of the said month, in the morning, I went with ten more of our company, and two canoes, to fetch water from the land. Being come thither, and having filled our jars, we could not get back to the ship, by reason of a southerly wind, that blew from off the ocean, and hindered our return. Thus we were forced to lie still in a water hole, and wait till the wind was over for a safer opportunity. While the violence of the wind increased, our ship was forced to get under sail, and make away, not without danger of being forced ashore. Hereupon, we sailed out of the harbor, to seek another place of anchoring. At noon I ventured out, to try if I could follow the ship, but was forced in again by the wind and raging sea. Thus we lay still for some while longer, till the evening came on. This being come, we ventured out again, both canoes together; but the winds were then so high, that we were forced to throw all our jars of water overboard to lighten our boats, otherwise we had inevitably perished. I ought to bless Almighty God for this deliverance; for, in all human reason, the least wave of that tempest might have sunk us. Notwithstanding, we came that night to our place of harbor, where we expected to have found our ship, (called False Wild Harbor,) but found her not. Hereupon, not knowing what to do, we went ashore, and hauled up our canoes dry. Having done this, we went higher up into the island, along a gully, for the space of half a mile, there to clear ourselves of the noise and company of the seals, which were very troublesome on the shore. Here we kindled a fire, and dried our clothes, and rested ourselves all night, though with extreme hungry bellies, as having eaten very little or nothing all the day before. In the sides of the hill, under which we lay, we observed many holes like coney-holes. These holes are the nests and roosting-places of multitudes of birds that breed in this island, called by the Spaniards *pardelas*. One of these birds, as we lay drying and warming ourselves, fell down into our fire.

The next morning being come, very early before sunrise we went farther to the northward, to seek for our ship, which we feared we had lost; but we were not gone far when we espied her at sea. Hereupon we passed a point of land, and entered a certain bay, which was about a mile deep, and not above half a league over. In this bay we put, and instantly made a fire, thereby to show the ship whereabouts we were. Here we found good watering and wooding close to the shore. In this bay we also saw another sort of amphibious animal, which I imagined to be the same that by some authors is called a sea lion. These animals are six times bigger than seals. Their heads are like that of a lion, and they have four fins not unlike a tortoise. The hinder parts of these creatures are much like fins, but are drawn after them, as being useless upon the shore. They roared as if they had been lions, and were full of a short, thick hair, of a mouse color; but that of the young ones was something lighter. The old ones are between twelve and fourteen feet long, and about eleven or twelve feet in thickness or circumference. A seal is very easily killed, as we often experimented; but two of our men with great stones could not kill one of these animals.

That day, in the afternoon, there came a canoe, from on board the ship, with provisions for us, they fearing lest we should be starved; also the launch came with men to cut wood. They told us that the ship came to an anchor in the other bay; but that within half an hour the cable broke and they were forced to leave their anchor behind them, and get out to sea again. Night being come, we made our beds of fern, whereof there is great plenty upon this island; together with great multitudes of trees like English box, the which bore a sort of green berries, smelling like pimento, or pepper. All this day the ship was forced to ply off at sea, not being able to get in.

December 30th. The morning of this day we employed in filling water, and cutting down wood; but in the afternoon, eight of us eleven went aboard the ship, all in one and the same canoe, sending her ashore again with provisions for the men that were there. This day, in like manner, we could not get into the harbor; for no sooner came the ship within land, but the wind, coming out of the bay, blew us clear out again. Thus we were forced to ply out all that night, and great part of the following day.

Next day, having overcome all difficulties, and many dangers, we came to an anchor, in the afternoon, in fifteen fathom water, at the distance of a cable's length from shore. Here it was observable, that we were forced to keep men ashore on purpose to beat off the seals, while our men filled water, at high-water mark, because the seals covet greatly to lie in fresh water. About this island fish is so plentiful, that, in less than an hour's time, two men caught enough for our whole company.

Saturday, January 1st, 1680. This day we put up a new main-top, larger than the old one; and we caught craw-fish that were bigger than our English lobsters.

The next day, being January 2d, died a chief man of our company, whose name was John Hilliard. This man, till our weighing anchor from the port of Coquimbo, had been our master all the space of this voyage; but from that time we chose John Cox for the starboard, and John Fall for the larboard watch. He died of the dropsy. That evening we buried our dead companion, and gave him a volley for his funeral, according to the usual custom.

January 3d, we had terrible gusts of wind from the shore every hour. This day our pilot told us, that many years ago a certain ship was cast away upon this island, and only one man saved, who lived alone upon this island five years before any ship came this way to carry him off. The island has excellent land in many valleys belonging thereto. This day, likewise, we fetched our anchor which we left in the other bay when the ship broke her cable.

Tuesday, January 4th, 1680. This day we had such terrible flaws of wind that the cable of our ship broke, and we had undoubtedly been on shore, had not the other held us fast. At last it came home, and we drove outwards. By the way it caught hold of a rock, and held some time; but at last we hauled it up. And the wind came with so much violence, that the waves flew as high as our main-top, and made all the water of a foam.

January 5th. Notwithstanding these great gusts of wind had continued all the night past, yet this day, at noon, it was brave and calm. But in the morning the anchor of our ship gave way again, and we drove to the eastward more than half a mile, till at last we happened to fasten again in the depth of sixty fathom water. In this bay, where we rode at anchor, ran a violent current, sometimes into, and at other times out, of the bay; so that all was uncertain with us. But our greatest discomfort was, that our men were all in mutiny against each other, and much divided among themselves. Some of them being for going home towards England, or our foreign plantations, and that round about America, through the Straits of Magellan, as Captain Sawkins had designed to do; others of them being for staying longer, and searching farther into those seas, till such time as they had got more money. This day, at noon, our anchor drove again; whereupon, to secure us from that dangerous place, we sailed into the west bay, and anchored there in twenty-five fathom water, and moored our ship a quarter of a mile from shore.

Thursday, January 6th. Our dissensions being now grown to a great height, the mutineers made a new election of a person to be our chief captain and commander, by virtue whereof they deposed Captain Sharp, whom they protested they would obey no longer. They chose, therefore, one of our company, whose name was John Watling, to command in chief, he having been an old privateer, and gained the esteem of being a stout seaman. The election being made, all the rest were forced to give their assent to it, and Captain Sharp gave over his command; whereupon, they immediately made articles with Watling, and signed them.

The day following, being the 7th, we burnt and tallowed the starboard side of our ship. In this bay we found a cross cut in the bark of a tree, and several letters besides. Hereupon, in another tree, up the gully, I engraved the two first letters of my name, with a cross over them. This day, likewise, William Cook, servant to Captain Edmund Cook, confessed that his master had oftentimes buggered him in England, leaving his wife and coming to bed to him; that he had also done the same in Jamaica, and once in these seas before Panama. Searching his writings, we found a paper with all our names in it, which it was suspected he designed to have given to the Spanish prisoners. For these reasons, this evening our captain thought it convenient to put him in irons, which was accordingly done.

January 8th, we finished the other side of our ship.

Sunday, January 9th. This was the first Sunday that ever we kept by command and common consent since the loss and death of our valiant commander, Captain Sawkins, who would throw the dice overboard, if he found them in use on that day.

January 10th, the weather was very clear and settled again. We caught every day, in this bay, great plenty of fish; and I saw this day a shoal of fish a mile or more long.

Next day, being the 11th, we filled our water, and carried our wood on board the ship. Our two canoes went to the other side of the island to catch goats; for on the barren side thereof are found and caught the best, and by land it is impossible to go from one side of the island to the other.

Wednesday, January 12th. This morning our canoes returned from catching of goats, firing of guns as they came towards us to give us warning. Being come on board, they told us they had espied three sail of ships, which they conceived to be men-of-war coming about the island. Within half an hour after this notice given by our boats, the ships came in sight to leeward of the island. Hereupon, we immediately slipped our cables, and put to sea, taking all our men on board that were ashore at that time; only one William, a Mosquito Indian, was then left behind upon the island, because he could not be found at this our sudden departure. Upon the Island of Juan Fernandez grow certain trees called bilby trees. The tops of these trees we used as we do cabbage in England. Here fish abounds in such quantites, that on the surface of the water I have taken fish with a bare hook. Abundance of fish is taken here of twenty pound weight; the smallest that is taken being almost two pound. Very good timber for building of houses, and other uses, is likewise found upon this island. It is distant from the main continent the space of ninety-five leagues, or thereabouts, being situate in 33° 40′ S. The plats of the islands lie N. W. and S. E.

Being got out of the bay, we stood off to sea, and kept to windward as close as we could. The biggest of these Spanish men-of-war, for such they proved to be, was of the burthen of 800 tons, and was called El Santo Christo, being mounted with twelve guns; the second, named San Francisco, carried 600 tons, and ten guns; the third carried 350 tons, whose name I have forgot. As soon as they saw us, they instantly put out their bloody flags; and we, to show them that we were not as yet daunted, did the same with ours. We kept close under the wind, and were, to confess the truth, very unwilling to fight them, by reason they kept all in a knot together, and we could not single out any one of them from the rest; especially considering that our present commander, Watling, had showed himself at their appearance to be faint-hearted. As for the Spaniards themselves, they might have easily come to us, by reason we lay by several times; but undoubtedly they were cowardly given, and peradventure as unwilling to engage us as we were to engage them.

The day following, being January 13th, in the morning, we could see one of the afore-mentioned men-of-war, under the leeward side of the island; and we believed that the rest were at anchor thereabouts.

At noon that day, we stood in towards the island, making as if we intended to be with them. But in the afternoon, our commander propounded the question to us, whether we were willing, now that the fleet was to windward, to bear away from them. To this we all agreed with one consent. And hereupon, night being come, with a fresh wind at S. S. E., we stood away N. E. by N., and gave them handsomely the slip, after having outbraved them that day, and the day before.

CHAPTER XL.

The Buccaneers depart from the Isle of Juan Fernandez to that of Yqueque. — They take several Prisoners, and get Intelligence of the Posture of Affairs at Arica. — Cruelty to one of the Prisoners, who had rightly informed them. — They attempt Arica a second Time, and take the Town, but are beaten out of it again without Plunder, and with a great Loss of Men, many of them being killed, wounded, or taken Prisoners. — Captain Watling, their chief Commander, is killed in this Attack, and Captain Sharp presently chosen again, who leads them off, and through many Difficulties makes a bold Retreat to the Ship.

Having bid our enemies adieu, as was said in the precedent chapter, the next morning, being January 14th, we bore N. E. We reckoned this day a N. N. E., one quarter S. way, and by it, thirty leagues. We were four leagues eastward from the Isle of Juan Fernandez, when I took our departure.

Saturday, January 15th, we had hazy weather. This day

we made by a N. E. by N. way, eleven leagues. The same hazy weather continued the 16th, but about ten in the morning we had a perfect calm. Our reckoning was a N. E. by N. way, and thirty-six leagues.

On the 17th, we had a soft gale, and a clear observation. We found by it latitude 28° 47′ S., easting seventy leagues. The next day we had likewise a clear day, and we reckoned by a N. E. by N. way, thirty-one leagues by observation, latitude 27° 29′ S.

Wednesday, January 19th, we had a clear day, as before, and reckoned a N. E. by N. way, and thirty-five leagues and two thirds. By observation, we took latitude 25° 0′ S. This day we put up our top-gallant masts and sails, which we had taken at the Island of Juan Fernandez, when we thought to have gone directly from thence for the Straits of Magellan. But now our resolutions were changed, and our course was bent for Arica, that rich place, the second time, to try what good we could do upon it by another attempt, in order to the making our fortunes there. In the evening we saw land at a great distance.

January 20th. About midnight past we had a small land wind that sprang up and reached us; at break of day we could descry land again, at the distance of about nine or ten leagues. This day was very hot and calm, easting ninety-two leagues.

On the 21st, we had very little wind, and all along as we went we could descry a barren high land. We sailed N. by E. and N. N. E. along the coast of the continent.

Saturday, 22d, we had very hot weather. This day we sailed N. and N. by E. and looked out continually for the Island of Yqueque, which our pilot told us was hereabouts. We kept a just distance from the land, for fear of being descried by the enemy.

The day following, Sunday the 23d, we sailed in like manner N. N. E. along the coast, which seems to be very full of bays hereabouts. By observation this day, we took latitude 21° 49′ S.

Monday, January 24th. This day we had an indifferent gale of wind, and we stood N. and by E., the wind being S. S. E. We found latitude by observation 21° 2′ S. our whole easting being ninety-two leagues and an half. In the afternoon, Captain Watling, our commander, and twenty-five men more, departed from the ship in two canoes, with design to seek for, and take the Island of Yqueque, and there to get intelligence of the posture of affairs at Arica. We were at the distance of twelve leagues from shore when they went from the ship.

The next day, by a clear observation, we found latitude 20° 40′ S. At four in the afternoon returned one of our canoes, bringing word that they could not find the island, though they had searched for it very diligently. At night came the other, being brought back by a wrong sign given us by the first canoe. This second canoe had landed upon the continent, and there found a track, in which they followed for some space. Here we found a dead whale, with whose bones the Spaniards had built a hut, and set up a cross. There lay also many pieces of broken jars. They observed likewise, that hereabouts, upon the coasts, are many bays, good landing, and anchoring for ships. That evening, about seven o'clock, a fresh gang went from the ship to seek the same island: meanwhile we lay becalmed all night, driving about a league to leeward.

Wednesday, January 26th. We had extreme hot weather. This day the Spanish pilot told us, that on the continent over against us, a very little way within the land, are very rich mines of silver; but that the Spaniards dared not open them, for fear of an invasion from the enemy. We sailed north, at the distance of about two leagues from shore. At noon, we had an observation, and found latitude 20° 21′ S. At four o'clock we saw a smoke made by our men, close by a white cliff, which proved to be the island. Hereupon, we immediately sent away another canoe with more men, to supply them in their attempts. But in the mean while the first canoe, which left us in the evening before, came aboard, bringing with them four prisoners, two old white men, and two Indians.

The other canoe, which set out last, brought back molasses, fish, and two jars of wine. To windward of the said island is a small village of eighteen or twenty houses, having a small chapel near it, built of stone, and for ornament sake, it is stuck full of hides, or skins of seals. They found about fifty people in this hamlet, but the greatest part of them made their escape at the arrival of the canoe. To this island barks frequently come from Arica (which is but at a little distance) to fetch clay, of which they have already carried away a considerable quantity. The poor Indians, natives of this island, are forced to bring all the fresh water they use full eleven leagues from thence, that is, from a river named Camarones, to leeward of the island. The bark wherein they used to bring it was then gone for water, when our men landed upon the place. The surface of this island is all over white, but the bowels are of a reddish sort of earth. From the shore is seen a great path leading over the mountains into the country. The Indians of this island love to eat a sort of leaves that are in taste much like our bay leaves in England, insomuch that their teeth are dyed of a green color, by the continual use thereof. The inhabitants go stark naked, and are a very robust and strong people; nothwithstanding, they live more like beasts than men.

Thursday, January 27th. This morning, on board the ship, we examined one of the old men who were taken prisoners upon the island the day before. But finding him in many lies, as we thought, concerning Arica, our commander ordered him to be shot to death, which was accordingly done. Our old commander, Captain Sharp, was much troubled in his mind, and dissatisfied at this cruelty and rash proceeding; whereupon he opposed it as much as he could. But seeing he could not prevail, he took water and washed his hands, saying, "Gentlemen, I am clear of the blood of this old man; and I will warrant you a hot day for this piece of cruelty, whenever we come to fight at Arica." Which fell out accordingly, as you will see hereafter.

The other old man being under examination, informed us, that the Island of Yqueque before mentioned belonging to the governor of Arica, who was proprietor thereof; and that he allowed these men a little wine, and other necessaries, to live upon for their sustenance. That he himself had the superintendence of forty or fifty of the governor's slaves, who caught fish and dried it, for the profit of the said governor; and he sold it afterwards to the inland towns, and reaped a considerable benefit thereby. That by a letter received from Arica, eight days ago, they understood there was then in the harbor of Arica three ships from Chili, and one bark. That they had raised there a fortification, mounted with twelve copper guns. But that, when we were there before, they had conveyed out of the town to the neighboring stations all their plate, gold, and jewels, burying it in the ground, and otherwise concealing it; which whether it were now brought again or not, he could not tell. That there were two great places, the one at ten, the other at twenty-five leagues distance from Arica, where lay all their strength and treasure. That the day before had passed a post to declare our having been at Coquimbo. That the embargo laid on all vessels going to the northward was now taken off, so that a free passage was allowed them. That by land it was impossible to go from hence to Arica in less than four or five days, forasmuch as they must carry water for themselves and horses for the whole journey. Lastly, that those arms that were brought from Lima to Arica, as was mentioned above, were now carried from thence to Buenos Ayres. All these things pleased us mighty well. But, however, Captain Sharp was still much dissatisfied at our shooting the old man; for he had given us a very true information, namely, that Arica was very well fortified, and much better than before, but our misfortune was, that we looked upon his information as a trick only.

The leaves, of which we made mention above, are brought down to this island in whole bales, and then distributed to the Indians, by a short allowance given to each man. This day we had very hot weather, and a S. W. sea. By observation, we found latitude 20° 13′ S. Besides the things above mentioned, our prisoners informed us, that at Arica the Spaniards had built a breastwork round about the town, and one also in every street, that in case one end of it were taken they might be able to defend the other. We stood off and in for the greatest part of the day. In the afternoon we were eight leagues and a half from shore, with a fresh wind. That morning we took the bark that was at the river of Camarones, to fill water for the island.

Friday, January 28th. Last night, about midnight, we left the ship and put ourselves aboard the bark before mentioned, the launch, and four canoes, with design to take Arica by surprisal. We rowed and sailed all night, making in for the shore.

Saturday, January 29th. About break of day we got under shore, and there hid ourselves among the rocks all day, fearing lest we should be descried by the enemy before we came to Arica. At this time we were about five leagues to southward of it, near Quebrada de San Vitor. Night being come, we rowed away from thence.

Sunday, January 30th, 1680. This day, (sacred to the memory of King Charles the martyr,) in the morning, about sunrise, we landed amongst some rocks, at the distance of four miles or thereabout, to the southward from Arica. We put on shore in all ninety-two men, the rest remaining in the boats, to keep and defend them from being surprised by the enemy, to the intent we might leave behind us a safe retreat in case of necessity. With these men we left strict orders, that if we made one smoke from the town or adjoining fields, they should come after us towards the harbor of Arica with one canoe; but in case we made two, that they should bring all away, leaving only fifteen men in the boats. As we marched from our landing-place towards the town, we mounted a very steep hill, and saw from thence no men, nor forces of the enemy, which caused us to hope we were not as yet descried, and that we should wholly surprise them. But when we were come about half way to the town, we spied three horsemen, who mounted the lookout hill, and seeing us upon our march, they rode down full speed to the city, to give notice of our approach. Our commander, Watling, chose out forty of our number to attack the fort, and sent us away first thitherwards, the rest being designed for the town. We that were appointed for the fort, had ten hand grenadoes amongst us when we gave the assault, and with them, as well as with our other arms, we attacked the castle and exchanged several shots with our enemies. But at last, seeing our main body in danger of being overborne with the number of our enemies, we gave over that attempt on the fort, and ran down in all haste to the valley, to help and assist them in the fight. Here the battle was very desperate, and they killed three, and wounded two more of our men from their outworks, before we could gain upon them. But our rage increasing with our wounds, we still advanced, and at last beat the enemy out of all, and filled every street in the city with dead bodies. The enemy made several retreats to several places, from one breastwork to another, and we had not a sufficient number of men wherewithal to man all places taken; insomuch, that we had no sooner beat them out of one place, but they came another way and manned it again with new forces and fresh men.

We took in every place where we vanquished the enemy a great number of prisoners, more indeed than peradventure we ought to have done, or knew well what to do withal; they being too many for such a small body as ours was to manage. These prisoners informed us that we had been descried no less than three days before, from the Island of Yqueque, whereby they were in expectation of our arrival every hour, knowing we had still a design to make a second attempt upon that place. That into the city were come four hundred soldiers from Lima, the which, besides their own, had brought seven hundred arms for the use of the country people, and that in the town they had six hundred armed men, and in the fort three hundred.

Being now in possession of the city, or the greatest part thereof, we sent to the fort, commanding them to surrender; but they would not send us any answer. Hereupon we advanced towards it, and gave it a second attack, wherein we persisted very vigorously for a long time. Being not able to carry it, we got upon the top of a house that stood near it, and from thence fired down into the fort, killing many of their men, and wounding them at our ease and pleasure. But while we were busied in this attack, the rest of the enemy's forces had taken again several posts of the town, and began to surround us in great numbers, with design to cut us off. Hereupon we were constrained to desist the second time, as before, from assaulting the fort, and make head against them. This we had no sooner done, but their numbers and vigor increasing every moment, we found ourselves to be overpowered, and consequently we thought it convenient to retreat to the place where our wounded men were, under the hands of our surgeons, that is to say, our hospital. At this time our new commander, Captain Watling, both our quarter-masters, and a great many more of our men, were killed, besides those that were wounded and disabled from fighting. So that now the enemy rallying against us, and beating us from place to place, we were in a very distracted condition, and in more likelihood to perish every man, than escape the bloodiness of that day. Now we found the words of Captain Sharp true, being all very sensible that we had a day too hot for us, after that cruel heat, in killing and murdering in cold blood the old Mestiso Indian whom we had taken prisoner at Yqueque, as we mentioned before.

Being surrounded with difficulties on all sides, and in great disorder, having nobody to give orders what was to be done, we were glad to have our eyes upon our good old commander, Captain Bartholomew Sharp, and beg of him very earnestly to commiserate our condition, and carry us off. It was a great while before he would take any notice of our request, so much was he displeased with the former mutiny of our people against him, all which had been occasioned by the instigation of Mr. Cook. But Sharp is a man of an undaunted courage, and excellent conduct, not fearing the least to look an insulting enemy in the face, and a person that knows both the theory and practice of navigation as well as most do. Hereupon, at our earnest request and petition, he took upon him the command in chief again, and began to distribute his orders for our safety. He would have brought off our surgeons, but they having been drinking while we assaulted the fort, would not come with us when they were called. They killed and took of our number twenty-eight men, besides eighteen that we brought off, who were desperately wounded. At this time we were all extreme faint for want of water and victuals, whereof we had none all that day; we were likewise almost choked with the dust of the town, being so much raised by the work that their guns had made, that we could scarce see each other. They beat us out of the town, and then followed us into the savannas, or open fields, still charging as fast as they could. But when they saw that we rallied again, resolved to die one by another, they ran from us into the town, and sheltered themselves under their breastworks. Thus we retreated in as good order as we possibly could observe in that confusion. But their horsemen followed us as we retired, and fired at us all the way, though they would not come within the reach of our guns; for theirs reached farther than ours, and out-shot us above one third. We took the sea side for our greater security, which when the enemy saw, they betook themselves to the hills, rolling down great stones and whole rocks to destroy us. Meanwhile those of the town examined our surgeons, and other men whom they had made prisoners. These gave them our signs that we had left to our boats that were behind us, so that they immediately blew up two fires which were perceived by the canoes. This was the greatest of our dangers; for had we not come at that instant that we did to the sea-side, our boats had been gone, they being already under sail, and we had inevitably perished every man. Thus we put off from the shore, and got on board about ten at night, having been involved in a bloody fight with the enemy all that day.

CHAPTER XLI.

A Description of the Bay of Arica. — They sail from hence to the Port of Guasco, where they get Provisions. — A Draught of the said Port. — They land again at Hilo to revenge the former Affronts, and took what they could find.

Our attempt at Arica being over, January ult., we plied to and fro in the sight of the port to see if they would send out the three ships we had seen in the harbor, to fight us; for upon them we hoped to revenge the defeat and disappointment we had received at the town the day before. But our expectations in this point also were frustrated, for not one of those vessels offered to stir.

The houses of this town of Arica are not above eleven feet high, as being built of earth, and not of brick or timber. The town itself is four-square; and at one corner stands the castle, which may easily be commanded, even with small arms, from the hill which lies close to it. This place is the *embarcadero*, or port-town of all the mineral towns that lie hereabouts, and hence is fetched all the plate that is carried to Lima, the head city of Peru.

On Tuesday, February 1st, we had a clear observation, and by it we found latitude 19° 6′ S. This day we shared the old remains of our plate, taken in some of our former booties. Our shares amounted only to thirty-seven pieces of eight each man.

N. B. Here I would have my reader to take notice, that from this day forwards I kept no constant diary or journal, as I had done before, at least for some considerable space of time, as you shall see hereafter; my disease and sickness at sea being the occasion of intermitting what I had never failed to do in all the course of this voyage till now: only some few memorandums, as my weakness gave leave, I now and then committed to paper, the which I shall give you as I find them, towards a continuance of this history. Thus: —

Monday, February 14th. This night between eleven and twelve o'clock, William Cook died on board our ship, who was servant to Captain Edmund Cook, of whom mention hath been made in this journal. He desisted not, even at his last, to accuse his master of buggering him, as before was related: moreover, that his master should say, it was no sin to steal from us, who thought it none to rob the Spaniards.

February 16th, 1680. This day we found ourselves in latitude 27° 30′ S. We had a constant breeze at S. E. and S. S. E. till we got about two hundred leagues from land: then at the eclipse of the moon, we had a calm for two or three days, and then a breeze at north for two days; after which we had a calm again for two or three days more.

March 1st, we found latitude by observation 34° 1′ S. At this time begins the dirty weather in these seas. We lay under a pair of courses, the wind being at S. E. and E. S. E., with a very great sea at S. S. E.

March 3d, all hands were called up, and a council held; wherein, considering it was now dirty weather, and late in the year, we bore up the helm, and resolved to go to the main for water, and thence to leeward, and so march over land towards home, or at least to the North Sea. But God diverted us from following this resolution, as you shall hear hereafter. We being thus determined that day, we stood N. E., with a strong wind at S. E. and E. S. E.

March 5th, died our Coquimbo Indian. The seventh we had a west wind, our course being E. by N. The eighth of the said month we were put to an allowance, having only one cake of bread a day.

March 10th, we had a strong south wind.

March 12th, we fell in with the main land, something to leeward of Coquimbo. Within the Island of Paxaras are double lands, in whose valleys are fires for melting of copper, with which metal these hills abound. Off to sea-board is a rocky land, and within, sandy. About the distance of eight leagues to leeward is a rocky point, with several keys or rocks about it. About half a mile to leeward of this point turns in the port of Guasco; right against the anchoring are three rocks, close under the shore.

Being arrived here, we landed threescore men of our company, with design to get provisions, or any thing we could purchase. The people of the country ran all away as soon as they saw us. There was building on the shore, in this port, a fire bark, of sixteen or eighteen tons burthen, with a cock-boat belonging to it. We took one Indian prisoner, and with him went up the space of six or seven miles into the country, to an Indian town of three or fourscore houses; from thence we came back to the church, which is about four miles from the sea-side, and lodged there all night. Here are multitudes of good sheep and goats in the country adjoining to this port, and it is watered with an excellent fresh water river; but the getting of water is very difficult, the banks being very high, or otherwise inaccessible. However, we made a shift to get in five hundred jars of water; furthermore, we brought away one hundred and twenty sheep, and fourscore goats, with which stock we victualled our vessel for a while. As for oxen, they had driven them away farther up into the country. The jurisdiction of Guasco itself is governed by a teniente or deputy governor, and a friar, and is in subjection to the city of La Serena above mentioned, as having a dependence thereon. Here grows both corn, pease, beans, and several other sorts of grain; and for fruits, this place is not inferior to Coquimbo. Here we found likewise a mill to grind corn, and about two hundred bushels thereof ready ground; the which we conveyed on board our ship. Every house of any account hath branches of water running through their yards or courts. The inhabitants had hid their wine, and the best of their goods, as plate and jewels, having descried us at sea before our landing; so that our booty here, besides provisions, was inconsiderable. However, we caught some few fowls, and eat five or six sheep, and likewise a great hog, which tasted very like our English pork. The hills are all barren, so that the country that beareth fruit is only an excellent valley, being four times as broad as that of Hilo above mentioned. These people of Guasco serve the town of Coquimbo with many sorts of provisions. We gave the Indian whom we had taken his liberty, and I took the port of Guasco thus.

Tuesday, March 15th, 1680. This morning we departed from the port of Guasco, afore mentioned, with very little wind, having done nothing considerable there, except only the taking in the few provisions above related. We were bent therefore to seek greater matters, having met with ill success in most of our attempts hitherto. We had now very dark weather all along the coast.

March 21st, we were west from the Bay of Mexellones. The point of this bay, one league upwards, represents a sugar-loaf exactly.

March 22d. This day our boats and canoes went from the ship, being well manned, to find the River Loa. They went also about two leagues to leeward of it, to a fishing village, but could find no place fit for landing; whereupon they returned without doing any thing. The next day another canoe of our company went out upon the same exploit, but found the same success. Notwithstanding, here Sir Francis Drake watered, and built a church, as we were told by our pilot. This church is now standing on the sea-side by the river, whose mouth is now dry. There are several huts to the windward of it; and from the said church or chapel goes a great path up the hills, which lead to Pica.

Thursday, March 24th, we found latitude by observation, 20° 10′ S. This day also we saw land, at about eighteen leagues distance.

Sunday, March 27th, we saw Mora de Sama and La Cumba at some distance. The same day we had an observation, and found it latitude 18° 17′ S. That evening we parted from the ship with our boats and canoes, towards the coast of Hilo, upon which we now were: we landed and took the village of Hilo undescried, they scarce suspecting we could have any design upon that place a second time. We caught the friar who was chaplain to the town and most of the inhabitants asleep, making them prisoners of war. Here we heard a flying report, as if five thousand English had taken Panama a second time, and were in possession of it. But this rumor proved to be a falsity, as it then seemed. At this time the river came out, and was overflown, it being near the time of the freshets. Here the prisoners told us, that in Arica ten of our men were still alive, whereof three were surgeons, all the rest being dead of their wounds. The Spaniards sent word to Hilo that we had killed them seventy men, and wounded three times as many of their forces. But here the inhabitants said, that of forty-five men sent to the relief of Arica from hence, there came home only two alive. We filled what water we pleased here, but a small boat that we brought from Guasco broke loose from us, and was staved to pieces on the rocks. Here we took eighteen jars of wine, and good store of new figs. On Tuesday following we went up to the sugar-work, mentioned in our former expedition against Hilo, and found all the fruits just ripe and fit for eating. There we loaded seven mules downwards with molasses and sugar. The inhabitants told us further, that those men who came to fight us when we were here the first time, were most of them boys, and had only fifty firearms amongst them; they being commanded by an English gentleman who is married at Arequipa. Likewise that the owner of the sugar-works afore mentioned was now engaged in a suit of law against the town of Hilo, pretending it was not the English who robbed him, and spoiled his *Ingenio*, when we were there before, but the townsmen themselves. This day in the evening we sailed for Hilo, with dark weather and little wind, which continued for several days afterwards.

CHAPTER XLII.

They depart from the Port of Hilo to the Gulf of Nicoya, where they take down their Decks, and mend the Sailing of their Ship. — Forty-seven of their Companions leave them, and go home overland. — A Description of the Gulf of Nicoya. — They take two Barks and some Prisoners there. — Several other Remarks belonging to this Voyage.

From the time that we set sail from tne port of Hilo, till Sunday, April 10th, 1681, nothing happened to us that might be accounted remarkable; neither did I take any notes all this while, by reason of my indisposition afore mentioned. This day we could hear distinctly the breaking of the seas upon the shore, but could see no land, the weather being extremely dark and hazy. Notwithstanding, about noon it cleared up, and we found ourselves to be in the bay called De Malabrigo. The land in this bay runs due east and west. By an observation made we found this day 6° 35′ S. We saw from hence the leeward Island of Lobos, or Seals, being nothing but a rocky, scraggy place. On the S. W. side thereof is a red hill, much frequented by the Indian fishermen. It is situate in latitude 6° 15′ S. This day, likewise, in the evening, we saw the point called Aguja.

On Saturday, April 16th, we came within a league distance

of the west end of the Island of Plate, above described. The next day, being Sunday, April 17, 1681, our mutineers broke out again into an open dissention, they having been much dissatisfied all along this voyage, but more especially since our unfortunate fight at Arica, and never entirely reconciled to us since they chose Captain Watling, and deposed Sharp, at the Isle of Juan Fernandez, as was related above. Nothing now could appease them, nor serve their turn, but a separation from the rest of the company, and leaving us. Hereupon, this day they left the ship, to the number of forty-seven men, all in company together, with design to go overland, by the same way they came into those seas. The rest, who remained behind, did fully resolve, and faithfully promise to each other, that they would stick close together. They took five slaves in their company, to guide and do them other service in that journey. This day we had 1° 30′ southern latitude. We sailed N. N. W. before the wind.

Next day after their departure, April 18th, we began to work about taking down one of our upper decks, thereby to cause our ship still to mend her sailing. We now made a N. W. by N. way, and had latitude, by observation, 25° N., the wind being at S. W.

April 19th, we made a N. W. by N. way. This day our observation was latitude 2° 45′ N. In the afternoon we had cloudy weather. The following day, likewise, we made the same way, and by it seventy miles, according to my reckoning.

April 21st. In the morning we had some small showers of rain, and but little wind. We saw some turtle upon the surface of the water, and great quantity of fish. We caught twenty-six small dolphins. By a N. W. by N. way, we reckoned this day forty miles.

April 22d. This day we caught seven large dolphins, and one bonito. We saw, likewise, whole multitudes of turtles swimming upon the water, and took five of them. We had an observation that gave us latitude 5° 28′ N. Hereabouts runs a great, strong current. This day we lowered the quarter deck of our ship, and made it even with the upper deck.

The day following we had but small wind, and yet great showers of rain. Hereupon every man saved water for himself, and a great quantity was saved for the whole company. In the morning we caught eight bonitoes, and in the evening ten more.

April 24th, we had both cloudy and rainy weather. By an observation we had latitude 7° 37′ N. Meridian difference was ninety-two leagues. This morning we caught forty bonitoes, and in the evening thirty more. In the afternoon we stood north, the wind being at S. W. by S.

Monday, April 25th. All the night before we had large gusts of wind and rain. At break of day we were close in with land, which, upon examination, proved to be the Island of Cano. To westward thereof is very high land. About noon this day it cleared up, and we had latitude 8° 34′ N. In the evening we sent a canoe to search the island. In it they found good water and even ground, but withal an open road. At night we stood off the first watch, and the last we had a land wind.

The day following, at daylight, we stood in, and about noon we came to an anchor at the east side of the island afore mentioned, which is not above one league over. In the afternoon we removed from our former anchoring place, and anchored again within shot of the N. E. point of the island. All over this isle grow abundance of cocoa-trees. On the north side thereof are many rivulets of good water, to be found in sandy bays. We saw some good hogs on shore, whereof we killed one, and two pigs. Here are great numbers of turtle doves, and huge store of fish, but withal very shy to be caught.

April 27th, we had some rain and wind the fore part of the day, but the afternoon was fair. The next day, in like manner, we had great quantity of rain.

On Saturday, the 30th, about seven o'clock in the morning, we weighed from the aforesaid island with little wind, and stood N. W. That day fell much rain, with great thunder and lightning.

Monday, May 2d. This day we observed, and found latitude 9° N. The coast all along appeared to us very high and mountainous, and scarce six hours did pass but we had thunder, lightning, and rain. The like continued for the two days following.

May 5th, we had an indifferent fair day, and at evening we were right off the Gulf of Nicoya.

Friday, May 6th. This morning we saw the cape very plain before us. N. by E. from it are certain keys, at eight leagues distance, close under the main. We steered N. N. W. towards the biggest of them, at whose E. S. E. side are two or three small rocks. The main eastward is fine savanna, or plain and even land, through which goes a very great road, which is to be seen off at sea. At noon the port of Caldero, commonly called Puerto Caldero, bore north from us, at which time the ebb forced us to sound in the middle of the gulf, where we found fourteen fathom water. After this we anchored nearer the eastern keys, in the depth of nineteen fathom, where we had oozy ground.

Saturday, May 7th. The night before was very fair all night long. In the morning we went in a canoe, being several in company, to seek for a place to lay our ship in. Amongst the islands along the shore we found many brave holes, but little or no water in them, and therefore not for our purpose. On one of the said islands we found a hat, and many jars of water, by which we knew that people had lately been there. About eight in the evening our ship weighed anchor, at young flood; and about three in the afternoon we anchored again in five fathom water.

Sunday, May 8th, 1681. The night before we had much rain, with thunder and lightning. The morning being come, our commander, Captain Sharp, left the ship in two canoes, with twenty-two men in his company, out of design to surprise any vessels or people they could meet hereabouts. Meanwhile, in the evening, we drove up with the tide (there being no wind) in the ship, two or three leagues higher, till we found but three fathom high water; here we backed astern. At this time we saw one of our canoes coming off from the island that was at head of us, (which was named Chira,) calling for more men and arms, saying there were two sail of ships higher up the gulf. Hereupon, eight of us went with them ashore, whereof two joined the party afore mentioned, and the six remaining were appointed to guard the prisoners they had taken: to these we showed ourselves very kind, as finding they were sensible of the cruelties of the Spaniards towards them and their whole nation. Here we found to the number of eight or nine houses, and a small chapel standing. These people have been, in former times, a considerable and great nation, but are now almost destroyed and extinguished by the Spaniards. We ascended a league up a creek of the sea, or thereabouts, and took by surprisal two barks, which were the two sail they had told us of before. One of these barks was the same we had taken before at Panama, of which I made mention at the beginning of this history.

The Monday following, we weighed anchor with our barks, and drove down the creek, with the tide at ebb, towards our ship. The prisoners we had taken here informed us, that when we were to westward in these seas before, there lay one hundred men at the port of Santa Maria. That our men, who left us at the Island Cayboa, as was mentioned above, met the other bark that we lost at sea, as we were sailing thither, and so went all overland together. That in the North seas, near Puerto Velo, they had taken a good ship, to be revenged of the Spaniards, who stop up the mouth of Santa Maria, with design to hinder others from passing that way. At night, our captain, with twenty-four men, went from the ship into another creek, and there took several prisoners, among whom was a shipwright and his men, who were judged able to do us good service in the altering our ship, those carpenters being actually building two great ships for the Spaniards. Having taken these men, they made a float of timber, to bring down the tools and instruments they were working withal; they also put several tools, and a considerable quantity of iron-work, into a doree, to be conveyed down the river, which sunk by the way, as being overladen with iron; and one of our company, named John Alexander, a Scotchman, was unfortunately drowned in her.

Thursday following, May 12th, we sent a canoe from the ship, and found the doree that was drowned: that evening likewise drove down the body of our drowned man afore mentioned; hereupon we took him up, and on Friday morning following threw him overboard, giving him three French volleys for his customary ceremony. Both this day and the day before, we fetched water from a point near the houses, on the Island of Chira afore mentioned; from the ship also we sent away a Spanish merchant, whom we had taken among the prisoners, to fetch a certain number of beeves, that might serve for a ransom of the new bark taken here. This day the weather was fair, but on Sunday following it rained from morning till night.

Monday, May 16th, we began to work all on our ship. Tuesday, an Indian boy, named Peter, ran away from us; he belonged to Captain Sawkins, and waited upon him as a servant. Wednesday, died an Indian slave, whose name was Salvador. Thursday, we heard thirty or forty guns fired on the main, which made us think these would also turn to Hilo beeves. Friday, we caught cockles, which were as large as both our fists. At night there fell such dreadful rain, with thunder, lightning and wind, that, for the space of two hours, the air was as light as day; the thunder not ceasing all the while.

Saturday night, we had more thunder, lightning, and rain. Sunday we continued our work.

Wednesday, May 25th. This day we finished our great piece of work, viz., the taking down the deck of our ship: besides which, the length of every mast was shortened, and all our work finished, insomuch that it would seem incredible, should I here give an account how much work we did in a fortnight or less. The same day, likewise, we set at liberty our Spanish carpenters, who had been very serviceable to us all this while, the old pilot, the old Spaniard taken at the Isle of Yqueque, and several other of our Spanish prisoners and slaves. To these people, but chiefly to the Spanish carpenters, as reward of their good service, we gave the new bark, which we had taken at this place: but the old bark we thought fit to keep and sail her in our company, as we did, putting into her for this purpose six of our own men and two slaves. The next day, we fell down as low as Vanero, a place so called hereabouts, and would have sailed away again that very evening, but that our tackle gave way in hoisting our anchor, which made us lie still. In the Gulf of Nicoya, we had commonly a fresh breeze, and at night a land wind.

Friday, May 27th. This day likewise we drove down with the tide as low as Cavallo, another place in the gulf. Here we staid and watered that day; and one Cannis Marcy, our interpreter, ran away from us.

May 28th, in the morning, we sailed from thence, and came within twenty-nine leagues of that rich and rocky shore: yet, notwithstanding we had but seven fathom water here, I saw a white porpoise. Behind this island is a town called New Cape Blanco. At Puerto Caldero, above mentioned, is but one storehouse. We came to an anchor in the depth of seven fathom water, at the distance of a league from shore, and caught five turtles.

May 29th. This day we saw Cape Blanco. Both this day and the day following, we continued turning it out of the gulf against a south wind.

CHAPTER XLIII.

They go from Nicoya to Golfo Dulce, where they careen their Vessel. — An Account of their Sailings along the Coast. — The Spaniards force the Indians of Darien to a Peace, by a Stratagem, contrived in the Name of the English.

Wednesday, June 1st, 1681. This day we had very fair weather, yet but little wind; hereupon the tide, or current, drove us to the westward of Cabo Blanco. Off of this cape, and at the distance of two miles within the sea, is situate a very bare key.

The coast here along runs N. W. half W., and grows lower and lower towards Cape Guyones: this cape now mentioned at seven leagues distance, and at N. W. by N., at first sight appeared like two islands. The latter part of this day was cloudy, which hindered our prospect.

June 2d. This morning we saw land, which appeared like several keys at N. W. by N., and at seven leagues distance: it was the land of Puerto de Velas.

This evening our captain called us together, and asked our opinions of the course we should steer: having discussed the points by him proposed amongst us, we all resolved to bear up for Golfo Dulce, and there to careen our vessels: this being done, we concluded to go from thence to the cape, and cruise thereabouts under the equinoctial. We observed this day that our bark, taken at the Gulf of Nicoya, sailed much better than our ship.

Friday, June 3d. The night before was very fair, and we had a fresh wind, our course being W. and W. by N. In the evening we stood N. E., and descried land at the distance of about twenty-four leagues from Cabo Blanco.

Sunday, June 5th. Last night we lay by the greatest part thereof: this morning we saw the Island of Gano, above described, which bore E. S. E. from us. We saw multitudes of fish, but they would not bite; also, water-snakes of divers colors.

June 6th. All the night past we had rain, with little wind, scarce enough to carry us clear off from the island afore mentioned. Towards morning we had a fresh wind at N. N. W.; so we stood out S. till morning, and then we stood N. E. by E. The land runs, from Punta Mala to Golfo Dulce and Punta Borrica, E. S. E. half S. At nine leagues distance we laid the Island of Gano.

The west end of Golfo Dulce is very high land, and a high rock lies close off it, besides which, two other rocks lie further out, the outermost of which is a mile distant from the shore. The east side is also high, but breaks into small points and bays, growing lower and lower to Punta Borrica. We came about a mile within the mouth of the gulf; then we anchored in eight fathom and a half water. The mouth of the gulf is almost three leagues over.

The next day, being June 7th, we weighed anchor again at young flood, and got about two leagues higher. At evening, we came again to an anchor, in the depth of seven fathom and a half water. It rained so hard this day, till eight o'clock, that the drops could not be distinguished one from another.

Wednesday, June 8th. At daybreak we weighed anchor again, with a fresh sea breeze; the higher up we went, the deeper we found the gulf, and at last no ground, even with thirty fathom line. This day we sent our canoe away to seek water, and a good place to lay our ship in. Having landed, we found one Indian and two boys, all which we made prisoners, and brought aboard. We used them very kindly, giving them victuals and clothes, for they had nothing but the bark of a tree to cover their nakedness withal: being examined, they informed us that a Spanish priest had been amongst them, and had made peace with their nation, ordering them strictly not to come near any ship or vessel that had red colors; for they were Englishmen, and would certainly kill them. Being asked where the priest was, they answered he was gone to a great Spanish town, four sleeps up in the country. After this, the Indian left the two boys, his children, with us, and went to fetch more Indians to us, from a plantain wall or grove, situate by a river about a league off. We came to an anchor in a bay close by one of the Indian keys, where two fresh rivers were within a stone's throw of each other, in twenty-seven fathom and a half water, and at a cable's length from the mark of low water. The Indians, whom our prisoner went to seek, came to us several times, selling us honey, plantains, and other necessaries, that we usually bought of them, or trucked for with other things. We also made use of their bark logs in tallowing our ship, in which case they did us good service. Their darts are headed with iron as sharp as any razor.

Here one of the prisoners which we took at the Gulf of Nicoya informed us by what means, or rather stratagem, of war, the Spaniards had forced a peace upon the Indians of the Province of Darien, since our departure from thence. The manner was as follows: A certain Frenchman, who ran from us, at the Island of Taboga, to the Spaniards, was sent by them in a ship to the river's mouth, which emptieth itself from that province into the South Sea. Being arrived there, he went ashore by himself in a canoe, and told the Indians, that the English, who had passed that way, were come back from their adventures in the South Sea. Withal, he asked them, if they would not be so kind and friendly to the Englishmen, as to come aboard and conduct them on shore. The poor deceived Indians were very joyful to understand this good news; and thus forty of the chiefest of them went on board the Spanish vessel, and were immediately carried prisoners of war to Panama. Here they were forced to conclude a peace, though upon terms very disadvantageous to them, before they could obtain their liberty.

These poor and miserable Indians of Golfo Dulce would come every day in our company, and eat and drink very familiarly with us, all the time we were there. We laid our ship on ground, but the water did not ebb low enough to see her keel. While we were careening our vessel, we built a house upon the shore, both to lodge and eat in; and every day we caught plenty of good fish.

Sunday, June 12th. The work of careening our ship going on in due order, we came to cleanse our hold; and here on a sudden both myself and several others were struck quite blind with the filth and nastiness of it; yet soon after we recovered our sight again, without any other help than the benefit of the fresh air.

June 14th, we had a great and fierce tornado, with which our cable broke, and had it not then happened to be high water at that instant, we had been lost inevitably; however, we had the good fortune to shore her up again, and by that means secure ourselves from further danger.

June 21st, we weighed anchor again, and went a league higher than the former place. Here we watered, and in the mean while left men below, to cut wood.

Thursday, June 23d. This day ran away from us two negroes: the name of one of them was Hernando, who was taken with Don Thomas de Argandona, upon the coast of Guayaquil, as was mentioned above; the other was named Silvester, taken at the town of Hilo; following the example of those afore mentioned.

Monday, June 27th, that is, four days after, two more of our prisoners endeavored to make their escape, both of them slaves: one of these was named Francisco, who was a negro, and had been taken in the cocoa ship mentioned before; the name of the other was also Francisco, an Indian born, taken at Panama. Their attempts to escape succeeded not, for we caught them both again, before they got on shore.

Tuesday following, I went and sailed up and down the gulf, in a little bark belonging to our ship, and viewed all the parts of Golfo Dulce. Our captain gave this gulf the name of King Charles's Harbor.

CHAPTER XLIV.

They depart from Golfo Dulce, to go and cruise under the Equinoctial.—Here they take a rich Spanish Vessel, with thirty-seven thousand Pieces of Eight, besides Plate and other Goods.—They take also a Packet Boat bound from Panama to Lima.—An Account of their Sailings, and the Coasts along.

Our vessel being now careened, and all things in a readiness for our departure, Tuesday, June the 28th, in the afternoon, we weighed anchor to go to sea again, turning out towards the mouth of Golfo Dulce. Our design was to cruise under the equinoctial, as had been concluded upon before, thereby to get what purchase we could by sea, seeing the greatest part of our attempts upon land had proved hitherto very unsuccessful to us.

Wednesday, June 29th. Both the night last past and this day we had rainy weather. About three in the afternoon a fresh gale sprung up at S. W. and S. S W., our course being S. E. and S. E. by S. At five this evening the gulf bore N. W. by W., being seven leagues distant, and Punta Borrica three leagues and a half distant.

Thursday, June 30th. All night past we enjoyed a fresh gale at S. S. W. We sailed in the bark where I was better than the man-of-war—for so we called the Trinity vessel—notwithstanding she was newly cleansed and tallowed. This day we had hazy weather, and I reckoned myself from Punta Borrica S. S. E. eighteen leagues and a half.

July 1st, 1681. Last night we had two or three tornadoes. I reckoned this day a S. S. E. way, and by a clear observation, found latitude 6° 10′ N. We saw great quantities of fish, as we sailed this day.

July 2d, we made a S. E. way, and our reckoning was 64 miles by it: by observation, I found latitude 5° 20′ N. At noon the same day, we had a fresh gale at S. W., with some rain.

July 3d, we had hazy weather. We made a S. S. E. by S. way, 37 miles.

Monday, July 4th. The night past was windy, with rain, which forced us to hand our topsails. Our reckoning this day was a S. E. way, and a hundred miles.

July 5th. We had a clear night the last past, and withal, a fresh gale; by this we made a S. E. way. Our latitude this day gave us 2° 20′ N. This morning we saw land southward of us, lying in low hammocks: it was the Point of Manglares.

Wednesday, July 6th, we turned up along shore, and by observation took this day latitude 2° 2′ N. Hereabouts every new moon is a windward current. In the evening we were close in with low land; we had windy weather, and a great sea.

Thursday, July 7th. This day, by observation taken, we found latitude 1° 48′ N. In the evening we lost sight of the said ship.

July the 8th, we saw the ship again, for loss whereof we began to be in some doubt. This day we made very high land all along as we went, and the port, or rather bay, of San Matteo, or St. Matthews, appeared like several islands.

Saturday, July 9th. This morning we stood fair in with the port of Tucames. Off of the highest part of the land there seems to be a key.

This day at noon we had a clear observation, which gave us latitude 1° 22′ N.

Sunday, July 10th. Last night we stood off to sea, thereby to keep clear of the shore. This day's observation showed us latitude 1° 31′ N. About noon the same day, we happened to espy a sail, which we immediately gave chase to. We bore up to the point of the compass, thereby to hinder her lasking away; notwithstanding, in the evening we lost sight of her. However, our great ship got up with her, and about eight of the clock at night, made her a prize. She proved to be the ship named San Pedro, which we had taken the last year, being then bound from Truxillo to Panama, and laden with wine, gunpowder, and pieces of eight, whereof mention was made before. We took her twice, in less than fourteen months. She had on board her now twenty-one thousand pieces of eight, in eight chests, and in bags sixteen thousand more, besides plate.

Monday and Tuesday, the 11th and 12th of July, we made in for the shore. Our prize was so hard laden, that she seemed quite buried in the water. She had forty men on board her, besides some merchants and friars. On Tuesday, an observation gave us latitude 1° 20′ N.

Wednesday, July 13th. This day we dared not adventure into the Bay of San Matteo, because we saw some Indians who had made a great fire on shore, which, as we judged, was designedly done to give intelligence of our arrival. Hereupon we bore away for the River of San Iago, about six leagues north-east from the bay before mentioned. Thursday, Friday, and Saturday following, we spent in taking out of our prize what parcels of cocoa-nuts we thought fit; she being chiefly laden with that commodity. This being done, we cut down the mainmast by the board, and gave them only their mainsail, and thus turning the ship loose, sent away in her all our old slaves for the good service they had done us, taking new ones from the prize, in their room. One only we still detained, who was Francisco the negro, that attempted to run away by swimming ashore.

Sunday, July 17th. This day we went from the ship, and found the River of San Iago, before mentioned. At the mouth of this river we staid Monday and Tuesday following, to take in water, which we now much wanted. On the sides of the river we found good store of plantains. Our fresh water we fetched four miles up the river. We saw several Indians, but could not speak with them, they were so shy of us, being forewarned by the Spaniards not to come near us.

Wednesday, July 20th, we shared our plunder, or rather, made part of the dividend of what we had taken, the rest being reserved to another day. Our prisoners being examined, informed us that the Spaniards had taken up our anchors and cables, which we left behind us at the Isle of Juan Fernandez. Also, that they had surprised the Musquito Indian, that we left behind us there on shore, by the light of a fire which he made in the night upon the isle.

Tuesday, July 21st. All the four and twenty hours last past, we stood off and in. The next day we shared the rest of our things taken in the prize, as also the money that was in the bags; the rest we laid up to divide upon another occasion, especially when we were got through the Straits of Magellan. Our dividend amounted to the sum of two hundred and thirty-four pieces of eight a man. Our prisoners informed us this day that a new viceroy of Peru was arrived at Panama, and that he dared not adventure up to Lima in a ship of twenty-five guns, that was at Panama, for fear of meeting with us at sea, but had chosen rather to stay till the armada came down from Lima to conduct him thither.

July 23d, we had a fresh breeze at S. W., and the next day a clear observation, which gave us only latitude 14′ N. This day we saw Cape St. Francisco, N. E.

Monday, July 25th. This day we observed latitude 1° 20′ S., and we had a S. W. wind.

July 26th. This morning we had a very great dew fallen in the night last past. The weather in like manner was very close.

On Wednesday, July 27th, we were at S. S. W. of Cape Passao, and at six leagues distance.

The same morning, about seven of the clock, we spied a sail

E. S. S. from us, under shore. We presently gave her close chase, and about noon came up with her. But several of her crew got on shore and made their escape, viz., a friar, who was either a passenger or chaplain to the vessel, and five negroes. She proved to be a *barco de aviso*, or packet boat, that was going with letters from Panama to Lima. In this bark we took, among other prisoners, two white women, who were passengers to the same place. These and the rest of the prisoners told us they had heard at Panama that we had all gone out of these seas homewards overland, and that made them adventure now up towards Lima; otherwise they had not come. This day and Thursday following we spent in rummaging the packet boat, in which we could find nothing of value, they having scarce brought any thing with them but the packet. They told us moreover, that the new viceroy of Peru, of whom we made mention above, was setting forth from Panama, under the conduct of three sail of ships — one of sixteen, another of eight, and a third of six guns; that a general peace was all over Europe, except only that the English had wars with the Algerines by sea, and the Spaniards by land. Having got what we could out of the prisoners and the vessel, we gave them their liberty and sent them away in the same bark, as being desirous not to encumber ourselves with more than we could well manage. That night we stood out to sea all night long, most of our men being fuddled.

CHAPTER XLV.

They take another Spanish Ship, richly laden, under the Equinoctial. — They make several Dividends of their Booty among themselves. — They arrive at the Isle of Plate, where they are in Danger of being all massacred by their Slaves and Prisoners. — Their Departure from thence for the Port of Paita, with Design to plunder the said Place.

Next morning, after we had turned away the packet boat before mentioned, the weather being very close, we spied another sail creeping close under our lee. This vessel looked mighty big, so that we thought she had been one of their chiefest men-of-war, who was sent to surprise or destroy us. Notwithstanding, our brave commander, Captain Sharp, resolved to fight, and either take her, though never so big, or she us. In order thereto, coming nearer her, we easily perceived she was a merchant ship of great bulk, as most Spanish vessels are, and withal very deeply laden. Being up with them, they fired three or four guns at us first, thinking to make their party good against us; but we answered them briskly with a continual volley of small arms, so that they soon ran down into the hold and surrendered, crying aloud for quarter. We killed in that volley their captain and one seaman, and also wounded their boatswain. The loss of their commander so daunted them, he being a man of good repute in those seas, that they surrendered immediately. Captain Sharp, with twelve more of our company, entered her first. In this vessel I saw the beautifullest woman that ever I saw in the South Sea. The name of the captain of the vessel was Don Diego Lopez, and the ship was called El Santo Rosario, or the Holy Rosary. The men we found on board her were about forty.

Having examined our prisoners, they informed us that the day before they set sail from El Callao (from which port they were going towards Panama) our men, whom they had taken prisoners at Arica, were brought into that place; and that they had been very civilly entertained there by all sorts of people, but more especially by the women. That one of our surgeons, whom we suspected to be Mr. Bullock, was left behind, and remained still at Arica.

We lay at anchor from Friday, July 29th, which was the day we took this prize, till Wednesday following, under Cape Passao, the place we anchored at before. Here we sunk the bark we had taken at the Gulf of Nicoya, being willing to make use of what rigging she had, and also to contract our number of men. In the mean while we took a great deal of plate out of the prize, and some money ready coined, besides six hundred and twenty jars of wine and brandy, and other things. Thus, leaving only the foremast standing in the vessel, we turned her away, as we had done the others before, together with all the prisoners in her, giving them their liberty, not being willing to be encumbered with them; and withal, being desirous to spare our provisions as much as we could. We detained only one man, named Francisco, who was a Biscanier, because he told us himself he was the best pilot in those seas. This being done, we shared all the plate and linen taken in her, and weighed from thence, standing S. S. E., with a fresh wind.

Friday, August 4th. This day we shared the ready money taken in the Rosario, our last prize. Our dividend came to ninety-four pieces of eight a man. We were now at N. E. of Cape Passao, under which all these prizes were taken.

The land runs S. E., and is, for five leagues together, to windward of this cape, all mountainous and high land.

Next day, being August 5th, we completed our dividends, sharing this day all our odd money ready coined, and plate, and some other things.

Saturday, August 6th. This day, perusing some letters taken in the last prize, I understood by them that the Spaniards had taken prisoner one of the last party of our men that left us; also, that they were forced to fight all their way over land as they went, both against the Spaniards and Indians; these having made peace with the Spaniards since our departure, as was mentioned above; that our Englishmen had killed, amongst other Spaniards, the brother of Captain Assientos, and Captain Alonso, an officer so named. Moreover, that ten sail of privateers were coming out of the North Sea, with intent to march over land into the South Sea, as we had done before, but that they were prevented, being forced back by the great rains that fell near the islands called Zemblas.

August 7th. We had very fair weather, and notwithstanding, sometimes strong winds from shore, and a strong current to leeward. This ran so fierce against us the next day, August 8th, that in four and twenty hours we lost three leagues.

Tuesday, August 9th. We saw the port and town of Manta; being only sixteen or seventeen straggling houses, with a large and high brick church belonging to it. What we got in the day by the help of the wind, we lost in the night by the current. The same fortune we had the next day, for we still gained no way all this while.

Thursday, August 11th. All the night past we had but little wind. This day we had a violent current to windward, as before, with some gusts of wind. However, by the help of these, we made shift to get to windward of the Isle of Plate.

August 12th, in the morning, we came to anchor at the aforesaid isle. We sent our boat ashore with men, as we had done formerly, to kill goats, but we found them extremely shy to what they were the last year. Here it was that our quartermaster, James Chappel, and myself, fought a duel on shore. In the evening, our slaves agreed among themselves, and plotted to cut us all in pieces, when we were asleep, not giving quarter to any. They conceived this night afforded them the fittest opportunity, by reason we were all in drink. But they were discovered to our commander, by one of their own companions; and one of them, named San Iago, whom we brought from Yqueque, leaped overboard; who, notwithstanding, was shot in the water by our captain, and thus punished for his treason. The rest laid the fault on that slave, and so it passed, we being not willing to inquire any farther into the matter, having terrified them with the death of their companion. We lay at this isle till Tuesday following, and in the interim gave our vessel a pair of boots and tops, being very merry all the while with the wine and brandy we had taken in the prize.

Tuesday, August 16th. In the afternoon, we weighed from thence with a S. W. wind.

Wednesday, August 17th. We got east of the island this morning, two leagues and a half distance.

All the day till next morning we had a leeward current, but then I could not perceive any.

Thursday, August 18th. This evening we were to windward of the Island of Solango. In the night before, we had a continual misty rain. At noon, the aforesaid island bore N. by E. of us, at three leagues distance.

About three leagues from Solango are two rocks, called Los Abercados. They appear both high and black. Besides this, N. N. E. from point St. Helena, is a high rock, which to windward thereof runs shoaling for the space of half a mile under water. It is distant about eight leagues from the said point, and is called Chanduy. At this place, and upon this rock, was lost the ship afore mentioned, that was ordered from these seas to the aid of Charles I., king of England. This ship had on board, as the Spaniards relate, many millions of pieces of eight; being sent as a present to him, he being then in his troubles, by the merchants of Lima. The rock afore mentioned lies about two leagues distant from the main.

August 29th. This day our pilot told us, that since we were to windward, a certain ship that was coming from Lima, bound for Guayaquil, ran ashore on Santa Clara, losing there in money to the value of one hundred thousand pieces of eight; which otherwise, peradventure, we might very fortunately have met withal. Moreover, that the viceroy of Peru had beheaded their great admiral, Ponce, for not coming to fight and destroy us, while we were at Gorgona. This evening we saw the Point Santa Helena ten leagues to S. S. E. from us.

August 20th. This day we had both misty and cold weather. In the afternoon, we saw La Punta de Santa Helena, at N. E. by N., and at about seven leagues distance.

On Sunday, August 21st, we had a fair and clear day. I reckoned myself to be about twenty-five leagues to the southward of Santa Helena.

August 22d. This morning, about two o'clock, we came close in with the shore. We found ourselves to be leeward of a certain point called Punta de Mero, which is only a barren, rocky point. Here runs an eddy current under the shore.

Tuesday, August 23d. This day, in the morning, we had but little wind. At noon it blew fresh again. We made all day but short trips, and reefed topsails.

Wednesday, August 24th. This morning a great dew fell. At noon we were west from Cape Blanco. We found by observation latitude 4° 13′ S. We resolved now to bear up to Paita, and taking it by surprisal, if possible, thereby to provide ourselves with many necessaries we wanted.

CHAPTER XLVI.

They arrive at Paita, where they are disappointed of their Expectations, as not daring to land, seeing all the Country alarmed before them. — They bear away for the Straits of Magellan. — An Account of their Sailings towards the Straits afore mentioned.

Thursday, August 25th. Wednesday night we stood off to sea for fear of the shore, lest we should be descried from the coast of Paita, which we were now pretty nigh. About noon this day we began to stand in again, and saw the homing of land, though with hazy weather. The next day, being August 26th, we had cold winds, great dews, and dry weather.

Saturday, August 27th. All this day, especially in the morning, we had a great fog. In the afternoon, we saw La Silla de Paita at W. S. W., being about five leagues from it.

Sunday, August 28th. Last night, about ten, we were close in with land, at about half a league to leeward of the Island of Lobos. We continued our course all that night, and about break of day found ourselves close under Pena Horadada, which is a high and steep rock. From this place we sailed with a land wind, and sent from the ship two canoes, well manned and armed, hoping we should take the town of Paita undescried. But it seems they had already got news of our coming, or being upon that coast; and supplies of forces were sent them from Pitura, twelve leagues up the country. These supplies consisted chiefly of three companies of horse and foot, all of them armed with fire-arms. Besides this, they had made, for the defence of the town, a breastwork along the sea-side, and the great church which lies at the outermost part of the town. From these places, as also from a hill that covers the town, they fired at our men, who were innocently rowling towards shore with their canoes. This untimely firing was the preservation of our people. For had the Spaniards permitted our men to come ashore, they had assuredly destroyed them every man; but fear always hindereth that nation of victory in most of our attempts.

Our men perceiving themselves discovered, and the enemy prepared for their reception, retreated, and came aboard the ship again, without attempting to land, or do any thing else in relation to the taking of the place. We judged there could be no less than one hundred and fifty fire-arms, and four times as many lances upon the shore, all in a readiness to hinder our people from landing. Within the town, our pilot told us, there might be about one hundred and fifty families.

Being disappointed by our expectations at Paita, we stood down the bay towards Colan, three times as big as Paita. It is chiefly inhabited by fishermen, who send fish to most inland towns of Peru, and also serve Paita with water from the river Colan, not far from the town. It is about two leagues from the town of Paita, before mentioned, to Colan, and from thence to the river one league, although the houses of Colan reach almost to the river. The town of Colan is only inhabited by Indians, who are all rich, because they will be paid in ready money for every thing they do for the Spaniards. But the town of Paita is chiefly inhabited by Spaniards, though there be also some Indians; but the Spaniards do not suffer the Indians to be any great gainers, or grow rich under them.

About ten o'clock a small breeze sprung up, and with that we stood away west, and W. by S. In a little time it blew so fresh, that we were forced to reef our topsails, the weather being very dark and hazy.

Monday, August 29th. All our hopes of doing any further good upon the coast of the South seas being now frustrated, seeing we were descried before our arrival wherever we came, we resolved unanimously to quit all other attempts, and bear away for the Straits of Magellan, in order to our return homewards, either for England, or some of our plantations in the West Indies. This day we had a great dew, and I reckoned myself W. S. W. from Paita thirteen leagues and a half, with very little wind; so we stood east.

The next day, August 30th, we had misty weather. We made a W. S. W. way, and by it five leagues and one third. In the afternoon, the wind freshened again, having been but little before, and we stood E. S. E.

The last day of August we had very fair weather. I believe now that the wind was settled S. E. and S. S. E. We made a S. S. W. way, and twenty-one leagues and two thirds.

September 1st. The night past was very cloudy, but withal we had a fresh gale. Our reckoning was a S. W. way, and that we had made sixteen leagues and two thirds.

September 2d. We reckoned a S. W. way, and by it twenty-six leagues and two thirds. This day we had an observation, and found latitude 7° 40′ S.

September 3d brought us both cloudy and misty weather. We made a W. S. W. way, and fourteen leagues.

September 4th. This day the wind was at E. S. E. and sometimes E., coming in many flaws. We had a S. W. by S. way, and reckoned twenty-three leagues and two thirds. We had a great sea from the south.

Monday, September 5th. We had great winds, and a high and short sea. Our way was S. S. W. and half W., by which we reckoned twenty-eight leagues and two thirds of a league.

September 6th. We had a very fresh wind at S. E. by E., with an indifferent smooth sea. By observation we found this day latitude 12° 0′ S. We made a S. W. by S. way, and twenty leagues and one third.

Wednesday, September 7th. We had a very fresh wind. We reckoned a S. W. by S. way, and thirty-six leagues. We observed latitude 13° 24′ S. We make now each mess a plum-pudding of salt water and wine lees.

September 8th. We had a fresh gale of wind, but hazy weather. Our reckoning was a S. W. by S. way, and hereby twenty-five leagues, and one third of a league.

September 9th. We made a S. W. by S. way, and twenty-one leagues and a third. In the afternoon, the wind came about something more southerly, allowing us a S. W. course.

Saturday, September 10th. All the night past and this morning the wind was very fresh at east. Our way was S. S. W. and by our reckoning thirty-five leagues and one third. The weather was now warm. An observation this day gave latitude 16° 40′ S.

September 11th. We had whiffling winds, a S. W. half S. way, and thereby twelve leagues and two thirds. By an observation we made, we found 17° 10′ S. Now we had a very great sea, so that we took in our spritsail.

September 12th. All the night before we were under a pair of courses: yet this morning we heaved out our main top-sail. We made a W. S. W. way, and seventeen leagues and one third. By observation we found latitude 17° 30′ S.

September 13th. The night past we had great and huge storms of wind. In the morning our goose-head gave way, so that about noon we were forced to lie by till four in the afternoon, to mend it. Our course was S. W. half W., and our reckoning twenty-nine leagues and two thirds of a league. Latitude by observation 18° 12′ S.

Wednesday, September 14th. This day we had very hazy weather. We made a S. S. W. way, and twenty leagues.

September 15th. This day likewise we had a S. S. W. way, and reckoned twenty-three leagues and one half. Our observation, taken this day, gave us latitude 20° 9′ S.

September 16th. We had a clear day, a S. W. half S. way, and made sixteen leagues and two thirds. We found, by observation, latitude 20° 48′ S.

September 17th, last night was very calm, also this day, being a full moon. We reckoned a S. W. way, and only (by reason of the calmness of the weather) nine leagues and one third of a league. We had an observation, which afforded us 21° 8′ S. latitude.

Sunday, September 18th. Last night a wind sprung up at S. S. E., which this morning freshened at S. E. We made a W. S. W. way, and by it eighteen leagues. This day likewise we had a clear observation, that showed us latitude 21° 30′ S.

September 19th. All the night past, we had a very fresh wind; but this morning it came about to E. by S. and E. S. E., with hazy weather. I reckoned a S. W. by S. way, and twenty-two leagues.

September 20th. This day gave us a fresh wind, hazy weather, and a S. by W. way, and hereupon twenty-three leagues and one third.

September 21st. This day also the fresh gale continued, with cloudy, and sometimes misty, weather. Our reckoning showed us a S. by W. way, as the day before, and by it twenty-eight leagues and one third. By observation made, we found latitude 25° 15′ S.

Thursday, September 22d. This day we had a very fresh wind: we reckoned a S. half W. way, and by that twenty-nine leagues and two thirds. An observation taken, gave us latitude 26° 42′ S. We observed this day a north-east sea, which was very strange to us.

The next day we had several showers of small rain. My reckoning was a S. by W. way, and thereupon twenty-six leagues. We found, by observation, latitude 27° 57′ S.

September 24th, we had hazy weather, and the wind not so fresh, at E. S. E., with a smooth sea. We made a S. S. W. way half westerly, and twenty-three leagues and two thirds. This day also an observation gave us latitude 28° 57′ S. I reckoned now that we were distant from Paita three hundred and two leagues and two thirds.

Sunday, September 25th. This day we had not much wind, and withal hazy weather. At noon the wind came E., then E. N. E., and then again N. E. by E. We reckoned a S. by E. way half easterly, and fifty-five leagues.

Monday, 26th, we had hazy weather, and a fresh wind at N. E. We reckoned a S. E. half S. way, and twenty-four leagues. In the afternoon we experimented a N. N. E. sea, and then a N. N. E. wind; after this a N. wind, and that but a little.

September 27th. All the night, before this day, we had a fresh wind at N. N. E. About eight this morning, it came about again to N. N. W. We made a S. E. by S. way, and thirty-eight leagues. By observation, I found latitude 32° 30′ S. Now we enjoyed a very smooth sea, and fair weather.

Wednesday, September 28th. The night past we had a very fresh wind at N. N. W. and N. W. At break of day we had a wind at ——, heaving us aback at once. At noon again, the wind was at S. W., our course being S. E. This morning we took down our topgallant-masts. We made a S. E. by E. way, and on this road twenty-seven leagues and two thirds. We found by an observation made, latitude 33° 16′ S.; a S. W. sea.

September 29th, we had very windy and hazy weather, with some rain now and then. All last night we handed our main topsail. We made a S. E. by E. way, and thirty-two leagues and two thirds. We had a S. W. sea and wind.

Friday, September 30th. This day we had fresh winds between S. W. and W. We reckoned a S. E. half south way, and thereupon forty-four leagues. By observation, we found latitude 35° 54′ S.

October 1st. The wind this day was not very fresh, but varying. My reckoning was a S. E. half S. way, and twenty-four leagues. An observation gave us latitude 36° 50′ S. This day I finished another quadrant, being the third I finished in this voyage. We had a S. W. sea, with showers of rain and gusts of wind.

Sunday, October 2d. The wind this day was hanging between W. N. W. and N. W. by N. We made a S. E. by S. way, and thirty-three leagues and two thirds. By observation we found 38° 14′ S. About noon we had a fresh wind at N. W. and S. W.

October 3d. The last night in the fore part thereof was clear, but the latter was rainy; the wind very fresh at N. W. by N. But this day we had little wind, and cloudy weather, a S. W. by W. wind, and a S. E. by S. way, by which we reckoned thirty-three leagues and one third of a league.

October 4th. We had a clear night, and a very fresh wind. We reckoned by a S. E. by E. way, and thereby forty-three leagues. An observation taken, showed us that we were in latitude 41° 34′ S. This day also fell several showers of rain.

October 5th. We had a windy night the last past, and a clear day. We reckoned a S. S. E. half E. way, and forty-four leagues and two thirds. By an observation made, we found latitude 43° 26′ S. The weather now was very windy, causing a huge tempestuous sea. The wind at N. W. and N. W. by N., blowing very high.

October 6th. This day the wind was still at N. W., and yet not so fresh as it was yesterday; the weather very foggy and misty: as for the wind, it came in gusts, so that we were forced to hand our topsails and spritsail. We reckoned a S. E. half S. way, and thereby forty-three leagues and one third of a league. The seas now were not so high as for some days past. In the evening we scudded away under our fore course.

Friday, October 7th. Last night was very cloudy, and this day both dark and foggy weather, with small rain. We made a S. E. way, and thirty leagues and two thirds: a fresh wind at N. N. W. and N. W. We kept still under a fore course, not so much for the freshness of the wind, as the closeness of the weather.

October 8th. We had a clear night the night past, and withal a strong gale, insomuch that this day we were forced to take in our foresail, and loosen our mizzen, which was soon blown to pieces. Our eldest seamen said, that they were never in the like storm of wind before; the sea was all in a foam: in the evening it dulled a little. We made a S. E. half E. way, and eighteen leagues, with very dark weather.

Sunday, October 9th. All the night past we had a furious W. N. W. wind. We set our sail a-drough, and so drove to the southward very much, and almost incredibly, if an observation had not happened, which gave us latitude 48° 15′ S. We had a very stiff gale at W. N. W., with a great sea from W., which met with a S. S. W. sea as great as it. Now the weather was very cold, and we had one or two frosty mornings. Yesterday, in the afternoon, we had a very great storm of hail. At noon we bent another mizzen.

Monday, October 10th. This day brought us a fresh wind at N. N. W. We made a S. E. half E. way, and by it forty-four leagues. By observation, we found latitude 49° 41′ S. I reckoned myself now to be east of Paita, sixty-nine leagues and a half.

Tuesday, October 11th. Last night we had a small time

calm. This day was both cloudy and rainy weather. The wind at S. W. and S. S. W., so furious, that at ten this morning we scudded under a mainsail. At noon we lowered our fore-yard, while we sailed. We made a S. E. by E. way, and thirty leagues.

CHAPTER XLVII.

The Buccaneers arrive at a Place unknown to them, which they new-name the Duke of York's Islands. — A Description of the said Islands, and of the Gulf or Lagoon wherein they lie, so far as it was searched. — They remain there many Days by distress of Weather, not without great Danger of being lost. — An Account of some other Things remarkable that happened there.

Wednesday, October 12th. All last night we had many high winds. I reckoned an E. S. E. way, and twenty leagues; for our vessel drove at a great rate. Moreover, that we were in latitude 50° 50′ S; so that our easting from Paita by my account ought to be one hundred and one leagues or thereabouts.

This morning, about two hours before day, we happened by great accident to espy land. It was the great mercy of God, which had always attended us in this voyage, that saved us from perishing at this time; for we were close ashore before we saw it, and our fore-yard, which we most needed on this occasion, was taken down. The land we had seen was very high and towering, and there appeared to be many islands scattered up and down. We steered in with what caution we could, between them and the main, and at last arrived at a place, or rather bay, where we perceived ourselves to be land-locked, and, as we thought, pretty safe from the danger of those tempestuous seas. From hence we sent away our canoe to sound and search the fittest place for anchoring. At this time one of our men, named Henry Shergall, as he was going into our spritsail top, happened to fall into the water, and was drowned before he could have any help, though we endeavored it as much as we could. This accident several of our company did interpret as a bad omen of the place; which proved not so, through the providence of the Almighty, though we were not clear of dangers neither, as I shall relate.

We came to an anchor in about forty fathom water, at a stone's cast only from shore. The water where we anchored was very smooth, and the high lands round about all covered

with snow. Having considered the time of the year, and all other circumstances, we resolved that, in case we could find a sufficient stock of provisions here, we would stay the longer, that is, till the beginning of summer, or something longer, before we prosecuted our intended voyage homewards through the Straits of Magellan, which now we began to be careful how to find. That day we anchored in this bay we shot six or eight brave geese, besides some small fowl. Here we found many hundreds of muscle banks, all which were very plentifully stocked with that kind of fish. We buried our dead man on the shore, giving him several volleys for his funeral rites, according to custom. At night our anchor came home, so that we were forced to let go a grappling to secure ourselves. But still every flaw of wind drove us. Hereupon we set our spritsail, and ran above a mile into another bay, where we anchored again. The first anchor, which was the biggest in our ship, we lost by this accident, the cable being cut by the rocks. These islands afore mentioned our captain new-named his royal highness the Duke of York's Islands.

Thursday, October 13th. This day we began to moor our ship, she driving, as we easily could perceive, with every flaw of wind that blew. The tide flows here full seven feet up and down. We moored our vessel in a rocky point, being a key, whereof there be many in the circumference of this bay. The ground of the bottom of the bay we found was hard and sandy, being here and there rocky. This evening we brought on board great store of lamperts, of which we made a kettle of broth, more than all our company could eat.

Friday, October 14th, we killed several geese, as also many fowls like an eagle, but having a bigger beak, with their nostrils rising from the top of the middle of their beak by a hand trunk: this fowl liveth on fish. Yesterday, in the evening, fell a great fleet of snow on the hills around about the bay, but none where we were at anchor. This day in the evening we caught lamperts in great quantities, three times as many as we could eat. Our men, in ranging the key for game, found grass plaited above a fathom long, and a knot tied to the end thereof. On the other keys they found muscles and lampert shells. Hence we concluded these countries were inhabited, and that some Indians or others were to be found hereupon.

Saturday, October 15th. The night past we had much rain, with large hailstones. About midnight the wind came to north with such great fury, that the tree to which our cable was fastened on shore gave way, and come up by the roots. All those gusts of wind were mixed with violent storms of rain and hail. We fastened again to other trees; but here it happened that our ship coming up to the shore, our rudder touched, and broke our goose-neck. Great was now our danger, and greater it would have been, if it had not pleased God to send us better weather. Scarce a minute now passed without flaws of wind and rain.

Sunday, October 16th. All night past was rainy, as before. About nine o'clock our biggest hawser gave way and broke. All this day likewise we had rain, with several showers of hail, and but little wind at N. W.

Monday, October 17th. Last night, till five this morning, it ceased not to rain; then till ten it snowed; on the hills it snowed all the night long. This day we hunted on the shore many tracks of people, but could find none, they having fled and concealed themselves for fear of us, as we supposed.

October 18th. The night past we had much rain and hail; but the day was very clear and pretty warm. Hereupon we made an observation, which gave us latitude 50° 40′ S.

October 19th. The night past was clear and frosty. This day was hazy, and something windy from the north quarter. Every day we had plenty of lamperts and muscles, of a very large size.

October 20th. The night past was rainy, and this day great gusts of wind at N. N. W. till the afternoon. Then we had wind at N. W., being very fresh, and in gusts.

October 21st. All the night past was tempestuous, with great gusts of wind and showers of hail. Yesterday in the evening we carried a cable ashore, and fastened it to a tree; this being done, at midnight our biggest cable broke in the middle. Towards morning we had much snow; in the day, great gusts of wind, with large hailstones. We caught great plenty of lamperts.

October 22d. Last night we had strong gusts of wind from N. W., together with much hail and rain. This day we killed a penguin, and began to carry water on board.

October 23d. For twenty-four hours past we had much rain; the wind was but little at W. and W. S. W.

October 24th. All this time till noon, nothing but rain. At that time it held up for half an hour, or thereabouts, and then it rained again all the rest of the day.

October 25th. All this while we had not one minute fair. Towards evening it held up, but the weather was cloudy, and withal much warmer than when we came hither at first.

Wednesday, October 26th. All night past, and this forenoon,

we had fair weather, but after noon it rained again. We found cockles like those we have in England.

Thursday, October 27th. Last night we had much rain, with very great gusts of wind all night. Notwithstanding, this day proved to be the fairest that we had had since we came into this place. In the evening, our canoe, which was gone to search the adjacent places for Indians, or what else they could find, returned to the ship with a doree at her stern. They had gone, as it should seem, beyond the old bay where we first anchored, and thereabouts happened to meet with this doree. In it were three Indians, who perceiving themselves nigh being taken, leaped overboard to make their escape. Our men in pursuing them did unadvisedly shoot one of them dead; a second, being a woman, escaped their hands; but a third, who was a lusty boy about eighteen years of age, was taken, whom they brought on board the ship. He was covered only with a seal's skin, having no other clothing about him. His eyes were squinted, and his hair pretty short. In the middle of the doree they had a fire burning, either for dressing of victuals, or some other use. The doree itself was built sharp at both ends, and flat-bottomed. They had a net to catch penguins, and a club like our bandies, called by them a tom-ahunks. His language we could not understand, but withal he pointed up the lagoon, giving us to understand that there were more people thereabouts. This was confirmed by our men, who also said they had seen more. They had darts to throw against an enemy, pointed with wood.

The next day, being October 28th, in the evening our canoe went from the ship again to seek for more Indians. They went into several lagoons, and searched them narrowly; but they could find nothing but two or three huts, all the natives being fled before our arrival. In the evening they returned to the ship, bringing with them very large lamperts, and muscles which were six inches and a half long. Our Indian prisoner could open these muscles with his fingers, which our men could not so readily do with their knives. Both the night past and this day we had very fair weather.

October 29th, we had in like manner a very fair day, and also a very smooth wind at S. S. E. Our Indian this day pointed to us, that there were men in this country, or not far from hence, with great beards. He appeared to us by his actions to be very innocent and foolish; but by his carriage I was also persuaded that he was a man-eater. This day likewise we caught lamperts enough to suffice us for the morrow.

Sunday, October 30th. This day was fair, and there blew a small S. S. E. wind. In the morning we sent a canoe over to the eastward shore, to seek either for provisions or Indians. I myself could not go, as I desired, being, with two or three more, at that time very much tormented with the gripes. I am persuaded this place is not so large an island as described by some hydrographers, but rather a collection of smaller islands. We saw this day many penguins, but they were so shy, that we could not come near them: they pad on the water with their wings very fast, but their bodies are so heavy that they cannot fly. The sun had now made the weather very warm, insomuch that the snow melted apace.

October 31st. Both last night and this day were very fair. At noon our canoe returned from the eastern shore, bringing word they had found several good bays and harbors, that were deep, even close to the shore; only there were several rocks sunk in them, which we had also where we were: but these rocks are not dangerous to shipping, by reason they have weeds which lie two fathoms in circumference about them. This morning blew a small wind at N. N. E.

November 1st. This day was also fair, and we had a small wind as before, at N. N. E.

November 2d. Last night I took the polar distance of the south star of the cock's foot, and found it to be 28° 25′. I observed also the two Magellan clouds, of which I made mention in this journal before, and found them to be as followeth, viz.: the lesser 14° 5′, and the greater 14° 25′. In the morning we hoisted on end our topmast, and brought too a main-topsail, and foresail, and finished our filling all the water we needed. At the same time the wind hung easterly, and I was still troubled with the gripes as before.

November 3d. This morning we hanged our rudder, the greatest piece of work we had to do, after those violent storms above mentioned. In the afternoon we hauled in our two biggest hawsers, and also our biggest cable from the shore. For three days last past, we had a very great and dark fog between us and the eastward shore. We had now very little wind in the cove where we were, but abroad at sea there blew at the same time a stiff gale at S. S. E. We could perceive now, the stormy weather being blown over, much small fry of fish about the ship, whereof we could see none before. This evening was very clear and calm.

November 4th. Both last night and this day we had very calm weather; only a small breeze in the morning sprung up at N. and N. N. E., which afterwards wheeled about to S. and

S. S. E. This morning we hoisted our main and fore yards, and likewise fetched off from the shore our other hawser and cable, into the depth of eleven fathom water. Our resolutions were now changed for a departure, in order to seek the mouth of the Straits of Magellan, seeing we could not winter here, for want of provisions, which we could not find either on the continent, or about these islands afore mentioned. The weather now was very warm, or rather, hot, and the birds sung as sweetly as those in England. We saw here both thrushes and blackbirds, and many other sorts of those that are usually seen in our own country.

Saturday, November 5th. This morning brought us a wind at N. N. E. Hereupon we warped to a rocky point, thereby to get out of the cove where we lay: for our anchor came home to us, as we were carrying our warp out. At this time a second breeze came up very fresh in our stern, so that we took the opportunity thereof, and went away before it. By noon we hoisted in our canoes, and turned loose our Indian doree; as for the Indian boy whom we had taken in the said doree, we kept him prisoner, and called him Orson. When we were come out into the channel, the weather grew quite calm; only now and then we had a small breeze, sometimes from one quarter, and then from another. By this slackness of wind we observed, that the current hoisted us to the southward. On the east side of this lagoon, we perceived the Indians to make a great smoke, at our departure.

We had a very fair day till six in the evening; when we got without the mouth of the gulf, it blew so hard, that in an hour it forced us to hand our topsails. Having now a fit gale at N. W. and N. N. W., we stood S. W. by W., to clear ourselves of some breaks, which lie four leagues from the gulf's mouth, at S. and S. S. E. Hereabouts we saw many reefs and rocks, which occasioned us to stand close hauled.

CHAPTER XLVIII.

They depart from the English Gulf in Quest of the Straits of Magellan, which they cannot find. — They return Home, by an unknown Way.

Sunday, November 6th. This morning we lost sight of land, so that we could see it no more. All the night past, and this day, we were under our two courses and spritsail; the weather this day was hazy. My reckoning was a S. W. half S. way, and by it twenty-one leagues. We had now an indifferent high sea, and a fresh wind at N. N. W.

November 7th. Last night was both rainy and foggy, but in the morning it cleared up. The wind for the most part was at W. and W. N. W., but at noon it came about at W. S. W. Our reckoning was a S. W. by S. way, and by it twenty leagues. We found, by observation, latitude 52° 3′. We now steered away S. S. E., the wind being at that time at W. S. W. In the evening I found a variation of the needle to N. E., to the number of 15°, or better. I was still troubled with the gripes, as I had been before.

November 8th. We had a fair night the last past. About midnight the wind came to N. N. W. This day early, at break of day, we all were persuaded that we had seen land; but at noon we found our mistake, it being only a cloud. The wind was now at N. My reckoning was at S. E. half E. way, and thirty-two leagues aud one third of a league. We had an observation that gave us 53° 27′ S. The whole day was very fine and warm, and we saw great numbers of fowls and seals.

November 9th. Yesterday in the evening the weather was cloudy; hereupon we lay by under a main course. After midnight we sailed E. and E. by N., with a fresh wind at W. N. W., and not any great sea. The day itself was cloudy, and towards noon we had some rain; so at two in the afternoon, we lay by under a main course, the wind being fresh at N. W. I reckoned an E. N. E. way, and thereby twenty-eight leagues.

Thursday, November 10th. All night past we lay under a main course, with a mere fret of wind at N. W. and N. N. W. Day being come, the wind rather increased, insomuch that about noon our sail blew to pieces: hereupon we were forced to lower the yard and unbend the sail, lying for a little while under a mizzen; but that also soon gave way, so that all the rest of this day we lay a hulk in very dark weather, foggy and windy, with a great sea, which sometimes rolled over us. In the afternoon it seemed to abate for some space of time, but soon after it blew worse than before, which compelled us to lower our fore yard.

November 11th. All the night past we had furious, windy and tempestuous weather, from the points of N. W. and N. N. W., together with seas higher and higher. In the evening we set our mizzen, at which time the sun appeared very waterish; but the wind now abated by degrees, and the seas also.

November 12th. This morning little wind was stirring, only some rain fell. About ten it cleared up, and by an observation then made, we found latitude 55° 25′. The sea was now much fallen, and a fresh wind was sprung up at W. and W. S. W. We experimented also a very great current to the S. W. In the afternoon we set our sails again, and resolved, unanimously, to make for the Straits of St. Vincent, otherwise called the Straits of Fernando de Magellan. We had a fresh wind at W. N. W., our course being S. S. E., under our spritsail, foresail, and fore-topsail. This day we saw many fishes, or rather fowls, who had heads like Muscovy ducks, as also two feet like them. They had two fins, like the fore fins of turtles, white breasts and bellies, their beaks and eyes being red. They are full of feathers on their bodies, and the hinder parts are like those of a seal, wherewith they cut the water. The Spaniards call these fowls *paxaros ninos*. They weigh most commonly about six or seven pounds, being about a foot long. Our commander, Captain Sharp, was so dexterous as to strike two of them. In the evening we set our mainsail, the wind now coming to W. and by S.

Sunday, November 13th. All the night past, we had a fresh wind between S. W. and W. N. W., with sometimes mists of small rain. In the evening we had a fine leading gale at W. N. W., together with clear and wholesome weather. We made a S. E. way, and by it forty-two leagues and two thirds. This day an observation gave us latitude 56° 55′ S. We still found a great S. W. current. In the afternoon we steered E. S. E., and in the evening had whiffling winds.

November 14th. Both last night and this morning, we had cloudy weather. About eight it cleared up. My reckoning was a S. E. by E. way, and by it thirty-two leagues. Our observation gave us latitude 57° 50′ S. This day we could perceive land, and at noon were due west of it. In the evening we stood E. by S.

November 15th. All the night past was very cloudy. We judged now that we should be close in with the land we had seen the day before; but the morning being come, we could see none. In the night much snow fell, and in the day we had great fleets thereof, the weather being very cold and cloudy. I reckoned an E. S. E. way, and hereby twenty-nine leagues and two thirds; moreover, that our latitude was 58° 25′ S. The wind was now so fresh at N. that we were forced to lie under our two courses and spritsail.

November 16th. Most of this time we had still rain and snow, but now no night at all, though the weather was dark. The wind was various, but from midnight before it was at S. E. and S. S. E. We now lay E. N. E. I reckoned a N. E. by E. way, and twenty-three leagues. About four in the afternoon two of our fore-shroud bolts broke, but withal, were presently mended. This afternoon also we saw a very large whale. In the evening we handed in our fore-topsail, and lay under our pair of courses and spritsail, the evening being very clear.

November 17th. In the night there was a very hard frost. At four this morning we saw two or three islands of ice, the distance of two or three leagues southward of us. Soon after this we saw several others, the biggest of them being at least two leagues round. By an observation made this day, we found 58° 23′ S. We had now a vehement current to the southward. At noon I saw many others of these islands of ice afore mentioned, of which some were so long, that we could scarce see the end of them, and were extended about ten or twelve fathom above water. The weather in the mean while was very clear, and the wind cold. I found variation of the needle, 18° to the N. E.

November 18th. All the night past was very fair; (I must call it night, for otherwise it was not dark at all.) The sea was very smooth, and the wind at N. and N. N. W. I reckoned a N. E. by N. way, and by the same twenty-two leagues. At ten it fell quite calm, which held all the afternoon. But at night we had a wind again at N. and N. by E.

November 19th. This day was cloudy, with snow, and a frosty night preceding it. The wind now was so fresh at north, that we were forced to take in our topsails, and lie all day under our courses and spritsail. We made, by an E. S. E. way, eighteen leagues and two thirds.

November 20th. We had a cloudy night the last past, together with mizzling rain and snow. This morning fell so great a fog, that we could scarce see from stem to stern of our ship. From ten o'clock last night we had also a calm, and very cold weather; but what was worse than all this, we were kept to a very short allowance of our sorry victuals, our provisions growing very scanty with us. About ten this morning we had a very small breeze at N. Several of our men were not able to endure the cold, it was so piercing; whereby they were forced to lie and keep themselves as close as they could. We made an E. way, and by the same sixteen leagues. This day, at noon, I reckoned myself to be east from the gulf, from whence we last parted, two hundred and five leagues, and two thirds of a league.

Monday, November 21st. Last night we caught a small land-fowl, and saw two or three more. This sight gave us good hopes we were not far from some coast or other; yet we could see none all this long and tedious voyage. In the night past we had a calm, and all this morning a great fog, with much snow and rain. We reckoned an E. by N. way, and ten leagues. At one in the afternoon, we had a fresh gale that sprang up at E. and at E. by N.

November 22d. Most part of this day was calm. Meanwhile we observed our ship drive east. My reckoning was an E. N. E. way, and thereby thirteen leagues and one third. At one in the afternoon we had a small gale at W. S. W., our course being N. N. E. and N. E. by N.

November 23d. This day we had a gale at N. W., freshening by degrees, so that we were forced to take in our topsails and spritsail. The wind was not a settled gale, but often varied from point to point. At noon it came at N. E., and our course was then N. N. W. By a north way, we reckoned sixteen leagues.

November 24th. Both the night past and this morning was foggy weather, with some calms between whiles; but at eight in the morning the sun broke out, yet it was not a clear day. By a N. N. E. way, we reckoned fifteen leagues. This morning the wind came about to E., and at noon it was again at N. E. We had a clear evening, and a fresh gale.

November 25th. All the night past we had a fresh wind at E. and E. N. E., insomuch that at eight in the morning we took in our topsails. But at noon the wind was not so fresh as before. I reckoned a N. N. W. half W. way, and by the same twenty leagues.

November 26th. Last night the wind was not altogether so fresh as before, but this morning it was again very high. The weather was dark and cloudy, with sometimes rain and snow. We made a N. N. E. way, and hereby thirty leagues; the wind all along E. by S. and E. S. E. In the evening we had fair weather again. We found for the ten days last past a great western sea, and saw in the same time several seals.

Sunday, November 27th. All the night past we enjoyed a

fresh gale, and clear weather. I reckoned thirty-six leagues by a N. E. by N. way. By an observation made, we now found latitude 52° 48′ S. And I judged myself to be east from the gulf, two hundred and eighty-five leagues. In the evening we had a very exact sight of the sun, and found above 30° variation of the needle. From whence ought to be concluded, that it is very difficult to direct a course of navigation in these parts; for in the space of only twenty-five leagues sailing, we have found 8 or 9° difference of variation, by a good Dutch azimuth compass.

November 28th. All last night, we had a fresh wind at E. S. E. Towards morning we had but little wind, all the day being hazy weather. This day we saw a whole flight of such land-fowls as we killed one of before. This sight gave us further hopes we were not far from land, yet we found none in all this voyage. We made by a N. N. E. way, thirty-three leagues. Yesterday in the evening we set a new spritsail, and about three this morning we also set our mainsail. At one in the afternoon, the wind came about at N. E. and N. N. E. which in the evening blew very fresh, with cloudy weather.

November 29th. The night proved very cloudy, and the wind blew very fresh at E. N. E. and N. E. by E. This morning it was E., both with snow and hail. Towards noon the weather cleared up, and we found, by an observation taken, latitude 49°. 45′ S. Our reckoning was a N. way, and thirty leagues. This day we had a short eastern sea, and withal a very cold evening. I took the sun, and hereby I found variation 26° 30′ to the N. E. This night the wind came about W. and W. N. W., continuing so all the night.

November 30th. This day the wind was N. and N. N. E., with some clouds hovering in the sky. At this time we had already almost four hours of night. The morning of this day was very fair and clear. Hereupon, to give myself satisfaction in the point, as fearing the truth of Spanish books, I worked the true amplitude of the sun, and found his variation to be 26° 25′ to the N. E., being very conformable to what I had read and experienced before. Hereabouts also we found a current to the northward. This day also we saw much rockweed, which renewed our hopes once more of seeing land. We reckoned a N. E. way, and by the same twenty-two leagues. By an observation made, we found latitude 48° 53′ S. This day also we saw several of these fowl-fish afore described, called *paxaros ninos* and these of a larger size than any we had seen before. In the afternoon the wind came about at N. N. E., whereby we stood N. W. by W. with a fresh gale, and smooth water. The weather now began to grow warmer than hitherto, and the evening was clear.

Tuesday, December 1st. The latter part of the night past was very cloudy, and sometimes rainy. About midnight we had a violent tornado, forcing us in a moment to hand in our topsails. At five in the morning we set them again, and at eleven we had another tornado, forcing us to hand our topsails a second time. We made a N. N. E. two thirds east way, and thereby thirteen leagues, and two thirds of a league. The afternoon of this stormy day proved very fair, and the wind came to W. S. W., our course being N. E. by N. In the evening the wind freshened, with cloudy weather.

December 2d. Last night we had a very furious whirlwind, which, notwithstanding, it pleased God, passed about the length of our ship to westward of us. However, we handed in our topsails, and hauled up our lowsail in the brails. After the whirlwind came a fresh storm of large hailstones, in the night, and several tornadoes; but, God be thanked, they all came large of our ship. We now made a great way under a fore course and spritsail. At four this morning our foresail split, whereby we were forced to lower our fore yard. At half an hour after ten we hoisted it again, with a furious S. W. wind. We made a N. E. by E. way, and by the same forty-seven leagues and a half. By observation, we now had latitude 46° 54′ S. We reefed our topsail, with respect to the violence of the wind. But in the evening this rather increased, and we had a very great sea. Our standing rigging, through the fury of this gale, gave way in several places, but was soon mended again.

December 3d. The wind all the night past was very fresh, with severe flaws, both of wind and rain, at S. W. and S. W. by S. We enjoyed now very warm weather. This morning we set our fore-topsail. Our reckoning gave us a N. E. half E. way, and forty-five leagues. We found latitude by observation 45° 28′ S. This day, at noon, a large shoal of young porpoises came about our ship, and played up and down.

December 4th. All the night past we had a fresh gale at W. S. W. The night was clear, only that now and then we had a small cloud affording some rain. In the morning, from four till eight, it rained; but then it cleared up again, with a S. W. wind, and a very smooth sea. We made a N. E. one quarter N. way, thirty-nine leagues. By observation we found latitude 44° 1′ S. At noon the wind came to S. S. W., our course then being N. N. E. This day we agreed among ourselves, having the consent of our commander, to share the eight chests of money which as yet remained unshared. Yesterday, in the evening, we let out the reef of our foresail, and hoisted up our foreyard. This evening I found variation 17° N. E.

Monday, December 5th. All night past, a clear night, and this a fair day, with a fresh wind at S. S. W. We reckoned a N. E. 5° N. way, and by the same forty-two leagues. An observation gave us latitude 42° 29′ S. This afternoon we shared of the chests above mentioned, three hundred pieces of eight to each man. I now reckoned myself to be E. from my departure four hundred and seventy-one leagues, and one third of a league. At night again we shared twenty-two pieces of eight more to each.

December 6th. We had a clear starlight night the last, and a fair morning this day, with a fresh gale at S. W. At noon we took in our fore-topsail. We reckoned a N. E. half N. way, and hereby fifty leagues and two thirds. An observation taken afforded us 43° 31′ S. This evening was cloudy.

December 7th. The night was both windy and cloudy. At one in the morning we took in our topsails, and at three, handed our spritsail, and so we scudded away before the wind, which now was very fresh at W. This morning a gust of wind came and tore our mainsail into an hundred pieces, which made us put away before the wind, till we could provide for that accident. My reckoning was a N. E. three quarters E. way, and by the same thirty-three leagues. By observation we found latitude 39° 37′ S. We had now a great sea, and a fresh wind. At three in the afternoon we set another foresail, the first being blown to pieces. At the same time we furled our spritsail. At five the wind came at W. S. W., with very bad weather. This day our worthy commander, Captain Sharp, had very certain intelligence given him, that on Christmas day, which was now at hand, the company, or at least a great part thereof, had a design to shoot him; he having appointed that day some time since to be merry. Hereupon he made us share the wine amongst us, as being persuaded they would scarce attempt any such thing in their sobriety. The wine we shared fell out to three jars to each mess. That night the wind increased.

December 8th. The night past was both cloudy and windy; the wind very often varying between the N. W. and S. W. points. This morning it varied between W. and N. W. by W. About noon this day we brought a new mainsail to the yard, but did not set it then, by reason there blowed too much wind. I reckoned a N. E. half N. way, and by the same thirty leagues. By observation made, we found latitude 38° 29′ S. In the afternoon we had one or two squalls of wind and rain; but the violence of both fell at stern of us. In the evening it blew again very hard. I observed this day the rising and setting of the sun, and found the exact variation to be 12° 15′ N. E.

December 9th. The night was starlight, but withal very windy. About break of day, the wind came to N. W., and at seven we set our fore-topsail, and stood N. N. E., with not much wind. We made, since our last reckoning, a N. E. quarter E. way, and twenty-nine leagues. We found, by observation, latitude 37° 30′ S. The sea was much fallen, but our ship began to complain of several leaks, through our tedious and long voyage. This afternoon we hoisted up our main yard, and set up back-stays and main-swifter, whose ring-bolt gave way, but was mended. In the evening of this day we had but little wind.

December 10th. The night was very clear, but till ten o'clock this forenoon, we had no wind. Then a small breeze sprang up at N. by E. We made an E. N. E. one third N. way, and hereby twenty-one leagues. An observation gave us latitude 37° 1′ S. In the afternoon our chief surgeon cut off the foot of a negro boy, which was perished with cold. Now it was like to be bad weather again. Hereupon we furled our topsails, and lay under a pair of courses. But in the evening we lay under a foresail and mizzen, with misty weather.

Sunday December 11th. All the night past we had a fresh wind at N., and sometimes at N. N. W. The weather was very cloudy, with drizzling rain. We made an E. way, and thereby twenty-five leagues. This day brought a great sea. About ten in the morning one of our main shrouds gave way. In the evening fell some small rain.

December 12th. All the night past we had misty rain, and but little wind; yea, in the morning a perfect calm. At noon came up a small gale at E. S. E. and S. E., bringing with it cloudy weather. We reckoned a N. E. by E. way, and by the same eighteen leagues. Yesterday died the negro boy whose foot was cut off by our surgeon, as was mentioned the day before. This afternoon also died another negro, something bigger than the former, named Chepillo. The boy's name was Beasero. All this evening but small wind.

December 13th. All night the wind was at E. S. E., our course being N. N. E. At three in the morning it came about at S. S. W., and at nine at E. by N. I reckoned a N. E. by N. way, and fifteen leagues. The weather was hazy. In the afternoon the wind was at N. E., our course being N. N. W. We had now a very smooth sea, and saw multitudes of grampuses, whales, and porpoises every day, as we sailed along.

December 14th. The evening past was cloudy, as also the

night foggy ; hereupon we took in our topsails. At half an hour after three this morning we stood N. E., the wind being then at N. N. W. At five we put out our topsails again. At seven we saw a turtle floating upon the sea. We reckoned a N. N. E. way. This day's observation afforded us 34° 32′ S. At this time we had very hot weather, and great dews in the night. My whole easting I reckoned to be now six hundred and seventy-seven leagues and one third of a league.

December 15th. We had a fine night the last past, and a great dew. The wind in the interim was between N. and N. W. I reckoned a N. E. half E. way, and by the same thirty-one leagues. We had an observation that gave us latitude 33° 46′ S. At noon the wind came about at N. N. W., our course being N. E. We had this day a very clear evening, and at the same time a fresh wind.

December 16th. We had a fair night and wind at N. N. W. and N. W. by N. This morning I took the sun at its rising, and found N. E. variation 20° 30′ S. My reckoning was a N. N. E. way, and thirty-six leagues and one third of another. By observation, I found latitude 32° 9′ S. At noon this day the wind came about to N. W.

December 17th. Most part of the last night, the wind was at N. W. as before; but towards morning a fine and easy gale sprang up at W. N. W. This morning we saw several dolphins playing upon the sea, which made us hope they would at last befriend us, and suddenly show us some land or other. We reckoned a N. E. by N. one third N. way, and by the same twenty-five leagues. An observation gave us now latitude 31° 4′ S. A fair evening.

December 18th. We had a clear night past, together with a smooth gale at N. W., which this morning was at W. by S. We had now a smooth sea for several days past. Our reckoning was twenty-five leagues, by a N. E. by N. way. By observation we perceived latitude 29° 48′ S.

December 19th. A clear night the last past, and a fresh breeze at S. S. W. and S. W. by S., lasting until nine in the morning. Then sprung up a wind at S. E. by E. I reckoned this day a N. N. E. half E. way, and upon the same thirty leagues. By observation made, we took latitude 28° 29′ S. The day was very fair, and a smooth sea, with weather that was very hot. My whole easting I reckoned now to be seven hundred and sixty leagues. This evening I found variation 2° 50′ N. E.

CHAPTER XLIX.

The Buccaneers continue their Navigation, without seeing any Land, till they arrive at the Caribbee Islands, in the West Indies. — They give away their Ship to some of their Companions that were poor, and disperse for several Countries. — The Author of this Journal arriveth in England.

December 20th, 1681. The night before was something cloudy, but the weather was fair, and the wind but little. At noon the wind came about N. by E., our course being W. N. W. We made a N. N. W. way, and thereby, as I reckoned, twenty-two leagues. By observation made, we took latitude 27° 25′ S. The evening was cloudy, and now and then there fell a shower of rain.

December 21st. At eight o'clock last night, the wind came N. W. by N., but withal with dark weather, that we were forced to take in our topsails. The night was something rainy, and the weather this morning calm and rainy. About ten we had a small breeze at N. W. We reckoned a N. by E. way, and by the same sixteen leagues. The afternoon was calm and still.

December 22d. We had a fair clear night the last past, which produced this day a smooth sea, and extreme hot weather, and very little wind near the sun, so that no observation was made.

December 23d. The night was very fair. At midnight, or thereabouts, a fresh gale sprung up at S. E. and E. S. E., which sometimes was E.; this freshened by degrees. We had in the day very hot and clear weather. By a N. way, I reckoned fifteen leagues.

December 24th. Last night we had both a fresh gale, and a clear night. The wind was at E. by S. We reckoned a N. E. by E. way, and by it thirty-one leagues.

Sunday, December 25th. This day being Christmas day, for celebration of that great festival, we killed yesterday, in the evening, a sow. This sow we had brought from the Gulf of Nicoya, being then a suckling pig, of about three weeks old, but now weighed about fourscore and ten pounds. With this hog's flesh we made our Christmas dinner, being the only flesh we had eaten since we turned away our prizes under the equinoctial, and left the Island of Plata. We had this day several flaws of wind, and some rain, but the weather otherwise was pretty clear. I reckoned a N. by E. way, and thirty-three leagues by the same. It was now also extremely hot weather, as was signified before.

December 26th. We had this day several gusts of wind, which forced us to stand by our topsails; yet they were but very short, and all the rest of the while we enjoyed an indifferent fresh gale at E. and E. by S. We reckoned a N. by E. way, and twenty-eight leagues.

December 27th. We had fair weather and a fresh wind at E. and E. by S. I reckoned a N. by E. way, and upon the same thirty-two leagues. The evening of this day was cloudy.

December 28th. Last night was cloudy, with a fresh wind. We reckoned a N. E. way, and by the same forty-six leagues. We found, by an observation made, latitude 15° 30′ S. My whole easting I reckoned this day to be eight hundred and twenty-five leagues. Now we saw much flying-fish, with some dolphins, bonitoes, and albicores; but they would not take the hook.

December 29th. All last night was cloudy, with a fresh wind between E. and E. S. E. The weather all the afternoon was hazy. I reckoned a N. by E. way, and hereupon forty leagues and one third. In the afternoon we had a S. E. by E. wind, which blew very fresh. The evening was clear. At sunset I found variation to N. W. 4° 19′.

December 30th. The night past was cloudy. Towards morning the wind came about at E. At six it came E. S. E., and at ten to S. E. by S. We made a N. by E. way, and forty-three leagues. By an observation, we found latitude 11° 3′ S. The evening of this day was clear.

December 31st. We had a cloudy night the last past, but the morning was hazy. We came now to a strict allowance of only three good pints of water each day. We made a N. by E. way, and found latitude, by observation, 8° 55′ S. In the afternoon we had an E. S. E. and S. E. by E. wind. My whole easting I reckoned now to be eight hundred and eighty-four leagues and one third. At noon we stood away N. W.

Sunday, January 1st, 1681. All the night past was cloudy, as this day also, with some showers of rain. We made a N. W. one eighth N. way, and forty leagues. In the afternoon came about a fresh wind at S. E. and E. S. E.

January 2d. The weather this day was both dull and cloudy. We reckoned a N. W. one quarter N. way, and by the same thirty-two leagues. By observation, we found that our latitude now was 6° 6′ S. The wind came pretty fresh at S. E.

January 3d. We had several squalls of wind, and some rain; but withal a fresh wind at S. E. and E. S. E. Our reckoning was a N. W. one quarter N. way, and thirty-four leagues. The afternoon was clear, but the evening cloudy.

January. 4th. All the night past was very cloudy ; but this forenoon it cleared up. Yesterday we put aboard our main-topsail studden-sails, but took them in at night. At four this morning, we set our larboard studden-sail, and before noon fitted up topgallant masts and yard. We made a N. W way, and by it forty leagues and two thirds. By observation, we had now latitude 3° 9′ S. This afternoon also we set up our topgallant-sail, being forced to make out all its running rigging. The wind was pretty fresh at S. E. and S. E. by E.

January 5th. Most part of the night past was clear, and starlight, though with some rain towards morning. This being come, we put out our topgallant-sail, and both our topsail studden-sails. At noon, likewise, we put up our fore topgallant masts and yard. We caught an albicore this day, weighing about one hundred and twenty pounds weight. The wind was at S. E. by S. and S. S. E. We made a N. W. way, and reckoned thereby thirty-five leagues. By observation, we found latitude 2° 3′ S. We had now mighty hot weather.

January 6th. Yesterday, in the evening, we caught another albicore, which weighed only eight or nine pounds. We made a N. W. way, and reckoned thirty-five leagues, as before. Now, by an observation made, we could perceive only latitude 49′ S. The evening of this day was very clear.

January 7th. The wind was variable between S. S. E. and S. S. W., though not altogether so fresh as before. Our reckoning was a N. W one quarter N. way, and thirty-six leagues by the same. This day, an observation gave us 32′ N. of the equinoctial, which now we had passed again. In the afternoon we caught another albicore, which weighed more than the first ; that is, between one hundred and thirty-five and one hundred and forty pounds. But little wind stirring this afternoon.

January 8th. The evening past we had almost a calm. At nine this morning, we had a fresh wind at S. S. E., with dark weather, so that we thought it convenient to take in our main-topsail. But at noon we set it again, and also, our larboard top studden-sail, with both topgallant-sails. We made a N. W. way, and by it thirty-four leagues. By an observation made, we found latitude 1° 55′ N. We had now extreme hot weather, and a very small allowance of water.

January 9th. Last night we took in our topsails all night, the wind then whiffling between S. and W. points. We had notwithstanding, for the most part, very little wind. The morning was rainy, so that we providentially saved a bompkin of water. There was now a great rippling sea rising very high.

It is reported, there is an enchanted island hereabouts, which some positively say they have sailed over. I reckoned a N. W. by N. one quarter N. way, and twenty-five leagues. This afternoon we had very dark and calm weather, looking as though we should have much rain. Now reckoning up my meridian, I found myself E. from my departure, seven hundred and two leagues. In the evening we had very rainy weather, and a cockling sea.

January 10th. All the night past was cloudy. About midnight sprang up a small breeze varying all around the compass. At five this morning we had a breeze at S. E., and a very clear sky, which afterwards continued to freshen, with the same clearness as before. We made a N. W. by N. one quarter N. way, and by the same two leagues and two thirds. By a clear observation, we had now latitude 3° 16′ N. At four this evening, the wind was at E. S. E., the weather being violently hot, insomuch that our allowance of water being short, it was very tedious. At the same time we had an indifferent smooth sea from the E.

January 11th. All the night past we had little or no wind; but about two in the morning, the wind freshened again at E. N. E., and brought both a clear and hot day. We made twenty-three leagues, by a N. W. one quarter W. way This day's observation gave us latitude 4° 6′ N. In the afternoon we had a shower of rain, and after a fresh wind at E. N. E. But the evening grew dull.

January 12th. In the night past we had two or three squalls of wind, and some showers of rain. In the mean while the wind blew fresh at N. E. and N. E. by E., as it also continued to do in the day. I reckoned a N. W. way, and forty-four leagues and one third. Our observation this day gave us 5° 49′ N. Yesterday and to-day we set our main-topsail. Now I could not find much variation of the needle.

January 13th. We had a fresh gale all the last night, but more northerly than before; for now it was N. E. by N. We reckoned a W. N. W. way, and thereupon — leagues and two thirds. An observation taken showed us latitude 6° 41′ N. We had a N. N. E. sea, and very clear weather.

January 14th. We had a clear night the last, and a fresh wind at E. N. E. We made a N. W. one fifth W. way, and thirty-eight leagues. By an observation, we found latitude 7° 46′ N. We had a smooth sea, and now we were come to only three horns of water a day, which were in all but a quart allowance for each man. The evening was clear, and we had a fresh wind.

Sunday, January 15th. The night past was clear, and the wind fresh at E. N. E., and again at N. E by E., very fresh. About eleven at night died one of our companions, named William Stephens. It was commonly believed that he poisoned himself with manzanilla in Golfo Dulce, for he never had been in health since that time. This forenoon was cloudy. We reckoned forty-four leagues, and a N. W. way. An observation gave us this day 9° 18′ N. All the night we kept out our top-gallant-sails. We saw hereabouts many large flying-fish. This morning, also, we threw overboard our dead man, and gave him two French volleys, and one English one. I found now again very small variation.

January 16th. We had a clear night, and a very fresh wind at N. E. and E. N. E., with a long homing sea. My reckoning was a N. W. one seventh W. way, and thereby forty-eight leagues and one third. The observation made this day gave us latitude 10° 48′ N. I reckoned myself now east from my departure five hundred and fifty-three leagues. We had a cloudy evening.

January 17th. All the night past we enjoyed a fresh wind, and so this day, also, at N. E. by N. We made a N. W. half W. way, and thereupon forty-seven leagues and one third of a league. By observation we found latitude 12° 19′ N. We had now a long north sea. At noon this day we steered away N. N. W. The day was very hot, but the night both cool and dewy.

January 18th. All the night past was both cloudy and windy. At six this morning our spritsail-topmast broke. I reckoned a W. N. W. way, and forty-eight leagues by the same. We found, by observation, latitude 13° 12′ N. At noon we steered away west, the wind being at N. E. fresh, with a clear evening.

January 19th. We had a clear night the last, and fresh wind at E. N. E., which sometimes came in pushes. Our reckoning was a W. half southerly way, and by the same forty-six leagues. We found, by observation, latitude 13° 1′ N. Yesterday, in the evening, we put up a new spritsail-topmast, with a fine, smooth gale at N. E. by E.

January 20th. The night past was clear, and not very fresh, but at daybreak it freshened again. Last night we saw a great shoal of fish, whereof we caught none, by reason the porpoises frightened them from us, as they oftentimes had done before. Yesterday, in the evening, we saw a man-of-war fowl, and that gave us good hopes we should ere long see land. These hopes, and the great desire we had to end our voyage, gave us

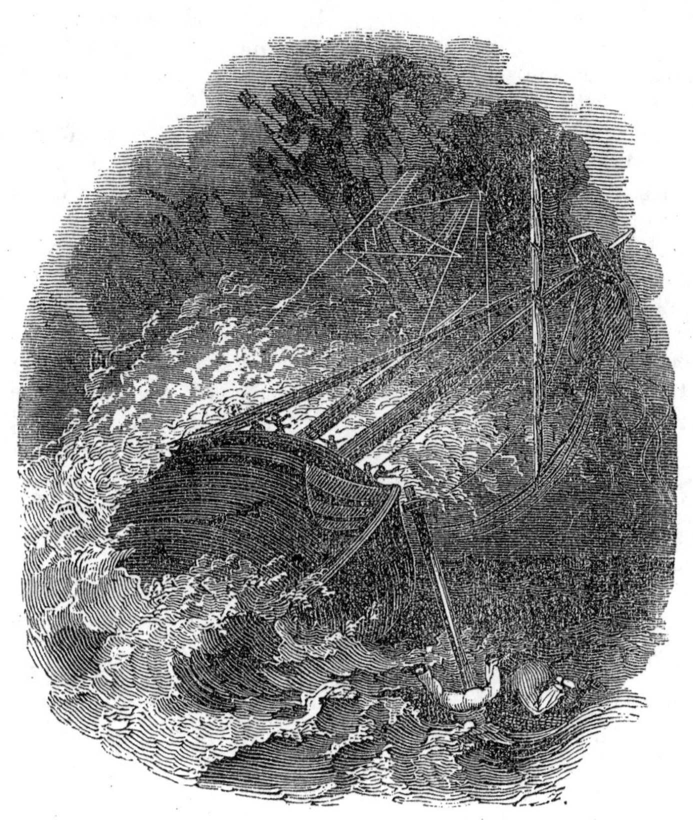

occasion this day to put in, or stake down, each man of our company, a piece of eight for a reward to him that should first discover land. We reckoned a W. one sixth northerly way, and by it thirty-eight leagues. An observation gave us this day latitude 13° 11′ N. The wind was at N. E. and E. N. E. This day we passed over many ripplings, and saw abundance of fish, but we could take none for the porpoises.

On January 21st, we made a W. way, and reckoned forty-seven leagues. By observation, we found latitude 13° 7′ N. The wind was at E. N. E., and from thence came a long sea. The evening was very clear.

January 22d, we had a fair and a clear day, the wind being at E. We reckoned a W. by N. one third W. way, and forty-leagues. An observation showed us latitude 13° 17′ N. We had a clear evening, and a fresh wind at E. N. E.

January 23d. This day was both clear and hot, with a fresh wind at E. N. E. My reckoning was a W. way, and forty-six leagues. Our observation, made this day, afforded us latitude 13° 15′ N. In the evening we had some rain.

January 24th. This day brought us likewise clear weather, such as the day before. I reckoned a W. way, and forty leagues and one third. By observation, we found latitude 13° 12′ N. The afternoon was cloudy, and we had some rain, the wind freshening at E. N. E. and E. by N. I reckoned now that I was E. from my departure three hundred and eleven leagues. We had a cloudy evening.

January 25th. Both last night and this morning the weather was cloudy. This morning we saw several tropic birds of diverse sorts. Our reckoning was a W. three quarters N. way, and forty-three leagues. We found, by observation, latitude 13° 29′ N. This afternoon we saw a booby flying close aboard the horizon. The weather was hazy. And now we began to look out sharp on all sides for land, expecting to see it every minute. I reckoned myself to be eastward of my departure two hundred and sixty-eight leagues.

January 26th. The night past was indifferently clear; yet notwithstanding this morning we had a smart shower of rain and wind. Hereupon we furled the spritsail, the weather being very hazy to the westward. We reckoned a W. way, and thereby forty-six leagues and one third. By observation taken, we found latitude 13° 17′ N. At noon this day we had a very fierce tornado, and rainy together, but withal a clear afternoon. We had a high E. N. E. sea, and saw multitudes of flying-fish; also several fowls, and amongst these two or three boobies. The evening was hazy.

January 27th. All night past we had a fresh wind and clear weather. This morning our fore-topmast-backstay gave way, and at daybreak the starboard sheet of our fore-topsail broke. We had several tornadoes this day, and dark weather. Our reckoning was a W. way, and forty-eight leagues by the same. We had a clear evening, and a dark night. This day, also, a certain bird, called a noddy, came on board us, which we took for a certain token that we were not now very far from land.

Saturday, January 28th. We had a very clear night the last past. About an hour before day one of our company happened to descry land, which proved to be the Island of Barbadoes, at S. S. W. from us, and at about two leagues and a half distance from Chalky Mount, standing S. W. by S. As we sailed, we saw several ships at anchor in Spike's Road. Soon after a shallop passed by, between us and the shore, but would not come within call of us. Hereupon we stood in within a mile of the shore, and made a whiff to a pinnace which we saw coming out of the road before mentioned. She came close aboard, and was the barge belonging to his Majesty's frigate, the Richmond, then lying at the Bridgetown at anchor. They told us of a peace at home, but would not come on board us, though often invited thereunto. Neither dared we be so bold as to put in at Barbadoes; for hearing of a frigate lying there, we feared lest the said frigate should seize us for privateers, and for having acted in all our voyage without commission. So we stood away from thence for the Island of Antego.

Here I cannot easily express the infinite joy we were possessed with all this day to see our own countrymen again. They told us, that a ship, which we saw in the offing to leeward of the island, was a Bristol man, and an interloper; but we feared that same vessel to be the frigate before mentioned. I reckoned a way of twenty-five leagues, so that I was now, by my account, to eastward of my departure one hundred and fifty-one leagues. Now we stood N. by W., and, by observation, found latitude 13° 17′ N., we being then N. W. from the body of the Island of Barbadoes between seven and eight leagues. This afternoon we freed the negro, who was our shoemaker by his trade, giving him his liberty for the good service he had done us in all the course of this voyage. We gave, also, to our good commander, Captain Sharp, a mulatto boy to wait on him, as a free gift of the whole company, in token of our respects to him for conducting us safe through so many dangerous adventures. This being done, we shared some parcels of money that had not as yet been touched of our former prizes, and this dividend amounted to twenty-four pieces of eight a man.

At one of the clock this day, from our fore yard we descried the Island of Santa Lucia, being one of the western islands, not far distant from that of Barbadoes. I had omitted to tell a passage which happened in our ship on Thursday last, which was 26th day of this month, and just two days before we made the island before mentioned of Barbadoes. A little Spanish shock-dog, which we had found in our late wine prize, taken under the equinoctial, and had kept alive till now, was sold at the mast by public cry, for forty pieces of eight, his owner saying that all he could get for him should be spent upon the company at a public merriment. Our commander, Captain Sharp, bought the dog, with intention to eat him, in case we did not see land quickly. This money, therefore, with one hundred pieces of eight more, which our boatswain, carpenter, and quarter-master had refused to take at this last dividend, for some quarrel they had against the sharers thereof, was all laid up in store till we came to land, in order to be spent on shore, at a common feast, or drinking bout. At sunset the Island of Santa Lucia bore W. S. W. from us, and was at ten leagues distance. Also the Island of Martinica bore N. W. by W. of us, at twelve or thirteen leagues distance. We had this day a very clear evening.

Sunday, January 29th, we had a clear night, and a fresh wind at E. by N. and at E. N. E. Our reckoning was at N. N. W. half W. way, and hereby forty-six leagues. By observation, we took latitude 15° 45′ N. At noon this day we saw the island named La Desseada, or the Desired Island, which then bore N. W. from us, and seemed to be at about eight leagues distance. At six in the evening, we saw Marigalante, another of the Caribbee Islands, at S. W. by W. from us, and that of Guadalupe, streaking itself in several hammocks of land, both westward and northward; as also La Desseada above mentioned at S. E., which from thence shows like table-land, and at each end hath a low point running out. At six this evening it was W. S. W., and at five or six leagues distance from us. At the same time we saw the Island of Monserrat, at a great distance, and making three round hammocks close together. This evening we caught an albicore of twenty pound weight.

Monday, January 30th. We had a fair night all the last past, and a fresh wind. Hereupon all night we hauled up our mainsail in brails, standing at the same N. by W., with the wind at E. N. E. At midnight we stood N. W. At three in the morning we lay by till five. Then we stood away W. N. W. till six; and then stood W. At eight of the clock we saw the Island of La Antigua, called by us Antego, to the southward of us, making three round hammocks of land, and a long high hill to northward. Hereupon, we stood W. S. W. for it. At noon we found latitude 17° N., the island being then just W. from us.

We came about to the south of the island, and sent a canoe ashore to get tobacco, and such other necessaries as we wanted, as also to ask leave of the governor to come into port. The gentry of the place, and common people, were very willing and desirous to receive us. But on Wednesday, February 1st, the governor flatly denied us entry; at which all the gentry were much troubled, showing themselves very kind to us. Hereupon we agreed among ourselves to give the slip to those of our company who had no money left them of all their purchase in this voyage, having lost it at play; and then put ourselves on board two ships bound for England. So I myself, and thirteen more of our company, went on board Captain Robert Porteen's ship, called the Lisbon Merchant, and set sail from La Antigua February 11th, and landed at Dartmouth, in England, March 26th, A. D. 1682.

CHAPTER L.

A Journal of a Voyage made by the Freebooters into the South Sea, 1684, and in the following Years.*

'It is no very uncommon thing for a child, that is a native of Paris, to go and seek his fortune abroad, and to entertain a fixed design of becoming a man engaged in hazardous adventures. This city, within which most of the wonders of the world are contained, and which is perhaps the greatest that can be met with, ought, in my opinion, to have the preference of any other upon the face of the earth. But who is he that can penetrate into the secrets of Nature, and give a reason for some sort of inclinations she works in the minds of mortals? As for myself, I confess I am not able to give an account of the depth of my desires; and all that I can say is, that I have always had a most passionate disposition for travel. Scarce was I seven years old, when, through some innate notions, whereof I had not the mastery, I began to steal out of my father's house. It is true, my first rambles were not far, because my age and strength would not allow them to be so; but they were so

---

* *A Certificate given by the Governor of St. Domingo to the Author of this Journal, concerning the Service.*

The Sieur de Cussy, his Majesty's Governor of the Tortoise Island and the Coast of St. Domingo.

We do certify, That the Sieur Ravenau de Lussan hath served in a company of fourscore and four men with the Sieur Lawrence de Graff, in the quality of an ensign against the Spaniards, his Majesty's enemies; and that, having gone into the South Sea, he fell into the company of other freebooters, from whence not being able to return, but by the force of their arms, he has given upon those occasions signal proofs both of his zeal and courage. In testimony whereof we have given him this certificate, to which we have affixed our seal, and ordered our secretary to countersign the same.

Given at the Fort of Port Paix, May 17, 1688. De Cussy.

By the Governor's command,

Boyer.

A Copy of a Letter written by Monsieur De Cussy, his Majesty's Governor of the Tortoise-Island and Coast of St. Domingo, to Monsieur de Lubert, Treasurer General of the Marine, upon the Subject Matter of this Author's Journal.

Sir: — I have taken notice from those letters you have done me the honor to write unto me the preceding years, that you interest yourself in the affairs of the Sieur Ravenau de Lussan; wherefore, sir, I have thought it my duty to inform you of his return from the South Sea, with two hundred and sixty of his comrades, who got clear out of that country by the performing of wonderful actions, the particulars whereof I shall not enter upon, since he will have the honor to give you an exact and faithful account of them himself, being the only person of all the company that has kept a journal.

I was in hopes to have got him embarked in the king's ship called the Marine, which was to be gone in two days, and Monsieur De Beaugeau, the commander, promised me to give him his table upon your account; but the said Sieur De Lussan, thinking

much the more frequent, and I have often given my parents the trouble to look after me in the suburbs, and that place we call La Vilette. However, as I grew up, my excursions were the larger, and by degrees I accustomed myself to lose a sight of Paris.

This rambling sort of humor was accompanied with another, which I dare not dignify with the name of a martial one, but was such as wrought in me an ardent desire to see some siege or battle. I could not hear the noise of the drum in the streets without those transports of mind, the remembrance whereof does still operate a kind of a vigorous heat and joy in me. It so fell out at length, that I met with an officer, with whom I had but a slender acquaintance; but my warlike genius quickly inclined me to make him my friend. I looked upon him as a person who could be very serviceable to me in my designs; and it was with this prospect I applied myself to manage him. The siege of Conde being happily commenced at this time, and he being obliged to serve there with his company, I made him the offer of a sword that had hitherto done neither good nor harm to any man, but which I was passionately desirous to make use of. Here it was that he gave me the first instances of his friendship, for he took me freely along with him, and

---

the frigate to be gone, staid with me at Port Paix, to wait an opportunity of meeting with another ship that should be bound directly for Dieppe. I heartily wish, sir, I could meet with an opportunity of serving you in these parts. I should do it with exceeding pleasure, as being, with all deference and respect imaginable, sir,

Your most humble and obedient servant, DE CUSSY.

AT THE CAPE, *May* 7, 1688.

A Copy of another Letter written by the said Monsieur De Cussy to the Father of the Author of this Journal.

SIR:—I cannot let your son be gone, without testifying to you how much concerned I am in the satisfaction and joy you will have to see him return from so long and toilsome a voyage, as I am confident of your being sorry at present that I had not sent him home to you at the time you desired, which yet I should not have failed to do, had he not been absent; and at whose return I delivered him one of your letters, which I always preserved safe with those of Monsieur De Lubert. He has no occasion to make use of me, though I have made him an offer of my utmost service. I may say, without vanity, that he has made the greatest and finest voyage in our age, and that he has seen countries which a great many people in the world content themselves to view in maps, without desiring any other sight of them, though they had all the riches thereof bestowed upon them for their pains. Besides the pleasure you will have to see your son again, you will have also that of hearing him discourse, pertinently enough, of his voyage and adventures; there being no other besides himself of all the company that can give an exact account thereof, as having all along applied himself to keep a very punctual journal of all transactions, which I am confident will be pleasing to my Lord Marquis De Signelay. I have myself the honor to write to him concerning it, that so I might engage your son to go and present it to him, which perhaps otherwise he would not have adventured to do, out of the little esteem himself has of his own work. This is what offers itself at present for me to write to you, assuring you, I should take a deal of pleasure to find myself in any condition to serve him, and that I am, sir,

Your most humble, and most obedient servant, DE CUSSY.

AT THE FORT OF PORT PAIX, *May* 18, 1688.

kept me all the campaign; at the breaking up whereof I returned with him, no ways discouraged, or weary of war, as the greatest part of them are, who have had but just a taste of it. And this I tell you was my first adventure.

The second was not quite so good in regard to the success that attended it, though it was alike agreeable to my palate, and according to my heart's desire. I happened to become a cadet in the marine regiment, but I fell into the hands of a captain who was wondrous skilful to drain children of good families of their money; so that this campaign, wherein I hoped to have done the king some service, was worn away in expenses. My father gave more than he should, or I deserved, to get my discharge, and to set me once at full liberty to take what I liked best; it was not perhaps his inclination I should do so, but it was mine, and I was not long to seek.

God, who, it seems, was not willing to make me out of conceit with the trade, was so much the better guide unto me at this time, as I was so ill guided before, for Monsieur the Count d'Avegean, whose personal merit has sufficiently distinguished him in the body of the French guards, took me along with him to the siege of St. Guislain, where I failed not to meet with new pleasures in the use of arms, though it were never so hot. There were a great many men's lives lost at this siege, which yet did not cool the desire I had to hazard my own. And though my parents, who could not well brook this my gadding humor, were in hopes the fatigues of war would cure me of it, they were mistaken in the matter, for I was no sooner got upon the stones of Paris, but I grew weary of being there. I had nothing but voyages in my head, and those that were longest, and most accompanied with dangers, appeared to me to be the best. For a person never to get out of his native country, and to be ignorant how the rest of the earth stands, appeared to me a matter that should be appropriated to a woman only. Whereas it was my judgment, that a man should never be confined to one place, and that nothing could suit him better than to make himself acquainted with all those of his own species. To travel by land, I thought both long and difficult, and therefore I concluded I could sooner and more safely accomplish my designs by betaking myself to the sea; and now you find me ready to go on board.

There was nothing omitted on the part of parents, that were full of tender affections for an extravagant child, to divert me from my resolution. But as to young men, such as I was, it may be said, as is usually done of womankind, that *what they will, God wills;* and to say the truth, I was overruled by my inclination herein; wherefore when they perceived that absolutely to oppose my humor would make me but the more opiniative, they proposed I should take a voyage for St. Domingo, where I should find friends and protection in case of need; and as this exactly suited both with my desires and designs, and that provided I could get to sea, I did not care whither bound, I very readily obeyed.

Dieppe was the place where I embarked, and from whence I parted on the 5th of March, 1679, with greater satisfaction of mind than I am well able to express. That element, which to the generality of men seems very frightful, appeared to me the most amiable and delightful of any in the world. The winds, if I may say so, wrought in me some delight, for I found that almost every little blast brought us happily onwards on our way. And I was so overjoyed to find myself in so desirable an island, that I thought no more of the hazards my voyage made me liable to. Let no man therefore be amazed thereat, if he finds none of them contained in my journal. And seeing there are other persons who have been particular enough in their relations given of this passage, I have this only to say, that I safely arrived, through the mercy of God, at St. Domingo, and if any one has the curiosity to follow me in my remaining expedition, he must begin from thence.

I continued there, however, for above three years, not only to see the country, but through such conjunctures as would not admit me to go out of it. I found myself chained there to a Frenchman, that was so far from deserving the name of one, that his hardened malice much better became a Turk. But what misery soever I have undergone with him, I freely forgive him, being resolved to forget his name, which I shall not mention in this place, because the laws of Christianity require it at my hands; though as to matter of charity he is not to expect much of that in me, since he on his part has been every way defective in the exercise thereof upon my account. But my patience was at last quite worn out, being weary of those cruelties, whereof I saw no end. I made my complaints to Monsieur de Franquesnay, the king's lieutenant, who acted as governor since the other's disease, and whose generosity proved to be a sanctuary to me. He readily consented to take me to his own house, where I staid six whole months.

I had borrowed money in the mean time, and I thought it was the part of an honest man to repay it. My parents would have been perhaps very willing to have paid my debts, but they could hear nothing from me, nor I from them; and the letters they sent me passed through such officious hands, that they spared us the charge of postage. I was therefore necessitated to seek out some other way to free myself; and this I found in meeting with that which satisfied the natural inclination I had for travelling. I bethought myself of making one of the freebooters' gang, to go a voyage with them, and to borrow, for the payment of my debts, as much money as I could from the Spaniards. Now these sorts of borrowings have this advantage attending them, that there is no obligation of repayment, as in our country, they being esteemed the product of a just war; and seeing the place of action is beyond the line, there is no talk there of making any restitution; besides which we may also observe in this place, that there was then a rupture between the two crowns, and that we had a formal commission from my lord admiral to infest the Spaniards.

There was no question to be made, but I could find a captain that would receive me; and I was not long in making the choice, since there were not many of them at that time to pitch upon. Laurence de Graff was the man I most fancied, who would make a special corsair; and though he had not been long arrived, all that he wanted was to be gone as well as I. We were in a few hours' time satisfied with each other, and became such friends as those are wont to be who are about to run the same risk of fortune, and apparently to die together. This last indeed we should have reckoned upon with the most appearance of reason, but it was what we least thought of. My departure took up all my thoughts. I furnished myself with arms and other small necessaries, at the charge of Monsieur De Franquesnay, who was very ready to advance me some money, which I have paid him since, and whose kindness I shall never forget. At last the day came, and I must freely say, it was, in my opinion, one of the best in the course of my life.

On the 22d of November, in the year 1684, we departed from Petit Gaves, on the coast of St. Domingo, to the number of one hundred and twenty men, on board a prize taken, some time before, by Captain Lawrence de Graff, from the Spaniards, which they sent as an advice boat from Carthagena, on the *terra firma* of America, to Spain.

Our design was to go and join ourselves with a fleet of freebooters, which we were in hopes to meet with before the Havana, a great city in the Isle of Cuba to the N., and about fourteen leagues distant from St. Domingo.

We anchored on the 4th of December, at the Tortoise Island, to take in water, and on the 6th sailed away, in order to return to the coast of St. Domingo, which is but three leagues off, where we arrived the 12th, and casting anchor at Cape Francis, we took in our full store of water and wood. We left this place on the 17th, and were taken with a N. wind two leagues from the road in such a manner, that we lost our shallop, which was too big to be put upon our gibbet. Towards evening we sailed back to a place of safety, whereby we were obliged to stay two days waiting for a canoe we had sent to buy at the cape, from whence we came, such things as we wanted for making up the loss of our shallop.

On the 20th, we made ready to endeavor to rejoin the Victorious, a ship that came with us from the cape, belonging to Nantes, and bound to the Isles of the Wind, which had on board the commander of St. Lawrence, lieutenant general of the French islands and the coasts of the *terra firma* of America, and Monsieur Begon, intendent of justice, policy, and the finances of that country, to whom we served as convoy, lest they should have been attacked by the Spanish periaugues that cruise thereabouts. And indeed we had a great deal of reason to be concerned for the safety of those gentlemen, who were in much esteem with all the colonies of these islands, because of the good orders they kept, the exact justice they administered, and the tranquillity the people enjoyed under them; but we could not possibly set sight on this ship, as not knowing what course she steered.

On the 23d, we steered our own course, and in the evening discovered a ship to leeward of us, to whom we gave chase; but she braced to, to wait for us; and when we were come up with her, we found it was Captain Le Sieur, of Dieppe, who commanded a flute called the Aramantha, whom we quickly left, keeping our own course. But on the 25th, which was Christmas day, we had a great calm till next day, when the wind, proving contrary, obliged us to put back to the port of Plata, on the coast of St. Domingo, where we staid to the end of the month.

On the 1st of January, in the new year 1685, we doubled Cape St. Francis, and next day, by ten in the morning, did the same by Cape Cabron, as we doubled that of Savona towards noon, they being all situated on the same coast; and that day one of our men died.

On the 4th, we sailed in sight of La Mena; next day, coasted the Isle of Porto Rico, and La Savona, and then steered S. E. and by S., till the eleventh, when we discovered the Isles of Ave, towards which we bore till the evening, and doubled them on the twelfth about eleven in the morning, keeping still the same course till we came to the Isle De la Roca; where there was also another rendezvous of our men-of-war to be, which we were going to seek out.

On the 13th, at seven in the morning, we discovered the main land of America, and were becalmed next day, which continued to the 15th, at noon, when we had a fresh gale, and steered N. N. E. till the 17th, when about moon-setting we descried two ships and four boats to windward of us, about a cannon's shot distance, that had the cape of us, which brought us upon deck to make all ready.

One of those boats, on the 18th, by break of day, being a tartane, commanded by Captain John Rose, as not knowing us, presently came up and hailed us; and as our captain had a commission from the lord high admiral of France, the count of Tholouse, we made answer, from Paris, and put out our flag; but Rose, who would not know us so, believing we had no other intention, in feigning ourselves to be a king's ship, than to get clear of him, gave us two guns to make us strike; insomuch that taking him really for a Spaniard, we knocked out the heads of two barrels of powder, in order to burn ourselves, and blow up the ship, rather than fall into the hands of those people, who never gave us quarter, but were wont to make us suffer all imaginable torments, they beginning usually with the captain, whom they hang with his commission about his neck. But one of the two ships came up with us in a moment, and knowing what we were, gave us a signal, which was so much the more satisfaction to us, that instead of enemies, which we took them to be, they proved to be not only friends, but those very ships we were in quest of, which obliged us to put in at the cape, and spend that day to visit one another.

One of these two ships belonged to Captain Michael Landresson, and was called the Mutinous, but formerly the Peace; and the other to Captain Lawrence de Graff, whose name was the Neptune, but once the St. Francis, and which he had quitted, when he went in his prize to St. Domingo to get a new commission of the governor, his own that he had being then expired. The first of these ships carried fifty pieces of cannon, and the other forty-four, and had both of them been two Spanish armadillas, who, the year before, coming out of Carthagena, to take the ships commanded as well by the Captains Lawrence and Michael, as those of Captains John Quet and Le Sage, were themselves taken by those whom they were about to become masters of. And as for the four boats, they were commanded by other captains, whose names were Rose Vigneron, La Garde, and an English traitor from Jamaica; by them we were informed that they were watching in that place for the Patach, of Marguerita, and a squadron of Spanish ships, which they expected would sail that way, in order to take them.

On the 19th, we resolved to quit that post, and did all we could to get up with the Isle of Currasso, a great part whereof belongs to the Hollanders. We sailed in sight of those of Bonnara and Roube; and about two in the afternoon of the same day, we chased a Flemish boat that came from the port of Guaira, on the continent, and was returning to the town of Curasso, two leagues to leeward of which we anchored that evening in the port of Sancta Barba.

On the 20th, we sent away a boat under the command of La Garde, to the town, to ask the governor leave to buy us masts for Captain Lawrence's ship, that had lost them in a hurricane near the Isle of St. Thomas; but this he absolutely refused, and shut up the gates against us. Upon the boat's return, and relation given us of the governor's refusal, I carried him a copy of our commission, hoping to engage him by that means to grant us our request; but he still persisted to deny us, while a part of our crew scrupled not in the mean time to go ashore, and enter the town, after having left their swords behind them at the gate.

On the 23d, our ships weighed anchor, in order to sail for Santa Cruz, which stands seven leagues to leeward of this town; and in our passage by the fort we saluted it, and they returned us gun for gun; but the governor, finding we were two hundred men of us in the town, informed us, on the 24th, by beat of drum, that it was his pleasure we should be gone, and return forthwith on board our ships, and that he would give us shallops to carry us thither, provided we paid him two pieces of eight a man. I presently discerned it was his will we should not go back by land, because we must for that purpose cross a lake that stands at the foot of the fort, which he had forbidden us to pass; and this made me go and tell him, we gave him thanks for his shallop, that if we were minded to go by sea to rejoin our ships, we had periaugues to carry us thither; and that we had no other design to get to them by land, but for a walk's sake. To which he answered, that the inhabitants there scrupled to let us see their island; but for all that, he would not let us pass over the lake, and so we were two days before we could reach Santa Cruz, where our ships were waiting for us.

We came afterwards to know the reason of the governor's displeasure against us, which was, that Captain Lawrence and Captain Michael's ships had taken two Dutch ships before the Havana, that were freighted for the Spaniards, having two hundred thousand pieces of eight that belonged to their company, which the freebooters meddled not with, being at peace with that nation; and they easily persuaded their principals that all had been taken from them, and so we were punished for the knavery these Dutchmen practised towards their own people.

Though this Island of Curraso be well enough known in France, I cannot but take notice, as I go along, that the temperature of its air is the same with that of St. Domingo, and produces the same sort of fruits; and the land is almost level throughout, and the country very naked, because of the little wood that grows there, being almost barren in several places, and produces little to the owners besides maize and small millet; yet it is watered with several springs and rivers. The town that stands upon it is small, but very neat, being encompassed with a high though very thin wall. There is a good and safe port belongs to it, and the fort that commands it, as well as the town, is very regularly fortified. The inhabitants are of several sorts of religions, the exercise thereof being free; the chief of which is that of the Dutch, of the Jews, as well as of others; each of whom have their respective places of worship in the town. The chief of their trade consists in sugar, that grows there, and of wool, which comes from the sheep which breed upon the place in great numbers, besides the skins of those animals, as also of a great many oxen and cows which they keep in the lowest and best watered grounds of this island, where it abounds in pasture. They are altogether affected to the Spanish nation, with whom they have the main of their trade.

On the 27th, we made ready and steered our course for Cape La Vella, which is on the continent of America, where we designed to fix ourselves in order to wait for the Patach, of Marguerita, whereof I have already spoken. The same day Captain Vigneron's boat left us to return to the coast of St. Domingo, because they had not men enough to make any thing of the enterprise, there being no more than twenty on board her.

Being come to the cape by the 30th, we anchored there; and our next care was to set some sentinels, to the number of fifteen upon the top of it, to give us notice when they discovered the Patach; but next day we thought it more advisable to pursue this following method to get intelligence. We sent, on the 1st of February, Captain Rose's boat to the mouth of the River La Hache, on the continent, inhabited by the Spaniards, and about twenty leagues distant from the cape where we then were, under pretence of trading with them, but in reality with a design to make some prisoners, that so we might be informed whether the Patach was passed by that way or no; for it was usual for her to take in part of her lading in that river.

While we waited for the return of this boat, I and some others went ashore to view and observe the country about the cape. I understood it was inhabited by a most cruel, barbarous, and savage Indian nation, who are neither friends to, nor have any society with, any other people whatsoever, no, not even with the Spaniards themselves, who live round about them. They eat without any distinction whatever they can catch, and are afraid of nothing but swords and the like weapons; but as for fire arms they matter them not at all. We were satisfied to have a sight of them as we returned, without having the curiosity to make a trial of their teeth, by going farther up into the country where there was nothing to be got.

I am not able to forbear in this place to give a strange example of what I am speaking, and of what this people can do, whom I take to be the oldest freebooters of America. The marquis of Maintenon, governor of the Isle of Maragalant, who had the command of one of the king's frigates called the Witch, having taken a prize of fourteen guns, which he went on board, and finding himself one day separated from his own ship, was constrained, in order to take in water, to cast anchor at Boca del Drago, on the *terra firma* of America, which was inhabited by the same Indian people as live at Cape La Vella. He brought his ship as near the shore as he could, and bringing all his cannon to bear on one side, he sent under the covert of them his shallop, with two and twenty armed men, to fill their casks with water. Now those savages lying in ambush upon the sea-side, did not give the shallop time to land, but throwing themselves headlong into the water, and rushing upon them, in spite of the continual fire made upon them from the cannon of the man-of-war, they carried her, with the two and twenty men, for above fifty paces to land, where, after they had killed them, every one took his man upon his back, and moved them off; then they returned, and swimming to cut the cables of the ship to make her drive ashore, they hoped also to serve those on board the same sauce; but as good luck would have it, they had time to loose their sails, and to make ready to put farther off from the shore.

On the 2d, we put our ships into a careening posture, and on the 8th, Rose's boat returned to us, and gave an account, that as soon as they had anchored at the mouth of La Hache, they sent a small canoe, with six Englishmen in it, ashore, they being of our crew, and at peace then with the Spaniards, who agreed with them, that next morning, about sunrising, they would fire a gun, to give the other notice to come on board to traffic with them; — that in the night they had put thirty men ashore to surprise those of the Spaniards that should pass to and fro, but that the Spaniards, having discerned the snare that was laid for them, fired all night, which gave all the inhabitants the alarm; — that next morning our people fired their cannon of signal, according to the agreement, and put out English colors; but it was to no purpose, for the Spaniards, according to all appearance, had no inclination for those goods they supposed we would trade with them in; so that our men finding their design had miscarried, weighed anchor, and sailed away to join us.

As we were of opinion, at last, that there was no hope the Patach would pass that way, we held a council on board our ship about forming another design; but not being able to agree with Captain Lawrence, (who was owner of two thirds of the Neptune,) because he would have imposed upon us, there were fourscore and seven that quitted the ship and went on board the prize in which we came from St. Domingo, and so left him on the 13th. He weighed and steered his course thitherward. Captain Michael and Captain John Rose weighed also, and sailed for Carthagena; and we, who were irresolute what way to take, followed the latter.

On the 25th, we had a hard easterly breeze, which carried us beyond a river that runs on the *terra firma*, and is by the Spaniards called Rio Grande, where we should have taken in water, which continues sweet within the sea for three or four leagues from the mouth of it, for all it rains so little, and provided you take that which runs on the superfices. About three of the same day, in the afternoon, we saw *Our Lady De La Poupa*, which is also on the continent, and the 26th anchored at the Isles of St. Bernard, from whence we parted in the evening with three periaugues only, in order to get to windward of Carthagena, to endeavor to seek us some provision, which they continually carry to that place; and our design had in effect the desired success.

We returned on the 18th, with seven periaugues laden with maize, which we made good prize. By the Spaniards that were in them, we understood that there were two galleons at Carthagena, and that the Spanish flota was at Porto Bello, and that two ships, one carrying twenty and the other twenty-four guns, would quickly set out from thence; but we did not think fit to wait for them, because they could not assign to us any determinate time when they should sail.

On the 22d, at noon, we weighed, and towards evening

discovered Point Picaron, on the continent, and the Isles of Palmas. About two hours within the night, we doubled the greatest point of these islands. The next morning, which was the 23d, we found ourselves separated from Captain Michael and Captain Rose; and then it was we took a resolution of attempting to cross over the continent, to the end we might get into the South Sea: in order to which, we sailed to the Bay of the Isle d'Or, which is inhabited by the Indians of Sambes, that so we might know of them (who were our friends) what success the other freebooters met with, who, we had been told, were gone thither some months before.

From the 23d at night to the 24th, we kept to the cape, being afraid of entering into the Gulf of Arian; and that morning, by break of day, we made nearer the shore, to discover where we were, and upon trial we found it to be a point of the wind in that gulf, which the currents made us to double.

Between this gulf and Cape Matance, happened a very remarkable adventure. We had on board our ship a soldier belonging to the Spanish galleons, whom we had taken to windward of Carthagena, in one of the periaugues, whereof we found the maize before spoken of, who out of despair to find himself made a prisoner, though he was very kindly used, took a resolution, as appeared by what followed, to throw himself into the sea, to which end he went five or six times upon deck without being able to put his design in execution, and that in all likelihood out of a secret resistance he found within himself to do it; but at last, after several attempts, he effected the same, which exciting my curiosity to inquire into the circumstances thereof, I found that, contrary to what usually happens in such cases, the body which fell down with full force into the water, floated a long time upon the back, by the ship's side, though to our apprehension he did all he could to drown himself; but when out of compassion, to save his life, we threw out some of our tackle for him to catch hold on, he not only refused to make use of them, but turned himself upon his face, and plunged to the bottom.

On the 25th, at eleven in the morning, we arrived and anchored at the Isle d'Or, or Golden Island, and at the same time fired a gun to give the Indians notice of our coming. Then we went ashore, to know what that flag was we discovered at a distance from us, where we found three men belonging to Captain Grognier and Captain Lescuier's crews, who told us that they tarried there because they would not go with the other freebooters, who were on their journey to the South Sea, under the conduct of those two captains; and that as soon as ever they saw us, they had set up that flag, as a signal for us to come up to them.

On the 26th came some Indians, with letters, on board us, which were directed to the first freebooters that should anchor in that road, to give them notice that they were gone, to the number of a hundred and seventy men, to that sea, and some small time before them, a hundred and fifteen English; besides which, they also sent us some instructions how to demean ourselves towards the Indians through whose territories we must pass, wherewith we were fully confirmed in the project we had already formed of undertaking this expedition. And though we were but fourscore and seven men, yet we made ourselves ready to be gone. In the mean time, some other Indians came also on board us, by whom we were informed that Captain Grognier and Captain Lescuier were still in their territories, and not yet gone to the South Sea, which made us write to them by one of those two Indians, to let them know that we were coming to them.

On the 27th, at noon, we saw Captain Michael, and Captain Rose, turn into the same port, which made us go presently on board, to know what made them come in and anchor in that road. They told us they had been in chase of a Spanish ship named the Hardy, come from St. Jago, on the coast of Cuba, and bound for Carthagena; but not being able to come up with her, they were come into this port, as being the nighest, to take in water. Then we showed them the letters we had received, which wrought a desire in many of them to come and increase our number, insomuch that a hundred and eighteen men quitted Michael's ship, and the whole crew of Captain Rose, being sixty-four men, who burnt their vessel, when they had paid the owners the price of it. We were not then for delaying, but, on the 29th, quitted our ships and and went ashore, where we encamped to the number of two hundred and sixty-four persons. But as to the ship belonging to our particular crew, we left her in the hands of Captain Michael, rather than burn her.

CHAPTER LI.

Our Passage across the Continent of America, to go to the South Sea.

Sunday, the 1st of March, in the year 1685, after we had recommended ourselves to the Almighty's protection, we set out under the command of Captain Rose, Captain Picard, and Captain Desmarais, with two Indian guides, and about forty more of that nation, whom we took along with us for the ease of those who were most burdened among us. We could not travel above three leagues that day, and encamped by a river side, after we had passed through a country that presently discovered a terrible aspect to us, and then proved very difficult to travel in, because of the mountains, precipices, and impenetrable forests, whereof it is full. And the difficulty of the journey was still the more increased by the great rains that fell all the next day. To say nothing that in our ascending the mountains, which are of prodigious height, we were clogged with the weight of our ammunition, arms, and other iron tools we carried with us. Upon our coming down upon these mountains, we got into a plain, which, though it was without any tracts, or ways, yet appeared very easy to us; but that we were obliged no less than four and forty times, in the space of but two leagues, to cross the same river, which, because it ran between very slippery rocks, gave us a great deal of trouble to get over it, being always in danger of falling.

On the 4th we lay in an Indian carbet, which is a spacious sort of a lodging, but almost like a barn, wherein the people are wont to meet together; there we staid next day to go a hunting, where we found great numbers of deer, and all sorts of birds. Amongst others we saw a kind of animal which the Indians call manipouryes, and we trefoil, because as they go along, each of their feet leaves the print of this simple in the ground. This animal is as big as a small bullock, but his hair is not so long, and more sleek. His legs are short, he has the head of an ass, but a sharper nose, and walks in the bottom of the water, as well as on dry land. They have here also a sort of hogs, which they call vents, because of an opening place they have in the form of a navel upon their backs. We may further take notice of those beasts they call agoutils and ovistitils, which both the one and the other of them are very like those we call Indian pigs in France, but much bigger. The monkeys of this country are almost as big as sheep, live in forests, and seldom come down from the trees, where they always find their food. They are so hardy, that though you shoot them with a fusil in the head, or through both shoulders, they shall not fall to the ground; and many times for all what you can do, they have so much cunning in their fall, as to twist their tails, which are very long, about the branch of a tree, where they hang and waste away, without any possibility of coming at them, because they generally make choice of the tallest trees for the places of their retreat.

I cannot without smiling call to mind what I have done to one of these animals, which, after I had made several shots at him with my fusil, that carried off part of his belly, insomuch that his guts came out, held himself, by one of his paws, or hands, (if you will,) by the branch of a tree, while he put his entrails with the other into that part of his belly that still remained whole.

There was another of them whom I shot with a small bullet across his nose, and who, finding himself blinded with the blood that gushed out, had so much industry as to wipe it off with the leaves of the tree whereon he stood. Here also we found harats, which are a sort of birds as big again as parrots, to whom they are very like, even to the note they have; but their feathers are infinitely more fine, for their wings and tail, which is very long, are of so lively and bright flaming color, that you cannot for some time fix your eye upon them without being dazzled. Here we saw those fowls called oecos, which are pretty like unto our Indian turkey-hens, but with this difference, that they have a small tuft of feathers upon their heads, that resembles a cock's comb, and a round of yellow about their eyes. They differ from one another in color, the male's feathers being inclinable to red, whereas the female's are blackish, but are never found asunder. Their partridges are larger than our Europeans, and their flesh is whiter, but not so good, and their note is different from ours. As to their pheasants, they are smaller than those in Europe, and their flesh nothing near so palatable, but their note is much the same. Besides these, there are in this country a multitude of other birds, with whose names I think it needless to swell this journal, because, as the islands of America are full of them, there is already an exact account given of them in those relations that have been made of these countries, and it is enough that I give a description of such as are not to be found in these islands, or of another kind. Yet I shall say this further, that lizards breed here in abundance, and there are different sizes of them. They are animals that resemble pretty nearly those whom we call cayements, of whom I shall have occasion to speak hereafter. Their flesh is good to eat, and their eggs, which are as big as pigeons' eggs, have an excellent taste, and are much better than our hens' eggs. This hunting bout was a great relief to us, against that hunger we had endured, because it was the first repast we had met with since our journey; but this I reckoned nothing in comparison of the miseries which we were to suffer in a vast number of other adventures.

At last, after six days' painful and wearisome travelling, even beyond all that can well be imagined, we got to the river which the Indians and Spaniards call Bocca del Chica, that discharges itself into the South Sea.

On the 7th, the Indians of that place carried us to see trees that were proper to make our canoes of, in order to get down that river into the South Sea. We presently fell to work upon them with our utensils and iron tools, which we had brought along with us, after we had agreed with the captains of these Indians for furnishing us in the mean time with victuals, which consisted in maize, potatoes, bananoes, and magniot roots, till we had done our work, upon condition that we gave them cloth, knives, thread, needles, pins, scissors, hatchets, bills, combs, and such like small wares, which are in great esteem with them; though the savages are not ignorant of the advantage that doth arise to them from these things.

It was partly with these toys that we lived, and kept a good correspondence with them during our passage through their country; but what made the conjuncture still more favorable unto us, was the resentment they had at that time of the ill usage they had received at the hands of the Spaniards, against whom they were so incensed, that they begged our assistance to be revenged on them. And had it not been for this, it would have been a very difficult task for us, if not impossible, to cross the country against their will, not only because of their numbers, which made them infallibly much stronger than we, but also by reason of the many forests and difficult passages their country is encumbered with, which we could not have gone through without we had some of themselves for our guides. But for all this, we did not think ourselves so safe amongst these men, but that we kept continually upon our guard, because we were well assured they were such wretches, as were at the service always of those that gave them most; and that though they appeared one minute to be our friends, they might become the next the Spaniards', who are nearer neighbors to them. Their treacherous dealings have proved fatal to some freebooters, who have put too much confidence in them. When a small number of them were passing through their country, these people gave notice thereof to the Spaniards, and that they might give an exact account of their number, they took them in a defile, and as they marched along, they put a corn of maize into a calabash for every man that passed by, and when they had done, carried the calabash to the enemy, who thereupon took their measures accordingly.

There is no sign of religion or of the knowledge of God amongst them, they holding that they have communion with the devil; and in short, when they would know any thing, they spend the night in the woods in order to consult him; and they sometimes foretold us some things, that have been true in the event in every particular circumstance of the relation they had given us. They lead a wandering and vagabond life, and fix their abode in no certain place. They generally erect their ajaupas or barracks upon a river side, where they continue till they have spent what sustenance they find thereabouts, and when this is done, they go and do the same things upon another river, and in this manner spend the term of their miserable lives. They go naked, except it be that they cover a part of their privities with a bit of silver or gold that is made like a candle extinguisher; and were I but satisfied that they had ever seen such a thing, I should think they took their model from it.

When they feast, or hold other solemn meetings, they put on a cotton robe, all of one piece, and it is usual with them, in a vaunting manner, to have a bit of gold or caracolay of an oval form hanging at their nose, which is bored through, and with this they think themselves as fine as any in the world. As for the women kind, they cover themselves from the waist downwards with an herb or cotton cloth, which they make themselves; and that they may appear finer, they color their faces with roccou, which is a small grain that dyes a brown red.

On the 22d, as we had finished the building of our canoes, we had news brought us by an Indian, who was returned from conducting the one hundred and fifteen English before spoken of to the South Sea, whither they were gone before us, that they had taken, under the command of Townsley, their captain, two ships, laden with provision, coming from Lima. He brought along with him a man of Captain Grognier's crew, who was lost in the woods a hunting, while his comrades were making their canoes in the same river where we were building ours.

On the 28th, we received news again by an Indian captain, who had conducted Captain Grognier, and Captain Lescuier into the South Sea, in a letter which they sent us, that they would stay for us at King's Islands, and desired us to lose no time, but to come and have our share in taking of the fleet of Peru, which they waited for. But for all the expedition we could use, our canoes could not be finished before the last of March, when we drew them into the river.

April 1st, we parted with fourteen canoes, carrying about twenty oars apiece, guided by twenty Indians, who made use of this opportunity in order to participate of the booty which they thought we were about to take from the Spaniards, as soon as ever we got again into the South Sea.

We rested on the 4th, to tarry for our men, who were behind, and to mend our canoes that were damnified by the rocks and flats we met with all along that river. It cannot be believed what pains we had to bring them to the great water, (as I may call it,) for we met with places where they rested dry, so that we were in a manner forced to carry them. This day died one of our men of the bloody flux, which was very rife amongst us, because we were forced to fast so long, and by reason of the hard feeding we had, and our continual dabbling in the water.

On the 5th, we put on, and about evening found the river deeper, but so full of, and encumbered with, trees, which the floods had carried thither, that our canoes were in danger every minute to be lost; and this day died two of our men.

On the 6th, we got to the great water, where the river is wider and deeper; and that day we spent on the banks of it to dry our sacks, which were wet through with the great rains that fell the day before. Another of our men died this day.

From hence to the 11th, we did all we could to get quickly to the mouth of the river, where we were informed by an Indian that was come in a small vessel to meet us, that the English and French freebooters had sent ashore, in a little bay called Bocca del Chica, (that stands at the mouth of that river,) some corn for our refreshment, when we should get down thither; for they could gather very well by themselves, who had been so straitened there for provisions, whereabouts we must be; and indeed we had so little, that we were reduced to a handful of raw maize for each man a day.

The same day we received further news, and by other Indians, who gave our guides notice to tell us, that a thousand Spaniards being informed of our descent, mounted up along this river by land, with a design to lay an ambuscade for us. Hereupon we resolved not to stir, but in the nighttime, and that without noise, that so we might shun them; and this succeeded accordingly. But we fell into another encumbrance, and that was, we being strangers in this country, and knowing no more than our guides how high the tide flowed in this river, we were surprised with the coming in of it, and it drove us and our canoes very far, so that one of them was overset with a great tree that had fallen into the river, and upon which the swiftness of the current threw it, but it luckily fell out that no one was drowned; they quitted it for the arms and ammunition that were lost; which could not but work some trouble in us, to see our men disarmed in a country where we could not go, but must have much use for them; but to deliver us of this inquietude, God was pleased to dispose of some of us, who left their arms to those that had lost their own.

When we got clear of these dangers, our guides advised us to row gently, for fear the Indian Spaniards, who were our enemies, should hear us, and who lay in wait to attack us, some leagues this side the mouth of the river, in a place called Lestocada. We took their council, and when we were got over against the said place, where the river is very broad, we disposed of our canoes in such a manner, that by the favor of the night they appeared to be much less than they really were. Now these Indian Spaniards having some glimpse of us, asked who was there; and our guides having answered, that what they saw was nought but a few boats belonging to them, with which they were going to fetch salt into the South Sea; by this wile we were spared the labor of engaging with those rascals.

On the 12th, in the morning, we cast anchor, because the tide came in, and was against us, and about ten made ready, but towards noon the heavens were overcast to that degree, that you could scarce see a man from one end to the other; and this was followed with such excessive rains, that we were afraid every minute of being sunk, though we employed two men in each canoe continually to throw out the water; and during that time one of our men died.

The same day at midnight we got to the mouth of the river, and entered into the South Sea, from whence we made directly for the Bay of Bocca del Chica, to see for the provision which we were told was there, and which we found accordingly; but before this, we met with a canoe of Captain Grognier that waited for us, and two barks at anchor. They had been purposely sent by the English, both to tow our canoes to the place where the freebooters were, and to bring us more provision.

On the 13th, in the morning, we carried our sick on board the two barks for their better accommodation, and then weighed anchor, in order to sail all together to an island four leagues distant from the mouth of that river, where we refreshed ourselves two days with the provision the English had sent us, which was a mighty comfort to us.

On the 16th, we went off in order to find out the English and French fleet, whose rendezvous was to cruise either before Panama, or at the King's Islands, which are not far from this river.

We arrived at those islands on the 18th, which stand thirty leagues to the east of Panama, where we found the largest of them to look more like the continent than an island, so spacious and mountainous is it. The same is inhabited by those negroes whom they call marons, or fugitives from the Spaniards, who, upon making their escapes from their masters at Panama, and the adjacent places, have made this a place of refuge. This day one of our men died.

We entered into this sea at a very bad time, for about this height, there are some years wherein it rains every day for the space of six months, and we happened to come thither exactly at such a season.

I should think it would have been proper in this place, before I proceeded to give a relation of our adventures, to give a large and exact description of the South Sea, and this fourth part of the world, with which it is washed, and to set forth the longitude and latitude of the places. But as it is my design to write of nothing but what was transacted by us there, and that this country is well enough discovered by the geographical charts that have been made of it, let the reader, when he has occasion to be informed herein, have recourse to them. I shall content myself with taking notice only, that all the continent that respects the South Sea, stands E. and W., and most of the islands N. and S. of it; and that it runs from E. and S. E. to S. and S. W.; and from the W. to W. N. W. and to the N. W.

The Spaniards are the only foreigners that possess these countries, since the unjust usurpation they have made of them from the aborigines, over whom they made themselves masters by such tyrannical and cruel methods as have been heard of throughout the world. They have good towns upon the seaside, which reach from the height of the Islands of Don Fernandez, that are situated at the mouth of the Gulf of Magellan, or rather from Chili, to the middle of a strait that is between the *terra firma* and the Isles of California, which the Spaniards call Mar Bermejo, through which it is believed a communication may be had between the Northern and Southern seas, without going about by the Strait of Anien. The chief of these towns begin from the south, and are Arica, Sagna, Nasca, Pachacama,

Lima, Cidade de los Reys, the port of Callao, (which is the place of embarking for this last, and where the king of Spain's ships anchor, that is, the fleet of Peru,) Truxillo, Paita, Queaquilla, La Barbacoa, (which is an open mine, from whence the Spaniards get a great deal of gold,) Panama, Realeguo, Tecoantepequa, Acapulco, and several others, that are as well maritime as inland places.

It is about ten years since the Spaniards, who dwell on all this continent, have not known what war was. Here they lived in a profound tranquillity, and fire-arms was hardly in any use amongst them. But since the time that we found out a way to go and visit them, they brought the Englishmen from Jamaica amongst them. But though they have a pretty many of them at present there, yet the sequel of this discourse will show they are not much more warlike than they were before. But the white Indians that inhabit a part of Chili have been always their enemies; and these are a people of prodigious bulk and tallness, who almost infest them with continual war, and when they happen to take any of them, they take off the plate of their breasts, as we do by a tortoise, and cut out their hearts.

On the 22d, which was Easter day, their fleet, who were gone before us into these seas, arrived at the King's Isles, where we were. They consisted of eight sail, which, together with the two barks they had sent to wait for our arrival, made up in all ten vessels; of which take the following account:—

The first served as admiral, and was a frigate carrying thirty-six guns, commanded by one Captain David.

The next was instead of vice admiral, had sixteen guns, and was under the command of one whose name was Sammes.

The third and fourth were two ships commanded by Captain Townsley.

The fifth was a ship that could have carried thirty guns, but had none, and was commanded by Captain Grognier.

The sixth was a small ship commanded by Brandy.

The eighth was a long bark commanded by a quarter-master, with a detachment of men drawn out of the fleet.

And the ninth and tenth were the two barks that came to meet us, whereof the one was commanded by Peter Henry, and the other by a quarter-master.

Of all these commanders, Captain Grognier was the only Frenchman, all the rest being Englishmen, except David, who was a Fleming. As to the whole number of our men, they were computed at about eleven hundred, when they divided into two fleets. It remains therefore now that I should say, according to the information I have received from all that were engaged in this enterprise, how all these ships fell into their hands, by what means, and at what time, they came into this sea.

In pursuance therefore to the order before observed, I am to declare that the English were the owners of our admiral, who in the year 1682, on the coast of St. Domingo, surprised a long bark belonging to a French captain, whose name was Tristan, who was then, with some of his ship's crew, ashore, waiting for a fair wind to sail together, to make war upon the Spaniards, by commission from Monsieur Povansay, who was then governor of that island. The English, who were superior in strength, drove the French out of the bark, with which they sailed to the Isle de la Tortille, whither a great many ships go every year to take in salt. The next thing they did was to take a Dutch ship, on which they went all on board, and sailed afterwards to the coast of Guinea, where they took several prizes more ; but they reserved none of them save the Dutch ship, which served as admiral, and wherein they sailed, when we left the South Sea, and was supposed to have been a ship belonging to Hamburg.

These English became pirates under the conduct of a captain of their own, and grew so notoriously wicked by a great many odious actions, performed not only towards strangers, but even those of their own nation, when they met with any of them, that, to avoid being chased, which they would infallibly have been, they passed from the North to the South Sea, by the Straits of Magellan.

They kept company for about eight months with a little frigate of eighteen guns, which they met with there in a short time after their arrival, and whose crew consisted of English, French, and Flemings. But their good correspondence with the corsair was of no long duration, for happening to have some difference with him, as he was one morning giving the other the good morrow, according to the English mode, he saw all his crew come upon deck ; whereupon the little frigate, who sailed much better than the pirate, came up with him, and having brought all his guns to bear, gave him a broadside, accompanied with a volley of small shot, and then bore away, having slain the captain and twenty of his men, in whose stead, the rest of the crew chose David, before mentioned. That little frigate of sixteen guns got into the South Sea some time after the other, as also by the same Straits of Magellan. I was told by one of the engineers on board her, that she belonged to his royal highness the duke of York; and that, under pretence of coming to treat with the Spaniards, she was sent upon no other account than to take a plan of those parts, the situation of the cities and seaports. Now Captain David meeting with her, made Captain Sammes come on board him, and threatened to take him, unless he would go and make war with him ; so that, finding himself too weak to resist, he chose rather to comply with the pirate than be taken : and these two together took a great many prizes, which, after they had taken out what was for their turn, they burnt.

About a year after, Captain Townsley came over land with a hundred and fifteen English into those seas, and, at the King's Islands, took two ships laden with provision and other refreshments, whereof I have already spoken, coming from Peru.

About a month after, the captains Grognier, and Lescuier, went also thither overland with two hundred and seventy men ; and who, being informed that the English fleet was before Panama, put ashore one night at Tavoga, an island two leagues off, from whence they discerned a ship on fire, and by break of day they saw the English under sail.

They went on board them, and came to understand that Captain David had taken a ship called the St. Rose, laden with corn and wine, bound from Truxillo for Panama ; the president of which last place had sent him to buy her, and in order thereunto, gave him a meeting at the Isles of Pericos, that are a league distant from the port. But instead of sending him the money they had agreed upon for the ship, he sent a fire-ship to burn him ; but the same, through the cowardice and ignorance of the commander, spent herself without doing the other any hurt ; and this made Captain David give the St. Rose to Grognier and Lescuier's ships' crew, who had already lost their captain.

As for the other five ships, commanded by Brandy, Sammes, Peter Henry, and two quarter-masters, they had also been taken from the Spaniards in these seas by the two first frigates, who reserved them for those who came thither over land. But of all our ships, there were none but the first two that had guns ; the other eight had none, they having been merchant ships, that had made use of none in the South Sea, where nobody but themselves had sailed a long time. And now having told you what passed before this fleet came together, we shall now proceed to give an account of our adventures since our junction.

On the 25th of April, we took an advice boat, going to the fleet of Peru, which was then at anchor in the port of Callao, that was carrying some packets from Madrid to Panama, and letters from the viceroy of Lima, wherein there was an account given, how many men-of-war, fire-ships, and merchantmen, the fleet consisted of, and about what time the same might arrive at Panama. Next day we examined the commander of the advice boat, but we could get no particulars out of him, saving, that when he saw himself like to be taken, he had thrown the king of Spain's packets, and a casket of jewels, overboard.

On the 27th, we put the same questions to the pilot, who, according to the example of his commander, would make no discovery, because they had taken an oath together, rather to lose their lives than to divulge any secret, or to let the said packet fall into the hands of the freebooters. On the 28th, two of our men died.

On the evening of the same day, we departed with two and twenty canoes, manned with five hundred men, in order to go and take La Seppa, which is a small town seven leagues to windward of Panama; and on the 29th, about ten in the morning, we discovered two ships bearing up to us, which, when they came near, we found to be two periaugues, manned with Greeks, which are a people composed of divers nations, to whom the Spaniards gave this name, and who serve them in their wars. These they brought sometime before, from the North Sea, to this coast, to defend them against us, because they look upon them to be better soldiers than themselves. We presently sent out two of our best sailing canoes, manned with twenty men each, to attack them.

These Greeks, who quickly took us to be really what we were, i. e. freebooters, made no delay to save themselves upon one of those islands that stand on the Bay of Panama; but upon their going ashore, they lost one of their periaugues, that split in pieces, and left us the other; then they got upon a rising ground, with their arms, and as much ammunition as they could save, and fought stiffly against us under a flag of defiance. And as the place where we landed was exposed to their fire from the ground where they had posted themselves, and that the ascent on that side where we stood was very difficult, we were forced to take a great round to come at them another way, where we found our passage much easier. At last, after we had fought at least for the space of an hour, we constrained them to flee for shelter in the woods, took two of them prisoners, besides their colors, and found between five and thirty slain upon the spot.

We were informed by the two prisoners, that those who had escaped could not be above an hundred men at most; that we might easily master them if we pleased, there being many wounded amongst them. They also told us, that they had an account at Panama of a reënforcement that was come from the North Sea to the fleet of freebooters. That the president of the town had thereupon sent an advice boat to Lima, to engage the viceroy to detain the merchant ships in port till further order, and with all speed to send a fleet of men-of-war to fight ours, and drive us out of those seas. But the relation given by these two prisoners we could not rely upon, since their party had put up a flag of defiance, they being three times the number of us.

After this advantage, and our rejoicing, with the rest of our canoes, we continued to prosecute our design upon La Seppa; but as we were obliged before we could come at it to go about two leagues up a very fine and large river of the same name, and on whose banks they have *vigies* sentinels always set, we could not choose but be discovered, and find the town alarmed, and ready to defend itself. Yet for all that we fell furiously on, and took it, with the loss only of one man; but finding no great matter of booty there, because they had saved most of their effects, we returned to our canoes again.

As I shall have frequent occasion to make mention of the word *vigie*, it will not be improper, in this place, to take notice, that by *vigier* is no other thing meant than to set a sentinel upon land or sea, and those persons who are thus set they call *vigies*. The Spaniards maintain a great number of them; for all their cities, towns, and villages, and even single houses, have persons on purpose, whom they send to all the rising ground round about, and river sides, where they have their horses ready night and day, so that, as soon as they discover an enemy, they hasten to give the Spaniards notice of it, who forthwith prepare themselves, not to fight, but to save their effects.

On the 1st of May we rejoined our ships, who waited for us at a very pretty island, called Sippilla, about a league distant from the mouth of the River La Seppa, which makes up a kind of canal that forms the Bay of Panama, and do, as it were, make a bar all along, that divides the channel into two parts, one to the east and the other to the west. Those pleasures we met with in these parts justly deserve a remembrance, whereof I shall give a little description in this place.

All these islands are so curious and delightful, that they are usually called the Gardens of Panama, and with very good reason, seeing all people of note in that city have each of them one of these islands for themselves, and their houses of pleasure there, also, with curious orchards, watered with a great many springs of running waters, adorned and embellished with a wonderful variety of flowers and arbors of jessamine up and down, and full almost of an infinite number of all sorts of the fruits of the country, among whom I have taken particular notice of four of them, which are called sappota, sappotilla, avocata, and las cayemites.

The first is a fruit almost like unto our pears, of a different size, whose rind is greenish, and contains, in the midst thereof, two kernels of an oval form, appearing pretty polished and sleek, and are each of them, in the largest of these fruits, somewhat bigger than an ordinary nut. When this fruit is ripe, it is very soft, and when the paring is taken off, the pulp is of a pure red color, very sweet, and of an admirable taste.

The second is of the same form as the other, but no bigger then a russet pear. It has an admirable taste, and under the rind is of a whitish color.

The third is of the same form as our quinces, saving that the rind is greener. This fruit must be fully ripe, and very soft, before it becomes good food, and then it is that you find the pulp of it as white as snow. The Spaniards eat it with spoons, as we do cream, and indeed the taste thereof is mostly the same.

The fourth is like a large damson, and very savory.

Besides these, and a great many more wherewith this country is peculiarly blessed, it produces also a great many of those fruits that are common to Europe, as apricots, pomegranates, goyaves, juniper, cocoa, bananas, figs of Provence, French and Spanish melons, all sorts of oranges, citrons, and lemons, of which I shall give no description, no more than of the trees that bear them; but those who would satisfy their curiosity herein, may do it in reading the History of the Antilles, written by Monsieur De Rochefort, in the year 1668, who was skilled therein, and gives a very good account of them. All these rich presents of fruits and pure water, of which Nature made us an offer in these islands, were a wonderful relief to us, after these fatigues we had undergone in our passage over the continent, to say nothing of the plentiful harvest we had of maize and rice, wherewith we found these islands covered, and which the Spaniards, I believe, did not sow with an intention we should enjoy them. But these same islands, that afforded us so many delights, wrought also afterwards some sorrow in us, of which by and by.

On the 8th of May, in the morning, we sailed away, and passed by the old and new city of Panama. The old one was that taken by General Morgan, in the year 1670, whose churches and houses seemed to us to be finely built, as far as we could judge of them at such a distance. There is none but the new town that is fortified, being defended with a good wall and several other works, but that is only to the seaward. This city is attended with an inconveniency, that as it is situated at the bottom of a bay, and that the sea ebbs very much in this country, great ships are left dry there, if they anchor nearer than a league to the place. We got as nigh it as we could with our colors and streamers loose, and from thence went to anchor at Tavoga, which appeared to us as if it were a little enchanted island, so agreeable and delightful are those houses and gardens that are upon it.

On the 9th, we caulked all our ships, and next day sent our long bark to cruise, in order to give us notice when the Spanish fleet appeared in sight of us; and on the 13th, we made choice of those ships that should engage it. Captain David and Captain Grognier were to board the Spanish admiral, Captain Suam and Captain Townsley the vice admiral, Captain Peter Henry and one of Townsley's prizes the Patach; our fire-ship was to keep herself under the quarter of our admiral. Our other ships were to attack the rest of their fleet according to their strength, and our armed periaugues were to keep off the enemies' fire-ships.

We heard this day a great many cannon fired at Panama, the cause whereof we could not guess at; and on the 14th, we put ashore, upon the Island of Tavoga, forty prisoners, who were very cumbersome to us, and then weighed, to go wait for the fleet at Cape Pin. But this was much out of season, since the fleet who was willing to spare us this trouble, as well as that of attacking her, was already, without our knowledge of it, arrived at Panama, having got in under the covert of one of those pleasant islands, through one of the two channels, which I said was formed by them, and which hid them from us while we cruised in the other channel, through which we thought they would have sailed.

As we knew nothing hitherto of this matter, and that, upon the return of our long bark, she told us she had discovered no ships pass, we went and anchored at Kings Islands, where the whole fleet took the usual oath, that we would not wrong one another to the value of a piece of eight, in case God were pleased to give us the victory over the Spaniards. On the 17th, one of our men died.

On the 19th, we weighed and anchored between the great island, and those in the east channel, through which we thought the fleet we expected would pass. On the 28th, another of our men died. Next day we made ready, and sailed for Cape Pin. On the 31st, we gave chase to two ships, whom we lost in the night, and which brought us back, in the pursuit of them, to the little Islands of Panama, where we anchored on the 1st of June; and the same day we surprised two Greeks, upon the island, where we had beaten them, when we went to take La Seppa.

On the 4th, we sent two canoes to the Isle of Sipilla, to endeavor to take some prisoners, that we might learn some news from them. There they took a ship laden with boards, which the Spaniards were carrying to Panama to build two periaugues instead of those we had taken. The men told us, that their fleet was got into Panama on the 12th of May; that on the 13th, they fired off a great many guns for joy; and that as soon as they were refreshed, careened, and manned, they would put out to fight us, and would be ready in a short time.

On the 7th, at noon, Captain Grognier, who had anchored farther from the island than we, gave us a signal, that he descried the Spanish fleet, consisting of seven sail; and this he did by lowering and raising his flag seven times. We also on our part made ready, and in doubling the point of the island where we had anchored, we discovered seven great ships coming up towards us, with a bloody flag in the stern, and a royal one on her masts. Now it was that the hopes which our crew had lost, when they understood the fleet was got into Panama, revived again, and the desire they had to enrich themselves, at the others' cost, animated them to that degree, that most of them threw their hats into the sea, as thinking they had the Spaniards already in hold. We put our ships in order, and then disputed the wind with them, which was at that time got to the west. About three in the afternoon, we all, except Captain Grognier, got the weather-gage of them, and he failed, because he waited for the coming up of his canoe from the shore, and cast about twice. Our admiral, finding himself to windward of the Spanish vice-admiral, who was separated from his own admiral, gave us the signal to follow him for to board him, in order to which, we lengthened our spritsail; but our vice-admiral took in his flag, as a token he would defer the engagement till next morning, hoping that Grognier would get the weather-gage in the night. Towards sunsetting, the Spanish vice-admiral, who was to leeward of us, saluted us with seven guns without ball, which was answered by our admiral with a whole broadside with ball. But night coming on, the Spaniards cast anchor, being better acquainted than we with the currents that run between these islands, and they sent a small vessel, that carried the lantern, to anchor two leagues to leeward of us, in order to amuse and cause us to take false measures;

and indeed we lay by all night, that we might next morning be to windward of the lantern, which we took to be the whole fleet.

On the 8th, early in the morning, we discovered our error, and were all of us strangely amazed to find ourselves to leeward of the enemies fleet, except Captain Grognier's ship, and that of Captain Townsley, and his prize, which were to windward. But it unhappily so fell out, that they were ships without cannon. The Spanish fleet having cast anchor again an hour after sunrising, we did all we could to get the weather-gage, but their vice-admiral, who had his anchor a-peak, and his sails but very slightly furled, quickly plied to the wind, which proving favorable to him, he bore immediately upon our admiral. Our vice-admiral did all he could to come to his assistance, for the Spanish guns had already incommoded him very much; but his coming up obliged the enemies' ships to bear off to windward, which we endeavored to gain all that day, though to no purpose; while the Spaniards, in the mean while, under whose cannon we found ourselves, mauled us terribly; and this made our admiral and vice-admiral to keep close together, and to resolve to die valiantly fighting, rather than suffer any one ship of the fleet to be taken, though they could both of them have saved themselves if they pleased, they being much better sailors than the Spaniards.

Captain Townsley, towards the afternoon, being to the windward of the enemies fleet, sent his periaugue on board our admiral, to receive his orders, while he that commanded it had both his legs shot off by a cannon ball. About two, the Spaniards sent out a ship of eight and twenty guns to hinder Captain Grognier to join us, as understanding, by some Spaniards who had been our prisoners, that he was the strongest in small arms of any in our fleet, and that they were so much the more fearful of him, when they came to know his crew consisted of Frenchmen. At last, finding ourselves towards evening much battered with their cannon, (for the Spaniards would not come to boarding,) we veered, by the favor of a gale of wind, to go and board the Spanish vice-admiral, that was the best sailor, and did us most harm. But we were no sooner unmoored, than the wind came about, which did us much damage; for we were just come upon the enemies' ship, who not observing the wind, by which we sailed, bore still upon us, so far, that when we returned the second time, she was so near us, that she was constrained to furl the end of her mainsail, for fear of bringing her foremast upon our counter; and this made us put out our canoes, which were upon the tow, that we might go better, and in this manner we defended ourselves till night approached.

Peter Henry's ship, wherein I was, having received above a hundred and twenty cannon shots, was forced to make the best of her way, which our admiral and vice-admiral perceiving, they put their periaugues under sail, which they had all along braced to windward during the fight, in order to attend us, because they saw we were in an ill condition. The enemy, observing our working, sent one of their small ships in pursuit of us, but as we bore back upon her, she gave us eighteen guns, and rejoined their own fleet.

Our long bark, having, during the action, been sorely handled, her crew was forced to leave her, and not having time to sink her, threw some guns, which our admiral had put on board her, into the sea, and then saved themselves on board of one of our other ships. Now the Spanish prisoners, whom we left behind, finding they were now at liberty, plied to put themselves into the hands of the Spanish admiral, but he, taking this bark for our fire-ship, sunk her with his cannon before she came near him, not thinking their own people were on board her.

On the 9th, we could see neither our own nor the Spanish fleet, which made us steer for the Isle St. John de Cueblo, four and twenty leagues to the west of Panama, where, by the favor of an easterly breeze, we arrived on the 14th : we ran ourselves presently ashore, and it was high time, for we had all along, from the time of the fight, five foot of water in the hold. We lost no time to put ourselves in a condition to get up again before Panama, that we might know what became of our fleet, about which we were in great pain, which we were put out of on the 26th, when we saw them coming to an anchor in the same place where we were, who told us they did not fight any more after our departure from them. That the Spanish fleet, upon the 9th, in the evening, had anchored within cannon shot of ours, and that, both the one and the other having made ready on the 10th, the Spaniards sailed away for the port of Panama. That Captain David had been hard plied by the Spanish cannon, especially with two shots that carried off half his rudder, but that he had no more than six of his ship's crew wounded, and only one killed; that Captain Sammes was no less put to it ; that almost all his poop was swept off, that he had received several shots between wind and water; that his mate had his head shot off with a cannon ball, and that he had no more than three men wounded. And that, in short, the other lesser vessels had not lost a man, and had but very few wounded. Here I may truly say, and without exasperating the matter, that it was a strange thing, and next to a miracle, that we, who were so few in number, and had such pitiful ships of our own, should be able to bear the fire of, withstand, and fight, so considerable a fleet, in comparison of our own, consisting of such good ships, and manned so well as that of the Spaniards' were, whose admiral was a vessel of seventy guns, though she had but *fifty-six* mounted, because she was too old. Their vice-admiral had forty, though she was bored to carry sixty guns: she was a very fine ship, and an excellent sailor, but also old. The Patach was a vessel of forty guns, though she had no more than eight and twenty mounted. The Conserve had eighteen guns, but was built, as well as the Patach, to carry forty. The other three were almost as big; besides they had the advantage of fire-ships, on board of which they had planted cannon, to the end that we might not take them to be really what they were, and that so they might come near, and the more easily surprise us, than if we were aware of them.

If we had met with this fleet, as we were in hopes we should, before they got an addition of strength in Panama, or that we had had but only the wind of them, when we attacked them, I do not question but things would have appeared with another face than now they did, and that we should have possessed ourselves of their ships to bring us back through the straits, with wealth enough to live at ease, which would have freed us all at once, after a continued succession of fatigues and troubles, which we were forced to go through for three years longer, as well in those places as in our return over land to the North Sea, but divine Providence had otherwise ordered it.

On the 29th, we parted from the Isle of St. John, to the number of three hundred men, in five canoes, in order to go and surprise the town of Pueblo Nuevo, that was six leagues off, thinking we should get some provision there, whereof now we began to be in need. Being landed on the 31st, we took a sentinel, but another escaped, which was the occasion of our being discovered. We were obliged, in order to get at this town, to go up a very fine river two leagues, and to make use of the flowing of the tide for that purpose. Before we came at it, we found a retrenchment made for its security, but ill guarded. The town is none of the best situated, though it stands upon the river side, being surrounded every way with marshes. We found neither people nor victuals there, and so we left it on the 3d of July; and next day, as we returned with our canoes to rejoin our fleet, we gave chase to a bark, which we took, and on the 5th, we got to our ships.

The English and we had a difference in the descent we made upon this town, for they, being more numerous than we, would take the advantage of us, and be masters of the whole, and that so far, that Captain Townsley would have taken Captain Grognier's ship away, which Captain David had given him, and give him his own for her; but as he found he had to do with men, who, though inferior in number, would not tamely be thus put upon, he was forced to give over his pretensions; yet we finding still that they continued to pretend to the same dominion over us, we separated ourselves from them to the number of a hundred and thirty Frenchmen, without reckoning Captain Grognier's crew, who were two hundred more, and, after having banded ourselves apart, we landed upon the island.

One of the chief reasons that made us disagree, was their impiety against our religion; for they made no scruple when they got into a church to cut down the arms of a crucifix with their sabres, or to shoot them down with their fusils and pistols, bruising and maiming the images of the saints with the same weapons, in derision to the adoration we Frenchmen paid unto them. And it was chiefly from these horrid disorders that the Spaniards equally hated us all, as we come to understand by divers of their letters that fell into our hands, which I have got rendered into French, as may be seen by and by.

On the 9th, the English weighed, and came to anchor about five or six leagues to leeward of the place where we were building our canoes, to fit up others for themselves in lieu of those they had lost as well as we, during the fight with the Spanish fleet. We laid out for trees fit for our purpose, and to that end went into a wood, which in these parts grows near to the sea, of which we chose the largest, which commonly are those trees called *mapou*, and *acajou*, and are withal very tender and easy to be wrought; among them we found some so large, that the single trunk, after being hewn and made hollow, could carry fourscore men.

While we were building our canoes, a sentinel, whom we had set on a very high tree, growing on the sea-side, in our island, as well for discovering lest the English, who knew we were employed about our canoes, should come to take away our ship, as to observe if any Spanish ship should sail between the main land and the island whereon we were, came to tell us, on the 15th, that he saw a ship out at sea, steering S. W. and by W., which put us presently upon making ready to come up with her. We found her to be a small vessel, commanded by Captain Willnet, an Englishman, whose crew consisted of forty English and eleven Frenchmen, of whom we had never heard any thing till now. But they told us, they had a long time ago passed over land into these seas, and that lately they had taken a ship laden with corn, out of the port of Sansonnat, which is on the continent, and the place of embarking from Guatimala, thirty leagues to the east of the Isle of St. John; and that going from thence towards the south coast, they understood that the viceroy of Lima had sent a Spanish fleet, on purpose to chase and beat the freebooters, which gave them to understand there were others besides them in these seas; and that upon the good news they were come in quest of us, in order to have a share in taking of that fleet, which they believed infallible, but that they understood, when they came before Panama, where they were in hopes to meet with us, that the fight was already over, and that we were gone to the Isle of St. John. The other English, who, as I have already said, were gone to anchor about five or six leagues to windward of us, had also sent out a canoe to know what this bark was, which came up with her as soon as we, and this made us very uneasy; for, this bark being laden with provision, those English influenced these new comers so far, that they took them to anchor in the same place where they were, except the eleven Frenchmen, who left them and staid with us.

This Island of St. John Cueblo is about twelve leagues in circumference, standing east and west, and north and south, five leagues distant from the main land, and separated by a narrow channel, (which is, indeed, no other than an arm of the sea running in between two lands.) It is not inhabited, very mountainous, full of wood, and watered with very fine rivers. It stands in no stead to the Spaniards, besides supplying them with masts for their shipping, which they have here in great abundance. When we stopped upon that island, we were in hopes to have fared well, so well stocked it was with deer, monkeys, agoutills, lizards, and banks full of tortoises; but we were deprived of these advantages by two inconveniences we labored under; the first whereof was, that the English, in less than fifteen days, had made such a destruction of these tortoises, that but very few of them landed; the other respected our hunting, which, after we had followed for a few days at first, we were bound to decline; for, having staid in this place longer than we designed, we were under a necessity of preserving our powder, for fear, should we have spent it, the Spaniards would have been quickly upon us, so that we staid a whole month upon this island, to the number of three hundred and thirty men of us, with eating no more than two tortoises, in eight and forty hours, and in seeking some fruits in the woods wherewith to subsist, and with the eating of which some of us died, as not knowing the nature of them.

There are a sort of serpents upon this island, whose stinging is so dangerous, that if any one has not a certain fruit by him, which he is to chew, and presently to apply to the wound, there is no escaping present death for him, as we found by experience, by some of our men whom we lost in this manner, and who, in their dying, endured terrible pains, through the activity and violence of that fire which this poison kindled in their bodies. The tree, on which this fruit grows, is to be found upon the same place, as well as in the other parts of this country, being, as to its leaves and height, very like unto our almond-trees; but its fruit resembles sea-chestnuts, though it is of a grayish color, and of a somewhat bitter taste, enclosing a whitish almond in the midst thereof. It is chewed altogether before the application is made, and is known by no other name than the serpent's seed.

Here, also, about two or three leagues up the country, you have a great many cayemans, which are a kind of crocodiles, that live both in the sea, rivers, and on dry land, and are of that ravenous nature, that some of our men have been devoured by them.

On the 27th, the English, who had left us, sent a quartermaster to us, to know whether we would join ourselves with them, as supposing they were too weak, to go and take the town of Leon, on which they had formed a design. And here we must acknowledge, that extreme misery is so terrible a thing, that it is almost impossible, when an opportunity presents itself of being delivered, that it should be let slip, notwithstanding all the repugnancy of our reason to the contrary. We had left the English by reason of their impieties, which we could not endure, and now we were ready to comply with the proposals they had made us of rejoining them again. The provision was on their side, and this was a charming bait for people that were ready to perish with hunger. We presently asked them for some victuals; and as we had but one ship, that could not hold us all, that they should give us another, because we were not willing to be dispersed on board their ships, as before; but this they would not agree to. In the mean while, as we were resolved not to recede herefrom, famine forced thirty of our men to join themselves with the English, as being unable to bear with the fasts we were forced to keep. And on the 4th of August, four of our men died.

On the 9th, when we knew the English were gone, we embarked, to the number of a hundred and twenty men, on board five canoes, commanded by Captain Grognier, and left two hundred on board our ship, and upon the island, whom we ordered to build more canoes, and afterwards to cross over to the continent.

Having made a descent there on the 13th, we came to a hatto, which is a kind of a farm, where the Spaniards breed their cattle. It was in the neighborhood of a town called St. Jago, which is twenty leagues distant from St. John's Island. The people we found in this hatto we made our prisoners, among whom was the master, who showed and conducted us to take a sugar plantation, in the River of St. Jago, where we were discovered. We sounded our prisoners, one after another, in order to know whether they understood any thing of our separation from the English, by telling them we came from the North Sea, and that they should show us where the freebooters were, which they said were come into these seas. They answered, they were gone to St. John's Island, to repair the damage the fleet of Peru had done them, together with other circumstances, which we knew better than they, without telling us one word of what had happened between the English and us. Hence we conjectured they knew nothing of the matter, and we could have been very well content that all the Spaniards knew as little as they, for fear our disjunction might render them more forward to attack us.

After this intelligence, we despatched away a canoe, which we had taken in this river, to carry our men some victuals, which we had found in this hatto, and to acquaint them that we were going towards Panama, to see whether we might meet with an opportunity of seizing some barks, that so we might get out of St. John's Island; because, as I have already said, our ship was not big enough to hold us, and that, as soon as the canoes were ready, they were to go and take Pueblo Nuevo, in order to get some provision, wherewith to subsist till our return.

On the 15th, we went ashore forty leagues to leeward of Panama, and, though we had no guide, we got, by cock-crowing, to a very pretty *estantia*, as they call it, which was a lone house, and where we took fifty prisoners, of both sexes. Among these, there was a young man and woman of quality, who promised we should have a ransom for them, and whom we carried to the Island Ignuana, a league's distance from the great one, and where there is no other but rain water to be had, which stands in the cavities of the rocks.

We staid for the fore-mentioned ransom till the 28th, when it was duly paid us, and then went off, being first informed that, about eight leagues to windward, there was a river, wherein were two barks laden with maize, which on the 29th, in the morning, we boarded and took. From thence we resumed our course to go and rejoin our men in St. John's Island, where we arrived on the 3d of September. Here they told us, that a hundred of them, whereof ninety-eight were come back, had gone on the 25th of the preceding month to Pueblo Nuevo, as we had ordered them, where they arrived on the 27th; and, though they were discovered by the sentinels of the town, they made themselves masters of it, and staid there two days, for all the continual and various attacks made upon them by the Spaniards. That the commander of the place came with a trumpet to speak with them, and asked why they carried white colors, seeing they were English, (so he took them to be,) but without satisfying his curiosity in the point, they constrained him to be gone from whence he came. That, eight of them being gone some distance from the place of arms, there were two of the number massacred by a hundred and fifty Spaniards, who, seeing so small a company together, bravely fell upon them; but, with all the advantage they had, they could not hinder the other six to recover their main guard, who fought retreating with extraordinary vigor.

On the 4th, we put out with six canoes, and a hundred and forty men on board, whereof we detached two to go to the hatto we had taken on the 11th of August, to look after the ransom of the master, whom we kept prisoner, and with the other four returned to that sugar plantation in St. Jago, in order to get some sugar cauldrons, whereof we had occasion. There we were informed that the governor of St Jago came thither, after our departure, the first time we took it, with eight hundred men. We staid in this place till the 9th, expecting the answer of a prisoner whom we sent to the governor, and by whom we sent him word, that, if he were minded to advance with his eight hundred men, we were ready; but, hearing no news of him, we departed thence, after our two canoes had rejoined us; and on the 11th, arrived on board our ship and the two barks, at the Island of St. John.

On the 5th, we careened our ships, and took in water and wood; we would have left this island, had it not been for the continual rains that fell and lasted eighteen days, and such bad weather, that it was impossible for us to appear upon deck, having never seen the sun all this time: and for this reason it is, that the Spaniards call the distance between the Bay of Gurgona and the Island of St. John the droppings of the South Sea. You have but four months of good weather here throughout the year, and they are December, January, February, and March ; the other eight months are incommoded with great rains, which fall almost without any intermission, and which, besides the bloody flux it brings, is so pernicious, that if a man has been wet with it two or three times, if he do not presently shift himself, it breeds large worms between his skin and his flesh, in form somewhat like unto a quill, and about half a finger long.

The weather clearing up on the 4th of October, we mended our sails, which were almost rotten, and made ready to be gone. And the same day we had one of our men stung in the leg by a serpent, who died of it presently, as not having taken care to provide himself with the remedy we have spoken of.

On the 8th, we made ready and sailed for Realeguo, which is both a port and town a hundred and fourscore leagues to the west and by north-west of the Isle of St. John, and two hundred and sixty west of Panama. We had a small south-east wind till the 11th, and on the 12th and 13th we steered west-north-west, and that evening descried land. On the 14th, we had a boisterous south wind, which made us take in all our sails, till midnight, and then came a calm till the 17th, when towards noon we were surprised with a south-west blast, attended with great rains, which separated us from our two barks. It blew so very hard, that the sea appeared presently very frightful, and put us so to it, that we began to be very apprehensive we should be all cast away. But the weather (as God would have it) proving fair again, we spent the 19th to set our vessel in order, as well as to mend our sails with our shirts and drawers, wherewith we were already but very indifferently provided. Towards evening we discovered land, and knew it to be the Bay of Caldaira, whereof I shall give an account by and by. On the 20th, we sailed in sight of that of Colebra. From thence we had moderate weather, and a south-east wind ; and on the 21st, we got to the height of the Morns, which the Spaniards call Papegayas.

On the 22d, we found ourselves over against Realeguo, a place very remarkable for the high mountains that surround it ; and especially for a high sulphurous hill that burns continually, and whose smoke reaches a great way ; but the tides next night put us twenty leagues to windward of it. On the 24th, we put out four canoes, with a hundred men in them, in order to take some prisoners, that we might receive some information concerning this coast, where we never were before.

On the 25th, we put to the shore and landed, and after a

march of three hours, came to a hatto, where we surprised the people, who gave us to understand that the English had taken the town of Leon, and burnt that of Realeguo. That the inhabitants of Legoria, Granada, Sansonnat, St. Michell, St. Salvador, and Villa Nueva, which are neighboring towns to the two fore-mentioned ones, had sent a considerable reënforcement of men to those of the town of Leon, who yet durst not attack the English, who staid there three whole days; during which time they had sent several messages to these reënforcements to require them to fight in the race savanna, which the other still refused, saying, they were not yet all come together; that is, they were hitherto no more than six to one, and that they staid till they were doubly increased.

On the 26th, one of our quarter-masters, who was a Catalonian by birth, fled to the Spaniards, which hindered us at this time from going to take the town of Granada, of which I shall speak in its due place, for we did not doubt but that he had given them an account of the design we had formed upon that place.

On the 27th, we went on board our canoes again, and made for the port of Realeguo, where the rendezvous of our ships was to be. We could land nowhere all along the coast, because the sea breaks with so much violence there, when it is a southerly wind, that it is impossible to come near it. However, six of our men swam with a design to fill some casks with water, which we were in want of, but they could not do it, for the Spaniards followed us by land all along the bank, and so it fell out that one of our men was unfortunately drowned.

On the 1st of November, we arrived at the port of Realeguo, where we found our ship at anchor. There are two passages to this port, whereof that to windward is best. It is very narrow, and, besides this, has two *mornes*, or little mountains, that form the two points thereof, upon one of which the Spaniards had a design to build a fort. There is a very fine river runs into this haven, that bears the same name with the town. It is safe from any winds, and contains within it five islands that are very good to careen ships in; there are but three leagues from thence up the river, before you come at the town. But, before we got there with our canoes, we met three very strong intrenchments, that had been made for its security, upon the river's side, about a quarter of a league distant one from another, and which the English had half burnt. About a musket shot from the town, the Spaniards had very fine docks, where they build their ships. It is washed with this river, and stands in a very fine country, watered with several other rivulets; and both its churches and houses, though then half burned, appeared to us to have been beautiful enough. We are also further to take notice, that that river we have spoken of has eight arms, by which you may conveniently convey any thing to the villages, sugar plantations, and hattoes, whereof this country is full, and which belongs to the burghers, as well of this town as of the neighboring ones, of which Leon, that is not above four leagues off, is situated in a very curious plain. On the 2d, we went to take two of those hattoes, from whence we carried some victuals on board for those who were careening our ships.

On the 6th, we departed, to the number of a hundred and fifty men, to go and seize the sentinels of the town of Leon, and having surprised them on the 8th, they informed us there were two thousand men in the place, who, yet not trusting to their numbers, had taken all their movables, and carried them to a place of safety. We returned on board on the 9th, and next day set out to go to a great sugar plantation, two leagues distant from this city, where we arrived at midnight, but found no soul living there, the people being gone for their security to the town, upon the report that was spread abroad that we had taken some sentinels. But as we were upon our return from this sugar plantation to go on board again, our vanguard met with a detachment of horse, upon whom they fired, and made them fly, but the captain was made a prisoner, who, upon our questioning of him, told us that he had heard of us a long time since, but not knowing what language we spoke, we had been taken for a company of two hundred and fourscore mulattoes, who were looking out to fight us, knowing we were ashore, and who would be at that sugar plantation that evening. We asked the captain what they were he had headed, and he answered they were a troop of horse, who guarded the embarking place belonging to that sugar plantation, and that the governor of the town, coming to know we were come to the port of Realeguo, had given them orders to retire in such a manner, as gave us to understand that our enemies kept a very good guard, when they had nothing to be afraid of, and that they would draw off as soon as ever they saw us near, and, in effect, we found them to be exactly the very same as represented to us: for, surely, if they had had but any thing of resolution and courage, being as numerous as they were in respect to us, they could have easily cut us off, as often as we made any descent upon them; and thus many times we found our safety to proceed from their cowardice, as much as from our own courage.

On the 13th, the same company of a hundred and fifty men

left our vessels to go to take a borough town, three leagues above the city of Realeguo, whose name was Pueblo Viego. We passed through this place, which we found to be quite deserted by its inhabitants, because of the excommunication they had thundered out against themselves.

Some, perhaps, will be surprised to hear of this extravagant humor; but there is nothing truer, than that, when the freebooters have several times taken the same place from them, their prelates, after excommunicating and cursing the same, quit it entirely, and will not bury even their dead, whom we killed, as supposing them, for the aforesaid reason, unworthy of Christian burial.

On the 14th, in the morning, we arrived at Pueblo Viego, from whence their sentinels had discovered us since the 13th, in the evening, so that we found the enemy intrenched in the great church, and about a hundred and fifty horse upon the place of arms. We presently fell to work, and, after some discharges, we put them to flight; but those that were within the church held it about half an hour longer, and then made their escape through a door that was behind the vestry, which we had not secured. We staid a day and a half in this place, and carried away all the provisions we could lay hands on, upon the horses which we had, and our own backs, and on the 16th arrived on board our ship. On the 18th, we returned to take an *estancia*, which was a league and a half from the said town, and the master, whom we took prisoner, told us, that, the day we went away, six hundred men lay in ambush for us, on the way by which we were to pass; but that, without knowing it, we had returned by a different road. On the 21st, we went on board with our prisoner, who promised us some provision for his ransom; and next day we put another prisoner ashore to endeavor to procure it for us with all expedition.

On the 24th, came a Spanish officer, who brought us a letter from the vicar general of the province, (and in all appearance,) by order of the general of Costa Rica, who sent us word there was a peace made between the crowns of France and Spain, for twenty years; that they were joined together to make war upon the infidels; that therefore we ought to commit no further hostilities; and that, if we had a mind to return to the North Sea, we might come safely unto them, and have our passage into Europe, in his Catholic majesty's galleons. We gave them an answer suitable to their proposal, being well enough acquainted with the evil disposition of the Spaniards towards us, who, by this false pretence, thought to have seduced us to come the more readily among them, who understood the extreme misery we had endured by one of our people, of whom we made mention before, and who ran away to them to be freed from the long fasts he was forced to with us.

On the 24th, we careened our ships, and the next day put thirty prisoners ashore, part of whom we gave their liberty to, and on the 28th we made ready to return and go in quest of our two barks, whom we had appointed to rendezvous at the Isle of St. John de Cueblo, in case we were separated from one another. As we were going out of the port, the Spaniards gave notice, by the fires they made all along the coast, what course we steered. On the 3d of December, we found ourselves got above a hundred leagues out at sea, whither a north-east breeze had driven us; we bore again towards land, and on the 5th went ashore. We sent out three canoes furnished with seventy men, to cross the Bay of Colebra, and to endeavor to get some provision along the coast, as also to discharge our ships of so many mouths, there being but too little victuals left for those who remained behind, and who went to the Isle of St. John. For as to the provision we were able to get together, while we were ashore in the port of Realeguo, there was no great quantity of it, for the Spaniards, knowing of our coming, had carried it up far into the country, whither we durst not go and fetch it with so few men as we had with us, as not being yet sufficiently acquainted with their cowardice.

From Realeguo to Panama there are a great many little ports which you must be well acquainted with before you can find them, for the mouth of them is very obscure, and if you once do miss them, it is absolutely impossible to get ashore along the coast, the sea being there always boisterous, and very high upon the blowing of the least south-east and south-west winds upon it.

I have observed this difference betwixt this sea and that of the north, that let the wind be ever so violent, as soon as it ceases, this sea proves as calm as if it had never blown; whereas in the other, for all the wind is allayed, it continues several days in the same violent agitation as when it blew hard. I have also taken notice, that the windy storms, that are formed to leeward, are much more dangerous in the former than those that come from the windward; but in the other, it is contrary, where a ship generally esteems not herself to be in danger, but from those that arise to windward of her, at leastwise, if the wind be not subject to a very great variation; to which we may add one difference more, that the South Sea is pacific enough upon the main, and very turbulent upon the coast; and that of the North is oftentimes very impetuous far out, and almost always calm near the shore.

The South Sea breeds, in divers parts of it, a very great number of serpents, in color like spotted marble, and are generally about two feet long ; their sting is of so venomous and killing a nature, that when a man is once stung by them, there is no human remedy that can secure him from a sudden death ; and that which is indeed very surprising, in regard to these creatures, is, that when the sea by the boisterousness of its waves throws them upon some bank or other, though they do not go out of the water, yet they no sooner touch the sand, but they presently die.

On the 9th, having still kept our course along the coast, we put fifty men in three canoes ashore, to go and take the town of Esparso, which is three leagues from Caldaira, and is the place that serves for a port to it ; we took the sentinels about the third part of our way, who told us, that, besides the inhabitants of the town, there were five hundred men, whom they had sent for, to come to their assistance, from Carthage, upon the alarm given them by our two barks that had anchored in this bay, from which they were but just gone. Upon this intelligence, we bethought ourselves, considering the smallness of our number, to put off this expedition to another time, and so returned with all speed, but in such want of provision, that we were forced to kill and eat the sentinels' horses, after four days' strict abstinence ; and this sort of fasting, which was not the first that we had used, did not prove to be the last.

Caldaira is a bay that bears the name of six magazines that stand about three leagues to the east of the mouth of it, and upon the bank of the place of embarking, belonging to Esparso. This bay, which by some geographers is called Nicoya, is one of the finest ports in the world, though the mouth of it be large, yet, in lieu of that, it is at least twelve leagues within land, and comprehends a great many islands of different sizes within it. There is none but an easterly wind that can hurt it. The bottom of the bay is open, by means of very fine rivers that run into it, and by which you may ascend to several villages, hattoes, and sugar plantations, whereof this country is full. You may chose your place of anchorage, according to the length of the cable, that is, from six fathom, increasing to a hundred, and the bottom is very good. I forgot to observe, that the six magazines of Caldaira, whereof I have spoken, were partly built by the inhabitants of Carthage, who make use of that for their port, for facilitating the traffic they drive with those living on the coast of Peru, before we came to terrify them.

Having, on the 10th, gone on board our canoes, we went to a great bananery that stood in the same bay ; it is a set of fruit-trees which they call bananiers, and the fruit thereof bananas, with which we loaded our canoes for our subsistence. As we went ashore, we took the sentinel of the little town of Nicoya, from which, finding ourselves at some distance, we did not then think fit to go up to it, and so we directed our course for Point Borica, where we arrived on the 14th. That is a very pleasant and delightful place, and among other things, we could not but admire a walk consisting of five rows of cocoa-trees that run along the bank for above fifteen leagues in length, and that in so orderly a manner, that though the same be no more than the bare work of nature, without any additional help from art, they seem as if they had been all planted on a line.

This fruit, which upon several occasions were so delightful to us, grows upon the stock of a tree, that is a kind of palm, twenty or five and twenty foot high. It is like a nut, but without making any comparison of the bigness of it, for there are some of these fruits that weigh twelve or fifteen pounds. The shell is very hard, and thick enough; it is wrapped up in a kind of thick covering, made up all of filaments, with which the Spaniards used to caulker their ships, it being much better than tow, which rots in the water in less than a year's time, whereas the other is fed by it, and waxeth green. If you bore a hole in this nut, there runs out a quantity of greenish liquor, which somewhat resembles the color of whey, but of a sharpish taste, and pleasant enough; and when the shell is broken, we find under it a kernel, or what is equivalent thereto, of the thickness of a man's finger, very white and nourishing, which sticks very close to the inside. We left this place on the 20th, keeping our course still all along the continent.

On the 22d, having no victuals to eat, we put sixty men in our three canoes ashore, to go seek some for us; and after travelling the space of a league, we took a very curious hatto with two prisoners, who told us we were within a league and a half of the little town of Chiriquita, and that there were six hundred men in it, which made us seize with all expedition upon as much victuals as we could, to carry it to the place where we had left our canoes; but in our return thither, we found four hundred horse in the way, whom we fought with all along, retreating, till we came to the sea-side. They challenged us again and again, and defied us in threatening language to go to their town, which we did not fail to do some days after. In the mean time, we bore away for the Isle of St. John, where, arriving on the 1st of January, 1686, we found our ship and two barks at anchor.

CHAPTER LII.

The Freebooters' Voyage to the South Sea, in 1686.

On the 5th of January, in the new year, we parted to the number of two hundred and thirty men in eight canoes, to go and face the townsmen of Chiriquita, and to give them the visit they had defied us to do. And so it was, that this Island of St. John being about twenty leagues from them, we went ashore on the 6th, about ten or eleven o'clock at night, without being discovered; but as we had no guide with us, we marched on till daylight without seeing any body. We hid ourselves on the 7th, all the day, in a wood; but as soon as night approached we came out and put on, without discovering any body, till the 8th, in the morning, when we concealed ourselves again in another small wood, and spent all the day in that place, during which time we came to know that we had mistaken our measures, by going ashore on that side of the river, whereas we should have gone on the other. This was cold comfort to people so fatigued as we were; however, as soon as it was night, we made no more-ado than to return to our canoes, wherein we passed that river. When we were got on the other side, we took the town watch, by whom we were informed that the Spaniards had conveyed away all their effects, upon our being at their hattoes.

On the 9th, we got to Chiriquita two hours before day: we surprised all the inhabitants, who were for two days at variance with one another, about going the rounds, and after we had secured our prisoners, we told them that belonged to us, and that we were come to spare them the labor. We surprised also their court of guard, where they were at play, and as soon as they saw us amongst them, they flew to their arms to defend themselves, but as it was a little too late, we eased them of that trouble also. Of them we learned that there was a small frigate up the river, which, having touched in going out upon a bank of sand that lay at the mouth thereof, was forced to go back, and so put the provision, which was her lading, ashore.

About two in the afternoon, we perceived some Spaniards in a house at some distance from the town, which made us send five of our number to fetch them out; but when we drew near those whom we had seen, having showed themselves for no other purpose than to draw us out, disappeared, and presently about a hundred and twenty more came out of a little nook, where they had concealed themselves, and beset us in such a manner, that, finding no likelihood of escaping, we resolved never to be taken alive, but to sell our lives as dear as we could; to which end we immediately stood back to back, that we might face the enemy every way, and in this posture we fought them above an hour and a half, at the expiration whereof there being no more than two of us in a condition to fight, God was pleased that some of our men who were upon the guard should come to our relief, being driven thither by the firings, for they thought, before they heard these cries, that we were exercising ourselves at shooting at a mark. When the enemy saw this reënforcement come, they made such haste to go away, that it was impossible to overtake them. This succor, coming in so seasonably, did infallibly save our lives, for the enemy having already killed us two men, and disabled another, it was impossible we should hold out against such a shower of bullets as were poured in upon us from all sides. And so I may truly say I escaped a scouring, and that without receiving as much as one wound, but by a visible hand of protection from heaven. The Spaniards left thirty men dead upon the spot, and thus we defended ourselves as desperate men, and, to say all in a word, like freebooters.

We burnt all the houses in the town this day, lest under the covert of them our sentinels might be surprised, and that the enemy might come to insult us in the night. When we had so done, we retired into the great church, where they durst not come to attack us, but contented themselves to give us some musket shot from time to time, and that from a great distance.

Chiriquita is a small town that stands in a plain of savannas, from whence the sight is bounded almost every way with no other than small, but very pleasant thickets. There are several rivulets that traverse it in divers places, and afterward gently glide into these savannas to water them. It is surrounded with a great many hattoes, and they drive no other trade but in tallow and leather. The port or embarking place belonging to it is on a pretty large river, from whence you must ascend about a league to come at it. There is but one way to come in at its mouth, and the Spaniards themselves, without a buoy, will not venture to enter it; there are three leagues by land from this embarking place to the town, and that through so pleasant a way, that none but such as we were could be weary of it, who had no other thoughts than to get victuals to satisfy our hunger, which bore hard upon us, when we were going to take this town, having eaten nothing from the 5th, when we left our vessels, till the 9th, that we took it.

On the 10th, we left the place, taking our prisoners along with us, to wait for the ransoming of them upon an island that is within the same river, making choice rather of these places for that purpose than of the continent, and where, being obliged for a long time to stay for the money, we should give the Spaniards thereby an opportunity to gather all their forces together, and to pay us all at once, by overpowering us with numbers; whereas, these islands to which they could not come any other way than in shallops, and that openly, put us out of care to reëmbark, according to the measures they took by land. When therefore we returned to our canoes, which waited for us at the port of Chiriquita, we found the inhabitants of that town had laid an ambuscade for us; but we beat them off, and after the enemy had quite retired, they sent us a person to demand their prisoners, whom they said they would recover, or perish in the attempt. We told the messenger we were very ready to give them up, if they would come and meet us in the race savanna, to take them; and that, if they fired one single bullet at us, they should have no quarter, which so humbled their pride, that we saw no more of them.

As soon as we were got to the fore-mentioned island, we sent part of our canoes to look after the cargo of the small frigate which the Spaniards of Chiriquita gave us information of, where they found above a hundred men intrenched; but they could not hinder our men from possessing themselves of what they went in search for. Among the baggage, they found some letters, that, among other things, gave us to understand that the admiral of the Peru fleet, who was returned to Lima, had been burnt, with all her crew, which was at that time four hundred men, by a thunderbolt; and this was so much the more surprising and admirable, that no man living could remember to have heard any thunder in that country, no more than to have seen it rain.

On the 16th, the ransom for our prisoners came, and after we had set them at liberty, we returned aboard our ship, which rode then at anchor at St. John's Island. On the 20th, we concluded among ourselves it was necessary we should build large periaugues, seeing we could make no further use of our ship, for want of sails, and we had nothing left to make them with, and still were less able to take ships from the Spaniards, on this western coast, where they had put an entire stop to their navigation since we were come thither. On the 22d, we made choice of tall trees to make our canoes and periaugues of, upon the banks of a curious river, which we knew to be in the island.

On the 27th, we descried seven sail of ships out at sea,

which made us fit out five canoes to go and see what they were, and as we doubled one of the points of the island, we discerned twelve periaugues, and three long barks, who coasted it all along. We took them presently to be the fleet of Peru that was come in quest of us; we gave our men notice of it without delay, and at the same time resolved to put all we had on board our ship into our bark, and to go into that river where our docks were, there to wait the coming of our enemy, where they could not come to attack us, without losing a great many men. This project we put forthwith in execution, and after we had abandoned our ship, which could not be brought into that river, we ran her ashore, lest the Spaniards should have any benefit of it, and put her into a sailing condition, being very well assured of ourselves, that they did not want sails, as we did, for that purpose.

On the 28th, our sentinels came to give us notice, that six periaugues plied along the shore, which made us at the same time put a hundred and fifty men to lie in ambush on both sides the river, and then we set out, with two of our canoes, from whence, after we had seen them, we feigned to go away, by going back, to engage them to give us chase; but they, suspecting a stratagem in the case, bore directly upon our ship, that was run aground, upon which they fired very furiously, though there was none left within it but only a poor cat, which they perceiving, they bravely boarded and burnt her, for the sake of the iron work that belonged to her, which is a commodity as rare as it is dear in some parts of Peru. On the 1st of February, the Spanish fleet sailed away, and left us at ease to finish our work, upon which we spent the remainder of the month.

We understood, afterwards, that the admiral of this fleet had orders to put some field-pieces ashore, to demolish those fortifications which they thought we had made upon the island, being induced to believe it was so by the report the prisoners, which we sent them, made of our intentions; and we, to impose upon them, having asked whether there were any masons among them that could do our work, and sometimes obliged them to give us brick for their ransom, though we had no need of them. There were no less than fourteen of our men died in the month of February.

On the 14th of March, we departed from the Isle of St. John, with our two barks, a half galley of forty oars, ten great periaugues, and ten small canoes, all built of mapou timber, except our two barks. We gained the windward point of the island, to take a review of our men, and found ourselves weaker by no less than thirty persons, since our separation from the English. But we formed a design anew at the same time, which had been put by for above four months, which was to go and take the town of Granada, distant now from us about two hundred leagues. To effect this work, it was necessary we should be furnished with provision wherewith to subsist us during the voyage; and we having none, this made us send away our half galley and four canoes, to seek for some at Pueblo Neuvo, while the rest of the company went to tarry for us at the Isle of St. Peter, which is two leagues to windward of the River Chiriquita, and to finish somewhat that was still wanting to the complete equipment of our canoes.

On the 6th of April, about three hours before daylight, we got near to the River of Pueblo Nuevo, and by a clear light of the moon, we discerned a small frigate at its mouth, as also a long bark, and a periaugue. We came within pistol-shot of them, as supposing them to be our English freebooters, from whom we had separated. But we found ourselves quickly mistaken, for, after we had hailed them, they answered us with an entire volley of great and small shot, which made us now conjecture that they were, and it was too true, a detachment left by the Spanish fleet in that place, when they left us at St. John's Island, as a guard to two small ships, which we knew they were lading with provisions, at the port of this town, in order to transport the same to Panama. Our mistake was the reason that we had twenty men disabled to fight, by this first discharge of the enemy, before we knew well where we were. But after we were a little recovered of the surprise this adventure put us to, we fought them stiffly for the space of two hours, though we had the use of no other arms than our fusees, and not one cannon to discharge upon them; and they, on their part, defended themselves so much the more vigorously, in that they believed we, after such a surprise as we had been exposed to, would quickly slacken our courage, and give way. They did all they could to make ready during the fight; but we hindered them, and no man could appear in the shrouds, but we brought them down, as well as their grenadiers from their round tops. But finding the light of the moon now gone, we put off out of the reach of their cannon, as well to take care of our wounded men, which amounted to thirty-three, besides four who were killed outright, as to wait for daylight, in order to terminate this affair, which we were not willing to leave undecided. But the enemy did in the mean time retire under the covert of an intrenchment, which I have said already they had upon the banks of this river, where the country people, who had heard the noise of the fight in the night, were also come, which made us conclude, that if we went to attack them in that place, we could not have that advantage there we had resolved to take of them; so upon approach of day we steered our course to go and rejoin our canoes at the Isle of St. Peter, where we arrived on the 8th.

On the 9th, we found ourselves in great want of victuals, having now nothing at all to eat; and this put us hard to it, more especially our wounded men, whom we sent by our half galley (for their better conveniency) on board our two barks, whom we had appointed to rendezvous in the Bay of Boca del Toro. When this was done, we went ashore to a town ten leagues to leeward of Chiriquita, where finding none, we left it, and on the 11th, in our return to our canoes, we found, in order to strengthen us under the languishment which hunger had reduced us to, a regale of an ambuscade of five hundred men laid for us, against whom, for all our weakness, we made so good a defence, that we obliged them to leave us free passage; but yet not without the loss of two of our men. We went on board in the evening, to go join our barks in the Bay of Boca del Toro, where we arrived the 13th, and went ashore, spending our time to the 16th in hunting, more especially for the subsistence of our wounded men; and here we found the same sort of deer and birds, as I have taken notice of in our passage over the continent, in great plenty.

On the same day, we departed for the Bay of Caldaira, after having renewed our enterprise upon the little town of Lesparso, of which I have already spoken. On the 19th, being arrived in the bay, we went ashore two hours before daylight, and reached the town. About eleven in the morning, we found the place was in a manner entirely abandoned from the time we had taken the sentinels, who, as I have already observed, diverted us from going thither, by the account they gave of the reënforcement that was come to them from Carthage. However, we took some prisoners, who told us all the people were retired to this last town, which is twenty-four leagues off; so that, finding our endeavors all frustrated, we returned, on the 20th, to the sea-side, to rejoin our canoes.

Lesparso is reckoned to be three leagues distant from the sea-side, and the way thither very bad; you cannot travel the length of a gunshot in even ground, but the same is every where rugged, and full of little mountains and hills, though beyond them the country appears to be very good and delightful. The town is built upon an eminence, from whence one may easily see all that comes in and goes out of the bay. This town is in a manner encompassed with a rivulet that runs round it. Between it and Carthage are very curious plains, with royal ways made through them, and that as well as any in Europe.

On the 21st, we victualled ourselves with the fruit of a bananery in this bay, wherein our two barks came to join us; and next day we summoned our people ashore upon this island, as well to consult how we should attack the town of Granada, which we had a design upon, as to take an account of what powder they had, as fearing many of them might use it in hunting. Here we enacted orders, whereby those were condemned to lose their share of the booty got in the place that should be found guilty of cowardice, violence, drunkenness, disobedience, theft, and straggling from the main body without orders. When this was over, we left the bay the same evening, and a strong easterly wind, surprising us in the night, separated our vessels from one another. At break of day we told thirteen sail, wherewith we were amazed, knowing we had no more than a dozen, and this made us give our canoes the signal to chase, as well as we, that vessel that did not belong to us: but when we had continued the chase for about an hour's time, we perceived five more; and having come up with the foremost, we understood it was Captain Townsley, come from the coast of Acapulco. He had left his ship at the cape, over against the mouth of the bay, where we had been, and went with his five canoes to find out some bananas, having very little provision on board. He told us that Captain David, with his fleet, was on the southern coast, and that Captain Suams, with his ship, was gone to the East Indies.

We, finding ourselves now to be the stronger party, called to mind their former imperious dealings with us, and, to show our resentment of it, we made him and his men, who were in the other four canoes, prisoners. We boarded his vessel immediately, of which having made ourselves masters, we made a sham of taking it away; but, our design being only to frighten them, we left them for some time under the apprehensions of the danger they were in. Then we let the captain know we were honester men than he, and that, though we had the upper hand, yet we would not take the advantage of revenging the injuries they had done us, and that we would put him and his men in possession of what we had taken from them four or five hours before. This moderation which we exercised towards them, together with their being informed by some of our crew of a design we had upon the town of Granada, engaged them to desire we would take them in to be our associates in the enterprise; and, they being a hundred and fifteen in number, we readily consented to such a reënforcement, as must needs be useful to us.

On the 25th, we departed all together, French and English, in our periaugues and canoes, leaving their ship and our two barks under the covert of Cape Blanck, which is twenty leagues to windward of the place where we were to go ashore, and gave orders to those that were appointed to guard them, to sail away six days after, and to coast it till they came to an anchor, at the place where we should leave our canoes.

On the 7th of April, we went ashore on a flat coast, to the number of three hundred and forty-five men, under the conduct of a very good guide, who led us across a wood that we might not be discovered. We marched on night and day till the 9th, but, notwithstanding all the precautions we took, we could not hinder our being discovered by the inhabitants of the town of Granada, who were fishing in a river about fifteen leagues off; and, though they made all the haste they could to advertise the Spaniards of our march, they could not have been there time enough to have given the people notice to remove all their effects, considering the expedition we used to follow them, had not they had (unhappily upon our account) notice given them of us three weeks before by the inhabitants of Lesparso, who having seen the great number of canoes we had, as we passed by there, grew suspicious of our design.

The fatigue we had undergone during our march, together with the sharp hunger that pressed us, obliged us to halt and rest the 9th, in the evening, in a great sugar plantation, that is about four leagues distant from Granada, and was in our way thither. It belonged to a knight of St. James's, whom, upon our arrival, we failed to take prisoner, our legs being at that time much more disposed to rest than to run after him. On the 10th we set out, and upon our approach near the town, we observed an eminence above it about a league off, and two ships upon the lake of Nicaragua, that carried, as we were since informed, all the wealth of the town, into an island two leagues off. We took a prisoner in a village that was in our way, who told us the inhabitants of the town had intrenched themselves upon the place of arms, and compassed it with a strong wall, since our quartermaster, who had run away to them, had given information that we designed to come amongst them. He told us further, that the place was guarded with fourteen pieces of cannon, and six patereroes; and lastly, that they had detached six troops of horse to attack our rear, while our front should be engaged with the Spaniards, if so be we should come up to them.

This information, which doubtless would have terrified any other but freebooters, did not retard our design one minute, nor hinder us. About two in the afternoon of the same day, we came up to the town, where, at one entrance into the suburbs, we met with a strong party lying in ambush for us, whom, after an hour's engagement, we fell with that fury on, that we made our way over all their bellies, with the loss only of one man on our own side, and from thence entered the town, where we made a halt to wait for the answer of several of our company, whom we had detached to go round, and take observation of a fort which we saw in a direct line from the street, by which we entered. Presently after came a party to inform us, that it was a square fort, and that, beside the street we were in, they had also observed three more, that looked out to the other three sides of that fort, by which the enemy could discover whatever came towards them through those avenues, which were, moreover, all commanded by their cannon and small arms.

We were not long in debate what we should do; we could easily see we were too few to make our attacks by those different ways all at a time. Wherefore, after we had got together all those whom we had sent out to scout, who for some time had been detained by some light skirmishes, we made ourselves ready to fall on, through that street alone where we then were; and it was well we did so, for, if we had dispersed ourselves through the others, the horse, which were in the rear of us, and observed our motion, would not have failed to hem us in, which they durst not do while we kept all together.

After we had exhorted one another to fall on bravely, we advanced at a round pace towards the said fortification. As soon as the defendants saw us within a good cannon-shot of them, they fired furiously upon us; but observing that, at every discharge of their great guns, we saluted them down to the ground, in order to let their shot fly over us, they bethought themselves of false priming them, to the end we might raise our bodies after the sham was over, and so be really surprised with their true firing. As soon as we discovered this stratagem, we ranged ourselves along the houses, and having got upon a little ascent, which was a garden plat, we fired upon them from thence so openly for an hour and a half, that they were obliged to quit the ground, to which our hardy boys, who were got to the foot of their walls, contributed yet even more than the other, by pouring in hand grenadoes incessantly upon them, so that at last they betook themselves to the great church, or tower; but they wounded us some men. As soon as our people, who had got upon the same eminence, perceived that the enemy fled, they called to us to jump over the walls, which we had no sooner done, but they followed us. And thus it was, that we made ourselves masters of their place of arms, and consequently of the town, from whence they fled, after having lost a great many men. We had on our side but four men killed, and eight wounded, which in truth, was very cheap. When we got into the fort, we found it to be a place capable of containing six thousand fighting men. It was encompassed with a wall, the same as our prisoners gave us an account of. It was pierced with many holes, to do execution upon the assailants, and was well stored with arms. That part of it which looked towards the street, through which we attacked it, was defended by two pieces of cannon, and four patereroes, to say nothing of several other places made to open in the wall, through which they thrust instruments made on purpose, to break the legs of those that should be so adventurous as to come near it ; but these, by the help of our grenadiers, we rendered useless to them. After we had sung *Te Deum* in the great church, and set four sentinels in the tower, we fixed our court of guard in the strong built houses, that are also enclosed within the place of arms, and there gathered all the ammunition we could get. Then we went to visit the houses, wherein we found nothing but a few goods, and some provision, which we carried into our court of guard.

Next day in the evening, we detached a party, a hundred and fifty men, to go and find out some women, that we might put them to ransom, and some booty which we were told they had in the sugar plantation, a league off of the city. But they were gone by the time we got thither, as not believing themselves safe in that place, so that our party came back *re infecta.* The same day we sent a prisoner to the Spaniards, to require them to ransom the town, or else we would burn it ; whereupon they sent a monk to treat with us, who said the officers and inhabitants were in consultation about it, but that one of our men whom they had taken as he lagged behind, through weariness upon the road, without the officer, that brought up our rear, having taken notice of it, assured them we would not burn it, because our design was to pass some month after to the North Sea, by the lake there, and to furnish ourselves in this town with necessaries for our journey, which we should not meet with if we fired the place : so that, the said man having given them such assurance, they would no longer trouble themselves about giving an answer to the proposal we had made for their ransoming the town, which at last constrained some of us to set fire to the houses, out of mere spite and revenge.

The opportunity, which now offered itself unto us of passing through the lake to the North Sea, was not at this time over favorable, and we should not have failed to make use of it, if we had had canoes ready in this place to go and take two ships, and the wealth of the town, which the inhabitants had carried, for the better securing of them, into the island, which I have already said was in the said lake; which would have put a full end unto the trouble we had been in from the time we failed of seizing the flota before Panama. But the term of our dangers and miseries, which our destiny had still in store for us, being not yet come, we could not take the advantage of so favorable an opportunity to get out of those parts of the world, which, though very charming and agreeable to those who are settled there, yet did not appear to be so to a handful of men, as we were, without shipping, the most part of our time without victuals, and wandering amidst a multitude of enemies, against whom we were obliged to be continually upon our guard, and who did all that in them lay to deprive us of subsistence.

Granada is a large and spacious town, situated in a bottom, inclining to the coast of the South Sea, whose churches are very stately, and houses well enough built. They have several religious houses there, both of men and women: the great church stands at one of the ends of the place of arms. The country thereabouts is very destitute of water, they having no other there than only the Lake of Nicaragua, upon the side whereof the city is built, and round about which you may see a great many fine sugar plantations, which are more like unto so many villages than single houses, and, among the rest, is that belonging to the knight of St. James's, where we lay in our march to the town, where there is a very pretty and rich church.

On the 10th, we left the city, and took along with us one piece of cannon, with four patereroes, as not questioning but we should meet with opposition in our way, before we came to the sea-side, from which we were near twenty leagues distant; and therein we were not deceived, seeing the Spaniards waited for us, to the number of two thousand five hundred men, within a quarter of a league of the town, and presently charged us: but, not dreaming that we had brought any artillery along with us, they were so terrified when we had fired two cannon shot upon their first ambuscade, that they left us a free passage in this place only; for, though they saw a great many of their men sprawling upon the ground, they ceased not all the way, at certain distances, to lay new ambushes for us, where they had no more success than at first. We took one of them prisoners, who told us there was a million and a half of pieces of eight, long since ordered for the ransoming of their town, in case the same should be taken, and that the same was buried in the wall, so as that it could not be seen. But we had no inclination to go back in search of this money, seeing we found difficulty enough to rid ourselves out of the hands of so considerable a number of enemies as we had already to deal with.

We were forced that evening to leave our cannon behind us, after we had first nailed them up, for the oxen that drew them were dead for want of water, having travelled several leagues through very great heats, without one drop of water, and through such a dust as choked both man and beast. But we reserved our patereroes, which were carried by mules, who could better bear this inconveniency. At last, we lay in a very pretty village, called Massaya, that stands upon the side of the lake; but from hence to the water there is so great a descent, that a man of full growth appears to be no bigger than a child. We were received by the Indians in this place with open arms; but the Spaniards that had retired thither, knowing the extreme thirst wherewith we were afflicted, had spoiled all the water that was in the village, hoping thereby to reduce us to such necessity, that we might go by night to drink to the lake, that so they might lay some ambush for us. But these Indians, that came to meet and pray us not to burn their village, remedied this evil, in assuring us they would supply us with whatever we had occasion for, as long as we staid there, and particularly with water. Taken with this their submission, we granted them their request, so much the more willingly, seeing they gave us to understand, upon several occasions, that they were more our friends than they were the Spaniards.

All these Indians are a miserable people, whom the Spaniards endeavor to reduce and bring under their subjection by little and little, with a feigned gentleness practised towards them, to make them forgetful of those cruelties and tyrannies they had heretofore exercised in those parts, and which they are not wanting still to keep in remembrance. They have at present a pretty number of them there, whom they have enticed down from those mountains where they had taken refuge, and brought them to submit in this manner. They have given them places to build boroughs and villages upon, but all their labor redounds to the advantage of the Spaniards; so that, being used as slaves by them, they are so weary of their dominion, and the barbarity showed them, by being made use of as palisadoes by the Spaniards, when they fight us, that if we had been people fit to receive them, as often as they made an offer to take our parts, we should have formed a very considerable army; and it is certain, that if they had but arms and protection, they would have infallibly shaken off the yoke of their pitiful masters, being three times more in number than they.

We rested only one day in this place, to refresh our wounded men, where two died of the cramp, which contracted all their nerves: this is so malignant a distemper in this country, that, when it seizes upon a stranger that is wounded, it will certainly kill him. This same day came a father to us from the Spaniards, to re-demand another father from us, who was one of our prisoners, who had taken up arms against us, and had his pockets full of poisoned bullets. We required in exchange for him one of our men whom they had taken, which they would by no means agree to; so that we carried the latter along with us, as far as the sea-side.

On the 17th, we left this borough, and lay in another place three leagues beyond it, from whence we passed next day, and as we came out of a forest to enter into a plain, we discovered five hundred men upon an ascent, waiting for our coming, commanded by the above-mentioned Catalonian quartermaster, that had deserted us. They had put up bloody colors, to signify they would give no quarter, which obliged us to lay by our white colors, and display our red as well as they. We marched directly to the place where they were, without stopping, though they fired very thick upon us; and when we came within musket-shot, we detached our vanguard to beat them off their ground, which they did with wonderful bravery: here we took about fifty horses. The enemy, in their flight, cowardly left part of their arms behind them, besides their dead and wounded men, by which last, we understood that these people were the reënforcement which the inhabitants of the town of Leon had sent to the assistance of Granada against us, and who were returned home.

After we had rested about an hour, we continued our march, and lay at a little town, which the inhabitants had forsaken. On the 19th, we lay in a hatto, and the next day in an estancia, where we rested some days to refresh ourselves, and to salt our provisions to carry on board our ships, where we knew very well there could be no victuals left. I always went before, with an advanced party of fifty men, to go and inform those who looked after our vessels with our return. On the 26th, the rest of our men came to the sea-side, where we reëmbarked all together, and understood that four of our men, wounded in the fight at Pueblo Viego, were dead, but more for want of sustenance than their wounds.

On the 27th, we sailed for Realeguo, and on the 28th anchored in that port, where, upon our going ashore, the sentinels of Pueblo Viego discovered us, but that did not hinder us to proceed and arrive at the place about noon. The Spaniards, who had heard of our coming, fled every where ; but the heats are so excessive in these parts, that you cannot travel there this time of day ; and this made us go and see rather for some shade or tufts of grass whereof to set our feet, than to run after the enemy ; however, we took some prisoners. We tarried there but two days, and after we had gathered as much provision as we could find in the houses, we sent out a party to seek for some horses, whereof they brought us a hundred ; we departed on the 1st of May, and carried our provision to the river side, at Realeguo, where our canoes were, who carried the same afterwards on board our ships, while we went out to seek for more, that so we might get together a good quantity, and not be obliged to consume it as we brought it in.

On the 2d, we went to a sugar plantation, to fetch off six caldrons, which we brought away next day, and on the 4th, set out for a borough two leagues from Realeguo, which they call Ginandego, which some of the inhabitants a few days before prayed us by way of raillery to go and visit, as thinking themselves sufficiently secured by an intrenchment cast up at the avenue leading to it, and that was defended by two hundred men. We got thither on the 5th, by break of day ; but, being discovered by the sentinel, he carried the Spaniards notice thereof, who gave us no occasion to desire them to quit it, after they had given us a few musket-shot ; so that, to punish their rhodomontades, we burnt the place down to the ground. We took one of their people prisoner, by whom we understood that the corregidor of Leon, who was very desirous to drive us away from that coast, had ordered all the *tements*, as soon as we got to any place, to burn all the provision they had, which to our sorrow was but too well executed, not only here, but every where else, and was the cause also of that hunger and extraordinary toil which we were forced to endure in these seas, as long as we staid there.

The same day about noon, came about eight hundred men into a *savana*, from Leon, to fight us ; the sentinels, which we had placed on the top of the steeple, rung the alarum-bell, to give us notice to get together, and come out of the houses where we were dispersed : whereupon we marched in a body of a hundred and fifty men, with red colors, to fight them ; but as they could not endure to let us come within musket-shot of them, for they fled without any more ado, we were obliged to retire, and, on the 6th, went away to go on board our ships, which we careened next day, as we also cleaned our canoes.

On the 9th, we had a consultation together, about what way we should take, and here we found ourselves of two opinions; one party was for going up before Panama, being in hopes they had begun their navigation again, as knowing we were far enough from them; but the rest represented that many times they had such years on that coast, whereof that might be one of them, that eight months thereof was sad weather, in respect to excessive rains and southerly winds which reign there, and that therefore it would be more advisable to go lower westward, and winter upon some island or other, and there to wait for fair weather.

Now these different sentiments were pursued by us, and, every man having made choice of his side, next day our chirurgeons had orders to give in an account of those among the wounded, who were crippled, to the end we might make them satisfaction befere we divided. They told us we had four men crippled, and six hurt, to which we gave six hundred pieces of eight a man, and a thousand to those that were crippled, as it was our constant custom in those seas; and it was exactly all the money we had got together that was applied to that use. We made a division of the barks and canoes on the 12th, and found ourselves to be a hundred and forty-eight Frenchmen, ready to go up towards Panama (without comprehending the English under Captain Townsley) and the same number of French sailed also to the westward. Next day our provision was shared amongst us, and now it was that we divided into two parts; those who were for the westward put themselves under the conduct of Captain Grognier, and we, that were bound for Panama, were commanded by Captain Townsley, and then we went to anchor at an island, half a league distant from that we left, to take in water and wood. On the sixteenth, Captain Grognier sent us his quarter-master to desire us to put none of our prisoners ashore, for fear they should give the Spaniards notice of our separation, for, as he had a design to make a descent upon them, he was apprehensive that such a discovery would make them more resolute and hardy to oppose him.

On the 19th, we made ready, and sailed for Panama with Captain Townsley's ship and one bark. We steered E. S. E. to S. S. E. and to S. S. W. till midnight, when we were overtaken with a storm, which made us lie by till the 20th at noon; when the weather proved fair, then we steered E. S. E. to the 23d, when we anchored in the Bay of Colebra, to take in water. We spent that day there to take tortoises, which are to be found in great numbers in that little bay. They are of different sizes, and we found one sort of them so large, that one was enough for fifty persons to feed upon in a day. On the 24th, we put a hundred and fifty men ashore, in order to find out some town or borough, we having no guide with us that knew this country; and, after we had walked a league or thereabouts, we alighted upon three hattoes very near one another, where, finding edibles enough, we staid till the 26th, when we returned on board; then Captain Townsley proposed we should go and take the town of Villia, which is 30 leagues to the leeward of Panama, to which all of us agreed, and that evening we weighed, having a wind blowing from the land, which served us till the 27th at noon, when it blew very hard from the S. E., accompanied with rain till the 28th in the evening, when it began to allay; we were favored all the 29th with a westerly wind, and that evening were brought in sight of Cape Blanco. On the 30th, the weather was fair enough; but on the 31st, two hours before daylight, it grew very boisterous, so that we were forced to put in for that cape; we had a thunderbolt fell upon the end of our great sail-yard, which did no more than crack it. Having moderate weather on the first of June, we steered E. S. E., and, next day about noon, had a sight of land; but it was so hazy, that we could not tell where we were; however we steered E. by S. E., to come near. The weather being now somewhat cleared up, we found we were between the Bay of Boca del Toro, and the point called Barica, when we sailed S. and by S. E., to put out to sea, and then bore to the N. E., that we might reach the Isle of St. John de Cueblo.

On the 7th, we put in at the Isle of Montosa, six leagues to southward of that of St. John; we set out three canoes, with which we coasted round about this last, and our ships anchored at another little island, which is half a league to the east. While we were going round St. John's Island, with our canoes, we found nothing there but one of our prisoners, who having made his escape from us when we were there, and, being not able to get to the continent, returned to us. On the 10th, we went back to our ships, and next day took in our store of water and wood, and cleaned our ships. There arose the succeeding night a north wind that tore our cables, and made us think we should be thrown ashore; but, as good luck would have it, it came about, and gave us an opportunity to make ready, and to cast anchor farther from the shore. By the favor of the lightning we discovered our canoes, and found their ropes also broken, and that the waves were throwing them ashore also, unless we had saved them, though we could not hinder one of them from being staved to pieces.

On the 13th, we made ready, and sailed for La Villia, with a W. S. W. wind, made land on the 15th, and knew it to be the cape called Morne a Peurcos; then we bore off to sea with a hard wind till the evening, when the weather grew so very bad, that we did nothing till the 18th, but let our ships drive with a south-west wind, having a terrible rain all the while till noon, when the weather grew better; and, being cleared up, we discerned three rocks, which are called the Three Brothers, standing three leagues to leeward of the Bay of Villia, whither we were going. On the 19th, we saw the Point Mala, which is leeward of that bay. We sailed all night northward, to get to the shore; and next morning at break of day we found ourselves within five or six leagues of it, when we furled all our sails except our sprit-sail. Next evening we went on board our canoes, and put on all night, after we had given our ships orders to lie by and wait for us at the mouth of the bay where we were.

On the 21st in the morning, we discovered the place where we were to go ashore, and cast anchor till night came, as we also took down our masts, for fear they should be discovered from the shore, and then made ourselves ready to land, which we did on the 22d, an hour before day. But experience telling us we had not time enough before us to get to the place before day-light appeared, we put three leagues off where we anchored, having no where in this bay above fifteen fathoms water. That evening we made for the shore again, which we could not recover before midnight, because the currents were against us. After we had got footing, we marched to the number of a hundred and sixty men directly to the town, and took one of two Spaniards, whom we found on the way, who told us that he was sent by the alcaide major to watch on the sea-side, because he had seen a ship and a bark aloof off, which yet they were so little alarmed with, that they had increased their guard with no more than twenty men. We continued our march, and, for all the expedition we were able to use, it was an hour after sun-rising before we could get to the town, where we found no resistance, half of the people being then at mass. Of men and women we took three hundred prisoners, by whom we understood there were three barks in the river, on which the town was situated. We sent presently out a party to take them; but the Spaniards, having lost no time, sunk one of them, hid the sails and rudder of the other two, and cut down their masts by the middle; so that the party, going on further, gave notice to those of us whom we had left to take care of our canoes, which they found at anchor at the river's mouth, that we had taken Villia. We gathered together that day the merchandise which the fleet had left in this town, computed by the Spaniards to be worth a million and a half, and to the value of fifteen thousand pieces of eight in good silver, which was an inconsiderable prize to what we should have found there, if the Spaniards in all these countries, who are always apprehensive of the visits of the freebooters, had not hid their treasures out of our sight, many of whom chose rather to be killed than to discover the places where they had buried them.

On the 24th, we sent a party of fourscore men to conduct a like number of horses laden with bales of goods to the river side, where we knew there were two canoes belonging to the Spaniards, on board of which, after they had put them, they were to bring them to the river's mouth where ours were; but one of our men, sent upon this occasion, was taken by the enemy. The same day we sent a letter to the alcaide major, (as they called him,) in order to know whether he would ransom the town, and buy the effects we had seized. He sent us answer, that all the ransom, that he took upon him to give us, was powder and ball, whereof he had a great deal at our service; that, as to the prisoners we had taken, he committed them to the hands of God; and moreover, that his people were getting together as fast as they could to get the honor to see us. Upon the receiving this answer, which angered all our men, we fired the town, and went our ways to lie in a place where our booty was kept by our fourscore men, which was about a quarter of a league off. We were alarmed several times that night, and on the 25th, put the best and finest effects on board the two Spanish canoes, because we could not carry off all. For our own canoes, as we have said, were at the mouth of the river, on board of which we could have laden the rest; but they durst not come up thither, because of the ambuscades of the Spaniards who had already killed them a man, as they were endeavoring to come up to us, pursuant to the orders we had before left with them. Wherefore, having laden the two Spanish canoes, we put nine men on board them, and the rest guarded them by land, all along the river side, while six hundred Spaniards did the same on the other side, without being discovered by us, because of a great many trees, bushes, and thickets, that grew along the banks thereof. When we had marched on about a league, we came to a place so full of these trees and thickets, that we could not pass it, so that we were obliged to take a turn about, which brought us off from the river side about two hundred paces, which was the occasion, as you will hear, of the loss of all our booty, and the death of some of our men.

As we quitted the place where we lay, we ordered those who had the charge of our canoes to stop in this river, at a place where there were three Spanish barks, to the end we might endeavor to bring them away; but, when they came there, they were suddenly surprised with an ambuscade, of which the Spaniards were never niggard to us, and, as they defended themselves against them, the current of the river drove them beyond the three barks, and consequently far from us; which was exactly what they would have, for, as soon as they saw them in a place where we could not relieve them, they discharged sixty musket-shot at them, with which they killed four, and wounded one. The rest made their escape to the other side of the river, and abandoned their canoes, which a dozen Indians, who swam the river, carried to the Spaniards, who cut off the head of one of our men, who was only wounded, and set it on the top of a pole, that we might see it as we came down the river.

After we had finished the tour we had taken, we drew near the river again; and being to come to the place where the three barks were, and not finding our canoes, we thought they were still behind; but, about an hour after, we saw three of those who had the charge of them coming through the thickets toward us, who gave us a relation of the disaster that befel them, and said, that, as they passed the woods, they found the rudders and sails of those three barks, in two of which we embarked ourselves all together, and sent out constantly fifty men by land before us, to seek out those sails and rudders, giving them a signal, that we would fire off three guns, and that they should answer us with as many, to show where they should find us, to the end they might join us there. But, at the same time that we fired our three pieces, we heard the report of above five hundred, which made us immediately conclude our men were attacked, wherefore we delayed not to go ashore, in order to relieve them; but, by the time we came up, the engagement was over, and, had not the river been between them and us, the matter had not been ended so. We found one of our people in this place, who had escaped out of our vessels, after we had brought away the ship-tackle that were hid in the woods.

After we were embarked, we asked the captain of horse of Villia, that was our prisoner, where it was the Spaniards could lay other ambuscades for us; he answered it might be about the river's mouth, and not only so, but that we should mistrust all those places, which seemed to give them any advantage over us; and then we came to an anchor, because of the coming in of the tide.

On the 26th, we went ashore at a place where they had killed our men the day before; we found the two canoes dashed to pieces, and the bodies of our men whom they had wounded in several places after they were dead. One of them they had thrown into the fire, and put the other's head upon a pole, as we have said already. These objects so enraged our men, that they cut off, at the same time, four of their prisoners' heads, whom they set up also upon poles in the same place. Then we took the bodies of ours to bury them on the sea-side, and, before we got thither, we were forced three times to go ashore to break through the ambuscades laid for us all along the river, at the mouth whereof we found also that we were warned of by the captain of horse aforesaid; but we happily freed ourselves from it, though with the loss of three men, and one wounded. At last we rejoined our canoes, where one of our wounded men died soon after.

The River of Villia is very large, and at low water it breaks at the mouth of it as on a flat shore. About a league to windward, stands a great rock, which night and day, and at all seasons, is covered with a vast number of birds called *fregates*, *maubies*, and great *goziers*, that live altogether by fishing. Great ships cannot enter into this river, they being obliged to anchor within cannon-shot in the sea; but, for barks of about 40 tons, they can go up a league and a half within it. The port, or place of embarking belonging to Villia, is still a league and a half higher, and the town a quarter of a league distant from it; it is very well situated, but its churches are almost fallen to ruin, though they are very rich on the inside. Its streets are very straight, and the private houses pretty well built; on the outside of it are a great many hattoes, accompanied with very fine *savanas*. The town of Nata, which is the nighest, stands seven leagues distant from it.

On the 27th, came a person on board us to redemand our prisoners, with whom we agreed for ten thousand pieces of eight ransom, and threatened to cut off all their heads, if they did not send us the money by the 29th. But, instead of that, he returned to tell us, that the *alcaide major* had seized upon those of their people who were our prisoners, whom we had sent ashore to get wherewithal to ransom their wives; in revenge whereof we presently cut off the heads of two prisoners, and gave them the messenger to carry to the *alcaide*, telling

32 *

him, if he sent us no other answer, we would cut off the heads of the rest, and, after having put the women upon an island, we would go to take himself. The same person in the evening returned to tell us that all the ransoms would come, and that, besides them, they would bestow upon us ten beeves, twenty sheep, and two packs of meal, the least whereof usually weighed a hundred pound, every day as long as we staid.

On the 30th, they brought us back the man whom they had taken, in exchange for the captain of horse that was our prisoner; and, as they show themselves very fond of having French arms, they pretended to have lost them that belonged to our man, for which we made them pay four hundred pieces of eight. They proposed to buy them one of the barks we had taken from them, and agreed with us for six hundred pieces of eight, and one hundred pounds of nails, of which we stood in great need; whereupon we delivered her up, after we had first taken out her tackle and anchors. They also required a passport from us, that we would not retake the bark, in case we met with her out at sea, but only the goods wherewith she should be laden, which we also gave them.

Next day in the evening, they brought us the ten thousand pieces of eight, as had been agreed upon; then we weighed, in order to go anchor at a place that served as a little port to a hatto, where they were to give us a hundred and twenty salted beeves. We departed from thence on the fourth of July, and anchored at the Isle of Iguana, to see and get us some water, not daring to go and get us any on the continent that was guarded with four thousand men: but after we had cruised in some places, and found that the water was brackish, we resolved, rather than we would die for thirst, to make a descent with two hundred men on the *terra firma*, in order to procure us some in spite of the Spaniards, whom we found about a hundred paces from the sea-side lying upon the grass, and, after a short fight, put them to flight, seeing we were a people who would hazard all for a small matter. This being over, we presently filled some casks with water, and reëmbarked again.

On the 7th, we weighed anchor, and sailed for the King's Isles, and on the 9th anchored at *Morne a Puercos*, fourteen leagues to leeward of the Island Iguana, to take in more water, there being nobody there to oppose us: we departed on the 10th with a favorable west wind, and that day one of our wounded men died. On the 13th, we discovered an island called Galera, which is to leeward of all the King's Islands; and on the 14th we began to perceive the currents that reign all the year round between those islands, which made us put farther off to sea. On the 15th we had a north-west wind, a fresh gale which brought us near land, and three days after, which was the 18th, we discovered Cape Pin, and kept all day at the cape, for fear of being discovered by the inhabitants of those many islands that were round about us.

On the 21st, in the evening, we went on board our canoes, and landed at midnight; but, for all the precaution we had taken, we were discovered by the people, that were fishing for oyster pearls, which are to be found in great numbers sticking to the bottom of the rocks that are round about these islands. On the 22d, in the evening, we discovered, from one of these islands where we had made a descent, a ship under sail, to whom we gave chase, and came up with her two hours before daylight, whom, without any more ado, we boarded, and made ourselves masters of her. The men on board told us the inhabitants of Panama did not think we were so near, and that, as we had come from the taking of Villia, they believed we had chose rather to have gone and wintered at St. John's Island, where they thought still we had built a fort, grounding their persuasions upon those shams, I have before observed, we had formerly made, and still did as we found occasion. They told us also that six and thirty English and French were come from Peru in a bark, with an intention to pass by the way of the River Bocha del Chica to the North Sea; but that the Spaniards, having intelligence thereof from the Indians, with whom they had made peace, since they had granted us passage through their country by that same river into the South Sea, went out to meet them in great numbers, had defeated the greatest party, and brought one prisoner to Panama. Moreover, that two English parties consisting of forty men each, having an intention to pass from the North to the South Sea, had been all of them massacred but four, who were still prisoners at Panama; and, lastly, that there was a bark in the River of Bocha del Chica, that tarried for eight hundred pounds in gold, dug up in the neighboring mines, in order to carry it to Panama.

On the same day we returned on board our ships, and found them at anchor by the greatest of the King's Islands, and ordered our carpenters to make a half galley of the bark we had taken on the 26th. We put some questions afresh to the captain of the said bark, who told us they were in daily expectation at Panama of the arrival of two ships laden with meal, which were to carry also the pay of their soldiers from Lima; upon which information we sent out our half galley, which was now finished, to scout without the islands. On the 30th, we departed with our canoes, and went ashore upon one of these islands, where we surprised a person that was come from Panama, whose master was captain of those Greek *periaugues*, whereof we have formerly spoken, who came on purpose thither to be taken, to the end he might endeavor by artificial ways to lead us into a snare, of which I am ready to give an account. This man immediately pretended a great deal of sincerity, in telling us several things, which he knew we were not ignorant of, and some others, which we could not quickly and easily come to know; and among the rest, that there were in the river of Seppa two merchant barks, and a *periaugue* with sixty Indians on board, whom the Spaniards had armed since they made a peace with them; that besides, the governor of Villia had acquainted the president of Panama, that one of our men, whom they had taken, had assured him that thirty more of us, who had not been informed of the peace and good understanding there was between the Indians and the Spaniards, were about to pass from this sea to that of the north, by the same way we all of us had come into the South Sea; and that, upon this information, the president had sent a hundred men into the River of Bocha del Chica, to wait for them. But to compass his design, which was to draw us under the forts of Panama, he told us in the last place, that they had a little frigate which came laden into that port, and a galley that was sent out every evening upon the scout. We resolved to take the advantage of this information, which we took to be candid and real, and not to neglect this opportunity of getting some vessels for ourselves, whereof we stood in great need.

On the 1st of August, we sent our galley for this purpose into the River of Seppa, in order to take one of the barks our captain spoke of, and at the same time we departed also with four canoes to go and seize those ships in the port of Panama; being accompanied by our Greek intelligencer, who intended to be our guide upon this occasion. He brought us two hours before daylight before the town, and as the moon shone very bright, we staid for some cloud to obscure it, to facilitate our approach undiscovered to the ships in the port, whereof we saw one already, which, to our thinking, had her sails loose. And here was the lure and snare to which the captain led us; but by the effect of mere chance, or, rather, our own good fortune, we turned away to a ship which we unexpectedly saw going out of the port, and gave her chase, believing the same to be the galley that usually went out to scout, as we had been told. We took her without a gun-shot, and upon examination of the captain who commanded her, he discovered unto us that the president of Panama had sent us a Greek, who was to suffer himself to be taken by us, and to whom he had promised a very great reward, if he succeeded in the project he had formed of destroying us; that the means that had been agreed upon to effect it, were to bring us under the forts of that town, allured with the hopes of taking those ships there, wherewith he had amused us, and whereof that which seemed to us to have her sails loose was but a sham ship, a pistol-shot from the port, which was built upon firm land, of sorry planks ill set together, in which they had set up masts, and adorned her with some sails: and as this was the most apparent object, and the first that offered itself in sight, it was not to be questioned but that we, who must believe the same to have been on the water, being deceived with the darkness of the night, would not have failed (being so greedy as we were to take her) to row up to her, where our canoes must infallibly run far ashore, and that, in the time that must necessarily have been spent in getting them off, the Spaniards would have leisure to fall upon us, where they did not doubt but so great a number of men as they had in so considerable a town as that was, would quickly overpower and destroy us.

This information, which came so seasonably, that it saved us from the certain danger we were going to throw ourselves into, was not so advantageous to our Greek captain, who being known by the captain of the bark for the same person of whose treachery he had now advertised us, we paid him for his trouble, by sending him to the other world, where he designed to have sent us: after which we went to take the island of Tavoga, which had been reinhabited since we had left the coast of Panama.

From the 2d at night to the third, we left this island, and went to take that of Ottoqua, which is two leagues north and south from it, and which we found peopled again. We made ready on the 4th to go and join our galley, whom we had appointed to rendezvous at the Isle of Sipilla; but we found her, in our passage, with a prize she had taken, being one of the barks that were in the River of Seppa, from whence, in coming out, she had met with an ambuscade that had killed two of her men, and broke the arm of another.

On the 5th, we saw five sail between Tavoga and Panama; we presently bore up to them, and found they were our own ships, that had given chase to a bark come from Nata, laden with provision. The mastor thereof finding he could not defend it, threw himself into the water and swam ashore, after he had made some discharges with his small arms upon them. On the 6th, we went with our prizes to anchor at Tavoga, and from thence wrote to the president of Panama, that if he would not give up the five English and French prisoners he had in that place, we would cut off the heads of fifty Spaniards we had in our hands. But, hearing no news of him, on the 7th we weighed, and sailed for the King's Islands. We anchored on the 9th, to stop the leaks of our ships, and while that was doing, we departed with our galley and four canoes, for the River Boca del Chica, as well to be informed whether it was true that the Indians of Sambe had made peace with the Spaniards, as we had been assured, as to go and burn all that was built of the town called Terrible, upon this fine river, that it might be a defence to a gold mine they had near. We went also to fight the hundred men, which the Greek told us lay in wait for thirty of our freebooters that were to pass into the North Sea.

On the 11th, we arrived at the mouth of the River Boca del Chica: we lay at anchor there till midnight, when we weighed, and, as the sea swelled, we suffered ourselves to be carried up the river at the pleasure of the current. About two in the morning our guide, still believing we were far from the place whither he was conducting us, made us put on apace, which did us great harm, for instead of going to surprise others, we were surprised ourselves; for about a quarter of an hour after, we saw fire, but there was no going back now, for the river made a bow, from whence the rapidness of the tide coming in threw us, in spite of our teeth, upon these fires, which we came quickly to know were kindled by those hundred men we were in quest of, for they presently asked us from whence our canoes were bound, and being answered by our guide, pursuant to our order, from Panama, they asked again who was the commander; and we being long in pitching upon a Spanish name, they gave us a full volley. But two paterero-shot, which we made at them, having forced them to quit their ground, we passed on and anchored out of the reach of their arms, to wait for the ebb of tide, that we might get out again; for, as we could find no place to go ashore above them, for the country was full of marshes, except at the place where they were, we resolved to take them lower down; and so an hour before daylight, we went back before their intrenchment, and after we had put all our men under deck, and fired four paterero-shots, wherewith we saluted them so opportunely, that we wounded them a great many men, and they made no great firing upon us.

On the 12th, we took a small vessel upon this river, wherein were three Indians; then we went ashore, with an intention to attack the Spaniards from behind their intrenchments, which commanded the river only; but they presently sent out their *periaugue* to take ours which made us expeditiously return on board our vessels to defend them, and to alter the manner of our attack, by resolving to go to them before their court of guard, at the foot whereof we went ashore in spite of all the fire they made upon us, which lasted not long; for our paterero and musket-shot killed them a great many men, which made them quickly fly, and leave us their intrenchment, where we found a great many dead and wounded men, and took some prisoners, among whom there was one named Alfier. He was an Indian, who, out of a blind zeal he had for the interests of the Spaniards, took us for them as we were going on board our canoes, and reproached us highly; but we quickly disabused my gentleman, letting the traitor know to whom we had before been so kind in our passage by the same river, that we were become his enemies, since he was become ours, and then put him out of a condition ever to serve the Spaniards or to injure us.

Those whom we took prisoners informed us that we were discovered at the new town La Terrible, and confirmed the account we had before of the massacre of the three parties already mentioned, as well those who would have gone to the South seas, as the other who were minded to return by the way of that river to the north. Within this intrenchment we found a letter written by the president of Panama, to a camp-master, that commanded in the town La Terrible, which was as follows: —

"When the enemy took La Villia, one of their men was taken, who gave us information that thirty men were to set forth by way of the River Boca del Chica, to return to the North Sea, as believing there was still a good understanding between them and the Indians. I have sent you three hundred men to defeat those enemies of God and goodness; be sure to keep upon your guard, be afraid of being surprised, and your men will infallibly be gainers in defeating of them."

Here it may be said, that the prisoners whom we took were highly useful to us, as well by giving us means to subsist in these parts as to deliver us from a great many ambushes and dangers, whereinto, had it not been for them, we must have fallen. Witness this same, where the Spaniards would have spared our thirty men the pains of going to the North Sea. At last, when we had burnt their court of guard, we took their *periaugue*, with some pounds of gold dust we found there, and then went down the river. As for those three Indians whom we took in the boat, we sent them to tell their comrades that we had killed him who was with the Spaniards, but that we had given them quarter, because they were not amongst them; and this we did to endeavor to make them kind to us, and so disunite and separate them from the Spaniards.

Being got down on the 13th, at noon, to the mouth of the river, we met with one of our barks, whom we had ordered to come and attend us thither. Those within her told us, that, while they waited there, two Indian *periaugues* being deceived with the sight of three or four Spanish prisoners, whom they had put upon the deck for that purpose, came of their own accord, and delivered themselves up into their hands, with some pounds of gold they had found there; and that one of those Indians, who bore great sway amongst his own nation, had a commission from the president of Panama to arm several *periaugues*, and to make war upon us. We weighed that evening to go and join our ships that were cruising between Cape Pin and King's Islands, and there we waited for those of the Spaniards, who, we were told, were to come from Lima.

We got on board our ships on the 17th, in the morning, and that evening, in our passage by the King's Islands, anchored to leave our bark there to be careened. Our people, during our absence, had put forty prisoners ashore upon one of those islands, who accidentally happening to meet with some canoes, which the Spaniards had hid thereabouts, they made use of them to get off, and to go to Panama, to inform the governor of the course we were to take, and that the ships we had left there were but weakly manned; which induced the president to send some force to attack them: but God was pleased so to order it, that we were returned with them to the rest of our company.

On the 20th, we made ready to go to cruise about Tavoga, and that evening anchored before the port of Panama, in order to learn some news. We saw two ships in the road, whither the town canoes went and came all along, without intermission; but, not dreaming they armed them against us, we anchored on the 21st, at Tavoga.

On the 21st, by break of day, we descried three sail just upon us, which we could not discover before, because of one of the points of the island, which kept them out of our sight, insomuch that one of our ships, that had not time to weigh anchor, slipped her cable. As soon as they saw us make ready, they gave us some guns, and as they had the weather-gage, they did not spare to make use of the advantage they had over us. We made five tacks to get to windward of them, and they could not hinder us; but they lost the wind for want of resolution, not daring to pass between the Island Tavaguilla and a rock, where there was indeed passage for no more than one ship, but we ventured it, and at last got the weather-gage. We fought them till noon, and knew not on which side the advantage lay ; and, though they plied our decks very close, we still persisted to keep them clear of them, which was the occasion that they lost a grand opportunity of mending their tackling. We threw a great many grenades into their biggest ship, one of which had so good an effect as to set fire to some loose powder they had, which burnt a great many men, and this brought the fight to end sooner than otherwise could have been expected : for we came up at the same time with the said ship now all on fire, and boldly boarded her, where, notwithstanding the vigorous resistance they made from the stern, whither they had all retired, we at last forced them to beg for quarter, and made ourselves masters of the ship. At the same time one of our barks boarded one of theirs, and took it. The third, that was a kind of a galley, who staid to the last, before she began to make her escape, as trusting to her good sailing, seeing herself now pursued by our galley and two periaugues, ran herself ashore, where she presently staved to pieces, and but very few of her crew were saved.

They had in their little frigate fourscore men killed and wounded, out of a hundred and twenty that were on board. As for the bark, there were no more out of seventy, than eighteen unhurt; neither could we see above ten or a dozen in all that swam ashore from the other vessel that was staved. All their officers were either killed or wounded, and among others, the captain, who received five musket-shot. He was the same person that fought so stoutly at Pueblo Nuevo, where he had received five more, and that had also laid an ambuscade for us at La Villia : but this last engagement rid us of him, for he died some time after.

While we were busy in mending the rigging of those ships we had taken, and throwing the dead overboard, we discovered two sail more come from Panama, which bore up towards us, whereupon we interrogated our prisoners, in order to know what they should be. They said they did not question but this was the relief they sent them. At the same time we bethought ourselves of a stratagem, to amuse and make them believe we were taken, which was by putting up Spanish colors in our own ships, and in the prizes, with English and French ones under them. As soon as these two ships approached, they came up to our ship, who received them quite after another manner than they expected. Being thus surprised, they fired upon us with precipitation, and made off towards the little frigate, which they supposed still to be theirs, who calling to them to lie by, and the others not doing it, they threw some grenades into one of their barks, which sent her to the bottom, while one of our periaugues boarded the other, wherein they found four packs of cords, but all of the same length, which they had made ready to tie us up with : but they reckoned their chickens before they were well hatched, and these ropes was the occasion that no quarter was given to those in the bark where they were found. We afterwards read the commission of the captain of the little frigate, which imported he should chase us as far as St. John's Island, and that, when they boarded us, they should spare none they found upon deck, but only our surgeons, whom they were willing to save ; and that troops of horse should march along the shore, to take care that none of us made our escape to land, in any canoe.

On the 23d, as we sailed away to go to anchor at Tavoga, we discovered another sail going back to Panama, whom we chased and took ; she was a shallop, whom the president had sent to fetch off our anchor, which we had not time to haul up the day before, which he came to know by the means of a canoe, who, passing that way, saw the buoy. But, for all the fatigues we had undergone in these adventures, we could not but scoff and laugh at the president, who had sent us ropes to hang his men, and also sent away to take this anchor wherewith to anchor our ship in his port, which he believed his men would bring in. We anchored this evening at Tavoga.

We had but one man killed in all the fight ; but there were twenty of us wounded, among whom was Captain Townsley, who died most of them of their wounds. On the 24th, one of our men died, and the same evening we sent one of our prisoners to the president of Panama to carry him a letter, wherein we required his giving up the five freebooters who were his prisoners, and to send us some medicines for, as we said, the use of his own people, though, in truth, it was for our own ; we also complained heavily of the little quarter they had given to the three parties whereof I have spoken, whom they had inhumanly massacred. He sent to us that night the commander of Seppa, who spoke a little French, with the following letter : —

The President of Panama's Letter.

"Gentlemen : — I wonder that you, who should understand how to make war, should require those men of me that are in our custody. Your rashness hath something contrary in it to the civility wherewith you ought to treat those people that were in your power. If you do not use them well, God will perhaps be on our side on another occasion. And as for the little quarter you complain we have given, you see the contrary by those that have been in our hands for some time past. If you please to put our men you have in your power ashore, we will take care to have them cured of their wounds."

We ordered the said officer to carry him our answer by word of mouth, that, if they would not send us our prisoners, we would send them the heads of all the Spaniards in our possession. On the 25th we weighed anchor, and sailed away for fear they should, for an answer, send a fire-ship, as they had done by the English two years before, and burn us. On the 26th in the morning, we anchored at the Isles of Pericos, that are not above a league distant from Panama. Towards noon we discovered a ship under sail, and sent out our galley to know what she was: it was our own long bark that was come from careening, wherein were sixty men that were not present in the fight. This day two of our wounded men died, though all of them were but slightly wounded, which is no matter of wonder, for all the Spaniards' bullets were poisoned.

On the 27th in the morning, came one to us from the bishop, (who concerned himself much in this business, for he had stirred up the president to fit out ships against us,) who brought us a letter, which in substance was the same that follows:—

The Bishop of Panama's Letter.

"GENTLEMEN:—Though the president of Panama hath written to you very inconsiderately, I earnestly desire you to shed no more of the innocent blood of those that are in your power, all of them having been engaged by constraint to make war against you. The president obeys the king's orders, who forbids him to restore any prisoners of war: I'll do my endeavor to get the men released; take my word, and rest satisfied."

"I am to acquaint you that all the English are Roman Catholics, that there is now a church at Jamaica, and that those four that are with us, having changed their religion, are willing to live amongst us."

This we saw was only a pretence to detain our men, and this sly refusal, together with the trouble we were in, for the loss of those who died continually of their wounds, through the violence of the poison that had got into them, forced us, though with reluctancy, to resolve to send twenty of his people's heads to the president, in a canoe, and ordered him to be told, that, if by the 28th he did not send us all our men, we would send him the heads of all the rest of the prisoners. I confess this was a violent way of proceeding, but we had no other method left us to bring the Spaniards to reason; and we knew them to be a people who, without we had showed this resolution, would despise, and be so much the more bent to ruin us in a short time, by how much the more indifferent we showed ourselves; for they are usually no otherwise courageous, than when they believe their enemies are of a dastardly nature.

On the 28th betimes in the morning, came a person on board, who brought us our five men, whereof four were English, and the other a Frenchman, together with some refreshments for the wounded men, and a letter to this purpose: —

The President of Panama's Letter.

"I send you all the prisoners I had in my power, and, if there had been more, you should have had them delivered; but, as for those that are in your custody, I'll leave that to be managed according to your own honesty and the practice of war."

Hereupon we sent him a dozen of the most wounded amongst their men, and wrote to him the following letter: —

A Letter for the President of Panama.

"Had you used us in this manner when we sent to you for the releasement of our five men whom you sent us, you would have saved the lives of those wretches whose heads we have sent you, and whose death you have been the occasion of. We give you a dozen men by way of exchange, and require twenty thousand pieces of eight for the ransom of those that are still behind. But, in default thereof, we shall put them out of condition to send us poisoned bullets again, which is so manifest a contravention of the laws and maxims of a just war, that if we were minded to punish according to the rigor of those rules prescribed thereby, we should not have given one man of them quarter."

Our five men, whom the Spaniards gave up to us, further confirmed us in the account we had of the massacring of the three fore-mentioned parties in the River of Boca del Chica, whereof they themselves were eye-witnesses. About twelve o'clock of the same day, which was the 28th, we weighed, and anchored again at Tavoga to take in water. And whilst matters were concluded on between the Spaniards and us, in respect to the ransoming of their people, we required they should come to a treaty with us, which they consented to, and sent us daily divers canoes full of merchandise and other refreshments; all which we had dog-cheap of them, except meal, biscuit, meat, and other provisions which they kept back, the reason whereof might be easily guessed at.

On the 29th their messenger returned, who gave us an account that he had been about the city to get the ransom, and that they had not got above six thousand pieces of eight together; but as we were eager to be gone, we told them they must send us ten thousand pieces of eight, or else we would go into the city to fetch them. The effect of this blustering was that, on the 1st of November, came a canoe to tell us that a bark would bring us next day the sum we demanded; and on the 2d, two of our men died.

As we saw nothing coming from Panama, we made ready and entered into the port, and, when we had hung out our main flag, we fired a gun; they answered our signal by putting up a white flag upon one of the bastions of the fort, to give us notice that the money was not yet ready, which made us put out again, and lie all night at the cape before the mouth of the port. Next day came to us a knight of Malta in a bark, wherein he brought us ten thousand pieces of eight, and received the prisoners from us. On the 5th we anchored at Ottoqua, in order to victual our ships; on the 7th, two of our men died.

On the 8th, the Indians who had been our guides in our passage from the North to the South Sea, and who kept close with us ever since, were taken or murdered by the Spaniards upon this Island of Ottoqua, in revenge for the service they had done us. On the 8th in the morning, we put fifty men ashore, to see if they could find the place whereunto the Spaniards had withdrawn themselves, whom we could not find in their habitations, that we might know what they had done with those Indians; but we could find nothing, save their money and baggage, which they had hid in a vault.

The same day, at noon, Captain Townsley died of his wounds. We threw his body into the sea, according to his desire, with such ceremonies as are usual upon these occasions. On the 10th we weighed, and came to an anchor at King's Islands, and, two days after, died one of our wounded men. On the 17th we put out with the little frigate and long bark, to sail to the port of Panama, to see whether they had any ships there that might come to insult us, while our vessels were careening. We had a north-west wind, so that we could not reach the Isles of Pericos before the tenth, when we found ourselves under the forts of that town. We furled our low sails, and, as the Spaniards saw us bring to, they gave us three guns, after they put up the Burgundian colors upon the windward bastion. But when we understood there was no ship in that place whereof we might be afraid, we went out cruising between Tavoga and Sippilla, we being resolved to watch those two ships that were to come from Lima, and in the mean time we sent one of our periaugues to bid our men careen the vessels with all expedition, and that they need fear no danger from Panama. We had very bad weather in this channel; it blew round all the points of the compass with such violent whirlwinds, that the sea grew very boisterous. But, on the 28th, the weather proving more moderate, we discovered a ship sailing all along the coast of the main land, after which we sent two periaugues in chase. She would have entered into the port of Panama, but they firing upon her from the fort, as believing she was one of our ships, she passed by, and our periaugues took her. She came from Nato, and was laden with provisions and sugars, which she was carrying to our enemies, who had the charity to put her back to us.

On the 11th, being not able to see any thing of what we waited for, we sailed for the King's Islands, and, as the moon shone bright, we found the currents very strong there also, which obliged us to anchor in the channel, with all the tides contrary to us, from twenty to forty fathoms of water. We arrived on the 16th, at the island where our ships were careening, and found them already done.

The sea round about these King's Islands, whereof I have spoken so much, is full of a great many very large whales, who are infested by a fish they call espadon, that assaults them continually with a kind of fish-bone, like unto a sabre, fastened to their heads; and this makes those monstrous animals to give such leaps and rebounds, that they raise themselves continually above the water. But to return from a great fish to a small one, I shall say, that, besides pearl oysters, which are to be found in those parts in great numbers; there are also others that are exceeding good, and so large that they are forced to cut them into four parts to eat them, and they are, when roasted, exceeding white.

We departed on the 18th, and sailed for those islands that are in the main, where we came to an anchor on the 19th in the morning, and on the 20th put out with our galley and two periaugues to go to a sugar plantation, which stands two leagues to leeward of Panama, giving orders at the same time to our

ships to come and anchor there three days after us. We possessed ourselves of the said plantation, and seized all the people belonging thereto, who told us there was a courier come from Chiriquita to Panama, who reported he had seen two ships, and as many barks, belonging to the freebooters, anchor at the port of that town, who came for provision there; wherewith we were somewhat surprised, and could hardly believe those freebooters would have left so good a coast as that of Peru was, (whither we knew they were gone,) to come thither, which is much worse; which difference arises from no other than the abundance and quality of the provisions that the former produceth, whereof I shall give you an account hereafter. We were also informed by these prisoners, as it was very true, that a galley, which we knew well enough was in building at Panama, was finished; that she carried fifty-two oars, five pieces of cannon, and forty patereroes; that there were, what with those come from Carthagena and Porto Bello, five hundred men come to go on board her and two periaugues, and that they watched the opportunity of our passing before their port, as we had used to do, to the end they might put out in the night, and surprise us during the absence of our other ships, whom they supposed to be still careening. On the 24th we anchored at Ottoqua, to gather mace and rice that was still standing on the ground; and next day being apprehensive, according to the report of our prisoners, that there might be freebooters at Chiriquita, we sent a bark thither to give them notice, if she found it to be really so, that we would come up to them as soon as we had taken in some provision along the coast. We put nineteen prisoners, on the 29th, ashore, and made ready to depart with an easterly wind. We were got, on the 30th in the morning, over against the Bay of La Villia; we straightened our round top, being afraid to come by it. We embarked in the evening on our canoes, and on the 31st at midnight went ashore. We were quickly discovered by a party that went the rounds, which made us use all the diligence imaginable in order to get into the town, before they had time to make themselves ready. But our guide having led us out of the way, another party making the round passed by, who no sooner saw us, but they made all the haste they could to get away, yet we fired upon them presently, which dismounted three of them, and one we took prisoner, who told us we were still three leagues distant from La Villia, and that we were gone out of our way; that all the people there were at their arms, and that they had had a reënforcement of six hundred men sent them from Panama. Upon this information we stopped short, and were forced to return back again, because we knew very well that we were discovered, and that so we lost all our labor. Before we went on board, we went to eat to an estancia that was half a league off from the seaside, from whence the Spaniards brought us back, by charging our rear from time to time, till that we had rejoined our canoes, whereon when we had reëmbarked, we found ourselves so weary and fatigued, that we deferred till next day to go and join our ship, and this being perceived by the Spaniards, they fired so furiously upon us, that we were constrained to lie at anchor farther from the shore.

On the 2d of November we rejoined our ships that were cruising in that bay. In the evening we anchored between the Island of Iguana and the continent over against some hattoes we saw there, with a design to go and see for some provision; to which end we went ashore on the 3d at noon, where we found the Spaniards got together, with whom we fought for half an hour; they killed us one man, and wounded another. But they could not hinder us to go to the next hatto, where we found no sort of cattle, for the Spaniards had carried away and drove them before them; here we lay this night, but the Spaniards being unwilling to let us have any rest, we were forced at midnight to march out against them, and made them quit the field to us.

On the 4th we returned on board our vessels, having brought only some little refreshments along with us to our wounded men, and that evening sailed away with a west wind, keeping out to sea to the 5th at noon, when we returned to land; at midnight we steered S. S. E., as near the wind as we could till the 6th, that we were brought back to the shore; about the middle of the following night we discovered a vessel under sail, and joined her. It was the bark that we had sent to Chiriquita, who, meeting with very bad weather, was constrained to put back under the Morne or Cape of Puercos. On the 7th, being not able to double the Morne, because of the contrary west winds, we sent our galley to Chiriquita, instead of our bark; we could not double the Morne before the 12th; and we had a blast of wind on the night, that, in itself, was favorable enough for our course, but the currents carried us so to leeward, that we were still on the 13th six leagues to leeward of the Morne. We steered W. N. W., bearing upon the Isle of Tigers, the which stands six leagues north and south from the continent, between the River of St. James and this Morne or Cape of Puercos. On the 14th at night, we were apprehensive, lest we should be driven too near the shore.

On the 16th we arrived at St. John's Island, where we met

with our galley returned from Chiriquita, having found nothing of what she sought for in that place; which still increased the suspicion we had already entertained, that the president of Panama had caused a false report to be spread abroad, that some freebooters had been there, that so he might get us to quit his port, and make way, by our absence, for those ships that were expected from Peru to enter into Panama; and this so much the more heightened our courage, in that we came to understand, one day after another, the cowardice and dastardly nature of this proud nation, who, with her three-decked ships, mounted each of them with eighteen pieces of cannon, and having four hundred men on board, were afraid of pitiful barks who had but four guns and some patereroes in all, with which, however, we waited for them.

On the 18th, we brought our galleys and canoes ashore, in order to clean them: two days after, we departed with an intention to take some prisoners, from whom we might obtain certain intelligence of the truth or falsehood of any freebooters having been at Chiriquita, for they might have been gone before we had sent thither; and upon our departure, we appointed our ships to rendezvous at the Isle of St. Peter, there to tarry till we returned. On the morning of the 24th, we went ashore two leagues to the leeward of the River Pueblo Neuvo, where, after we had travelled till about four in the afternoon, to discover some houses, we saw two horsemen, one of whom we dismounted, but he made his escape, and took the other, of whom we asked where we were; and being informed that there was, about half a league from thence, a borough called St. Lorenzo, we went that way, and arrived there in the twilight. Here we took a great many prisoners, who told us they had heard of no freebooters from the time we had taken Chiriquita, which now fully confirmed us in a belief of the amusement the president of Panama had entertained us with. On the 26th, we returned to the seaside with our prisoners, and discovered our ships that were sailing to the place of rendezvous, to whom we sent a canoe, to give them notice to come and anchor at an island which is over against, and three quarters of a league distant from, the port of St. Lorenzo.

This borough stands a league and a half within land, and is in my opinion no more than a village; it is inhabited partly with Spaniards, and partly with Indians, who, as I have already said, have been reduced by degrees, and submitted themselves to the Spaniards. It is a very open country, and a man is so far from being sure of what place he is in, that he would believe himself to be at Chiriquita when here, so like is the one to the other, as well in respect to the borough and places adjacent, as for the course and disposition of the rivers, wherewith it is watered.

On the 26th, in the evening, we went on board our ships with our prisoners, and agreed with them upon what quantity of provision they were to give us for their ransom: on the 27th we sent the father or curate of the place ashore, to despatch the sending of it. On the 28th, the English, who made part of our fleet, desired us to come together, in order to make a division of the ships and artillery we had taken, as being desirous to be in a ship by themselves; which was presently done. On the 1st of December we sent a canoe to the continent, and the men that were in her told us they had seen a troop of horse, who threatened them at a distance with their cutlasses, which made us at night, to the number of a hundred men, go ashore to see them. On the 2d, we waited for them in their town of St. Lorenzo, but nobody appearing, we burnt it. As soon as the Spaniards saw the fire, the commander of the place came to offer us a sum of money for the ransom of the prisoners, which we refused, because we had much more need of provision. We told them, if they did not send us the same, pursuant to the agreement we had already made with their people, they should have no more to do than to send for their heads away from the island. In the said commander's house we found the following letter, written by the Tenient of Chiriquita, —

A Letter from the Tenient of Chiriquita to the Commander of the Town of St. Lorenzo.

"Sir: — I have sent you, by way of reënforcement, all the men which I could get together. Use your endeavors to take one or other of the enemy, to the end we may know what they design to do, about which our generals are mightily concerned. Order the cattle to be drove away from the seaside, and put them into a place fit to lay an ambuscade, to the end that the enemy, severing from one another, according to their usual manner, in order to kill them, it may be so much the more easy for you to secure some one of them. But if you cannot do that, lay an ambuscade at a place where you think they will put our prisoners ashore, and let them show you those persons whom they have observed to be most respected on shipboard; so that if God gives us the advantage over them, do not you cut them off, but send them to me. Especially interrogate the women, that you may know whether they have met with some weak fellow that hath made any discovery unto them."

This letter made us keep more upon our guard than otherwise we would have done, and we returned on board our ship that evening. On the 3d, we went in a canoe ashore, to see whether they had brought the provision agreed upon for the ransom of their people; but instead of that, we saw them busy in raising an intrenchment near the place where they expected we should make our descent, which gave us to understand they pursued the orders prescribed to them by the aforesaid letter. On the 4th, we put those prisoners ashore upon the island where we had anchored, and left them there, without any further expecting of their ransom, so that we might secure ourselves against that ambuscade whereinto we must have fallen, had we sent them to the same place where we took them.

In the evening we weighed and sailed for the Bay of Boca del Toro, with an easterly breeze that put us forward. On the 5th, we doubled the point of Porica, which is ten leagues to leeward of that bay; at the height whereof, we were becalmed till the 10th; when, towards evening, a small wind blowing from the sea arose, which brought us to the mouth of the bay. But the same was followed by so terrible a tempest, that our ship lay for an hour in such a manner, that she was under water as far as her great scuttle; and what amazed us was, that our ropes, sheets, and clewings were cut so cleverly, as if the same had been done with a hatchet. However, this tearing of our rigging served us in good stead, for had it not been for that, we had quickly gone to be meat for fishes; for our sails, being held by no other than the wind and arms alone, the sail-yards yet stretched themselves out along the masts, and our ship by little and little happily recovered herself. The wind was allayed in the dusk of the evening by a great deal of rain that fell, wherewith we were becalmed; and on the 11th, we had a southerly wind, which brought us to an anchor in the bottom of the bay.

The mouth of this Bay of Boca del Toro is about four or five leagues in extent from one point to another, and eight in depth. If you would enter it with safety, you must keep the whip of your rudder to starboard, because it is dangerous to keep to the east side. Here is good anchorage every where, and also a covert; one may anchor in the bottom of the bay, within pistol-shot of land.

There are four islands contained in it, that stand very near unto the main land to the east and north-east; but it is not safe to lie near them, because of the many rocks that are there. Several fine rivers discharge themselves into it, and lead us up them to divers Indian carbets, who have neither peace, nor are in amity with any people whatsoever, no more than those whom I have mentioned when I spoke of Cape La Vella and Boca del Drago, which yet does not hinder the Spaniards from passing their caravans through the midst of their country, when they come from Costa Rica to Panama: but then they must be very well guarded, and the great road, through which they pass, is not above six leagues from the sea-side.

On the 12th, we went to find out trees fit both to make canoes of for carrying our water, and canoes of war. On the 25th, being Christmas day, after we had, according to custom, said our prayers in the night, one of our quarter-masters, being gone ashore, in order to take care about our eating some victuals, (for our ships being a careening, all our provisions were then put out,) one of our prisoners, who served us as cook, stabbed him with a knife, in six several places; wherewith crying out, he was presently relieved, and the assassin punished with death.

CHAPTER LIV.

The Freebooters' Voyage to the South Seas in 1687.

On the 1st of January, 1687, our canoes being ready, we left this bay and sailed for that of Caldaira, that we might victual there, and make an end of careening our ships. We left them there on the 2d, after we had given orders to those who had the charge of them, to come and join us in the bay, and we embarked two hundred men in our canoes, to cross over to La Cagna, which is a small island very inconvenient to draw near to, and stands about a league north and south from the main land, between Boca del Toro and Caldaira. We were six days in our passage before we could get thither, having only put forward in the night, for fear of being discovered. Being come on the 6th at night into the bay, our guide made us put in under a covert, and told us that, to prevent our being discovered, we should go ashore in that place; which we had no sooner done, but we were conducted into a marish, in the soundest places whereof we sunk in the mud to the very middle, insomuch that five of our men, of whom we could see no more than their heads, did not give us a small trouble to pull them out with cords we made fast to mangles, which are trees of that name growing in this marish. So that, not knowing how we should be able to free ourselves from this wretched place, we lifted up our guide to the top of a tree, to endeavor, by the help of moonlight, to discover how far we might be from sound land. But he, finding himself now at liberty, skipped like a monkey from tree to tree, and railed all the while at us, who could neither see him, nor do any more than threaten him, which I believe he little mattered: We spent the rest of the night in making about a hundred steps in this sweet place, where we exactly went the rounds, and from whence we could not come out till break of day, and not then neither, without being bedaubed all over from top to toe, and having our arms laden with mud. When we were in a condition to reflect a little upon ourselves, and that we saw two hundred men in the same habit, and so curiously equipped, there was not one of us who forgot not his toil, to laugh at the posture he found both himself and the rest in. At length, after having inveighed against our guide who had so cunningly saved himself when he saw us stuck fast in the mire, we went into our canoes again, where we cleaned ourselves as well as we could, as we did also our arms, and, after having left our covert, we met with a very pretty river, whereinto we entered, and went up it about two leagues, where we landed at an intrenchment. There we found the remains of the two ships which the Spanish had burnt, when an English freebooter, whose name was Betsharp, came to careen in this bay, which made us suppose, according to the relation that had been given us concerning it, that it was the embarking place belonging to Nicoya. We followed the road we found there, and marching about two leagues, at the end of them we entered, by the help of the barking of the dogs, into a borough called Sancta Catalina, where we took all the inhabitants prisoners. Now as we were informed by them there, that there was no more than three leagues to Nicoya, we mounted sixty men on horseback, in order to go thither; but we met half way with horsemen, whom we could not reach, and who, returning back with full speed, gave the inhabitants notice of our march towards them, insomuch that, by the time we got thither, they had already hid all their effects, and were expecting our coming upon the place of arms, from whence we drove them, after we had sustained their first discharge, with which they neither killed nor wounded one of our men. While we were gathering what provision we could together, we sent out small parties into the neighboring places, who brought us some money, and, among other things, the governor's plate, and all his movables.

On the 8th we left the town, and went to rejoin our people at Sancta Catalina, where we staid the remainder of that day

At night came two of the enemy's sentinels thither, one of whom we killed; for they, not knowing we were in the town, were come to give the Spaniards notice that they saw three sail of ships enter into the bay, and that they were enemies. But this intelligence came too late. On the 9th we left this place to go and join our canoes again, on which being embarked, we left one of our prisoners ashore to go and raise the ransom of those we carried along with us; and, on the 10th, we got on board our ships that lay at anchor in the bay. We had found among the governor of Nicoya's papers three letters, which are these that follow: —

The Governor or General of the Province of Costa Rica, his Letter to the President of Panama, dated May 2, 1686.

"SIR: — This letter is to let you know of the taking of our dear town of Granada by pirates, on the 10th of the last month. They came ashore at a place where we had no sentinels, we supposing there was no occasion for it, because the sea is so high there; they passed on across a wood like so many wild beasts. We had the good fortune to have notice of it by our fishermen, though we were already upon our guard ever since the news we had concerning them from Lesparso and Nicoya. They lay on the 9th at the fine house of Don Diego Ravalo, knight of St. James; we were very well prepared to receive them, but the way of fighting practised by these men did so much astonish ours, that we could not make that resistance we had promised ourselves we should do. They fell on briskly, singing and dancing, as if they had been going to a feast; at length, after we had been fought bravely by them, they won the place of arms, with the loss of thirty of their men, according to the estimate of Don Antonio de Fortuna, a person of good experience in war, who came to us some months before. We are also of opinion that they have lost their general, for we saw a man, that distinguished himself from the rest by his habit, fall.

After they had staid for the space of four days in our fort, they sent to require us to ransom the town and prisoners they had taken; but, we being not very forward to return an answer to their proposal, they burnt it, and went their ways. Seignior Don John de Castilla, serjeant-major, went out to observe them with his men; but not knowing they took away our artillery, he attacked these enemies of God and goodness about a mile from the town; but they, being resolved to make their way through, or to die upon the spot, slew so great a number of his men, that the rest fled, and left their commander alone.

We have taken one of their men, who told us they came to our province upon no other design than to know the strength of it, though it is not to be doubted, if they had found our vessels at anchor, but they would have made use of them to pass by the way of our lake to the North Sea, and have abandoned their comrades, who looked after their ships, and their way would have been infallibly by Carthage. Monsieur, the governor, takes his measures thereupon, and continues to fortify his entrenchment. I shall give you a more ample account of this business by the first caravan."

The President of Panama's Letter to the Governor of Costa Rica.

"SIR: — This is to give you notice of the advices I have received from Carthagena, by the way of Puerto Bello. The king of France, supposing he had received some affront from our nation, sent eighty sail of all sorts before Calix, to demand contribution; and, seeing there was so vast an inequality of force upon this occasion, we agreed to give him half a million to withdraw his ships, and return to their ports.

"You know that my lord bishop, on the 22d of August, forced me to send out three ships to fight the pirates, that still continued before our port and took all the barks and canoes that were coming on. Our ships surprised them at break of day, which made one of the pirates slip his cable; and this was done, not for to fly away, but through the skill of the commander. I saw the fight from my ramparts, the honor whereof I thought infallibly to have appertained unto us. Having seen them draw near the shore, I sent a shallop to bring away the anchor of that vessel that had slipped her cable, in order to fasten her in our port. As soon as ever I saw them ungrappled, I despatched away two long barks or galleys, to go and learn the news, and to bring those of the enemy that survived before me, though my orders were, that no quarter should be given to any that were found upon deck, to the end we might rid the world of these enemies of God and his saints, who profane his churches, and destroy his servants. In the evening they sent one of our men to require me to give up five men of theirs, that I had prisoners in my town, and, as my prince forbade me to do so, I refused it; but these new Turks sent me twenty heads, and I bethought myself, that, for the preventing of the slaughter of so many Christians, I ought to send them their men, with ten thousand pieces of eight, for the ransom of ninety of our people, that were almost all wounded, which they sent us out of three hundred and thirty they had taken with them. Thus you see how God is pleased to afflict us on all sides — let us take all for the sake of his sufferings for us."

The Tenient of Sansonat's Letter to the President of Panama.

"Captain Francis Grognier is separated from his fleet at Realeguo, and gone ashore with a hundred and fifty men upon the Isles of Napalla. We took three of their men, who told us, that those of them, that were gone up towards Panama, had a design to return to the North Sea. The peace we have made with the Indians will do us more hurt than good : we were concerned, at least, to observe their motion, and stop up that passage. Those people, seeing no place whereunto to retire, became as so many enraged dogs. We had no need of that, for wherever these irreligious wretches set their feet on land, they always win the victory. If you please, let them have free passage, that we may be at rest. They came ten or a dozen times ashore, without knowing what they wanted. Send us a man who understands the way of sea fighting, for I am of opinion they will never be able to get off from these islands, and so it will be convenient to go and take them there."

On the 12th, as we saw no ransom come, we set out to go ourselves to Nicoya, to fetch it, where we arrived next day ; we sent out several parties also in search of some victuals, which the people had hid, and sent one to treat with them about the ransoming of their town. The tenient told us the governor was gone for relief to Costa Rica, and that he had no orders to pay any ransom, further than what had been agreed on for the prisoners, which was all ready, and that he would not have us be impatient, if we received not the same as soon as we desired it, because they having no canoes, whereby to send the money to us by sea, which might have been done in half a day's time, (the passage was so short that way,) had been obliged to have it carried on mules' backs by land, which was four days' journey. When we had received this answer, we sent again to tell him that our intention was to have been gone next day, but that however, seeing he waited in expectation of succors, we would wait also ; but at length, growing impatient that things were so long retarded, we went our ways on the 17th.

Two days after, being the 19th, they came to the sea-side,

over against the place where our vessels lay at anchor, and brought us the ransom they had promised for the prisoners, whom we sent ashore at the same time. We gave them a letter, which we wrote to the governor, wherein we sent him word, if he would let us know when his reënforcement came, we should not fail to attend him ; and that in the mean time, if he did not send us so many horse-load of biscuit and mace, as we required of him for the ransom of the town, he might assure himself we should go and burn it.

On the 20th, we weighed anchor, and went to one of the islands in this bay to careen our vessels. On the 22d, we went off in our canoes, leaving no more men with our ships than were necessary to careen them, and sought out some hattoes, where we might get necessary subsistence, to the end we might lay by, and keep in store those provisions we had got together on board, and whereof we should have occasion in the execution of an enterprise we had formed upon the town of Queaquilla. On the 22d, at night, we went ashore at Caldaira, where we were discovered by the sentinels, who, as they made their escapes, set fire unto the savannas, in order to stop our passage ; however, this did not hinder us to reach the little town of Lesparso, which had been almost entirely abandoned since the time of our being there before.

On the 23d, we had the curiosity, or rather humor, to pursue the first road that offered itself to our view at our departure ; and after we had marched about a league on, we discovered about two hundred horse upon our flank, and in our rear. A Spaniard, who was advanced before the rest, made a thousand mouths at us, and reviled us as much, which gave us an occasion to hide five of our men that were behind the rest, in the grass, that was exceeding high upon both sides of the way, and leave our main body to march on ; so that when our Spaniard, who still followed our people, went to pass forwards, he was quickly dismounted, and we made him make a grimace in good earnest. We questioned him according to our usual ceremony, that is to say, by putting him on the rack, about the place where we were. He told us we were on the highway of Carthage, and that all places were quite forsaken from thence to this town, which was no less than twenty-seven leagues, out of an apprehension his country had, lest we should go and force them to grant us passage to the North Sea, as their chief officers had caused it to be reported among them. He also gave us information, that they had four hundred men making their rounds, whereof the two hundred we saw were of that number, being detached to observe the time of our landing, that so they might retire to a strong entrenchment they had six leagues on this side the town, for to beat us back, in case we made that way. Being thus pre-admonished, we thought it not convenient to go any further, our design being no other than to know the country, and to get us some victuals; so we returned to Lesparso, and on the 24th, rejoined our canoes.

On the 26th, we went ashore under the guidance of our new prisoner, who brought us to a sugar plantation, where we divided into two companies to go to two hattoes, and took all the people we could meet with there, who informed us, that several other hattoes and sugar plantations in the neighborhood had all together sent out two hundred armed men, who were gone in the evening to beat back the crew of three of the enemy's canoes, that had landed at Colebra, where they had killed and wounded divers Spaniards. We presently imagined it must have been Captain Grognier, that was come up that coast, and therein we were not mistaken; we immediately returned back to the sea-side, to go with our canoes to meet him, and in our way heard the noise of several cannon-shot and small arms, towards the place where we had left our ship careening, which made us double our pace, and reëmbark in our canoes.

As soon as we were got on board our ships, we found Captain Grognier, with three canoes there, who with his crew, had been conducted to the said place by one of our canoes, whom they had fortunately met in crossing this bay; and the firing we had heard, was made by the one and the other, for joy of their meeting together.

Grognier told us, that he came up this coast with an intention to find out an uninhabited place, to the end he might land without opposition, and to fetch a compass across the country, to get to the North Sea. We laid the danger whereunto he must necessarily expose so small a number of men before him, (they being no more than sixty in all,) that if he were resolved to undertake so dangerous an enterprise, it were better he would stay with us until we found a favorable opportunity to repass together to that sea, as being better able conjointly to surmount those difficulties which we might be exposed to thereby. Being overcome with our reasons, he staid with us; and after we had given him an account of the adventures we had had since our separation from him, he also, in his turn, entertained us with a recital of his, and told us, he had made several descents in the Bay of Napalla, with various success, and that among other things, in one of those descents, the Spaniards had taken three of his men, who had been exchanged some time after for other prisoners; but that the Spaniards had so far corrupted those three men with the fine promises they made them, while they were in their custody, that upon their return, they insinuated into their comrades, in order to betray them, a design of going to a very considerable gold mine, which was fourteen leagues off from the sea-side, and as many from Tinsigal, and that being prepossessed of making their fortunes there, they had left the island where they were, to the number of a hundred and twelve men, and went ashore upon the continent, with an intention to go to that mine, under the guidance of the prisoners, who knew the way, and towards which they journeyed only in the night time, for fear of being discovered; that those three men who had been exchanged, and sold their friends to the Spaniards, pretended they were weary, and had occasion to rest, that so they might not go with the rest; that for all this, they departed two hours after, bringing to the Spaniards, who waited in a convenient place for them, all the prisoners that were ashore in the said bay, and, after some time, carried off the arms and ammunition of all the rest of our company that staid behind upon the island, who had no mistrust of them, whereof they laded a canoe; but that the treachery, in the mean time, had not had all the projected effect, and that he and his men got to the mine without opposition, because the Spaniards, who had made all things ready for massacring of them, when going ashore, got thither later than they should have done, and that through the fault of our renegadoes, who had too much precipitated the departure of their comrades, whom they thus saved by pressing them on to their ruin. That they had got no great purchase at the mines, because there had been orders given before for saving their treasure; though, after all, it was not above an hour's space that they had got away four hundred and fifty pounds of gold, that was already prepared. That yet they found some pounds still left, and took some prisoners, who were surprised by them, as not expecting their company so soon, and that they also did believe they had been defeated by the way, as the design had been formed against them.

That when they had staid two days at this mine, and being intent upon returning with his men to the sea-side, he met with a body of Spaniards on the way, waiting his coming, and making a mean, as if they would, now upon his return, make amends for the fault they had committed, in not preventing his descent. Their commander sent a trumpet to Captain Grognier, to know if he were minded to fight; who being answered that he desired nothing more, the Spaniards sent a second time to tell him, that, if he would give up his prisoners, they would grant him free passage; but he boldly answered, that, if they desired to have them, they must come and fetch them by the help of their arms; and, as for the passage, he would open his way through in spite of them. That, having made themselves ready, the Spaniards had not the courage to stay for them, contenting themselves only with firing a few muskets at a distance, and so fairly took to their heels, while he pursued his march towards his canoes, which had, as good luck would have it, been left in a place where the renegadoes could not show them to the enemy.

He told us moreover, that, some time after his return from that mine, they had been at Pueblo Viego, by the way of a river that runs not above four leagues, and discharges herself into the Bay of Napalla; that they had surprised the town, and that, after having rested there for some days, as they were coming back to rejoin their canoes, they had met with an ambuscade, laid for them under the covert of an entrenchment, guarded by six hundred men out of the garrison of Realeguo, which began to be inhabited again, with whom they had fought a long time. But, finding the Spaniards stood to it more tightly than ordinary, they threw themselves into their entrenchment, where, killing all about them that made any resistance, they wrought a great slaughter amongst them; that one part of them continued prisoners, while the other fled without any more ado, and forsook their entrenchments as well as the three colors that they had set up there. That the freebooters had lost no more than three men, but that the Spaniards in the heat of the action killed several prisoners of the one and the other sex, which the other had brought away from the town, who after this went on board their vessels. That some months after, not concurring with a design which fourscore and five of his men had taken, of going down towards the Isles of California, he had resolved with the sixty that remained with him to go up towards Panama, where happening, as I have told you, to meet us, we gave both him and his men room in our ships, where we learned this whole relation from them.

On the 30th we quitted our ships, and went in our canoes into several rivers which discharge themselves into this Bay of Caldaira; and, amongst the rest, into a very fine one, whereon we went up ten leagues, in all which space we always found her of the same depth and breadth. Several Spaniards told us, that, a matter of forty or fifty leagues higher, there was a mountain, from whence arises the spring of this river; and, on the other side of the same mountain, arises also a spring, from which runs the River St. John, that discharges itself into the North Sea at the White Point.

We took a large canoe, laden with tallow, in this river, which some time after was of great use to us, by way of food, as we went to Queaquilla. We also found some hattoes on this river's side, where we refreshed ourselves till the 6th of February, when we returned on board our ships. On the 12th we departed, in order to go the third time and visit Nicoya; we arrived there next day in the evening, and presently detached several parties to get us intelligence concerning the Spaniards, who never appeared since they had threatened us with their succors, instead of the ransom we required of them for saving their town, which they still refusing to satisfy us for, we burnt it this third time, and, on the 17th, went our ways.

But though we were forced to chastise the Spaniards in this manner, we showed ourselves very exact in the preservation of the churches, into which we carried the pictures and images of the saints which we found in particular houses, that they might not be exposed to the rage and burning of the English, who were not much pleased with these sorts of precautions; they being men who took more satisfaction and pleasure to see one church burnt, than all the houses of America put together. But, as it was our turn now to be the stronger party, they durst do nothing that derogated from that respect we bore to all those things.

Nicoya was a small town, pleasant enough taken altogether; its churches are very fine, and the houses as ill built; they have a pretty river there, that runs about one half of the town round; but, when one is within, you cannot know which way it is you have entered, nor how to go out, because of the height of the mountains wherewith it is surrounded every way.

We were no sooner gone from this town, but the Spaniards sent to set fire to the roads through which we were to pass, which yet we happily escaped, because they had but just begun to do it. We took one of their men who was hemmed in between us and the fire, and who conducted us to several estancias, from which we did not return before the 20th. And, on the 22d, we put forty prisoners ashore, who were too chargeable to be kept on board with us.

Some men, perhaps, may be amazed at what I have said concerning the burning of the roads, but they would be much more so, had they seen it as we have done. There were two sorts of places where this burning was wont to be practised, to wit, in the savannas and woods; when the former were set on fire, whose grass was almost as high as our heads, and also as dry, in a manner, as powder, we found ourselves so besieged on the right and left side of the road with the flame, that it made us feel it to some purpose, though the same were of no long duration. But when these roads lead through covert and woody countries, as in the present occasion whereof I am speaking, and that once fire be set thereunto, one may see, according to the course of the wind, the country for several leagues burnt in a little time, to which the dryness of things doth very much contribute, the sun being exceeding hot at that season.

On the 23d we sent our quarter-master on board the English, to make an agreement with them. We proposed to go in conjunction with them to take Queaquilla, (where the Spaniards drove a great trade by sea,) upon condition that, if we took two ships, we should cast lots who should choose, and that, in case there were but one taken, that then we would put fifty men of each nation on board her, till such time as we could take another, which they would not agree to, as inflicting upon the first choice. So that, seeing we could not bring them to comply, we parted as well from them as from Captain Grognier, and fifty of our men who staid on board him; so that they had a hundred and forty-two men in their ship, and we a hundred and sixty-two in our frigate and long bark.

On the 24th we weighed, and set sail for Queaquilla, which is the first maritime town on the south coast, as you go thither from Panama; we made all the sail we could to get thither before the English, who had formed the same design as we had done. We lay by till the 25th, to get out of the bay, and, in passing from the White Cape, we steered S. S. W., S. and by S. W., and directly south to the 28th in the evening, that we had on our starboard side a W. N. W. wind, bearing us to the south, which lasted till the 29th, when we were becalmed in the night. On the 1st of March towards noon, arose a pretty fresh gale from the north, which made us bear S. S. W. and S. S. E., till the 4th in the morning, when an easterly breeze took us, and made us bear south; on the 5th arose a north-west wind; and on the 8th at noon we passed the equinoctial line, leaving the Isles of Galapa, which are below to the west, a dozen leagues to leeward.

These are eight islands that stand north and south of the White Cape, and east and west from Queaquilla; they are full of sea tortoises, that land there every hour of the day, and you cannot find a place to tread on or walk along in the woods, for the great number of land tortoises, lizards, and agoutils, that retire thither. The sea thereabouts is also so fruitful in the production of fish, that they come to the very sands to die there; but these advantages, on the other hand, are encountered with the want of water, whereof these islands are entirely destitute.

The wind, towards evening, came to N. N. E., and made us bear E. and by S. E., to keep to the continent; the weather, on the 10th in the morning, grew very dark, and, we having a southerly blast, bore E. and E. by S. E., till the 11th, when we were becalmed. On the 13th arose an east wind, and we bore to the S. S. E., upon a tack, and N. N. E., and then lay by for some time, because we did not know the currents. On the 14th, having a north-east wind, we bore E. S. E., and accordingly, as it blew fresh, we steered E. and by S. E., and E. On the 15th, two hours before day-light, we had a storm, and then a south wind; we steered east all that day, but we had such bad weather the following night, that we could not carry our sails; next day about noon the weather grew better, and an easterly breeze presented; we lay by till the 18th at noon, when we discovered a ship to the windward of us, to whom we gave chase till the evening; she proved to be the English ship that had parted from us when we came out of the Bay of Caldaira, who, knowing who we were, put into the cape. We came to leeward of her, but she spread out her sails, and got to leeward of us. After we had given one another this salutation, we put out for two hours to see which sailed best; but knowing at last they were the better sailers, and fearing they might reach Queaquilla before us, we desired them to join with us in our design, to which when they agreed, we set sail together. We found ourselves much perplexed to know what latitude we might be in, since we had not seen the sun for ten days together. But it happily fell out, that it appeared on the 19th; our pilots computed we might be about twenty-five leagues to windward of Queaquilla, and sixty leagues from land; but the winds varied to that degree, that we could make no way, and many times went contrary.

On the 20th we had a west wind, and steered E. and by S. E. till the 21st, when we were becalmed. On the 24th arose a south wind, and on the 26th an easterly breeze; at last, the wind persisting to be contrary, we were reduced to great want of victuals, for we had already been upon our passage longer than our provision would allow us; to which we may add, that fish had, till now, been so scarce, and hard to catch, that we had but little support from them. So that, having on the 28th taken an account of the remainder of our victualling, we were forced to retrench ourselves so far, as to eat but once in forty-eight hours. We also wanted water, and, had it not been for the help of rain, we had certainly died of thirst; but what made us amends for one part of our wants was, that we found ourselves, all of a sudden, in a kingdom of large fishes, such as emperors, tunnies, germons, galdenies, negroes, bonitoes, and several others, to whom we gave no quarter, no more than to the sea-wolves, who, for all their ill smell, could not escape us. During that time we bore to the north-east, the wind not allowing us to keep on our designed course, that, if the worst came to the worst, we might, by this course, reach the Isle of St. John, pursuant to the design we had formed, upon meeting with this contrary wind, of putting in there, in case the same continued all the way. On the 29th, after we had taken the latitude, our pilots computed us to be opposite to the Isle of Platta, thirty leagues to leeward of Queaquilla. On the 30th, being Easter day, we were but one degree north latitude; in the twilight the wind began to blow fresh, and bore us E. N. E. Next day the wind came S. S. W., we steering E., E. and by S. E., and E. S. E. On the 3d of April we were becalmed; and, as we had for the space of two days, by the computation of our pilots, sailed towards land, they were of opinion that the currents deceived them, of which we made ourselves satisfied by the following manner: On the 4th, the weather being very calm, we furled our sails, and put out one of our periaugues, about whose forecastle we spun sixty fathoms of our smallest rope, made fast unto a grappling iron, and, from that coast she made from, the tide ran along her side with as much swiftness as the current of a river, and bore to the north-east. On the 5th we caulked our ships; towards midnight a south-west wind presented itself, and we bore south-east.

On the 6th in the morning, we discovered land both to windward and leeward of us; we veered to, lest we should be brought too near, and steered south. On the 8th, we were about four or five leagues off, and our coasting pilots knew the place to be Cape Pastao, which is under the line, thirty leagues to leeward of the Isle of Platta; we had all hands aloft, and steered south. On the 9th, we bore to the S. S. E. till the evening, and to the S. W. till ten at night, when we steered to the S. S. E.; and, on the 11th, we were got to the height of the Isle of Platta, eighteen leagues out at sea.

On the 12th at noon, we saw the point of Sancta Helena, which is fifteen leagues to leeward of Queaquilla, and forms the beginning of the bay that bears the name of that town. On the 12th at night, we saw fire to windward of us; we lay by till break of day, when we discovered a ship three leagues to windward of us, and, as we were becalmed, we sent three periaugues to know what she was; they found her to be a prize, laden with wine and corn, which Captain David had taken as she came out of Nasca, and which was separated from him; he had put eight Englishmen on board to conduct her, who were to have their rendezvous, in case of separation, at the Isle of Platta. These men told us, that, after they had left St. John's Island, they made several descents, and in several parts of that country, among others, at Sagua, Arica, and Pisca; that, in the last of these places, a relation of the viceroy of Lima came at the head of eight hundred men, to attack them with sword in hand, but that they were vigorously repulsed; that they had also taken a great many ships, which, when they had pillaged, they let go again; so that, finding they had got to the value of five thousand pieces of eight a man, they had resolved to return to the North Sea, and that, as they sailed away for the Straits of Magellan, they fell to gaming, whereat many lost all they had got; that they had anchored in the road that leads to the Isles of Don Fernandez, that stand upon the brink of the strait, to which place came Captain Willnet, an Englishman, who had left them long before, and was come thither upon the same design with themselves, of repassing into the North Seas by the same straits; but that Captain David had altered his resolution, for that those of his crew who had lost their money, were not willing to leave those seas, nor the ship, till they had taken another. That, as for those who had won, they went on board Captain Willnet, out of which ship went also, at the same time, such of his crew as were without money, in order to go and get some with Captain David, and that so they were come back into the South Sea, to the number of sixty English and twenty French, as Willnet was gone through the strait for the North Sea; that Captain Peter Henry was gone for the East Indies, presently after Captain Suams; and lastly, they told us (though we had been informed thereof before) that the Spanish fleet was a careening at Puerto Callao, which, as I have already said, is the place of embarking that belongs to Lima.

As these eight Englishmen did not think that Captain David's frigate would rejoin them so quickly at the place of rendezvous, they proposed going with us to Queaquilla; which we so much the more willingly agreed to, in that they gave us a share of their victuals and drink, and a little revived amongst us that usual merriment, that had now for some time been exiled from us, by the abstinences we were forced to undergo, wherewith we were extremely weakened; then we sailed all night in their company, steering S. E. and by E.

On the 14th, we furled all our sails for fear of being discovered from land, near unto which we were. About two, arose a fog, by favor whereof we made use of our main sail of all, as well to come ready rigged into the bay, which is thirty leagues in length, as to get to windward of the River Queaquilla, and to spare ourselves also the labor of rowing so much, for, being so extraordinarily weak, we had not strength to do it.

We steered all night S. E., and, on the 15th, discovered the White Cape, which is the windward cape of this bay; about ten in the morning, we embarked to the number of two hundred and sixty men on board our canoes, after having given our ships orders to lay by in the bay, till they heard news from us. We steered all day long for the Island of Sancta Clara, with which we came up at sunsetting. This little island is in reality nothing else but a rock, standing east and west, six leagues distant from the continent; we were obliged to cast anchor with all the tides contrary to us, it being impossible to put into this bay against the currents, where we found six fathoms of water; and, on the 16th, we found ourselves between Sancta Clara and La Puna, about five leagues from the shore.

La Puna is a very pretty island, and may be discovered at a great distance at sea, because of the form of it, resembling a cardinal's cap; it is twenty leagues in circumference, and stands east and west, two leagues from the continent, and over against the mouth of the River Queaquilla. There is a large borough built upon it, where, in former times, were kept the king of Spain's magazines. Great ships, that is, such as are two or three decked ones, that cannot come into the river, anchor between it and the island. We hid ourselves in this island all day, and that with the good luck of not being discovered by the sentinels, who were there to the number of forty of them, though we knew nothing of it; we departed in the evening, and got more southerly, that we might not be discovered from the continent.

On the 17th, we hid ourselves again in a covert place upon the same island; where, after we had got an exact account from our prisoners of the state, situation, and disposition of the town of Queaquilla, which we were about to go and take, we disposed of our forces in the following order: There were fifty men making the forlorn hope, led by Captain Picard, who commanded our frigate, to attack the great fort; fourscore grenadiers, commanded by the captain of our bark, were to be in the nature of reserves, and to serve any where, as there should be occasion for them; Captain Grognier with the main body was to make himself master of the town and port; and Captain George Hewit, who was commander of the English ship, with fifty of his men, was to attack the little fort, and a thousand pieces of eight was promised to any one of the ensigns, whereof

I was one, that should pitch the first colors upon the great fort Things being thus regulated, we left our covert in the evening, believing we might be able to enter into the River of Queaquilla that night, before day-light appeared; but, for all that, all we could do was to gain one of the points of the island, which is over against the river, for we could have the advantage of the tide's coming in but for three hours; which was the reason that on the 18th, as we put off again, that we might the more readily get under the covert of the island, day overtook us, and so discovered us to a sentinel, who set a cottage on fire as a signal to the other sentinels, that were posted at convenient distances on both sides of the river, that he saw us, that so these same might advertise the town of it. As soon as we got ashore, we marched across a wood to get to the said fire, where we found some of those that had kindled it; whereof two were killed, as they fled to save themselves, and a third was taken, but we could get no intelligence from him, for he was but a little boy.

This day we discovered a ship entering into the river; we let her pass, being unwilling to come out from under our covert to fall upon her, for fear of being discovered by those on the main land, who, we supposed, knew nothing of us, because the inhabitants of Queaquilla had not answered the fire signal which the sentinel of La Puna had given them. Upon the approach of night, we made ready, and entered into the River of Queaquilla by one of the two mouths we found there, and by which goes in and out with the tide so rapid a current, that it is enough to carry a canoe two leagues in an hour, so that we made four in the space of two hours.

There are two very fine islands in the two largest parts of this river, (which may be about a half a league over,) under the covert whereof we hid ourselves on the 19th, all day long. We made ready in the evening, and had the pleasure to be carried up by the current, without the use of our oars, for fear lest the sentinels, who are always placed on this river's sides, should hear the noise of our rowing. The design of our guide was to pass by and land beyond the town, because he knew it was weaker, and worse guarded on that side than on the other; but his project failed him, for the tide, now going out, was as injurious to us, as it before had been favorable, and forced us to go ashore, two hours before day, within cannon-shot on this side of the town, from whence we discovered a great many lights, which they usually keep in their houses all night long.

This place, where we landed, is a country full of water and shrubs, across which we were forced to cut our way with our sabres; but we did not know we were unhappily landed over against a sentinel, nor that, half an hour after that, one of our men, who was left behind to look after our canoes, struck fire to light his pipe with, which he rashly did, contrary to the express prohibition we had given him; which being perceived by that sentinel, he made no doubt but there must be enemies near, because the Spaniards, upon pain of death, forbid their people to strike fire in the night; insomuch that he presently discharged a small paterero, to give the fort notice of it, who readily answered the same with a whole discharge of their cannon. Being overtaken at that instant of time with a storm of rain, we were obliged to put in for shelter into a great house we found before us, to light the grenadiers' matches, and wait till day appeared; during which space the enemy fired continually from the town, to frighten and let us understand they were ready to receive us.

On the 20th at break of day, we marched out in order towards the town, with our drums beating and colors flying; and upon our approach, found ourselves stopped by seven hundred men, who attacked us from under the covert of a wall four feet and a half high, and of a ditch, wherewith the same was encompassed towards the river's side, which made us presently suppose it to be their fort, having had no good intelligence of the situation of the place. They did all they could to repulse us, and presently killed some of our men. Being encouraged with this little advantage, they had the boldness to sally out upon us with sword in hand; but, seeing we gave them a most vigorous reception, they fled without any more ado, and contented themselves with breaking down the bridges, to hinder us from advancing; but this could not prevent our crossing the ditch, and getting to the foot of the wall, whereof we rendered ourselves masters, in spite of all the resistance made by them, who were not proof against our grenadoes, that drove them into the very houses, which are all of them built on purpose for places of defence, in case they be attacked, and from whence in a short time we also drove them. They fled to the place of arms, and entrenched themselves in a strong caze, which we call a redoubt, and which, when they had defended for an hour's time, they were all forced to abandon, insomuch that we pursued them from fort to fort, till we came to a third, which is the greatest and most considerable of them all. Here they defended themselves a long time; for they fired continually upon us, by favor of the smoke of their cannon, which hindered us from seeing them. When we were got to the foot of the palisadoes, they sallied out again with sword in hand, and, having wounded some of our men, they took one of them prisoner; but we quickly made them leave him, and to run back into their fort, after they had lost a great many men. At last, being weary with about eleven hours' fight, and our powder being now almost spent, we redoubled our efforts in such a manner, that we broke in upon them, and made ourselves masters of this last fort, but not without loss on our side, since we had nine men killed, and a dozen wounded. We sent out several parties at the same time to pursue those that fled, who were still in sight of us, while the other Roman Catholics went to sing *Te Deum* in the great church, after we had first put a garrison into the fort.

The town of Queaquilla is almost built round about a little mountain, whereon stand those three forts, two whereof are commanded by the third, which is the largest, and all of them command the town. The greatest, which is that against which we had most to do, is nowhere strong, but to the river-ward, and the two lesser ones are upon the descent of a hill, which also looks towards the river, and are each of them surrounded with a thin but very high wall on the outside; we found none but patereroes to defend it. There is a communication between these last two, and the other by a covert-way, on each side whereof are two rows of palisadoes filled with earth, and defended also with patereroes. In the great fort, which is also beset with palisadoes, we found seven pieces of cannon, carrying from twelve to eighteen pound ball; but they could not, because of the elevation of the place, bring their guns to bear low enough to incommode those that were in the town, unless, by thundering against the houses, they should be buried in the ruins of them. The magazines of powder stand in the middle of the fort, and are slightly enough built. The town, as I have observed, is to the river-ward, encompassed with a wall, four feet and a half high, and three feet thick. The streets are very straight. The parish churches, as well as the convents, are very curiously built; the houses are almost all built with boards, and founded upon piles, for that in the rainy time of the year, which continues from the beginning of January to the end of April, they are so incommoded, as to be forced to make bridges, and raise banks of earth in all the streets, to keep off the water and mud. Their chief commodity is cocoa, of which they make chocolate. We took seven hundred prisoners of both sexes in this place, and among the rest was the governor and his family. He was wounded, as were several officers and men of quality, who fought more bravely than five thousand other men that defended the place.

We found in the place several sorts of merchandise, a great many pearls and precious stones, a prodigious quantity of silver plate, and seventy thousand pieces of eight at least; though there were three millions among them when we came thither. But, as we were all wholly taken up to make ourselves masters of the forts, they laid hold of that opportunity to make their escape along the river, with the greatest part of their most valuable movables. When our canoes were come to anchor under the town, we were not backward to send four of them away, in pursuit of the shallops that carried the said riches of the town away; but then it was too late. They only took twenty-two thousand pieces of eight, and a vermilion eagle gilt, that had served for a tabernacle to some church, weighing sixty-eight pounds, and was exceeding rare, as well for the workmanship as two great rocks of emeralds, wherewith the eyes of it were made. There were fourteen barks in the port, with the galleys against whom we fought at Pueblo Nuevo, and two of the king of Spain's ships upon the stocks, almost finished. We agreed with the governor in the evening about the price of the ransom of his family, the town, fort, cannon, and the ships, they being to give us a million of pieces of eight in gold, and four hundred sacks of corn; and, in order to forward the payment of the said ransom, which was to be brought from the town of Quito, eighty leagues off, he desired us to release their vicar general, who was a man of great authority and credit amongst them.

We found this governor's house so richly furnished and filled with such precious movables, that nothing in Europe could be more magnificent. The women of this town are very pretty; but most of the fathers or monks live here at great ease, and in such familiarity with the fair sex, that is far from being a good pattern and example unto others. The fathers hated us to that degree, that they persuaded the women, who had never seen any freebooters, we were altogether unlike them, that we were not even of human form, and that we would both eat them and their children; which made them conceive so much horror and aversion for us, that they could not be dispossessed thereof, till they came to know us better. But then, I can boldly say, they entertained quite different sentiments of our persons, and have given us frequent instances of so violent a passion as proceeded sometimes even to a degree of folly.

It is not from a chance story that I came to know the impressions wrought in these women, that we were men that would eat them; for, the next day after the taking of the town, a young gentlewoman that waited upon the governess of the place, happening to fall into my hands, as I was carrying her away to the place where the rest of the prisoners were kept, and to that end made her walk before me, she turned back, and with tears in her eyes, told me, in her own language, *Senior pur l'Amor de Dios no mi como;* that is, Pray, sir, for the love of God, do not eat me. Whereupon I asked who had told her that we were wont to eat people; she answered, the fathers, who had also assured them, that we had not human shape, but that we resembled monkeys.

On the 21st, some of our men, who had made a fire in the day-time, in one of the houses of the town, came to the court of guard in the evening, without extinguishing of it, so that at night it set the town on fire; but the fear we were in, lest the same should reach our court of guard, wherein was lodged all the powder in the place, and part of the merchandise and riches of the town, we were obliged to get all carried on board the barks that were in the port, and to bring all our prisoners into the fort; and, when that was done, we endeavored to put a stop to the fire, which yet burnt down one third of the town, notwithstanding all the pains we took to put it out.

We returned on the 22d in the morning to our court of guard, and fearing lest the Spaniards might refuse to pay the ransom agreed on for the town, because of this accident, we having promised by our treaty with them not to burn it, we took upon us to believe they were the cause of it, and sent them a letter, wherein we gave them to understand we were much surprised at their manner of procedure; that they should, after our agreement with them, come with a mischievous intention to burn the merchandise and corn that were of so much use to us, and that we repented we had not left all the town to be burnt; that, if they did not pay us what we had suffered by the fire, we should send them fifty of the prisoners' heads. They thereupon excused the matter to us, saying they must be some rascally spiteful people that had done this, and they would take care to satisfy us.

On the 23d, the governor furnished us with a coasting pilot, whom we sent in one of our canoes to see for our ships, (to whom we had given orders they should lie by in the bay,) to bring them to anchor at the Isle of Puna, whither we were to go at our departure from Queaquilla, to wait for the promised ransoms. On the 24th, finding one of our men was sick with the stench which the dead carcasses, to the number of above nine hundred, lying up and down the town, occasioned, we went our ways, after we had first dismounted and nailed up the cannon in the fort, and carried five hundred prisoners, being the best of the inhabitants, along with us, into our barks; wherein we arrived with them on the 25th at Puna, where we found our ships ready to cast anchor.

On the 2d of May, Captain Grognier died of the wound he had received that day we took the town, when the seven hundred Spaniards opposed our entering the fort, and the same day died four of our men also. On the 4th we sent our galley to the Isle of Platta, to see if Captain David's frigate was come to rendezvous there.

The time allowed for the payment of the ransom of Queaquilla being expired on the 9th, we granted them four days longer; but then we began to be weary of this delay, when a Spanish bark, that was wont to carry us provision, brought an officer in her, who desired us not to be impatient, for the ransom would be quickly paid. Now this dilatoriness made us begin to suspect very much that there was some treachery in the case, and that they entertained us with hopes for no other end than to amuse us, till such time as the enemy were reënforced. And our guess was right enough, as will appear hereafter, insomuch that we were constrained to use such severity towards our prisoners, as we knew would strike a terror into our enemies. We made them throw dice for their lives, and, the lot falling upon the heads of four, we cut them off presently, and sent them to Queaquilla in the same vessel that had brought the said officer unto us, by whom we let the tenient understand that, if the ransom did not come within four days, we would send them the heads of all the rest of the people that were in our power.

Our galley on the 14th returned from the Isle of Platta, and related that she had been chased about the Point of Sancta Helena by two ships, but she could not discover what they were; and this made us that evening send out one of our canoes that sailed well, to see what those ships might be. On the 16th, she found they came to join us, they being Captain David's frigate and a prize he had taken after the other had been separated from them, which we met before we went to Queaquilla: they came with full resolution to make a descent at Paita, in order to get some refreshments for their men, who had been wounded in a fight they had had with a Spanish ship called Catalina, which they met fifty leagues to leeward of Lima, and was one of those that we had for so long a time waited for before that town.

This ship Catalina was separated from two more with whom she was returning to the port of Callao, when, unfortunately for her, she met with Captain David's frigate, that sailed much better than she, and could have taken her, without making, as he did, two days' fight of it, had it not been that the greatest part of his crew, being continually drunk, failed twenty times to come up close to board her, and suffered themselves to fall to leeward, because of their ill rigging, as often as they found themselves to windward of her; which being observed by the Spaniards, they thought, by putting up a bloody flag, they would be quickly brought to strike; but therein they were mistaken, and the quite contrary fell out. For David's people growing sober on the third day, and putting their tackle and rigging into better order than before, the Spaniards were so terrified thereat, that they ran ashore, where their ship did not keep whole two hours. David's men, in a canoe, went to save two Spaniards, who were about swimming to land, and now, having escaped the danger of drowning, told them that their captain, having had his thigh shot off with a cannon-ball, had desired his lieutenant, before his death, to lose no time, but to go without tarrying, to acquaint the viceroy of Lima of the dangerous estate the frigate was reduced to, that he might send without delay to her assistance.

Our canoe, which on the 22d came to rejoin us, and gave the aforesaid information, brought also along with her Captain David's prize, which he had sent to desire us to get a mainmast to be brought him from Queaquilla, as somewhat of our ransom, his having been very much damnified in the last engagement; and that, till it came, he would cruise without the bay to prevent our being surprised by the Spaniards.

I forgot to take notice that this ship's crew had, at Paita, surprised a courier that was going from Queaquilla to Lima the third time, to carry the following letter unto the viceroy; which clearly made out unto us the suspicions we had entertained before, that the Spaniards deferred to pay us the promised ransom, that they might have time to prepare themselves to come and pay us in a sort of coin we had no occasion for, and which we did not require at their hands.

A Letter of the Tenient of Queaquilla to the Viceroy of Lima.

"SIR: — I am to inform your excellency, the second time, that the English and French are still at Puna; it is several days since the term they had allowed us for the redemption of our prisoners is expired; I have done it on purpose that your excellency might gain time. They have sent me four of our people's heads. I will amuse them with some thousands of pieces of eight from time to time, (though they have no reason to be weary,) while your excellency may please to come; and, though they should yet send me fifty heads more, I shall esteem that loss to be much less prejudicial to us, than to suffer such evil-disposed people to live. Now, sir, we have a brave opportunity to get rid of them, provided your excellency lose no time to do it."

We could not have received a more certain testimony of the thoughts and designs of our enemies than those discovered by this letter unto us; so we took our measures accordingly.

CHAPTER LV.

The remaining Actions of the Freebooters in the South Sea, during 1687.

THE best winter quarters which we had met with in these seas, and that of longest duration, was that of the time of our sojourning upon this Island of La Puna, where, for the space of thirty odd days that we staid here, we lived mighty well; for, besides the victuals which the Spaniards brought us daily from Queaquilla, we had brought thither ourselves a great many refreshments. Neither did we want charms for our ears in this place, for we had all the music of the town among our prisoners, which consisted of lutes, theorvoes, harps, guitars, and other instruments, I never saw any where else, wherewith they made a very fine concert.

Some of our men grew very familiar with our women prisoners, who, without offering them any violence, were not sparing of their favors, and made appear, as I have already remarked, that, after they came once to know us, they did not retain all the aversion for us that had been inculcated into them, when we were strangers unto them. All our people were so charmed with this way of living, that they forgot their past miseries, and thought of no more danger from the Spaniards than if they had been in the middle of Paris.

Amongst the rest, myself had one pretty adventure. Among the other prisoners we had a young gentlewoman lately become a widow of the treasurer of the town, who was slain when it was taken. Now this woman appeared so far comforted for her loss, out of a hard-heartedness they have in this country one for another, that she proposed to hide me and herself in some corner of the island till our people were gone, and then she would bring me to Queaquilla to marry her; that she would procure me her

husband's office, and vest me in his estate, which was very great. When I had returned her thanks for such obliging offers, I gave her to understand that I was afraid her interest had not the mastery over the Spaniards' resentments; and that the wounds they had received from us were yet too fresh and green for them easily to forget them. She went about to cure me of my suspicion, by procuring secretly from the governor and chief officers under their hands, how kindly I should be used by them. I confess I was not a little perplexed herewith; and such pressing testimonies of good will and friendship towards me, brought me, after a little consultation with myself, into such a quandary, that I did not know which side to close with; nay, I found myself at length much inclined to close with the offers made me. And I had two powerful reasons to induce me thereunto, one of which was the miserable and languishing life we led in those places, where we were in perpetual hazard to lose it, which I should be freed from by an advantageous offer of a pretty woman and a considerable settlement; the other proceeded from the despair I was in of ever being able to return into my own country, for want of ships fit for that purpose. But when I began to reflect upon these things with a little more leisure and consideration, and that I revolved with myself, how little trust was to be given to the promises and faith of so perfidious as well as vindictive a nation as the Spaniards, and more especially towards men in our circumstances, by whom they had been so ill used; this second reflection carried it against the first, and even all the advantages offered me by this lady. But, however the matter was, I was resolved, in spite of the grief and tears of this pretty woman, to prefer the continuance of my troubles (with a ray of hope I had of seeing France again) before the perpetual suspicion I should have had of some treachery designed against me. Thus I rejected her proposals; but so, as to assure her I should retain, even as long as I lived, a lively resentment of her affections and good inclinations towards me.

On the 23d, we sent one of our canoes to Queaquilla, to carry one of the fathers thither, they being a people as much obeyed and respected by that nation, as the viceroys themselves. The governor gave this man a full power to act as he pleased, even in opposition to the obstructions which the tenient made against the payment of the ransom afore-mentioned. After his departure came a bark which brought us four and twenty sacks of meal, and to the value of twenty thousand pieces of eight in gold. They desired us, moreover, to grant them three days time for the payment of the rest; which we allowed them, but withal threatened, upon their failure therein, we should seize upon their fort and burn their town and ships.

Our canoe returned on the 25th, who gave us an account they would pay no more than two and twenty thousand pieces of eight for the rest of the ransom, and that the tenient would pursue his prince's orders, who forbade the payment of any; that he had five thousand men at hand, with which he waited to see if we would put our threats in execution. Upon this fierce and bold answer, we had a consultation together whether we should cut off the heads of all the prisoners. The plurality of voices, together with mine, was, that it were better we should go and look after the two and twenty thousand pieces of eight, than shed any more blood; seeing also, that, our design being to leave these seas, we had no further occasion for these executions to make us be feared; and that, after all, we were but too well assured, by the tenient's letter, that the Spaniards were setting all things in order, to come and act their utmost efforts against us, which, perhaps, would administer matter of repentance unto us, if we still persisted in our resolution.' That therefore we ought to accept the offer, and to give up unto them no other than the meanest of the prisoners, without divesting ourselves of those of quality, who would be a security unto us for the rest. That, while we waited for them, it was our best way to take them along with us, and put off from the shore, steering towards the point of St. Helena, where we should be out of danger of the surprises of our enemies, whose motions we could every way discover at a distance. Things being thus concluded on, we sent our canoe to Queaquilla, who returned again on the 25th, and told us, that next day the Spaniards would, without fail, bring us the two and twenty thousand pieces of eight to the Isle of Puna, where we then were.

We put, the same day, fifty of our best prisoners on board our ships; and, at the same time, weighed anchor, and quitted our good winter quarters, where we left the rest of our prisoners, with two canoes to guard them, and to wait for the money promised us; giving our men orders to tell those who brought it, that they should send us the remainder of what was agreed on, to the point of St. Helena; and, upon default thereof, that they should see the people no more. Our canoes, on the 26th in the evening, came to join us, as we lay by to get out of this bay, and brought us the two and twenty thousand pieces of eight.

Next night the English frigate's prize, who thought we still lay at anchor at La Puna (from whence she met us about eight leagues) came to give us notice, that two Spanish armadillas waited our coming out of the bay, and that David's frigate lay by, as they did, to stay for us. On the 27th by break of day, we discovered them between the Isle of St. Clara and the point of St. Helena, to the windward of us. Captain David's frigate, upon sight of us, made up presently to us, and, having got all together, we consulted what we were best to do. We put fourscore of our men on board of him, because he had not number enough of his own to manage his guns; and, as we had not men enough to manage our prizes, we reserved only but two ships and a long bark, and sent the rest with our periaugues upon the flats, where the Spanish ships could not come, as drawing more water than they did. We lay by till noon, to get the weather-gage, which yet we could not do, because at this time of the year the winds blow from the sea, and are very fixed, and that besides, as we came out of the bottom of the bay, we could not well hope to gain it, the Spaniards being at the mouth thereof.

About noon our enemies came upon us, and so we fought till the evening with our cannon, which the Spaniards call gallant fighting, without much hurting of one another. We cast anchor upon the approach of night, as they did also about a league to the windward of us. We fired a gun for our prizes to come up, which they did, and cast anchor near us, for their greater security.

We sent them back about an hour before day-light to their former station, and, as soon as ever light appeared, we made ready, and the Spaniards did the same; but no sooner were we got under sail, but we were becalmed. Unhappily it fell out that we were without our periaugues to row us to the windward, because we had sent them back with our prizes, to avoid the trouble they might have caused us, and therefore all we could do, now, was to make use of our little canoes, which we had still with us; the Spaniards also rowed to the windward to dispute the matter with us; however, with much ado, we got a cannon-shot to the windward of them; but, as they knew better how to bear close up to the wind in these seas than we, in half an hour's time they recovered the weather-gage of us. We lay by till two in the afternoon, and seeing we could do no good with them, we put in to the cape, to wait for two of our ships that were behind. In the mean time these armadillas bore up to us, and, when they had got within a good cannon-shot, we fought till it was dark night; they very much shattered us, yet wounded but one man; we anchored in the evening, as we had done the day before, and they did the same also to the windward of us.

We remained at anchor on the 29th, as well as they, till three in the afternoon, when they weighed to go and attack the biggest of our prizes, because she had anchored only on the side of the shallows, and we made ready to defend her. We came to such a close fight with them, that all our small arms, as well as great guns, came into play on both sides; yet we lost not one man, though they on their side had a great many killed, which we knew by the blood that ran out of their scupper-holes; and at our parting they cried, "*A la manana la partida*," that is, To-morrow to it again.

On the 30th, both they and we prepared to put out of the bay, and the Spaniards, who were still to windward, did all they could to hinder us to get the weather-gage. We came to an anchor towards noon, to disarm one of our prizes that sailed very badly, and to fit up another in the room of her, which Captain David gave us, as well as the twenty Frenchmen that made part of his crew, and were minded to leave him. We wrought all night to unrig her, and when we had so done, we sent her into the bottom. We put ourselves under sail on the 31st, and about two in the afternoon came to an anchor, because of the tide's being against us. Presently after, the two armadillas came up with us, which made us weigh, and then to put in to the cape, to wait for one of our prizes that was far from us, which not being able to join us as soon as the enemy, her crew left her, and went into her periaugue, wherein they came to throw themselves on board one of our men-of-war. They had left four Spaniards in that same prize, who, by the favor of a good wind, put back into the River of Queaquilla, where they made their escape, and what was worst of all, took along with them almost all our provisions that were in her.

When we were got within half cannon-shot of our enemies' ships, we fired upon one another, and that without intermission, till an hour within night. We received several cannon-shot in our sides, during this engagement, had almost all our tackle spoiled, and our sails sifted, because the Spaniards did all that ever they could to bring our masts by the board; and indeed, the foremast of the frigate received five cannon-shot, and the mainmast three; but they came only slanting, and as good luck would have it, we had not one man killed nor wounded.

We saw the enemy on the 1st of June, by break of day, a league's distance from us; we were not slow to do all we could to put out. About ten they lengthened their boltspring sails, and returned upon us; but as we saw them bear up towards our frigate, we thought they intended to board her, and this made us presently put into her the crew of our long bark, by way of reënforcement. As soon as ever the Spaniards were come up, they put out their Burgundian colors, having till then put out none. When we were come pretty near, they gave us a volley of musket-shot, together with a discharge of their cannon, laden with cartouches; but we got clear of them, so that they could not come to grapple with us.

After we had left them to make all the fire they could, we gave them a discharge of all our cannon, and a full volley with our small arms in our turn, and then we were ready to board them; but they, finding themselves much damaged, very readily got aloof to hinder us.

They took up an hour's time to refit, then bore up to us again, renewing the fight, which lasted till night; but they had been so well banged, that they had no mind to feel us this time so near; and that day we had three men wounded.

On the 2d, by break of day, they were still to the windward of us, at about two leagues distance, and bore up to us; we having a fresh gale, put into the cape, and when they were come within a good cannon-shot of us, they plied us very tightly with their great guns, and then approached within a musket-shot of us, as believing we were now out of condition to make any long resistance: but as we had a better advantage of using our fusils, we made so great a fire upon them, that they were forced to close up their port-holes, and bear up to the wind. We received sixty cannon-shot this day in our sides, whereof two thirds were between wind and water; besides which, all our rigging was torn, and we had two men wounded, whereof myself was one.

About two hours within night, they made a show of coming to board us, but, finding we were as well prepared to receive them by night as by day, they bore upon the wind. We spent some part of this night at anchor, to stop up our cannons' mouths, which otherwise might have sent us into the deep.

We were astonished next morning at break of day, that we could not set sight on the two armadillas, with whom we had made ourselves ready to renew the fight; and in all appearance, they grew weary of it before us, though they had so great an advantage as that of the wind, which yet, as we heard since, could not secure them from losing a great many men, and having their ships at least as much shattered as ours. So that supposing well with ourselves, that they had steered their course to Port Callao, we steered ours for the Isle of Platta, where we anchored in the evening, and continued there two days to caulk our ships.

36 *

We had, during these several engagements, brought up upon our decks the governor of Queaquilla, and the other chief officers that were our prisoners, that they might be witnesses of the vigor with which our men fought, and the cowardice of their own people, who durst not enter our ships, though they came board and board with us twice.

We weighed on the 6th, and sailed along the coast, that we might find a convenient place to take in water. This coast is very level, safe, and very good to land upon, which is the reason that the same is throughout, as far as Barbacoa, inhabited by the Spaniards. We anchored between Cape Pastoa and that of St. Francisco. On the 10th, we put our prisoners ashore, and gave them their liberty, being not able to go to the point of St. Helena, to see whether their ransom was come, which I suppose would have been to little purpose, for those two armadillas had been sent to pay us with cannon-ball.

On the 11th, we went about dividing the gold, precious stones and pearls we had found in Queaquilla ; but as these things could not be divided, nor easily valued, the gold not being coined, and the stones of different value, we put up all by way of auction, that those who had silver might bid for them, and so every man have his part according as he bade ; and as there were several among us who, having got considerable sums of money at play, were sure, and if it pleased God, they should once get safe out of these seas, their way must be no other than over land, where the weight of their silver must hinder or retard their going ; they bid for those jewels that kept but little room, and weighed not much, so excessive a price, that the gold alone that was coined was worth eighty and a hundred pieces of eight an ounce, and each pistole fifteen of the said pieces. But though these things were sold so dear, we made no more a division of the booty of that town than what came to four hundred pieces of eight a man ; the whole might amount to about five hundred thousand pieces of eight, or fifteen hundred thousand livres ; which money, as we were out of hopes to carry along with us, served us to play for on board our ships for our diversion : so that in the descents we made, we sought now for nothing but gold and precious stones, which we did not find so plentifully as silver ; of which, I must be plain, we made so little account, that we thought it not worth our while to take along with us a great quantity of plate, and other things, whereof the town of Queaquilla was full. We also neglected to send a canoe after the hundred caons of coined silver, each consisting of eleven thousand pieces of eight, which the Spaniards had sent away to the other side of the river, when we were engaged with them, and which were yet in sight of us when the fight was over. There is such a vast quantity of that rich metal in this country, that most of those things we make in France out of steel, copper and iron, are made by them in silver. This indifference in us gave some of their people many times occasion to intermix with us, to pillage from their own fellow-citizens what we neglected, and of which they were not so squeamish as we, or rather so put to it for the carriage of them, they being in their own country, and we far from ours.

On the 12th, Captain David's frigate left us, he designing to go and careen at the Isles of Galapas, and then to sail away for the Strait of Magellan, in order to return to the North Sea; but as for us, our vessels were so small, and withal so bad, that it was impossible we should get up higher than the coast of Peru; neither could they also contain such a quantity of water as we had occasion for, which is very hard to come by on that coast, where you must go two or three leagues up the country before you can meet with any. These difficulties made us resolve to return to the western coast, that so we might endeavor to find out a way also to return to the North Sea, but that must be other than over land.

Before I leave this coast, I cannot but take notice that Peru is one of the richest countries in the world, not only in respect to the great quantity of gold and silver which the Spaniards dig out of the mines they possess there, but also upon account of the great fertility of the earth, that produceth to the tillers of it three crops every year, as well of corn as wine; and that besides those fruits that are peculiar to all America, you have also many of those here which grow in France, insomuch that this great diversity of species is the occasion that you have continual supplies of fresh fruits in all the seasons of the year.

The inhabitants of this country reckon but two seasons, which divide the whole year into a summer of nine months, and a winter of three; during which it freezes oftentimes very hard on the mountains, though the same is hardly discernible in the plains. Amongst their other cattle, they breed sheep, that weigh two hundred and fifty, or three hundred pounds weight. These animals are of great use to them, having the very same instinct as camels. They make them carry jars of water, oil, or wine, which are a sort of earthen ware made like sugar-pans, two of which hold about five and thirty quarts, and when empty, weigh as much as the liquor that fills them. When they are minded to fill them, these sheep will kneel down, and as soon as they are full, get up very gently; when they are come to the place whither they are to carry them, they lay them down in the same manner, and continue till they are discharged of their burden.

We weighed on the 13th, and on the 15th anchored twenty leagues to the windward of Point Mangla; we put ashore in a canoe, where we surprised a watch of fifteen Spanish soldiers, who were set upon the side of a curious river. The entertainment we gave them forced them to own unto us, that they were to guard the river, which they called Emeralda, because of the many rocks, or great pieces of emeralds, which their countrymen take up there; and that we might, in the space of eight hours, go very easily from the mouth of it in our canoes, to surprise the town of Quito, but not so by land, because then we must fetch a compass of fourscore leagues, through a country full of inhabitants, who would not fail to oppose us; and for these reasons it was, that they endeavored all they could to keep from strangers the knowledge of these advantages. This town of Quito is well peopled, and was formerly the capital of the kingdom that bears its name, but now it depends upon the government of the viceroy of Lima.

On the 17th, we got ready and sailed away for the Isle del Gallo, which stands at the mouth of the little Bay of Barbacoa, a hundred leagues to the leeward of Queaquilla. On the 19th, we discovered, by break of day, a ship whom we chased, and towards ten in the forenoon, took her: she was a bark come from Panama to go and buy negroes, which the English in Jamaica send them by the way of Puerto Bello, and which they were going to trade with at Paitas; they get very considerable by these blacks, for the English sell them to the Spaniards for four and five hundred pieces of eight a man, and are worth three and four hundred with them. We anchored on the 20th at the Isle of Gallapo, where we examined the prisoners we had taken in the said bark, who told us, that the galley of Panama was gone into the Bay of Mapalla, in quest of the Frenchmen that were gone ashore upon those islands, which, I have already said, are there; and that, in her return, she was to carry the president of Guatemala and his wife to Panama.

On the 25th, we weighed and sailed for the Isle Cocas, which stands north and south of Realeguo, a hundred leagues distance. We had a S. W. wind, and sailed W. N. W. On the 30th we discovered land; we pinched upon the wind, that we might know what place it was: we found towards evening, it was the Isle of Mapalla, that stands forty leagues southwards of that of St. John's, and from thence we sailed to the Bay of Mapalla, instead of going to the Isle of Cocas, from whence the wind blew, and consequently was contrary to us.

From this day forward to the 11th of July, we had the same south-west wind, which allayed not, but when it blew from the east and south. On the 13th we took our latitude, and found we were thirty leagues out at sea from Realeguo, and steered north to get to land. On the 16th, at noon, we discovered the mountains, and put into the cape for fear of being discovered. On the 17th, we sent two of our canoes to endeavor to take some one prisoner, that so we might know how things were before we brought our ships into the bay.

In the evening our canoes having discovered what coast it was, returned, and told it was St. Michael's Bay, whither the currents had driven us in making the cape, and which we took for that of Mapalla, whither we would have gone, and which stands fourteen leagues to windward of the former, which might the more easily have been mistaken from the sea, in that the mountains of these two bays are very like one another. We lay by to windward of it in the night; and on the 18th, put out our canoes, and continuing at the cape till the 20th, we made use of them to go and join our friends at one of the islands. As we entered in on the 23d, we were taken with a breeze of wind that separated us from one another; and of five sail, whereof our fleet consisted, we had no more than two of the least and weakest of our ships left together: but we did not lose sight of the other three, though they were got very far to leeward, and overtaken with a calm. In the mean time, we anchored at the Isle of Tigers, which is the nearest to the mouth of it.

On the 24th, about eight in the morning, we discovered three sail of ships, that doubled the point of Harina, which is to the windward of that bay, and ten leagues to the leeward of Realeguo; we presently fired a paterero, to call in our canoes, who were ashore to take in water. As soon as they were come on board, we made ready and bore up to those ships with a full wind, though we had then but very little of it.

Those three vessels, which were a galley and two periaugues, bore also towards us, though they saw us not; but, as soon as we were got out and discovered by them, they doubled the cape upon us with their sails and oars, and the two periaugues, that sailed better than the galley, got behind us, and fired fifteen cannon-shot upon us; but as our arms could reach them, these periaugues were forced to fall astern, and to wait for their galley. When she had joined them, they held a council, and then put out to attack us; our ships not being able to give us any relief, put to the cape to wait for us. We fought them all along till we had rejoined our vessels, which we did about two in the afternoon, when the Spaniards left us to go bury their dead upon the island where we had been to take in water, when we first discovered them. They did us some damage in our mainmast and rigging, and wounded few of our men. Towards evening a wind arose from the sea, and we sailed in quest of them, but they kept to the shore.

On the 25th, we passed round the island in search for our canoes, which the enemy's galley sought for also, rightly imagining they were ashore, as not having seen them with us during the action. About two in the afternoon, they discovered us, and coming out from under their covert, gave us the signal, which we on our part answered : they had hid themselves there for four hours, expecting our coming, and had a full sight of the engagement, but could not possibly, any more than the rest of our ships, come in to our assistance. The Spaniards, who saw us take them with us, durst not hinder it, though they were at anchor very near them ; then we attempted with one of our ships to board the enemy's galley, but she saved herself upon the flats, where our ships could not come near her. On the 26th, we anchored at an island in the bay, where we put two of our vessels to careen, while the other three guarded them. On the 28th, we saw a canoe under white colors, crossing from the main land to the islands, where one of ours met and took her. It was a Spanish captain, who believing us to be his own people, came to congratulate the commander upon the victory, which he, from the shore, thought they had got over us. We put him upon the rack, to know whether he came not by some wile or other to draw us into a snare laid for us by the galley, as the Greek captain had formerly done ; but he solemnly protested it was not so, and informed us, that there was a periaugue with thirty men, in the same bay where we were, who were gone ashore sometime since, and had fought in the race of savannas against six hundred Spaniards, whose captain, called Don Albarado, who was accounted the bravest and most valiant man in the province, they had killed ; and that, when we had met with their galley and two periaugues, there had eight hundred armed men come, not with a design to look after us, but to fight those thirty Frenchmen, who could not be conquered by his six hundred countrymen ; an admirable instance of the valor of the Spaniards in those parts !

The Bay of Mapalla is a very curious place, and full of divers great islands, not inferior in beauty to those of Panama. They were formerly inhabited, and there are still three boroughs there which the people have forsaken, by reason of the descents of the freebooters. As for anchorage, it is very good here, but no good shelter to be found in this place from any corner of the wind, great blasts whereof come over those great mountains that are at the bottom of it, so that there are very few cables that are proof against them.

On the 6th of August, one of our men, who was hunting upon the island where we were careening, found two men who had been there for the space of eight days to observe our motions, and who, taking us to be Spaniards, durst not come near us. They were two Frenchmen belonging to the periaugue, of which the fore-mentioned officer spoke to us, and who had defended themselves so valiantly against the six hundred Spaniards; we found them to be of the number of fourscore and five, who had separated themselves under Captain Grognier, to go to California; they presently gave notice to the other eight and twenty, who came and joined us, and of whom we learned that they had saved themselves upon this island, after they had been chased a whole night by the Spanish galley, that did not sail so well as their periaugue. They told us also, that they had gone down a matter of forty leagues to the windward of Acapulco, without being able any more than once to go ashore; and that then they ran a great risk, so boisterous is the sea in those parts, wherewith they were so discouraged, that they had forsaken fifty-five of their companions, in order to come and find us out, and left them to continue their course to California. Having made an end of our careening on the 10th, we made every thing ready for our departure, after we had given those thirty men room in our ships. We sailed from the coast of Acapulco, with a design to find out the other fifty-five men spoken of, who were to make a descent there, and to rid them from a miserable state, whereunto, in all appearance, they had gone to plunge themselves, without any hopes of retrieve; being too small a company to find out provisions (whereof they stood in great need,) in the best peopled country upon the continent, where also it could not be believed they could arrive, having but a little sorry bark under them, that could not carry them far without splitting in two.

We had, at our departure, an easterly breeze, wherewith we were favored till we came to the height of Sansonat; from the 15th to the 21st, we were becalmed all along in the day-time, and the winds were so high in the nights, that we could not carry our sails; on the 22d we had a pretty good gale from the south-east; and, on the 27th, we drew near land, to know where we were. We found ourselves to the windward of the Bay of Tecoantepequa, and put out our canoes to go in thither, while, at the same time, we appointed our ships to rendezvous in the port of Vatulco, which is twenty leagues to the leeward. We came very near land in the evening, but the sea runs so high along that coast, that it was impossible to go ashore.

On the 29th we found an embarking place, where there was a very strong entrenchment, guarded by a considerable number of Spaniards, and, supposing it would cost us dear to go ashore in that place, we sailed two leagues to the leeward, where the sea was somewhat more pacific, but found here also about three hundred men upon an eminence waiting for us. We detached fifty of ours to go and meet them; but the Spaniards, after having made a foolish discharge, fled. However, we took two of their number, and asked them whither that way led, upon which we were; they told us it would bring us to the town of Tecoantepequa, according to whose name that bay was called, and that we had but four leagues to it. We lay next night upon the road, under the canopy of heaven, according to our usual custom; next day, which was the 30th, we resolved to go to the said town, and directed our course that way, in such a manner, that, about two in the afternoon, we had a sight of the place from an ascent, which was about half a league off.

As it is encompassed and beset every way with eight suburbs, it seemed to be so large, that we were a long time deliberating with ourselves whether so small a number as we were ought to go thither, as being no more than a hundred and fourscore men, whereas there were three thousand of the enemy in the place. In the mean time the extreme necessity we were reduced to, for want of provisions, pressed us to advance, and would not let us deliberate long upon the danger that lay before us, so that, all our apprehensions being reduced to the fear we had of starving to death, we pursued our march to go and confront our enemies.

When we had marched about half an hour, we found ourselves near the town, and upon the brink of a great and very rapid river, which separates it from four of the suburbs that adjoin to it; this river we crossed over, being up in the water to the middle, in spite of the Spaniards, who were entrenched on the other side, to dispute the passage with us, which they were forced to leave open for us, after a good hour's sharp dispute. As soon as we were masters of the entrenchment, we entered the town, where, after we had fought hand in hand with the enemy, like men enraged with hunger, we became masters of the place of arms about four in the afternoon. But our work was not yet done, for the enemy, having again entrenched themselves in a very fine abbey, built in the manner of a platform that commanded the town, we went, to the number of fourscore men, to dislodge them, which was so readily executed, that, having chased them thence, we made our court of guard of it, and then every one endeavored to satisfy that hunger wherewith we were extremely pinched.

When we were got into this town, we found it yet much more spacious and larger than it appeared to be unto us, from the fore-mentioned ascent; its houses are well built, the streets very straight, and the churches exceedingly stately and ornamental. Tbe abbey of St. Francis, from whence we drove the enemy, appeared more like unto a fort than a religious convent, and it was built to serve for that use in case of need.

On the 31st we sent to require them to ransom their town, or else we would burn it. We had no answer returned, which made us conjecture they had a mind to come and attack us; for which they had so much the more advantage, in that the river, which began, from the time we had passed it, to overflow, was about to hem us in; wherefore we decamped, and lay in one of the suburbs that stands on the other side, where we continued to the 3d of September; when we departed to return to our canoes, without reaping any advantage by the taking of this town. We reëmbarked on the 5th, and went to join our ships in the port of Vatulco, where we arrived the 9th. On the 15th we went off again in our canoes without a guide, and, having landed, marched ten or a dozen leagues up the country, where we took divers villages, and in one of them the old governor of Marida with his family, who was retired to this place, and who promised us a quantity of provisions for his ransom; in expectation whereof we carried him on shipboard, where we arrived on the 25th. The same day, about ten in the morning, we discovered a ship, and put out with our canoes to know what she was; she bare to the cape, and put up Spanish colors; but as the sea ran very high, and that our canoe could not well weather it, we returned again into port. Now this ship believed it was her colors that hindered us to come on board her, wherefore she took the same down, and put up a white flag in the room of them; we at the same time fitted up our galley to go and hail her, but she could never get out of the port; whereupon she sailed away, and, as our ships were much out of order, we could not follow her. She was undoubtedly a frigate built in the North Sea, but it was impossible for us to know what nation she belonged to.

The sea being calm on the 26th, we went with our galley about twenty leagues to the windward of Acapulco, to see if the above-mentioned ship were not put into port, we judging by her rigging she wanted to put in somewhere to land; but we returned without any news of her. We waited till the 4th of November for the ransom of the governor, which we did not overmuch press for, as finding in this port, and parts adjacent, plenty of victuals, particularly of tortoises, which we had there in great numbers, and hattoes, that are to be met with up and down frequently here, furnished us with all other necessaries; beside that, we had here a place of security from the insult of the Spaniards.

It is impossible to go ashore from Sansonat to Acapulco, unless it be in the ports or bays; and though that which they call the salt-pits be difficult of access, because of the smallness of it, and that the sea there runs very high, yet they esteem it a bay for all that. It is the next you meet with after Sansonat, and stands twenty leagues to the windward of that of Tecoantepequa, which the Spaniards set down also for a bay in their charts, though it be so far from being deep, that it can scarce be distinguished from the rest of the coast. There is a lake at the bottom of this last place bearing the same name, with which it had formerly a communication, but whose mouth at present is stopped up by a bank of sand which the waves have drove thither. This lake hems in three islands that are not far distant from one another, and all of them very near the mouth thereof. Some years since the hourqua of Acapulco, that went to the East Indies, in its return entered into this lake through the bay, and we understood that some Spaniards had entered by the other end of it into the river of Vastaqua, that discharges itself into a bay of New Spain, and consequently to the North Sea.

When the hourqua returns from the Philippine Islands, where the Spaniards drive a great traffic, it is one of the richest vessels that sails upon the ocean; it is of a prodigious bigness, and built so strong, that she is afraid of nothing but land and fire. She is provided with forty pieces of cannon, whereof one half are of no use to her, for her lading makes her sink so deep in the water, that her battery between the two decks is rendered useless. She goes out yearly from the port of Acapulco, convoyed with a patach of twenty-eight guns, and laden with several sorts of merchandise that she carries to the inhabitants of those islands, who, by way of barter for the same, give a great deal of those curious China and Japan ware we see in Europe, and, what is yet more valuable, pearls, gold dust, and precious stones.

This ship had great advantage in making this voyage, that is, that, in making choice of a proper season, she goes and returns in a twelve months' time, comprehending the while they stay in that country, without being put to the trouble of veering about, and shifting the sails; and it is beyond dispute, that she cannot be met with by any that wait for her before the port of Acapulco, at a certain season of the year, which I shall take no notice of here, for reasons I have spoken of in the beginning of this journal.

I shall not forget also to remark in this place, that it will be so much the more easy to take her, in that when she returns from those parts with the patach, all her crew are in so sickly and dying a condition, that of four hundred men that make up the complement, there are not one fourth of them in a condition to defend it; and this distemper, which they call *scorbutus*, never fails them in their return from the Philippines, insomuch that a ship, which goes from the North Sea with a design to look after this hourqua, might, in less than eighteen months' time, abating the perils and accidents which she might be liable to at sea, return with immense riches.

About twenty leagues to leeward of the bay of Tecoantepequa stands the port of Vatulco, so small, that it cannot contain above ten or a dozen ships; but yet they must have an anchor fore and aft, for, if they had no more than an anchor out at the forecastle, they would fall foul upon another, in endeavoring to avoid it upon the change of wind or tide.

At the entrance into the port, which is very narrow, there is a whirlpool to the leeward, which the Spaniards call *bosadera*, whereinto the water enters in so violent a manner that it makes a noise that may be heard above four leagues off.

Four leagues lower there is another port, where you cannot anchor with safety, because of the rocks, whereof the bottom of it is full. In the passage to it stands a great rock, called the *fourillon*, which is all over as well as continually so covered with those sorts of birds which we had before seen in the River of Villia, that there remains nothing of the surface of it to be seen; and a little further is an island called Sacrifice.

About eight leagues lower there are three small ports of a league's distance one from another, whereof that called the Angels is the best; it is no difficult matter to find the passage to it, provided you sail along the shore, but it is impossible to perceive it from the main. There is a rock stands at the mouth of it that has a hole therein resembling a large gate. From this port to Acapulco, which is sixty leagues off, we have no harbor.

The country, which extends itself from the Bay of Salt Pits as far as Acapulco, is that upon the South Sea that is best peopled, and where there are moreover several famous and very rich towns; more gold mines are also found there than in Peru, though the metal is not so fine; and those of Tinsigal alone are more valued by the Spaniards than the mines of Potosi; and therefore it is not without reason that this western coast is called by the name of Costa Rica, though, in our geographical maps, they bestow this name only upon a small part of this vast tract of land.

On the 7th we went to make a descent upon a little town called Muemeluna, which is eight leagues to the windward of Vatulco, and six up the country, about four leagues from the sea-side, and two from the town. We found a very strong entrenchment made upon a rock that stands upon the river; but the Spaniards therein made no great resistance, no more than in the town where we completed our victualling. The prisoners we took told us, that, about a month before they had seen a frigate pass by, that sent a small canoe with seven or eight men in it to their embarking place, where they found some Spaniards, who made them embark again with so much precipitation, that one of their men was drowned, and whom indeed we found dead upon the shore, whither the sea had thrown him, with his fusil lying some paces from him, which would not have lain so long there, no more than the dead carcass, if the Spaniards had espied it. For they believe themselves revenged when they cut into pieces or burn the dead body of an enemy; and we were assured that, when we buried any of our men in their country, they dug them up when we were gone, if they knew the place, for to exercise their cruelty upon those carcasses, which, when alive, they could not make us feel.

We returned on the 16th aboard our ships, and on the 20th, not being able, all along the coast, to hear any news of the five and fifty men we were in quest of, we weighed anchor, and directed our course for the Bay of Mapalla, where we were minded to agree upon the place by which we were to repass to the North Sea. On the 21st we had a north wind that carried us to a certain latitude where the west winds reign; and this continued to the 23d, when we were becalmed. On the 1st of December at night, we had a storm which separated us one from another, and thus we continued alone, and without any water, for all our casks were run out, whereby we were reduced to the greatest extremity, though we were but two leagues from the shore. But it was impossible for us to go ashore, for it is a bank of sand that reaches from the bar of St. Mark as far as Sansonat, for the space of about fourscore leagues, where the sea breaks with great violence. Believing ourselves on the 6th to be to the windward of this bank, we armed our periaugue to go near the shore, and look out for a place where the sea was calmer. Next day one of our men, being more impatient than the rest, and urged on with drought, that had tormented him four days, swam to land; but thinking to return in the same manner, he was drowned, without our being able to succor him, notwithstanding all the cry he made unto us to save him. On the 9th, in the beginning of the night, we thought to have seen a little bay, before which we anchored, that we might know in the morning what it was, during which time we heard the firing of about six hundred muskets on the land. As soon as day-light appeared on the 10th, we saw that what we took for a bay was a kind of a covert that stands fifteen leagues to the leeward of Sansonat, where we could see no likelihood of entering in. In the mean time we saw a very pretty ship upon the stocks in that place, which made us conclude there must of necessity be a passage for her to come out. We anchored pretty near the rock, to wait for a tide, during which time a wind blew from the sea, and we adventured with the help of our sails and oars to get in, where we were saluted with three waves that had filled our periaugue in the very sight of the Spaniards, who watched our entering in.

We put up to one side of the said covert, and fired for the space of half an hour upon their magazines, built by the side thereof, without their returning us one single shot; but at last, we being tormented with violent drought, which we were desirous to allay, whatever it cost us, we hoisted up our sail, and run up our periaugue before them, who, believing we were going to their town, that was but half a league off, they went off. But as we were no more than two and twenty men, instead of running after them, we improved their flight in filling our casks with water, and to furnish ourselves with what provisions we found in the magazines, and some of that ship's rigging, which were more necessary for ours; but not daring all at once to laden our periaugue with them, for fear of sinking in her passage out, we spent the night on the other side of those magazines, that we might be under covert from the surprises of our enemies, for we computed very well, by the six hundred musket-shot we had heard, that there were a great many armed men in that place.

On the 11th we departed from under the covert, to go and join our ship, which we found on the 12th in the morning, lying at anchor eight leagues to the windward of Sansonat, where she had found the sea somewhat more favorable. We spent that day to take in water, and sent twenty men to take a village that was about half a league from the sea-side, from whence we returned the same day with some refreshments, that put life into our ship's crew, now much weakened with the thirst they endured, as well as we who were in the periaugue, as also with hunger, which failed not to waste us away, though we had victuals to satisfy the same; but we durst not eat for fear of being made dry. We weighed anchor in the evening, with a west wind, and on the fifteenth arrived in the Bay of Mapalla, where we found the rest of our vessels at anchor near one of those islands that lie within it.

I am to observe, that as long as we were going up this coast, continually in the night time there blew winds from the land, which were very favorable to sailors, provided they were not far out at sea, for ten leagues off there could be but very little of it felt; and there are certain reasons when it blows so violently that they are obliged to lower their sails, and even to furl. On the 17th, we had a consultation together, about what passage, according to the prisoners' relations, was less dangerous for us to return to the North Sea, over land: it was thought our best way was by Segovia, seeing we had no more than sixty leagues to go before we came to the head of a river, upon which they told us we might go down to the North Sea, whereunto it discharged itself; and that, in the way we were to take by land, we could have no more than five or six thousand men to deal with, and that the way was very good to carry our wounded and sick men along with us. But we were not fully convinced of the sincerity of this advice; we sent two of our canoes to shore, to take some other prisoners, that so we might see whether they should confirm or contradict this information, and thereby be the more fully instructed concerning those things that might be an obstruction to our passage, and others that might facilitate the same.

We went ashore on the 18th, to the number of seventy men, and marched all day long without meeting one soul, as we did also the next day till noon, without any more discovery than in the preceding one, wherewith we were so fatigued, that we resolved to return back again; and here we may add, that the greatest part of our men were not over content to repass by land to the North Sea, because of the five or six thousand men wherewith we were threatened; wherefore we left those that were minded to return to their canoes, and eighteen of us, who found ourselves less weary than the rest, staid behind. We followed a great road which we met with soon after they had left us, and had not walked above an hour, when we took three horsemen, who, when we had asked where we were, told us, that about a quarter of a league off there was a little town called *Chiloteca*, wherein there were four hundred white men, besides negroes, mulattoes, and Indians, and assured us we had not yet been discovered. We had a mind to run after our men to acquaint them with this account, and engage them to go back with us to the town; but the apprehensions we were under of being discovered, and thereby giving the inhabitants time to put themselves into a posture of defence, hindered us to do so, and made us undertake, perhaps, the boldest, most resolute, and if you will, the rashest action, that could be thought of; which was, that, being no more of us than eighteen men, as I have said before, we should adventurously enter that town, where we surprised and frightened the Spaniards to that degree, that we took the tenient and other officers, to the number in all of fifty persons, including the women, prisoners. They were seized with such a panic fear, supposing us to be far more numerous than we were, that all the rest would doubtless have been taken and bound by us, had it not been for their horses, which are always at hand, which they mounted to ride away upon. And so it was, as we would have it, for if they had had courage to stay behind, they might have cut out work for us, whereof we had already but too much, which was, to watch our prisoners.

We asked the tenient where the galley of Panama was, who made answer, she lay at anchor in the embarking place of Carthage, which is Caldaira, where she waited for us, as hoping we would pass that way to go to the North Sea, and that the king of Spain's ship, the St. Lorenzo, was in the port of Realeguo, mounted with thirty pieces of cannon and four hundred men on board, to hinder us to come near that place, which they began to settle in again. As we had a desire to lie in this little town where we now were, we further asked him what number of men we should have occasion for to guard us, if we should stay there; he told us, there would be six hundred men next day there, but that they had no more fire-arms than for two hundred. The Spaniards, who, during this time, were a little recovered of their astonishment, being got together, entered into the town again; and after we had several times conflicted with them, we entrenched ourselves in the church where we had put our prisoners, who, seeing us go in with precipitation, believed their people pursued us close, and were just upon falling on us; which made them so bold as to run to the swords and other arms we had got together, wherewith they wounded us one man. We presently got to the doors, and from thence fired upon them so long, till there were no more than four men and their wives, left alive of them. At the same time we mounted the horses which we had taken, and with our four prisoners, of each sex, went away with as little noise as we could, which the other Spaniards observing, they sent one to treat with us; but we refused, and fired upon him, for fear if he came too near us, he should come to know how few we were. Next day, which was the 20th, we rejoined our other people, who had rested themselves at a hatto they had met with in their return, and who gave us assistance against six hundred of those Spaniards who followed in the rear of us; then we gave the women prisoners their liberty. On the 21st we went on board our canoes, and next day reached our ships, where we interrogated our four new prisoners concerning the passage we had projected; but they laid so many difficulties before us, that we grew almost out of conceit with it. But yet, when we considered we must either make our way through, or end our days miserably in a horrible want of all convenient necessaries, and in an enemy's country, where we grew weaker every day by the loss of our men, we resolved to hazard all to get out of it: insomuch that being no longer daunted at the dangers we were in, in this passage, and being persuaded it would be better for us to die with our swords in our hands than to pine away with hunger, we made all things ready for this journey; and to the end we might cut off from the most timorous any desires they might have to return to their ships, if their minds should alter, in reference to their going along with us, we ran our vessels ashore, except our galley and periaugues, which we reserved to carry us off the island where we were to the continent.

On the 25th, we formed four companies, consisting of seventy men each, making all together two hundred and fourscore; and as for the forlorn hope, we agreed for to draw out ten men out of each, and to relieve them every morning. We also made a contract among ourselves, that those who should be lamed in the encounters we might have with the enemy in our way, should have the same recompense as formerly, that is, a thousand pieces of eight a man; that the horses we should take should be divided between the companies for the ease of all our men, and for those that were incommoded above any of the rest; hat those that straggled and should be lamed, should have no recompense made them; and that violence, cowardice and drunkenness should also be punished as formerly.

Before I leave these seas, I will spare the reader the trouble of asking how we came to endure so much hunger, miseries, and fatigues in these parts, since I have said upon several occasions, that the country is so good and pleasant, as well as fruitful in the production of all things necessary for the support and comfort of human life; as to this, there needs no more than observing, that since our separation from the English at the Isle of St. John, we were all along so ill accommodated with shipping, that we were forced to keep continually to the coast; and by consequence, in sight of the Spaniards, who discovering even the least motions we made, had almost always time to remove all their effects out of the way, before we made our descent, and left us nothing but what they could not carry away, which was many times very inconsiderable; whereas, had we had but one good ship to put out far to sea, they could not have discovered us, and we should have surprised them continually in our descents, where we could have wanted nothing, not only that was necessary, but also pleasurable, besides the wealth we must have carried away in a short time.

This want of shipping under which we labored, was so advantageous to our enemies, and the consequence thereof they knew so well, that the people of Peru sent no more ships to the western coast where we were, for fear some of them might fall into our hands, and traded with one another no otherwise than by land.

The same reason also hindered us to go up to the coast of Peru, where we could not have failed of having ships, seeing they sailed up and down there every day, and drove a great trade with one another, as knowing we were not so near unto their country; so that it is easy, from what I have remarked, to conjecture that for want of these helps, which were of so much importance to us in these seas, we must also very often stand in need of all those things which we could not but with the greatest difficulty have without them; wherefore, to make any thing of it in these climates, and to raise a considerable fortune without much danger and sufferings, there needs no more than to be provided with a good ship, and for the better conveniency victualled for some time, that so there may be no necessity of going ashore to seek it.

On the 27th, we discovered a ship passing along between the islands, which made us send our galley and periaugue to see what she was. She put up a white flag, but, as soon as we came within musket-shot of her, she took down the white flag, and put out Spanish colors, and withal gave us ten or a dozen guns; we returned to the shore to give our people notice of it, not doubting, but if that ship came to an anchor in the same place, she would destroy our periaugues. We sent them with our baggage and prisoners up to the flats that are behind the island, where we were.

This vessel, about noon, came in with the tide, and anchored within half a cannon-shot of ours that were run ashore, under the covert of which we fought against them with two pieces of cannon, till it was night; but as the enemy had no other aim than to ruin our ships, they put them this first day out of a condition to sail, which was what ourselves had a mind to, and then put farther off from the shore.

On the 28th, in the morning, they drew nearer again, and began to fight us, which made us shelter ourselves behind the points of the rocks that run out into the sea, from whence our arms carried aboard them; upon this, they were forced to send their shallop under the favor of their cannon, to take away an anchor that was nearer to shore than their ship; but being prevented therein, they cut off the cable that held it, and put off again. At last, concluding with ourselves that this ship would not leave us so hastily, we sent a hundred men in the evening to the continent before us, that they might endeavor to take some horses, on which we might lay our disabled men, with orders afterwards to return and wait for us upon the sea-side, in the same place where they went ashore, (which was a kind of a port we had assigned them,) in case they had returned before our arrival there. And for fear the Spanish ship should suspect, from the running of ours aground, the design we had to go to the North Sea, and that the men on board her would send to the continent to give the people notice to put themselves in a readiness to hinder us, we counterfeited all night long the caulking of our ships, that so we might fully possess them with a belief that we were careening them, which wrought so effectually upon them, that in the morning they failed not to come up, to destroy with their cannon the work they fancied we had been doing during the night.

On the 29th their ship took fire, which made them put farther off, where they extinguished it. On the 30th, we made use of a new stratagem to amuse our enemies, and take away all manner of suspicion from them that we designed to be gone, which was to charge our guns, grenades, and four pieces of cannon, whereunto we tied lighted matches of different lengths, that so, having their effect in our absence, one after another, the Spanish ship's crew might still believe we were upon the island, from whence we parted in the twilight, as secretly as ever we could, with all our prisoners, whom we reserved for no other use than to carry our surgeon's medicines, carpenter's tools, and the wounded men we might have in this passage.

On the 1st of January, in the year 1688, we arrived on the continent; and on the evening of the same day, the party which we had sent before to look for horses, came thither likewise. They had taken sixty-eight, with several prisoners, who, without any violence offered them, told us, they did not think it advisable we should travel through Segovia, because the Spaniards had intelligence we had made choice of that province to pass through; but as we had already resolved upon the matter, and that our ships could be of no longer use unto us, all that they could say to the contrary did not hinder us to persevere therein. All our people, at the same time, packed up every man his charge, and put their silver into bags, which they thought they could carry with their ammunition. Those who had too much of the former, gave it to those who had lost theirs at play, for to carry, conditioning with them, that they should return the one half back to the owner, in case it should please God to bring them safe to the North Sea.

As for myself, I must say I was none of the worst provided, and though my charge was lighter than others, yet it was not, for all that, less considerable for the value, seeing I had converted thirty thousand pieces of eight, into gold, pearls, and precious stones. But, as the best part of this was the product of luck I had at play, some of those who had been losers, as well in playing against me as others, being much discontented at their losses, plotted together, to the number of seventeen or eighteen, to murder those that were the richest amongst us. I was so happy as to be timely advertised of it by some friends, which did not a little disquiet my mind, for it was a very difficult task for a man, during so long a journey, to be able to secure himself from being surprised by those who were continually in the same company, and with whom we must eat, drink, and sleep, and who could cut off whom they pleased of them, in the conflicts they might have with the Spaniards, by shooting us during the hurry, which yet they executed in another manner, as may be seen in due place. The apprehensions I had of this conspiracy did not hinder me to retain so much judgment and presence of mind, as to fall presently upon such methods as I thought most rational and secure for the preservation of my life, and which effectually saved it; which was to deposit some of what I possessed in the hands of divers persons, and that, in the presence of all the rest, upon condition they should restore unto me such a proportion as I agreed with them for, when we were come upon the coast of Domingo. By this means, I rid myself of the care I should continually have had of keeping upon my guard, without exposing them much neither, who carried my effects, the which being divided diversely and to different persons, they had to do with too many people to compass their ends. It is true, I paid dear for this precaution ; but what will not a man do to save his life ?

CHAPTER LVI.

The Return of the Freebooters from the South to the North Sea, over the Continent, by another Way than that by which they got thither.

On the 2d day of January, in the morning, after we had said our prayers, and sunk our periaugues, lest the Spaniards should have any benefit of them, we set out, and lay that night by the sea-side ; we stopped next day about noon, at a hatto, to bait. On the 4th, we lay upon a platform that extends itself upon the tops of several high mountains, where the Spaniards, notwithstanding all the precautions we had taken, were advertised of our departure, and failed not to let us have their company, keeping themselves always in our flanks and rear.

On the 8th, we lay at another hatto, belonging to the tenient of Chiloteca, about which place the enemy began to barricade the ways. We rested on the 6th for an hour and better, at an estantia to bait ; and upon a bed, in a hall there, we found the following letter, directed unto us, in these words : —

" We are very glad that you have made choice of our province for your passage through, homewards ; but we are sorry you are no better laden with silver ; however, if you have occasion for mules to carry your baggage, we will send them to you. We hope to have the French General Grognier very quickly in our power, and we will leave you to consider what is like to become of the soldiers. "

We saw clearly by this letter that they knew nothing of the death of Grognier, since they believed he was still our commander ; and that they had no knowledge of him, but by the account that had been given them by the three men that had run away from him to them, when they failed of getting the gold of the mines of Tinsigal.

On the 7th, we met with an ambuscade of the enemy, whom

our vanguard forced to retire, and lay in the evening at a hatto. The Spaniards, who left no means unattempted to destroy us, burnt all the provision that was in our way, and also when we entered into any savannas where the grass was very dry, they went to the windward of us to set it on fire, whereby we were very much incommoded, and our horses were even stifled with the smoke. As we were sometimes obliged to stay till the fire had burnt up all, to go forwards, this very much retarded our march ; and this was the chief thing the Spaniards aimed at, that the men might have leisure to finish an entrenchment, whereof I shall quickly have occasion to speak, which they erected unknown to us, at some distance off from our road, to which also the work they cut out for us to remove the barricades of trees, wherewith they had encumbered the way, contributed very much ; insomuch that, not being able to penetrate into their designs, we persuaded ourselves that they did all this with no other intent than to chagrin us only, as being not able to do worse unto us, or I should have rather said, having not the courage for it.

On the 8th we passed on to a very fine sugar plantation, and, as we were very desirous to take some prisoners who might inform us of what was done, all our company filed off, and twenty of us staid behind in a house, after they had set it on fire, to oblige the Spaniards to come and put it out, when they saw our men at a distance from them, and this they failed not to do. But our impatience being the means of discovering us too soon, they thereupon fled ; yet we, firing upon them, wounded one, and took him, by whom we understood that all their reënforcements were coming together to dispute our passage, and that we were going to meet them that came from Tinsigal, who consisted of three hundred men.

When we had done with this wounded man, we rejoined our main body, who had halted to wait for us, and then jogged on till we came to a great borough, where we found those three hundred men, who afterwards were our continual guard, for they gave us, morning and evening, the diversion of their trumpets ; but it was like the music of the enchanted palace of Psyche, who heard it without seeing the musicians ; for ours marched on each side of us, in places so covered with pine-trees that it was impossible to perceive them.

We lay this evening about a quarter of a league from the said borough, upon an ascent, according to our usual manner, who never encamped but upon high ground, or in the race of savannas, for fear of being hemmed in. We decamped on the 9th in the morning, after we had reënforced our advanced guards with forty men more, who were appointed to fire their muskets at the entries or avenues of the woods, that we might have a sight of the Spaniards, in case they laid any ambuscades for us. In the mean time, about ten in the morning we passed on to a place that was so thin set with wood, that we might see a considerable distance from us, and, seeing no enemy appear, we did not fire at all. But we did not dream that we were seeking for that far before us, which we had at the sides of us, for the Spaniards, who were ranged to the right and left of our way, lying on their bellies, made their discharges with so much precipitation, that there was no more than one half of our advanced guard who had time to answer their firing. They killed us two men presently, who were turned out of the way to pass undiscovered of the enemy; after which we went to refresh ourselves in a little town that was in our way, and lay half a league beyond it.

We met with another ambuscade on the 10th, wherein we were beforehand with our enemies, and made them leave us their horses; then went to bait at another borough, and lay a little farther.

On the 11th, as we drew nearer unto the town of Segovia, we met with a new ambuscade a little on this side it, and, when we had forced them with our fusils to retire, we went into the said town, being resolved and disposed to fight stoutly, as believing, if the Spaniards were minded to try us, they would use their greatest effort in that place; but they contented themselves with firing only a few musket-shot at us from under the covert of some pine-trees that grew upon the ascents which encompass the town, whither they had retired. We found nothing there to eat, because they had burnt all the provision in the place.

By good luck we took a prisoner to conduct us to the river we sought for, and which was still twenty leagues off, forasmuch as those who had been our guides as far as Segovia knew not the way any farther.

This town lies in a bottom, and is so surrounded with mountains, that she looks as if she were laid up in prison. The churches here are but very indifferently built, and the place of arms is both very considerable and very fine; it is an inland place forty leagues off from the South Sea. The way that leads to it, from the place where we were, is very difficult, being all mountains of a prodigious height, to the tops whereof we must creep with great danger, and the valleys consequently are so very narrow here, that for a league of even ground you pass over, you have six leagues of mountains to go. When we had passed these mountains we felt a very sharp cold, and were taken with so thick a fog, that, even when day appeared, we could not know one another otherwise than by our voices; but that lasted not till above ten in the morning, when the weather cleared up, and the fog went entirely off; and the heat, which succeeds the cold, becomes there very great, as well as in the plains, where none of this cold is felt till you come directly to the foot of the mountains. Thus we were forced to endure such contrary seasons, as well when we travelled, as when we reposed ourselves, that they exposed us to very great inconveniences; but the hopes of getting once into our native country made us patiently to endure all their toils, and served as so many wings to carry us.

On the 12th we departed from this town, and went up other mountains, where we had incredible trouble to clear the ways of those works the Spaniards had prepared to barricade them up with. We went to lodge in a hatto, where they fired very much in the night into our camp.

On the 13th, an hour before sunrising, we mounted along an eminence, that seemed to us to be an advantageous place to encamp on; from whence we saw, upon the edge of a mountain from which we were separated but by a narrow valley, twelve or fifteen horses, which we took for some time for cattle that fed there, whereat we much rejoiced, as being in hopes we should next morning have good cheer at the cost of these animals; and, that we might be the more assured of the matter, we sent forty men thither, who told us, at their return, that what we took for beeves were all saddled horses, and that they had observed three entrenchments in the same place, about pistol-shot one from another, which, rising by degrees towards the middle of the same side of the mountain, fully barricaded the way through which we were to pass next day, and commanded a small stream that ran along the said valley, into which we must necessarily descend first, there being no other way, nor any likelihood of our going on one side thereof. They saw also a man, who, as soon as he discovered them, severely threatened them with his cutlass, which he held naked in his hand.

These sad tidings were a mighty alloy to our joy, and the transformation of those pretended beeves, on whom our pining appetite had depended so much, affected us to a great degree; but these thoughts were at present to be laid aside, to make room for to consider how we should disentangle ourselves from that place, and that without delay, because the Spaniards, who were gathering together from all the adjacent provinces, would quickly fall upon our small company, who must of necessity be overborne by them, if we staid for them. The means to effect this were not easily found, and perhaps it would have appeared an impossible thing to any other than such as we were, who, till then, had been successful almost in all our undertakings; and, to be plain in the matter, we found ourselves now hard put to it. For, as I observed to the rest of our people, ten thousand men could not be able to force their way through that entrenchment, without being cut to pieces, as well because of the advantage of the place, as the number of Spaniards that defended it, which we might compute by that of their horses; and, seeing a single man could hardly pass on one side of it, there was no likelihood we should be able to do it with our horses and baggage, so rough was the country. And indeed, saving the road itself, all the rest was no other than a thick forest, without either ways or paths, full of sharp rocks in some places, of quagmires in others, and embarrassed with a great many trees that had dropped down to the ground with age. And, though after all, we should have found out a way to escape across so many obstacles, there was still an indispensable necessity that we should fight with the Spaniards, that we might be at quiet for the rest of our journey. This they all agreed to; but, as they objected unto me, that it was to no purpose to represent these difficulties, which of themselves were but too apparent, without proposing some method to surmount them, nor to give counsel without facilitating the execution thereof, I told them, that, for my part, I could not see what else we could do but go across those woods, precipices, mountains, and rocks, howsoever inaccessible they appeared to be, and endeavor to surprise the enemy in the rear, and to gain the advantage of the ground from them, by getting above them, where surely we were not expected; and that I would answer for the success of the same at the peril of my life, if they would undertake it. That, as for our prisoners, horses, and baggage, wherewith we were encumbered, we ought not to leave them defenceless to the discretion of those three hundred men, who always kept close to us in our march, and encamped every evening about a musket-shot off. That we ought to leave fourscore men to guard them with all necessary precaution, as you will hear by and by, and that such a number was enough to fight with so many Spaniards four times told.

We took some time to deliberate hereupon; and, at length, these expedients, how hazardous soever they were, being found the most suitable to the condition we were in, and I may say the only ones we had left us, we resolved to lay hold of them, and put the same in execution.

Scarce had we projected the design, and considered the ascent where we were, the situation of the opposite mountain, where the Spaniards had made their entrenchments, but that above the highest of them we saw a road, which we took to be the continuation of that which they had shut up against us, and, turning to the right, went winding about the side of the same mountain; which yet we could not discover but with difficulty, and by lights peeping in between the trees, which would allow us to see but some traces at a distance from one another.

As we had not hitherto resolved upon which side to pitch, in order to get behind those entrenchments, whether the right or left, this way decided that point, being well satisfied that, if we could but once cross it, it would bring us directly upon the enemy. But yet, that we might not engage ourselves inconsiderately in this enterprise, where all things went for us, we sent twenty men, while we had any daylight left, to a place that was somewhat higher than that where we were, to cover another party, whom we had known by experience to have been very ingenious and expert upon several occasions, that so they might pitch upon those places by which we might, in the night, the more easily get up as far as that road, thereby to go and charge the enemy in the rear, by break of day.

As soon as our men were returned and gave us an account of what they had observed, we made all things ready for our departure; but we first made that station, we were leaving, a place of arms, where we left our baggage, all the prisoners we had, and fourscore men to guard them, and this, that the three hundred Spaniards who continually followed us, as well as those who were behind the entrenchments, might be persuaded we had not left our camp; and we gave the officer that commanded order to make every sentinel he set or relieved in the night-time, to fire his fusil, and that he should beat the drum at the usual hour. We told him, moreover, that, if God gave us the victory, we should send a party to bring him off, and that if, about an hour after he heard the firing at an end, he did not see any body from us, he should provide for his own safety as well as he could.

Things being thus disposed, we said our prayers as low as we could, that the Spaniards might not hear us, from whom we were separated but by the valley we have spoke of. At the same time we set forward, to the number of two hundred men, by moonlight, it being now an hour within night; and, about one more after our departure, we heard the Spaniards also at their prayers, who, knowing we were encamped very near them, fired about six hundred muskets into the air to frighten us. Besides which, they also made a discharge at all the responses of the litany of the saints which they sung. We still pursued our march, and spent the whole night (in going down, and then getting up) to advance half a quarter of a league, which was the distance between them and us, through a country, as I have already said, so full of rocks, mountains, woods, and frightful precipices, that our posteriors and knees were of more use to us than our legs, it being impossible for us to travel thither otherwise.

On the 14th, by break of day, as we were got over the most dangerous parts of this passage, and had already seized upon a considerable ascent of the mountain, by clambering up to it in great silence, and leaving the Spaniards' entrenchments on the left, we saw their party that went the rounds, who, thanks to the fogs that are very rife in this country (as I have already said) till ten o'clock, did not discover us. As soon as they were gone by, we went directly to the place where we saw them, and found it to be exactly the road we were minded to seize on. When we had made a halt for about half an hour to take breath, and that we had a little daylight to facilitate our march, we followed this road by the voice of the Spaniards, who were at their morning prayers, and we were but just beginning our march, when unfortunately we met with two out-sentinels, on whom we were forced to fire; and this gave the Spaniards notice, who thought of nothing less than to see us come down from above them upon their entrenchment, since they expected us from no other way than from below. So that those who had the guard thereof, and were in number about five hundred men, finding themselves on the outside, when they thought they had been within, and consequently open without any covert, took the alarm so hot, that, falling all on upon them at the same time, we made them quit the place in a moment, and make their escape by the favor of the fog.

This so much unexpected morning music disturbed the whole economy of their designs, and so thwarted their whole contrivance, that those of the other two entrenchments drew all without the lowermost, where they prepared to defend themselves. We fought with them a whole hour from under the covert of the first entrenchment which we had got of them, and which exactly commanded them, because of its elevated situation upon the mountain. But as they gave no ground, we began to think that the shot we discharged did not reach them, because of the fog which hindered us to discover them, and that we could not fire but according to the discharges that came from them ; so that being resolved to lose our aim no longer, we advanced and fell directly upon the places from whence they fired. There we fought them stoutly, and they did not quit the place till such time as they saw the butts of our muskets, and that near them, the sight whereof the mist had till then taken from them. But then, being much terrified, they left us all, and ran that way which was before their entrenchments, which proved very incommodious for them, because, that being the only place by which they thought we could come at them, they had cut down all the trees that grew there and in the adjacent parts as well because they might obstruct their sight in this bottom, as hinder us to come on under the covert of them. And thus the precaution, which they had taken against us, by a quite contrary effect was turned upon themselves, insomuch that we had so clear a view of them from the entrenchments we had taken, that we did execution almost with every piece we shot. We pursued them after that for some time, still beating them; but at length being weary both of running and killing, we returned to the entrenchments where the five hundred men whom we had put to flight at first, being come back, endeavored to break in upon those whom we had left to guard them; but we made them, like the rest, quickly run away. We were also fatigued mightily in pursuing of them; for, besides that the ground was so extraordinary bad and hard to pass, they also augmented the difficulties by making use of the trees which they had felled down, to barricade and stop up even the least avenue that was near the place round about.

We found these Spaniards had so little mind to give us quarter, if they should have the upper hand of us, that even when we took any of them, they would not as much as ask it at our hands, and to some of them we gave quarter in spite of their teeth, though they did otherwise all that ever they could to save themselves out of our hands. But at this no man ought to wonder; for it is a maxim amongst them in these parts, and whereof we have had experience upon several occasions, whether it proceeded from pride or natural fierceness of temper, or because of an oath they take before their commander, before they go to fight, that they will never submit to ask quarter of those to whom they have sworn they would give none. But we in the mean time, being affected with compassion upon sight of the great quantity of blood we saw running down into the rivulet, spared the rest, and went a second time into our entrenchments, having lost all this while but one man, and two only wounded. The Spaniards, among others. lost their general, who was an old Walloon officer, who had given them the plan of this entrenchment, that would infallibly have prevailed against us, had we attacked them by the way they expected. In the mean time another old captain had advised him to secure their rear, but he saw so little likelihood of danger on that side, that he answered, we must be either men or devils; that if we were men, he defied us to get over any way in eight days' time; but if we were devils, though he should take never so much care of himself, he must still be taken.

However, at the solicitation of the said officer, he sent a party that way to go the rounds, and to post the two sentinels we spoke of, as they thought most convenient. The general being searched, there were several letters found in his pockets, which had been written to him by the governors of the province, that set forth particularly the number of men they had sent him; and one among others, from the general of Costa Rica, who expressed himself as follows: —

A Letter written by the General of the Province of Costa Rica to the Commander in Chief in the Entrenchments, dated January 6, 1668.

"Sir: — I thought I had made a good choice, when I committed to you the conduct of an affair which ought to reëstablish our reputation, if you have the better of the enemy, as you induce me to believe you will. I was preparing to send you eight thousand men, if you had not sent me word that fifteen hundred was enough. I do not doubt but a person that hath served so long as you have done, will take care of your men, especially since you have to do with a people from whom there will no honor redound to you by overdoing them.

"According to the relation you have given me of your entrenchments, it is impossible but those people, with the help of God, must be destroyed. I advise you to put a thousand men into them, and two hundred near unto the river by which they hope to get unto the North Sea. In case any of them save themselves across the mountains, Don Rodrigo Sarmado, the new governor of Tinsigal, ought to be at the head of three hundred men, to fall upon the rear as soon as ever they are engaged, for certainly their baggage must be there. Take good measures, for those devils have a cunning and subtlety that is not in use amongst us.

"When you find them advance within the shot of your arquebusses, let not your men fire but by twenties, to the end your firing may not be in vain; and when you find them weakened, raise a shout to frighten them, and fall in with your swords, while Don Rodrigo attacks them in the rear. I hope God will favor our designs, since they are no other than for his glory and the destruction of these new sort of Turks. Hearten up your men, though they may have enough of that according to your example; they shall be rewarded in heaven, and if they get the better, they will have gold and silver enough, wherewith these thieves are laden."

After we had sung *Te Deum* upon the field of battle, by way of thanks unto God for this victory, we mounted sixty men on horseback to go and give notice to our other people of the success the Almighty was pleased to give us. We found them ready to begin another engagement against the three hundred Spaniards whereof we have spoken; who as soon as they heard that action at the entrenchments begin, and saw how few men we had left behind in our camp, were easily induced to believe we had made our attack by that disadvantageous way I have spoken of, as supposing it impossible for us to do it in any other place, and that therefore our ruin must be inevitable; insomuch that instead of entering directly into the place, which considering their number, they could have carried in a moment, they had so little courage that they contented themselves to send an officer to our men that guarded the baggage to parley with them, whom they stopped for a time, in expectation of some news from us, that so they might return an answer conformable to the intelligence they received. And thus the platform I had laid whereon to ground the sufficiency of fourscore of our men for that work, or rather the cowardice of the enemy, was fully confirmed.

They told us that as soon as we had begun the fight, those three hundred Spaniards advanced a little, and having got upon an eminence that commanded our camp, they alighted and sent them the said officer to make the following harangue to them: —

"I come hither from my general. You say you do not question but you have force enough, and that you are men of courage, which you have let us know whenever you have been minded to make yourselves masters of our country; yet you are not to doubt but the great numbers of men we have got together will overpower you. We are to let you understand there are a thousand men in that entrenchment against whom they are gone to fight, where they are worsted; that we are three hundred men in this place, and that two hundred are posted near to the river you go and seek, to wait for those of you who escape out of the fight. Wherefore, if you will give yourselves up prisoners of war into the power of our general, who is a man of honor, we will be friends, and we will let you pass to your own country. But as to those of your men whom ours have taken alive, their almoner yesterday after prayers begged quarter for them, for the honor of the holy sacrament and glorious Virgin, which has been promised unto them."

Our men, hearing him talk at this rate, were already somewhat alarmed, as fearing what he said was true; but as soon as they saw us come at a distance, they took courage, and returned him as fierce an answer, like men who had no fear upon them, to this purpose: —

"Though you had had force enough to destroy two thirds of our number, we should not fail still to fight with the remaining part; yea, though there were but one man of us left, he should fight still against you all.

"When we put ashore and left the South Sea, we all resolved to pass through your country or die in the attempt; and though there were as many Spaniards of you as there is grass in this savanna, we should not be afraid, but look upon you always in our opinion cowards, and we will pass on, and go where we will, in spite of your teeth."

The officer being dismissed upon our arrival, mounted his horse to return from whence he came, and observing we were booted, and mounted upon his companions' horses who guarded the entrenchments, he shrunk up his shoulders by way of amazement, and rode as fast as he could to carry the news to his own party. As soon as he was got to them, who were not above a musket-shot off, we advanced and fell upon them, to put them out of condition all at once to follow us any more. We received their first firing, to which we made no return otherwise than with our pistols and cutlasses, and that unhappily for them who had not yet got upon their horses; for we cut a great many of them to pieces, insomuch that God crowning all the advantages we had had in the rest of our engagements by the success we had in this last, we let the rest go, detaining only their horses; and when we had broken all their arms, we with our baggage rejoined our main body, who staid still upon the place to guard the entrenchments. We had no more than one man killed in this engagement, (as it was in the other,) and two maimed.

We asked some of the prisoners whom we had taken several questions, and they told us, among other things, that we should still meet with another entrenchment upon the road, about six leagues distant from those we quitted, which made us fear with very great reason lest the fugitives should go and possess themselves of it, with a design to dispute our passage once more. And indeed, we saw fire upon the top of a great mountain, which they had made for a signal to gather their scattered troops together, and those who out of the fear they were in, might perhaps hide themselves for eight days together, had it not been for this, as believing us still at their heels. But we prevented their design, for we lay two leagues from thence to cut off their passage, there being no other way than this by which they might get thither, and whose sides were still less accessible the farther you went on, than they were behither the same. We had cut the hams of nine hundred of their horses before, that so they might be made unfit to pursue us; we took much about the same number of them with us to ease our journey, till we came at the river we were in quest of, and to kill and salt them upon our arrival, that so they might serve us for food in that long passage.

On the 15th we passed by the fore-mentioned entrenchment, which was not yet finished, without any resistance, this proceeding in all appearance from the terror which the noise of our victory had struck into the people, and lay at a hatto three leagues beyond it. On the 19th we lay at another, six leagues farther; and at last, on the 17th, which was the sixteenth day since our setting out, we came to the so much desired river, and presently entered into the woods that grow upon the banks thereof, where every one fell to work in good earnest to cut down trees to build piperies, wherein we might go down the same.

Some perhaps may think that these were some commodious vessels, wherein to carry us with ease down the river; but there was nothing less than that in it. What we called piperies, were four or five stocks of one kind of tree, which they called *mahot*; it is a light, floating sort of wood, which after we have taken off the bark, we join and tie together, instead of cords, with a sort of lines that grow in these woods and cling like ivy unto every thing that is near them, and especially to trees, to the height whereof they mount; and when these pieces are set together, they put two or three men upon them, according to the bigness of the pipery, and this is all the equipment we make thereof.

The surest posture we can find ourselves to be in, is to stand upright thereon, though they sink two or three feet under the water; and you may judge by what follows, whether the continual apprehensions of danger we were in were well or ill grounded.

We built ours no bigger than to hold two men, that so they might the more easily pass between those very narrow rocks we foresaw, by those that already presented themselves to our view, we must meet with before we got unto the sea-side. When this pretty *flota* was in a condition to put out, we dragged it to the river-side, after we had furnished ourselves with long poles, to keep us from being driven too violently upon the rocks, where we were apprehensive we should be carried by the violence of the stream, as it came also frequently to pass.

This river springs in the mountains of Segovia, and discharges itself into the North Sea at Cape Gracias a Dios, after having run a very long way in a most rapid manner across a vast number of rocks of a prodigious bigness, and by the most frightful precipices that can be thought of, besides a great many falls of water, to the number at least of a hundred of all sorts, which it is impossible for a man to look on without trembling, and making the head of the most fearless to turn round, when he sees and hears the water fall from such a height into those tremendous whirlpools. In short, the whole is so formidable, that there are none but those who have some experience can have right conceptions of it. But for me, who have passed these places, and who, as long as I live, shall have my mind filled with those risks I have run, it is impossible I should give such an idea hereof, but what will come far short of what I have really known of them.

It was therefore upon this dangerous river that we went down, suffering ourselves to be carried along at the will of the stream, in these pitiful machines, whereof the greatest part was under water, as has been said before, two or three feet, insomuch that we were almost always up to the middle therein. But this was nothing in comparison of the rapidity of it, which many times hurried us, in spite of all the resistance we could make, into the publings of foaming water, where we now and then found ourselves buried with our pieces of wood, which made many of our men tie themselves thereon, as being in hopes the wood that floated would bear them up still upon the water; but in this some of them were mistaken.

But as for those great falls, they had, to our good fortunes, at their entrance and goings out, a great basin of still water, which gave us the opportunity to get upon the banks of the river and draw our piperies ashore, to take off those things we had laid on them, which, as wet as we were, we carried with us, leaping from rock to rock, till we came to the end of the fall, from whence one of us afterwards returned to put our pipery into the water, and let her swim along to him who waited for her below. But, if he failed to catch hold (by swimming) of those pieces of wood, before they got out of the basin below, the violence of the stream would carry them away to rights, and the men must then be necessitated to go and pick out trees to make another.

We thought at our setting out to go down the water all together, to the end that, in case of any accident, one might give assistance to the other; but, at the end of three days, when I knew the danger we exposed ourselves to in this way of swimming together, which had already been the occasion of our losing many piperies, I set myself against the design of our continuing thus together, by demonstrating to all our men, that, now we had no Spaniards in these parts to conflict with, but only the difficulties of this dangerous river, it was convenient on the contrary to allow every crew of us to advance a little before the other, and to keep, as it were, in a line successively; and so, in case the first were carried (as indeed it came to pass) by the violence of the stream upon the rocks on the brink of the water, whereof the river is full in an infinity of places, they might have time at least to get off before the arrival of the next pipery, which had already wrought so much disorder by the wrecks that had been occasioned by their falling foul on one another, that all of us were in manifest danger of perishing.

I afterwards found, as well as several others of our people, who had made trial hereof, that this foresight was not useless to us; for my pipery happening to be cast upon such a place, I was forced to untie the pieces of wood, and to straddle upon one piece, while my companion did the same upon another, and so leave ourselves to be carried down in this manner at the pleasure of the stream, till it pleased God that we should meet with a place, as we did indeed, that was not so rapid, where we could go upon the bank of the river, which we could not have done, if others had immediately followed us. I also advised that those, who went down first, should take care to set up in the most dangerous places a flag or banner at the top of a long pole, that so we might discern it afar off, not so much to give notice to those who were hindermost that there was a fall in such a place, for these would make themselves to be heard almost a league off, but to signify to them what side they were to put to land, which should be that where the flag stood. These methods being put in practice, saved the lives of a great many men, though, for all these precautions, several were also lost.

The many bananas which we found along the banks of this river were almost the only food that kept us from starving; for, our arms being continually wet, and our powder all spoiled, we could not possibly go a hunting, though there is very good game there; for, as to the horse-flesh which we had salted, we were forced to throw it away in two days' time, for it could not keep in the water any longer.

These bananas have partly been planted by the Indians, who dwell along the sides of this river, and partly by the overflowing of the waters, which, having dragged them along, and then left them dry, took root again, and so have multiplied.

Some days after we found, when we began to go down the river, some carbets of an Indian nation called Albaouins, whom we chased to get their victuals; there are a multitude of others, who dwell farther from the brink thereof on the opposite side to the former, and those of the one bank have neither war nor commerce with those of the other.

It was in this place that those of our men, who had lost their money by gaming, put their cruel design in execution, and where I came to know that the warning formerly given me was too true. For these wretches, being gone before, went and hid themselves behind the rocks that are upon the brink of this river, by which we must necessarily pass. As every man endeavored to save himself as well as he could, and that for the reasons already given, we went down the river at a distance one from another, and without any mistrust, they had but too much time and conveniency to pick out and murder five Englishmen, whom they knew to be some of the best furnished with booty, of which these assassins entirely deprived them. My companion and I found their bodies upon the river's side; and I must freely confess, that such a spectacle would have struck no small terror into me, if I had still been the bearer of my winnings; I bless God with all my heart, that inspired me with a design to quit my treasure, being then exposed in going down the river, as I was last after the English, to the treachery of those villains, where I must infallibly have run the same risk as they had done. None of our people knew any thing of this murder; but when we were got all together farther down, I told them what I had seen, which was fully confirmed, as well by the absence of the dead men as by that of the assassins, who durst not come and rejoin us, and whom we never saw from thence forward.

On the 20th of February we found the river larger, and more spacious than before, and met with no more falls therein; but the same was so encumbered with trees and bamboes, which the floods carried thither, that our wretched machines could not be kept from overturning; but the depth of the water in these parts being a means to moderate the rapidness of it, there were not many drowned.

At last, when we were gone down some leagues farther, we found the river very good, the stream very gentle, and no likelihood of our meeting any more rocks or trees, though we had still above sixty leagues to the sea-side. Wherefore, now finding ourselves freed from those perils and dangers which we had been exposed to in such terrible places, where death, in the most frightful shape, presented itself continually to our view, every one began to resume fresh courage, and conceive good hopes of the remainder of the voyage; insomuch that, being now all of us assembled together in the same place where those who had gone before, staid for them that came after, and that we had now before us how we should go quite through with the rest of our voyages, we agreed to divide ourselves into several companies, each consisting of sixty men, to build canoes out of mapou wood, which sort of trees grow in great numbers upon the banks of the said river.

Having, with wonderful diligence, finished four canoes by the 1st of March, for the use of a hundred and twenty men that were of us in one canton, we put them into the water, and embarked thereon, without staying for a hundred and forty more, who were finishing theirs; the ardent desire we had to be, as soon as possible, satisfied whether we should really be able to reach the North Sea, egged us mightily to put on; for, according to the idea we had conceived of our passage, we were apprehensive of being carried back into that of the South, as not being able to think we could be so happy as to recover the sight of a sea, by which we might be carried home to our native countries, and which we had for so considerable a time longed for.

The English, who would not make any canoes, had got in their piperies before us to the sea-side. Here they met with an English boat from Jamaica, at anchor, whom they were very forward to press to go and ask leave of the governor of that island for their safe coming thither, because they had gone out without any commission; but that vessel being unwilling to go thither, without they laid down 6000*l.* sterling, by way of advance, and they being not in a condition to run the hazard of such a sum, because many of them had lost their money, as several amongst us had done, which they would have carried with them, by the oversetting of the piperies, they staid with the Moustic Indians, that dwell some leagues to the windward of the mouth of this river, and who are very kind to them, because of the trinkets they bring them from Jamaica.

Thus, that boat proving to be of no use to these English, they politicly bethought themselves to send us word hereof, as hoping we, in acknowledgment of this kindness, would obtain leave of the governor of St. Domingo for them to retire, and be protected in that island. This news we received by two Moustic Indians, whom in a boat they sent to meet us forty leagues up the river, and who told us, that there should no more than forty men only come down, because that ship could contain no more by reason of the smallness of it, and its scantiness of provision. But for all this, the one hundred and twenty that made up one of our companies, went down together, for every one pretended to be of the number of the said forty.

Though this river we are now leaving is by some Spanish maps made to run directly eighty leagues, and then to fall into the North Sea, yet we have computed the same to run above three hundred, being almost always carried to the south-east, for to go to the north.

We happily arrived on the 9th at the mouth of the river, at Cape Gracia de Dios, and entered into the sea, which with much satisfaction we knew to be that of the north, where we were obliged to wait for the English ship that was at the Isles of Pearls, which are a dozen leagues distant from that cape to the east. Here we staid till the 14th with the mulattoes that live in these parts, and who fed us for some days with fish.

This cape, which stands on the continent, hath been inhabited for a long time by these mulattoes and negroes, both men and women, who have greatly multiplied there since a Spanish ship, bound from Guinea, freighted with their fathers, was lost by coming too near the shore, which is very dangerous in these parts. Now those who had escaped the shipwreck were courteously received by the Moustic Indians living about this canton, who were well pleased with the loss of that ship and of the Spaniards, their enemies, that were in it.

Those Indians assigned their new guests a place to grub up, where they built themselves cottages in the finest country of savannas, that reach along the river from the mouth of it for five or six leagues upwards. Here, for their sustenance, they plant maize, bananas, and magniots, which the Indians gave them; they also taught them to make a most nourishing sort of drink, which they call *hoon;* they prepare the same of a fruit that is produced on the top of a kind of a palm-tree, which grows naturally in these woods, and never exceeds ten feet in height. Each of these trees bears no more than one bunch of grapes, but most of them are a full load for one man. Its grain is of the same form and thickness as an olive; some of them are yellowish, others reddish, and containing in a very hard stone an exceeding oily kernel. They pound the fruit, stone, and kernel all together, boiling the same afterwards in water, and this makes up the composition. When the same is grown cold, or but lukewarm, they put what quantity they are minded to drink, into a calabash pierced through with small holes like unto a skimmer. This drink, besides that it is very nourishing, and fattens very much, is also a pleasanter liquor than any that is to be met with among the other Indians, the same being only peculiar to this nation.

The mulattoes are all a very tall people, and go altogether naked, saving their privy parts, which they cover, nature having provided for them upon that account a kind of grayish stuff, which they pull from a tree called the bastard-palm, the top of whose stock is wrapped up in some fathoms of it, from the first rising of its branches some feet downwards, according to the thickness of each of these trees. This stuff is also a great help to them to make coverlets, wherewith to cover them in the night; and some of those people who live more at ease, wear shirts and drawers, which the English bring them from Jamaica. They are the boldest people in the world for expossing themselves to the perils of the sea, and undoubtedly the most expert in the art of fishing. They will commit themselves to the waves in these little boats, or such like, which an able seaman will scarce venture to do; and here they will stay for three or four days together, being no more concerned, let the weather be what it will, than if they were made of the same piece as their boat; and provided they can but once set sight on the fish, though swimming never so low in the water, they will not fail to take him, so dexterous are they at this work.

They many times do our freebooters a kindness, when they take them on board with them, upon condition of letting them have a share of what booty is got, which must be exactly performed unto them. For if you once deceive them, you must no longer expect their assistance; and this temper is peculiar almost to all the Indian nations in these parts, that they will never go again when once you have broke your word with them.

The ancient Moustics, who gave these men I have spoken of, entertainment, live about ten or twelve leagues to the windward of Cape Gracia a Dios, in those places they call Sambay and Sanibey. They are very slothful, and neither plant nor sow but very little, and lie all day on their *amacks*, which are a kind of moving beds in their *ajoupas* or barracks, while their wives wait upon them in every thing as far as they can serve them; and when they are pressed with hunger, they go a fishing in their boats, at which they also are very skilful, and when they have taken any, they eat them, and go not out any more, till hunger returns upon them again.

As for their clothing, it is neither larger nor more sumptuous than that of the mulattoes at the cape. There are but a few amongst them that have a fixed abode, most of them being vagabonds, and wandering along the river side, and having no other house to shelter themselves in but a latanier leaf, which they manage so, that when the wind drives the rain on the one side, they turn their leaf against it, behind which they lie, and this skreens them against the weather. When they are inclined to sleep, they dig a hole in the sand, where they lie and then cover themselves therewith; and this they do to keep themselves from the stinging of the moustics, wherewith the air is generally very full. They are little flies, that are sooner felt than seen, and have so sharp and venomous a sting, that where they alight, they seem to have fiery darts wherewith to prick men. These poor people are so tormented with those mischievous insects, when they see them not, that their bodies appear like lepers, and I can assure it for truth, as knowing the same by my own knowledge, that it is no small pain to be attacked with them; for besides that they caused us to lose our rest in the night, it was then that we were forced to go naked for want of shirts, when the troublesomeness of these animals made us run into despair, and such a rage as set us beside ourselves.

When these Indians go a journey, though ever so short, they take their wives, children, dogs, and fawns, which they breed tame, all along with them. It is a custom I have observed to be held among all the Indian nations on the *terra firma* of America; and these I speak of live as brutishly as any of the rest, yet they are not so cruel and savage, because of the society they have with the English, who have no other aim than to endeavor to bring them under, and master their country, where they have a great many habitations already.

On the 14th the vessel, which I said was gone to the Isles of Pearls, arrived at the place where we were, and came scarce to an anchor, but we all crowded to go on board, because we were to draw lots who should embark; but about fifty of us, for all that, being more vigilant than the rest, made a shift to enter her; who thinking it unadvisable to go ashore again, to commit to chance a thing we were already in possession of, and for to prevent a greater number from entering in, we being already piled as it were on the top of one another, we weighed anchor and departed.

The master would have carried us to Jamaica; but we, not knowing how matters stood between France and England, whether it were peace or war, engaged him to carry us to St. Domingo, for forty pieces of eight a head. We went to take in water at the Isle of Pearls, and on the 16th left the same. On the 17th we doubled the island of Catalina or Providence, as the English call it, where the Spaniards had formerly a very fine fort and small town, which were taken by the French and English, under the colors of the last. On the 18th we went to cross the channel, though it blew a strong easterly breeze. On the 24th we came to land at Los Jardinos, which are a great many small islands near unto that of Cuba. And on the 29th we took in water at Port Portilla, (in the Isle of Cuba,) which is not inhabited. On the 30th we anchored to the S. S. E. of the borough of Baracoa, in the same island, where we surprised the hunters belonging to that place, whom we obliged to sell us the victuals they had took, by giving them their own price for it. But this our liberality towards them proceeded from another cause, and that was, that we were uncertain whether our nation was at peace or war with the Spaniards, since we had no intelligence here, or from any French country, how things went with them.

On the 6th of April, we touched at Nippas, which is a small borough on the coast, seven leagues distant from Petit Guavis, that so we might hear some news of our own country, while we rode at anchor there. There were some of our people so infatuated with the long miseries we had suffered, that they thought of nothing else but the Spaniards, insomuch that when from the deck they saw some horsemen riding along the seaside, they flew to their arms to fire upon them, as imagining they were enemies, though we assured them we were now come among those of our own nation. We left this port on the 4th, and went to anchor in the port of Petit Guavis, from whence we had departed almost four years before; and before we came near the fort, I went to Monsieur Dumas, the king's lieutenant, to require him to grant us protection and indemnity in the Governor Monsieur de Cassy's absence, by virtue of an amnesty the king had been pleased to send to those that made war upon the Spaniards since the peace, which being concluded on since our departure, it was impossible we should come to know it in such remote places, and where we were thought to have been entirely destroyed.

Lastly, when we were got all ashore to a people that spoke French, we could not forbear shedding tears for joy, that after we had run so many hazards, dangers and perils, it had pleased the Almighty Maker of the earth and seas to grant a deliverance, and bring us back to those of our own nation, that at length we may return without any more ado to our own country; whereunto I cannot but further add, that for my own part I had so little hopes of ever getting back, that I could not, for the space of fifteen days, take my return for any other than an illusion; and it proceeded so far with me, that I shunned sleep for fear, when I awaked, I should find myself again in those countries out of which I was now safely delivered.

CHAPTER LVII.

A Relation of a Voyage made by the Sieur De Montauban,* Captain of the Freebooters on the Coast of Guinea, in the Year 1695. With a Description of the Kingdom of Cape Lopez, the Manners, Customs, and Religion of the Country.

SINCE I have so often felt the malignant influences of those stars that preside over the seas, and by an adverse fortune lost all that wealth which with so much care and trouble I had amassed together, I should take no manner of pleasure in this place to call to mind the misfortunes that befel me before the conclusion of the last campaign, had not a desire of serving still both the public and particular persons, as well as to let his majesty know the affection and weddedness I have always had for his service, made me take pen in hand to give M. de Pheli-

---

* *A Letter to Monsieur* ———

"SIR: — A relation of the voyage made by Captain Montauband, commonly called Montauban, is at last come to my hands, and I have sent you the same in print. There is no doubt, but you will admire, as well as I, how much his prudence and courage have been instrumental to deliver him from many unhappy accidents, where another must have infallibly perished. You will remember, as soon as you begin to read, to have seen some of his men at Bourdeaux, in the year 1694; from thence it was he departed the following year to undertake the voyage you are here presented with. He gave chase to several ships he met with in his way; he fought with a frigate carrying thirty-four guns, at Cape Verde; he met with an English ship of twenty guns, at Cape St. John, which he took after a short fight; after which he took a Brandenburgh caper, and sailed away for Angola. Near the shore he met with an English guard-ship, being a frigate carrying fifty-four pieces of cannon. This ship he fought for five or six hours, and both of them very bravely boarded one another; and as he was about to make himself master of the said ship, the English captain set fire to his powder, and so both the ships blew up into the air with a terrible crack.

"You will have the pleasure to contemplate, in the perusal of this book, as if you stood upon the sea-side, this tremendous shipwreck; as also see how the Sieur de Montauban, together with fifteen or sixteen of his men, were saved. He suffered hunger for above three days together, and at last arrived at Cape Lopez, from whence he went to visit the king of that country, of whose court and kingdom he has given us here a description. He speaks also of his reception, and advances a project how to settle the Roman Catholic faith in those parts. He stood for surety at the bap-

peaux an account of such observations as I have made; wherein he may also find with what eagerness I have penetrated to the remotest colonies of our enemies, in order to destroy them and ruin their trade.

I was not willing to swell up this relation with an account of all the voyages I have made, and all the particular adventures that have befallen me on the coasts of New Spain, Carthagena, Mexico, Florida, and Cape Verde, which last place I had been at twenty years ago, having begun to use the seas at the age of sixteen.

I could also have added hereunto the campaign I have made in 1691, when, being commander of the ship called the Machine, I ravaged the coasts of Guinea, entered into the great Serelion, and took a fort from the English, where they had four and twenty pieces of cannon, which I caused to be split, that they might be of no further use unto them.

But I am desirous to confine myself to give an account of my last voyage, because it is the nearest, and that which is yet fresh in the memory of the public; notice and some information having been given thereof by the noise made in France and elsewhere of the burning of my ship, and the terrible crack it made in the air.

In the year 1694, after I had ravaged the coast of Caracca, I went up to the windward towards St. Croix, where I understood that there were some merchant ships, with a convoy, to come from Barbadoes and Nevis, and bound for England; and upon the same information I resolved to sail up to the height of the Bermudas, hoping to take this small fleet, and so to make

---

tizing of a son of Prince Thomas, the aforesaid king's son. He went on board a Portuguese ship, in order to his passage to Europe. An Englishman, that was his friend, took him aboard his vessel, and carried him to Barbadoes, where he was confined to his chamber by Colonel Russel, who was governor of those islands. He was freed from thence, and went to Martinico, where he saw M. de Frontenac, general of the French islands. From thence he got into France, being very uncertain whether he shall return to sea again. But, sir, all these adventures are set forth in so natural and easy a style, that you cannot but infallibly observe the sincerity and generosity of the author. It is true, our seafaring men are not so polite as those who live on shore; and that proceeds from want of society and conversation. But to make amends for that, they are a hundred fold more sincere than the other. And thus, sir, do not think a seafaring man will impose upon you. For myself, I have several times heard Montauban, in person, give a relation of this same voyage, but I could never observe that he varied in any one thing at any time; and the free and generous air wherewith he delivered those brave actions he has performed in fight, would persuade you of the truth of what he hath related. It is not for any ostentation that he has written this account; he has in the very beginning thereof declared openly enough, that he had no other end in doing it, than to give a minister of state an account (as he calls it) of his campaign. In short, if you are dubious in respect to the fight where the Sieur de Montauban was shipwrecked, you may recollect yourself, and find you have read the same in the gazettes of September and October this present year.

I am, Sir, your most humble, and most obedient servant,

B——."

a good booty of it. I was scarce got thither, but that I saw them appear, and sailing directly towards me, without any apprehensions of danger upon them. But I presently attacked their convoy, called the Wolf, and took her, with two more of the merchant ships laden with sugar, the rest having made their escape during the fight. As I was carrying my prize into France, I met with another English ship of sixteen guns coming from Spain, and bound also for England, that after a short fight struck, and which I carried to Rochelle, where the admiralty judged the same to be good prize. When I had sold this ship, I carried my three other vessels to Bourdeaux, where I arrived in September, 1694; and these last being also condemned as good prizes, I made it my business presently to find out merchants that would buy them.

In the mean time, my freebooters, who had not seen France for a long time, finding themselves now in a great city where pleasure and plenty reigned, were not backward to refresh themselves after the fatigues they had endured, while so long absent from their native country. They spent a world of money here, and proved horribly extravagant. The merchants and their hosts made no scruple to advance them money, or lend them as much as they pleased, upon the reputation of their wealth, and the noise there was throughout the city of the valuable prizes whereof they had a share. All the nights they spent in such divertisements as pleased them best, and the days in running up and down the town in masquerade, causing themselves to be carried in chairs, with lighted flambeaux at noon-day, of which debauches some died, while four of my crew fairly deserted me. So that now, seeing I lost my men, notwithstanding all the care I had taken, and strict injunctions I had laid upon them, I thought it advisable for me to be gone from thence as soon as I could, that I might keep the rest together.

In the first place I supplied the room of those whom I had lost with as many Bourdeaux young men, who in a short time became as expert as the old ones; for you are to observe, I made it my continual care and business to teach my men to shoot; and my so frequent exercising them rendered them in a short time as capable of shooting and handling their arms as the oldest sea freebooters, or the best fowlers by land.

When I had revictualled my ship, that carried no more than thirty-four pieces of cannon, I left Bourdeaux in the month of February, 1695, with an intention to go and cruise on the coast of Guinea, in Africa. I got up to the Azores, which are thirty-seven degrees north latitude, and cruised thereabouts for the space of eight days without any purchase. From thence I passed to the Canary Islands, which are in twenty-five degrees north latitude. We discovered the Peak of Teneriffe a great way off, which they say is the highest mountain in the world. They report these mountains had their names from dogs, which the Latins call *canes*, and which the Portuguese found here in great numbers upon their first arrival. I cruised round about them for fourteen days, in expectation of meeting with some Dutch ships which I was informed were to come that way, and it proved to be really so; for the said ships came thither, but they got into the port before I could reach them; and this made me sail away for the White Cape and the Isles of Cape Verde, that are between fourteen and eighteen degrees north latitude. Upon my arrival there, I found two English ships lying at anchor in the road of the Isle of May, which made me put out my shallop to know what they were, and the same informed me that they were two interlopers, carrying about thirty guns each. I resolved to board and take them; to this end I lay by to come nearer them; but as we bore upon one of the points of this island, these ships did not think fit to tarry for my coming up; but smelling my design, they made all ready, and left their cables and anchors in the road at which their shallops lay.

I pursued them all day; but night coming on, I lost sight of them, and returned to the road from whence they were gone, in order to take away the cables and anchors, and to sink the shallops fastened by them. When I had so done, I sailed away for the Isle of St. Vincent, to calk my vessel in that place, and to take in water and wood. This island also is one of those of Cape Verde. Here I staid for the space of eight days, at the end whereof, understanding by a Portuguese bark that there were two English ships, carrying from twenty to thirty guns, at the Isle of Fuego, one of which was refitting there, because of a fight she had been engaged in with some other ships, I presently weighed anchor, and sailed away for the said island, which is not far distant from that of St. Vincent, being in hopes to meet with the enemy in that place. But upon my arrival, I understood by a Portuguese, that they were gone away four or five days before, in the night, without saying any thing of the place whither they were bound, from the said Island of Fuego, or Fire Island. I thereupon steered my course for the coast of Guinea, and first discovered the Cape of Three Points, where I met with the guard-ship, which was a Dutch frigate, carrying thirty-four guns, and cruised out at sea. She quickly discovered me, and made directly towards me, in order to know what I was. As I had also on my part perceived her, and was in hopes to come close and fight her, I hung up Dutch colors, that I might not frighten her away, but give her an opportunity to come up within cannon-shot of me. When I saw her near enough, I put up French colors, and gave her a signal to strike; but instead thereof, she, without any more ado, very bravely gave me a broadside, and at the same time received one from me. We continued to fight one another in this manner from morning till four in the afternoon, without my being able to get the weather-gage, or come up near enough unto her to make use to any purpose of my fusils, which are the chief arms in such ships as ours be; nor to hinder her, by the favor of the wind which she had of me, to go and anchor under the port of the Cape of Three Points, where there were two Dutch ships more fitted out for men-of-war, one whereof carried fourteen, and the other twenty-eight pieces of cannon. I presently thought these three ships had joined together, in order to come out and fight me, which made me lie by thereabouts for a whole day, in expectation of them. I anchored also within a league of the shore, hoping at length that they being spighted at my insulting them in this manner, would be eager for revenge. But all this to no purpose, and in all appearance the guard-ship had already found herself so ill-treated that she had no occasion for a second fight. A small Portuguese ship, that passed by soon after, told me these ships were the same that had forced the Sieur Rey, captain of the king's flute called the Deep, to leave that coast; which also was confirmed afterwards unto me by the Sieur Rey himself, at the Prince's Island, where I met him.

Seeing therefore that the enemy would not fight, and considering with myself it was not advisable for me to attack them under the cannon of the fort, I resolved to go to Cape Lopez, and to Prince's and St. Thomas' Isles. In my passage I discovered Cape St. John, that stands on the continent of Guinea, as well as the Cape of Three Points, and I happened to meet with an English ship of twenty guns, and that had three hundred and fifty negroes, elephants' teeth, and wax on board it, which did not cost me much pains to take her. The captain told me he was come from Ardra, where he had taken five hundred and fifty negroes on board, but that they had slain some of them, because they had mutinied against his ship's crew; and that some more of them had made their escape to land in his shallop, which they secretly stole from him. Ardra is one of the principal towns in Guinea, standing upon the sea-side, and the usual residence of a prince who governs a great country in this part of the world.

From thence I went to Prince's Isle, in sight whereof I took a small Brandenburgh caper, mounted with eight pieces of cannon, and carrying sixty men. She cruised about this latitude, and took all the barks she could light on, without distinction of nation or colors. When I had done this, I went into the port, in order to clean my ship, which was foul enough; and that I might clear myself of the English prize I had taken, I sent her away to St. Domingo in America, to have the same condemned, under the command of the Sieur de Nave, and a sufficient number of men in her, whom I picked out of my own crew. But some time after, I understood she was taken by some English men-of-war that were before Little Goara.

In the mean time, that my men might not be idle, I gave my officers orders to have my ship careened, while I myself with the Brandenburgh caper which I had taken, and ninety men whom I had put on board her, went out to cruise, and continued at it for six weeks, upon the coast of Guinea, or about the Prince's and St. Omer's Islands, without meeting any enemy. Whereupon I returned back into the road of the first of these isles, where I revictualled my ship as soon as possibly I could; and when all things were ready, I weighed anchor, and sailed directly for the Isle of St. Thomas, there either to sell, or truck the caper I had taken; which last I chose to do for some provisions, because I had not enough to go and cruise long upon the coasts of Angola, whither I had resolved to go and spend five or six months, in order to avoid the English ships they were fitting out at the same town of Guinea, which consisted of three men-of-war and a fire-ship, and were designed to go in quest of me, cruising about St. Thomas, where they thought I should continue.

As I left St. Thomas, I saw a ship at anchor. I sailed towards her, and gave her chase a long time; but I could not prevent her getting to land at the Isle of St. Omer, and staving to pieces. In striving to take her, I lost a hundred and fifty pounds of gold dust, which this Dutch interloper had got in trading on this coast.

This being over, I sailed for the coasts of Angola, which is two hundred and fifty leagues on the other side of the line. There I arrived on the 22d of September, and understood, when I came within three leagues of the port of Cabinda, that there were two English ships with negroes on board in that place. As I was to leeward of that port, I bore out to sea, in hopes next day to have a south-west wind, that usually blows from the seaward, to help to recover the port. When day appeared, I saw a ship under English colors bearing upon me,

whom I presently did not take to be a man-of-war. But some time after, I discovered she carried no less than four and fifty guns. I used all the art I could to amuse her; and for that end I hung out Dutch colors, that I might also the more easily come near her; while she on her part was not backward to amuse me, and by the guns she fired from time to time, to assure me of her friendship, endeavored to come up with me. When I perceived my enemy's design, I took upon me to make a show of waiting for him, and sailed but very slowly, that I might make him believe my ship was heavy laden, or that I was encumbered for want of sails and hands. We kept in this manner from break of day till ten in the forenoon. He gave me a gun from time to time without ball, to assure me what he was, and as he supposed, my friend; but finding at last I did not answer him on my part in the same manner, and that we were now within cannon-shot of one another, he gave me one again with ball, which made me presently put up French colors, and answer him with another. Hereupon the English captain, without any more ado, gave me two broadsides, which I received without returning him one again, though he had killed me seven men; for I was in hopes, if I could have got something nearer to him, to put him out of condition ever to get away from me. I endeavored to come within a fusil shot of him, and was desirous to give him an opportunity to show his courage in boarding me, since I could not so well do the same by him, as being to the leeward. At last, being come by degrees nearer, and finding him within the reach of my fusils, which for that end I kept concealed upon the deck from his sight, they were discharged upon him, and my men continued to make so great a fire with them, that the enemy on their part began quickly to flag.

In the mean time, as their ship's crew consisted of above three hundred men, and that they saw their cannon could not do their work for them, they resolved to board us, which they did with a great shout and terrible threatenings of giving no quarter, if we did not surrender. Their grappling irons failing to catch the stern of my ship, made theirs run in such a manner, that their stern run upon my bowsprit and broke it. Having observed my enemy thus encumbered, my men plied them briskly with their small shot, and made so terrible a fire upon them for an hour and a half, that being unable to resist any longer, and having lost a great many men, they left the sport, and ran down between decks, and I saw them presently after make signals with their hats of crying out for quarter. I caused my men therefore to give over their firing, and commanded the English to embark in their shallops, and come on board of me, while I made some of my crew at the same time leap into the enemy's ship, and seize her, and so prevent any surprise from them. I already rejoiced within myself for the taking of such a considerable prize; and so much the more, in that I hoped, that after having taken this vessel that was the guard-ship of Angola, and the largest the English had in those seas, I should find myself in a condition to take still better prizes, and attack any man-of-war I should meet with. My ship's crew were also as joyful as myself, and did the work they were engaged in with a great deal of pleasure; but the enemy's powder suddenly taking fire, by the means of a match the captain had left burning on purpose, as hoping he might escape with his two shallops, blew both the ships into the air, and made the most horrible crack that was ever heard. It is impossible to set forth this horrid spectacle to the life; the spectators themselves were the actors of this bloody scene, not knowing whether they saw it or not, and not being able to judge of that which themselves felt. Wherefore leaving the reader to imagine the horror which the blowing up of two ships above two hundred fathoms into the air must work in us, where there was formed, as it were, a mountain of water, fire, wreck of the ships, cordages, cannon, men, with a most terrible clap made, what with the cannon that went off in the air, and the waves of the sea that were tossed up thither; to which we may add the cracking of masts and boards, the rending of the sails and ropes, the cries of men, and the breaking of bones; I say, leaving these things to the imagination of the reader, I shall only take notice of what befell myself, and by what good fortune it was that I escaped.

When the fire first begun, I was upon the fore deck of my own ship, where I gave the necessary orders. Now I was carried upon part of the said deck so high, that I fancy it was the height alone that prevented my being involved in the wreck of the ships, where I must have infallibly perished, and been cut into a thousand pieces. I fell back into the sea (you may be sure,) giddy-headed enough, and continued a long time under water without being able to get up to the surface of it; at last, falling into a debate with the water, as a person who was afraid of being drowned, I got upon the face of it, and laid hold of a broken piece of a mast that I found near me. I called to some of my men whom I saw swimming round about me, and exhorted them to take courage, hoping we might yet save our lives if we could light upon any one of our shallops. But what yet afflicted me more than my very misfortune was, to see two half bodies who had still somewhat of life remaining in them, from time to time mount up to the face of the water, and leave the place where they appeared all dyed with blood. It was also much the same thing, to see round about me a vast number of members and scattered parts of men's bodies, and most of them spitted upon splinters of wood. At last, one of my men, having met with a whole shallop, among all the wreck that swam up and down upon the water, came to tell me that we must endeavor to stop some holes therein, and to take out the canoe that lay on board her. We got to the number of fifteen or sixteen of us who had escaped, near unto this shallop, every man upon his piece of wood, and took the pains to loosen our canoe, which at length we effected. We went all on board her, and after we had got in, saved our chief gunner, who in the fight had had his leg broke. We took up three or four oars, or pieces of boards which served us for that purpose; and when we had done that, we sought out for somewhat to make us a sail and a little mast; and having fitted up all things as well as possibly we could, we committed ourselves to the Divine Providence, who alone could give us life and deliverance.

As soon as I had done working, I found myself all over besmeared with blood, that ran from a wound I had received in my head at the time of my fall. We made some lint out of my handkerchief, and a fillet to bind it withal out of my shirt, after I had first washed the wound with urine. The same thing was done to the rest that had been wounded, and our shallop in the mean while sailed along, without making land, or our knowing where we were going. And what was still more sad, was, that we had no victuals, and we had already spent three days without either eating or drinking. One of our men, being greatly afflicted with hunger and thirst at the same time, drank so much salt water that he died of it. Most of our men vomited continually, whether it were that they were incommoded with the water that got into them when they fell into the sea, as it will happen if they drink of it out of mere necessity. As for myself, I was incommoded for a long time. I afterwards swelled up mightily, and my excrements came from me in the form of small buttons; and I attribute to a quartan ague, that seized on me soon after, the cure of my dropsy, and recovery of my health that by degrees returned to me. I make no enumeration of the other inconveniences which so dangerous a fall brought upon me, such being unavoidable to a man that fell into so great a fire. All my hair, face, and one side of me, were burnt with the powder; and the same fate attended me as usually does bombardiers at sea, and that was to bleed at the nose, ears, and mouth. I do not know whether this be the effect of the powder or no, by swelling up those vessels which contain the blood in our bodies to such an extraordinary degree, that the ends of the veins open and let it out; or that the great noise and violent motion that is wrought in those organs make the same happen. But let it come which way it will, since there is no room here for a consultation of physicians, as long as we were dying of hunger, nor to inquire what became of the English, when we had so much difficulty, and could hardly save ourselves, we continued our course up the current with the help of our oars, because we knew the same came from the port of Cabindas. But as the wind was against us, we could never get thither, and were forced to be satisfied to get to the Cape of Corsa if we could, which stands a dozen leagues from that of Cathersna, where we could not land, because of a bar that renders the coast inaccessible. That was our design, but hunger hindered us to put the same in execution, and we were forced even to overcome the obstacles which nature laid in our way, by running ashore in spite of the bar. This we performed at last, (after much difficulty,) being in hopes to find there some negroes that might furnish us with victuals. One of our company presently landed, in order to go and seek out somewhat to satisfy our hunger, and by good fortune found in a pond, sticking to the branches of trees, some oysters, whereof he gave us presently notice. We went all up to the very pond along a channel of the sea, where we were no sooner come, but we eat lustily of the oysters with a very good appetite. We opened them with a few knives we found in our pockets, lending the same from one to another very charitably and readily. When we had spent two days in that place, I divided my men into three small companies, and sent them up into the country to seek for victuals and houses, with orders to return again in the evening to the shallop. I went out myself also as the rest did; but we could find neither any houses, nor the least sign of any men in those parts. All that we could see were great herds of bufflers, as large as oxen, who fled so fast from us, that we could not possibly come near them. Wherefore having spent all the day in this manner, and got nothing, we returned to our shallop to eat oysters again, and resolved next day to leave this place, and go to Cape Corsa, to the leeward of which there is a large port, where ships that sail that way put in to furnish themselves with water and wood. The negroes that live in the country having notice of the coming in of ships by firing of cannon, come thither also with provisions, and barter the same for brandy, knives and hatchets. They are forced to live remote from the sea, because all the coast is very marshy. As soon as we were got to the said cape, we heard a great noise made by the negroes who came thither to sell wood to the ships that lay at anchor in the port. I looked amongst them to see if I could find any one whom I knew, for as they had often brought me some wood, and other refreshments in the course of my former voyages, I was in hopes to find some or other that would know me again. But though I knew several of them, it was impossible for me to persuade any of them that I was Captain Montauban, so much was I disfigured with my late misfortune; and all of them took me for a man that would impose the belief of it upon them. I thought fit to tell them in their own language, whereof I understood a little, that I was ready to die with famine, and prayed them to give me somewhat to eat; but it signified nothing. So I desired them to carry me to Prince Thomas, who is son to the king of that country, as hoping he might call to mind the favors I had formerly showed him.

I carried all my company with me to that prince. We were first brought to the dwellings of those negroes, where they began to be a little more tractable, and gave us some bananas to eat, which are a sort of figs longer than a man's hand. Next day we got to the prince's habitation; but I was in so pitiful a condition, that I could never, by the signs I gave, make him know me, though I spoke to him in his own language, as also in the Portuguese tongue, which he understood very well. It fortuned one day, that going to bathe ourselves, he saw a scar upon my thigh, that was the effect of a wound I had received with a musket-ball. He told me that he must immediately know whether I was Captain Montauban or no; and that if I were not the man, he would cut off my head. He asked if ever I had a scar with a musket-shot upon my thigh, which when I showed him, he presently embraced me, and said he was exceeding sorry to see me in that condition, and immediately caused victuals to be distributed among my men, and divided them into several habitations, with strict orders to the negroes, with whom they were quartered, to take the greatest care they could of them. As for me, he kept me with himself, and made me always eat at his own table. When I was a little brought into order, he said he would carry me to see the king his father, who lived five or six leagues off, that is about ten or a dozen from the sea-side. I let him know how great the favor and honor was he did me, and prayed him at the same time that I might have the liberty to let my freebooters go along with me, and grant us some pieces of stuffs to put ourselves in as good equipage as we could, in order to appear before so great a prince; all which he allowed me, and three days after, we went all together in a great canoe, and passed by the River of Cape Lopez, because the country is so full of marshes that you cannot go by land.

Being arrived at the king's habitation, which is a village consisting of three hundred booths, covered with palm-leaves, wherein the king keeps his wives, family, relations, and some other negro families, whom he loves best, I was lodged in Prince Thomas's house, and all my men were distributed into other habitations. We found all the people in great lamentation, because the chief of their religion, whom they call *papa*, had died that day, when they were to begin the funeral obsequies, which were usually to last for seven days for priests of that quality. This same person was had in great esteem and veneration by all the people, they looking upon him to be a holy man. As the king is in mourning, and sees nobody all the while that this funeral ceremony lasts, Prince Thomas bid me have patience, and not to go out of my lodgings for to see the king, because that was the custom of his nation.

However, I could not forbear going to see the funeral solemnity, where I saw nothing else but a great concourse of people standing round the dead corpse. I was in the mean time very well fed by Prince Thomas's orders, who was gone to see his father. They did not let me want bananas, elephant's flesh, and river fish, though all of it came without either bread or wine, as you may well suppose. My men were treated in the same manner in their respective quarters all the time we staid there.

At the eight days' end, Prince Thomas came, in order to carry us before the king. He is a large negro, well enough made, and about fifty years old, who to do me the greater honor, according to the relation given of me to him by his son, came out of his house to receive me, and advanced some steps to meet me. He was supported by four or five women, which gave him a kind of an air of grandeur in a very cumbersome and fantastic manner. He was guarded by several negroes, who were armed with lances and fusils, which they discharged from time to time with no great order. There were several trumpets and drums marched before him, at the head of which company there were several standards carried, alike in color to those used in Holland. He had no other clothes than a piece of cotton stuff, streaked with white and blue, wherewith part of his body was covered, the same being several times folded round about him.

He gave me many demonstrations of his friendship; he also stretched out his hand to me, saying it was the first time he had ever done so to any man before me. Being come to his house, he sat at his door, and made me take place on the one side of him, as his son did on the other. He asked me several questions concerning the greatness and power of the king my master; and when I had told him that he alone waged war against the English and the Dutch, whom himself knew, as having seen them often at the Cape of Lopez; that he also warred against the Germans and Spaniards, who were more potent nations than the English and Dutch; he also told me he was pleased with my account, and that he would drink the king of France's health. Presently they brought him up some palm wine, which is not unpleasant to drink, and his wives served him in a great crystal glass. As soon as he began to take the glass, the negro men and women lifted up their right arm, and held the same in that posture very silently till he had done drinking. But when it was over, they made a great noise with their trumpets and drums, and discharged all their muskets, or I should rather have said fusils.

Prince Thomas then asked me, what was the king of France's name, and having told him, Lewis le Grand, he said he had a mind I should hold a child of his, of about seven or eight months old to baptism, and that I should give him the name of Lewis le Grand, which made me smile a little at the humor. He told me also, that the first voyage I should make into his country, he would give me the child to carry to France for a present to the king, to whose service he devoted him, being very desirous he should be brought up according to the custom of the country and court of so great a prince. I also promised on my part, that the first time I came to the coast of Guinea, I should not fail to come and put him in mind of his promise, that so, upon my return into France, I might be capable of making the greatest present that could be unto the king, in presenting him with the son of Prince Thomas. And assure him, said the same prince, that I am his friend, and that if he has occasion for my services, I will go myself into France with all the lances and fusils belonging to the king my father; which was as much as to say, with all the force of the kingdom. The king presently pursued the discourse, and assured me he would go thither in person, if there was need for it; and with that all the negro men and women raised such a shout as much surprised me; and this was scarce over, when the fusileers made a general discharge of their arms; the drums and trumpets went to it again; and those who carried the lances set themselves running from one side to another with such horrible outcries as frighted me. I was really ignorant of the meaning of all this, and could not be satisfied till I saw the king drink the French king's health a second time, with the same ceremonies as at first. Prince Thomas drank it also, and all of us were commanded to do the same. This being over, the king ordered two wax cakes to be brought, whereof he made me a present, desiring me to accept them as a token of his friendship, and then he went into his house.

The audience being thus over, Prince Thomas carried me along with him into all the parts of the village, whither he went to visit his friends; and we went on the succeeding days to see several other villages that are scattered up and down the country, about five leagues distant from each other.

These people, the greatest part of whom had never been at the sea-side, and consequently had not seen any white people, ran from all quarters to see us, and brought us more fruit, with bufflers and elephants' flesh, than we could eat. As for the elephants of this country, they are not altogether like unto those in the East Indies, whereof they are a different species; as are also those of Cafala, near Zanguebar, on the eastern coasts of Ethiopia. The negroes eat of their flesh with a good appetite, and like the same better than any other; hereof they provide their best feasts, and those who were minded to honor us most, brought it unto us instead of that of bufflers, which I prefer much before it.

As they were not able to comprehend the difference there was between the color of their faces and ours, they would frequently put their hands upon our faces to see if the white color would go off; and it was the fortune of many of us, to meet with hands scrubbed with knives, so as that many times we were hurt with them, which yet we durst not complain of. Prince Thomas, when he saw that, commanded all the attendants that they should suffer none to come and rub and scrape us with their fingers in that manner, and spoke aloud to all the people who came to see us, that all strangers were white as we were; and that if the negroes went into another country, they would seem to be as odd colored there as we were in Guinea. He laughed also from time to time to see the people run in that fashion after us, as if we had been some unknown animal; and I am not certain whether he were sorry to see us thus incommoded with the importunities of those negroes, or that he took some pleasure to see the folly of his countrymen, as I have done many a time, to behold all their extravagant humors.

At last, after a journey and diversion together of three days, the prince brought me back by another way to take my leave of his father. The king caressed me a thousand times, after a most obliging manner, according to the custom of his country, and made me promise I should give him a visit the first time I returned into Guinea. Then we embarked in our canoes, and next day came to Prince Thomas's village, where he continued to treat us after the same manner he had been used to do. Here he spake to me again, that he would have me stand witness for his son at his baptism; which I did with so much the more pleasure, in that I was helping to make a Christian, and sanctify a soul.

But as I was dubious whether the priest of the town knew how to baptize a child, or that he could remember the words he ought to say at the administration of that sacrament, I desired the prince to send for a priest out of one of the Portuguese ships, which he presently did, to Cape Lopez; so that one came from thence in two days' time. The Portuguese were the people that brought the Christian religion first into these countries. It is true, they have not kept the same up there as they ought to have done; but the difficulties that obstruct that good establishment proceed, without doubt, from hence, that men must dwell in a country that is no better than savage, where the air and the victuals are not so agreeable to strangers. To give religion a sure footing in these regions, it is necessary that the Europeans have fixed habitations, or build towns there; that they instruct the negroes in the truths of the Christian faith, and that they send out missionaries from time to time among these poor wretches. This might very easily be done, because the people are very docile, and readily apprehend the truths which you would teach them, as having lived without any faith at all, or any idea of another religion, for a long time. These negroes being once become Christians, you might make priests among them of their own nation, who might be furnished with books for the ceremonies of the church, and a catechism for the rule of their faith, until they were capable to read the New Testament. It is necessary also, that a bishop were constituted in this town, who should take care to send priests to the dwellings of the negroes, up and down the countries, and to build oratories in the most populous places. The Christian religion might in this manner be settled in Guinea, and so become less subject to be ruined by the wars which strangers make there. The Christians also who dwell in the kingdoms of Fez and Morocco might be reformed, and a correspondence settled between the priests of that nation, and those of Guinea, that so they might be assisting to one another for the keeping up of religion on all the coasts of Africa. It was in a manner not unlike unto this, that Christianity established itself among the gentiles, who were a hundred fold more averse to our faith than the negroes of Guinea. The priests of this country are for the most part no priests at all, as having never been ordained by any bishop, and constituted themselves in the room of those that were deceased in their country. And thus it is that they have nothing in a manner that savors of Christianity, though they have ceremonies enough, and some appearance of a sacrifice.

But to return to our baptism. The Portuguese priest being come, Prince Thomas's son was baptized, and named Lewis le Grand, in pursuance to the intention of his father. A negro woman, and one of his relations, served as godmother, and I for godfather. I was told this lady was called Antonia, and that she had been thus named by the wife of a Portuguese captain at her baptism.

Two or three days after this ceremony was over, which was performed with all the magnificence the negroes were capable of, Prince Thomas's guards, which he kept at Cape de Lopez to give him notice of the arrival of any ships, came to tell him there was an English ship come thither. I desired him to let me go on board her, that I might return to my own country, to free myself from those many inconveniences I still labored under. But he would not have me commit myself into the hands of my enemies, and desired me to have a little patience till the arrival of some Portuguese ships, with which he would let me go. In the mean time the prince went to Cape Lopez, there to exchange elephants' teeth, bees' wax, and negroes for iron, arms, and brandy, and returned from thence in ten or twelve days.

He told me, when he came back, that there was a Portuguese ship come to anchor at Cape de Lopez, and that I should go down in his canoe in order to go on board her; that he had recommended me to the captain, and that I should want nothing that was necessary for my voyage into Europe.

I presently gathered my men together, except two whom I did not think fit to wait for; for they were gone up into the country five or six days before, and I knew not where to find them. We therefore embarked on board this prince's canoes, after I had taken my leave of him; and upon our arrival at Cape Lopez, I found the Portuguese commander to be one of my friends, with whom I had contracted acquaintance at the Isle of St. Thomas. I went on board him, and three days after we anchored at the said island, the governor whereof showed me and my men a thousand civilities during a month's space that we were forced to tarry in that port. At the expiration of that time, came in an English ship that had been out upon the Gold Coast. I made acquaintance with the captain, and we grew to be such friends, that I thought myself obliged in honor to accept of the offers he made me. He prayed me to go on board his ship, and assured me I should find all the help imaginable at Barbadoes, whither he was bound, because there were very good Jewish physicians of that island of his acquaintance. I embarked therefore in his ship, with all my men, notwithstanding all the reasons given me by the governor of the island to make me suspicious of the Englishman, who was undoubtedly as honest a man as any of his country. He was so civil as to give me his own cabin, with all the pleasure and diversion he could think of, for the solacing of my spirits under the afflictions I had from time to time endured.

Ten days after our departure from St. Thomas, a blast of wind unhappily made us lose our rudder, in the room whereof we were forced to set up a spare top-mast; and this proved very detrimental to our voyage, which lasted no less than three months.

Provisions began to be scarce before our arrival at Barbadoes; so that when we came there, we had no more than what would have served us for three days longer; insomuch that the captain, being concerned that he had taken our men aboard, ordered our allowance to be lessened three fourths of what it should be. When we were got to port, the captain went to wait upon Colonel Russel, who is general there, related to him my whole adventure with the guard-ship of Angola, and was much blamed for bringing me to Barbadoes. When the captain returned on board his ship, he told me what the governor had said, who had forbid him upon pain of death to let me go ashore. However, he said nothing to me of this prohibition, but contented himself with only desiring me not to go ashore, that it might create no suspicion in the governor; which I promised exactly to perform, having no great concern upon me of seeing a place again that I had known so long ago, and being unwilling to create my captain any trouble.

Next day, several Jews that had been driven away from Martinico, having heard of my arrival, came to see me, and finding I was very crazy, and much out of order, they sent some physicians of their nation to me, who said I could not be cured, if I were not carried ashore, and thereupon offered to solicit the governor on my behalf, for giving me leave to go and lie in a house in the town. I drew up a petition to him, praying him to grant me that liberty, and promising I would not stir out of the chamber where I was placed, till I were to reëmbark to go for Martinico.

The physicians themselves were obliged to be my securities, and I was at length carried to Mr. Jacob Lewis's house, where I was very well looked after all the time I staid there. Three days after I was brought thither, the major general came to see me from Colonel Russel, the governor. He very civilly offered me his protection, and all those things that could be conducive for the recovery of my health. The same major, as also the captain of the garrison, came also to visit me from time to time, though I apprehended they came not so much to inspect into the state of my health, as to see if I were in a condition to be transported out of that island. Colonel Russel, about ten or twelve days after my arrival, came to see if I were as bad as they said I was. He came again about seven or eight days after in the evening, and caused me to be carried out of the Jew's house where I was, to an English merchant's. He told me I should be better accommodated there than at Jacob Lewis's; but I thought it was to the intent I might be watched more narrowly, and not converse with many people. He came to see me the next day, and asked how I liked my new lodgings. I rendered him many thanks for the civilities and kindnesses he showed me, and that he might have no occasion to suspect my men, I prayed him to shut them up in the citadel, that they might not run about the island, and to prevent their making of their escape.

He said he would take care of it, but that I was to understand they were prisoners of war as well as myself. I made answer, I knew that, and that I thought myself a happy man to have fallen into his hands; but that the English captain, who had brought me to Barbadoes, had given me his word I should not be detained, nor any of my men; that it was upon his faith given me, and the tenders of service he made, that I had embarked, as firmly relying upon those testimonies of his friendship he had given me. Then I desired him to grant me and my men our liberty, promising I should be ever mindful of the favor done me, whether it were by restoring of the prisoners I might take belonging to the islands, or paying him such a ransom as he required.

No, said the governor, I will have neither your ransom, nor your prisoners, and you are too brave a man for me to have no compassion upon your many misfortunes; I desire, on the contrary, that you would accept of these forty pistoles, which I present you with, to supply your present occasion. He gave them me in a purse, which he had doubtless brought along with him for that purpose; and when he left me, he said he went to give orders for to bring my men together. Next day he sent me two of them, who said they knew not what was become of the rest, and that they had orders from the governor to stay with me. I had the liberty to send them abroad to get me necessaries; and at last, finding myself somewhat recovered by the care my landlord took of me, I told the officer that came daily to see me, that I desired the governor to let me go on board the first vessel that was bound to Martinico.

Three days after came a bark, which the Count de Blenac, general of the French islands, had sent thither about the exchange of prisoners. Colonel Russel sent me word she was come, and that I should prepare to be gone. Then it was I had the liberty to go to his house to render him thanks for all the civilities he had showed me. He told me he was sorry that by the laws of war he was bound to allow me no more liberty than I had, and that he prayed me to use the English kindly that should happen to fall into my hands. This being done, I went on board the French bark, which was commanded by the Sieur Courpon, formerly an inhabitant of St. Christopher's, and I could never find any more of my freebooters than those two I have spoken of, whom the governor sent me.

We went ashore at Port Royal in Martinico, and I went with my men to the town to wait upon Monsieur de Blenac, who was then sick of that distemper he died of. I gave him a relation of all my adventures, and I am sure he was surprised to hear the particulars of so many misfortunes. As he would have me stay at his house all the time I tarried in Martinico, he made me every day repeat unto him the manner of my fight with the English man-of-war; and at last finding an opportunity of getting me transported into France, he sent for the captain of the ship who was bound thither, and recommended me to him. He would also have written letters by me to Monsieur Phelipeaux, to recommend me to some employ; but the day before my departure he was taken so very ill, that he could not write, and that day, which was the 10th of June, in the evening he died. I was mightily troubled at his death for several reasons. He was a person that took delight in serving every body; who had great compassion on such as had been persecuted by an evil fate, as was my case; who went forwards with what he knew; who of himself made an offer of those favors he was minded to bestow, before they were asked of him; and who, in short, was brave as to his person, skilful in maritime affairs, a good seaman, knew all the coasts and heights of land in America, was in great esteem with the king for his integrity, wisdom, justice, and for all the great services he had done the government in the way of commerce and discovery of islands. The next day after his death I embarked on board the Virgin, a ship belonging to Bourdeaux, and which had been built there, in which port, after a passage of not many days, I arrived at last, with many different thoughts and contrary sentiments within me. I do not know whether I have bid the sea adieu, so much has my last misfortune terrified me; or whether I shall go out again to be revenged on the English, who have done me so much mischief, or go and traverse the seas with a design to get me a little wealth, or rest quiet and eat up what my relations have left me. There is a strange inclination in men to undertake voyages, as there is to gaming; whatever misfortunes befall them, they do not believe they will be always unhappy, and therefore they will play on. Thus it is as to the sea; whatever accidents befall us, we are in hopes to find a favorable opportunity to make us amends for all our losses. I believe whoever reads this account will find it a hard task to give me counsel thereupon, or to take the same himself.

www.ingramcontent.com/pod-product-compliance
Lightning Source LLC
LaVergne TN
LVHW020924110826
845150LV00004B/764

* 9 7 8 1 4 2 5 5 5 4 3 4 7 *